Essentials of Aviation Management:

A Guide for Aviation Service Businesses

Sixth Edition

J. F. Rodwell

KENDALL/HUNT PUBLISHING COMPANY
4050 Westmark Drive Dubuque, Iowa 52002

Book Team

Chairman and Chief Executive Officer Mark C. Falb
Vice President, Director of National Book Program Alfred C. Grisanti
Manager, Editorial Development Georgia Botsford
Senior Developmental Editor Angela Willenbring
Prepress Project Coordinator Sheri Hosek
Prepress Editor Carrie Maro
Permissions Editor Colleen Zelinsky
Cover Design Manager Jodi Splinter
Cover Designer Suzanne Millius

Formerly published as Essentials of Aviation Management:
A Guide for Fixed Base Operators
J. D. Richardson, J. F. Rodwell, P. Baty

Internet Link Access
Link directly to the Internet sites listed in the appendix by going to www.kendallhunt.com and search for author 'Rodwell.' The links are located on the book description page.

ISBN 0-7872-9762-3

Printed in the United States of America
10 9 8 7 6 5 4 3

To my life partner,
Vern Curtis,
who kept me sane during the writing of this book
and solved my computer problems.

Contents

List of Figures

Preface

Essentials of Aviation Management was first published in 1977. Since that edition, developed by JD Richardson as a result of his work with small dealerships, the US general aviation industry has changed in many ways. Industry ownership has been evolving, with the "mom and pop" operation less common, and larger Fixed Base Operators (FBOs) with multiple locations becoming the norm. These companies provide much more internal training and upward career mobility to their employees than can a small operator.

As the industry moves into the twenty-first century, certain types of flying will continue to grow. In particular, an increase in sport, experimental and homebuilt personal flying can be predicted based on the growth of aircraft ownership in that segment. Increases in business and executive travel are anticipated, especially in heavier and more sophisticated aircraft. Owning a general aviation aircraft is increasingly a luxury, rather than an inexpensive toy. Those who fly purely for the love of it may be from different socio-economic strata than in the past. The flow of pilots up from general aviation to the airlines may slow as those companies increasingly struggle with cost control and market shrinkage. However, this is not a stable industry and shows few signs of becoming so. Aviation operators must continue to be flexible in addressing needs and opportunities.

The general aviation manager of the future must be a businessperson first and an aviation enthusiast only second. *Essentials of Aviation Management* seeks to provide the analytical tools of basic business practice with a focus on the aviation service business. It serves several levels of audience including the technical, vocational, graduate, and undergraduate levels as well as the individual in industry. For an in-depth study, it should be supplemented with additional trade and industry materials, of which there is a growing flood. A new appendix is provided in this edition, which lists many of the key aviation web sites. This should be the starting point for any inquiry into greater depth on the issues within these covers, and provides a framework for analyzing the many issues that face the ever-volatile general aviation industry. Link directly to the Internet sites listed in the appendix by going to www.kendallhunt.com and search for author 'Rodwell.' The links are located on the book description page.

In the larger environment in which aviation businesses operate, the single most pervasive major external change appears to be globalization—more international business, more foreign travel, overseas manufacturing and worldwide instant communications changing our perception of ourselves and our place in the world.

This has been vastly facilitated by the advent of the worldwide web and the Internet, which together with individual desktop computers have changed how virtually all companies are run and have access to information. For the average aviation business owner, the web is increasingly how he or she learns about industry actions and trends, how data is gathered, how communication takes place with clients, and how potential clients find the company. Within the company, a computer likely sits on every desk, used for scheduling, billing, and many other functions. Computer literacy is a job requirement in aviation as it is in almost every other industry.

World economic and population growth lead to an increasing concern with fossil fuel depletion, global warming, and the need for effective environmental protection. The aviation industry is extremely affected by these issues.

The need has become more apparent in the past decade for all companies to focus on standards of ethics and corporate integrity, not just to "do the right thing" but also to stay within the law.

Within the industry, airports themselves are increasingly threatened. Few other businesses are so dependent for their very physical facilities—runways and taxiways—on landlords that are rarely committed only to the cause of aviation. Many municipal airport tenants discover to their cost that elected officials are more influenced by airport residents, who vote them in and out of office, than by airport pilots and business owners, who may not live in the same jurisdiction as the airport. It is essential, with the US now losing dozens of airports per year, that aviation businesses play an active role in ensuring a positive business climate for their own and other airports. The FBO manager must budget substantial time for these external relations.

The advent of the rapidly-expanding fractional aircraft ownership industry means changes for FBOs as they explore providing contracted supplemental lift to fractional companies. FBOs may also be able to develop maintenance contracts with fractional companies.

The terrorism attacks of 9/11/2001 may change for many decades the attitude toward aviation in the US. First, it has been brought home to this country more dramatically than before, that all technology can be used for either good or evil. Whether used to fly into a building or spray disease spores from the air, aircraft large and small, like any technology, can be either a threat or an asset. In practical terms, there is the simple hardship that the ban on much GA flying directly after 9/11/01 caused for many operators. The long processing times at scheduled service airports have more and more companies looking at charter and fractional or full aircraft ownership as alternative methods of getting their employees around. Airport security requirements at even small airports may add to inconvenience and cost for small aviation businesses. Paperwork needs more attention so that inappropriate aliens do not get approvals to remain in this country and study flying.

The book's structure has not changed from the 5th edition; new materials are woven into the existing chapters; however, instructors should note that some chapters have old sections in a new order, and new sections. Many valuable suggestions were incorporated that came from students and instructors who use the book; such suggestions continue to be welcome at any time.

As with any "how-to" book, there are differing opinions on the best way to approach a problem. Many opinions presented here are synthesized from the teachings of experts in the various fields. Others are derived from my twenty-five year career as an aviation educator and consultant. Many forms of assistance went into this edition, and many people made input. My thanks are due especially to the National Air Transportation Association (NATA) for generously sharing several publications, and to Bill de Decker, Diane Paholke, David Worrels, and Christine Wolf for advising on how the book needed to be updated, providing key materials, and reviewing drafts. Nevertheless, the author takes full responsibility for the book's facts and opinions. Facts change constantly in this rapid-paced industry, and while every attempt has been made to provide current information, practioners should consult current legal and other advice to expand on topics offered by this book, necessarily an overview.

I hope this book will continue to be valuable to students and practitioners in the general aviation industry.

Julie F. Rodwell
Julie.cfd@ccountry.net
Ashland, Oregon, 2003

1

The Role of the General Aviation Service Center or "Fixed Base Operator" in the National Aviation System

OBJECTIVES

- Explain the term "FBO," and the functions such businesses fulfill in the general aviation community.
- Discuss the historical development of powered aircraft and why some believe we have come "full circle."
- Describe some of the aviation trends and issues relative to the fixed-base operator/airport service business.
- Increase the reader's awareness of external and non-aviation issues facing general aviation and impacting its future.

Introduction

Terminology

This book is a small business text for the management of United States general aviation service centers or Fixed-Base Operators (FBOs), which are the service stations of the general aviation system. It addresses two audiences: the aviation student who is seeking a basic managerial training, and the fixed-base operator owners, managers, and staff who are practitioners in the field with varying levels of formal business training.

In 1911 when a pilot by the name of Calbraith P. Rogers made the first transcontinental flight across the United States, it is reported that a special train was sent ahead of him with parts and repair facilities, thus a "mobile" service support system made his flight possible.[1] Although the history of the "fixed-base" operations aviation service system is not well documented, it must have gone hand-in-hand with the development of powered flight and of the airport system, for without fuel and repairs, aircraft could not fly very far. Therefore, as aviation developed, "fixed-base" operator services must also have grown in number.

"Fixed-base" operator (usually shortened to FBO) is an elusive term applied to almost any general aviation business existing on an airport. Over the years, there has been considerable industry discussion about the idea of changing the name "FBO" to some other term more meaningful to the non-aviation public. "General aviation service center" or "aviation service business" is probably more descriptive. However, old habits die hard and within the industry, "FBO" is well understood, therefore in this book we interchange the terms "FBO," "general aviation center," and "aviation service business." The reader should assume they are synonymous; for the purposes of the book, "FBO" does not necessarily mean a full-service organization, as defined by FAA or others, as discussed elsewhere in the book.

Scope of Book

This book places the aviation service business in context as part of the national aviation system. It reviews from an aviation standpoint, current small business practice and theory in areas such as business planning, marketing, financial strategy, human resources, and administration and information systems. It explores the principal areas of general aviation center activity; namely, flight line and front desk, flight operations, and aviation maintenance. The regulatory context of each area is summarized in its pertinent chapter. Physical facility planning for general aviation center areas and other parts of the airport and environs is discussed. Finally, the book examines likely future trends affecting general aviation and general aviation center services.

Various appendices, chapter notes and references for further reading provide additional technical data, including a new appendix on aviation web sites (Appendix I). For ease of use, Appendix I is also available on Kendall/Hunt's web site at www.kendallhunt.com and search for author 'Rodwell.'

Aviation's Early Economic History

Aviation Pioneers and Economic Milestones

Aviation's history in the US intertwines the development of new technologies with their practical application to serve the economy. The first part of the 20th century saw an extraordinary rate of aeronautical experimentation and development that has changed how not only the US, but also the whole world, interacts and does business. The technological advances, new records, and feats of endurance in aviation and space that have occurred have led quickly to market applications. This history is well documented in numerous texts, one of which, *Air Transportation*, is used heavily as a reference here.[2] What follows is a very brief overview.

When human beings first began to build flying machines, particularly when they began to build powered craft, their primary preoccupation was to understand and master aerodynamics; potential markets for the technology were a secondary consideration. Orville Wright, even ten years after Kitty Hawk, felt there was almost no chance of successfully completing a transatlantic flight.[3]

Yet, some, even in the very early days, understood the economic and transportation role of aviation. Experimenters such as Samuel Langley succeeded in getting financial backing from people interested in the large-scale practical uses of aircraft.[4] With Lindbergh's solo transatlantic flight in 1927, and the huge public acclaim that accompanied this feat, the perception of the market potential of aviation began to change. From around this time, passenger flight became a market reality.

For airmail, it changed much earlier. From 1911 mail was carried by air in the United States in a system that must have had as many challenges and risks as the Pony Express in the preceding century. Mail does not present the same risk as human cargo in a crash, and it can more readily withstand delay and rerouting. The American public, therefore, waited for evidence of safety and reliability in airmail service before entrusting themselves as aircraft passengers. By the mid-1920s, especially in the United States, the capabilities of the heavier-than-air planes were apparent. Passenger service began to be popular in the 1920s and 1930s. Between 1911 and 1927, the post office handled airmail in its own aircraft. However, the Airmail Act of 1925 enabled passenger air carriers to contract for mail service.

By early 1926, twelve contract airmail routes had been awarded. In 1927 the Boeing Aircraft Company received a bid award (later transferred to Boeing Air Transport) and in the first two years of operation carried about 6,000 passengers as well as 1,200 tons of airmail. However, the wider acceptance of aircraft as passenger carriers did not occur until the 1930s after several legislative changes designed to strengthen national airmail routes and encourage financially viable carriers. This was a stormy period in the development of commercial aviation; however, by the end of 1936 the air carriers were finally making more revenue from passengers than from mail.

Some earlier acceptance of air travel had resulted from nineteenth and twentieth century European lighter-than-air flying machines. Henri Giffard built the first controllable dirigible as early as 1852, and in 1909 Count Zeppelin started the world's first airline called DERLAG.

During World War I, the Germans used dirigibles extensively for bombing. In the 1920s and 1930s several other nations became active in the development of passenger and military airships. The passenger airship era ended after a series of crashes. The last one was the explosion and crash of the Hindenburg in 1937. After this, airships were used only for military purposes.

The Jet Engine: New Horizons

World War II military necessity gave the jet engine its impetus, although experimenters in this area had been working on it for decades.[5,6] The commercial jet's greater speed and range opened up significant new horizons for aviation, especially in larger countries such as the United States and Canada. During World War II, jet technology became refined, and after the war commercial jet applications began. The implications of jet aircraft travel relate not only to speed but also to:

> Range of flight without refueling;
> Higher noise levels (with a few exceptions);
> Runway length requirements;
> Fuel type requirements;
> Fuel consumption; and
> Traffic mix in the flight pattern.

The *subsonic* jet is now state-of-the-art for most air transportation. Decreasing transatlantic or transcontinental travel time down to about seven hours and eliminating refueling stops were highly significant achievements for most of the flying public.

Although *supersonic* transports are still in service in various parts of the world, and the Concorde was reinstated in service after a dramatic crash in the 1990s, there continue to be serious questions in the United States about the acceptability and financial feasibility of these aircraft. Time savings of a few hours (time for which the passenger generally cannot account later!) must be weighed against the cost and environmental impacts of supersonic transports. Nevertheless, at least one US company, Gulfstream, believes a supersonic business jet to be a next evolution of aviation technology.[7]

Rotorcraft: New Functions

The concept of a flying machine that could hover, land almost anywhere, and perform operations without even needing to land was a dream for many aircraft inventors over the years.[8] Its development has evolved to the design and use of very sophisticated machines with range, speed, and load capacity close to midsized, fixed-wing aircraft. Because of their ability to operate from a site as small as a rooftop, increasing numbers of corporations are turning to the use of rotorcraft. Their use has been of major importance in the development of offshore oil resources and servicing of rigs, in forest fire-fighting, in pipeline laying and patrol, in construction of tall buildings, and in search and rescue. They have also been important in activities such as logging, which otherwise requires the construction of roads for access. Rotorcraft, though not a major portion of the total aviation fleet, do comprise a rapidly growing one.

With the downsizing of the military in the late 1980s and early 1990s the supply of helicopter-rated pilots available to meet the growing need by industry continues to be an issue.

Rotorcraft technology is also being updated. According to a recent source:[9]

> "An even more radical aircraft (than new biz-jets) that will be offered for business use is the Bell/Boeing Model 609 tilt-rotor. This six-to nine-passenger, twin-engine aircraft can take off and land vertically like a helicopter yet has the speed and range of a turboprop aircraft. The pressurized $10m aircraft, with an operational ceiling of 25,000 feet, is to be certificated instrument flight and operations in known icing conditions and will have an advanced cockpit and fly-by-wire flight controls."

This tilt rotor aircraft has no current timetable for production; however, it is a major advance in technology that will transform the rotorcraft segment of the industry once it becomes commercially available.

The Full Circle: Ultralights and Homebuilts

It has been said that if the Wright Brothers had had Dacron and aluminum tubing, they would have invented the ultralight. Certainly the appearance and handling of the first generation of ultralights (such as B1-RD and Kasperwing) is very similar to the aircraft in which the Wrights first undertook powered flight.

There has been a tremendous surge of interest in recent years not only in ultralights, but also in related heavier aircraft including the new category of Primary Aircraft approved by the FAA in 1993. Interest has surged in a great array of experimental and homebuilt aircraft. The FAA Recreational Pilot certificate, for ultralight pilots, was supplemented in the late 1990s by a new proposal for a sport license and if this is enacted, could remove one of the significant barriers to becoming a pilot; the Notice of Proposed Rulemaking (NPRM) is pending.[10]

Market Changes of Recent Decades and Their Implications for Aviation

1990s New Wealth

Owing to the booming stock market in the US in the late 1980s and 1990s, and to the major fortunes made by many younger people in computer-based businesses (colloquially known as "dot-coms"), a new generation of younger wealthy people emerged as individuals with discretionary income. According to one source, current wealth levels in the US are as follows:[11]

Households with net worth of:	Number
$1-$5m	16,000,000
$5-25m	500,000
Over $25m	100,000

Some of these people turned to flying as an outlet for their energies and their wealth, and as a business tool, giving a boost to an industry that had seen shrinkage in many areas for over a decade.

9/11/2001—Aviation and Terrorism

Not only were aircraft used directly as weapons of mass destruction on 9/11/01, but also, it appears that potential terrorists had considered additional use of general aviation aircraft—for example, the exploration of aerial application aircraft to spread diseases such as anthrax. The repercussions for flight schools and for GA flights in most areas continue to be substantial. General aviation businesses may experience frustrating new security measures at airports, which while important, may make customer access to the business more difficult. On the other hand, the new security requirements at airline airports may cause a growth in business flying for reasons of speed and perceived safety. Last but not least, the economic damage to the airlines from 9/11/01 has trickle-down impacts to the entire industry, as it is the airlines, through passenger ticket taxes (and Passenger Facility Charges) that pay the majority of the costs for airport improvements to the federal Airport Improvement Program (AIP) and for the operation of the FAA. A decline in airline prosperity affects airport improvements at airports used by GA operators too.

Computers and Exponential Growth in Information

In the larger environment in which US aviation businesses operate, the single most pervasive external change appears to be the advent of the world wide web and the Internet, which together with individual desktop computers have changed how virtually all companies are run and have access to information. For the average aviation business owner or employees, the web is increasing how people learn about industry actions and trends, how data is gathered, and even how communication takes place with clients. It's often also how potential clients find the company. Within the company, a computer likely sits on every desk, used for word processing, accounting, scheduling, billing, training, and many other functions. Computer literacy is a job requirement in aviation, as it is in almost every other industry.

Computers have changed the world in some other ways. First, information travels much more rapidly around the world and the hierarchy of power is being changed now that virtually all levels of employee can access the same data. Second, this technology perhaps even more than most other new tools, has first been used to do better what people were already doing, and second, to do much more. For example, back in the mid-1980s if an aviation industry official or lobbyist gave a speech, it might have been reported in the trade press, and that was it. Now, in the 21st century, that speech is on the web, the trade magazine is on the web, and there may even be a web chat room discussing what was said. Thus, students and practioners alike are at risk of being deluged with information of all types. Furthermore, web information may be more opinion than fact yet with no easy means of determining which is which.

Globalization of the Market

The world is moving rapidly to a global economy and has been doing so for some time. At the macro level, the gross annual output of a number of "transnational" corporations is larger than the gross output of many nations. At the consumer level, one can buy a Coca Cola, Pepsi or fast food hamburger in a great number of countries for which this is not the native fare. Vastly increased global flows include commodities such as money, manufacturing production, imports, information, cultures, and workers. For aviation, the globalization trend means several things: more international business flight in corporate aircraft; more FBO chains looking at establishing overseas operations, and more need to conform with international airspace regulatory bodies, meaning more complex education for pilots making international flights and a tendency to standardize in the US to meet international requirements.

Aviation Milestones of Recent Decades

Industry Development

In the beginning all aviation was experimental. But even before the 1920s there was evidence of market segmentation in the United States. Airmail flights were gradually becoming more sophisticated, thus triggering the development of coast-to-coast air navigation and airfields in the United States. This was the commercial development of the infant industry. Then there were the stunt flyers and barnstormers, who helped to popularize aviation by flying all over the country with their daring feats. The aircraft manufacturers persisted in seeking better and safer designs with more practical applications. The military use of aircraft played—and still plays—a major role in the research and development of new aviation technology. Then there were the airlines, which first developed the airmail business and then eventually developed passenger transportation and carried other cargo. During the 1920s and 1930s (with the support of the Works Progress Administration (WPA)), there was a great deal of activity to develop the airport system. Without this network, no amount of aircraft technology and market development would have led to a viable air transportation system.

In the discussion above about the jet era, the impact of World War II on aviation was touched upon. Post World War II the US economy boomed for three decades, albeit erratically, and general aviation flourished.

Airline Deregulation

The Airline Deregulation Act of 1978 was a major economic milestone in the history of U.S. aviation. By unshackling airline services to be a virtually free-market operation, it eliminated the industry's protected status and most of its subsidized role as an "infant industry." Deregulation permitted the scheduled airlines to abandon unprofitable small points they were formerly required to serve. New, competitive subsidy processes for these small points were established under "Essential Air Service." Many commuter carriers have been successful in bidding for this small community service and receiving federal subsidies to assist them. While the Essential Air Service Program is now substantially reduced in scope, it provided an important boost to small carriers in the years after deregulation.

At the same time, rapid fuel cost increases, fare increases, intensive competition and, in some cases, over ambitious expansion have resulted in major stresses for many of the larger carriers. This has led to numerous mergers and several bankruptcies. As a result, other new markets have opened up for commuters and former air-taxi operators. In the decades since deregulation, fewer and fewer scheduled service points in the United States continue to have nonstop service. This is primarily due to the airlines' development of hub-and-spoke route systems. The economic impact of the deregulation act seems likely to continue and to result in new opportunity for not only scheduled commuters, but also for the traditional FBO charter and air-taxi services.

One of the success stories resulting from the Airline Deregulation Act has been Southwest Airlines. With a "no frills" service and marketing strategy, the company has steadily increased its market area. Beginning as a regionally based carrier, operating primarily in the southwest, it has now expanded its routes to include over half the US.

A unique management style, designed to be both customer and employee oriented, has led to its success. Reducing operating costs by offering a snack only, eliminating boarding passes, and providing quick turn-around times at the gate were all factors. Other more established carriers initially thought Southwest would not survive long. Many of those same airlines are now trying to duplicate the successful strategies initiated by Southwest, and it is also being emulated overseas, for example in the UK where British Airways announced early in 2002 its plans to start a similar service.[12]

The start-up of several new companies since deregulation has helped to keep fares low. Stiff competition has also led to the demise of several companies and has resulted in several mergers. The airline industry continues to be fast changing and volatile due in part to deregulation, and this situation continues to create opportunities for the general aviation industry, as has the 9/11/01 terrorism attack and its aftermath.

Market issues for airport service businesses are discussed more fully in Chapter 3, Marketing.

General Aviation Revitalization Act of 1994 (GARA)

One of the major milestones of recent decades for general aviation is GARA. The GA aircraft production industry had been crippled by a difficult economy and insurance claims with no statute of limitations and with all parties who had ever been involved with an aircraft being at risk for lawsuits in the event of accidents. Product liability insurance was becoming an ever-increasing percentage of the cost of each new aircraft, pushing up prices, and resulting in lower sales. Thus, the insurance costs of aircraft production had to be spread over an ever-decreasing volume of aircraft, resulting in even higher total costs and a higher percentage of the final cost being for insurance. The figures for US new aircraft production hit their lowest in 1978. The result of this downward spiral was, as mentioned, that the nation's GA producers were virtually unable to stay afloat. The industry lobbied for product liability time limits, or tort reform, and finally in 1994 a bill was passed. A news article three years later reported as follows:

> "On August 17, 1994, President Clinton signed into law the General Aviation Revitalization Act (GARA) in order to breathe life into an industry that had lost over 100,000 jobs and experienced a 95 percent decline in production. Today, over three and a half years (sic) after the bill was signed into law, it is clear that GARA has been a tremendous success.
>
> "Thanks to GARA the general aviation industry is in better shape today than it has been at any time in well over a decade. Employment at general aviation manufacturing companies has increased every single year since enactment of the statute of repose. Overall employment at general aviation manufacturing companies has increased over 46 percent since the legislation was signed into law.
>
> "The production of general aviation aircraft in the United States has also increased every single year that GARA has been in existence. The total increase in general aviation production since enactment is over 69 percent. Production of single engine piston-powered aircraft, the type normally associated with the entry-level market, has increased over 103 percent.
>
> "Without GARA many of the positive things that are now happening in the general aviation industry would never have taken place. For example, the world's two largest producers of piston-powered aircraft—Cessna Aircraft Company and The New Piper Aircraft, Inc.—would not be building piston-powered airplanes. Exciting new computer based training programs for the student pilots would not have been developed. And GA Team 2000, the largest "learn how to fly program" in civil aviation history, would not have been launched.

"Clearly, the general aviation industry is in a much different position now than it was before passage of GARA—it has been revitalized. Companies have once again begun investing in general aviation, the industry is growing, and its future outlook is bright. And that, after all, is what GARA is all about."[13]

Since that time, aircraft production has picked up and continues to grow year by year.

The "Revenue Diversion" Issue

Beginning in the FAA Authorization Act of 1982 and repeated with growing emphasis in the acts of 1987, 1994 and 1996, has been strong emphasis on the issue of not diverting airport revenue for non-aviation needs. For example, one small community that was having budget problems wanted to use its airport revenue surplus to support most of its law enforcement budget. The federal position against such revenue diversion, and indeed, against much smaller revenue diversion attempts, is based on the outlook that federal aviation funding is scarce, and thus airports seeking federal funds must first make full use of local funds. Airlines also strongly oppose revenue diversion; at air carrier airports, many have used what is known as the "residual" method of budgeting, meaning that airport administration and improvement costs are recovered to the extent possible from lease, parking and concession revenues, with the remainder or "residual" being collected from landing fees set precisely to cover the residual amount. It is in the airlines' interest for this residual amount to be as low as possible, to keep landing fees low. Thus, the airlines add to FAA's voice in saying that all airport revenues must go back into the aviation system and not elsewhere. Over the years, the focus has not just been on diversion of normal revenues, but on making sure that income is at market or reasonable levels and that no historic "sweetheart" lease or concession deals are sustained that mean revenue is foregone. For example, a Chamber of Commerce had a lease on non-aeronautical airport land for $1 per year. When it was time to renew the lease, the airport authority brought the lease rate up to a market level.

The revenue diversion issue does not directly affect FBOs nearly as much as it affects airport managers and operators. However, all airport businesses need to understand the stringency with which FAA and the USDOT Inspector General are addressing this issue, and where the FBO is also the public airport operator/manager, he or she has a direct need to understand and comply with this situation.

Threat of Airport Closures

In recent remarks, Jim Coyne, President of NATA, indicated that an airport is shut down every week in the US.[14] FBOs are in a most unusual position of being totally dependent on other agencies as their landlords and providers of the essential facilities—runways and taxiways—that make their business possible. If an FBO faces closure of his airport, it is as if a retail merchant is under constant threat of having the access road to his store closed down. The uncertainty can be almost as damaging to business as the actual event. The inventory of airports is not being replaced at anything like the loss rate, and indeed it is usually extremely difficult to make even modest expansions of existing airports. Thus preserving what already exists is a more effective strategy than creating new fields. Strategies for countering the airport closure trend are discussed in Chapter 12, Physical Facilities.

Airport Improvement Funding

Despite a longstanding system of collecting aviation user fees through passenger ticket taxes, fuel fees and other sources of revenue, Congress has traditionally not funded airport improvements to the extent that is either needed or possible. Part of the reason over the years has been because inclusion of the Aviation Trust Fund balances made the national budget look better even though these funds cannot be used for non-aviation purposes. Another problem is that over the years, progressively more of the cost of running FAA, now 100 percent of the cost, has come out of the Fund as opposed to being taken from general revenues. The Aviation and Investment Reform Act for the 21st Century of 2002 may be able to achieve higher funding through a variety of changes in how revenues are raised and spent. This will strengthen the airport system.

Fractional Aircraft Ownership

The ability to own as small a portion as 1/32, 1/16 or 1/8 portion of a business aircraft and have the use of it 25, 50 or 100 hours a year is changing the face of general aviation business travel. One industry specialist suggests that it is the single biggest development in general aviation since World War II.[15] The cost for flying in one's "own" fractionally-owned plane begins to compare extremely favorably with using the airlines. This trend is likely to continue because 9/11/01 means that airline travel is increasingly slow and inconvenient. The full impact of fractional ownership has barely begun to show up in the marketplace and this type of ownership is growing at an extremely rapid rate of 40-50 percent or more per annum. This topic is discussed in greater depth in Chapter 3, Marketing.

NASA's Involvement in General Aviation

NASA has been developing a small aircraft program, SATS, with planes that can use shorter runways, and if this becomes a marketable product, then possibly smaller communities with small landing strips will seek to use their airport as a basis for economic development and growth. However, as one article says:

> "NASA's vision of a future full of aerial taxis depends on airports that are under siege and rapidly disappearing.
>
> "With the introduction of a fleet of automobile-sized, high-tech, on-demand jet-powered aerial taxis and various airspace enhancements, NASA says business travelers could be taking daylong regional jaunts for about the price of coach airfare by the end of the decade.
>
> "Advocates say the Small Aircraft Transportation System (SATS) will be a pressure relief valve for the congested hub and spoke transportation system, a tool that will boost business productivity by cutting travel time in half or more. Not only that, but communities connected to such a point-to-point transportation system—those with an airport—would prosper, in theory."[16]

Transportation Security Administration

One result of the 9/11/01 terrorist attacks is that a new federal security organization was created by Congress—the Transportation Security Administration, which came into being in fall, 2001. This adds a new layer of regulatory requirements to those being transferred from FAA and will increase the complexity, and, no doubt, cost, of tasks that FBOs must undertake.

Revolution in Avionics Technology

The trend continues to smaller, cheaper, and better-computerized gadgets, many of which aid aviation. Examples include Global Positioning Systems (GPS), flight computers/trip planners, transceivers and accessories, cell phones, and CDs, video and DVDs for training and flight simulation. At the same time, the increased amount of controlled airspace and advent of Microwave Landing Systems (MLS), to name just two trends, mean that pilots may be required to have more gadgets to enter certain areas and perform certain maneuvers.

Components of the Modern Aviation Industry

Summary

Today's aviation system has evolved into a number of distinct areas:

> Pilots-at all levels of rating;
> Other aviation support personnel;
> The airport system;
> The air navigation system;
> Aviation manufacturers;
> Scheduled air carriers;
> General aviation, including aviation service centers;
> Aviation interest groups; and
> The governmental regulatory system.

The following sections provide a brief description of the national aviation system. Chapter 13, The Future, offers a more in-depth discussion of key issues, problems, and opportunities likely to affect certain aspects of the system.

Pilots

Pilots in the early 1900s entered aviation from an enthusiasm for testing the new technology of powered flight. World War II and subsequently the Korean, Vietnam and Gulf wars have created generations of pilots trained through the military and later becoming civilian pilots. General aviation is the "low man" on the pilot totem pole, starting with the private license, moving up to higher ratings including the instrument rating and for some, the Air Transport rating. Today, many militarily trained pilots are nearing retirement, and the military system is not supplying aviation with as many people as in years gone by. Also, until the 1980s it was possible to get ratings beyond private pilot through the GI bill, and after this ceased, another source of trainees diminished. Thus general aviation businesses today must look to their own ability to attract pilots into the system. A simpler sport aviation license may increase the numbers of people who then go on to more advanced piloting skills. Nevertheless, GA is likely to continue to see its best-qualified individuals advance up the career ladder from flight instructors to charter to air taxi to corporate, fractional company or commuter and airline employment. GA trains the pilots (and others) and the more sophisticated areas of aviation often benefit.

Other Aviation Support Personnel

The pilot may be the most visible person that the member of the traveling public observes when flying. However, the small aviation business pilot's function would not be possible without the support of the maintenance and parts crews, the fueling person, the reservations and front desk staff, the aircraft and parts factory workers, and numerous administrative, secretarial and bookkeeping personnel. Whether a large business or a small one, these functions are necessary in some degree. In the typical FBO, all these support functions are poorly paid compared with what a qualified person can get elsewhere in aviation, and FBO aviation maintenance technicians suffer perhaps the most from low pay levels.

More on personnel issues is provided in Chapter 5, Human Resources.

The Airport System

The US airport system is the most extensive and sophisticated in the world. It varies widely in its physical quality and the type of traffic it can handle. Over 3,000 airports are designated as essential to the national air transportation system, and are listed in the National Plan of Integrated Airport Systems (NPIAS). These airports vary from major international facilities with several runways and many services, to the single short runway with limited or no services. Nationally there are over 18,000 landing facilities. However, most of these are small private airstrips, or fire fighting strips with very limited facilities and are for use by permission only. Most of them do not have any public services and may only have tie-downs. Of an estimated 5,350 public-use airports, almost half are privately owned and operated directly by the owner or through a contract with an FBO.

The nature of airport usage varies greatly. The most densely populated states are well served by scheduled service airports such as the Kennedy-LaGuardia-Newark trio in the New York area and the Los Angeles International-Long Beach-Burbank-Ontario-Orange County system in southern California. Rural parts of the country depend more heavily on general aviation airports; the most extreme example is the bush areas of Alaska, where many communities have no road access and hopping into a small plane is as natural as driving. In this instance the local airport may be a seaplane facility with floats used in summer and skis in winter.

Airports in the NPIAS have had a reliable funding source for several decades through the Airport Improvement Program (AIP). Funds go into this from airline ticket taxes, aviation fuel taxes, and other sources for redistribution to the various classes of airport in the NPIAS.

Airports are classified in a variety of ways, depending on whether their function or their physical facilities are under discussion. General aviation airports are functionally classified as such and may also be designated as "reliever" airports, meaning they relieve nearby airline airports or the system at large, of general aviation traffic. This increases the capacity and safety at the larger fields by separating out the smaller, slower aircraft from the large jets with their dangerous wake turbulence, and is a major reason why the air carrier system subsidizes the general aviation system thought the AIP's formulas.

The national airport system, as backdrop to the individual airport location of a particular aviation

Rural parts of the country depend more heavily on general aviation airports. Photo courtesy of Skinner Aviation.

business, is discussed in more depth in Chapter 12, Physical Facilities.

The Air Navigation System

The US civil airspace and its management come exclusively under the purview of the FAA.[17] While the Transportation Security Administration (TSA) is currently part of FAA, it will in due course move to Homeland Security. Nationwide, there are 21 Air Route Traffic Control Centers (ARTCCs) that keep track of all traffic flying on Instrument Flight Rules. The ARTCCs transfer traffic to individual air traffic control areas, usually tower areas. En route airways and navigational aids of various types are in place as well as rules for en route and airport vicinity flying.

Flight Service Stations provide information to pilots and enable them to file flight plans. The number of Flight Service Stations has been decreased. Remaining Flight Service Stations have been automated by use of computers and telephone voice systems. Pilots may now receive current weather information for their arrival, departure, and en-route phases of flight without speaking to a "live" briefer. The option of a personal briefing is still there for those who want further clarification or who prefer the ability to converse with an FAA representative.

After several years and many hundreds of millions of dollars, a project to upgrade the FAA air traffic computer system was abandoned in the late 1990s as it was behind schedule and progress was not adequate. Part of the decision to halt the project was also due to discussion, still at a conceptual stage, of privatizing the air traffic control system in the US. However, the newest concepts in airspace safety provide the individual pilot with much greater control and options through the use of high tech tracking systems.

Aviation Manufacturers

The General Aviation Manufacturers Association (GAMA) represents many of the general aviation aircraft manufacturers and their suppliers. Membership includes Cessna, The New Piper Company, Beech, Lear, and others. With McDonnell Douglas being absorbed by Boeing in the mid-1990s, the large US aircraft companies now include Boeing and Lockheed-Martin; the latter focused more on aerospace, and on aircraft engines and parts. Makers of avionics and aircraft components are another important group. Much US aircraft component manufacturing is now taking place overseas because of lower labor costs and the requirements of aircraft sales agreements with overseas buyers.

In terms of total new aircraft sold, general aviation hit its post-WW II *volume* peak in 1978 with the largest number of general aviation aircraft shipped. This represented a high number of low priced aircraft. Today, the dollar value of sales is higher although the number of aircraft is smaller than this peak year figure. Much higher priced aircraft are being sold, to a different segment of the market—business and corporate end users—than was in place in the 1970s. In 1977 a total of 17,811 aircraft were shipped from the manufacturers, compared to an all time low of only 941 in 1992. With the passage of the General Aviation Revitalization Act (GARA) "Tort Reform" bill in 1994 and the growth in fractional aircraft ownership, an upward trend has been developing. In 2001, a total of 2,999 GA aircraft were shipped worldwide as shown below in Figure 1.1.

US military aircraft production added another 54 units in 2001. As may be seen by the average prices of the smaller GA planes shown in Figure 1.1, the need by the flying public for cost effective aircraft is still valid. Interest in general aviation continues to soar as evidenced by the attendance annually at aviation events around the country. For example, the annual convention sponsored by the Experimental Aircraft Association in Oshkosh, Wisconsin generally attracts close to one million participants and over 12,000 aircraft from around the world.

Scheduled Air Carriers

Since the Airline Deregulation Act of 1978, the hierarchy of air carriers has changed both in nomenclature and in role. Industry giants such as

Figure 1.1 » 2001 General Aviation Aircraft Shipments

Company	Number	Value	Value per aircraft
Airbus	5	$180,000,000	$36,000,000
American Champion	56	N/A	
Aviat Aircraft	57	$10,500,000	$184,210
Bellanca	1	N/A	
Boeing Biz Jets	16	$650,000,000	$40,625,000
Bombardier	182	$3,295,134,695	$18,104,395
Cessna Aircraft	1,202	$2,547,548,489	$211,942
Cirrus Design	183	$51,567,936	$281,792
Commander Aircraft	11	N/A	
Dassault	75	$1,963,500,000	$26,180,000
Fairchild Dornier	4	$56,000,000	$14,000,000
Gulfstream	101	$3,201,675,000	$31,699,752
Lancair	27	$9,000,000	$333,333
Maule Air	57	$6,487,786	$113,821
Micco Aircraft Co.	10	$2,350,000	$235,000
Mooney Aircraft	29	$11,675,481	$402,603
Piaggio	12	$56,340,000	$4,695,000
Pilatus	70	$219,150,000	$3,133,071
Raytheon Aircraft	364	$1,441,481,000	$3,960,113
Socata	96	$88,300,000	$919,792
The New Piper Aircraft	441	$243,185,807	$55,144
TOTAL	**2,999**	**$14,033,896,194+**	

Source: General Aviation Manufacturers Association (GAMA), 2002

Braniff and TWA have gone bankrupt or been merged; smaller new carriers have emerged such as Air Tran and Jet Blue. As shown in Figure 1.2, large jet airline aircraft, including all-cargo in 2001 involved 5,108 aircraft, comprising only 2.28 percent of the civil aircraft fleet. Commuters and regionals accounted for 2,427 aircraft, or 1.08 percent. The distinction between these two levels of carriers, which started in 1969, is fast disappearing. The new nomenclature for the carriers is majors, nationals, large regionals, medium regionals, and small regionals. Nevertheless, airlines comprise, by the numbers (not by seats) only a very small proportion of the civil aircraft fleet, as shown in Figure 1.2.

General Aviation

As Figure 1.2 indicates, general aviation aircraft will continue to dominate the civil aircraft fleet, shrinking from 96.5 percent in 1990 to a mere 95 percent by 2013, according to FAA's FY 2002 forecasts. General aviation comprised 96.63 percent of the civil aircraft fleet in 2001, roughly the same percentage as it has been for decades. While the number of seats per GA aircraft, and the range tend to be much smaller, these GA proportions illustrate the huge dimensions of the GA portion of the national transportation system—a portion that is often ignored except by those familiar with the industry. Many corporate aircraft departments and fractional companies have fleets larger than those of some of the smaller scheduled airlines. NBAA describes the business component of GA flying thus:[18]

> "Many companies use business aircraft for transporting priority personnel and cargo to a variety of far-flung locations, including sites overseas. Often, business aircraft are used to bring customers to company facilities for factory tours and product demonstrations. Some individuals, such as salespeople and doctors, use business aircraft to cover regional territories. While the overwhelming majority of business aircraft missions are conducted on demand, some corporations have scheduled operations, known as corporate shuttles, which are essentially in-house airlines."

As shown in Figure 1.3, general aviation also constitutes a very major portion of the system in terms of hours flown.

As is indicated in Figure 1.4 below, the other elements of general aviation flying are also quite diverse and complex.

The most interesting comparison between the scheduled airlines and GA would be seat-hours flown, a data item that is not available from FAA.

Figure 1.2 » US Civil Aircraft Fleet, 1995 to 2013

Type	1995 (Actual)		2001 (Actual)		2013 (Forecast)	
	#	%	#	%	#	%
Large jet air carriers	**4,721**	**2.42**	**5,108**	**2.28**	**7,165**	**3.02**
> passenger	3,897					
> cargo	824					
Regionals/commuters	**2,109**	**1.08**	**2,427**	**1.08**	**4,457**	**1.88**
> turboprops	2,031		1,731		1,563	
> jets	78		696		2,894	
General aviation	**188,100**	**96.50**	**216,200**	**96.63**	**225,300**	**95.09**
> Pistons	152,800		169,000		172,700	
> Turbine	9,600		12,900		16,800	
> Rotorcraft	5,800		7,200		7,500	
> Experimental	15,200		20,400		21,400	
> Other	4,700		6,700		6,900	
TOTAL	**194,930**	**100.00**	**223,735**	**100.00**	**236,922**	**100.00**

Source: Table created from data in FAA aerospace forecasts, FY 2002-2013[17]

Figure 1.3 » Thousands of Aviation Hours Flown, FY 1995 to 2013

Type	1995 (Actual)		2001 (Actual)		2013 (Forecast)	
	#	%	#	%	#	%
Large jet air carriers	12,000	28.29	14,500	30.60	19,400	34.80
- Passenger & cargo combined						
Regionals/commuters	3,817	9.00	3,805	8.04	6,519	11.10
General aviation	26,600	62.71	29,000	61.30	32,900	55.90
- Pistons	20,300		20,500		22,300	
- Turbine	2,900		4,700		6,500	
- Rotorcraft	2,000		2,200		2,400	
- Experimental	1,200		1,200		1,400	
- Other	300		400		400	
TOTAL	42,417	100.00	47,305	100.00	58,819	100.00

Source: Table created from data in FAA aerospace forecasts, FY 2002–2013[19]

Additionally, although also less readily quantified, general aviation industry sources estimate that general aviation carries about one quarter of all air passengers in the United States. This segment of aviation appears to be growing rapidly.

The nation's fixed-base operators provide the airport services to this major segment of the aviation system as well as servicing airlines at a number of the country's major airports. General aviation is a complete array of types of users and varieties of activity. Figure 1.4 suggests a method of organizing general aviation into a meaningful system. It divides general aviation activity into (1) methods of travel and (2) methods of undertaking an operation from the air. This second role of general aviation is a key distinguishing characteristic because airlines provide only transportation whereas GA provides aerial functions of diverse types, many of which are very important to the economy.

Aviation Industry Groups

Many pilot and industry groups represent aviation interests today dedicated to the growth and support of general aviation. As a part of the business plan and marketing efforts of a fixed-base operator, a working knowledge of those organizations and how they might support the goals of the local business can be a strategic part of the overall plan. Appendix I contains a web site listing and brief description of many of these groups and more can be found through links from this database as well as through web searches for specialized topics. The diverse general aviation industry groups are fairly influential given the diverse nature and interests of the industry. Congress, particularly the Senate, tends to be very conscious of the value of general aviation in particular, since given this country's vast size, most of them cannot campaign effectively without using general aviation. Thus, given the relatively small number of aircraft in private ownership compared with autos and trucks (under 200,000 of the former and well over 200,000,000 of the latter), general aviation through its various interest groups, succeeds somewhat effectively in getting attention to its issues. It could probably be even yet more effective if it communicated more successfully with that vast proportion of the American public that as yet knows little to nothing about the industry and may only have been disturbed by a noisy night flight or an air show.

Here is a summary of a number of these organizations.

Aircraft Owners and Pilots Association. AOPA represents 300,000 general aviation aircraft owners and pilots who use their aircraft for noncommercial, personal, and business transportation. AOPA members constitute 60 percent of the active pilots in the nation.

Figure 1.4 » A Taxonomy of General Aviation Flying

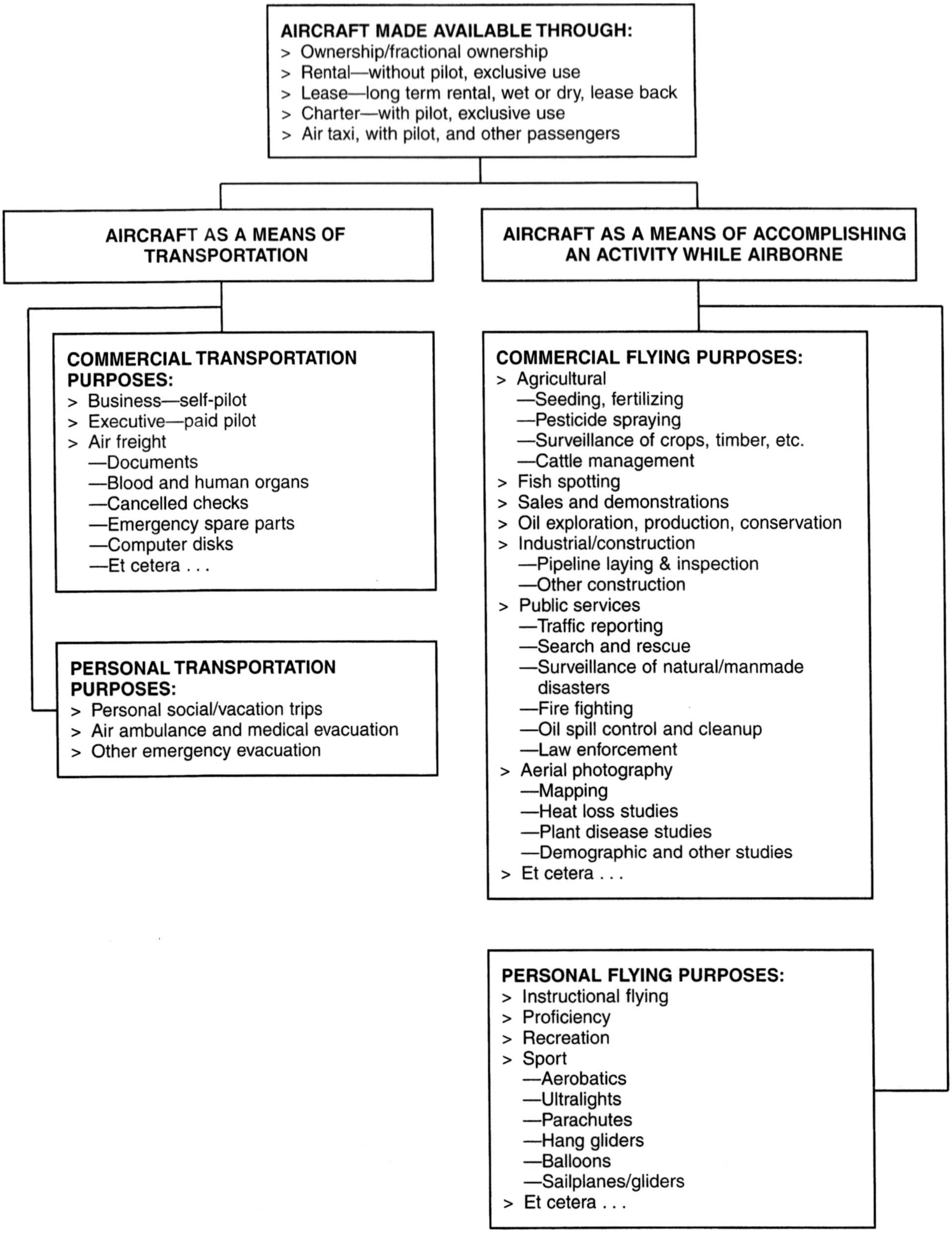

AIRCRAFT MADE AVAILABLE THROUGH:
> Ownership/fractional ownership
> Rental—without pilot, exclusive use
> Lease—long term rental, wet or dry, lease back
> Charter—with pilot, exclusive use
> Air taxi, with pilot, and other passengers
AIRCRAFT AS A MEANS OF TRANSPORTATION
AIRCRAFT AS A MEANS OF ACCOMPLISHING AN ACTIVITY WHILE AIRBORNE
COMMERCIAL TRANSPORTATION PURPOSES:
> Business—self-pilot
> Executive—paid pilot
> Air freight
—Documents
—Blood and human organs
—Cancelled checks
—Emergency spare parts
—Computer disks
—Et cetera . . .
PERSONAL TRANSPORTATION PURPOSES:
> Personal social/vacation trips
> Air ambulance and medical evacuation
> Other emergency evacuation
COMMERCIAL FLYING PURPOSES:
> Agricultural
—Seeding, fertilizing
—Pesticide spraying
—Surveillance of crops, timber, etc.
—Cattle management
> Fish spotting
> Sales and demonstrations
> Oil exploration, production, conservation
> Industrial/construction
—Pipeline laying & inspection
—Other construction
> Public services
—Traffic reporting
—Search and rescue
—Surveillance of natural/manmade disasters
—Fire fighting
—Oil spill control and cleanup
—Law enforcement
> Aerial photography
—Mapping
—Heat loss studies
—Plant disease studies
—Demographic and other studies
> Et cetera . . .
PERSONAL FLYING PURPOSES:
> Instructional flying
> Proficiency
> Recreation
> Sport
—Aerobatics
—Ultralights
—Parachutes
—Hang gliders
—Balloons
—Sailplanes/gliders
> Et cetera . . .

Source: Julie F. Rodwell, 2003

American Association of Airport Executives. AAAE is a professional organization representing the men and women who manage general aviation airports as well as scheduled service fields that enplane some 90 percent of the passengers in the United States.

Experimental Aircraft Association. EAA is a sport aviation association with a worldwide membership of over 132,000 aviation enthusiasts, pilots, and aircraft owners. The organization includes an active network of over 800 chapters.

General Aviation Manufacturers Association. GAMA represents over 40 US manufacturers of general aviation aircraft, engines, avionics, and related equipment.

National Air Transportation Association. NATA represents the business interest of the nation's general aviation service companies providing fueling, flight training, maintenance and repair, and on-demand charter service by more than 1,700 member companies with more than 100,000 employees.

National Agricultural Aviation Association. This is the voice of the aerial application industry. NAAA works to preserve aerial application's place in the protection and production of America's food and fiber supply. Aerial application is one of the safest, fastest, most efficient and economical ways to apply pesticides.

National Association of State Aviation Officials. NASAO represents the state government aviation service agencies in all the states, as well as the aviation departments of Puerto Rico and Guam.

National Business Aircraft Association. NBAA represents the interest of over 3,200 companies which operate general aviation aircraft as an aid to business. NBAA members earn annual revenues in excess of $3 trillion and employ more than 16 million people worldwide.

Professional Aviation Maintenance Association. PAMA is a national professional association of aviation maintenance technicians, with some 4,000 individual members and 250 affiliated company members.

Helicopter Association International. The not-for-profit trade association for the civil helicopter industry. Its mission is: "To provide our membership with services that directly benefit their operations and to advance the civil helicopter industry by providing programs to enhance safety, encourage professionalism, and promote the unique societal contributions made by the rotary flight industry."

Women in Aviation, International. WAI is a professional organization representing the interests of women in all facets of aviation—general, commercial, and military. The organization provides networking opportunities, educational outreach programs, and career development initiatives.

Aviation Regulation

Introduction

The aviation industry is extremely heavily regulated. All aspects are under regulation by FAA-aircraft production, pilots, airspace usage, airport planning, design and construction, and aircraft repair and maintenance. While passenger airlines operating under Federal Air Regulations (FAR) Part 121 are under more stringent controls than the rest of the system (mainly due to rules about pilot duty hours and passenger safety), the entire system must budget time and resources for understanding of and compliance with regulations.

It would be impossible to describe all requirements here; they do change from time to time also. This section summarizes the main considerations and indicates how to get more information.

Federal Aviation Administration (FAA)

The Federal Aviation Administration regulates virtually all aspects of aviation: flight, pilots, aircraft, airports, and the airway system. A list of its aviation regulations is contained in Appendix II. In addition to the Federal Air Regulations, FAA issues "Advisory" circulars on numerous topics, updated from time to time. These are shown in Appendix III.[20] These updates are generally treated like new rulemakings and are published in the federal register for comment, as are new FARs. To the extent possible, each chapter touches on the pertinent FAA or other regulations.

At first glance it may seem confusing as to why FAA regulates different types of flights under three sections of the FARs—part 121, part 135 and part 91. In its discussion about appropriate regulation for fractional aircraft companies, the Fractional Aircraft Ownership Aviation Rulemaking Committee (FOARC) convened to develop a rule succinctly summarizes the differences:[21]

> "In general, airline passengers exercise no control over, and bear no responsibility for, the airworthiness or operation of the aircraft aboard which they are flown. Because the traveling public has no control over, or responsibility for, airline safety-of-flight issues, an optimum level of public safety is provided by the FAA's imposition of very stringent regulations and oversight under part 121 and the sections of part 135 applicable to scheduled service.
>
> "In general, on-demand or supplemental air charter passengers exercise limited control over but bear no responsibility for the operation of the aircraft aboard which they are flown. On-demand or supplemental air charter passengers negotiate the point and time of origin and destination of the flight, and may have the ability (subject to the pilot's supervening authority) to direct or redirect the flight. Under these circumstances, the optimum level of public safety is provided by the FAA's imposition of stringent regulations and oversight under part 121 or part 135.
>
> "In general, aircraft owners flying aboard aircraft they own or lease exercise full control over and bear full responsibility for the airworthiness and operation of their aircraft. Under these circumstances, the optimum level of public safety is provided by the FAA's imposition of general operating and flight regulations and oversight under part 91.
>
> "These policies and differing levels of responsibility were reflected in the development of part 91, subpart D, subsequently subpart F, which governs most business aviation today. On July 25, 1972, the FAA promulgated Amendment 91-101 to 14 CFR part 91 (37 FR 14758, July 25, 1972). This Amendment added to part 91 a new subpart D, applicable to large and turbojet-powered multiengine aircraft. Subpart D was the predecessor to the current subpart F of part 91 (54 FR 34314, Aug. 18, 1989). Section 91.181 of subpart D was the predecessor of current § 91.501 (54 FR 34314)."

National Transportation Safety Board (NTSB)

The NTSB reports directly to Congress on safety and accidents, and provides interpretations of "probable cause" for serious/fatal accidents and incidents. NTSB delegates to FAA and sometimes National Aeronautics and Space Administration (NASA) to help with accident investigations. The NTSB reports also provide recommendations on corrective actions aimed at preventing similar problems in the future. Due to this, FAA and NTSB are often at odds. More on NTSB is in Chapter 11, Safety, Security, and Liability.

Transportation Security Administration (TSA)

The TSA was established in late 2001 as a result of concerns raised by the 9/11/01 terrorist attacks. It has taken over FAA's security regulations, and builds on work by the prior administration, notably the Gore Commission on aviation security. It will have similar powers to FAA in requiring compliance. The agency is too new to evaluate.

Fixed-Base Operators

Fixed-Base Operators: Their Role

For many, the term "fixed-base" operator conjures up images of a gas station for aircraft. While providing quality fuel is a key service, it is far from the only contribution FBOs make to general aviation. They provide the avionics, airframe and powerplant repair and overhaul services needed by the aviation community, not only for routine maintenance but to meet the demands of aircraft that experience problems enroute. They perform major overhauls in specialized locations. FBOs also provide other services, such as aircraft hangaring, flight training, air taxi, and charter services, which help stimulate interest in general aviation and add to the public's understanding of another important segment, business aviation.

The industry has been changing a good deal. The following excerpt from a 1997 article interviewing Paul Meyers, an industry consultant, and Jim Coyne of NATA, sums it up well:[22]

> "The FBO business reached its peak in terms of size in 1980 (sic) when almost 18,000 GA aircraft were delivered in this country and FBO operators totaled 10,000 companies . . . Changes in the economy and regulatory requirements since then, however, have led to the prediction that only 2,000 FBO companies would survive by the year 2000.
>
> "'With the turn of the century looming, it now appears that this dire prediction probably won't happen,' Meyers said. Although estimates vary, some 4,000 FBO companies still exist following a wave of consolidations and business failures that has left the remaining operators on more stable ground economically. That fact, coupled with the improvement in the nation's economy, means that 'overall, things have probably improved in the (FBO) industry,' Meyers said.
>
> "While consolidation has reduced the number of FBO companies over the past decade, other trends are reshaping the traditional profile of this industry as well, according to Jim Coyne, president of the National Air Transportation Association, a public policy group representing aviation businesses, such as FBOs, air charter operators, flight schools and others.
>
> "'Many small GA airports have lost their only FBO over the past few years,' Coyne said, since GA traffic wasn't increasing and fixed costs to the FBO were rising. 'It's not a mystery that many of these companies have been forced out,' he commented. 'Many of them have been in business a long time, but the family (owners) won't keep it going.'
>
> "Another trend in the FBO sector is the decision by some small airports to contract with the FBO to take over management of the airport. 'In those cases, the FBO can survive,' Coyne said. 'It receives revenue from managing the airport as well as from fuel sales.'
>
> "With these economic forces at work, Coyne predicts that by the turn of the century the number of FBOs will drop by another 500, to level off at about 3,500 companies."

The first companies labeled fixed-base operators were easily distinguished from their counterparts known as the field hopping, post World War I "barnstormers". Although exciting and colorful, these transient characters had no fixed base of operations and were pilots first, last, and always. Those who started the first FBOs were also generally pilots. Those who survived financially of necessity became businesspeople committed to providing stable, professional flight and ground services to all customers from a permanent, or fixed, base of operations.[23]

There is great diversity in services provided. Many airports define how many of the following services MUST be provided for an aviation service business to be defined as a full-service FBO at that airport. The array of possible aeronautical services listed by the Federal Aviation Administration is as follows:[24]

- Charter operations;
- Pilot training;
- Aircraft rental and sightseeing;
- Aerial photography;
- Crop dusting/aerial application;
- Aerial advertising and surveying;
- Passenger transportation;
- Aircraft sales and service;
- Sale of aviation petroleum products;
- Repair and maintenance of aircraft; and
- Sale of aircraft parts.

Specifically excluded by the FAA's definition are ground transportation (taxis, car rentals, limousines); restaurants; barbershops; and auto-parking lots—although, of course, an FBO may operate such items.[25]

One Cessna dealer lists the following array:

Transportation:

- Air ambulance;
- Aerial pick-up and delivery service;
- Air cargo in;
- Air cargo out;
- Emergency medical supply;
- Fishing and hunting trips;
- Holiday and vacation travel;
- New business calls;
- Out-of-town conventions and meetings;
- Personal transportation to special events;
- Plant-to-plant company transportation;
- Regular sales calls;
- Transportation of dated articles; newspapers, mail, reports, proposals, retail merchandise;
- Transportation of perishables;
- Trouble-shooting with tools;
- Transportation to hub air terminals;

> Ski trips; and
> VIP passenger service for clients, customers or prospects.

Aerial Functions:

> Aerial inspection and patrol;
> Aerial mapping;
> Aerial photography; and
> Management field inspection.

Scale and Prospects of the Industry

There are still many individual airport service companies. In a 1998 survey of FBOs in Illinois, it was found that they typically provide nine separate aviation services.[26] This study also found that the Illinois operators thought local numbers of FBOs in business would stay the same while state and national numbers would shrink slightly, in the next five years. For the future those surveyed also saw increased FBO specialization, more focus on corporate jet customers, and single FBOs joining chains as the three most likely changes nationally. The existing small number of very large FBOs, such as MillionAir, Piedmont Hawthorne, Signature, Raytheon, AvJet, JetCenters, and Air Kaman with branches or franchises at many airports, (the largest being Signature with over 30 outlets) may increase.

Airport Management

FBOs who also have the responsibility for the management of the airport have a challenging, multi-faceted role. The best interests of the FBO and the (publicly owned) airport may not always coincide; conflict of interest situations are easily developed. Little is documented about aviation businesses that wear dual hats; however, it appears that about half the public use airports (often the smaller, non-NPIAS half) are run by FBOs. These figures do not distinguish between FBOs running airports for either a private or a public owner.

FBO Industry Trends and Issues

Maturity and Professionalism

Early aviation managers or businesspeople no doubt found themselves faced with many technical problems associated with simply keeping the plane airborne. The challenge of the job and the associated thrills may have kept them fully occupied, with little focus on business administration. There appears to have been a historical tendency for the general aviation businessperson to have been primarily a flyer or aircraft mechanic who allowed love of aviation and preoccupation with technical problems to override sound business practices. Conventional wisdom indicates, almost without exception, that inventors and other creative geniuses make poor businesspeople, no matter what the field of endeavor. The early decades of technical genius in aviation were indispensable, but the industry has matured and needs other skills.

The 1980s may have been the decade that first showed signs of being a transition era in the management of many aviation enterprises. The early flyer-turned businessperson, often a retired military pilot, was now becoming a manager with more awareness of the need for a businesslike approach. In many instances, the manager simply acquired this additional insight through training and the necessity for survival. In other situations the second generation in a family business influenced the business and accomplished changes. Additionally, there has also been and continues to be an influx of new professional managers who are bringing new ideas to the general aviation field. Last but far from least, the original post World War II and Korean War "mom and pop" businesses are largely disappearing, bought out by large FBO chains and franchises that have more streamlined central management procedures and training.

When viewing the general aviation business scene, one should bear in mind that most fixed-base operators are nevertheless still very small businesses in a very competitive, volatile, highly regulated industry. Despite this smallness, the FBO manager is called upon to provide a complexity of skills and services common to much bigger enterprises. It is hard to be a manager in any industry—a post that requires wearing many hats and dealing with many types of problem solving; being a manager in an aviation service business is perhaps one of the hardest managerial roles of all.

An examination of many general aviation businesses reveals four unsound business practices:

> Continued investment of money in a business because of a love of flying rather than because of profitability;
> Low rates of return for costly qualification training, capital investments, and operating expenses;
> Lack of adequate record keeping and procedures for monitoring and evaluating performance; and
> Weak marketing and promotional activities.

The anticipated growth in general aviation, the need for high-quality aviation services and the competition for qualified labor are likely to mean that in order to survive in future years, FBOs will become more professional and based less simply on the love of flying. That is, a passion for aviation is a necessary, but not a sufficient condition for aviation business success.

Public Awareness

When the various aviation markets are examined, it seems each acquires a different image. The airlines, at least until 9/11/01 have been commonly accepted forms of transportation, and over 81 percent of the adult population has flown at least once, as shown in Figure 1-5.[27] Air cargo traffic is beginning to be perceived by the public as a vital service, particularly as express package delivery grows in importance. But general aviation still seems to have the silk-scarf-and-goggles image of the barnstorming days. Even major general aviation airports have been referred to by airport commissioners as "just marinas for planes." Some elements of the flying community may heighten this frivolous image by taking unnecessary chances that can result in spectacular accidents and incidents. The negative image may also be heightened because general aviation airports are often located in smaller communities. In such locations, people expect a quiet living situation. Possibly there may be a larger percentage of people who lack basic trust in aerodynamics and who lack awareness of general aviation's key role in the transportation system. As population growth has continuously for the past 50 years brought residential neighborhoods in contact with airports, the negative responses of airport-area populations have almost universally been exacerbated by aircraft noise.

Figure 1.5 » Expanded Market for Flying

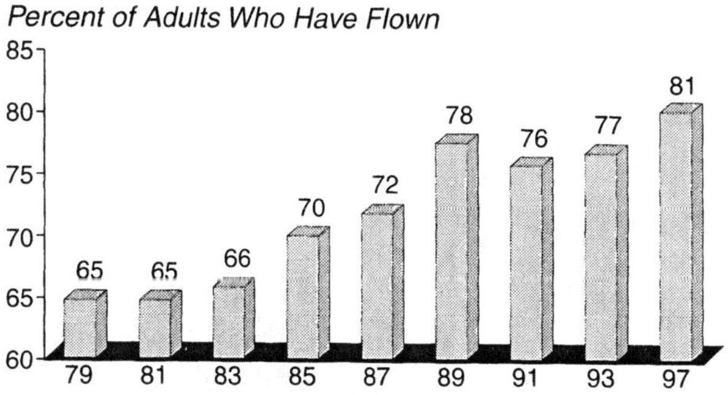

Source: Air Transport Association

As mentioned, the US is losing one airport per week. Nearly all such losses are of GA airports that are the basis for FBOs' livelihoods, since air carrier airports get more support from their neighbors and users who can see a direct personal benefit from having the airport available to them. Furthermore, it is increasingly difficult to site new airports and expand existing fields. For example, a decade-long effort was made in Washington State to find a "satellite" airport to assist Seattle-Tacoma International airport (Sea-Tac) and siphon off 5–10 percent of its flights. Some thirty possible locations were considered, which is in itself a challenge as each must have many precise qualities including flat land, reasonable access to the population to be served, relatively unobstructed approaches, and so on. The 30 were narrowed down to 12, and then narrowed further. Not a single site was found to be feasible, because of community opposition and an effective political protest effort at the state level. The project was abandoned, and no further efforts have taken place to find any relief for Sea-Tac, which like most other major airports in the US has an available capacity through at most 2020 or 2030. This topic is discussed in Chapter 12, Physical Facilities.

The public awareness questions affecting general aviation's future, and thereby the future of the FBOs, include:

> Pollution;
> Noise;
> Land use including encroachment of runway protection areas by development, and addition of noise-sensitive activities in airport surrounds;

Existing airports are increasingly close to full capacity and need relief.

> Community safety;
> Transportation availability;
> Allocation of the costs of the airway system in equitable fashion;
> Access to the airport system for all users;
> Product liability and other legal issues; and
> The image of general aviation.

These issues are discussed in greater depth in Chapter 13, The Future, and touched on below.

Many organizations have campaigns attempting to introduce more people to aviation. Of particular note are the BE A PILOT program, Young Eagles program, Learn To Fly, and Project Pilot.

BE A PILOT is a GA industry sponsored program to increase understanding and knowledge about general aviation and to encourage people to learn to fly. Participating BE A PILOT flight schools offer introductory flights for $49 and BE A PILOT runs TV commercials, print ads and a media campaign to let people know about the flights and the reasons to learn to fly.[28]

The Young Eagles program, initiated by the Experimental Aircraft Association in 1992, intends to introduce one million young people (ages 8-17) to the world of aviation by the year 2003, commemorating the 100th anniversary of powered flight. The full program teaches youth to build their own aircraft. Members of the Association volunteer their time and aircrafts to take the youngsters on an introductory aircraft flight.

The Learn to Fly program, now under the auspices of the National Air Transportation Association (NATA), hopes to encourage more adults to learn to fly. NATA sees a definite advantage to its members, FBO owners and managers, by increasing not only their flight instruction business but also potential sales of new and used aircraft.

The Aircraft Owners and Pilots Association (AOPA) has been promoting its "Project Pilot" program, begun in 1994. Members of AOPA are asked to bring their friends to the airport, take them for a flight, and bring them to a local pilot's meeting, in hopes of bringing another new person into aviation.

All of these programs are efforts to help market aviation to the general public. Obviously, the hope is that many of these individuals will go on to obtain pilots certificates and ratings, becoming "consumers" of aviation. But, the other benefit is an educated pro-aviation citizenry; local members of the community who will not complain about aircraft noise or block expansion of their local airport, etc.

Technical Issues

Fuel prices and availability will periodically be major concerns for general aviation, as they will be for all transportation systems. The possible transfer to alternative fuels appears less easily achieved than for stationary fuel consumers. More fuel-efficient engines and lighter aircraft will continue to be major technical objectives. Quieter aircraft engines present another major technical challenge, although much has already been done in this area. Improved navigational safety and greater crash survivability seem likely to be substantial issues of the coming decades. The pioneers tackled the basic aerodynamic problems leading to successful flight, and the same kinds of innovation and technical skill will be needed to enable aviation to play its full role in the transportation system of the future.

Conclusion

The nation's fixed-base operators are central to general aviation as well as serving many airlines. The skill of their pilots and the FBO's sensitivity to the concerns of the non-flying public, as well as the way they bring new users and advocates into the system, will have much to do with the prosperity of general aviation in coming decades. Failure to develop a more understanding and enthusiastic general public will likely lead to more restrictive zoning, more lawsuits about noise, failure to pass needed bond issues and appropriations, restrictive leases, closure of airports, lack of business support in the community, and limited access for general aviation to the nation's airports and airspace.

Thus the nation's fixed-base operators have more than just the challenge of running a profitable business in a tough economy. They have the wider obligation concerning:

> Technical improvement in the performance and safety of flight vehicles and equipment;
> Improved standards of professionalism and business orientation throughout the industry;
> Reduced fragmentation of the industry; and
> Wider public understanding and acceptance of the general aviation industry and its benefits to the public as a whole.

In sum, the typical FBO owner/manager should be budgeting only about 70 percent of his or her time for internal running of the business, and about 30 percent on outside liaison and education.

Summary

A brief review of aviation history reveals a background of tremendous individual accomplishment in overcoming aviation, technical, and aeronautical problems. The civil aviation industry

DISCUSSION TOPICS

1. What did the Wright brothers achieve that was unlike previous successful flights?
2. Where does the term "Fixed Base Operator" come from? Can you think of a better term?
3. What five aspects of aviation would you feel should be most focused on for the centenary of powered flight? (Kitty Hawk, December 17, 2003).
4. What aspects of aviation are encompassed by the term "general aviation"? Can you think of a better term?
5. What is the future growth potential of the general aviation fleet? Why?
6. Why would a businessperson remain in a low-profit aviation activity?
7. What are the major elements of the U.S. aviation industry?

began to divide in the 1920s into scheduled passenger service and "general aviation." Particularly since the Airline Deregulation Act of 1978, airlines have functioned similarly to other big business by focusing on market opportunities and the bottom line. They have developed management practices as specialized and sophisticated as most other large organizations. By contrast, general aviation is still closer in spirit and functions to the exciting days of barnstorming and record breaking. The industry went through rapid growth until the late 1970s when a variety of factors caused a decline. Since that time, the surviving operators have achieved success largely because of their ability to evolve from aviation enthusiasts to professional managers. As the general aviation industry matures, these trends will likely continue, although there may and should still be a strong experimental and innovative aspect in general aviation design that will affect the whole industry. In short, general aviation will be predominantly a business activity, but there will also be a segment that fly just for the enjoyment.

Endnotes

1. Kane, Robert M. *Air Transportation.* Dubuque, IA: Kendall/Hunt Publishing Company, 2002.
2. Kane, op. cit.
3. Kane, op. cit
4. Kane, op. cit.
5. Constant II, Edward W. *The Origins of the Turbojet Revolution.* Baltimore, MD: John Hopkins University Press, 1980.
6. Serling, Robert J., and the Editors of Time-Life Books. *The Jet Age.* New York: Time-Life Books, 1982.
7. Allen E. Paulson, Chairman Emeritus of Gulf-stream Aerospace Corporation, quoted in Searles, Robert A. and Parke, Robert B. *NBAA's Tribute to Business Aviation.* Washington D.C.: NBAA, 1997.
8. Delear, Frank J. *Igor Sikorsky—His Three Careers in Aviation.* New York: Dodd, Mead and Company, 1976.
9. Searles, Robert A., and Parke, Robert B., see 6 op. cit.
10. For a discussion of the various ways to get licensed for sport flying, see *http://www.aero-news.net/columns/sa/ULAv8r/jthornburgh2000g.htm.*
11. Telephone conversation between the author and Bill de Decker, May 13, 2002.
12. AAAE news article about British Airways, April 2002.
13. *http://www.generalaviation.org/gara/index2.html.*
14. As quoted in "The Evolution of FBO's: Seeking the Perfect Mix," *Airport Magazine,* March 4, 1997.
15. Telephone conversation between the author, Bill de Decker, de Decker and Conklin, May 13, 2002.
16. *Aviation Week and Space Technology,* April 15, 2002.
17. See *http://www.api.faa.gov/clientfiles/CONTENT.htm.*
18. See 6, op. cit.
19. See 17.
20. See *http://www.faa.gov/arp/150acs.htm.*
21. Regulation of Fractional Aircraft Ownership Programs. The Recommendation of the Fractional Ownership Rulemaking Committee (FOARC), presented to FAA on February 23, 2000. See also NATA comments on Docket #FAA-2001-10047: Notice No. 01-08, Regulation of Fractional Aircraft Ownership Programs and On-demand Operations, November 16, 2001.
22. *Airport Magazine,* March 4, 1997. Op. cit.
23. NATA: "Trends Affecting Aviation Service Providers," Prepared by Northwestern University, March 2002.
24. 150/5190-5, Exclusive Rights and Minimum Standards for Commercial Aeronautical Activities makes available to public airport owners, and to other interested persons, basic information and guidance on FAA's policy regarding exclusive rights at public airports on which Federal funds, administered by FAA, have been expended.
25. See above.
26. Worrells, D.S., Ruiz, J.R. and NewMyer, D.A. "The Scope and Status of the Fixed-General/General Aviation Service Industry in Illinois," *The Journal of Aviation/Aerospace Education & Research 9 (3)*(2000). 33-53.
27. Air Travel Survey: Conducted by the Gallup Organization for the Air Transport Association, this detailed 1998 survey describes current trends in air travel demographics, including a breakdown by purpose of trip, number of trips taken annually and destination data.
28. The best way to find more out about the program including all the flight schools who participate- is to go to the BE A PILOT web page at *http://www.beapilot.com.*

2

Management Functions

OBJECTIVES

- Identify the "four functions" of management as they are traditionally set forth, how they specifically relate to the operation of an FBO, and what else management involves.
- Recognize some of the common managerial errors found in business today and how to correct them.
- Describe the elements of a successful business plan.
- Understand the dos and don'ts of delegation.
- Show how good time management techniques relate to good business practice. And, demonstrate good time management concepts that you can implement now.

"Some are born managers, some achieve management, and some have management thrust upon them."[1]

Introduction

The Four Traditional Functions of Management

Management is defined as getting things done through others. This means that a manager's (or supervisor's) primary responsibility is to keep his or her staff effectively occupied on the priority activities of the department or company, reserving to him or herself those tasks that only he/she can do. Its successful accomplishment may require different techniques of delegation for different tasks and people. It appears to be both an art and a science. The FBO owner/manager may be the only manager in the company, depending on its size. In a larger organization the owner/manager will have other departmental managers reporting to him or her.

The basic philosophy of what management *is* derives from a French engineer, Henri Fayol, who in 1916 published a book called *Administration Industrielle et Generale.* This book was translated into English in the late 1940s and its basis was that management activities are divided into four functions:

1. Planning.
2. Organizing.

3. Directing and Coordinating.
4. Controlling.

Yet, it can be very difficult to divide the managerial functions this way. At the end of any given day the typical manager will not likely be able to say, "I spent three hours planning, one hour organizing, two hours directing, an hour coordinating and two hours controlling." Reality just does not work that way. A recent writer in the Harvard Business Review puts the challenge of management as follows:[2]

> "If you ask managers what they do, they will most likely tell you that they plan, organize, (direct), coordinate and control. Then watch what they do. Don't be surprised if you can't relate what you see to these words.
>
> "When a manager is told that a factory has just burned down and then advises the caller to see whether temporary arrangements can be made to supply customers through a foreign subsidiary, is that manager planning, organizing, coordinating or controlling? How about when he or she presents a gold watch to a retiring employee? Or attends a conference to meet people in the trade and returns with an interesting new product idea for her employees to consider?
>
> "These four (sic) words, which have dominated management vocabulary since the French industrialist Henri Fayol first introduced them in 1916, tell us little about what managers actually do. At best, they indicate some vague objectives that managers have when they work."

The article goes on to discuss what managers really do, which cannot be packaged so neatly as M. Fayol perceived. Peter Drucker has said that the purpose of business management is to get and keep customers profitably.[3] That being the case, then the functions of planning, organizing, directing, and controlling are simply tasks performed to accomplish these goals of happy customers and a profitable enterprise.

The typical manager is a problem-solver. He or she also needs to be a visionary leader, yet making sure there are followers! Some managers are caretakers, seeking to get and keep everything running smoothly. Such an approach may not have ever been possible, for there appears to be no time in US industrial history that the economy was in a steady state. Indeed, today a caretaking approach is unlikely to succeed because new and often unpredictable external events affect the general aviation business almost daily.

However, some framework is needed for discussing managerial work, and so these four traditional functions are used in what follows. The ways that these functions are interpreted and carried out will have major results on the success or failure of the enterprise. Management theory has been evolving rapidly in the last 30 years, and there are numerous books, articles, web sites, and professional associations that can assist the aspiring manager.[4,5] For example, there has been much emphasis in recent times on the manager as leader. Yet, if a manager is a visionary leader but impractical and disorganized, the vision will not come to pass unless subordinates take care of the practicalities—and are empowered to provide the consistency and persistence that are needed.[6,7]

The general approach to management tends to look at the internal operations of a company. In the aviation service industry, the typical owner/manager of an FBO will need to budget his or her time to spend perhaps as much as 30 percent of each week on external affairs. This external involvement includes dialog with local businesses about the merits of aviation and their potential use of that airport, time spent with community members concerned about airport noise, and time with local elected officials, especially the local jurisdiction that controls land use around the airport and receives noise complaints, and the airport owners and policy makers, who have it in their control to make or break your business by actions they take to support or limit the airport that you depend on for your livelihood.

Common Managerial Errors and How to Address Them

It is useful to consider the traits of the ineffective manager so that they can be avoided.

There are a dozen problem areas that managers must overcome if they are to be successful.[8]

1. Failure to Anticipate Industry Trends

We are part of a fast-changing economy, and new technology in some other field may affect part of our sales. For example, the facsimile machine has been available since the mid-1970s, but it did not offer good quality until the late 1980s. In the early

21st century, a fax machine is no longer thought of as new technology. Routinely, many information items are being faxed over telephone lines instead of being delivered by overnight small package air express. Any FBO depending heavily on the air courier market may have been significantly affected by this trend, as well as by electronic data transmission through e-mails and attachments, through web-based project management where several workers in different locations interact in real time on an evolving design or writing project, and through teleconferencing.

Managers can address this problem by staying abreast of industry literature, thinking "outside the box" about how new societal trends and technologies may affect their business, and by investigating and pursuing emerging markets early.

2. *Lack of Priorities*

We live in an increasingly overwhelming information environment, making it harder to decide what to read and do. Greater knowledge about the economy, about potential markets, and about new business tools can make the business owner feel indecisive about where to begin. Technology is changing faster than ever; obsolescence arrives before the machine is even paid for and sometimes before we even know how to use it properly. As many business owners have said, "I'm so busy doing the urgent things that there isn't time to do the important things."[9] Going in all directions causes exhaustion and lack of results.

Focusing first on the important and letting non-important and non-urgent matters fade to lower on one's list can help address this. This assumes the manager IS making some kind of priority list and working through it each day.

3. *Indecisiveness and Lack of Systems*

As some businesses grow, they resist the establishment of policies and procedures. The owner/manager thinks out how to proceed each time, even though similar situations arise again and again. Worse yet, the manager makes a decision, the staff starts implementing it, and a week or two later management revises it.

Companies of any size need rules about who can make what level of decision, and standard occurrences need standard procedures, manuals, and policy guidelines. It is a managerial task to break work down into steps and memorialize these written forms into written formats so that they do not have to be continually reinvented.

4. *Poor Time Management*

The average manager gets interrupted once every eight minutes. This means that even large tasks must be managed in less than eight-minute segments. The manager must expect and welcome interruptions because getting staff questions answered enables them to be fully productive and stay on task.

The manager must be extremely disciplined about getting back on task after each interruption. Failure to do so is the most time-consuming consequence of interruptions. It may be desirable to set up specific drop-in times where interruptions are invited, in order to prevent them from happening all the time. This topic is discussed in more depth below with many more suggestions for solutions.

5. *Poor Communication Skills*

Since the manager's results are manifested only through the work of his or her subordinates, then the ability to communicate clearly what one wants is crucial. This is discussed more fully in Chapter 5, Human Resources.

6. *Lack of Personal Accountability and Ethics*

Even though a manager delegates a task, he or she is still responsible for the result. If the delegatee failed to produce, it becomes the manager's responsibility, including finding a timely remedial action, so that the project can still be salvaged.

By modeling personal accountability and ethics, the manager encourages similar behavior among staff. The business ethics issue is discussed at greater length below.

7. *Failure to Develop, Train and Acknowledge People*

A knowledgeable manager may have a better understanding than any of his or her staff about what the proposed project should look like. Unless staffs are given a chance to grow to a comparable level of knowledge, understanding, and initiative, the manager will not get satisfactory results from them. More on how to "stretch" people is discussed below under "Delegation" and Chapter 5, Human Resources, reviews training and recognition. Also, even modest performers need appreciation and acclaim.

8. Failure to Support Company Policy in Public

When talking to one's team, an attitude that says, "We've got to do this even though we don't like it because the higher-ups say so," is more likely to engender reluctance than enthusiasm.

Good managers express their reservations and concerns to bosses in private, and sometimes they are persuasive enough to get their way. If they lose the argument they support the boss's decision gracefully (or quit).

9. Failure to Acknowledge and Accommodate People's Workstyles

Numerous testing instruments divide people into four or more types.[10] Each type has a vastly different style of learning, working, and thinking. The various types of people may have difficulty respecting other styles of thinking and problem solving than their own. This can create conflict and lack of forward motion on assigned work.

Effective bosses, regardless of their own style, carefully (and formally or informally) identify the styles of their people and use this knowledge both in what they assign to whom, and how they manage the assignees. A good manager knows this is the way to get the most out of everybody. Management also needs to teach people having the various styles, how to recognize and respect each other's strengths and perform teamwork with people completely unlike themselves.

10. Failure to Focus on Profit

Ignorance of business results and lack of awareness about the comparative success of one's different products and services can be a major downfall.

In most companies, sales and profits are the key objectives, and everything else undertaken must keep this in mind. Different workers may bring about profits in different ways; problems should be resolved primarily because lack of resolution will affect profits.

11. Failure to Recognize Needs People Fulfill from Working

There are diverse viewpoints about the needs people hope to meet from working. Chapter 5, Human Resources, discusses these in more depth. Many studies about motivation indicate that people want to do a good job and to be shown greater challenges by a supportive boss. The manager who behaves unpredictably, or who manipulates people for his or her own ends, who is dishonest about use of time, who is not accountable or who attempts to be a buddy with subordinates will generally create a counterproductive level of discomfort.

By contrast, a boss who sets out clear expectations, praises equal work with equal praise and in other ways plays fair will generally get more than adequate work from people.

12. Failure to Establish and Adhere to Standards

Lack of standards means that staff does not know how high the bar is set and what good performance is supposed to look like. Not knowing may mean not delivering.

Standards permit all staff to be treated alike. In recurrent task areas, they must be established and then all violators treated the same way (see the discussion of the "red hot stove" rule in Chapter 5, Human Resources). Incompetence must not be tolerated no matter who is the source.

Planning and Organizing

The Need for a Business Plan

The first two functions of management—planning and organization—should be a daily process for the manager. Much can also be gained by formally structuring these processes into a written business plan. The aviation manager wears the many hats of the entrepreneur and does so in an organization that has more than the average number of service lines, each with different levels of sophistication. The FBO manager must also cope with the very rapid rate of change that continually occurs in aviation. New equipment, changing regulations, advancing technology, and a volatile market all contribute to a rapidly changing environment.

A sound planning process is a necessity in this kind of environment. The effective utilization of a planning process becomes a way of life for the successful manager. Planning falls into two areas: objectives planning and operational planning. Objectives planning concerns the things the business owner wants to accomplish, the vision, the long range ideas and the business mission. Operational planning concerns the methods used to achieve them. Objectives planning deals with specific long- and short-range targets for the organization. It is the subject of the following paragraphs. Operational planning deals with the development of policy, procedures, rules, and standards used to run the business. This is the topic of Chapter 6, Organization and Administration.

Some business owners will argue that in a changing world it is impossible to plan effectively, so it is better to simply seize opportunities as they present themselves and not formulate any kind of plan. Here are some considerations in relation to this approach:

1. If the business has not specifically selected a market niche, it will tend to pursue all opportunities without priority. Time and energy may be wasted pursuing activities that are not central to the company's strength areas. In the meantime, more valuable opportunities may be overlooked. Furthermore, the company will present no clear image in the marketplace.
2. Customers who know the direction the company is going will tend to plan their own needs around the future availability of services. For example, a businessman thinking of learning to fly may choose a flight school based on the fact that starting next year it will be offering instrument instruction. The flight school needs to not only plan, but also let its plans be known.
3. Customers who know your business and service area priorities will refer customers who need those services to you.
4. Setting ambitions through expression of achievable goals is often a self-fulfilling prophecy. The very process of setting higher goals tends to shift the employees "comfort zone" of what is attainable. Well thought-out, well-expressed goals seem to create a synergy of their own, such that time after time, fortuitous occurrences will take place in support of these goals.
5. A business plan can be written for each and any new business project such as a new product line. The analysis required for a written feasibility study or plan will help to make it very clear what time and money commitments will be needed to get the new line into place on a profitable basis.
6. Last but not least, any business that may ever need outside financing must have a written business plan in order to attract suitable lenders.

A business plan is only valuable if it is examined and evaluated frequently and its results compared to the original objectives. It is a living process, not a beautifully bound report on a shelf.

Most business experts place great emphasis on a written business plan. Even for a new company or one that is in a very volatile market, such as general aviation, it should be specific, written and made available to all managers, and periodically reviewed and updated.

Business Plan Outline

A suggested outline for a full business plan is shown in Figure 2.1. The numbers after each section indicate a practical order in which to write the sections. It is vital to have a one or at most two-page executive summary with 1–2 figures. That may be all some audiences such as bankers may read!

Mission Statement

The mission statement should answer the questions "Who we are, what we do, and why we're different." It can be quite short, such as the following:

Figure 2.1 » Business Plan Outline

A. EXECUTIVE SUMMARY (12)
> *Mission Statement*—definition of business purpose, product and market. Method of sales and distribution.
> Values.
> Brief description of management team.
For Seeking Capital or Loans:
> Summary of financial projections.
> Amount, form and purpose of money being sought.

B. COMPANY HISTORY AND BACKGROUND (10)
> Date and state of inception, form of company.
> Principals and functions of each.
> General progress to date.
> Successful strategies to date.
> Most urgent issues to be addressed.
> Other general context.

C. INDUSTRY OVERVIEW (2)
> Current status and outlook for industry.
> Specific industry-related issues (economic, social, technological, regulatory).
>Areas of growth and opportunity.
>Performance of primary participants.

D. PRODUCT(S)/SERVICES (1)
> Description.
> Research and development.
> Future development.
> Environmental factors.
> Policies and warranties.

E. MARKETING ANALYSIS (3)
> Market definition.
> Market size.
> Market trends.
> Competition.
> Competitive advantages/disadvantages.

F. MARKETING PLAN (4)
> Potential target markets, estimated sales, market share.
> Strategies.
> Pricing.
> Sales and distribution.
> Suitable promotional methods and costs.
> Promotional mix and total budget.
> Evaluation/effectiveness plans.
> Stationery, logos and image.

G. LEGAL REQUIREMENTS (9)
> Legal structure of the business.
> Licensing, trademarks, patents.
> Certification.
> Insurance.
> Codes or zones affecting business.
> Anticipated changes affecting business.
> Company name.

H. PERSONNEL (6)
> Number and type of employees.
> Labor issues and compliance.
> Sources of labor.
> Changes anticipated.

I. OPERATIONS (7)
> Location.
> Plant and/or office facilities.
> Equipment.
> Methods of production and manufacture.

J. MANAGEMENT (5)
> Organization.
> Key people and resumés.
> Strengths and weaknesses.
> Professional advisors.

K. FINANCIAL INFORMATION (8)
> Funding requested (if appropriate).
> Desired financing.
> Capitalization.
> Use of funds.
> Future financing needs.
> Current financial statements.
> Financial projections.

L. APPENDIXES (11)
1. Goals.
2. Objectives.
3. Functional Schedules, Gantt Charts, etc.
4. Information Systems.

Source: Julie F. Rodwell, 2003

"To be the best quality repair, instruction, and flight service facility within a fifty-mile radius of xyz"; or

"To provide the lowest cost fuel and services and maximize transient traffic."

There can be different mission statements for each segment or profit center in the business. Another way of considering the mission statement is to answer the question "What business (es) am I in"? The functions enjoyed most by the owner may be neither the most needed nor the most profitable functions. The manager should consider why customers use aviation to meet their needs and whether the business is primarily service or product oriented.

Values

The most successful businesses seem to be those that (1) stay close to the customer and (2) operate with real concern for employees.[11,12,13] A value statement combining these two concerns might be "Our top priority in Xyz Company is customer satisfaction, and our only means of achieving it is through each and every employee. We want happy employees so that we will have happy customers."

Other values could apply, such as quality, durability, reliability, speed of service, and friendliness. The important thing is to spell out the paramount value or values so that all members of the firm know what comes first. Companies with a strong "corporate culture" have a better chance of dealing with difficulties.

Market Niche and Goal

This part of the business plan should discuss the total market for the company's products or services, and the precise niche or segment of that overall market that this company hopes to serve. It will include whatever ways the company's products or services differ from that available elsewhere and should relate closely to the mission statement.

Company History and Background

This section, primarily for readers outside the company, can also be useful for orientation of new employees.

Industry Overview

The FBO may be in the mainstream of industry trends or may already have one or more specialty niches that are atypical of the industry. Periodic evaluation of major factors and trends affecting the whole industry is important. Also, it may be valuable to examine national economic and demographic trends that do NOT at first appear to have much to do with aviation, (e.g., the aging of the population). Some open-ended brainstorming on such issues may yield both threats and opportunities. An example—an aerial application firm may want to assess in its market area what is the trend toward organic foods, which means fewer farms using pesticides and thus less demand for the aerial applicator's services.

Products

This section provides the opportunity to examine not just the present product and service mix, but also key technological, institutional, environmental, and market changes that may affect the product mix.

Marketing Analysis

The marketing analysis will likely be addressed separately for each product line. Some products and services may have a highly local market (e.g., a flight school). Others may have national markets, such as a maintenance shop certified to do major overhauls of specific types of aircraft engines.

Marketing Plan

Some new activities may not need much marketing. Perhaps something new is being offered based on "market research" in terms of customer feedback, which is an excellent way to find out what the existing client group wants. Then a way to market it may be simply to enclose a flyer with billings, tell each customer as they come in, and so on. But this may not be sufficient to spread the word and gain new customers. The choices of marketing and sales techniques are discussed more fully in Chapter 3, Marketing and the precise approach will probably need to be developed on a case-by-case basis. It is useful to keep track of what worked or didn't in a promotional campaign so that the plan can be more finely honed the next time. Again, the plan requires segmentation into individual tasks with deadlines, quotas, and staff assignments. One fundamental marketing element in today's world is a company web site with easy to find contact information and a summary of the various services offered.

Legal Requirements

In many cases, such as obtaining business licenses, legal requirements are a one-time process. However, the FBO should not assume that this is always so. A current example is the underground storage tank issue, where tough environmental requirements are causing FBOs (and others) to look very carefully at both past and future operations relating to fuel storage. The legal structure of the business should also be re-examined periodically as the business changes.

Personnel

Written organization charts and job descriptions are an important starting point, though in some cases they are only that. Staff in a small business may need to perform more than one job, and special task forces, quality circles, and the like are increasingly supplementing organizational structures. But even these more nebulous arrangements generally lend themselves to some kind of description and narrative. This topic is discussed more fully in Chapter 5, Human Resources, and Chapter 6, Organization and Administration.

Operations; Production Plan

This part of the business plan reviews physical requirements, supplies, materials, labor, office equipment, and other items needed to actually produce the goods and services. These areas are reviewed more fully in Chapters 8 through 10 and in Chapter 12. Plans describe the overall functions of each division of the firm, and tasks describe individual work assignments to that end.

Management

This may include a review of key people, strengths and weaknesses, and include on-going resources available such as a financial or management consultant used on a periodic basis. These topics are crucial to any business plan seeking outside investment, but should not be ignored even if the business plan is for internal use only.

Management information can have other uses such as selling company services to a major corporation and for public relations. A small brochure may be appropriate, especially one separate from the rest of the business plan document.

Ownership information may or may not be appropriate in a plan to be shared with all employees; in any case, it requires some consideration, especially in a very small and/or family-owned business where the sudden absence of key people might cause the firm to flounder. The succession needs to be spelled out clearly, and key-person insurance may be a consideration.[14]

Financial Information

In some cases it may be desirable to set up a financial plan for a period of 20 or 30 years, if this is the length of a new FBO lease or the anticipated retirement date of the owner. In other cases, a five-year period may be sufficient. In a new business, particularly one that is seeking financing, the first year should be presented on a month-by-month basis. In the case of a new project or firm, the financial plan should include a profit-and-loss statement, a balance sheet showing assets and liabilities, and a cash-flow analysis showing the break-even time. This will also show the cumulative amount of cash needed before a positive cash flow begins. Another useful feature of the financial plan can be criteria for new expenditures (e.g., those related to production or sales volume). These topics are discussed more fully in Chapter 4, Profits, Cash Flow, and Financing.

Strategy and Objectives

For a long-established firm, the strategy for becoming established in a market niche may already have been accomplished. However, new market opportunities arise constantly, and if a decision is made to pursue them, a strategy is needed. The strategy statement must discuss the new product in terms of its features, benefits, and pricing, its means of production, the sales and promotional activity, and the cost of getting it launched. Setting objectives means choosing specific, measurable targets with dates attached.

Growth Strategy

Once the target level of activity is reached for a product or service, several growth strategies are possible for successive time periods. For example, the sequence or choice of strategies might be:

1. No growth. (Note that in a growth market this necessarily means declining market share.)
2. Maintenance of market share, i.e. growth at the pace of the total market.
3. Growth to a specific, higher dollar volume or market share by a certain year, with annual rates of growth till then.
4. Growth till some perceived point of diminishing returns. For example, a repair shop might grow only until utilization of the repair hangar reaches the maximum point, stopping short of the need for and expense of a new hangar.

Growth will be limited by the competition, national trends in aviation, and by the business cycle. A detailed growth strategy will need to look carefully at the actual and potential profitability of each service or product, which is a topic discussed more fully in Chapter 4 Profits, Cash Flow, and Financing.

Functional Schedules

In the appendix section of the business plan, it may be appropriate to develop more detailed schedules than in the main text of the business plan by using PERT (flow diagram) and Gantt (timeline) charts as well as matrices that show the assignments of staff to tasks. Software such as Microsoft Project is available to produce these.

Information Systems

The best plan in the world is of little value if there is no way of telling whether it is being successfully implemented. Information on the competition, industry sales, new clients acquired, costs, productivity, profit by area, promotion results, and so on must be collected regularly and organized into quickly usable formats. As when flying a plane, the quicker you know you are off course, the easier it is to get back; the sooner you know that turbulent times are ahead, the easier it is to enact contingency plans that will keep you safely aloft. This subject is reviewed in depth in Chapter 7, Management Information Systems.

Directing, Coordinating and Controlling

Managing Versus Doing

Poor delegation is probably the typical manager's greatest weakness when it comes to the second two management functions-directing and controlling. The more one is a manager, the more one must obtain results through others and the less by doing things oneself. And yet, some technical knowledge and interest in specific aviation activities is what brings a person into the business, and indeed, equips them to delegate with some knowledge about what it takes to do the job. Also, particularly in the FBO business, employees tend to be promoted up the ranks and may well become managers and supervisors without ever having had any exposure or training in how to get work done through others, as opposed to doing it oneself.

Most individuals start off in the working world by acquiring a technical skill or specialty. Most aviation managers start with an interest in aviation and some professional qualifications. Their career track may have included being a corporate pilot, mechanic, flight instructor, aircraft production worker, or simply a private pilot and aviation enthusiast. When the opportunity came along, they moved into a managerial position, either as an owner or an employee. Such a move required that they begin performing different activities, such as planning, organizing, directing and controlling the work of others, rather than doing wholly technical or line activities. In an FBO this tends to mean more office work and less time in a plane or a hangar. This changing role requirement is illustrated in Figure 2.2.

Studies of successful and unsuccessful managers indicate that the successful ones are paying close attention to planning, organizing, directing, and controlling others. The less successful ones are spending most of their time doing other things. In a study by the Small Business Administration, the success of a business was found to be in direct proportion to the owner's possession of these talents:

> Alertness to change;
> Ability to adjust or to create change oneself;
> Ability to attract and hold competent workers;

Figure 2.2 » Managing Versus Doing

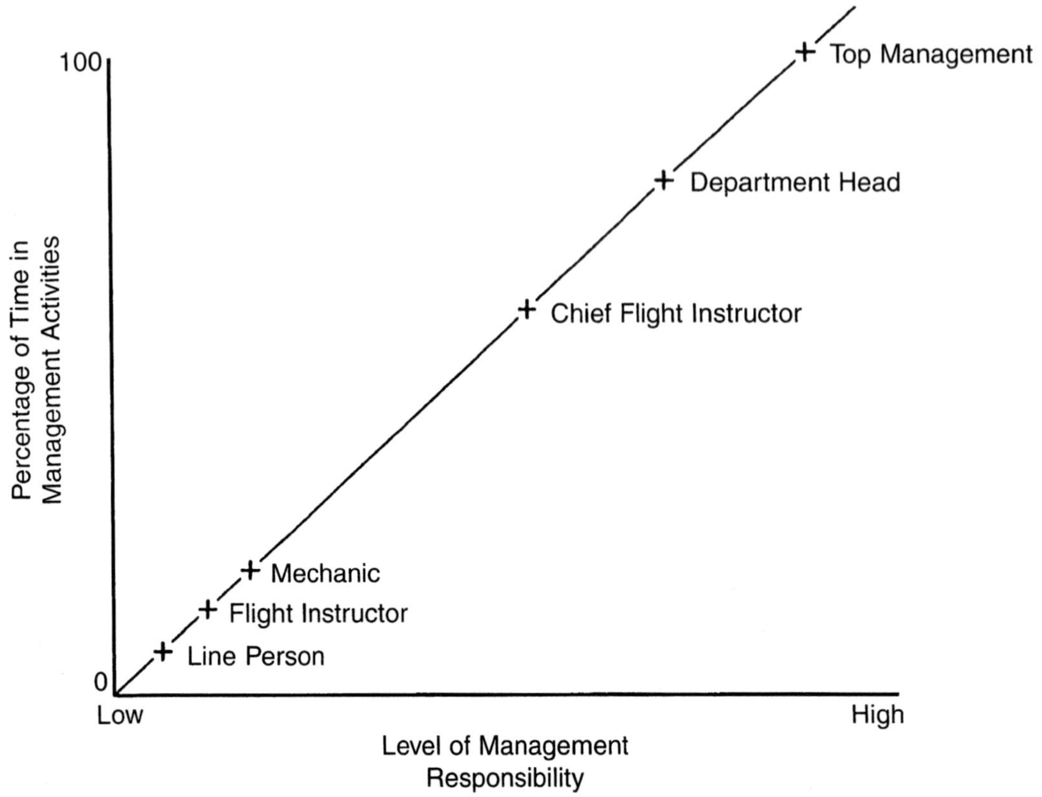

- 180-degree vision with respect to operating details; and
- Knowledge of the market—customers and their needs.

A difficulty for the FBO manager in a very small firm, one with ten people or less, is that he or she never will be able to devote 100 percent of the time solely to managing, but must generally spend part of the time in line functions. This is because of the long hours most FBOs must be available and the mixed array of services they offer. Managers in such a position may need to specifically divide each day into "doing" and "managing" times, make sure that the precious and limited managerial time is blocked out to minimize interruptions and assigned to top-priority important issues.

Style of Problem-Solving and Delegation

There are many styles of delegation, and any that gets both short- and long-range results is successful. Much has been written about whether the autocratic or the democratic approach is most suitable. The choices appear to be on a spectrum, as follows:

- The manager makes a decision and announces it;
- The manager "sells" a decision;
- The manager presents ideas/decisions and invites questions;
- The manager presents a tentative decision subject to change;
- The manager presents the problem, gets suggestions, and then makes his or her decision; or
- The manager—or another staff member—presents the issue and the entire work team brainstorms solutions and chooses how to proceed using consensus.

In general, U.S. management style appears to have shifted from the autocratic toward the participatory during the past four decades.

Leadership Styles

The successful leader is one who wants others to be successful in the business and who is a supercoach, most of the time, rather than a star player.

One myth of leadership is that leaders are born. People are born with a degree of health and intelligence, but leadership can be learned. The following is intended to be a basic introduction to some basic leadership styles and their definitions. It is by no means a comprehensive examination of this topic.

Authoritarian Leader. This type of leader claims power, not through personal endorsement, but through the position held. This is often referred to as "situational" leadership. Characteristics of an authoritarian leader include:

1. Adheres to a schedule.
2. Likes things in their proper place.
3. Planning is very important (everything worked out ahead of time).

The only creativity allowed is that brought in by the leader. The leader presents directives, not alternatives. Others are eliminated from making decisions. People who are insecure like this kind of leader.

Therapeutic Leader. This type of leader does not want to make anyone angry and fears hurting anyone's feelings. This leader is more concerned that people like him/her personally.

This leader would rather form a committee than make a decision personally. In the end no one may be satisfied. Characteristics of a therapeutic leader include:

1. Personable-wants to be everyone's friend and is usually well liked.
2. Spontaneous.
3. Adaptable to change (ideas are often those of the last person spoken with).

This type of leader does not concentrate on him or herself, but rather on subordinates. However, this is often due to poor self-esteem.

Charismatic Leader. Eleanor Roosevelt, John F. Kennedy, and Bill Clinton may be mentioned when listing people with charisma. There may be a tendency to narcissism, which will weaken the leader's influence. Characteristics of this type of leader include:

1. Invites others to identify with them.
2. Protects others (makes them feel strong).

Each of the three styles of leaders has implications for the decision-making process and for the manager's role as a change agent. No one person fits neatly into any one of these styles. There are fragments of all of them in all administrators. Any kind of leader is accepted by some and rejected by others. It depends on the needs of the followers or employees.

If the employees are in need of inspiration they will want a charismatic leader. If answers are needed the authoritarian leader will be preferred. And, if understanding is the major need, a therapeutic leader will be considered best. The good leader needs to fit all these needs. This is part of what makes it so difficult for a leader to be truly effective.

Objectives of Delegation

An autocratic view of management might be described as a system set up with only the manager's immediate personal needs in mind; thus, its objective is mainly to free the manager's time for other important tasks. The staff is to do the manager's bidding, preferably carrying out tasks as closely as possible to the manner in which the manager would carry them out. This manager is happier the more closely his or her subordinates are able to function as "clones."

An alternative perspective is that "freeing up" the manager is only a minor purpose of delegation. A fuller list of the purposes of delegation includes:

- Leaving the details to others;
- Getting the job done;
- Allowing key management staff to take initiative;
- Keeping things going in the boss's absence;
- Raising the level of employee motivation;
- Increasing the readiness of subordinates to accept change;
- Improving the quality of all managerial decisions;

> Developing teamwork and morale; and
> Furthering the individual development and growth in skills of employees.

The degree of delegation depends on the level of skill available, the central or peripheral nature of the task, its urgency, and the manager's other priorities.

Managerial Control

Delegation of authority for a task does not mean giving away control or accountability. A manager in delegating work must:

> Spread the work realistically among available aides;
> See to it that the job is done correctly;
> Have enough time to take corrective action should something go wrong; and
> Develop the subordinates' talents and abilities.

To accomplish these ends, a process of auditing the progress of the task is needed, but without constantly peering over the person's shoulder or being rigid about how the task is done. Methods for keeping track include:

> Verbal reporting at prearranged points or dates;
> Written reports on progress;
> Scheduled conferences;
> Setting deadlines for results;
> Checking results; and
> Measuring results in related areas (e.g., changes in the number of complaints).

When the task is clear from the outset, product inspection and deadlines, with some intermediate status reporting, may be successful. When the task itself still requires definition, the manager may assign various specific tasks to different people and schedule a conference at some reasonable future date to decide what the problem is and to design and assign a course of action. In the case of new problems or new employees, where untrodden ground is to be covered, it is advisable to delegate only small, highly specific tasks with short deadlines. Then one can evaluate quite soon the person's response to the issue, and whether supervision and other expertise are needed. Throwing people into the deep end to see how they do is usually unproductive and demoralizing. Also, it is easier to gradually give out more responsibility based on good results than it is to take it away once it has been given.

Choosing the Areas to Delegate

One of the most crucial questions for a small business is what areas to delegate on a consistent basis. Lower level managers constantly encounter the need for decisions ranging from a trivial to a serious nature. They would consume your entire day with questions if they did not have some basic guidelines. The general level of responsibility given to line managers must be tailored to each company, but some possible criteria include:

> The owner approves all decisions relating to spending the company's money (e.g., overtime, new promotions, equipment), or all decisions above some modest amount;
> The owner is the final decision maker on hiring and firing, or at least above a certain level of management;
> The owner decides about new services to be offered; and
> The owner makes or approves all public statements to the media, politicians, and so on.

Dos and Don'ts of Delegation

One of the biggest complaints of managers is that they cannot "get the monkey off their back," that is, the task delegated to a subordinate is brought right back and for various reasons becomes the manager's problem again. Successful delegation requires that the delegatee actually perform most if not the entire delegated task. How can this be accomplished? One useful rule-of-thumb is the 80:20 rule. Delegate tasks to people who are 80 percent ready to handle them. Give clear instructions and establish mechanisms and timelines for checking how things are going. There will seldom be anyone who is 100 percent capable of doing the task. The autocratic manager knows that he or she is the only one really competent to do it. At 80 percent readiness, the person will handle most of the assignment, will grow in the process, will ask some questions, and will generally advance to virtually 100 percent readiness for next time. At 50 percent readiness, a person will be intimidated, overwhelmed, and anxious, ask too often for help, and may make serious mistakes—or do nothing until right before the deadline. It is the manager's business to know how ready each employee is for specific new functions. Figure 2.3 offers some dos and don'ts for successful delegation.

The Decision-Making Process

In an established enterprise where basic authority has been clearly delegated to certain people for certain things, few if any questions should arise about who should decide what. Indeed, nothing but routine decisions should be taking place. Such periods of stasis are, however, the exception rather than the rule in small businesses and in aviation businesses in particular. The need to react frequently to rapidly changing conditions is what one author considers the crucial difference between entrepreneurs and executives. The latter are characterized as having a custodial role and temperament while caring for an existing empire.

A sound decision-making process involves seven steps:

1. Setting company goals and objectives as a context for the decision.
2. Diagnosing the problem or issue precisely—not the symptoms, but the causes.
3. Collecting and analyzing data about the problem or issue.
4. Developing an array of possible alternative solutions, including a do-nothing option.
5. Through brainstorming, mind-mapping, and the like, use the rule that "all ideas are good" at this stage.[15]

Figure 2.3 » Dos and Don'ts of Delegation

1. Select the right person for the job. Don't just dump it on the first person that comes to mind. The right person will depend on how urgent the job is and whether you can afford the time to give the assignment to a less experienced employee. Urgent tasks must usually be assigned to old hands.
2. Set the climate for a comfortable briefing. Don't delegate on the run. Encourage the delegatee to ask questions.
3. Encourage the free flow of information. Don't forget to impart everything you know about the assignment, including any existing materials.
4. Focus on the results, the *what*. Don't stress the *how*, unless there's absolutely only one right way.
5. Delegate through dialog. Don't do all the talking yourself.
6. Set firm deadlines, both interim and final. Don't leave due dates uncertain, but work them out with delegatee's input, given other projects and plans. Interim dates allow time to rescue the project if necessary.
7. Be certain the person is pointed toward all the necessary resources. Don't leave them wondering where to start.
8. Turn over the entire job to one person. Don't give bits of it to several different people.
9. Give the person the full authority to do the job and make this clear to others through staff meetings, memos, and phone calls to peers in other departments. Don't set them up to fail.
10. Offer guidance without interfering. Don't fail to point out the minefields. Don't cross wires by making your own contacts with people you have told the delegatee to consult.
11. Establish a system of controls beforehand. Don't do it as an afterthought. A written week by week schedule is desirable.
12. Support your people if they need help or in disputes. Don't leave them to succeed or fail on their own.
13. Follow up along the way. Set the task up to minimize surprises. Don't wait until deadline day to see if the job is done.
14. Give credit to the delegatee for a job well done. Put his or her name on the cover of the report; take him or her to the meeting with higher-ups to present the work, and praise the person to your bosses. Don't hog the glory.
15. The "Rodwell Rule" of delegtion: give away each and every task which someone on your staff is 80% ready to handle. Reserve for yourself only the tasks that you alone can do.

6. Evaluating and weighing the pros and cons of each alternative, quantifying wherever possible, and perhaps combining elements of several alternatives into a new one.
7. Selecting and implementing the alternative(s) that best fit(s) with objectives to solve the problem.
8. Feedback—did it really work?

The manager may choose to involve the staff in all or none of these stages, depending on his or her theories of effectiveness. However, the numerous studies of group dynamics in recent years, coupled with motivational analysis, suggest that much better results will be obtained by involving key personnel in the process. They may have other interpretations of the performance data so that the problem may ultimately be defined quite differently. Their staffs may need to be enlisted to help gather better data on the problem, requiring both an understanding of what is going on and a time commitment. The process of developing alternatives almost always goes through several iterations. The manager might develop what he or she considers to be a complete array of possibilities and in a management conference find new options proposed. Similarly, when everyone has digested the issues and perhaps chatted with outsiders (e.g., with spouses and customers if appropriate) and presented the options to their own departments, it is almost a certainty that constructive and creative new alternatives and sub alternatives will spring up on any big issue. In the task of quantifying the pros and cons of the possibilities, the staff's time and understanding may be needed. The manager may reserve the final selection of the best alternative; but if this is after a participatory process, then everyone will know why it is being selected, why certain alternatives were rejected, and what is going to be involved. After this groundwork it will be much easier to delegate the plan's implementation successfully.

The decision-making process just described can be accomplished in five minutes or five months, depending on the complexity and importance of the issue. One of its most difficult elements is the second step—being sure one has properly identified the problem, and one is not just treating symptoms. It is essential to define the root cause. Treating only the symptoms will not remove the problem. It is suggested that the problem-solving team seek to isolate the critical factor that has to be changed, moved, or removed before anything else can be accomplished.

The process of developing alternatives does not imply that these are necessarily "exclusive" possibilities. More likely they are "program packages" of compatible solutions to related issues. The selected alternative may include program elements from several other alternatives, as long as the program as a whole is internally consistent.

Decision-Making Tools

Some decision-making tools are straightforward and commonsense applications of knowledge in an aviation business. Figure 2.4 depicts some typical problem areas and available techniques for decision-making.

Other tools are more complex. The field of operations research is devoted to the study of management problem-solving tools. A few of the basic types of approach are summarized here.

Sampling theory involves the use of random samples to represent the population being considered. Sampling techniques can be of great value in an aviation business to conduct surveys of customer opinion regarding service, products, or potential business. Other applications include the sampling of inventory, work activity, or production quality.

Time distribution can be a useful piece of data when examining staffing shifts and hours of operation. Arrival time, service time, average wait time, maximum parking accumulation, and similar time-related data sampled over different days of the week and seasons can be a great help in making decisions about the best allocation of resources. A sign at the front desk about avoiding peak times of the week (as is sometimes done by the postal service and by transit systems) can even help customers with choices about their schedules.

Simulation of scenarios can be useful, particularly with today's computers (but even manually for certain issues). Simulation of scenarios alters one factor at a time in an analysis to examine "what-ifs." For example, an analysis of acquiring a new aircraft might examine the consequences of different interest rates on monthly repayments. A drop in prices could be tested using different assump-

Figure 2.4 » Practical Decision Tools for the Aviation Manager

Areas	Typical Problems	Available Techniques for Decision-Making
1. Human Resources	Selecting personnel	> Application blanks, interviewing guides, tests, reference checks, job specifications, job descriptions.
	Evaluating employee performance	> Job requirements, performance appraisal system and forms.
	Compensating employees	> Job evaluation program, job surveys, performance appraisal system.
	Disciplining employees	> Clear rules and regulations, positive discipline environment, progressive discipline system, grievance procedure.
	Organizing work activity	> Organization chart, manual; planning goals, organization.
2. Financial	Determining profitability	> Financial information system, financial analysis, goals and objectives.
	Capital investment problem	> Analysis by pay-back, rate of return, present value, company investment requirements.
	Departmental development and control	> Goals and objectives, budget, analysis of activity.
	Cash requirements	> Cash budget, short-term loan source.
	Accounts receivable	> Credit policies, credit application, account aging process, collection procedure.
3. Material	Supplies on hand	> Inventory system, information system, goals and objectives.
	Pricing material	> Pricing policy, pricing guidelines and procedures.
	Maintaining physical assets	> Maintenance policy, preventive maintenance procedure.
4. Aviation Operations	Marketing activity level	> Company goals and objectives, economic situation, product requirements, outside assistance with promotion.
	Flight activity guidelines	> Operating procedure manual, pilot training and flight standards.
	Maintenance quality control	> Statement of policy, guidelines and procedures, inspection check lists, inspector personnel.
	Fuel contamination	> Company policy, rules, procedures, fuel sampling, clear markings, training.
	Safety	> Policy statement, rules, regulations and procedures, reinforcement and recognition, involvement.

tions about elasticity to see what would happen to revenue in worst- and best-case situations. Using computer models or spreadsheets can be built to test the results of changing several variables at once.

Decide Something!

"Not to decide is to decide," as the saying goes. That is, the world will not stand still even if you do—there will be changes to deal with as a result of not making a decision. This generally seems to hold true except for the most compulsive type of manager, who may benefit once in a while from letting things run their course for a few days. Serendipity sometimes steps in and resolves things without any action on the manager's part. However, even this approach means making a decision to address the issue at a specific future date, if it hasn't resolved itself by the simple passage of time.

Time Management

"Work expands so as to fill the time available for its completion," says Parkinson's First Law. "Granted that work (and especially paperwork) is thus elastic in its demands on time, it is manifest that there need be little or no relationship between the work to be done and the size of the staff to which it may be assigned."[16]

While written in a whimsical vein, there is a very large measure of truth to these remarks. The converse is also true: work compresses to get done in limited time if that's all there is; an urgent or important project always seems to be done by the deadline no matter how few people are assigned to it. Witness how even the most lethargic organization regularly gets its paychecks out on time.

Sources of Time-Management Problems

Various studies and books available on time management seem to agree on the key causes of problems:[17,18,19]

> Procrastination—because you dislike a task or it is overwhelming;
> Telephone and other interruptions;
> Failure to get back to the task being done before the interruption;
> Meetings—too many, too long, too unspecific, no agenda, no decisions as to who will do what next;
> Reports—too many, too many contributors, too long;
> Unplanned visitors;
> Lack of delegation; poor delegation;
> Failure to make decisions on incoming items;
> Preoccupation with operational crises rather than preventive activities;
> Special requests—interruptions without adequate warning;
> Delays;
> Too much unfocused reading; and
> Lack of priorities.

Learning to plan time is one of the tasks that all workers need to do, but managers need it most because they are not on a production line or customer service position, with tasks coming at them constantly, but rather must exercise a choice about how to spend every minute of the day.

Time Management Strategies

In anything but a one-person business, clear delegation is the best means of gaining time. Moreover, all tasks should be delegated that someone else can handle, whether or not they can do them quite as fast, quite as well, or in exactly the same way as the manager would. As the mother whose three-year-old washed the supper dishes every night said, "Sure I could do it faster, but she enjoys it and has a sense of achievement; besides, it frees me up to do the things a three-year-old can't do, such as paying bills or vacuuming." It pains many managers immensely to delegate to people they sometimes feel have the competence of a three-year-old, but as long as the job gets done, the manager can get on with something else that only he or she can do. Also, the person given a task slightly ahead of their skill level will learn, feel pride, and be ready for even more difficult assignments. This is the 80 percent rule of delegation in action.

Other recommended methods of better managing time include:

1. Plan each day's activities; don't just stumble through.
2. Use a "tickler" file to organize papers relating to future dates and projects.
3. Sort tasks into urgent and important, not urgent and not important.[20] Aim to do two to three important tasks a day. Many of the other tasks will simply disappear, and fewer important tasks will be left till they become urgent.
4. Work out six to seven goals with your manager.
5. List the tasks that relate to the goals, along with start and finish dates.
6. Transfer tasks on to "today's to-do" list when their start date arrives.
7. Keep a notebook, pack of index cards, or pad for ideas or things to remember.
8. Eliminate avoidable distractions—set up a routine where someone working for you handles them.
9. Identify long-winded individuals in your work group, and set up short times to speak to them (e.g., just before a meeting or shift end, or shortly before you have another appointment).
10. Communicate with "chatterers" by e-mail instead of orally and have them do the same to you.
11. Use a desk needle or other simple organizer for messages and calls to be returned/ responded to.

12. Manage by wandering around and asking questions—forestall problems before they develop.
13. Don't interrupt others but plan your use of their time.
14. Stick to one task until it's done; try not to interrupt yourself.
15. Keep your bosses posted on your results before they have to chase you down and ask you.
16. Make sure your employees know their authority and discretion.
17. Set up a section/division procedures manual so everyone knows what he or she should be doing, how and who to go to for help; routine-ize the routine so that methods don't have to be thought out each time something comes up.
18. Use the phone instead of going to see people.
19. Use a written checklist for shift transfer issues.
20. Set up "red flags" for certain personnel or work groups on things they must get help on.
21. Graduate your people to fewer "red flags" as they learn new skills.
22. Take advantage of the POSITIVE side of deadline pressure by getting adrenaline going and allowing less time for others to change their minds.
23. For tasks that are done well under deadline pressure, set up more (artificial) deadlines to increase productivity.
24. If a task has to be stopped in the middle, try to leave it where you know exactly what you were going to do next; write yourself a note.
25. Coordinate and aggregate errands and tasks together whenever possible.
26. Delegate all possible tasks and set up reporting-back arrangements.
27. Set goals for your people with check-up dates.
28. Personal prime time—identify your best working time and block it out for no interruptions at least twice a week. Block out time several times weekly when you don't take calls or visitors except in dire emergencies. (If you were out of the office at a business meeting, people would put up with not being able to reach you, so be adamant.)
29. Don't put in too long at one stretch on high priority tasks.
30. Do low priority tasks at low-output periods of the day.
31. If unable to reach a decision, examine the need for more information and delegate getting it.
32. Divide overwhelming projects into small pieces and delegate parts.
33. Do a first, appealing, or random small task on a big project to develop momentum and ideas and to get over the intimidation that new project can create. Break big projects down into small manageable steps; delegate some parts.
34. Set intermediate milestones for big projects and acknowledge getting there.
35. Identify why you are putting off a project and tackle the cause.
36. Make all projects as simple as possible to get the job done—remember that *opportunity cost* is the cost of what doesn't get done while you are doing what you do.
37. To get you started, do the task first that you like best; it'll be easier then to do the distasteful part.
38. Use small parcels of time (e.g., while waiting to see someone) to check lists, add to lists, write someone a note, brainstorm a new assignment.
39. Be assertive—assert the right to refuse more assignments.
40. Exercise telephone discipline; be task-oriented.
41. Reduce paper flow to essentials. Handle correspondence only once, by assigning it to someone else, handling it, filing it or tossing it out
42. Be selective in reading.
43. Utilize travel time for catching up on projects.
44. Finish and put away one thing before starting another.
45. Relax and recharge occasionally by attending conferences and meetings away from the office.
46. Limit your reinvolvement in tasks already delegated.
47. Use your worst times of the day for trivial matters and low priority items.
48. Work somewhere else on key projects, away from the phone and visitors.

49. Write less and use the phone more. Not only do you get instant feedback, but also some things are better floated as trial balloons, discussed informally without being committed to paper. This is especially true today as e-mail is so easy to route to others, often causing confusion and misunderstandings.
50. If you get stuck in a useless meeting, work on something else to stay alert and productive.
51. Avoid meetings with ineffective chairpersons.
52. Since meetings can be considerable time-wasters, meeting management skills should be a goal of everyone who ever has to call a meeting. Figure 2.5 shows meeting management pointers.

Business Ethics

Good business ethics are essential.[21] In the early part of the 21st century there are some very public examples of non-ethical companies, such as the Enron case, where top management left the bankrupt company taking substantial pension and other benefits with them, while lower level workers lost their entire retirement, and many agencies that invested in Enron, such as state retirement funding organizations, also lost millions of dollars. By contrast are examples of highly ethical businesses such as:

> Malden Mills, inventor of Polartec fleece, whose owner paid over $25 m in salaries to his employees while the mill was being reconstructed after a devastating fire;[22]
> The Body Shop, which refuses to sell animal-tested products, works with small producers in third world countries to help villagers make a living and is involved in global issues of sustainability;[23]
> Ben & Jerry's Ice Cream, which gives a percentage of profits to charity and encourages employee activism;[24]
> And many more.

Whether the business owner considers that operating from high moral standards is the way he or she will operate because that is how his or her whole life operates, or whether the owner thinks simply that operating with integrity is enlightened

Figure 2.5 » Meeting Management

1. Don't hold a general meeting if two individuals can resolve the issue together.
2. Prepare a written agenda, get it out ahead of time, identify topics and OBJECTIVES of meeting on these topics. Consider specifying the time to be spent on each agenda item. Ask for missing items when the meeting begins, but reserve the right to save them for another time.
3. Call people 48 hours before the meeting to:
   a. Remind them of time and place
   b. Refresh their memory on their role
   c. Ask for any other agenda items from them.
4. Substantial handouts should be distributed by the person responsible for that agenda item, BEFORE the meeting. Be sure any needed audiovisual aids are working properly.
5. Keep meetings to no more than one hour and specify finish time on agenda.
6. Start on time. Have someone else take minutes. Record those present and absent in the minutes. Don't allow side conversations. End on time!
7. Listen to input but firmly steer discussion back to the subject if it wanders. Give the talkers tasks to do; invite involvement of the quiet ones.
8. Take action on every item, even if the action is not final. Assign responsibility for more research, for example, with products and deadlines.
9. Use a place with no chairs to speed up meetings, if necessary.
10. Get minutes out promptly; highlight each recipient's new tasks and deadlines.
11. If votes are required or other formal protocol, establish rules (*Robert's Rules of Order*, for example).

self-interest, the process can be almost the same. One company describes its ethics goal as follows:

> Fostering global business practices which promote equitable economic development, resource sustainability, and just forms of government.[25]

Ethics applies to at least the following areas: treating employees fairly and honestly; ensuring that the company's accounting and fiscal practices are legal and accurate; paying vendors on time; not using potentially substandard generic parts; ensuring that all company environmental practices are sound and legal, and being honest and straightforward with customers, especially if there is a disagreement about a product or service.

A strong ethical foundation for the business will have positive results, such as:

- Increase customer loyalty;
- Motivate employees to also operate from integrity;
- Build loyalty because it will be evident that the boss is committed to fair dealings within and outside the company;
- Keep the business out of legal trouble, which is potentially costly and time-consuming; and
- Create a business with higher resale value.

Summary

Management is defined as getting things done through others. It therefore involves planning, organizing, directing, coordinating, and controlling the work of others. The problem for most managers, especially those promoted up the ranks and not formally trained in management, is that despite their titles, they are also "do-ers." This has also become truer as the prevalence of computers has meant fewer secretarial positions. A business plan can help the manager lay out the long-range activities and rationale of the business. The plan will contain many elements of the manager's job. In so doing, he or she is constrained by time in how much "doing" takes place. In a small business a manager wears many hats and spends significant portions of time delivering the goods or services of the business; however, this activity should be delegated as much as possible. Various styles of delegation and levels of decision-making are available. The manager by these choices achieves good or poor use of not only his or her own time, but also the time of all the staff.

DISCUSSION TOPICS

1. Describe the manner in which a manager's functions will change as he or she advances up the promotion ladder.
2. Tasks should be delegated to the most junior staffer remotely capable of handling them. Discuss.
3. What subjects should a business plan cover? Why?
4. What are the pros and cons of preparing/not preparing a written business plan?
5. What are some of the choices about styles of delegation? How should a manager set about deciding which to use?
6. What are the pros and cons of decision-making by consensus?
7. What are the greatest causes of time mismanagement? How can they be dealt with?
8. Why should a business have an ethics policy and what should it say?

Endnotes

1. With apologies to William Shakespeare's Julius Caesar: "Some are born great, some achieve greatness, and some have greatness thrust upon them."
2. Mintzberg. *Harvard Business Review on Leadership* (Harvard Business Review Series). Harvard Business Review/Paperback/ Harvard Business School Publishing, August 1998.
3. Peter Drucker has been writing on the subject of business for 60 years. More about him can be found at various web sites such as *http://www.peter-drucker.com/ontheweb.html.*
4. For example *http://www.accel-team.com/human_relations/.*
5. See, for example *http://www.deming.org/.*
6. Goleman, Daniel, McKee, Annie and Boyatzis, Richard E. *Primal Leadership: Realizing the Power of Emotional Intelligence.*
7. Collins, James C., and Collins, Jim. *Good to Great: Why Some Companies Make the Leap . . . And Others Don't*
8. Brown, Steven W. *13 Fatal Errors Managers Make, and How You Can Avoid Them.* New York: Berkley Publishing Group, 1987.
9. Covey, Stephen R. *The 7 Habits of Highly Effective People.* ® Covey Franklin Publishers.
10. One if the most frequently used is the Myers Briggs personality styles system, which classifies people based on self-testing, into 16 major types. See *http://www.keirsey.com/.*
11. Bygrave, William D., and Bygrave, Bill. *The Portable MBA in Entrepreneurship, 2nd Edition.*
12. Collins, James C. and Lazier, William C. *Beyond Entrepreneurship: Turning Your Business into An Enduring Great Company.*
13. Drucker, Peter Ferdinand. *Innovation and Entrepreneurship.*
14. Brown, Deaver. *The Entrepreneur's Guide.* New York: Ballantine Books, 1980.
15. A right brain process of recording ideas, developed originally by Tony Buzan. See *http://www.buzancentre.com/TBuzan.html.*
16. Parkinson, C. Northcote. *The Law.* Boston, MA: Houghton Mifflin, 1980.
17. Morgenstern, Julie. *Organizing From the Inside Out: The Foolproof System for Organizing Your Home, Your Office, and Your Life.*
18. Lagatree, Kirsten M. *Checklists for Life: 104 Lists to Help You Get Organized, Save Time and Unclutter Your Life.*
19. Blanchard, Kenneth, and Johnson, Spencer. *The One-Minute Manager: The Quickest Way to Increase Your Own Prosperity.* New York: William Morrow and Company, 1982.
20. This is the basis of the time management skills taught by Covey. Non-urgent and non-important things either fall off the bottom of the list, or get done in the "interstices" of time. Important things must come before urgent things.
21. For resources, see the following: Business New Haven Consulting Group, Inc. offers customized workshops in business ethics and other related training at *http://www.nhcg.com; Integrity Interactive Ethics Courses:* the leader in online business ethics training for employees- offers courses in over 130 ethics and compliance topics at *http://www.integrity-interactive.com; Strategrity Consulting*: Strategrity offers business ethics training and analysis services at *http://www.strategrity.com.*
22. See *http://www.polartec.com/01_malden_mills/01_02_articles/01_02_malden.html.*
23. See *http://www.the-body-shop.com/global/values/index.asp.*
24. *http://www.benjerry.com/foundation/.* The mission of the Ben & Jerry's Foundation is to make the world a better place by empowering Ben & Jerry's employees to use available resources to support and encourage organizations that are working towards eliminating the underlying causes of environmental and social problems.
25. Mission statement of International Business Ethics Institute http://*www.business-ethics.org.*

3 Marketing

OBJECTIVES

- Describe some reasons why a marketing plan aimed at the mass market would not be beneficial to a general aviation business manager.
- Understand what forecasting sources are available to the FBO in planning for each market area.
- Show how businesses must be able to identify new prospects and relate that to customer needs.
- Discuss the differences between cost-based pricing and price-based costing.
- Realize the importance of location and promotion to a marketing strategy.
- Describe three elements of distribution and how they function.

Introduction

Need for Marketing in Aviation

The aviation industry has evolved from being an experimental, exploratory, and record-setting sport into being an important element in everyday business. In its early years, the excitement created by air travel and its stunts was often enough to attract huge crowds of patrons. In today's world, the general aviation business cannot wait for people to come to the business; he or she must seek them out. If the customers are business travelers, they will constantly be evaluating other travel modes such as the scheduled airlines, rail and the automobile. If they are recreational flyers, many non-aviation activities compete for their support and dollars.

Nor is the general aviation business in the position of having a captive audience. If the service is unfriendly or the desired fuel is not available, a pilot will certainly fly to another airport next time. Within metropolitan areas, studies have shown that pilots will travel some distance to hangar or tie down their aircraft at a favored field.

Aviation businesses must continually seek to improve their marketing skills if the business is to prosper. The most effective companies in the United States spend a good deal of time "staying close to the customer." A suggestion box may tend to gather only complaints, whereas training each and every employee to invite feedback will generate more discussion and ideas of a positive nature. Aviation customers, especially those who travel a good deal, are also excellent sources of information on innovations being tried elsewhere.

The entire business strategy must hinge upon anticipated sales. The money to run the business, make improvements, and to expand comes from gross sales. A realistic sales forecast must rest upon a planned schedule of daily and weekly marketing activities.

Modern aviation businesses are learning something the hard way: a specific marketing plan and its timely implementation are essential to a healthy business. This is an area of expertise where the manager and employees should be continually exploring and experimenting. Marketing is still as much an art as a science, and what works for one business or product may not work for another.

Marketing Orientation

Having a marketing orientation in a business means running the entire business with a focus on the customer.[1] It is a viewpoint that recognizes the dependence of the business upon customers and the sale of products and services to them. The manager without a marketing orientation makes no real effort to attract customers, and by many subtle and even oblivious indications, actually suggests that customers go elsewhere. Such a manager's employees are likely to be unconsciously mirroring and reinforcing the same message. By contrast, the manager with a marketing orientation is totally conscious of customers, their needs, and what it will take to attract and keep them, and spends considerable time emphasizing this in formal and informal staff training as well as constantly modeling it in his own behavior.

Such a manager recognizes that the business depends upon sales and that the first step is getting the customer inside the door. Once inside and face to face with a company representative, the customer should continue to experience the positive marketing orientation of the business all the way through the conclusion of the sale and in subsequent encounters, even—or perhaps most particularly—the handling of any problems. The marketing-oriented manager sees to it that every single one of his or her employees behaves likewise, whether their job calls for dealing with customers and whether or not they themselves know all the answers customers want.

Definition of Marketing

Marketing, as treated in this chapter, covers the entire process of identifying customer needs, purchasing or producing goods and services to meet those needs, determining the price and place to dispense the items, prospecting, promotion, and selling. In short, it deals with the four Ps: product, price, place, and promotion.

The marketing function in a company may be handled by the owner/manager, or each department may handle it. For example, the maintenance manager might be responsible for planning sales in his area and the used aircraft manager might be responsible in her area, and so on. In a large company, a separate department, as shown in Figure 3.1, may handle the marketing function. Whether these functions are handled by one individual as a part-time responsibility, or whether they are each handled by a separate person, they are all necessary functions in the marketing area.

FBOs and other general aviation businesses are unusual in at least two distinct ways. First, their entire function depends heavily on infrastructure over which they often have little or no control—the airport runway. Without this facility, there could be no aviation business. Its quality affects the general aviation business customers, even though there may be no direct quality control on the part of the business.

Second, full-service FBOs are sellers of both products and services, and both types of goods encompass a wide array of choices. Even the smallest FBO business generally caters to a variety of perhaps incompatible market segments (e.g., the corporate chief executive taking a charter juxtaposed with the euphoric sixteen-year-old in half a T-shirt who has just soloed). The ambience and facilities of the general aviation business must accommodate both of these ends of the spectrum and an array of markets in between.

Since services are one product of a general aviation business, the word "product" is generally used here to refer to both products and services.

Natural Markets

US aviation customer bases may be generally divided as follows:

1. The lowest-income 20 percent are viewed as having no discretionary income—and therefore should not be of concern to an aviation business.
2. The mass market—the top 21 percent to 88 percent of the population, that has discretionary income; some of these may be attracted to aviation but may not be able to afford to take their training or ownership of aircraft to a high level.
3. The young, upwardly mobile urban professional ("yuppie") market. This group is about 10 percent of the total market or the top 88 to 98 percent in terms of wealth.
4. Lastly, certain cultural subgroups, and the wealthy or highly specialized markets; the top 2 percent of the market.[2]

Each of these markets has different interests and needs, and lends itself to different types of promotion. For clarity, they break down as follows:

Percent of population	Aviation buying power/ discretionary income
Poorest 0–20	None
Middle 21–88	Mass market; modest aviation buying power
Upper 88–98	"Yuppie" market—good potential customers
Wealthiest or most unusual 98–100	Excellent aviation prospects

What, therefore, is the general aviation business's natural market using this way to slice the market pie? An evaluation of some of the national statistics suggests that general aviation businesses should generally target both the 2 percent market and the 88–98 percent market.

As was indicated in Chapter 1, the top assets in the US are shared as follows:

Households with net worth of:	Number
$1–$5m	16,000,000
$5–25m	500,000
Over $25m	100,000

The typical general aviation business is, however, less likely to tap the mass market. The 2 percent market figure is derived from the fact that only a small percentage (about 0.3 percent) of the total US population is actually pilots. About one person in a thousand or .01 percent owns an aircraft.

Non-pilots traveling by air are thought to use general aviation transportation about one quarter of the time. A recent speech indicated that less than 1.2 million people are interested in aviation, so with a population of nearly 300 million in the US, the understanding that this is not a mass market is key to how the business owner approaches selling.

By contrast, mass markets and mass marketing techniques may simply not be appropriate for general aviation businesses. The general aviation business is in the custom-tailoring business, at least

Figure 3.1 » Typical Marketing Department

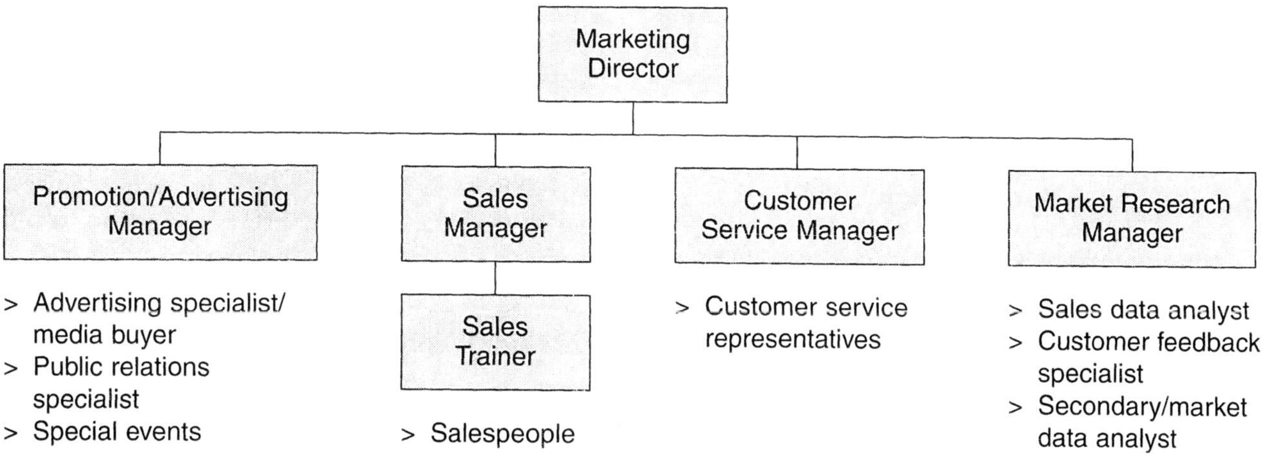

on the service side, so that each client is treated differently and has different needs met.

Market Research

Marketing and market research are often used synonymously, but they are by no means the same. Market research helps the business owner understand the trends—and the underlying factors causing them—that then can help him or her focus on what products and services to emphasize. Without market research, one's attempts to increase sales will tend to be scattershot. With market research, they can be closely targeted because one knows what is going on in each segment of the market.

Nature of Aviation Market Research

In the US as a whole, the last two decades of the 20th century saw a relatively continuous upward trend in prosperity. There were geographic areas, socio-economic groups and limited time periods that this was less true, but in general, discretionary income rose, consumer spending rose, and many new products and services arose to tap these funds. The aviation market operates in this wider context, but is also heavily influenced by matters unique to the industry.

National Trends That May Affect General Aviation

Introduction

General aviation has been a relatively volatile industry for the past 50 years or more. Thus, accurate interpretation of past causes of volatility is important because they can help to project future development. Chapter 1, Introduction touched on some of these issues; here some of the key ones are covered in more depth.

Terrorism and Its Aftermath

Recent milestones in general aviation include not only the Tort Reform act and the proposed recreational license, but also the events of 9/11/01 which for a period severely curtailed most GA activity and harmed many businesses. The resulting delays and periodic airport terminal evacuations that have occurred since then are encouraging many more companies to look at air taxi, charter and fractional or full aircraft ownership as a means of enabling their employees to make rapid business trips. This can be encouraging news for general aviation businesses seeking to serve these new customers.

The events of 9/11/01 have led to a massive increase in attention to airport security, at both large and small airports.[3] This, coupled with lost airline revenues, is placing a financial burden on the system that may mean other investments, which help aviation businesses—such as runway, and taxiway improvements, may be curtailed or delayed. In addition, new security measures for the typical GA airport many be a mixed blessing, as they tend to decrease ease of airport access for regular customers in the process of making access more difficult for undesirable characters. These problems may be resolved as new security technology is brought into use; it may take time for the necessary comprehensive security pans and related funding programs to take effect, however.

The events of 9/11/01 as well as vast improvements in teleconferencing technology are also triggering a new look on the part of many companies at whether travel—face-to-face meetings—should be talking place at all. An Airport Magazine article addresses this among other issues.[4] Researchers for several decades have been asking if telecommunications methods of various kinds would start to replace face-to-face gatherings, but only in the 1990s did technology really begin to be available that makes this widely possible. The author comments that today, almost every company has access to high speed data lines with transmission speeds up to 50 times faster than even as recently as 1998, with more speed being anticipated. "Virtual meetings" can take place on desktop equipment rather than requiring special conference rooms. The availability of the technology coupled with the post-9/11/01 time loss and security concern have led many companies to not only promote this technology but often, require a justification for why electronic communication would NOT work, before approving an air trip.

Fractional Aircraft Ownership

Fractional aircraft ownership companies and equally importantly, individuals, apparently now ac-

More often, companies are using corporate jets when their people need to travel.

count for more than 40 percent of all new corporate jet orders, according to a 2001 article in Airport Magazine.[5] The number of companies and individuals with fractionally owned aircraft jumped from 948 in 1997 to 4,900 by 2001 according to those tracking this fast-growing industry. The article states:

> "Now, private jet service can be cost-effective for companies with travel budgets of less than $200,000 per year, particularly if they are headquartered near a large city and travel to other large cities. In fact, the minimum aircraft hours in a fractional ownership contract has fallen to only 50 hours per year. Just as importantly, companies using NetJets and other large providers can now fly on four hours notice, with multiple staff to multiple destinations. Airport check-in time can be a mere 15 minutes at each end, with the return scheduled comfortably to eliminate connections and overnight stays."

The origins of fractional aircraft ownership lie with corporations owning aircraft and seeking to utilize them more fully to share costs. However, passengers for hire cannot be carried in a corporate aircraft unless it is certified to operate under FAR Part 121, which regulates air carriers, or Part 135, which regulates air taxi operators. The corporate flight usually operates under FAR Part 91. In October 1999, a working group, the Fractional Aircraft Ownership Aviation Rulemaking Committee or FOARC was convened by FAA to explore the issue of appropriate safety rules for fractionals.

FAA took FOARC's recommendations, which had been drafted as a preliminary Notice of Proposed Rulemaking (NPRM) almost verbatim. The main thrust was to add a new section to FAR 91 to address fractionals, and also make some similar changes to FAR 135. The rules will allow for as little as a 1/16 share of some aircraft and 1/32 share of others. Over 200 comments were received, and it is hoped although not expected (given other attention-requiring activities of FAA) that a final rule should be in place by the end of 2002.

The regulatory/safety debate however has not in any way slowed the development of the fractional market, which still operates today under the current FAR Part 91 requirements. The primary question for FBOs (and the reason that this topic is addressed most fully in this Chapter) is how will exponential growth in fractional aircraft ownership affect our business?

At first blush, one might think that FBOs would be hurt by the growth in fractionals. This is because the fractional management companies such as NetJets, Bombardier's Flexjet, Flight Options and others, operate their own flight departments and maintenance facilities and thus could mean less work for FBO pilots and mechanics, as well as enticement away to higher-paying jobs (ever the FBOs' lament, that they are at the bottom of the aviation "food chain"). Yet it appears so far that fractional aircraft operation is developing its own market niche. Its customers are coming to a small extent from charter operators, but according to NATA, it's still generally cheaper to charter than be a fractional owner.[6]

According to the aviation consulting firm IMG, fractional operations can be cost-effective for companies with travel budgets under $200,000 per year.[7] Another study indicates that an individual with an annual income of $10m or a company with gross sales of $30m would find fractional ownership cost-effective, and that the range of annual flight hours for which this mode is most useful is about 145 to 390 hours per year.[8] With a ½ share meaning 200 flight hours per year, needs can be met without owning the complete operation.

Fractional aircraft clients seem to be coming from three sources:

> Smaller corporate aviation departments which have closed down in favor of fractional ownership;
> Business people who have not previously used general aviation and are realizing its efficiencies. This group is no doubt increased due to 9/11/01, and the greater time burden imposed by security processes during airline travel; and
> Some frequent charter flyers switching modes within GA.

Benefits of fractional ownership include:

> Lower cost than running a corporate flight department and no managerial hassles of overseeing it;
> No aircraft maintenance responsibilities;
> Much lower travel times than using airlines;
> Wide choice of aircraft through the fleet pools owned by fractionals;
> NO direct payments for "deadheading" or aircraft positioning time; and
> Under the proposed new rule, more airports that can be accessed due to runway length requirements being made more realistic.

Aviation businesses should monitor the fractional station closely as it evolves, as it is still growing at 40 percent or more per year and therefore major change with implications for a specific FBO can occur in a relatively short time.

Encouraging New Pilots

The BE A PILOT program is having some success at encouraging individuals who never dreamed of flying, to try it out for a hobby or for business reasons.[9] Many flight schools are part of this program and it has had favorable press in business periodicals and elsewhere. According to a 2001 article in Business Week, new student pilot licenses issued by FAA increased 9 percent in 2000 over the previous year.[10] According to GAMA, for example, a 2001 Cessna survey found that 40 percent of the people buying their piston aircraft are new pilots.[11]

Recreational License

Another example is the proposed FAA rulemaking on a sport pilot license as shown in Figure 3.2, which would enable beginner recreational pilots to fly with fewer time and money barriers to getting qualified.[12]

Another positive trend in terms of flight training has been the increasing percentage of pilots who are adding advanced certificates and ratings. The percentage of pilots with instrument ratings now totals over 45 percent. This has been especially true of women pilots

Airport Closures

Another area where the government can influence the aviation market example is in protecting or not protecting "threatened" airports. Such airports may be encroached on by urban development, or may have severe noise complaint levels causing local government to favor the needs of the community at large over the needs of the aviation community. An aviation business located at such an airport needs to be aware of its situation and ideally, be proactive in creating a more favor-

Figure 3.2 » Proposed Sport Pilot License

The proposal would establish new FAA certification categories for:

Aircraft

Light-sport aircraft are simple, low-performance aircraft that are limited to 1,232 lbs. (56 kg) maximum weight, two occupants, a single non-turbine powered engine, stall speed of 39 knots, maximum airspeed of 115 knots, and fixed landing gear. Aircraft categories include airplanes, weight-shift-control aircraft, powered parachutes, gyroplanes, gliders, balloons and airships. Due to their complexity, helicopters and powered-lifts are not covered by the proposed rule. Light-sport aircraft standards meet the "Voluntary Consensus Standards" of *OMB Circular A-119.*

These are the two new airworthiness certificates that would be established:

> A new experimental light-sport aircraft airworthiness certificate for existing light-sport aircraft that do not meet the requirements of Part 103 (ultralight vehicles) of the Federal Aviation Regulations.
> New special, light-sport aircraft airworthiness certificates for light-sport aircraft that meet an airworthiness standard developed by industry.

Pilots and Flight Instructors

These are the new pilot and flight instructor certificates that would be established:

> New airmen certificates would include a student pilot certificate for operating light-sport aircraft, a sport pilot certificate, a flight instructor certificate with a sport pilot rating.
> Two new aircraft category and class ratings—weight-shift-control (with land and sea class ratings) and powered parachute.
> New training and certification requirements for these new ratings.
> A current and valid U.S. driver's license or an FAA airman medical certificate would be required to operate a light sport aircraft.

Repairman

This is the new repairman certificate and ratings that would be established:

> A new repairman certificate with a maintenance or inspection rating to maintain and inspect light-sport aircraft.

Source: www.faa.gov/avr/afs/sportpilot

able local climate for the airport as a whole and thus for that business in particular. This is discussed more fully in Chapter 12, Physical Facilities.

Technology

Technology is of key importance in aviation. As electronics become yet more sophisticated, this leads to changes in avionics that will affect the sale of parts as well as the avionics maintenance requirements that a business may seek to meet. It is also very important to keep the latest technology in mind when considering marketing strategies and continued long-term business. In the computer industry, a company on the cutting edge today can find their product basically obsolete in one or two years. The development of RNAV and Loran, which were the most advanced flight navigation systems in the 1980s are now considered "dinosaurs" by some in lieu of the latest GPS systems available.

Tort Reform

Since aviation is such a heavily regulated industry and relies for its facilities so heavily on government agencies, part of the market context is created by government actions. Being aware of both pending and new regulations, and of the federal and local budgeting and funding processes, can help shape marketing decisions. A prime example is the "Tort Reform Act" of 1994, which basically encouraged a rebound in small aircraft production in an industry that otherwise, might have virtually ceased to exist.[13] However, it was paralleled by the growth in fractional aircraft ownership, which also had a major impact on the new aircraft market.

While many feel that the turnaround in aircraft sales since 1994 is due primarily to the Tort Reform Act, others feel that the growth of fractional aircraft ownership is as much or more the reason, since almost half the new aircraft on order are destined for fractional aircraft companies. Figure 3.3 provides an alternative view of past industry trends in summary form, that can be reviewed in more detail if desired.[14]

Sources of Aviation Forecasts and Market Projections

For many years, FAA has been a leading source of aviation forecasts. These are produced primarily for its own use in forecasting workloads and facility needs for the airspace system, but are increasingly being tailored to also meet the needs of states and local users and industry itself. FAA now also produces a guide called "Forecasting Aviation Activity" which provides a how-to for any party wishing to prepare a forecast.

FAA forecasts appear in the following documents:

> The National Plan of Integrated Airport Systems (NPIAS)—an annual document that sets out airport needs and improvement plans;
> Terminal Area Forecasts—examining projected activity at towered airports; and
> National Aerospace Forecasts—examining projections in the national airport system as a whole.

FAA's web site should be consulted for the most current issue, which can generally be downloaded.[15] Figures 1.2 and 1.3 in Chapter 1 contained summaries of the most recent forecasts of fleet mix and flight hours. These forecasts are by no means cast in stone and are revised every year; however, they are a reliable backdrop to any one general aviation business's situation. Some key

Figure 3.3 » An Alternative View of GARA

Before 1979, the industry's growth was fueled by a number of factors that artificially boosted demand and led to a flooding of the market with new aircraft.

The general aviation industry's decline in the early 1980s was based on a number of economic factors.

After the early 1980s, while other industries bounced back, the small aircraft market—one segment of the general aviation industry—remained in the doldrums due to several factors other than product liability lawsuits, including the industry's own behavior.

> Limited Demand—the industry's success at building long lasting products

> Decline in Pilots.

> Other Factors—aircraft enthusiasts turned their attention and money to the experimental and kit aircraft market.

While the small aircraft market remained depressed, the general aviation industry began to grow on the strength of high-priced turboprop and jet aircraft.

AFTER GARA

Small aircraft prices have not dropped as the general aviation industry promised, because the industry has realized no product liability "savings" due to GARA. The small aircraft market has experienced a very modest revival over the last two years, but nothing that even approaches the robust demand of 20 to 30 years ago.

Because small aircraft prices have not dropped, this modest increase in demand can be attributed to other factors.

The effects of GARA cannot be isolated from the effects of other efforts by government, industry, and organizations of aircraft owners and operators to revitalize the industry.

Cessna's decision to resume single engine manufacturing in 1994 was not the result of any financial savings due to GARA, but because Cessna's Chairman, Russell W. Meyer, Jr., promised Congress that production would resume if GARA were enacted.

Source: Public Citizen Congress Watch

figures from the FAA 2002 forecasts, made by John Rodgers, Director of the forecasting unit are shown here in Figures 3.4 through 3.13.

More fine-grained analysis of the market can be obtained from other public studies such as the FAA'S Terminal Area Forecasts that contain airport-by-airport forecasts for every facility in the National Plan of Integrated Airport Systems. An example of the data provided is shown in Figure 3.14. Individual airports also periodically conduct airport master plans, usually with the help of a consultant. These plans may provide a guide not only to demand for growth at a particular airport, but also capacity limitations that could affect those plans.

Figure 3.4 » Results from FAA CY 2000 GA Survey

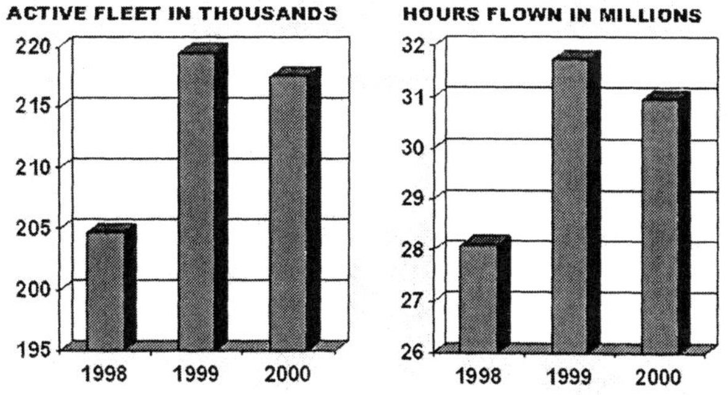

Source: FAA

Figure 3.5 » GA Hours Flown in 2000 by Type

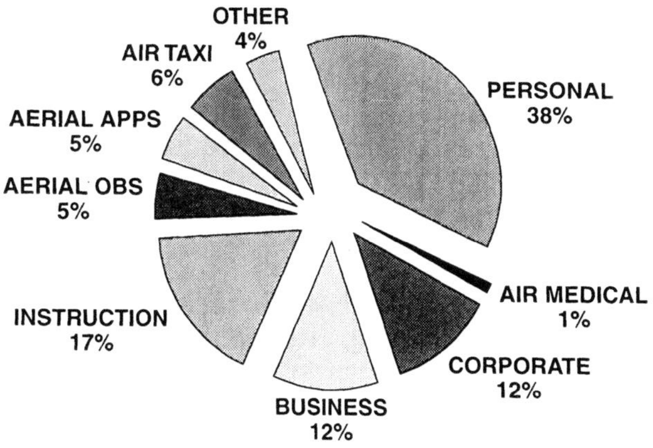

Source: FAA

Figure 3.6 » FAA's Assessment of Factors Affecting GA Trends Through 2013

Mixed News for GA in 2000–2001

- GA billings set a record for the fourth consecutive year
- Turbojet shipments were up for the fifth consecutive year
- Total pilot certificates held were up for the fifth consecutive year

But

- GA active fleet and hours flown were down in CY 2000 after five consecutive years of increase
- GA activity at FAA facilities down
- F/W piston shipments were down
- Student certificates were down in 2001 for third consecutive year

Uncertain Future Environment

- Recession in general economy in 2001/2002
- Lasting effects of September 11th
  - — Restrictions on GA?
  - — Restrictions on pilot training?
- How fast does GA recover from recession?
- Can fractional ownership maintain pace?
- Will "sport pilot/light sport aircraft" provide a measurable boost to GA?

Source: FAA

Figure 3.7 » Overall Interpretation by FAA of GA Activity Through 2013

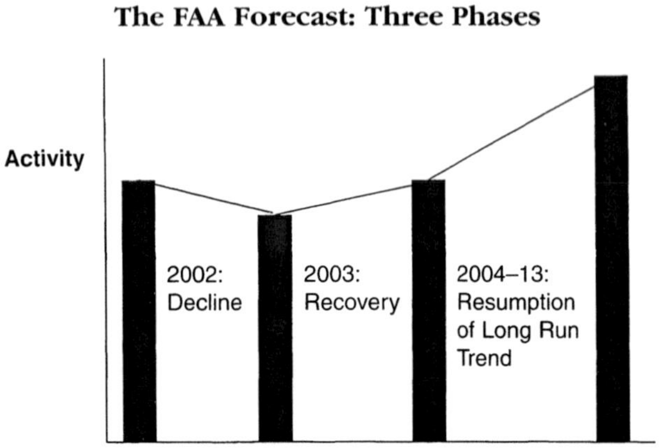

Source: FAA

Figure 3.9 » GA Fleet History and Forecast: 1996–2013

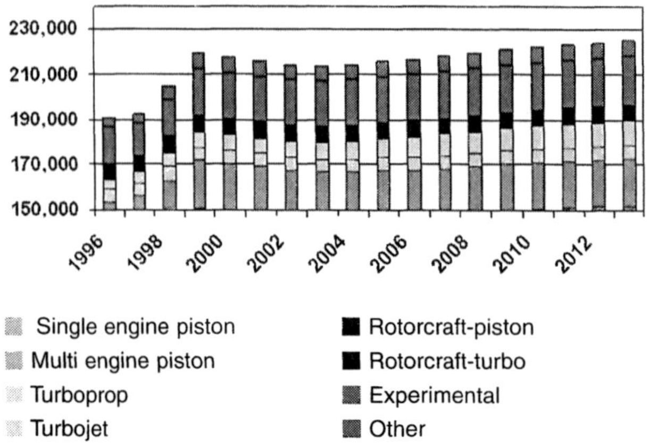

Source: FAA

Figure 3.8 » GA Fleet Forecast Assumptions and Forecasts

F/W piston
- Single-engine: contraction in fleet through 2003; no change in 2004; and resumption of growth in 2005

F/W Turbine
- Turboprop: slight decline through 2003; modest growth through 2013
- Turbofan/jet: modest to strong growth throughout the entire forecast period

Rotorcraft
- Decline through 2003; modest growth, led by piston through 2013

Source: FAA

Figure 3.10 » 2001-2013 Aircraft Utilization Assumptions and Forecasts

Piston
- "Aging" of piston fleet and decline in number of student pilots leads to lower piston utilization at end of forecast period

Turbine
- Increase in turbine utilization is largely due to increase in number of these aircraft in fractional ownership programs

Rotorcraft
- Utilization decreases slightly due to change in fleet mix and changing use patterns

Net Effect
- Overall 2.6% increase in utilization over forecast period

Source: FAA

Historic trends in one sector of aviation can be a useful backdrop to the individual general aviation business situation. For example, general aviation aircraft production and sales began to fall off in the late 1970s. It was predictable from that time—though not widely observed—that general aviation business in the early 1980s would fall off as a result.

In addition, almost all states produce aviation forecasts as part of their state airport system plans, and most local airports update their airport Master Plans every 5-10 years and include a forecasting section.

Beyond all these government sources, several industry organizations such as GAMA and AOPA produce industry outlook reports on an annual basis. Again, web sites should be consulted for the most current documents. See Appendix 1.

Every general aviation business needs to be aware of national trends in aviation. Air travel is generally a "derived" demand and triggered by some other purpose rather than being an end.

Figure 3.11 » Pilot Certificates Held, 1999–2003

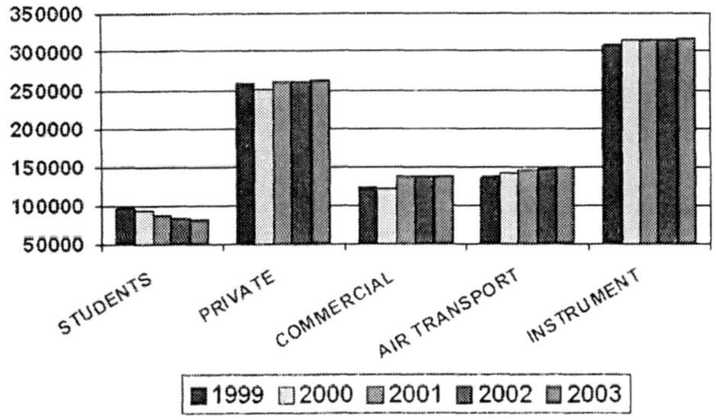

Source: FAA

Figure 3.12 » Instrument Rated Pilots, 1996–2013

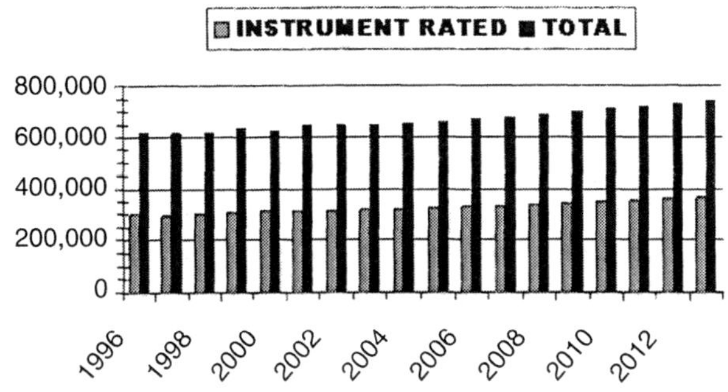

Source: FAA

Figure 3.13 » Factors Affecting Future GA Trends

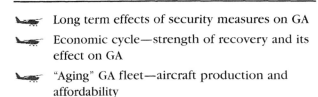

- Long term effects of security measures on GA
- Economic cycle—strength of recovery and its effect on GA
- "Aging" GA fleet—aircraft production and affordability
- Ability of airport and ATC system infrastructure to support growth

Source: FAA

The need for activities performed from the air, for example aerial photography or aerial application, is a function of the economic climate of that other industry, farming, or photography. This means general aviation businesses also need to be aware of overall business and recreational trends and competing products. Aviation tends to be substantially affected by the health of the overall economy. It has also been radically affected by the industry's insurance climate, most specifically, product liability insurance, which had resulted by the early 1990s in the insurance cost of a new aircraft being such a high proportion of total cost that the price for a new plane became almost prohibitive and production all but ceased. This issue is discussed more fully below. Suffice it to say that an aviation businessperson seeking to foresee the future for his or her business must have a grasp of the overall economy as well as of any unique phenomena affecting general aviation.

It would be impossible to review here the entire economy from the general aviation business standpoint; moreover, regional variations make such a task of doubtful value at the national level. However, the general aviation picture nationally is both well documented and a useful guide to local trends.

Understanding the Local Aviation Market

Trade magazines and newspapers provide a more detailed review of technology and market shifts. The major ones are listed in Figure 3.15.

Another shift in markets that general aviation businesses should anticipate is the "ripple effect" in metropolitan areas. As major airline airports become more congested, there is a tendency to encourage general aviation traffic to use reliever general aviation airports that in some cases lie further out in the suburbs of metropolitan areas. As these airports in turn become busier, the proportion of business traffic tends to increase, and the recreational and instructional flyers may prefer to go out to more rural airports where smaller, lighter aircraft dominate the pattern and where they are not constrained by the requirements of an air traffic control tower.

Figure 3.14 » Example of Data Provided in FAA Terminal Area Forecasts

Region State:	ACE-IA			**LOCID:**	DBQ	Contract Tower								
City:	DUBUQUE			**Airport:**	DUBUQUE REGIONAL								**Based Aircraft:**	
				AIRCRAFT OPERATIONS										
	Enplanements			Itinerant Operations					Local Operations					Total Instrument Operations
Year	Air Carrier	Commuter	Total	Air Carrier	AT & Comm	GA	Military	Total	GA	Military	Total	Total OPS		
Actual														
1996	727	34,559	35,286	70	5,882	18,857	71	24,880	11,848	20	11,868	36,748		12,643
1997	2,408	35,449	37,857	51	5,274	17,964	127	23,416	13,318	16	13,334	36,750		11,754
1998	453	41,266	41,719	17	6,062	20,500	90	26,669	17,960	14	17,974	44,643		12,695
1999	0	53,569	53,569	5	8,811	20,623	70	29,509	15,762	22	15,784	45,293		14,737
2000	39	57,848	57,887	4	9,587	23,862	94	33,547	13,500	28	13,528	47,075		15,305
Forecast														
2001	39	57,848	57,887	2	8,424	21,127	70	29,623	15,066	8	15,074	44,697		13,953
2002	39	60,008	60,047	2	8,573	21,555	70	30,200	15,352	8	15,360	45,560		14,211
2003	39	62,169	62,208	2	8,723	21,983	70	30,778	15,638	8	15,646	46,424		14,469
2005	39	66,490	66,529	2	9,022	22,839	70	31,933	16,211	8	16,219	48,152		14,985
2010	39	77,293	77,332	2	9,771	24,980	70	34,823	17,643	8	17,651	52,474		16,277
2015	39	88,096	88,135	2	10,520	27,121	70	37,713	19,076	8	19,084	56,797		17,570
Comments:														

Source: FAA. Note: Forecast prepared before 9/11/01 and under revision

Location will tend to determine the market of an airport, and a general aviation business must be prepared for these shifts and adapt to them, unless he or she desires and is prepared to work against the current. The process of working downwards from national trends to local and individual business prospects is described in Figure 3.16.

Forecasting Techniques and the Individual General Aviation Business

The individual general aviation business must examine the local and regional aviation market and determine what share of local sales will be captured for each area of service. As reviewed above, national events and trends play a role, as well as the policy of the general aviation business. For example, suppose a new market opportunity is observed. Suddenly this market area looks promising. How promising? How long until government rules supporting the new program are approved and underway? What are likely to be the plans of other general aviation businesses in the area? Is this a market that our general aviation business should pursue? Can our business be sufficiently profitable undertaking the new program?

Some research and analysis will be needed before deciding that new sales will be x dollars this year. A contingency plan may even be appropriate. "If the new federal program reaches such-and-such a state of readiness by July of this year, we can initiate our program in September and this means by December we will expect to have y results." Sales will be forecast under several different startup scenarios.

Such forecasting is not very sophisticated because of factors outside of the general aviation business's control. However, this may be the most specific level of prediction feasible.

Other areas of the business may be more predictable. For example, let's suppose the general aviation business has a well-established maintenance shop that has increased its business by 5 percent per year over the past 5 years. Is it reasonable to predict that sales will be up five percent this year, too? Yes and no.

First, you need to know whether that history of 5 percent growth includes inflation. If the cost of labor and parts also went up five percent per year, then the actual volume of business stayed the same, even though the dollar volume went up. If the price went up more than 5 percent in a

Figure 3.15 » General Aviation Publications

Aero Magazine, Macro-Comm Corp., P.O. Box 38010, Los Angeles, CA 90038. *http://www.boeing.com/commercial/aeromagazine/*

Ag-Pilot International, 10 N.E. Sixth, Milton-Freewater, OR 97862. *http://www.agpilot.com/*

Agricultural Aviation, National Agricultural Aviation Association, Suite 103, 115 D Street, Washington, D.C. 20003. *http://www.ag-aviation-online.com*

Aircraft Maintenance Technology Magazine, 1233 Janesville, Ave. Fort Atkinson, WI 53538. *http://www.amtonline.com/*

AOPA Pilot, 421 Aviation Way, Frederick, MD 21701. *http://www.aopa.org/pilot/*

The Aviation Consumer, P.O. Box 972, Farmingdale, NY 11737. *http://www.aviationconsumer.com*

Aviation Career, PO Box 550070, Fort Lauderdale, FL 33355. *http://www.aviationcareer.net/*

Aviation Safety, 1111 East Putnam Avenue, Riverside, CT 06878. *http://www.aviationsafetymagazine.com*

Aviation Week and Space Technology, Mc-Graw Hill, 1221 Avenue of the Americas, NY, NY 10020. *http://aviationnow.com/avnow/news/channel_awst.jsp?view=top*

AvWeb(online only) Publisher Tim Cole. *http://www.avweb.com/contact.html*

Flight International, Business Press International, Quadrant House, The Quadrant, Sutton, Surrey, England, SM2 5AS. *http://www.flightinternational.com*

Flight Training Magazine, 405 Main St., Parkville, MO 64152. *http://www.aopaflighttraining.org/*

General Aviation News & Flyer, 5611 76th St., W., Tacoma, WA 98467. *http://www.generalaviationnews.com*

In Flight USA, PO Box 620447, Woodside, CA 94062. *editor@inflightusa.com*

Pilot's Web, Pilot's Web editorial (631) 736-6643. *http://www.pilotsweb.com*

Plane and Pilot, Werner & Werner Corp., Ventura Boulevard, Suite 201, Encino, CA 91436. *http://planeandpilotmag.com*

Private Pilot, Macro-Comm Corp., P.O. Box 2432, Boulder, CO 80322. *http://www.privatepilotmag.com*

Professional Pilot, West Building, Washington National Airport, Washington D.C. 20001. *http://www.propilotmag.com*

Sport Aviation, Experimental Aircraft Association, Wittman Airfield, Oshkosh, WI 54903-2591. *http://www.eaa.org/benefits/sportaviation/index.html*

Customer Service for the following publications can be reached via email at the addresses below:

Aviation Week and Space Technology *p02cs@mcgraw-hill.com*

Business and Commercial Aviation *p02cs@mcgraw-hill.com*

Overhaul and Maintenance *p18cs@mcgraw-hill.com*

World Aviation Directory *p92cs@mcgraw-hill.com*

A/C Flyer *p93cs@mcgraw-hill.com*

Aviation Week Newsletters *awgnews@mcgraw-hill.com*

The following website has access to many publications on aviation:

http://www.aviationnow.com/

Source: Julie F. Rodwell, 2003

Figure 3.16 » Industry Market Research and Sales Planning Process

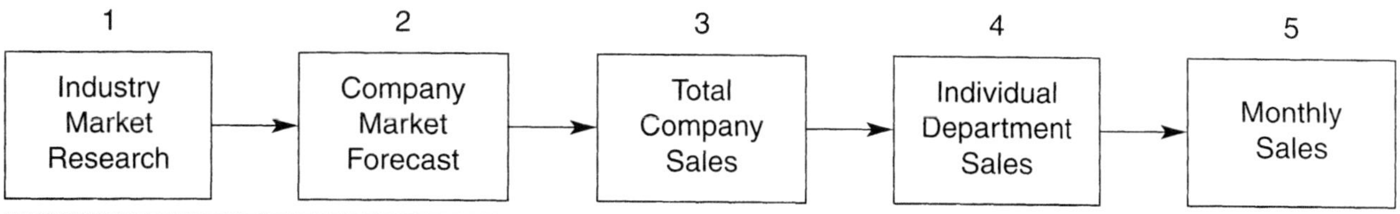

single year, then the volume of business actually declined.

Are there any reasons why the coming year might be other than "business as usual"? Is a competitor about to get into or out of the aircraft maintenance business? Why? Or does the general aviation business have a good chance of winning a new fleet maintenance contract for a commuter airline, fractional ownership company, or a corporate flight department? You must examine whether the total market "pie" is growing or shrinking in your market area and what share of that pie you can realistically expect.

It will be apparent from the above discussion that forecasting based on historic trends is a little superficial and risky unless some evaluation is made of the underlying causes of those trends and whether any of them will change. Nevertheless, predicting from historical trends if often done. This is most accurate at the large-scale level and least accurate at the individual company level. As has been said by one wit: "Trying to forecast the future by looking just at the past is like trying to drive a car by using only the rear-view mirror."

Market share is another method of forecasting. In looking at individual airport-based aircraft operations, one approach is to use national forecasts and using aircraft per capita population, disaggregate to the local or regional level. This method requires a reliable national forecast and does not allow for local variations in aviation activity.

The most sophisticated approach to forecasting is to build a multiple regression model. The factors contributing to historical activity are identified, as well as the scale of each factor's contribution. The relationships that held in the past are postulated to hold true in the future. Future values for the causal factors, such as disposable income, fuel prices, and population by age group, are identified from published sources, and predictions developed.

Such a method still has weaknesses, especially since relationships do change over time; therefore, the time period over which a factor is examined may not be representative, and good forecasts may not be available for the variables considered relevant. Moreover, such a method is difficult to use for such a small unit as an individual general aviation business; it will be much more accurate at the regional or national level.

In summary, there is no perfect way to do aviation sales forecasts. They should be developed with as much knowledge as possible about what the competition is doing, with as much understanding as possible about national aviation trends and their causes, and with company goals and policies in mind. Forecasts can often become self-fulfilling prophecies. They should be tracked against actual results and adjusted as new events occur.

Customer Needs and Identification of New Prospects

There are a number of ways to identify and sell to more customers, and for most businesses these ways must all be applied all the time. Every business continually loses clients through relocation, death, and changing needs. Therefore, every business requires new clients just to maintain current levels of sales. A growth plan requires more than just replacements. Growth of the client base is possible to achieve in the following ways:

1. Maintain market share; grow or decline in step with the total market.
2. Obtain a bigger market share, that is, take business away from the competition.
3. Offer new products to existing clients.
4. Offer existing or new products to clients not previously in this marketplace (e.g., new general aviation enthusiasts attracted away from the airlines or from other hobbies).

Effective ways of selling more or different items to the same clients include maintaining close rapport and seeking feedback in person, by surveys, by complaint forms, and by direct-mail advertising. It is recommended by most marketing experts that both a list and a wall map of existing clients be maintained.

Lists of prospective clients served by competitors are obtainable from many sources. In today's sophisticated direct-mail market, lists of pilots and aircraft owners; and lists by area, income, and industry type (and thousands of other classifications) may be rented from list brokers in all major cities.

To attract customers who are not currently involved with general aviation, new techniques may be needed. For example, there is substantial evidence of a growing reliance on executive travel among the top companies (Fortune 500). For example, for years *Business Week* magazine tracked the financial performance of the aircraft owning and non-aircraft owning companies in the Fortune 1000, and found that aircraft owners had higher performance on virtually every count. More recently, GAMA and NBAA commissioned an analysis by Arthur Andersen to investigate this issue in more depth.[16] The study found that of the 214 operators and 121 non-operators in their sample, operators earned 141 percent more between 1992 and 1999. The study states: "According to the CFOs interviewed, aircraft helped improve performance in the areas of greatest importance in today's fast-paced economy (e.g. identifying and executing strategic opportunities for new relationships and/or alliances, reaching critical meetings and closing transactions; expanding into new markets; and increasing contact with customers). Armed with some of the statistics correlating company performance and use of general aviation aircraft, a general aviation business might present the benefits to business people at Chambers of Commerce, Jaycees, Kiwanis, and Rotary clubs. Industry groups can assist in this respect.

To encourage recreational flying and instruction, a general aviation business may need to publicize the contests organized by the General Aviation Manufacturers' Association as well as use other approaches.

While the overall economic climate for general aviation in the past two decades or more has been discouraging, many enterprising general aviation businesses nationwide have developed healthy markets in such areas as:

> Corporate aircraft maintenance;
> Restoring antique aircraft;
> Airline flight training;
> Propeller balancing;
> Airport hotels and motels;
> Air charter;
> Servicing airline aircraft, including de-icing;
> Airport snow removal;
> Overnight package express;
> Air ambulance services;
> Airport barbershops;
> Pay telephones; and
> Retail merchandise.

For general public awareness of the benefits of the general aviation business's services and the airport, fly-ins, open houses, and air shows may be appropriate, although care should be taken not to present a barnstorming image if that is not the airport's target market. Appendix IV of this book presents a list of other suggestions.

Product and Service Definition

The starting point of any business is the identification of the product it wishes to sell. In the aviation business, this means the identification of several products, such as transporting passengers, providing landing facilities, servicing aircraft, renting space, and so on. It is extremely important that the manager clearly identify each of the products that he or she expects to include as part of the business. Each product or service offered by a business must be identified because decisions on other marketing variables, such as promotion, will depend upon identification and knowledge of the product. In addition the manager may want to identify services that will be offered if requested but will not be emphasized. What such items are, for any one general aviation business, is hard to predict. They will be things that take more trouble in terms of training and special equipment than will normally prove feasible or profitable. For many businesses such an item might be banner towing or aerial photography.

By the same token, there may be activities that are in demand but the general aviation business might want to refer to another specialist in the field. Some examples include specialized avionics, radio work, and the whole maintenance function. Some general aviation businesses do not pump fuel, except perhaps for their own use, because the municipality runs this operation or another general aviation business is better placed to do it profitably. Each general aviation business must decide its own service and product lines relative to what it perceives as its customers' desires and on the profit in each area.

Finally, there are some activities, that although non-aviation, are very profitable related areas. Examples include restaurants, car rentals, and limousines. A quality airport restaurant with good views of active aircraft may attract many non-flyers and help provide an introduction to the services and facilities at the airport as well as provide a positive public image.

Total Product

Even for consumer goods, the typical customer is not just looking for the product but for the experience of fulfilling a want. He/she is concerned with the total product, including the experience of obtaining it, as well as the assurance of related functional and aesthetic features. The typical customer is also concerned with necessary accessories, installation guidance, instruction, packaging, dependability, and assurance that good future service and maintenance is available. In making his or her purchase, he/she is looking for indications that all needs in regard to the item will be met.

Product Classification

Traditional marketing theory divides consumer goods into four categories:

1. Convenience goods are those the purchaser wants to buy frequently and with minimum effort; therefore, comparison-shopping is not employed. An example might be aviation fuel, unless there is a discount fuel operator in the area.
2. Shopping goods are those items that shoppers do compare. Examples might be a used aircraft or a flight instruction course. The general aviation business will have to offer some special features of quality or price to attract customers.
3. Specialty goods are those items where the customer wants one specific brand name or custom item and will go to great lengths to obtain it.
4. Unsought goods are those items that the customer is not seeking and may not have thought he or she needed. New products, the savings realized from preventive maintenance, and novelty items fall into this category.

The Competition

Convenience goods will be sold to local customers and to transients who are at that point a captive market. If you have what they need, they'll buy it. Shopping goods are the subject of strong competition and there may not be any customer loyalty for these. Specialty goods can help a general aviation business to establish a reputation either as carrying a good inventory, or as being known to go to any lengths to find what a customer wants. Unsought goods require skills to make a potential customer aware of the benefits of something new.

Market Niche

Based upon the total market in the area and the competition's share of it, each general aviation business must seek to determine its own market niche or share. This will also require review from time to time. Questions to address are "What do we do?" and "Why are we different?"

Price

There are three basic methods of pricing: cost-based, demand-based, and price-based. These are discussed in the following sections.

Cost-Based

Retail stores usually mark up wholesale prices about 100 percent; that is, an item costing ten dollars wholesale will be sold at twenty dollars retail. This markup is a cost-plus approach to pricing in which the overheads such as storage, retail showroom space, labor, bookkeeping, and financing costs are covered by a predetermined overhead rate. Assuming you purchase wholesale at competitive rates, and your overhead costs are within industry norms, you can price competitively using this method.

Cost-based pricing is a straightforward approach with a basic appeal to most aviation managers. There are, however, two typical difficulties that exist in many situations: (1) many managers are not aware of, nor do they have available, adequate cost data, and (2) even where some data are available, the manager may not adequately recognize the various ways that costs change. In order to use cost-based pricing, the manager must understand the following types of costs:

1. Total fixed costs is the sum of those costs that are fixed in total, regardless of output level. Typical fixed costs include rent, property taxes, insurance, depreciation, and adminis-

trative salaries. Such expenses must be paid even if business activity ceases temporarily.

2. Total variable costs is the sum of those variable expenses that are closely related to level of business activity. Variable expenses include materials used, wages paid, and sales commissions. At zero business, total variable cost is zero. As output increases, total variable cost increases.
3. Total costs is the sum of total fixed costs and total variable costs. With total fixed costs set, growth of total costs is dependent upon the increase in total variable costs.
4. Average cost is figured by dividing the total cost by the volume of business, the average cost per unit of business is then obtained.
5. Average fixed cost is when the total fixed cost is divided by the quantity of business.
6. Average variable cost is the total variable costs divided by the related quantity of business.

The following example illustrates the above cost structure for a line department engaged in aircraft fueling operations in an aviation business: Figure 3.7 illustrates the cost data for such an activity. Notice that the average fixed cost decreases steadily as the quantity of fuel increases and that the total variable cost increases when quantity increases. Note also that the average cost is decreasing continually. The behavior of the three average-cost curves (average variable, average fixed and average cost) have been graphed in Figure 3.17. The aviation manager could use this type of graph in setting prices. First, he must include an element for profit either as a fixed amount in the total fixed costs, or as a fixed amount per unit in the average

Figure 3.17 » Shape of Typical Fuel Cost Curves when Average Variable Cost Is Assumed Constant

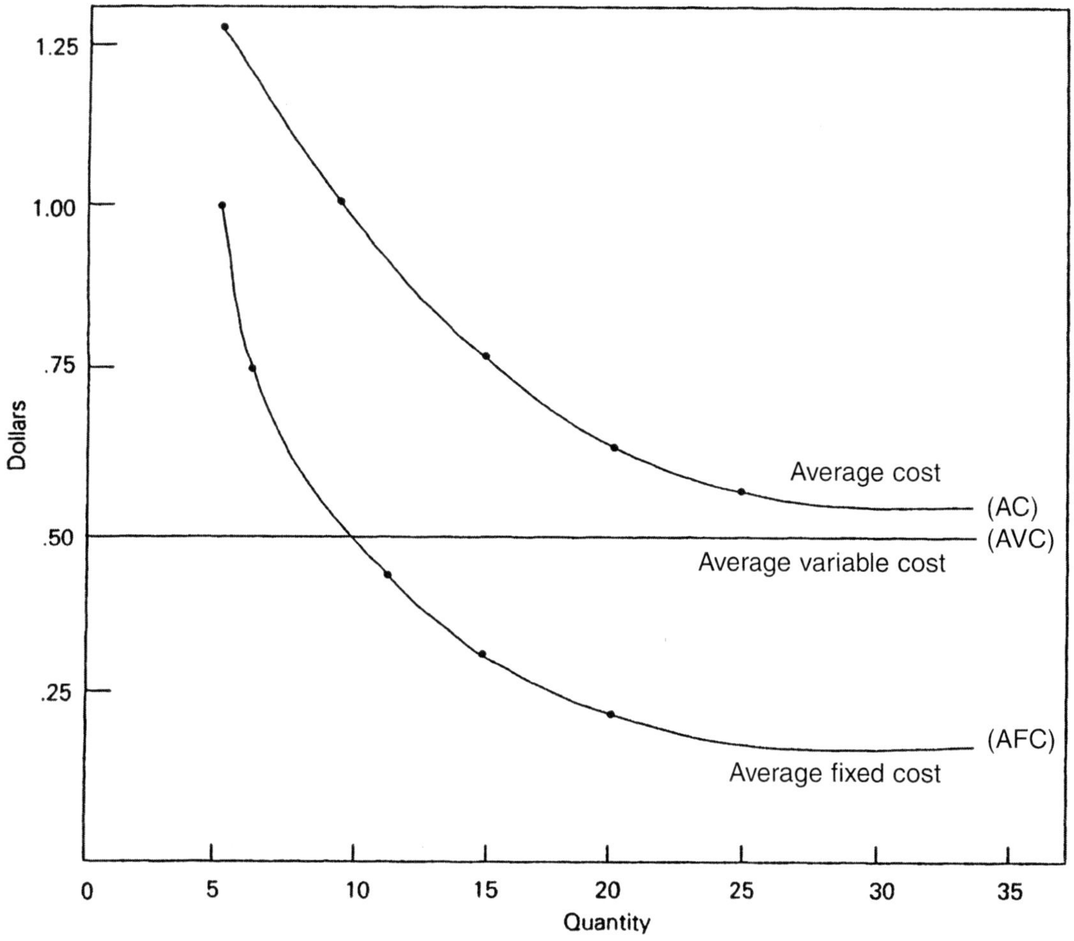

variable cost. The next step is to simply decide how many gallons of fuel the department will sell. If the goal is to sell 30,000 gallons, then by referring to the cost curve (Figure 3.17), the price is determined per gallon. Therefore, for whatever quantity is desired, the price can be identified. The quantity selected can be related to previous levels of activity or to target goals for future periods; thus, it becomes a useful managerial tool.

Demand-Based

Another method of pricing is simply to charge whatever the traffic will bear. As long as this is higher than the price arrived at by cost-plus, there will be a higher profit. For desirable or scarce items there will be a very considerable profit, which will bear little relationship to the actual cost of making that item available.

Price-Based

Price-based costing says that what the traffic will bear is going to be a result of the potential customer checking out your competitors and making a choice based on their prices compared with yours.[17] Therefore in order to be competitive, cost-based pricing will not work if your costs are higher than the competition's. Rather, you need to also check out the competitions' prices, and then figure out how to get your own prices down to that level. A small difference in price won't make a difference to most customers, but you would have to offer a huge and tangible difference in quality to entice a customer to pay much more than the competition wants, and such differences are hard to convey to a customer who is shopping around for the best price.

How to get one's costs down is then the challenge and will likely examine every component of cost that goes into that particular commodity or service.

Elasticity

Pricing that reflects what the traffic will bear conforms to the economist's true pricing theory. That theory states that price is determined as the point at which the seller's supply curve and the buyer's demand curve intersect. As price goes down, the buyer is assumed to want more; and as the price goes up, the consumer wants less. For a price increase of 1 percent, a drop in demand of 1 percent would follow under conditions described as unit-price elasticity. Price elasticity is less than one or less than unit if demand goes down less than 1 percent for a 1 percent price increase. For example, it appears that price elasticity for aviation fuel is fairly low. Where price elasticity is small, a seller would have to lower prices considerably to sell more to the same customer.

In theory, each buyer has his or her own demand schedule for each product at different prices. This is expressed most commonly as a curve, as shown in Figure 3.18. As a customer comparison shops for a product or service, it seems likely that his or her demand curve will shift depending on the asking prices of suppliers for various levels of quality.

The seller behaves in the opposite way. The higher the price of the product he/she is selling, the more he/she wants to sell. Such a supply curve is shown in Figure 3.19. Where the buyer's demand curve and the seller's supply curve intersect is the price, as shown in Figure 3.20. In practice most prices are not negotiated with each buyer but are predetermined and based on assumptions about regional aggregate supply-and-demand conditions. Moreover, in times of scarcity, when traditional economic theory would indicate raising price as the market's best form of allocating supply, there are usually regulations in effect about price gouging. Offering more of something for sale when prices go up is questionable because the profit margin probably will not go up at all. In order to remain competitive, a general aviation business most likely will pass on the higher cost to the customer. However, trying to make an exceptional profit when demand is high will probably alienate customers and be self-defeating.

Pricing is, therefore, an inexact science where basic economic theory must be combined with common sense and knowledge of the competition. Year-end or other sales to get rid of old inventory, as well as discount pricing for promotions, must be added to this complex picture before any calculations of revenue can be considered.

Figure 3.18 » Demand Curve for Aviation Fuel

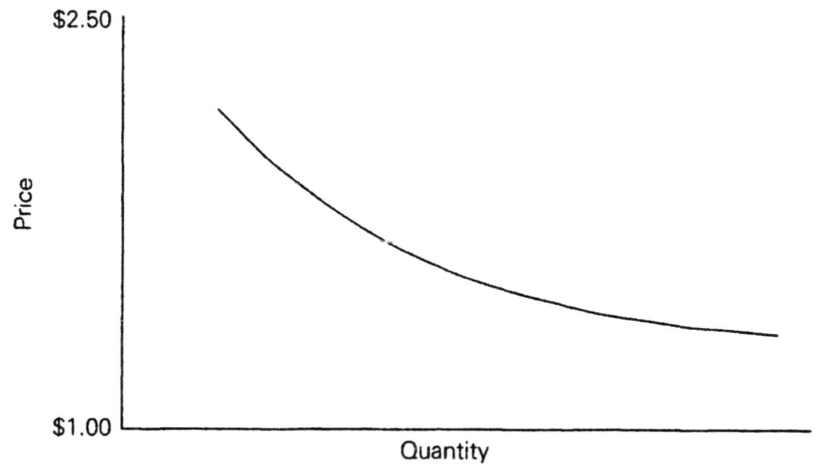

Pricing Policy

For the pricing practices of an organization to follow a logical pattern, for the employees to have a pricing guide to follow, and for the customer to experience understanding and goodwill toward the business, it becomes vital to have pricing policies on at least the following seven essential areas:

1. One price or flexible prices.
2. Price level with respect to market.
3. Pricing as related to the product life cycle.
4. Pricing product lines.
5. Promotional pricing policies.
6. Geographic pricing policies.
7. Marketing channel pricing policies.

Most businesses set their prices according to some guidelines rather than allow the daily market pressures to determine price. One policy option is one price to all customers versus a flexible-price policy where different customers may pay different prices. The second policy deals with the decision to price at above or below the market level. Many factors must be considered in making this decision and in reviewing it for necessary changes. The next area deals with picking a policy that cov-

Figure 3.19 » Supply Curve for Aviation Fuel

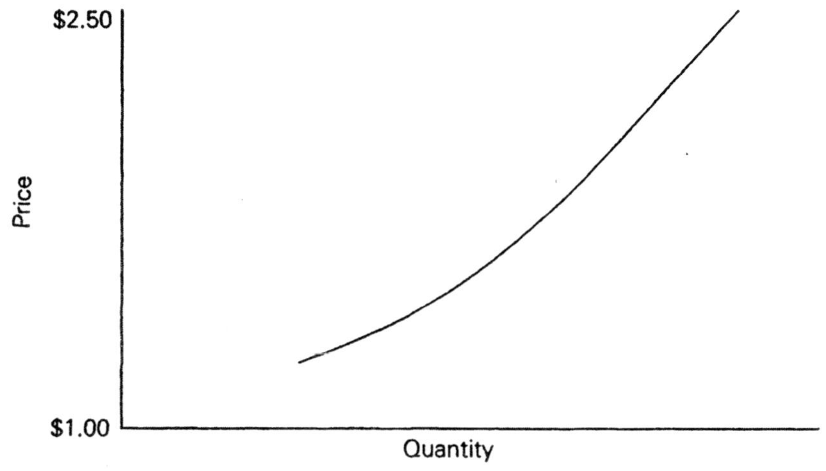

Figure 3.20 » Equilibrium of Supply and Demand for Aviation Fuel

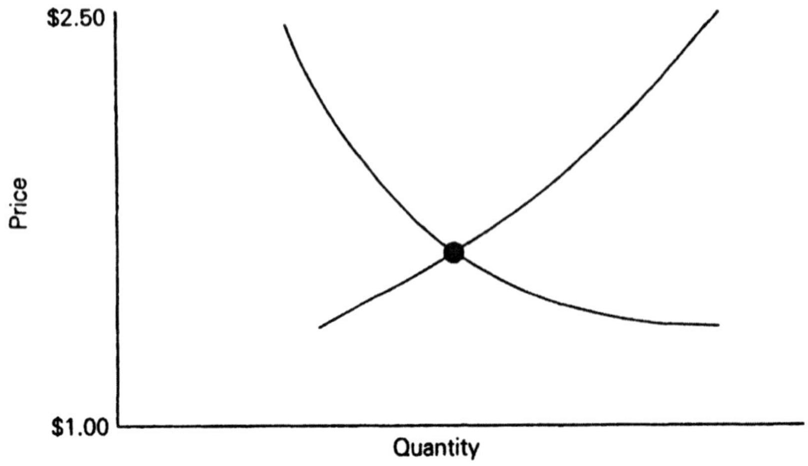

ers practices related to product life cycle. Will the prices be high initially in order to "skim" the market "cream" or will the prices be lower in order to "penetrate" the market and get a larger share? The fourth decision deals with creating policies in relation to the various product lines. Is the relationship between the various product lines a logical one? Are price classes to be set, rather than individual prices? The next policy area deals with promotional pricing, such as coupons, multiple unit pricing, loss leader pricing, and introductory price setting. The last two policy areas deal with geographic and channel problems and are not major concerns for most aviation managers unless they have widespread operations or strongly influence pricing throughout a marketing distribution channel.

In order to use pricing as a marketing tool, it is necessary to understand the need for pricing policies and to understand the operational opportunities in each of the above seven areas. The first policy area—fixed or flexible prices—can be applied to many aviation business activities. For example, let us consider the charter business. Will you charge $150.00 an hour for rental of a twin-engine aircraft, or will you promote a lesser rate ($125.00/hr) for the hours of midnight to five a.m. in order to enhance the utilization of the aircraft? Although some managers are reluctant to use flexible prices, others are quick to use such policies to their advantage.

Higher prices may well be associated with better quality products; lower prices with cheaper products. At the same time, the decision to price below market level may very well be influenced by the desire to increase the volume of business. Finally, your price level may well determine the level of support/services you may provide in your business for your products. For example, higher rates for maintenance labor may enable you to have better equipment and better-qualified mechanics.

Pricing as related to the life cycle of a given product means normally that when the product is new and in great demand, the price may be higher. Later, when the product is not as new, or when competition has become plentiful, the price may, out of necessity, become lower.

Pricing by product line may be hard to introduce in the typical aviation business. For example, pricing fuel lower than competitors may help establish a low-price image for the entire business.

Promotional pricing activities are a familiar feature of the aviation business world. Coupons and bonuses have been used at many airports. Airline special or promotional rates are commonplace and accepted. Introductory price cuts by new businesses are sometimes used to speed entry into the market.

Geographic pricing policies may not have to be made by many of the smaller aviation businesses, but they are frequently the targets of such policies set by large national distributors of aviation products. The main issue is who will pay the freight or how is it split between buyer and seller. FOB (Free On Board) pricing means that the closer you are to the source, the cheaper the product becomes. Zone pricing is used to smooth out the delivered prices in sections of the country. Uniform delivered pricing means that there is one price to all customers, wherever they may be. Freight absorption pricing is another example of geographic pricing policy. This technique is used by businesses that are shipping their goods considerable distances. In those distant markets they may absorb some of the freight costs in order to allow their salespeople to become more competitive.

The last pricing policy area deals with marketing channels activities. Most aviation businesses do not set channel policies, but they should be aware of the approach. By viewing a marketing channel as a unit, they can consider applying many of the above policies to the channel as a unit. The secret to the success of this approach lies in every member of the channel feeling that commensurate profits are being realized.

Place

No product is commercially valuable if it cannot be brought to the right place at the right time. The general aviation business is one in which the customer comes to the business, rather than the other way around. Therefore, the location of the business is critical. But in another sense, the location of a general aviation business is fixed and relocation is difficult if not impossible. Place is a given for the general aviation business. By contrast, aviation supply stores in shopping malls and mail-order avionics firms are much less tied geographically and have considerable advantage over a general aviation business in this respect.

Distribution Systems

Place also refers to the channels of distribution and the process that gets goods into the general aviation business's stock for use or sale. The channels between original producer and end consumer may involve no intermediaries (e.g., Beech Aircraft and Cessna sell factory direct and no longer use dealers). Or the process may require one or more wholesalers and the general aviation business as a retailer. Figure 3.21 shows these four basic channels of distribution.

The general aviation business as retailer must understand the distribution process for all the items sold, since it affects their cost, availability, and supply schedule. He or she must also be involved in merchandising, which means the display of retail

Figure 3.21 » Four Basic Channels of Distribution

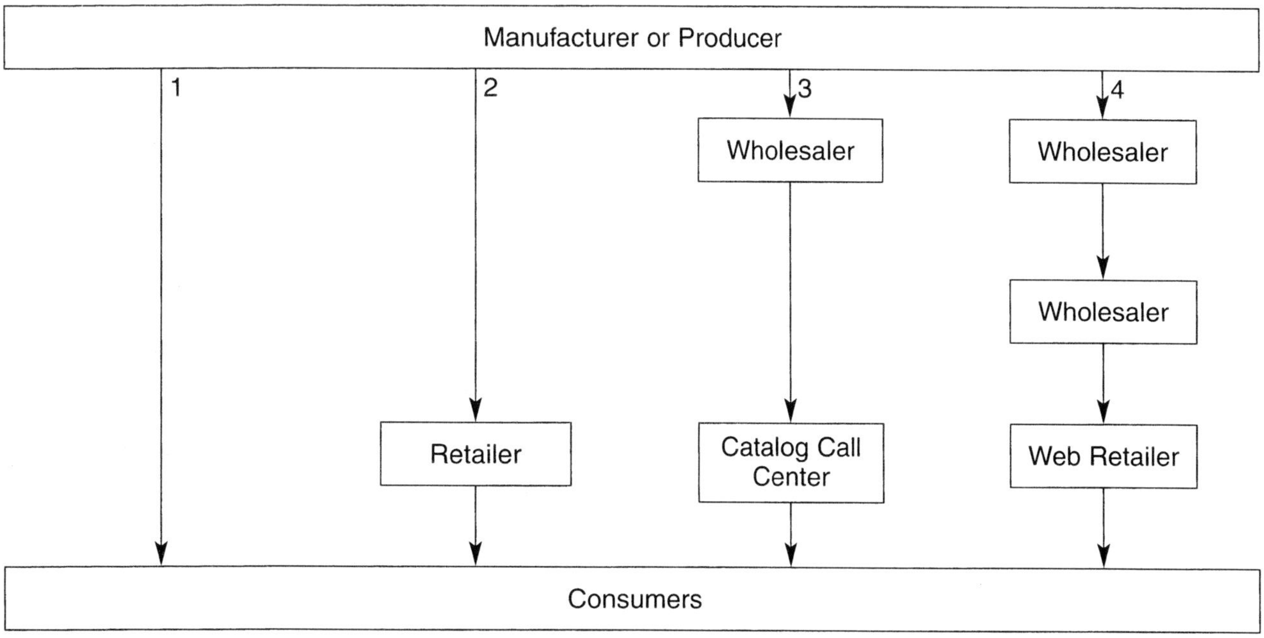

goods to best advantage, and inventory control, which means keeping track of fast- and slow-moving items and setting up appropriate reorder schedules. These functions to some extent will also be necessary in the parts department, where display and merchandising can perhaps produce many more sales than many parts and service managers realize. Chapter 10, Aviation Maintenance discusses how to calculate the "Economic Ordering Quantity" of a given item.

Computerized inventory control can in many cases be useful in keeping track of stock from the point of sale and preparing summaries of product turnover.

Promotion

The object of promotional activities is to inform, persuade, and remind existing and new customers about what the business offers them. Methods of promotion include television, radio, newspapers, trade publications, direct mail, novelty items, air shows, tours, signs, and referrals from happy customers (with or without incentives). Figure 3.13 shows a year-long promotional planning chart for a typical general aviation business.

Advertising

Advertising is but one method of promotion, and its cost-effectiveness is generally greater when it can be targeted more toward the right market. Thus, advertising in the mass media such as radio and television may not be very appropriate for general aviation, whereas advertising in aviation publications may be. A relatively new targeted mode of advertising is cable television, where detailed information is available on what types of audiences are watching what types of shows.

Direct Mail

For general direct mail, such as to all households in certain zip codes, a "rule of thumb" in the industry is that a good result is two percent for most kinds of mass merchandise. The use of aviation mailing lists and pre-selected business lists could be much more successful than general lists for aviation purposes. Carefully designed and targeted direct-mail advertising with a no-risk "offer" to encourage response can be an excellent source of leads. E-mail advertising has become a new form of "junk mail" that can cost less than traditional direct mail.

Referrals

Word-of-mouth and selling more to existing customers may be the most effective promotional tools in an aviation business. The individual general aviation business will need to test different concepts in limited ways before deciding which particular techniques work in each of his or her market segments. What appeals to the business market is more likely to relate to efficiency and quality, while price may be the overriding consideration for the flight instruction market. Follow-up with every customer should be a goal in order to identify negative feedback. With prompt follow-up, a negative experience for one of your customers can be turned around so that he makes positive referrals. If uncontacted, the unsatisfied customer will be persuaded by the competition the next time. Conversely, firms that get a reputation for dealing fairly and promptly with problems get good word-of-mouth press that can continually strengthen their client base.

Institutional Promotion

Institutional promotion or advertising means the promotion of a positive image about the business without stressing any particular product or service. In many cases it is very successful because people want to buy an experience and some assurance of ongoing service rather than a product per se. Institutional promotion can use mass media or targeted marketing, depending on the situation. As general aviation businesses begin to compete with airlines for business travel, they need to consider emulating airline institutional advertising techniques. A major step has been taken in this direction through the General Aviation Task Force's "GAME" plan that is promoting all aspects of general aviation flying through a national advertising campaign which supplies ad copy to individual general aviation businesses. Examples are shown in Figures 3.14 through 3.17.

Consulting as a Promotional Tool

In the aviation world a great deal of selling relates to the selling of aircraft, particularly to new business users that have been identified as a growth market. The general aviation manufacturers such as Beech, Cessna, and The New Piper offer to prospective buyers a pro forma analysis comparing current methods of travel for time and costs with travel by means of a corporate aircraft. The astute general aviation business can conduct this analysis on behalf of prospective buyers. The study helps the general aviation business achieve a better rapport with the prospective client and helps to specify exactly what type of aircraft will best meet the company's needs. Such a study will include:

> Current company travel patterns;
> Current travel costs (including overnight costs and time spent by personnel);
> Percentage of past year's travel that could have been made more efficiently by general aviation;
> Cost of making that travel by general aviation, including deductions for savings of time and overnight costs;
> Costs of aircraft ownership minus tax benefits; and
> Net positive or negative position resulting from use of corporate aircraft, annualized.

The study may be manual or computerized; the latter permits the testing of more assumptions. A general aviation business might offer to conduct such an analysis and refund its cost if the client buys an aircraft.

Sales

Needs Assessment

"Staying close to the customer" should be interpreted in part as listening to what problem the customer is trying to solve or what benefit he or she is seeking. Particularly for major purchases, a first discussion should likely focus only on needs and not on products.

Alternatives

A second, or second-stage discussion will present to the prospect some alternatives that the general aviation business has available to address the needs already expressed. The dialogue will give the buyer the opportunity to comment about each alternative.

Closing

Closing may involve satisfactorily addressing objections raised by the customer and presenting the best alternative in terms that suggest a purchase. Much has been written elsewhere about sales techniques and much of the necessary skill appears teachable if the salesperson has the right attitude. Selling should be a win-win proposition for the buyer and the seller, especially assuming that follow-up sales and service and positive referrals are desired. The same approach should be used whether the sale is large or small because the next purchase may be a major one.

Collecting

Payment is, of course, essential. Part of the sales process is to determine if the buyer is financially qualified for credit or is going to pay cash. Terms must reflect your costs of financing. Chapter 6, Organization discusses credit policies and procedures.

Marketing Controls

Marketing Plan

The marketing effort must be part of the overall business plan, for it is that portion of business planning that helps estimate sales and hence revenue to the business. Measures of marketing effectiveness may include sales volume, area coverage, new clients, product establishment, or all of these.

Contribution Analysis

Contribution analysis allows the manager to examine what contribution each sale makes to profit or overhead. For example, each sale might cost sixty cents and yield forty cents to pay commission, overhead, and profit. If a certain advertising promotion results in another 100 sales, the advertising cost per sale can be calculated and the contribution to profit compared with previous results. In this way the merits of more or less advertising for that product can be calculated in terms of the return yielded.

Performance Evaluation

An important area is the collection and analysis of sales data. Routine analysis of sales data for selected operating periods provides benchmarks that can be used to measure progress toward the selected goals of the firm as well as to analyze some of the fundamental assumptions used in setting these goals. The focus may be on sales territory, individual product, salesperson productivity, or cost analysis.

Quality Control

Some pilots who have flown in many parts of the United States comment that in some regions there seems to be more of a "pro-aviation" attitude. When a plane arrives, there is a "follow-me" van right there. And a red carpet treatment that offers to check everything, to obtain ground transportation, and to do whatever is needed in the way of service and information. In other regions, flyers say that it is difficult to even find line help and get the basics. Quality is a constant goal in the best businesses.

Budgeting

The marketing budget is part of the cost of doing business and must be set up by product or by division of the firm on an annual or quarterly basis. Chapter 4, Profits, Cash Flow and Financing discusses budgeting in more depth.

Information Systems

In order to keep track of the sales of numerous products and services and organize these data into useful monthly or other summaries, good record keeping and analysis are essential. A microcomputer can be very beneficial in this regard. This and other data systems are discussed in Chapter 7, Information Systems.

Integrated Marketing

In order to realize the maximum potential in a given business, the marketing effort should be developed as an integrated, consistent, and systematic approach. The first step is to clearly identify

This "follow-me" van is ready and waiting for a plane to arrive. Courtesy of Executive Beechcraft, Inc.

Figure 3.22 » Promotion Planning Chart for a General Aviation Organization

Planning Chart

ACTIVITY		January	February	March	April	May
LINE OPS	PLAN		check line needs			
	ACTION			Refurbish line, exterior paint, spruce		←
INSTRUCTION	PLAN	Plan Spring Learn to Fly Program Develop Prospect List Films - etc.			Flight School Air cond. June & July	Local Learn to Fly Promotion
	ACTION	Advanced Ratings →	Go Twin Learn to Fly Two Time	High School Promotion	← National Adv. $5, $88.	Learn to Fly → solo
FLIGHT SVCS	PLAN					
	ACTION	← Twin Invitational →				
ACFT SALES	PLAN			Plan for Arrow II		
	ACTION	National Adv. Business Twins Local Promotions Travel Analysis		→	← Arrow II Local Promotion PFC	Nat'l Adv →
PARTS	PLAN					
	ACTION			Promote Pilot Supplies		←
SERVICE	PLAN					Plan program- med maint. effort
	ACTION	Review Annual List	Promote Engine Work	Promote Radio Work		Promote Acft Clean-up
OTHER General	PLAN			Prepare Open House		
	ACTION	Review Plan for Year!!	Visit: News T.V.	Visit: Real Estate	Annual Open House	
OTHER	PLAN					
	ACTION					

Figure 3.22 » Continued

June	July	August	September	October	November	December
← Special Service Program →				Winterize & Safety Program		
	Plan Fall Instrument Rating Course	Plan PIP Trng. Fac.				
← Flight School—Air Cond. →		Follow Up Learn to Fly		Local Instr. Course Go Twin Natl. Adv.	PIP New Model Acft	← Ground School
			Order Calendars Navajo Now!		Plan local Twin Promotion	PFC Refresher
← Piper Nat'l Adv Fortune 500 →				Navajo now!	Calendar mailing	2003 material & literature
			Prepare Xmas List			
Promote Cleaning Materials →				December Gift Mailing		
Piper Nat'l Adv. For Programmed Maint. Local Program		Maint. Seminar				
Movie Showings	Airport Promotion			Fall Fly-In	Dealer Meeting!!	

the business goals, the products, and the market. All available tools should be utilized. Specific short-range objectives should be set. Budgeting may use a cost that is a percentage of past or forecast sales or may be based on other considerations such as matching competitors' spending or spending to achieve a certain sales goal.

Coordination of the marketing tasks to achieve the desired schedule is a key step. Work schedules, flowcharts, and similar tools may be helpful. Careful analysis at each step not only checks on progress, but also may suggest corrections and alternative marketing actions.

Marketing the Airport

Because of the general aviation business's dependence on the whole airport and not just on the part that he or she leases, the marketing function must address the question of creating and maintaining a positive image for the airport among nonuser neighbors who—as we have just seen—are likely to predominate over users. Even a privately owned airport must pay increasing attention to this because of:

> Land use and zoning decisions around the airport;
> Property tax questions;
> Availability of public federal funds for selected private airports;
> Public actions needed to protect airspace;
> The need for highway signs to the airport; and
> The need for support from the business community.

The general aviation business relies on a good public image for the total airport, whether he or she owns the field or is a tenant. The general aviation business can do much to create a positive attitude about the airport. For example, he or she can:

> Ensure that flight instructors and students know the noise-sensitive areas to avoid and the proper noise-abatement techniques for flight operations;
> Set up a documented complaint system for airport neighbors and meet personally with any who are the victims of buzzing or other inappropriate flight behavior;
> Invite airport neighbors to open houses and demonstration flights;
> Present the operation of the airport to business groups;
> Invite local public officials to visit the general aviation business and make presentations to flight school classes;
> Conduct tours for school children and others;
> Organize a fly-in or air show and invite the local community to attend; and
> Organize group meetings and seminars for local pilots or other groups including local business owners, letting them utilize airport facilities.

This topic is discussed further in Chapter 12, Physical Facilities. Such activities are a form of institutional marketing except that the general aviation business will be trying to convey the value of the airport as a whole, not just the part of it he or she may lease. Even if other general aviation businesses on the field are not willing to spend the time to do this, you should try to make it a priority. As a result goodwill will flow to the business.

Summary

The successful aviation manager develops a marketing orientation; he or she operates the business with a major focus on the customer. Specific target customers and markets are identified. The product and service, price, place and promotion mix is developed to meet customer needs. To accomplish this effectively, the first step involves the collection of information on the market and the many variables that affect business activity. From these data, a forecast must be developed that will enable the manager to formulate a marketing mix to satisfy buyer needs. The product element is concerned with firm identification of the "total" product and the market-related concepts of product categories, demand curves, supply curves, and product planning. Place deals with physical distributions: getting the right product to the target market in order to provide the customer with the right time-place-possession utility. Promotion activities are designed to inform, remind, and per-

» DISCUSSION TOPICS

1. Why is a "marketing orientation" important to the aviation manager and how can it be acquired?
2. Identify three key activities associated with a comprehensive marketing strategy.
3. Identify the "four p's" of marketing and discuss the ways in which they are different for general aviation businesses than for most other types of businesses.
4. Why are demand and supply curves useful in relation to market planning?
5. Describe three elements of distribution and how they function.
6. What methods would one select for (a) mass marketing, and (b) targeted marketing? How would each work?
7. How can one determine the effectiveness of promotional activities? Discuss two methods.
8. What are the pros and cons of setting prices based simply on your costs plus a profit margin?
9. Identify five types of market-related input that can be obtained from either sales records or customer feedback. How can each be used?
10. What is meant by "integrated marketing" and why does it matter?

suade target customers about the available products and services. This may be done through personal selling, mass advertising, direct mail, and other techniques. Price is based upon cost considerations tempered by pricing actions of competitors. Predicting market opportunities requires thorough study and constant vigilance for necessary adjustments resulting from economic and technological changes as well as changes in the competition. Marketing is more than sales; a sound marketing plan should guide the sales forecasting and implementation process through market research and strategy development.

Endnotes

1. Peters and Waterman. *In Search of Excellence—Lessons from America's Best-Run Companies.* New York: Warner Books, 1982.
2. Derived from Jerry Stoltenberg. *Determining Your Natural Market: Practical Market Research for Entrepreneurs In Fifteenth Annual Entrepreneurship Symposium.* School of Business Administration, University of Washington, May 12, 1984.
3. Discussed in more depth in Chapter 11.
4. Steckler, Steve A. "The Transformation of the US Air Travel Market," *Airport Magazine,* Fall 2001.
5. See above.
6. Telephone conversation on May 9, 2002 between the author and NATA's Jackie Rosser, who provided staff support to FOARC.
7. See note 6 above, op. cit.
8. Worrells, D.S., NewMeyer, D.A. and Ruiz, J.R. "The Evolution of Fractional Ownership: A Literature Review," *The Journal of Aviation/Aerospace Education & Research,* 10 (2001). 41-59.
9. A GA industry sponsored program to increase understanding and knowledge about general aviation and to encourage people to learn to fly. Participating flight schools offer a $49 introductory flying lesson and share in nationally developed media campaign materials.
10. Ante, Spencer B. "Up, Up and Away," *Business Week Online,* September 3, 2001.
11. Bolen, Edward M. "2001 Annual Industry Review," *General Aviation Manufacturers' Association,* February 13, 2002.
12. See *http://www.faa.gov/avr/afs/sportpilot/* for the full text of the Notice of Proposed Rulemaking (NPRM).
13. General Aviation Revitalization Act (GARA), August 17, 1994.

14. See *http://www.citizen.org/congress/civjus/prod_liability/general/articles.cfm?ID=562.*

15. See *http://www.api.faa.gov/pubs.asp* for a complete list of FAA forecasts. Also *http://www.api.faa.gov/conference/conference2002GA/GA-Over.htm* for the 2002 GA forecasting conference, which includes industry outlook information such as a speech by Drew Steketee, manager of the Be A Pilot program at *http://www.api.faa.gov/Conference/Conference2002GA/Steketee.htm.*

16. See *http://www.andersen.com/resource2.nsf/vAttachLU/9summer01_BusinessAviation/$File/9summer01_BusinesAviation.pdf.*

17. de Decker, Bill. "Price Based Costing-Gobbledygook or Good Business?" *AMT Online,* October 1999.

4

Profits, Cash Flow, and Financing

OBJECTIVES

- Describe the meaning of the word "profit."
- Enable the manager to distinguish between lack of profit and lack of cash flow and take appropriate corrective actions for each.
- Understand the relationship between social responsibility and profit in business decisions.
- Give examples of the differences between "fixed" and "variable" costs.
- Recognize methods of improving thc FBO's cash position.
- Realize the conditions needed for effective budgeting.
- Describe the benefits and disadvantages of extending credit to customers.

"Lack of cash can drive a firm into bankruptcy even though its products are first rate and its operations are profitable"[1]

Introduction

Historic Context

The economy of this country has been built upon entrepreneurs who started out small, provided a vitally needed product or service, made often very large profits, and plowed them back into the business to finance further growth. Profits were the key to a successful business. In former times, profits provided cash flow for two reasons. First, it was much more a cash economy, and customers expected to pay cash on the spot. Second, it was a tremendous growth economy so that demand was always outstripping supply and "supernormal" profits were often possible.

While this statement is a major simplification of the United States economy in pioneer days, it contains some important concepts. The main concept is that cash flow was not much of an issue. A second concept is that businesses were less likely than today to seek outside sources of financing to support growth, since internally generated funds arrived copiously and fast.

Profit and Cash Flow Today

Due to slower growth in most markets and to virtually instant communications about the competition, "supernormal" profits tend now to be only evident in new industries and then, evident only in the beginning. Due to the credit economy, cash flow lags are a major issue in almost every type of business. In many industries, customers expect at least thirty days to pay. Money has to be spent producing and delivering the goods well before the producer gets paid. Profits alone, when they are eventually collected, may not be sufficient to finance growth. Even when they are, financing may be needed to get a business out of seasonal or startup cash flow "holes."

One facet of cash flow is often not well understood: That the faster a company is growing today, the greater its cash flow problems are likely to be. It may be growing fast simply because it has found a highly profitable market niche. Nevertheless, more raw materials, people, and other inputs are generally needed to respond to the growth market with quality and promptness. Costs go up fast; and even though receipts will eventually come in, any lag can mean a cash flow "hole."

A successful small business will do well to consider, therefore, that both positive profit and positive cash flow are essential for continued operation. As indicated in the opening quote, the two do *not* necessarily go hand-in-hand. Each is a necessary, but not a sufficient condition, for the survival of the business. Large amounts of outside financing or funds obtained from selling off assets channeled into an unprofitable business will only delay, and not prevent, its demise. Borrowing to ensure a positive bank balance does not constitute an adequate financial survival plan. Having more money coming in than going out does not, alone, mean a healthy business if this situation appears only on financial statements (in terms of receivables) and not in the checking account (in terms of receipts actually received).

Figure 4.1 provides an illustration of the typical cash flow process in a small business and the ways that cash flow can be adjusted to keep the business solvent.

Figure 4.1 » Cash Flow Process in a Small Business

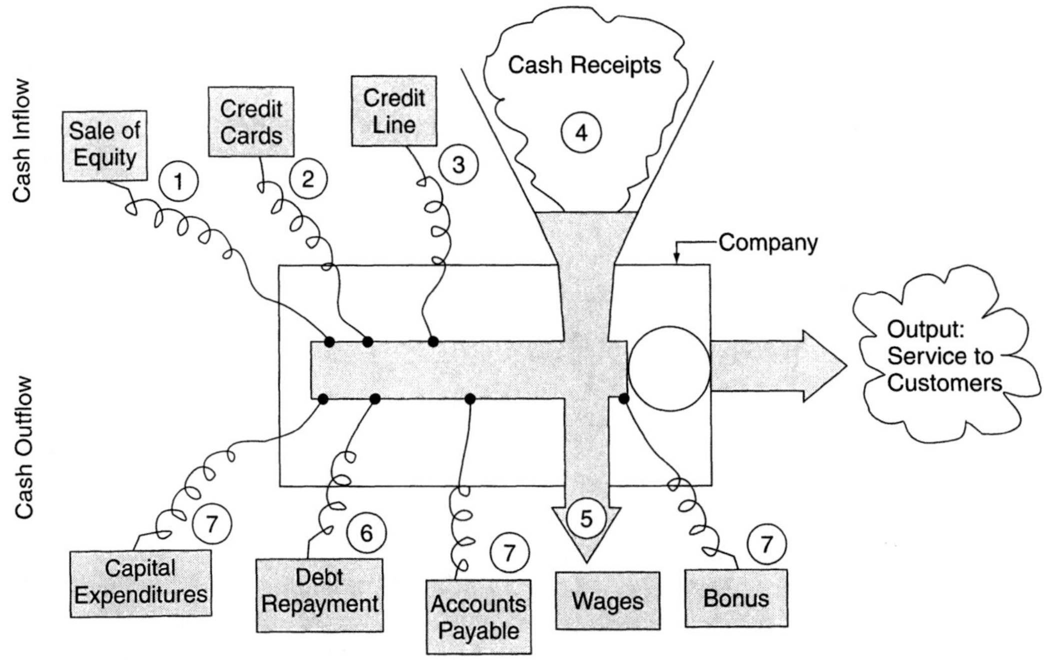

Notes:

1. Limited by ownership dilution.
2. Limited by debt/equity.
3. Limited only by capacity and sales.
4. Primary throughout.
5. Cannot be delayed.
6. Can be stretched to interest only (short term).
7. Can be delayed if insufficient cash (short term).

Source: Julie F. Rodwell and John Moore, 1984

This chapter examines how a financial plan for an FBO business can deal with both profit and cash flow in such a way as to provide the basis for long-term viability.

Definitions of Profit

Reward for Effort

Some business owners regard profit as being simply what is left after all the bills are paid. It is a bonus on top of their salary. Some do not even take a salary but look on profit, if there is any, to be their compensation. Yet the theoretical economist says that the very reason for anyone being in business is the "profit motive." Is the possible chance of something being left over when the bills are paid, a sufficient motivation?

Reward for Risk

A more precise definition of profit is reward for the risk of entrepreneurship. It therefore should be ranked with similar rewards from higher or lower risks that can be made with one's time and money. These range from speculating in highly risky but profitable investments to perhaps putting one's money in a passbook savings account at 5 percent or less.

Return on Investment

Profit measured in this way is examined as a percentage earned on the equity the owner(s) hold in the business. This ratio indicates whether the organization is realizing enough net profit in relation to dollars invested. A business owner should be able to get at least as high a return on total investment as he or she could by investing elsewhere, or have some acceptable reasons why not. To be in business at all, says this school of thought, an owner should not only be earning as much in wages as he or she would get from being on someone else's payroll, but should also be getting a reasonable pretax return on his or her investment in the business.

Profit to Sales Ratio

This ratio is calculated by dividing the net profits of the business by its total sales. It indicates whether profits are appropriate in relation to total dollars brought into the company through sales.

However, if an aviation specialist develops his or her own aviation service business rather than investing the funds elsewhere, it provides several other results in addition to a return on capital. For example:

- A full-time job and/or a vocation;
- A paycheck; and
- The opportunity to build a highly successful, profitable, and salable enterprise.

Profit ratios should be examined over time as well as used to compare the company with industry norms. As will be seen below, this is difficult to do, as the aviation service industry has tended to be an industry with few norms.

Profit Objectives

A business person has many possible choices regarding what plan for profits he or she wishes to pursue. The only inappropriate course, which happens more often than it should, would be not to plan for profit at all and just hope for the best.

Profit Maximization

In theory this is the only profit goal. The point of maximum profit can be calculated by examining the point of diminishing returns for the business's production; that is, that production volume at which the marginal cost of producing one more item exceeds the marginal revenue from selling it.

In reality, however, production functions tend to go in steps. That is, new economies of scale and higher rates of profit might be realizable by expansion. This expansion—such as a new maintenance hangar—tends to come in large units. Also, for any given set of production factors there is a point of diminishing returns. In a labor-intensive business, this might be the point reached when everyone has worked 15 hours a week overtime and is getting too tired. More output will require new hiring, and unit costs will go up again. Maximizing profit could mean doing less, not more.

Satisfactory Profit

More for the sake of more is increasingly less consistent with the lifestyle of many of today's managers, who may seek more leisure rather than more stress. Setting a profit goal in terms of a certain satisfactory dollar level, whether or nor it represents maximum profits, is a choice that many managers may want to make.

Non-Monetary Profit

A variation on the theme of modest profit is that many people in aviation are in it as much for the fun and excitement as for the money. There is an old joke about the couple that won the lottery. "What are you going to do with the winnings?" ask their friends. "We're just going to buy an FBO and run it till the money's all gone." This is fine except that it will not pay the bills and will not provide the return on investment one could get elsewhere. But a conscious lowering of profit goals because of enjoyment of the business is a possible approach. Some managers are forced to settle for this level of profits because their competition is setting profit low (and hence prices low) because of *their* love of flying.

Hobby/Business

A love of one's occupation to the point where profit is not a concern puts that enterprise in the category of a hobby rather than a business. If one's business is bordering on being a hobby, a consultation with a tax specialist would be in order. The requirements have been tightened up in relation to hobby businesses.

Social Responsibility

There is a body of opinion, which appears to be growing as a result of government program cutbacks, that says that business has a duty to support the needs of the community in a very broad way. Most managers do show considerable concern for the social environment that affects their employees and the community at large. Some of the things a good manager does perhaps cannot be justified on the grounds of profitability alone or even at all. However, they build loyalty and goodwill as well as help to ensure a long-range future for the airport. Such activities come under the topic of enlightened self-interest and are a cost of doing business. They do not need to erode profit, but the business' annual budget needs to set a ceiling for them.

Profit Levels

In planning for profit, what guidelines should an FBO use? In addition to what he or she could get by putting his money in the bank, he or she may want to know how others in industry set their profit goals or what they actually realize.

FBO Reports

When a number of FBOs were asked many years ago what their profits actually were, these were some of the replies:[2]

> "I'm lucky not to be losing money."
> "Hope to break even."
> "One to three percent."
> "Five percent."
> "Ten percent."
> "Fifteen percent."
> "Twenty-five percent."

The range of the replies and an analysis of the respondents suggest several things. Possibly some of these owners did not have good tracking systems and were guessing. First, one group felt that it was lucky to be breaking even. These people were in the 1 to 5 percent rate of return category. These may be new businesses, marginal operations, those experiencing temporary setbacks, or perhaps those that do not know their true profit.

Another group, in the 10 to 15 percent category, attempted to be realistic when comparing the aviation business with other possible investments for their money.

The last group (25 percent) was apparently concerned with the risky nature of the aviation business and felt that higher compensation for risk was appropriate.

The industry has become more business-like since this informal survey was taken; however, today it is difficult to obtain system-wide profit information on FBOs because of confidentiality, the competitive nature of the industry and the fact that some FBOs still do not even keep adequate records to determine their profit. However, when one considers that a person could invest his or her assets at 5 percent in a Certificate of Deposit (CD) and not work at all (assuming his principal is enough), this would indicate that 5 percent is not enough reward for all the hard work and worry that goes into running an aviation business. A person could invest in Mutual Funds and generate a 9–10 percent return over the long haul. The highest rates of return discussed here, 15–25 percent, is the rate that Fortune companies seek, and is only reasonable given the hard work and risk involved. So if a person does not think they can make at least 15 percent return on the business investment, then they should seriously consider whether to proceed. This is the profit level that the more effective aviation businesses are succeeding in making.

What one does with profit is a matter of choice: it can be taken as part of the owner's pay, passed on to employees, distributed to shareholders, reinvested in the business, used for corporate philanthropy, or a blend of all these.

What Is Your Profit?

It seems apparent from this discussion that there may have been successful FBOs making 20 percent or more profit. It also appears that lack of effort to ensure profit may contribute to the failure in reaching such a level. In addition to being the reward for risk, a solid profit margin has the added advantage of providing a cushion if extra expenses are suddenly required, as well as being available for planned long-term development of the business. Each business must make its own profit target and then, even more important, monitor to see if the desired results are being produced. Profit should be planned in the same way as fixed costs. Periodic cost surveys are performed by the industry and these may assist in developing budgets and planning for profit.[3]

Realizing Profit

Profit Orientation

Profit orientation refers to a positive attitude toward profit generation, the effective utilization of managerial tools and techniques in achieving desired profit levels, and the permeation of this orientation throughout the organization.

Key techniques used for staying focused on the dollar aspects of profits include cost control, break-even analysis, financial statement analysis, budgeting, and pricing. These are discussed in subsequent sections.

Cost Control

A major portion of profit orientation is cost containment orientation. The difference between profit and loss in a given time period may not be more volume of sales or different services, but simply reducing the cost of each unit of output through recycling, comparison shopping, thrifty approaches to getting work done, and minimization of overheads. These steps can be taken in major degree without harming quality.

Planning

Planning for profit is part of the overall business plan; and within the business plan, it is part of the financial plan, of which another part is cash flow planning. An adequate accounting system to track and report all financial activity in the firm is necessary for this purpose. Software such as "TotalFBO," "QuickBooks" or "FBO Manager" should be used and are discussed more fully in Chapter 7, Management Information Systems.[4]

Marketing Orientation

As discussed in Chapter 3, Marketing, a marketing orientation is also essential to a healthy business and to profits. It includes:

> The customer is always right;
> Knowing what the customer wants; and
> Service rather than product delivery.

Information System Design

A poor information system design can prevent profits because the manager is not getting information needed to answer certain questions. The manager needs the right information at the right time, though he does not need data collection on everything. With computerized financial management, analysis of even small time periods or small segments of the business is possible with very little work, and thus the manager should be able to keep needed profit data and trends at his fingertips. As mentioned, at least two "families" of FBO software are available; these are Total FBO and FBO Manager. This topic is discussed more fully in Chapter 7, Management Information Systems.

Records

Record keeping is the first step in implementation of the information system. Poor quality or absent records can be a hidden weakness in the system. Examples include:

> Fuel readings not taken and recorded;
> Sales slips not filed;
> Maintenance charges not entered for company aircraft;
> Accounts receivable not organized by age; and
> Balance sheets being available only many months after the period they cover.

With a completely computerized financial system, these problems should not arise.

Depreciation Practices

It is possible to treat depreciation of capital items in a number of ways with each having different long- and short-run tax implications that can affect income after taxes for a given year. The advice of an accountant who understands aviation is ideal.

Inventory

In calculating the business's assets and liabilities, inventory is often a major asset. However, it is important to know the true value of inventory, which may not be the same as what was paid for it. Replacement costs may change, and existing stock may deteriorate during storage due to obsolescence or decay. Storage and insurance costs must also be attributed to existing inventory.

Bad Debts

Not all accounts receivable—another major asset of most businesses—will be collected in full. Total losses and those where only a percentage is realized because a collection agency is involved must be subtracted from income. This can have a significant effect on profits. The manager will need to allow some estimate for the level of bad debts, based on past history and on policy.

Managerial Decisions

There are numerous other areas in which managers can affect profit without even realizing it. These may include:

1. Excess allocation of overhead could turn a profitable department into a loser.
2. A department receiving labor or supplies at cost is receiving a cash benefit. The department supplying it is losing because the same goods and services could have been sold outside at full markup.
3. "Pot mixing" or combining resources from several departments for a special project can make it hard to allocate overheads.

Cash Flow

The US has shifted to a credit economy. Customers expect this convenience and seek the protection that payment by credit card offers if there is a dispute with the seller. Using credit cards will cost the business owner a few percentage points, usually passed on to the customer, and will create a slight lag in payments compared with cash.

Allowing customers to have accounts that are invoiced monthly is a greater source of cash flow lags. When payments lag 30 to 90 days after delivery of goods and services, the resulting cash flow lag may require outside financing. If so, the cost of money can erode profits. However, some customers, longstanding and/or large, insist on company credit and you may still need to be prepared for this.

Setting Your Cash Flow and Profit Goals

Part I—Planning for Positive Cash Flow

Forecasting Sales and Revenues

For each product and service, an annual forecast of units sold must be made. This will be based partly on the past year's performance, partly on market research about needs and trends in the area, and partly on expectations about the economy. NATA periodically polls its membership about activity and plans and publishes findings. The aviation business manager should consider both national and local projections before deciding on the next year's volumes of business for each of his/her lines of activity, as was discussed in Chapter 3, Marketing.

After predicting volume for each item, the price must be multiplied by volume to get revenue for each line and total revenue must be calculated. (Pricing was reviewed in depth in Chapter 3 and will not be discussed here.) Sales by month should be estimated using seasonal factors common to the area. December, January, and February tend to be much slower aviation months nationwide than the rest except in certain resort areas, and most activity shows peaking over the summer months.

Forecasting Expenses

Expenses are generally defined as fixed, which have to be met merely for the business to open its doors, and variable, which go up as the volume of sales goes up. Fixed expenses or overhead include such items as:

> Rent;
> Utilities;
> Property taxes;
> Office supplies;
> Labor;
> Professional dues and publications;
> Janitorial and routine maintenance;
> Advertising (part);
> Inventory (part); and
> Insurance.

Of course, when inflation is more than zero, so-called fixed expenses also will tend to go up, and while some are predictable, such as rent, governed by escalator clauses in a lease, some are not. A worst- and best-case figure may be appropriate.

Some so-called fixed costs actually do go up because of growth. For example, more space or inventory may be needed. Heavy use of office machinery may cause it to wear out faster, or more inventory may be needed. More personnel often means new office furniture, another computer and other overheads, and if overhead costs are figured on top of the payroll cost of a new person, it may be two to three times his or her salary. The costs of expansion must always be calculated before deciding whether it is feasible. This is discussed in a subsequent section "Break-Even Analysis."

Expenses and sales of all types should be calculated at least on a monthly basis, and can readily be calculated more frequently if desired. This should be done allowing for seasonality of production needs and variations in overheads such as heating and air conditioning costs.

Month-by-Month Cash Flow Analysis

Particularly in a new business, but also in any business where cash flow lags or is erratic, a monthly cash flow for at least a year is a very valuable tool.

Figure 4.2 sets out a sample cash flow analysis for a very small company taking in $8,000 to $12,000 per month.

In Figure 4.2, the cash position shown in the bottom line tells whether and when the firm will get into a cash flow problem and how great the need for cash will be. It can also tell for a new business how many months will go by before the firm has a permanent positive cash flow. Some businesses swing from negative to positive cash flow and back each year. Such a case is the small airline serving an island resort. Practically all the revenue is made between May and September. The rest of the year the revenue is less because of much less activity producing much less income.[5] Borrowing and repayment are part of the year's plan.

Figure 4.2 provides a dramatic illustration of how a business can show a profit ($3,400 over seven months) yet still encounter serious cash flow problems (a cash flow "hole" of $4,750 by April).

In order to test a variety of cash flow scenarios, a spreadsheet program such as Excel may be used to change one figure at a time and automatically recalculate the bottom line. It is a good idea to make pessimistic assumptions about payment lags, bad debts, and costs in order to see the difference in cash position between that and the most likely case.

Improving the Cash Position

There are a number of ways that a firm can improve cash flow lags, including:

> Seek as many low rate credit cards as possible for the company and use these to be the company's "banker";
> Obtain cash on the spot for more services;

Figure 4.2 » Monthly Cash Flow Chart

	Jan.	Feb.	March	April	May	June	July. . .	7 months
Cash In								
Product 1	2,000	6,000	3,000	4,000	5,000	5,000	5,000	30,000
2	1,000	2,000	1,000	2,000	2,000	3,000	3,000	14,000
3	5,000	5,000	4,000	4,000	5,000	5,000	5,000	33,000
etc.								
Total cash in	$8,000	13,000	8,000	10,000	12,000	13,000	13,000	77,000
Cash Out								
Materials	2,000	2,500	1,500	1,000	1,000	1,000	1,000	10,000
Labor	3,000	3,000	3,000	3,000	3,000	3,000	3,000	21,000
Other inventory	500	600	700	400	500	500	500	3,700
Subtotal variables	5,500	6,100	5,200	4,400	4,500	4,500	4,500	34,700
Management	3,000	3,200	3,200	3,200	3,200	3,200	3,200	22,200
Rent	1,500	1,500	1,500	1,500	1,500	1,500	1,500	10,500
Utilities	250	250	250	250	250	250	250	1,750
Marketing/ads	200	1,000	1,000	750	1,000	250	250	4,450
Subtotal fixed	4,950	5,950	5,950	5,700	5,950	5,200	5,200	38,900
Total cash out	10,450	12,050	11,150	10,100	10,450	9,700	9,700	73,600
Net Cash Out	(2,450)	950	(3,150)	(100)	1,550	3,300	3,300	3,400
Starting Cash	-0-	(2,450)	(1,500)	(4,650)	(4,750)	(3,200)	100	-0-
Cumulative Cash or Deficit "hole"	(2,450)	(1,500)	(4,650)	(4,750)	(3,200)	100	3,400	3,400

- > Deposits and advance payments for a percentage of the cost (e.g., collect a deposit on a charter flight rather than waiting till the customer returns to get paid);
- > Larger deposits on aircraft sales;
- > Regular advance deposits from regular customers;
- > Memberships paid in advance of service delivery, such as annual flying dues;
- > Interest charges on accounts over 30 days past due;
- > Flight instruction courses paid in advance;
- > Factoring receivables—selling the accounts receivable at a discount; and
- > Borrowing against receivables.

A firm can also delay its own cash outflow by such techniques as:

- > Buying supplies on consignment—only paid for if and when sold; and
- > Negotiating more favorable terms for purchases including discounts and extended payments.

However, putting off payment will not cure the problems in a firm that never has a positive cash flow and is basically operating at a loss. Payments should only be deferred until the cash position is expected to improve.

Part 2—Planning for Profits

Profit Objectives

The desired profit in percentage terms should be converted into dollar terms for the year so that a precise profit figure is part of the budget.

Break-Even Analysis

Break-even analysis is the tool that identifies whether doing more business will result in more profit, or a loss. The first few units sold by a business probably do not bring in enough to cover even fixed costs. As sales go up, first variable costs, and subsequently fixed costs, are covered. The point at which all costs (variable plus fixed) are exactly covered (but no more) is the break-even point. Beyond that point, all revenue is profit as long as fixed costs do not go up. This is shown in Figure 4.3.

A break-even level of sales can also be calculated after insertion of a figure for profit. In this case, profit is treated just like any other expense:

Break-Even sales = fixed costs + variable Costs + profit

When a business owner is trying to decide whether to expand, it is apparent that any expansion requiring only higher variable costs will be profitable because each extra sale must cover only the extra or marginal cost of producing that sale, not the full cost. For example, the aviation manager plans to sell model planes at a convention. He can purchase the planes at $2.00 each on consignment (with the privilege of returning all unsold models). The booth rental is $800.00 and payable in advance. He feels that he can sell the aircraft models at $4.00 each. Assuming he is not going to count any labor costs, how many models must be sold to break even (zero profit)?

Break-Even sales = fixed costs + variable Costs + profit

Let x = number of units to be sold to break even

$4.00x = $2.00x + $800.00 + 0

2.00x = 800 + 0

X = 800 / 2

X = 400 units

Or in dollars:

X = $1600.00

Besides the Break-Even Point, three other important terms are the Contribution Margin, Unit Contribution Margin, and Contribution Margin Ratio. The Contribution Margin is what's left of revenue to contribute to fixed costs after variable costs have been subtracted:

Contribution margin = revenue − variable costs

The Unit Contribution Margin is the unit selling price less the unit variable cost. The Contribution Margin Ratio is the unit contribution margin divided by the selling price. In the case just described it was .5 ($2.00/$4.00).

The Break-Even Point (BEP) in dollars is (fixed expenses + profit)/contribution margin ratio.

Break-Even analysis can be used for a single product line or department or for the business as a whole. It can apply to:

> Fuel servicing activity;

> Billed service hours of a maintenance department;

> Instructional hours of a flight department;

> Activity volume of a parts department;

Figure 4.3 » Break-Even Chart

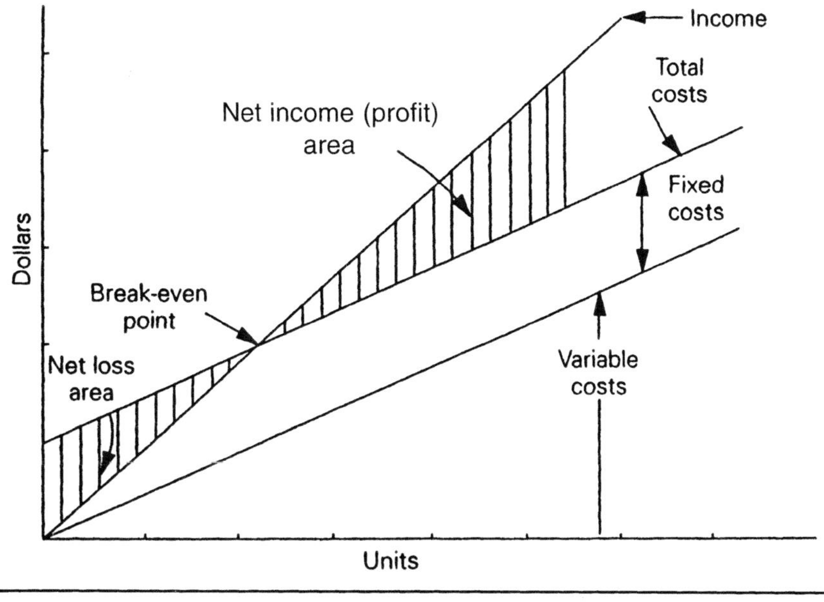

> Revenue hours of air charter or air taxi work;
> Route planning; and
> Acquisition of new operating equipment.

A more complex example is the decision of whether or not to start a new flight school operation. The FBO has the following estimates:

Fixed expenses:	
Building lease, utilities and taxes	$21,600
Aircraft insurance and depreciation	$18,000
Flight instructor base pay	$15,000
Subtotal fixed expenses	$54,600
Variable expenses:	
Aircraft operating expenses-$60/hr, for 2600 hours	$156,000
Instructor commission, $30/ flight hour	$78,000
Classroom time $30 per classroom hour, 200 hours	$6,000
Supplies/materials $300/student, 75 students	$22,500
Subtotal variable expenses	$262,500
Total Costs	$317,100
Estimated income	
Ground School, 75 students @ $1,050	$78,750
Flying Lessons, 2600 hours @ $135.00	$351,000
Instruction Kit, 75 @ $600	$45,000
Total income	$474,750

Using these figures we can examine the break-even point for each product:

Ground school selling price, $78,750/200 hours; per hour	$393.75
Average variable cost per hour	$30.00
Contribution Margin (Unit selling price of $393.75 less unit selling cost of $30)	$363.75

Break-Even Point = Fixed Expenses/ Contribution Margin
$54,600/$363.75 = 150.09 hours
150.09 hours x $393.75 = $59,099.44

Thus, the ground school alone could pay for all fixed costs and for its own variable costs if $59,099 worth of enrollments or 56 students were mustered, compared with an estimated sales potential of $78,750 or 75 students.

Suppose the FBO decides to examine just added flying lessons without the ground school.

Selling Price per Hour	$135.00
Average variable cost per hour ($60 + $30)	$90.00
Contribution Margin	$45.00

Break-Even Point = Fixed Costs/Contribution Margin
$54,600/$45.00 = 1,213 hours
1,213 × $135.00 = $163,755.00 income

Thus the flying lessons must make $164,000 (rounded) to break even compared with an estimated $351,000.00 in prospective sales.

Suppose now that all fixed costs are double the previous estimate, without changing the price:

Break-Even Point = Fixed Costs/Contribution Margin
$109,200/$45.00 = 2,427 hours
2,427 × $135.00 = $327,646

This is a much more marginal proposal because 93 percent of forecast sales must actually be achieved just to break even, which leaves very little room for sickness, bad weather, lack of demand, and so on.

Profitability Variations Among Product Lines

In the above example, the ground school was more profitable than the flying lessons because one instructor was handling one class of 75 students, whereas the flying lesson is a one-on-one situation with substantial aircraft and instructor costs. It is possible to take all fixed expenses and allocate them among the divisions of the business and estimate which areas are most profitable. For example, one FBO may decide that since there is ample extra space in the front desk area, he or she is going to emphasize the sale of aviation books and accessories, where the markup can be 100 per cent over wholesale for relatively little variable cost in handling. Another aviation business may see the strongest profit line in aircraft sales, where even a few percentage points in commissions can mean many dollars because of the high value of the item. An FBO may decide not to even compete in such areas as specialty avionics because there is another operator on the field and the cost of startup and getting established in the market would be so great for limited profit. Whatever the manager's inclinations, break-even analysis will provide the tools to find out whether something is really worth doing from a financial standpoint. Both breakeven and cash flow analysis should be applied to all prospective new ventures by using conservative assumptions. Keep in mind the "garbage in, garbage out" rule; i.e., one's results are only as useful as the quality of one's assumptions.

Profit Centers

Owing to different profitability levels, it may be desirable to divide the various functions of the business into separate profit centers, each having its own profit goal. This avoids hidden cross-subsidies among areas, and also permits conscious subsidy of certain items that may persuade people to make greater purchases (e.g., "free" washing of aircraft, coffee, air and other freely provided items).

In practical terms, setting up profit centers means that each revenue generating area of the business will be treated as its own mini-business. However, each must carry a share of the company's overhead or fixed costs—rent, heat and phones as well as those staff functions such as reception, computer administrator, CEO and bookkeeper who do not directly generate revenue themselves, although without whom, the business would fail. How this overhead is allocated should be examined from time to time, as annual budgets are set. Under the profit center model, one department performing work for another must also then be billed internally just as an external customer would be billed.

Profit and Loss Statement/ Income Statement

This is the operating income statement that represents the picture annually, monthly or quarterly. A skeleton income statement is shown in Figure 4.4:

The Gross margin is the funds taken in from sales before any of the internal or overhead costs (usually fixed costs) have been subtracted. The net profit (or loss) is what is left after all expenses have been taken out.

Balance Sheet

A balance sheet tells not only about the operating account, but also about the capital account, as shown in Figure 4.5. It tells "What you own and what you owe." Both the operating statement and the balance sheet need to be projected two to five years ahead. A company can have a healthy looking balance sheet and still have cash flow problems if its assets are tied up in plant and equipment

Figure 4.4 » Income Statement

George's Test Data
General Ledger Monthly Budget Review
For The Year: 1/ 1/2002 Through: 12/31/2002

		01/2002	02/2002	03/2002	04/2002	05/2002	06/2002	07/2002	08/2002	09/2002	10/2002	11/2002	12/2002	Total
Income														
4010.50	Fuel Sales - Line	500	500	500	500	500	500	500	500	500	500	500	500	6000
4060.01	PKG: Solo Rental Revenu	417	417	417	417	417	417	417	417	417	417	417	417	5000
4080.00	Charter Revenue	2083	2083	2083	2083	2083	2083	2083	2083	2083	2083	2083	2083	25000
	Total Income:	3000	3000	3000	3000	3000	3000	3000	3000	3000	3000	3000	3000	36000
Cost of Sales		01/2002	02/2002	03/2002	04/2002	05/2002	06/2002	07/2002	08/2002	09/2002	10/2002	11/2002	12/2002	Total
5010.10	Fuel Cost Of Goods Sold -	333	333	333	333	333	333	333	333	333	333	333	333	4000
	Total Cost of Sales:	333	333	333	333	333	333	333	333	333	333	333	333	4000
Expense		01/2002	02/2002	03/2002	04/2002	05/2002	06/2002	07/2002	08/2002	09/2002	10/2002	11/2002	12/2002	Total
7110.10	Salaries & Wages - Shop	833	833	833	833	833	833	833	833	833	833	833	833	10000
	Total Expense:	833	833	833	833	833	833	833	833	833	833	833	833	10000
	Net Budgeted Profit:	1833	1833	1833	1833	1833	1833	1833	1833	1833	1833	1833	1833	22000

Courtesy of TotalFBO Accounting and Business Management Software by Horizon Business Concepts, Inc.

Figure 4.5 » Balance Sheet

George's Test Data
General Ledger Balance Sheet Report
As Of: 5/31/2002
All Departments Consolidated

Assets			
	Current Assets		
1010	State Bank Checking #780017315	1,533.48	
1110	Petty Cash	425.00	
1120	Undeposited Receipts/Cash On Hand	18,757.19	
1200	Accounts Receivable	28,824.55	
1215	A/R Credit Cards	10,667.09	
1217	Contract Fueling Receivable	2,196.02	
1220	Employee Advances	440.00	
1300	Parts Inventory	17,078.64	
1310	Fuel Inventory	138,335.11	
1320	Oil Inventory	306.87	
1330	Aircraft Inventory	31,000.00	
	Total Current Assets	249,563.95	249,563.95
	Fixed Assets		
1540	Furniture And Fixtures	17,500.00	
1560	Automobiles	68,000.00	
1570	Computer System	17,000.00	
	Total Fixed Assets	102,500.00	102,500.00
	Intangible Assets		
1950	Computer Software Costs	3,989.00	
1980	Leasehold Improvements	18,900.00	
	Total Intangible Assets	22,889.00	22,889.00
	Total Assets:		374,952.95
Liabilities			
	Current Liabilities		
2000	Accounts Payable	225,085.16	
2010	Unearned Revenue (Customer Deposits)	1,520.13	
2030	N/P- Short-term	(645.96)	
2060	Suspense	(3,009.74)	
2070	Sales Tax 1 Liability	1,840.11	
2180	Salaries/Wages Payable	658.00	
2190	Employee Benefits Payable	1,588.15	
2200	Medicare Payable	362.80	
2210	FICA Payable	1,551.26	
2220	FIT Withholdings Payable	1,289.72	
2230	SIT Withholdings Payable	516.31	
2240	SUTA Payable	1,417.10	
2250	FUTA Payable	436.15	
2260	Worker's Comp Payable	9.23	
2330	Fuel Flowage Fee Payable	657.65	

Figure 4.5 » Continued

George's Test Data
General Ledger Balance Sheet Report
As Of: 5/31/2002
All Departments Consolidated

	2350	Charter Passenger FET Payable	1,550.64	
	2360	Charter Int'l Taxes Payable	56.10	
	2370	Charter Departure Tax Liability	192.00	
	2380	Landing Fees Payable	53.00	
	2390	Charter Per Segment Tax Liability	2.00	
		Total Current Liabilities	235,129.81	235,129.81
		Long-Term Liabilities		
	2520	N/P - Long-term	14,247.28	
		Total Long-Term Liab	14,247.28	14,247.28
		Owner's Equity		
	3600	Retained Earnings	(286,471.98)	
		Total Owner's Equity	125,575.86	125,575.86
		Total Liabilities:		(37,094.89)
Equity				
	3010	Owner Capital	500,000.00	
	3900	Current Earnings	(87,952.16)	
		Total Equity:		412,047.84
		Total Liabilities and Equity:		374,952.95

Notes:
All Departments Consolidated.

Courtesy of TotalFBO Accounting and Business Management Software by Horizon Business Concepts, Inc.

needed for the business operation and not readily liquidated.

Part 3—Budgeting

Introduction

There are some popular misconceptions about budgeting that have detracted from its use and effectiveness. Some individuals feel that a budget is a straightjacket; others feel that it is repressive; some people feel that it wastes time; and still others feel that it is a mechanical, futile activity. Many who have experienced the heavy end-of-year spending in order to make the budget appear accurate or to ensure they get at least as much in the next cycle ("use it or lose it") lack confidence in the process. Most of these misconceptions are the result of personal experiences in situations where budgeting was not handled properly or where the individual may have overreacted to the process.

Budgeting involves setting cost limits for each unit of the firm or cost center. These limits are based on the projected sales and profit desired for the line departments or with some reference to overhead as a percentage of business costs or sales for the administrative or staff departments. Budgets can be changed in the course of the year if circumstances warrant, and break-even analysis can help decide if a budget should be increased to capture a new business opportunity. The budget need not be a straightjacket but can achieve the following:

> Set specific goals for each department and the firm as a whole;
> Establish limits within which managers know they are to operate;
> Establish company needs and priorities during the budget period;
> Foresee potential operational problems and allow preventive action;
> Provide management with increased flexibility;
> Provide management with an early warning system if costs are getting too high or revenues too low;
> Inform line departments about improvements planned for later years;
> Provide standards to measure performance and results; and
> Enable intended profits to be actually realized.

Aviation Budget Development

Developing a budget for an aviation business, like any other business, is really profit planning. From a practical point of view, it is a technique for managing the business. It involves the formation of definite plans (budgets) for a limited future period. These plans are normally expressed in financial terms. A complete budget develops and includes standards to measure and evaluate the actual performance of management and the business.

In order for a budget to serve as an effective managerial tool, several conditions should exist. It is perhaps the absence of these conditions that creates the misconceptions and apprehension already mentioned. Advocates of the budgeting process suggest that the following are necessary:

1. There should be a suitable organization structure for the business activity.
2. An adequate accounting system should be in operation. Today that will be a computerized system.
3. The budget should have the interest and support of top management.

Preliminary preparations for the budget, much as already discussed in planning for profit, include:

> Forecasting business activity;
> Preparing budget proposals;
> Assembling and approving the budget;
> Using supporting budgets; and
> Budget operation and control.

Steps in Budget Development

Preparing for the budget. The first and most important preparations are setting goals, defining objectives, and creating long-range plans for the organization. As was discussed in Chapter 2 under planning, it is essential that the manager have a good grasp of the present organizational situation. He or she then develops a plan that is complete with goals and objectives. These goals and objectives should then be related to financial and other specific goals for the coming year. The objectives that are developed should express the desired results in specific measurable terms. Developing the long-range plan is considered an important prelude to the development of the budget, for there is obviously a very close correlation between the two. A budget may be considered the first year of a long-range plan—the implementation of that plan.

Forecasting business. Chapter 3, Marketing, discussed other business forecasting issues and sources of published aviation forecasts. What follows here is in brief.

Next, the manager develops some careful estimates or forecasts of business conditions that are expected to exist during the budget period. Although all external conditions are important, the critical task is the selection of conditions facing the individual business. Many managers feel that this is the chief difficulty in budgeting. They indicate major problems in: (1) obtaining meaningful figures in advance; and (2) making good use of the information available. Forecasting future business is a fundamental and necessary process that must be accomplished for all businesses. It is not, however, an activity approached enthusiastically by all managers, partly because of unfamiliarity with the procedure, and partly due to apparent failures of past attempts. It is much art as science, that is, the assumptions made cannot all be derived and defended technically. However, they should be based on solid research and spelled out. Then if conditions change, it will be clear what assumptions underlying the calculations need to be changed.

It is felt that more meaningful figures can be developed by using a procedure that considers:

> Identification of the general economic situation;
> Key regulatory factors that influence the business environment;
> Recent industry developments;
> Specific trend and forecast data that might be acquired;
> The evaluation of business opportunities that may exist;
> Local economic trends and factors; and
> Competitive elements facing the business.

Budget preparation. With the forecast data in hand, the manager's next (and very important) step is the preparation of the budget. The development of the detailed blueprints showing how the company intends to reach the desired goals and objectives in the business conditions identified by the forecast is best accomplished in the following sequence:

1. Set a timetable for activity.
2. Develop a sales budget.
3. Formulate a purchases budget.
4. Develop an expense budget.
5. Formulate the income statement budget.
6. Calculate a balance sheet budget.

Timetable. It is very important to prepare a timetable for the development of a budget. Such a schedule is necessary because budgeting is a planning activity and is very likely to be postponed if not established on a fairly regular schedule. The following illustrates a timetable for a small company budget based on a calendar-year cycle. Larger companies, with more review layers, will need to start earlier. (Note that many public agencies start their annual budget process in about April of each year, aiming at adoption by Thanksgiving). Of course, it should be recognized that a budget is a living, flexible document that must meet the variable conditions facing the business enterprise. The possibility and reality of change must become part of the timetable and the budgeting process.

Date	Activity
15 October	Develop plans and objectives
1 November	Complete business forecast
10 November	Develop preliminary budget
15 November	Final budget review
1 December	Budget acceptance and approval
1 January	Initial implementation
As required	Budget modification

Sales budget. The manager begins the development of this budget by working on the sales estimate. Since most of the activities of a business are geared to the level of expected sales, budget preparation begins with sales forecasting. The business forecasting procedures mentioned earlier should provide the basic material needed to start this first step. In some instances, it may even provide the exact information for a sales budget if the historical information is available and the forecast has been prepared in adequate detail. The initial step is a thorough market analysis. Normally, this is composed as an analysis of the overall marketplace (as is outlined in the earlier section on forecasting), salespeople's estimates of the market situation, general sales trends in the industry and the area, and a study of previous years' sales.

The second step is the development of the company market forecast. Using a great deal of the data acquired in step 1, a forecast is prepared for the company's market potential. The structure of the market in terms of types, units, time, and prices is set forth.

The third step involves pricing out the company forecast in order to acquire the expected total sales (revenue) of the business. Adjustments are made to reflect the goals and objectives of the business as well as the market situation.

The next step is the breakdown of total sales into the departments or work centers of the business. The expected incomes for parts, service, flight line, aircraft sales, instruction, and miscellaneous are estimated for the accounting year. Naturally, this reflects the forecast data used in the development of total sales.

The final step is the development of a monthly sales budget for each of the identified departments in the business. This enables the manager to identify and anticipate the monthly variations in sales due to seasonal and other fluctuations.

Figures 4.6 and 4.7 illustrate worksheets that may be used to calculate the sales budget for an

Figure 4.6 » Annual Sales Budget Worksheet

	Previous Year Budget	Previous Year Actual	Current Year Budget
Total Sales of Company			
Aircraft sales (300)			
Parts Sales (400)			
Service Sales (500)			
Flight Sales (600)			
Line Sales (700)			
Misc. Activity (800)			

Figure 4.7 » Monthly Budget Report

George's Test Data

One-Year Budget Performance Report

All Departments Consolidated

Account	For the Month Ending: 5/31/2002 Budgeted	Actual	Variance	Pct	Year-To-Date: 1/ 1/2002- 5/31/2002 Budgeted	Actual	Variance	Pct
Income								
4000 Parts Sales	0.00	0.00	0.00	0.0%	0.00	28.13	28.13	0.0%
4010 Fuel Sales	500.00	6,427.60	5,927.60	1185.5%	2,500.00	6,747.20	4,247.20	169.9%
4015 Into-Plane Fees	0.00	0.00	0.00	0.0%	0.00	500.00	500.00	0.0%
4060 Solo Aircraft Rental Revenue	416.67	572.40	155.73	37.4%	2,083.35	572.40	-1,510.95	-72.5%
4070 Dual Aircraft Rental Revenue	0.00	96.00	96.00	0.0%	0.00	186.00	186.00	0.0%
4080 Charter Revenue	2,083.33	5,520.00	3,436.67	165.0%	10,416.65	5,520.00	-4,896.65	-47.0%
4081 Charter Income - Aircraft Standby	0.00	20.00	20.00	0.0%	0.00	20.00	20.00	0.0%
4082 Charter Revenue - Pilot Standby	0.00	10.00	10.00	0.0%	0.00	10.00	10.00	0.0%
4100 Flight Store Revenue	0.00	134.60	134.60	0.0%	0.00	134.60	134.60	0.0%
4140 Instruction - Primary Revenue	0.00	22.40	22.40	0.0%	0.00	22.40	22.40	0.0%
4160 Ground School Revenue	0.00	25.20	25.20	0.0%	0.00	25.20	25.20	0.0%
4930 Miscellaneous Revenue	0.00	40.00	40.00	0.0%	0.00	90.00	90.00	0.0%
Total Income:	3,000.00	12,868.20	9,868.20	328.9%	15,000.00	13,855.93	-1,144.07	-7.6%
Cost Of Sales								
Total Cost Of Sales:	0.00	0.00	0.00	0.0%	0.00	0.00	0.00	0.0%
Gross Profit:	3,000.00	12,868.20	9,868.20	328.9%	15,000.00	13,855.93	-1,144.07	-7.6%
Expense								
5000 Parts Cost Of Goods Sold	0.00	87.50	87.50	0.0%	0.00	96.50	96.50	0.0%
5010 Fuel Cost Of Goods Sold	333.33	3,940.96	3,607.63	1082.3%	1,666.65	4,134.31	2,467.66	148.1%
7010 Lost Fuel Inventory	0.00	95,859.13	95,859.13	0.0%	0.00	95,859.13	95,859.13	0.0%
7110 Salaries/Wages Expense	833.33	658.00	-175.33	-21.0%	4,166.65	1,581.08	-2,585.57	-62.1%
7140 Taxes-FICA	0.00	0.00	0.00	0.0%	0.00	57.23	57.23	0.0%
7150 Taxes-Medicare	0.00	0.00	0.00	0.0%	0.00	13.38	13.38	0.0%
7160 Taxes-FUTA	0.00	0.00	0.00	0.0%	0.00	57.23	57.23	0.0%
7190 Taxes-Worker's Comp	0.00	0.00	0.00	0.0%	0.00	9.23	9.23	0.0%
Total Expense:	1,166.66	100,545.59	99,378.93	8518.2%	5,833.30	101,808.09	95,974.79	1645.3%
Net Income:	1,833.34	-87,677.39	-89,510.73	-4882.4%	9,166.70	-87,952.16	-97,118.86	-1059.5%

Courtesy of TotalFBO Accounting and Business Management Software by Horizon Business Concepts, Inc.

aviation business. Figure 4.6 deals with the total and departmental sales budget while Figure 4.7 shows the monthly budget report with budgeted activity, actual results, and variances (deviations) from that budget. In using Figure 4.6, the previous year's budget and actual sales are filled in for the total business and the departmental components. Using this as a guide along with the other elements for developing a forecast, the current year budget is projected.

Purchases budget. Next is the development of the purchases budget. In order to achieve the desired sales level, it will obviously be necessary to purchase the products that will be sold to meet the sales budget goals. Figure 4.8 illustrates a worksheet for developing a purchases budget. Note that in calculating anticipated purchases that it is necessary to consider dollar volume of sales first. Then, the number of units or quantity of material needed to arrive at the right sales volume is calculated by using the markups for the various product areas. These annual purchase figures (which are expressed in dollars and units of quantity) are then divided into monthly allocations.

Expense budget. The manager next constructs an expense budget. Figure 4.9 illustrates a worksheet that may be used in this process. In this instance, the expense budget categories are identified as employment, aircraft, occupancy, and other. These four major groups are divided into subcategories, which are the expense accounts contained in the ledgers of the accounting system. In general, these expenses are incurred by operating the business. The worksheet is com-

Figure 4.8 » Combined Annual and Monthly Purchases Budget Worksheet

Guidelines:

Includes those goods that are the basis for the sales budgets. Materials on hand, plus units required for sales, resulting in the desired ending inventory needed for each product, by month.

Procedure:

1. Determine the total amount for each activity area, that is, sales, parts, service, and so on as a portion of the total sales volume.
2. Allocate the amount for the twelve months, making adjustments for seasonal variances.
3. Determine the units required for each month where appropriate.
4. Adjust annual budget as required.

		Annual Budget	Jan.	Feb.	Mar.	Apr.	May	June	July	Aug.	Sept.	Oct.	Nov.	Dec.
Aircraft	$													
Sales	#													
Parts	$													
Sales	#													
Service	$													
Sales	#													
Flight	$													
Sales	#													
Line	$													
Sales	#													
Misc.	$													
Activity	#													

Figure 4.9 » Expense Budget Worksheet

EXPENSE BUDGET WORKSHEET

Procedure:
1. Fill in previous year annual expense figures
2. Based upon anticipated level of business activity, project the current year annual expense figures
3. Allocate the annual expense figures to months.

		EXPENSES:		Annual		Jan.	Feb.	Mar.	Apr.	May	June	July	Aug.	Sept.	Oct.	Nov.	Dec.
				Previous Year	Current Year												
6	EMPLOYMENT	Salaries – Officers	20														
7		Salaries/Wages – Employees	21														
8		Commissions	22														
9		Taxes – Payroll	23														
10		Employee Benefits	24														
11																	
12																	
13																	
14		TOTAL EMPLOYMENT															
15	AIRCRAFT	Aircraft Delivery	30														
16		Aircraft Miscellaneous	31														
17		Depreciation – Aircraft	32														
18		Fuel & Oil – Aircraft	33														
19		Insurance – Aircraft	34														
20		Interest – Aircraft	35														
21		Inventory Adjustment – Aircraft	36														
22		Maintenance – Aircraft	37														
23		Warranty	38														
24																	
25																	
26		TOTAL AIRCRAFT															
27	OCCUPANCY	Rent	44														
28		Depreciation/Amortization - Bldg.	45														
29		Taxes – Property	46														
30		Utilities	47														
31		Maintenance – Bldg./Land	48														
32																	
33																	
34		TOTAL OCCUPANCY															
35	OTHER EXPENSES																
36		Advertising	50														
37		Bad Debts	53														
38		Depreciation – Other	56														
39		Donations & Dues	59														
40		Freight & Postage	62														
41		Insurance – Other	65														
42		Interest – Other	68														
43		Inventory Adjustment – Other	71														
44		Maintenance – Other	74														
45		Professional Services	77														
46		Supplies	80														
47		Taxes–Other than P.R./Prop./Inc.	83														
48		Telephone & Telegraph	86														
49		Travel	89														
50		Vehicle	92														
51																	
52																	
53																	
54		Miscellaneous	98														
55																	
56		TOTAL EXPENSES															

pleted and filling in previous-year expense figures and then projecting the current-year expenses forms the budget. Of course, this projection is based upon anticipated sales and the effect upon expenses required to support the sales. The annual expense for each account is divided into a monthly expense item according to an appropriate system. It may be a straight percentage or it may be based on work load, number of people, borrowing schedule, marketing plan, or some other factor according to the elements that dictate or control the expenditures.

Income statement budget. The next key step in developing a complete budget is bringing the sales and expenses together into an income statement budget. Figure 4.10 suggests a budget worksheet. This form follows the income statement format and uses it for budgeting purposes with both previous year and current year figures. Sales, purchases, and expenses all come from the completed worksheets in those areas. The basic objective of this worksheet is to bring them all together with the primary focus on profit. At this stage, the goal is profit planning-budgeting for the desired net income for the operating period. This is the ultimate objective of budgeting: to identify planned operating profit.

Balance sheet budget. The final step in the budgeting process is to transfer the overall outcome of the operating budget to the balance sheet and to develop a projection for the total financial condition of the company. By using a worksheet comparable to those for sales, purchases and expenses, a budget can be constructed to show anticipated changes in assets, liabilities, and net worth. Desired business activities will influence accounts in each of these areas and a budget will assist in testing the feasibility of such action.

Budget assembly and approval. All the business activities should be represented in the budgeting process and in the various divisions of the budget. The final budget should be presented to identify clearly the organization's subdivisions and their assigned budget goals. The budget's figures should represent reasonable but not easily attainable goals. The personnel involved in and responsible for achieving business results should also be involved in the development of the budget. Back-up schedules should be developed as necessary features to augment the budget. The budget should not be developed with the expectation of cutting; rather, it should be considered a realistic contribution to achieving the overall company objectives.

In addition to these guidelines, the human aspects of budget building should be recognized and every effort made to create a structure as free from personal distortion as possible. Some of the likely distortions that might detract from the desired objectivity are:

- Preparing a low budget in order to play the role of the "successful, driving leader";
- Preparing a budget with excessive figures to get "my fair share" of the funds;
- Allowing personal biases for a favorite aspect of the business to have too great an influence;
- Allowing a "halo" effect associated with one department or business activity to distort the overall company budget beyond realistic expectations; and
- Distorting the sound budget concept into a game of trying to outguess the approving level of management.

Using supporting budgets. In developing and utilizing a budget system, a manager will undoubtedly need to establish and use several additional supporting budgets to meet specific needs. He or she may need one for cash, one for people, one for fixed assets, or for a variety of items already in the budget as a single line but in need of support. One such budget with universal application and of special interest is a cash budget or a cash flow projection. Since cash flow is so very important to a business, we will review the cash budget in some detail. It is a schedule over time of cash inflows and outflows. This is used in an attempt to pinpoint cash surpluses and shortages so that the manager can always be certain to have sufficient money in the bank to cover obligations or have a plan to invest surpluses. There are a variety of uses of the cash forecast, including:

- Determining operating cash requirements;
- Anticipating short-term financing needs;
- Investing excess cash;

Figure 4.10 » Budget Worksheet Used to Formulate Complete Budget

INCOME STATEMENT BUDGET WORK SHEET

LINE NO.			ACCT. NO.	PREVIOUS YEAR BUDGET	PREVIOUS YEAR ACTUAL	CURRENT YEAR BUDGET
1		TOTAL SALES				
2		COST OF SALES				
3		GROSS PROFIT				
4		Gross Profit – % of Sales				
5		EXPENSES:				
6	EMPLOYMENT	Salaries – Officers	20			
7		Salaries/Wages – Employees	21			
8		Commissions	22			
9		Taxes – Payroll	23			
10		Employee Benefits	24			
11						
12						
13						
14		TOTAL EMPLOYMENT				
15	AIRCRAFT	Aircraft Delivery	30			
16		Aircraft Miscellaneous	31			
17		Depreciation – Aircraft	32			
18		Fuel & Oil – Aircraft	33			
19		Insurance – Aircraft	34			
20		Interest – Aircraft	35			
21		Inventory Adjustment – Aircraft	36			
22		Maintenance – Aircraft	37			
23		Warranty	38			
24						
25						
26		TOTAL AIRCRAFT				
27	OCCUPANCY	Rent	44			
28		Depreciation/Amortization - Bldg.	45			
29		Taxes – Property	46			
30		Utilities	47			
31		Maintenance – Bldg./Land	48			
32						
33						
34		TOTAL OCCUPANCY				
35	OTHER EXPENSES					
36		Advertising	50			
37		Bad Debts	53			
38		Depreciation – Other	56			
39		Donations & Dues	59			
40		Freight & Postage	62			
41		Insurance – Other	65			
42		Interest – Other	68			
43		Inventory Adjustment – Other	71			
44		Maintenance – Other	74			
45		Professional Services	77			
46		Supplies	80			
47		Taxes–Other than P.R./Prop./Inc.	83			
48		Telephone & Telegraph	86			
49		Travel	89			
50		Vehicle	92			
51						
52						
53						
54		Miscellaneous	98			
55						
56		TOTAL EXPENSES				
57		Expenses – % of Sales				
58		OPERATING PROFIT				
59						
60		Other Income				
61						
62		Other Expense		( )	( )	
63						
64		INCOME – Before Special Charges				
65						
66						
67						
68						
69		INCOME – Before Income Taxes				
70		Provision For Income Taxes	290			
71						
72						
73		FINAL NET INCOME				

Procedure:

1. Using the sales, purchase and expense worksheets, complete the previous year budget and actual columns
2. Complete the current year column
3. Compare projected net income with selected business goals

> Planning reductions in debt;
> Scheduling capital payments;
> Taking advantage of cash discounts; and
> Supporting credit policies.

The primary method of developing a cash flow forecast is through the receipts and disbursements comparison. This procedure generally adheres to the following pattern:

1. Develop forecasts for sales, purchases, expenses and related schedules.
2. Analyze the forecasts carefully to identify the cash receipts and payments of each particular period.
3. Using the cash budget worksheet (Fig. 4.11), list the receipts and disbursements for the periods that cash actually changes hands.
4. Review the projected results of the worksheet. Note the periods requiring additional outside funds and periods providing excess funds for use in retiring obligations or for investment.

With the cash position identified, the manager can take action to control the cash flow through day-by-day transactions. Three such actions are (1) speeding up collections, (2) controlling payables, and (3) controlling bank balances.

Budget Operation and Control

Once a budget period begins, the function of budgeting becomes one of exercising control over business operations as they progress. The word

Figure 4.11 » Cash Budget Worksheet

Procedure:
1. Identify the cash receipts and payments expected throughout the year.
2. List receipts and disbursements for the periods that cash actually changes hands.
3. Note difference between cash available and that required.
4. Plan for the source of needed funds or the utilization of excess.

Item	Jan.	Feb.	Mar.	Apr.	May	June	July	Aug.	Sept.	Oct.	Nov.	Dec.
1. Cash Balance, Beginning												
2. Add Receipts from Customers												
3. Total Available												
4. Less Disbursements												
5. Payroll												
6. Aircraft												
7. Occupancy												
8. Misc.												
9. Income Tax												
10. Total Disbursements												
11. Difference between Cash Available and Required (Line 3 minus Line 10)												
12. Source or Utilization												

control, as used here, means making certain that actual performance is going according to plan. This usually requires:

> Periodic reporting of performance;
> Comparing performance with the budget (plan);
> Pinpointing reasons for variations;
> Taking action to correct unfavorable variances; and
> Reevaluating the original budget goals.

Frequently, an examination of a budget in operation will suggest problems in the operation. When the budget is examined closely, one or more of the following deficiencies may be noted:

1. There has been a poor determination of budget standards.
2. Not all key business activities have been included in the budget.
3. The budget has not been revised when the need is indicated.
4. There is a lack of understanding of the budget process throughout the organization.
5. There is a lack of acceptance of the budget by management and employees.

The budget area should not be closed without at least a mention of the flexible or variable budget. The budgets discussed thus far are static in that the plan is geared to a single target level of sales. A flexible budget is geared to a range of activity rather than one level and will supply a more dynamic basis for comparison than will a fixed budget. As aviation managers and organizations become better versed in budgeting, they might like to use flexible budgeting for some or all of their needs.

Part 4—Other Considerations

Tax Planning

As mentioned, tax planning can affect cash outlays in a given year and in the amount, especially in relation to depreciation and tax credits. Taxes are an expense like any other but their prediction requires the skills of an accountant who not only sees you once a year, but also may have helped to set up the books to collect the data needed for taxes and other purposes.

Competition

At all times an FBO must watch the competition and determine whether to match someone else's new service, reduce prices, or be innovative by trying something new. These contingencies should be allowed for in the business plan.

Retained Earnings

These are profits plowed back into the business or kept liquid for a rainy day. The cyclical nature of aviation suggests the desirability of retained earnings if only to even out the good and bad years.

New Revenue Sources

Many public airport owners are seeking new sources of revenue at airports and often finding that the most profitable ones are not aviation.

Related. The feasibility of each depends on the size and clientele of the airport, but an FBO might be able to tap these just as readily as an airport manager. These are some possibilities:

> Vending machines;
> Luggage lockers;
> Copying machines;
> Cash machines;
> Stores and newsstands;
> Latte stands, coffee shops and restaurants;
> Pay phones;
> Car rentals;
> Parking lots;
> Rental of unneeded space for commercial use;
> Agricultural (for example sale of hay, turf farming, worm farming);
> Video games; and
> Travel agent commissions.

While leases may preclude some of these, any way to increase profits should be given consideration if little or no expense is involved.

Financing

Types of Money

There are basically four types of money for running a business: short-term cash, long-term cash, equity, and employee ownership. Each has different conditions. The last two involve giving away some of the ownership, and probably control, to others in exchange for their cash or their willingness to forgo short-term cash.

Sources of Money

Family and friends. Many businesses start this way. It is important to be extremely specific about ownership, control, profit sharing, and inheritance where this approach is used. All loans should be written in as businesslike a fashion as if they were for strangers.

Accounts receivable financing. Accounts receivable financing, usually involving factoring, can help a business that is already operational but suffering from lags in collection. The factoring company normally takes title to invoices and collects directly from your customers. Rates charged by factors may be fixed or may vary with the collection period. However, your administrative costs can be cut or even eliminated; and once a relationship with a factor is set up, you can get cash at the time of invoicing.

Banks also from time to time finance accounts receivable. A bank will not buy the invoices; rather, it will loan a percentage of the face value of invoices to the business on the day that the invoices are sent out. The business owner pay receipts from them into a special account from which the bank first pays itself and then any remainder goes into a business checking account. This will normally cost less than factoring, but the business owner is still responsible for collection of any bad debt. A bank may want some collateral to set up this arrangement.

Leasing. Leasing and lease purchasing are good ways to keep monthly costs down when compared with buying outright. Lease purchase terms, especially where the lessor takes care of maintenance, may be extremely cost effective.

Venture capital. Venture capital sources grew in the 1990s, particularly for high-tech areas, but for an FBO they remain an unlikely source. This is because investors are looking for five to ten times their investment within five years; also, they usually will only consider large potential sales. The dramatic growth path of any product in its early years is ideal for venture capital. One drawback is that ownership of 40 percent or more of the business will pass to the venture firm.

SBA. Small Business Administration (SBA) loans are actually usually loan guarantees. Being turned down twice for regular bank financing makes one eligible. Points above prime are charged, making this a very costly source of aid. Owing to the paperwork and conservatism involved in the banking industry, it is uncommon for new businesses to get SBA loans.

Customers. A common practice among FBOs is to invite steady customers to place several hundred dollars on account with a small bonus of credit for doing so. This method can encourage a close rapport with a set of regular customers and keep the bank balance healthy. However, the true cost of this financing depends on how fast the customer uses up his credit account. If he uses it in a month, you may have provided a rather high annual rate of interest.

Banks. A bank will give a secured line of credit relatively easily for a few points above market rate. For an unsecured line of credit or a loan against receivables, they want to know everything about the business, its managers, and its performance. The more polished and detailed the presentation, the better chance of success. Also, it appears to pay to dress as a banker when making the request.

Public markets. Going public is complex and expensive, but some states have limited variations on full public ownership that could be feasible for an FBO.

Small Business Investment Companies (SBIC). These are companies licensed by the Small Business Administration (SBA) to provide equity capital or long-term loans to small businesses.[6] They are restricted to businesses with a limited net worth and net income. Rates and equity are determined by negotiation but the SBIC does not generally seek control.

Credit Management

Nature and Reason for Credit

Credit is derived from credo. This means "I believe" or "I trust." Today, credit provides a measure of the trustworthiness of an individual to receive goods and services while deferring payment to a definite future time. The seller (creditor) recognizes this confidence or trust by allowing the customer (debtor) to receive the goods immediately, but to postpone payment until later.

The individual consumer uses credit to:

> Raise his standard of living or increase his enjoyment;
> Realize the convenience offered by use of credit; and
> Meet the pressures of economic necessity.

The manager or the business uses credit to:

> Enable the business to sell more goods and services;
> Permit the business to purchase goods on terms that will normally allow the business to resell and thus gain funds for repayment and profit; and
> Provide the opportunity for cash loans from some financial institutions.

Creating a Credit Policy

The easiest way to grant credit is through the acceptance of credit cards. Numerous companies are now available to assist the small business not only to accept credit cards face to face, but also on-line through secured channels. Every aviation

Figure 4.12 » Sample Credit Policy

Credit Policy Statement

1. ***General policy.*** It is the policy of the company to extend credit and grant terms to customers in relation to the credit risks involved. The responsibility for implementation of this policy rests with the Vice President, Finance. Administration and control of this policy is centralized in the Credit Department.
2. ***Extension of credit and limits of authority.*** Credit may be extended to new customers as follows:

Extended value of each order	Authorized by
a. Up to $100	Any order-processing unit or salesperson
b. Up to $750	Division or Subsidiary Sales Managers
c. Up to $25,000	Credit Manager or his or her delegate in certain locations as specified
d. Over $25,000	Treasurer

3. ***Procedure***
   a. Credit approvals made by authorized personnel in paragraphs 2a and b must be reported to the Credit Department by memorandum, which will include customer name, address, class of trade, and amount of credit granted.
   b. Credit limits on specific customers will be established by the Credit Department and will be adjusted from time to time as conditions warrant.
   c. Orders received from customers with whom the company has had unfavorable credit experience must be cleared for credit approval through the Credit Department, regardless of the amount of the order, until such time as credit limits have been reestablished.
   d. Collection of accounts is the responsibility of the Credit Manager or his or her delegate. Other personnel may be asked to assist by the Credit Manager.
   e. Standard payment and discount terms are established by the Vice President, Finance and are published in sales literature and other documents. Deviations from standard payment and discount terms must have approval of Vice President, Finance or his or her delegate prior to granting such terms.
   f. All orders received from customers outside of the United States and Canada must be forwarded to the Credit Department for credit approval and determination of method of payment prior to release of the order for processing.

Courtesy of The Conference Board

business should also have a credit policy relating to charge accounts with that company that expresses the basic philosophy of the management and serves as a guideline for decision making throughout the organization.

Although it may have many possible variations, such a credit policy should consider the following areas:

> Authority for granting credit;
> Terms of the sale;
> Dealing with delinquent customers;
> Classification of risks; and
> Helping customers obtain financing.

In some cases, such as new and used aircraft sales, the FBO may simply provide loan search assistance to its customers and let various other lenders deal with the actual financing. However, should you decide to permit credit accounts, the following procedures should be a guide.

Functions of Credit Management

The purposes of credit management include:

> To maximize sales and profits;
> To minimize bad debt losses;
> To achieve efficient utilization of invested funds;
> To develop full coordination with the operating departments;
> To establish an effective credit policy;
> To set standards for credit operation;
> To collect information on credit activity;
> To analyze and evaluate credit activity information;
> To make decisions on credit issues and matters; and
> To carry out the credit process.

Credit Process

The total credit process in a business is made up of five elements:

1. Determining the acceptable credit risk.
2. Setting the credit limits.
3. Handling credit transactions.
4. Maintaining controls and efficiency.
5. Collections.

Acceptable credit risk. In determining acceptable credit risk, the manager needs to answer two questions: "Can the customer pay?" and "Will the customer pay?"

In arriving at an answer to these questions, the manager frequently considers four key factors, known as the four C's of credit. The credit risk is felt to be indicated by character, capacity, capital, and conditions (economic).

Credit Risk = Character + Capacity + Capital + Conditions

These four factors sound logical. Unfortunately, they are hard to determine in actual cases because they are difficult to identify through direct inquiry. There are, however, some credit qualities that can be investigated and used to infer a standing on the four C's. Among the typical items reviewed are:

> Payment record;
> Income level;
> Employment history;
> Residence: ownership and value;
> Marital status;
> Age and health;
> References and reputation;
> Reserve assets;
> Equity in purchases; and
> Collateral available.

In arriving at a decision on the acceptability of a credit applicant, the manager will normally make this decision based on information supplied by the applicant, information supplied by direct inquiry, and information supplied by in-house records.

The applicant must provide much of the credit evaluation data. The use of a credit application form similar to Figure 4.13 shows a great deal of the needed information and should be included routinely as part of the process. An interview can be used to expand and verify the data received in the application and from other sources.

The organization should routinely check each applicant by making direct inquiry of all appropriate sources. This inquiry may be made by mail or by telephone and should include references, bankers, business associates, and previous credit sources. Credit bureaus and groups should also be considered and used if appropriate. They are a ready source of credit information and are designed for that specific purpose by having established procedures and sources.

In-house records may be used in many instances to either verify or obtain additional insight regard-

Figure 4.13 » Credit Application Form Available to Piper Aircraft Dealers

APPLICATION FOR CREDIT

PIPER Management Services

______________________ Social Security Number

Full Name ______________________ Age ________

Spouse's Name ______________________ Single ________ Number of Dependents ________

Home Address ______________________ Own Rent ________

______________________ Tel. No. ________

______________________ How Long ________

Zip

Previous Address ______________________ How Long ________

____

____

Employed By ______________________

Address ______________________

Position ______________________ How Long ________

Monthly Salary $ ________

Former Position ______________________ How Long ________

Landlord or Mortgage holder ______________________

Address ______________________

Nearest Relative (other than Husband or Wife)

____

Address ______________________

____

Personal Reference: ______________________

Address: ______________________

____

Banks: ______________________ Regular Checking ☐

______________________ Savings ☐

Loans ☐

Make of Car ______________________ Year ________

CREDIT REFERENCES

Name	Address	Type Credit

The above information is for the purpose of obtaining credit and is warranted to be true. I agree to pay all bills upon receipt of statement or as otherwise expressly agreed.

Date ________ Signature ______________________

Courtesy of Piper Aircraft Corporation

ing the credit risk of an applicant. Records of previous business transactions (cash) are useful indicators to consider along with pertinent correspondence or business association.

One technique that has been found useful in evaluating an application for credit is the credit grading. By using a form such as the one illustrated in Figure 4.14, each credit element or quality is consciously and separately reviewed and given its proper appraisal. Thus a higher degree of objectivity is achieved and a better overall decision is obtained. Measurement of a number of specific factors is likely to be more accurate than a single overall judgment. Credit quality is a relative evaluation, not an absolute measurement.

Setting the credit limits. Based upon evaluation of the risk and other factors such as economic environment, company position, and supplier policies, the manager must set a credit limit for the customer. This is normally expressed as a specific dollar figure and is used to guide administrative or accounting personnel responsible for monitoring the credit program. It is difficult to recommend any one method of fixing the credit limit. Some use the technique of limiting the account to a certain time (e.g., a month's purchases). Another manager might start with a low credit limit and raise its level with experience. Some organizations encourage the customer to fix his own limits (within bounds, of course).

Handling credit transactions. The actual handling of credit transactions involves identification, authorization, recording, and billing. The first step is identifying the customer as an approved credit customer. This may be done through the use of a credit card, by signature, or by personal recognition. The approval or authorization of each transaction should be based upon the positive identification of the customer and a verification of the records indicating that he or she is an approved credit customer. This must be done by the salesperson at the point of sale.

Recording and billing are covered in Chapter 7, Information Systems.

Maintaining controls and efficiency. A successful manager should be concerned with maintaining positive control over the credit program to ensure that it is an effective one. There are a number of tests that can be applied by the manager in controlling credit activity. The generally accepted tests include:

> Review of bad debt loss record;
> Analysis of credit sales;
> Collection percentage records;
> Days required to collect charges;
> Turnover of receivables;
> Number of new accounts;
> Aging of accounts; and
> Cost analysis of credit program.

The use of these techniques will greatly assist the manager in working toward previously determined goals and objectives.

Collections. Normally, collection problems are not major if sufficient attention is paid to the investigation and analysis of a credit risk. If, however, the credit analysis is weak, collection problems will multiply. There is a need for close supervision and administration of the collection policy. In accomplishing this it is desirable to understand the different types of debtors, to have a systematic collection system, to use the appropriate collection tools, and to understand the reasons for slow payment by customers.

Debtors vary considerably, but the different types can be classified as those who are prompt to pay, those who are sure but slow, and those who are undesirable risks because they are either dishonest or unfortunate. The process of collecting requires a systematic approach (steps and procedures) and a schedule to ensure timely action. Many organizations have found that a tickler file is most useful to ensure correct follow-up action.

The most frequently used collection tools in their sequence of normal use are:

> Invoices on transaction;
> Statements on account;
> Collection letters;
> Follow-up notes;
> Telephone reminders;
> Possible a personal visit; and if necessary
> Sending the account to a collection agency.

Throughout the entire credit process there should be an awareness of credit problems and

Figure 4.14 » Credit Check Form

CREDIT CHECK FORM

____
Date

____
Name

____
Address

Credit qualities	GRADE			Verified:
	GOOD 1	FAIR 2	POOR 3	
Income				
Employment				
Residence				
Marital Status				
Age				
References				
Reserve Assets				
Payment Record				
Reputation				
Summary - Overall				
Appraisal				

Decision: Accept __________ Refuse

Limit: $ __________ Single Item

$ __________ Monthly

$ __________ Total

Special Conditions: __________ __________ __________

__________ __________ __________ __________

__________ __________ __________ __________

____
Signed

____
Date

Source: Dr. J. D. Richardson

every effort should be made to spot trouble as soon as possible and to adjust the credit exposure.

Terms and Definitions

There are a number of terms and procedures that should be understood by those involved in developing and administering a successful credit program.

Credit period is the length of time allowed the buyer before payment becomes due. Usually computed from the date of the invoice.

Example: Net 30 (payment of the full amount within 30 days).

Cash discount is the deduction from the invoice amount allowed the customer for payment within a specified time prior to the expiration of the net credit period.

Example: 1 percent 10, Net 30 (payment within 30 days with a 1 percent discount for payment within 10 days).

Prepayment terms include COD-cash on delivery, CBD-cash before delivery, CWO-cash with order.

Individual order terms are the stated terms applying to each order individually and start with the invoice date.

Lumped-order terms are used when sellers allow buyers to accumulate obligations over a period of time, usually one month, and submit one payment after the end of each period.

Example: 10 keys EOM (invoice on last day of the month, payment due on the 10th day of the next month) Net 10th Prox (payment of all previous month's invoices on the 10th of the following month).

Cash discount value is the value of a cash discount and can be equated to the annual interest on the money involved.

Example:

1/2 percent 10 days, Net 30	9 percent per annum
1 percent 10 days, Net 30	18 percent per annum
2 percent 10 days, Net 60	14 percent per annum
2 percent 30 days, Net 60	24 percent per annum
2 percent 10 days, Net 30	36 percent per annum

Collection period is calculated by

365 × receivables = average annual net sales collection period

In general, the collection period should not exceed the net maturity indicated in the selling terms by more than 10 to 15 days.

Cash or Credit Card?

With increasing frequency, however, many aviation businesses are giving their customers only two alternatives in paying for products or services—cash or credit card. This trend stems from the realization that a small business is not as efficient as a "lending" agency, as will be evident from the description just given above. Without training, experience, procedures and volume, the real cost of extending credit and billing clients monthly is relatively high for the benefit received. As a result, many businesses have turned to credit cards from a few selected sources, such as fuel companies, MasterCard, and Visa. Some organizations still provide open credit for local and carefully screened customers of long standing, but these are at a minimum. The tendency has been to give the credit business to the "experts."

It should be recognized, however, that it costs the aviation business to use a credit card service. Typically the charge is expressed as a percentage of the sales with the actual percentage based upon the volume of business. This cost will vary, but for the small business it is likely to be around 4 to 6 percent. The actual figure may be negotiable, so the prudent manager will explore options.

When using credit cards, it is necessary to train issuing personnel in the correct procedures in order to minimize delays in receiving payment or the chances of error voiding a voucher.

It appears likely that the number of fuel companies with fuel credit cards or those accepting cards of other companies will be smaller in the future. This trend will reduce the options available to aviation businesses for extending credit and place a heavier burden on the remaining sources.

Summary

Business profits should be planned for and not left to chance. Planning techniques include ratio analysis, financial statement evaluation, budget projection, break-even analysis, and cash flow projection. The sales planning, pricing, and marketing orientation discussed in Chapter 3 underlie sound profit planning. Net profit levels vary in aviation businesses; a goal of 15 to 25 percent is not unrealistic given the high-risk nature of the industry. Non-monetary profit measures such as

DISCUSSION TOPICS

1. What are some meanings to the word "profit"?
2. How should a business trade social responsibility against profit? Is it always an either/or situation?
3. Describe a manager with a "profit orientation."
4. What techniques should be used in profit planning?
5. What are the conditions needed for effective budgeting?
6. How should one distinguish between fixed and variable costs? Why does the distinction matter?
7. Why is cash flow important? How can it be improved?
8. What is breakeven point? How is it calculated, and what does it tell you about profit?

"satisfactory" profits, social goals, and personal satisfaction may, however, play an important part in setting the overall profit goal. The manager's job is to guide the organization to an explicit and acceptable level of profitability. In doing this he or she must also pay close attention to credit policies, bad debts, and the cost of finance.

Endnotes

1. Murphy, John F. "Sound Cash Management and Borrowing," Washington D.C.: SBA Management Aids #1.016, 1984.
2. Informal survey by Dr. J.D. Richardson, original author of 1st and 2nd editions of this book.
3. NATA: Operating Cost Survey, 2002. $25
4. *http://www.totalFBO.com* and *http://www.fbomanager.com/.*
5. This information was derived from New England Airlines, Block Island, Rhode Island and is typical of any resort or tourist area.
6. See *http://www.sba.gov/hotlist/sbic.html.*

5

Human Resources

OBJECTIVES

- Discuss labor market trends in aviation for the 21st century.
- Realize some of the legal implications involved in hiring practices due to federal statutes.
- Realize a variety of methods utilized in recruiting qualified candidates for aviation positions.
- Identify issues that should be covered in an exit interview.
- Relate Maslow's hierarchy of needs theory to leadership styles.
- Describe the importance of having a personnel policy manual.

Pipeline Concept

A common tendency of small business owners is to assume or hope that staffing can be done just once and that stability will follow. This is an illusion brought about by the many pressures of the job and in some cases, accentuated by the manager's discomfort in the personnel area.

A more realistic view, especially based on labor shortages, and the fact that general aviation is the lowest rung on the aviation career ladder, may be that most staff passes in a steady flow into, through, up, and out of the organization. Some degree of turnover is not only inevitable but can also be beneficial to both the company and the individual. Some individuals may not be adequate performers or may have insufficient interest in a career with a general aviation service business. Others may have ambitions beyond what an FBO can offer. In such cases, the employer is better off for the good of the company, when such employees choose to move on; managers may even have to terminate a person with poor attitude and lack of enthusiasm. An influx of new people means fresh ideas. The flow of personnel can be described as a pipeline with various spigots or control points along its length for the manager to operate. Controlling personnel matters is one of the many control functions that are an essential part of the management process. The pipeline is illustrated in Figure 5.1.

Control Points

In dealing with the personnel pipeline, the manager has key control points for successfully

Figure 5.1 » Human Resource Pipeline

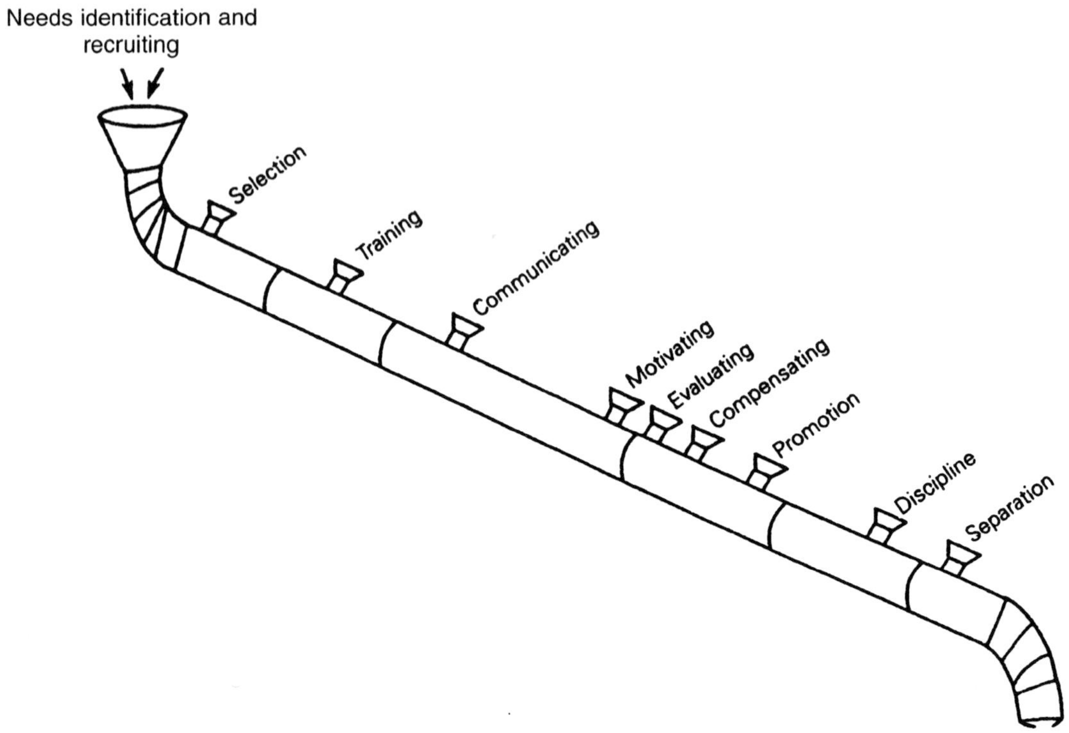

operating the personnel management program. These points are:

> Identifying human resources needs;
> Recruiting qualified candidates;
> Screening applicants;
> Selecting employees;
> Communications;
> Motivation;
> Orientation and training;
> Compensation;
> Evaluating employees;
> Promotion;
> Discipline; and, in some cases
> Separation.

This chapter discusses the elements of human resource management by considering all of these control points and the ways that they can be used to manage the flow of people through the company in the most beneficial manner.

The pipeline is a good description of the career course for some percentage of a company's employees, but it is neither desirable nor inevitable for all personnel. People work for reasons other than advancement and money. For example, they also work for a sense of belonging to a team that produces quality products and services. Shared values about the goals of the company and a perception of its overall direction and purpose, along with recognition and rewards, job security, and continued challenge can be reasons why a person might spend his entire working life in the same company.[1] Some of the ways in which these qualities have been developed in a company's staff include democratic, consensus-oriented decision making, interchangeability of most staff among the jobs in the business, and a willingness from top management to encourage the best contribution from even the less able workers in the firm. In a small business particularly, there may indeed be little choice but to run the firm this way. Its positive aspects need to be considered.

Scope of Chapter

This chapter also discusses personnel matters in the context of related laws and regulations. It discusses how the key control points are combined into a personnel policy manual and considers appropriate ways to handle employee organizations. For each of the topics, the manager needs to have information on currently accepted tools and procedures, which are referenced in the text and the sources provided.

Aviation Industry Trends

Labor Market Trends in Aviation

Smaller FBOs have a variety of pay systems that range from minimum wage for line personnel through hourly commissions for flight instructors and hourly wages for repair personnel. Some build in a bonus system for instructors so that they earn more per hour with more bookings. Many aviation service center employees wear several hats. People on the flight line may also work on front desk and maintenance assignments; the secretary may also pump gas, order parts, and do bookkeeping; and, of course, the owner/manager is often a jack-of-all-trades who fills in for anyone who is unavailable and solves problems, large and small, as they crop up.

Perhaps the single biggest issue in the area of FBO personnel matters is that many of the people in the business are in it for their love of aviation. They settle for low and sometimes erratic pay patterns for a few years until the need to be more financially established takes them into other areas of aviation. These other areas, such as corporate pilot or mechanic, airport manager, airline pilot or mechanic, and positions in aircraft manufacturing tend to offer better pay, substantially better fringe benefits, and often greater job stability and better working conditions. As the FBO industry becomes more mature and more professional, it is addressing the issues of pay levels in competing areas and the questions of high turnover and high levels of part-time involvement that have traditionally characterized smaller FBOs.

The Bureau of Labor Statistics (BLS) publishes reports on the job outlook in all industries in the US and is a good source of pay and other data.[2]

Recent studies suggest that qualified labor for the aviation/aerospace industry as a whole, and general aviation operators in particular, is in short supply and in future years will become even shorter. First, the number of current employees who will reach retirement age in this time period will be on the increase. Additionally, due to downsizing of the military over several years, that ready-made labor force, traditionally relied upon by the entire aviation industry, will not be available, at least not to meet the demand. On the other hand, the pilot job market may be softer. The following discussion addresses pilots first, then mechanics.

Pilots Employment Outlook. The BLS says:

> "Flight crewmembers make up about one-fifth of total civil air transportation employment, and include pilots and flight attendants. Pilots are highly trained professionals who fly airplanes and helicopters to carry out a wide variety of tasks. Although most are airline pilots, copilots, and flight engineers who transport passengers and cargo, others are commercial pilots involved in more unusual tasks, such as agricultural application, spreading seed for reforestation, testing aircraft, flying passengers and cargo to areas not serviced by regular airlines, directing firefighting efforts, tracking criminals, monitoring traffic, and rescuing and evacuating injured persons.
>
> ". . . . Under current standards, a civilian school graduate with 250 to 300 hours of flight time and a commercial certificate, multi-engine rating, and instrument rating has difficulty becoming employed by an air carrier until he/she has accumulated about 2,000 hours of flight time with perhaps 500 of those hours in multi-engine aircraft. Similar problems relate to career opportunities in corporate aviation.
>
> "Except on small aircraft, two pilots usually constitute the cockpit crew. Generally, the most experienced pilot, or captain, is in command and supervises all other crewmembers. The pilot and copilot split flying and other duties such as communicating with air traffic controllers and monitoring the instruments. Some aircraft have a third pilot in the cockpit—the flight engineer or second officer—who assists the other pilots by monitoring and operating many of the instruments and systems and watching for other aircraft. Most newer aircraft are designed to be flown without a flight engineer."[3]

Here's what the Future Aviation Professionals of America say about pilots:

> "Pilots are expected to face considerable competition for jobs through the year 2005 because the number of applicants for new positions is expected to exceed the number of openings. Aircraft pilots understandably have an extremely strong attachment to their occupation because it requires a substantial investment in specialized training and can offer very high earnings. In addition, the glamour, prestige, and travel benefits make this a very desirable occupation and pilots rarely change occupations. However, because of the large number of pilots who will reach retirement age over the next decade or so, replacement needs will generate several thousand job openings each year."[4]

A Blue Ribbon panel on aviation labor convened in the early 1990s provided projections related to the pilot population. The Department of Defense advised the panel that the 25,000 pilots and 95,000 technicians currently in the military would be reduced by 30 percent during the next five years. The military downsizing would adversely affect the air carrier pilot supply, because for some air carriers, 80 percent of the pilots are ex-military aviators who have undergone highly selective screening before their military training, are team-oriented, are knowledgeable of technically advanced equipment, have gained six to eight years of experience in mission-focused flying activities and, most importantly, require little extra investment.

The panel concluded, however, that there nevertheless are, and will continue to be, plenty of pilots who meet the FAA minimum requirements for a commercial rating. They indicated that a more pertinent issue is the question of quality and the need to update the minimum training standards to ensure knowledge of computers, human factors, aeromedical issues, etc., in light of increasingly sophisticated equipment.

Pilots Wages and Benefits. The BLS indicates as follows:

> "Earnings of aircraft pilots and flight engineers vary greatly depending whether they work as airline or commercial pilots. Earnings of airline pilots are among the highest in the nation, and depend on factors such as the type, size, and maximum speed of the plane and the number of hours and miles flown. For example, pilots who fly jet aircraft usually earn higher salaries than do pilots who fly turboprops. Airline pilots and flight engineers may earn extra pay for night and international flights. In 2000, median annual earnings of airline pilots, copilots, and flight engineers were $110,940. The lowest 10 percent earned less than $36,110. Over 25 percent earned more than $145,000. Median annual earnings of commercial pilots were $43,300 in 2000. The middle 50 percent earned between $31,500 and $61,230. The lowest 10 percent earned less than $24,290, and the highest 10 percent earned more than $92,000."[5]

General aviation must compete with some enticing fringe benefits in the airlines. According to the Bureau of Labor Statistics:

> "Airline pilots usually are eligible for life and health insurance plans financed by the airlines. They also receive retirement benefits and, if they fail the FAA physical examination at some point in their careers, they get disability payments. In addition, pilots receive an expense allowance, or "per diem," for every hour they are away from home. Per diem can represent up to $500 each month in addition to their salary. Some airlines also provide allowances to pilots for purchasing and cleaning their uniforms. As an additional benefit, pilots and their immediate families usually are entitled to free or reduced fare transportation on their own and other airlines."

Mechanics Employment Outlook. A growing population and rising incomes are expected to stimulate the demand for airline transportation, and the number of aircraft, and thus volume of repair work, are expected to grow. However, according to the Bureau of Labor Statistics (BLS), employment growth will be "restricted somewhat by increases in productivity resulting from greater use of automated inventory control and modular systems which speed repairs and parts replacement."[6]

Overall, aircraft mechanics, especially those with experience, are expected to have excellent job opportunities since the number of job openings is expected to exceed the supply of qualified applicants due to growth in demand for the services of aircraft mechanics coupled with an expected large number of retirements. The Bureau of Labor Statistics provides an overview:

"Aircraft mechanics and service technicians held about 173,000 jobs in 2000; fewer than 10 percent were avionic technicians. About two-thirds of all salaried mechanics worked for airlines or airports and flying fields, about 12 percent worked for the Federal Government, and about 9 percent worked for aircraft assembly firms. Most of the rest were general aviation mechanics, the majority of whom worked for independent repairshops or for companies that operate their own planes to transport executives and cargo. Few mechanics were self-employed."

The BLS job outlook continues:

"The outlook for aircraft and avionics equipment mechanics and service technicians should be favorable over the next 10 years. The likelihood of fewer entrants from the military and a large number of retirements, point to good employment conditions for students just beginning training. Job opportunities are likely to be the best at small commuter and regional airlines, at FAA repair stations, and in general aviation. Wages in these companies tend to be relatively low, so there are fewer applicants for these jobs than for those with the major airlines. Also, some jobs will become available as experienced mechanics leave for higher paying jobs with airlines or transfer to another occupation.

"At the same time, aircraft are becoming increasingly sophisticated in general aviation and in regional carriers, boosting the demand for qualified mechanics. Mechanics will face competition for jobs with large airlines because the travel benefits that these jobs offer attract more qualified applicants than there are openings. Prospects will be best for applicants with significant experience. Mechanics who keep abreast of technological advances in electronics, composite materials, and other areas will be in greatest demand.

"The number of job openings for aircraft mechanics in the Federal Government should decline as the size of the U.S. Armed Forces is reduced.

"Employment of aircraft mechanics is expected to increase about as fast as the average for all occupations through the year 2010. A growing population and rising incomes are expected to stimulate the demand for airline transportation, and the number of aircraft is expected to grow. However, employment growth will be somewhat restricted as consolidation within the air carrier industry continues and as productivity increases due to greater use of automated inventory control and modular systems, which speed repairs and parts replacement.

"Most job openings for aircraft mechanics through the year 2010 will stem from replacement needs. Each year, as mechanics transfer to other occupations or retire, several thousand-job openings will arise. Aircraft mechanics have a comparatively strong attachment to the occupation, reflecting their significant investment in training and a love for aviation. However, because aircraft mechanics' skills are transferable to other occupations, some mechanics leave for work in related fields."

Mechanics Wages and Benefits. The BLS also provides data on earnings:

"Median hourly earnings of aircraft mechanics and service technicians were about $19.50 in 2000. The middle 50 percent earned between $15.65 and $23.65. The lowest 10 percent earned less than $12.06, and the highest 10 percent earned more than $26.97. Median hourly earnings in the industries employing the largest numbers of aircraft mechanics and service technicians in 2000 were:

Air transportation, scheduled	$21.57
Aircraft and parts	$19.77
Air transportation, nonscheduled	$19.16
Federal Government	$19.11
Airports, flying fields, and services	$16.26

"Median hourly earnings of avionics technicians were about $19.86 in 2000. The middle 50 percent earned between $16.31 and $24.01. The lowest 10 percent earned less than $13.22, and the highest 10 percent earned more than $27.02."[7]

The BLS continues:

"Mechanics who work on jets for the major airlines generally earn more than those working on other aircraft. Airline mechanics and their immediate families receive reduced-fare transportation on their own and most other airlines."

Another source has the following comments:

"General Aviation is composed of many different types of organizations. These organizations are involved in all kinds of aviation activities from corporate transportation to agricultural application. Many aviation mechanics and technicians work for small FBOs or FAA part 145 Repair Stations that service and maintain the private/corporate aircraft fleet. The starting salary for these mechanics range between $18,000 and $24,000 a year. For avionics technicians the starting salary is between $22,000 and $28,000 a year. After 5 years a mechanic's salary range is between $25,000 and $30,000 a year. An avionics technician's salary is between $28,000 and $35,000 a year.[8]

In addition, airlines commonly offer starting salaries as much as 20 percent higher to people with scarce skills. As corporate and fractional aviation grow, competition already faced by fixed base operators seem likely to become more acute. However, the notion that FBOs are always at the bottom of the pay and benefits ladder should not be accepted unexamined. Aviation Maintenance Technician reports in its annual salary survey the following findings:

"The largest sector of respondents (42%) came from Air Carriers; and, overall, pay did improve as predicted due to this year's contract settlements. A closer look reveals that Air Carrier Line Mechanics' pay improved everywhere except in the Northwest Mountain and Western Pacific regions. The second largest group of respondents came from Corporate Aviation with 16.4%, followed closely by General Aviation with 15.2%. Some notable statistics for these two groups revealed that pay for the corporate sector in the Great Lakes, Southern, Southwest, and Western Pacific regions have decreased every year since 1997. Pay for A&Ps in GA in the Southern region also has decreased every year since 1997, while the Eastern region's GA A&Ps pay has increased each year. Helicopter A&Ps did not escape this trend either. New England helicopter A&Ps pay has decreased each year since 1997, but those of this sector in the Southwest, Western Pacific, and Great Lakes regions all show pay increases over four years.

"Sadly, the results again this year showed that more of you, 58%, an increase over last year's 55%, would not recommend Aircraft Maintenance as a career option to a child or friend. Reasons stated most often were lack of respect and pay not commensurate with amount of responsibility and training necessary to do the job, which were exactly the same reasons given last year, and the year before that. On the positive side, many of the respondents, 42 percent, love what they do and are happy to recommend aircraft maintenance as a career to others."[9]

Maturity and Professionalism

On the brighter side, tight labor markets spell good news for aviation students and suggest that working conditions and compensation must become more competitive. A career as an FBO may be a viable choice for even the best students, rather than just for the mediocre students or for those who find flying a paid avocation. Increased professionalism in terms of the quality of position and career ladder for employees is part of an increasing professionalism in the entire FBO industry.

During the 1980s, high insurance costs coupled with high costs of fuel and high interest rates caused stagnation in aviation activity. Many FBOs went out of business during this period, leaving an area of great opportunity over the next few years for the remainder. Not only will FBOs have to operate with the highest standards of professionalism in order to compete for scarce skills, but also certain markets for FBO services will be strong enough for them to do so. The business and corporate aviation markets are likely to be particularly strong. Good employees will be key to meeting the demands of the market.

Identifying Human Resource Needs

The Human Resources Component of the Business Plan

Like the rest of the business plan, the personnel issue should be considered when the manager first gets into the business and then should be updated periodically. In a fast-changing enterprise it will not be possible to predict needs more than a few months ahead; in a static operation more advance planning may be possible. In most small aviation businesses, the personnel function is complicated by the fact that many or all of the staff must have more than one function. The industry also tends to be characterized by extensive use of part-time labor and in many parts of the country by large seasonal variations. Nevertheless, at any given time the manager needs to know the likely personnel needs, the skills, certifications, and training required to meet these needs, the probable cost for each position, and some likely places to find new talent.

The overall company planning behind the human resources strategy includes:

1. Determine company objectives.
2. Formulate policies, plans, programs, and procedures designed to attain these objectives.
3. Develop a budget that will serve as a short-range plan of operations to meet the objectives.

With the plan, specific objectives, and the means for achieving goals established, the next step is the process of relating the selected plan to human resource needs. The following questions should be asked:

1. What types of personnel are needed?
2. What will each person be required to do?
3. What number of personnel is required? full-time? part-time?
4. What skills will be required of each employee?
5. When will the new staff be required?
6. How long will each position be required?
7. What potential for development is desirable?
8. Can the type of person needed be attracted?
9. Can the type of person needed be afforded?
10. Are the types and numbers of personnel desired available?

Permanent or Temporary Needs

Where a need for extra help may be short-lived, the business may benefit from using temporary help. This may be from a temporary agency, a nearby college, or simply by hiring with the understanding that the job is of limited duration. Depending on the workload, the tasks, and whether or not overtime is paid, an estimation of whether to hire from outside or have existing staff work longer may be worthwhile. Many companies are increasingly using contracted labor obtained through an agency. Such personnel are employees of the agency, not the place where they work. However, there have been several successful lawsuits in recent years (e.g. Microsoft, King County, WA) in which long-term "temporary" or seasonal workers claimed that their jobs were in fact really permanent and thus that they had experienced discrimination in terms of not being provided with the fringe benefits of regular employees (although pay levels were often higher). Microsoft has apparently resolved this issue in part by limiting "temporary" jobs to 365 days and requiring that the temporary worker take 100 days off between assignments for the firm. An employer considering the use of temporary workers needs to be familiar with these legal trends.[10]

Skills Required

The traditional approach to job skills is to look at the tasks performed by the organization, group them together into job descriptions, and seek people that appear to match them. Recent management literature suggests otherwise. In his book, *Entrepreneuring: The Ten Commandments for Building a Growth Company,* Steven Brandt presents the fifth commandment as "Employ key people with proven records of success at doing what needs to be done in a manner consistent with the desired value system of the enterprise."[11] In an aviation business a combination approach may be needed since some of the positions require specific license and certifications and the owner/manager cannot just hire people with good energy and values; they must have the technical credentials too.

In addition to a concern with values, an employer may also look at a prospective employee's transferable skills from other jobs. In a world that is going to change more and more rapidly, an ability to transfer one's experience into a new context may be more valuable than years of doing the same thing over and over. Such an approach does have implications for training, as discussed later.

Job Descriptions and Specifications

Each position requires specific tasks and definite functions that are all related to the overall plan. The following suggests an approach to be taken when determining the requirements of specific positions in an aviation activity.

Figure 5.2 describes the types of tasks that different aviation positions might require, Figure 5.3 describes skills required for the tasks in Figure 5.2, while Figure 5.4 describes briefly the training needed for aviation maintenance work.

Figure 5.2 » Tasks Required in FBO Positions

Mid-Manager This position is required to accomplish a wide variety of activities depending upon the size of the business, its specific functions, and its organizational structure. Typical situations could include:

1. Serving as the manager in his or her absence
2. Performing specific, delegated duties for the manager
3. Representing the manager at certain functions
4. Being responsible for assigned technical or functional areas of the business; for example, department head or area manager
5. Serving on coordinating, developmental, or special project committees

Accountant This position is typically required to establish a bookkeeping and information system, to ensure that the system is performing to the organization's needs, to develop the desired reports, and to provide information and guidance of a financial nature to management.

Office Manager/Administrator This position is responsible for directing the administrative activities of the organization. This includes filing, record keeping, duplication, lease administration, insurance programs, reports, and the various activities of a clerical nature that might also include personnel programs.

Front-Desk Manager This person is responsible for reception of visitors, answering questions and directing personnel, scheduling aircraft, and telephone answering. In meeting the responsibilities of dealing with the public, this person must be knowledgeable about the internal organization, services and activities of all departments.

Line Service Personnel These employees are responsible for meeting, directing, servicing, and seeing-off aircraft that land and taxi into the ramp area of the business. They are responsible for operating various aircraft support vehicles and equipment and dealing with aircrew personnel of visiting aircraft. They are usually responsible for fueling.

Flight Instructor This person is responsible for: (1) the type aircraft used for instruction, (2) the required maneuvers and flight information, (3) instructional techniques and testing, and (4) administrative and promotional activities relating to the functions of flight instruction. These responsibilities vary with the size of operations and the type of instruction, such as private, multi-engine, instrument, jet, helicopter, and so on.

Aircraft Pilot This person may be engaged in charter work, ferry, aerial application, cargo flights, forest or pipeline patrol, or other similar activities. Pilots are responsible for conducting flights safely and efficiently.

Aircraft Mechanic This position is responsible for a broad range of duties dealing with the inspection and repair of aircraft, maintaining records, completing administrative functions, and assisting customers.

Electronic Technician This person is responsible for servicing the various communication and navigation equipment used in aircraft. Also he or she is responsible for test equipment, necessary records, and administrative activities.

Engine Mechanic This position is responsible for the maintenance of reciprocating and turbine aircraft engines and related accessory equipment such as propellers, starters, generators, fuel pumps, carburetors, and fuel-injection systems.

Custodial Worker This person has a variety of duties that will be determined by the needs of an individual location. A typical worker would be responsible for a number of duties related to security, cleaning, upkeep, and repair, and, in some instances, vehicles, and support equipment.

Sales Personnel Sales personnel can be new or used aircraft salespeople, ticket salespeople, parts salespeople, flight training salespeople, or flight store sales personnel. They are responsible for functions associated with selling. These include product knowledge, determining customer needs, explaining benefits, closing sales, and the administrative, or support activities associated with selling.

Special Activities

In addition to traditional flight line, flight operations, and aircraft maintenance functions, there are many other and varied activities for aviation businesses, such as auto rental, property rental, insurance, airline baggage handling, airline fueling, limousine service, auto parking, coffee shop, or restaurant administration, and bar operation. Each of these activities calls for a separate position with individual responsibilities to fit the specific functional areas.

Most aviation managers in a small organization are well aware of the necessity for individuals to

Figure 5.3 » Skills Required of Various FBO Positions

Mid-Manager Knowledge of the overall business and the specific technical portion assigned. Managerial skills of planning, organizing, directing, and controlling to achieve specific objectives.

Accountant Technically qualified in training and experience to provide the level of accounting services required by the business. Includes normal accounting training, skills in aviation accounting, information system development, and financial reporting.

Office Manager Qualified to direct the administrative office. Normally requires skills in personnel programs, insurance, record keeping, filing systems, duplication, and perhaps lease administration.

Front Desk Manager Knowledge of the internal organization and the activities of all departments. Skillful in meeting and dealing with the public. Normally must possess a radio operator's license and be skillful in radio operation and dispatching.

Line Service Personnel Technically qualified to operate the assigned fueling and support vehicles. Knowledgeable about the systems and requirements of the aircraft to be serviced. Skilled in dealing with aircrew personnel of visiting aircraft.

Flight Instructor Must possess a certificate for the type of instruction assigned. Must be skillful in communicating with and training students.

Pilot Qualified in the assigned aircraft. Must possess the required operational experience and the technical knowledge of the type of flying, such as crop dusting, power line patrol, and so on.

Maintenance Skill requirements depend upon the level of maintenance accomplished by the organization. Generally it will include knowledge related to airframe, powerplant, electronics, propeller, and other specific qualifications. FAR Part 65 includes specific requirements for these and other positions.

Custodial Skill or knowledge requirements vary dependent upon the job as developed. Generally includes skills in minor facility repair, security, cleaning and painting, and after-hour duties.

Sales Personnel Must have knowledge of the specific product being sold, be skillful in selling and in the marketing and administrative activities related to selling.

Combination Positions Skills necessary to meet the minimum requirements of the various jobs most likely to be assigned.

have a high degree of flexibility and efficiency in order to perform several positions. There are simply not enough people employed to compartmentalize each activity neatly and positively. This problem should not, however, overshadow the need to think through each functional area and consciously plan for its satisfactory completion. It is not desirable to create artificial, impassable barriers around separate positions. Such barriers reduce the incentive of the personnel as well as the overall flexibility of management and the organization. Employees for the most part need to see a path or several paths open to them within the company as they advance in their careers.

Laws and Regulations

Introduction

Employment law has become increasingly stringent over the years, and workers' rights generally get a more favorable treatment in the courts than employers' rights. Any employer thus needs to not only know the laws, but also how to document a given situation so that the odds are improved of having the laws interpreted favorably in the courts. Employment law divides into three primary areas:

> Discrimination in the workplace;
> Workplace Safety; and
> Workmen's Compensation.

Since case law evolves rapidly, as well as new legislation coming into being, readers are advised to consult the Cornell web site mentioned below, and their own attorneys, for the most up to date information. What follows is a brief summary.

Employment Discrimination

The following overview of laws relating to employment discrimination is provided courtesy of the Legal Information Institute at the University of Cornell, a free legal web site.[12]

"Employment Discrimination laws seek to prevent discrimination based on race, sex, religion, national origin, physical disability, and age by employers. There is also a growing body of law

Figure 5.4 » Training Required for Aviation Maintenance Positions

- The FAA requires at least 18 months of work experience for an airframe, powerplant, or avionics repairer's certificate. For a combined A & P certificate, at least 30 months of experience working with both engines and airframes is required.
- Completion of a program at an FAA-certificated mechanic school can substitute for the work experience requirement. Applicants for all certificates also must pass written and oral tests and demonstrate that they can do the work authorized by the certificate.
- To obtain an inspector's authorization, a mechanic must have held an A & P certificate for at least 3 years. Most airlines require that mechanics have a high school diploma and an A & P certificate.
- Although a few people become mechanics through on-the-job training, most learn their job in 1 of about 200 trade schools certified by the FAA. About one-third of these schools award 2- and 4-year degrees in avionics, aviation technology, or aviation maintenance management.
- FAA standards established by law require that certificated mechanic schools offer students a minimum of 1,900 actual class hours. Courses in these trade schools normally last from 24 to 30 months and provide training with the tools and equipment used on the job.
- Aircraft trade schools are placing more emphasis on technologies such as turbine engines, composite materials—including graphite, fiberglass, and boron—and aviation electronics, which are increasingly being used in the construction of new aircraft. Less emphasis is being placed on old technologies, such as woodworking and welding.
- Additionally, employers prefer mechanics that can perform a variety of tasks.
- Some aircraft mechanics in the Armed Forces acquire enough general experience to satisfy the work experience requirements for the FAA certificate. With additional study, they may pass the certifying exam.
- In general, however, jobs in the military services are too specialized to provide the broad experience required by the FAA. Most Armed Forces mechanics have to complete the entire training program at a trade school, although a few receive some credit for the material they learned in the service.
- In any case, military experience is a great advantage when seeking employment; employers consider trade school graduates who have this experience to be the most desirable applicants.
- Courses in mathematics, physics, chemistry, electronics, computer science, and mechanical drawing are helpful, because they demonstrate many of the principles involved in the operation of aircraft, and knowledge of these principles is often necessary to make repairs.
- Courses that develop writing skills also are important because mechanics often are required to submit reports.
- FAA regulations require current experience to keep the A & P certificate valid. Applicants must have at least 1,000 hours of work experience in the previous 24 months or take a refresher course. As new and more complex aircraft are designed, more employers are requiring mechanics to take ongoing training to update their skills.
- Recent technological advances in aircraft maintenance necessitate a strong background in electronics—both for acquiring and retaining jobs in this field.
- FAA certification standards also make ongoing training mandatory. Every 24 months, mechanics are required to take at least 16 hours of training to keep their certificate. Many mechanics take courses offered by manufacturers or employers, usually through outside contractors.
- Aircraft mechanics must do careful and thorough work that requires a high degree of mechanical aptitude. Employers seek applicants who are self-motivated, hard working, enthusiastic, and able to diagnose and solve complex mechanical problems. Agility is important for the reaching and climbing necessary to do the job. Because they may work on the tops of wings and fuselages on large jet planes, aircraft mechanics must not be afraid of heights.
- As aircraft mechanics gain experience, they may advance to lead mechanic (or crew chief), inspector, lead inspector, or shop supervisor positions. Opportunities are best for those who have an aircraft inspector's authorization.

Source: BLS. See http://stats.bls.gov/oco/ocos179.htm

Figure 5.5 » Job Description Format

Date ______

Organization ______

1. *Job Identification:*
   A. Job Title ______
   B. Department ______
   C. Employee Type: Exempt Nonexempt
   D. Reports to ______
   E. Job Number ______
   F. Grade ______
2. *Work Performed:*
   A. Summary Statement: (A statement of the job duties sufficient to identify the job and differentiate the duties that are performed from those of other jobs.)
   B Major Duties: (Should indicate (a) what employee does, (b) how he or she does it and (c) why he or she does it. The description should indicate the tools and equipment employed, the material used, procedures followed, and the degree of supervision received. May also include relationship to other jobs.)
3. *Working Conditions:*
   (General physical environment under which the job must be performed. May include such things as lighting, degree of isolation and conditions such as hot, cold, dusty, or cramped. Job hazards identified.)
4. *Equipment Used:*
   (Identifies the equipment to be used in the performance of normal duties.)
5. *Job Requirements:*
   A. *Education:* (May include the minimum formal education, including special courses or technical training considered necessary to perform the job.)
   B. *Training and Experience:* (Minimum amount and type required in order that employee holds a job, expressed in objective and quantitative terms such as years and months.)
   C. *Initiative and Ingenuity:* (Identifies the degree, level and importance to the job and the relationship to others.)
   D. *Physical Demands:* (Identifies the amount of physical effort required and the length of time such effort must be expounded. Normally includes: walking, stooping, lifting, handling, or talking.)

This statement reflects the general details necessary to describe the principal functions of the job identified and shall not be construed as a detailed description of all the work requirements that may be necessary in the job.

Approved by: ______

Source: J. D. Richardson

preventing or occasionally justifying employment discrimination based on sexual orientation. Discriminatory practices include bias in hiring, promotion, job assignment, termination, compensation, and various types of harassment. The main body of employment discrimination laws is composed of federal and state statutes. The United States Constitution and some state constitutions provide additional protection where the employer is a governmental body or the government has taken significant steps to foster the discriminatory practice of the employer.

"The Fifth and Fourteenth Amendments of the United States Constitution limit the power of the federal and state governments to discriminate. The Fifth Amendment has an explicit requirement that the federal government not deprive individuals of "life, liberty, or property," without due process of the law. *See* U.S. Const. amend. V. It also contains an implicit guarantee that each person receive equal protection of the laws. The Fourteenth Amendment explicitly prohibits states from violating an individual's rights of due process and equal protection. *See* U.S. Const. amend. XIV. In the employment context the right of equal protection limits the power of the state and federal governments to discriminate in their employment practices by treating employees, former employees, or job applicants unequally because of membership in a group (such as a race or sex). Due process protection requires that employees have a fair procedural process before they are terminated if the termination is related to a "liberty" (such as the right to free speech) or property interest. State constitutions may also afford protection from employment discrimination.

"Discrimination in the private sector is not directly constrained by the Constitution, but has become subject to a growing body of federal and state statutes.

"The Equal Pay Act amended the Fair Labor Standards Act in 1963. The Equal Pay Act prohibits paying wages based on sex by employers and unions. It does not prohibit other discriminatory practices bias in hiring. It provides that where workers perform equal work in jobs requiring "equal skill, effort, and responsibility and performed under similar working conditions," they should be provided equal pay. The Fair Labor Standards Act applies to employees engaged in some aspect of interstate commerce or all of an employer's workers if the enterprise is engaged as a whole in a significant amount of interstate commerce.

"Title VII of the Civil Rights Act of 1964 prohibits discrimination in many more aspects of the employment relationship. It applies to most employers engaged in interstate commerce with more than 15 employees, labor organizations, and employment agencies. The Act prohibits discrimination based on race, color, religion, sex, or national origin. Sex includes pregnancy, childbirth, or related medical conditions. It makes it illegal for employers to discriminate in hiring, discharging, compensation, or terms, conditions, and privileges of employment. Employment agencies may not discriminate when hiring or referring applicants. Labor organizations are also prohibited from basing membership or union classifications on race, color, religion, sex, or national origin.

"The Nineteenth Century Civil Rights Acts, amended in 1993, ensure all persons equal rights under the law and outlines the damages available to complainants in actions brought under the Civil Rights Act of 1964, Title VII, the American with Disabilities Act of 1990, and the Rehabilitation Act of 1973.

"The Age Discrimination in Employment Act (ADEA) prohibits employers from discriminating on the basis of age. The prohibited practices are nearly identical to those outlined in Title 7. An employee is protected from discrimination based on age if he or she is over 40. The ADEA contains explicit guidelines for benefit, pension, and retirement plans.

"The Rehabilitation Act's purpose is to "promote and expand employment opportunities in the public and private sectors for handicapped individuals," through the elimination of discrimination and affirmative action programs. Employers covered by the act include agencies of the federal government and employers receiving federal contracts over $2500 or federal financial assistance. The Department of Labor enforces section 793 of the act, which refers to employment under federal contracts. The Department of Justice enforces section 794 of the act, which refers to organizations receiving federal assistance. The EEOC enforces the act against federal employees and individual federal agencies promulgate regulation pertaining to the employment of the disabled.

"The American with Disabilities Act (ADA) was enacted to eliminate discrimination against those with handicaps. It prohibits discrimination based on a physical or mental handicap by employers engaged in interstate commerce and state governments. The type of discrimination prohibited is broader than that explicitly outlined by Title VII.

> "The Equal Opportunity Employment Commission (EEOC) interprets and enforces the Equal Payment Act, Age Discrimination in Employment Act, Title VII, Americans With Disabilities Act, and sections of the Rehabilitation Act. The Commission was established by Title VII. Its enforcement provisions are contained in section 2000e-5 of Title 42, and its regulations and guidelines are contained in Title 29 of the Code of Federal Regulations, part 1614."

State laws also provide extensive protection from employment discrimination. Some laws extend similar protection as provided by the federal acts to employers who are not covered by those statutes. Other statutes provide protection to groups not covered by the federal acts. A number of state statutes provide protection for individuals who are performing civil or family duties outside of their normal employment.

Workplace Safety

Again, the Legal Information Institute of Cornell University provides a summary[13]:

> "Workplace safety and health laws establish regulations designed to eliminate personal injuries and illnesses from occurring in the workplace. The laws consist primarily of federal and state statutes. Federal laws and regulations preempt state ones where they overlap or contradict one another.
>
> "The main statute protecting the health and safety of workers in the workplace is the Occupational and Safety Health Act (OSHA). Congress enacted this legislation under its Constitutional grant of authority to regulate interstate commerce. OSHA requires the Secretary of Labor to promulgate regulations and safety and health standards to protect employees and their families. Every private employer who engages in interstate commerce is subject to the regulations promulgated under OSHA.
>
> "In order to aid the Secretary of Labor in promulgating regulations and enforcing them the act establishes the National Advisory Committee on Occupational Safety and Health. The Secretary of Labor may authorize inspections of workplaces to ensure that regulations are being followed, examine conditions about which complaints have been filed, and determine what regulations are needed. If an employer is violating a safety or health regulation a citation is issued. The act establishes the Occupational Safety and Health Review Commission to review citation orders of the Secretary of Labor. The Commission's decision is also subject to judicial review. The Secretary of Labor may impose fines with the amounts varying according to the type of violation and length of non-compliance with the citation. The Secretary of Labor may also seek an injunction to restrain conditions or practices, which pose an immediate threat to employees. The act also establishes the National Institute for Occupational Safety and Health, which, under the Secretary of Health and Welfare, conducts research on workplace health and safety and recommends regulations to the Secretary of Labor. Federal agencies must establish their own safety and health regulations. The regulations that have been promulgated under OSHA are extensive, currently filling five volumes of the Code of Federal Regulations.
>
> "Under OSHA states are not allowed, without permission of the Secretary of Labor, to promulgate any laws that regulate an area directly covered by OSHA regulations. They may, however, regulate in areas not governed by federal OSHA regulations. If they wish to regulate areas covered by OSHA regulations they must submit a plan for federal approval. The amount of state regulation varies greatly. California is an example of a state that has chosen to adopt many of its own regulations in place of those promulgated under OSHA."

Businesses with eight or more employees are required to record work-related illnesses or injuries. Other OSHA requirements are detailed, complex, and variable depending on the nature of the worksite and work. Consultation with OSHA or state department of labor representatives is advised. There are now at least 20 states or territories with, or considering, state-administered OSHA-certified plans including: Washington, Oregon, Alaska, Hawaii, Nevada, Utah, Arizona, Wyoming, Minnesota, Iowa, Michigan, Indiana, Kentucky, Tennessee, North Carolina, South Carolina, Vermont, Puerto Rico, the Virgin Islands, Virginia, and New Mexico. In these states, therefore, contact with the state labor department is recommended, as the implementer of the OSHA requirements.

Workers Compensation: An Overview

This material also is supplied courtesy of the Legal Information Institute of Cornell University.[14]

"Workers' Compensation laws are designed to ensure that employees who are injured or disabled on the job are provided with fixed monetary awards, eliminating the need for litigation. These laws also provide benefits for dependents of those workers who are killed because of work-related accidents or illnesses. Some laws also protect employers and fellow workers by limiting the amount an injured employee can recover from an employer and by eliminating the liability of co-workers in most accidents. State Workers Compensation statutes establish this framework for most employment. Federal statutes are limited to federal employees or those workers employed in some significant aspect of interstate commerce.

"The Federal Employment Compensation Act provides workers compensation for non-military, federal employees. Many of its provisions are typical of most worker compensation laws. Awards are limited to "disability or death" sustained while in the performance of the employee's duties but not caused willfully by the employee or by intoxication. The act covers medical expenses due to the disability and may require the employee to undergo job retraining. A disabled employee receives two thirds of his or her normal monthly salary during the disability and may receive more for permanent physical injuries, or if he or she has dependents. The act provides compensation for survivors of employees who are killed. The act is administered by the Office of Workers' Compensation Programs.

"The Federal Employment Liability Act (FELA), while not a workers' compensation statute, provides that railroads engaged in interstate commerce are liable for injuries to their employees if they have been negligent.

"The Merchant Marine Act (the Jones Act) provides seamen with the same protection from employer negligence as FELA provides railroad workers.

"Congress enacted the Longshore and Harbor Workers' Compensation Act (LHWCA) to provide workers' compensation to specified employees of private maritime employers. The Office of Workers' Compensation Programs administers the act.

". . . . California's Workers' Compensation Act provides an example of a comprehensive state compensation program. It is applicable to most employers. The statute limits the liability of the employer and fellow employees. California also requires employers to obtain insurance to cover potential workers' compensation claims, and sets up a fund for claims that employers have illegally failed to insure against."

Comparable Worth

The issue of comparable worth means equal pay for jobs of comparable difficulty. The concept had its start in the mid-1970s when a landmark study in the state of Washington reviewed state salaries and found that on average women earned 20 percent less than men for comparable jobs. In 1981 a Supreme Court ruling supported this finding. The criteria used by comparable worth studies may be of value in reviewing jobs for any purpose. They include:

> Skill, knowledge, and education required;
> Effort (e.g., mental demands, latitude, judgment and difficulty of problems);
> Accountability-scale of executive decisions; and
> Working conditions.

Each of these four factors is given a weight and the sum total of these weights ranks the job with all other jobs having the same weight, regardless of whether there is any similarity in jobs. Positions with extremely desirable ancillary conditions, such as free or almost free air travel if one works for the airlines, would get a negative weighting for that factor.

The first step in developing an equitable pay system for a business involves job definition.

One way to clarify what each employee's job actually is to have them fill out a simple form stating:

> Job title;
> Reporting relationship;
> Specifications;
> Primary function;
> Main duties;
> Other duties;
> Job requirements;
> Technical/administrative complexity;
> Responsibility for dollar results;
> Responsibility for supervision and training of others; and
> Unusual working conditions.

Some employees may turn out to be doing more or different tasks than thought, and more than one may claim primary responsibility for the same thing. These and other such issues may arise. The review process should also allow you to determine what functions may need to be covered by new staff.

Payroll Taxes and Deductions

In summary the likely items will include:

> Withholding of employee income tax;
> Social Security and FICA;
> Unemployment taxes; and
> Medicare taxes.

An FBO is advised to obtain the help of an accountant in establishing the books and maintaining the proper deductions. It is vitally important that the business and financial plan for the company include adequate funds for the required items.

Employee Access to Records and Fair Information Practices

Although there are no federal laws standardizing employee information practices, a number of states (e.g., California, Connecticut, Illinois, Maine, Michigan, New Hampshire, Oregon, Pennsylvania, and Wisconsin) in recent years have established laws in regard to employee access to, and ability to change, data in personnel files. There has also been increasing attention to the issue of employee privacy and the possible misuse of personnel data (e.g., in relation to credit, medical or other agencies). The personnel policy manual should contain a section on employee data, its use, and the company's policy on access to files by employees and their supervisors.

Recruiting Qualified Candidates

The recruiting function for an FBO business will vary in its scope and complexity with the degree of specialization involved. If the business needs a bookkeeper or file clerk, then local general business sources of candidates will be appropriate. If a very senior aviation technical position requiring current licenses is necessary, sources for bookkeepers will normally be inadequate and a more far-reaching search will be necessary, using specialized industry publications and contacts. While some positions require specific certifications and licenses and are thereby constrained, the manager should keep in mind that career paths can change radically and employees with good values and work habits should get a chance to move in unusual directions and learn new expertise. Considering existing employees is always an excellent place to start when there is a vacancy to fill, for it also assures staff that the company potentially offers an upward career track for all.

Industry Contacts

For a position requiring aviation skills and knowledge, likely sources of qualified candidates include:

1. Friends of existing personnel (some businesses value this approach so much that they will pay several hundred dollars to staff that provide contacts leading to a new hire).
2. Managers in competing businesses who may not be doing as well as you (the risk being that they will recommend their worst people).
3. Personnel offices and individuals in competing businesses.
4. Professional and business associations, either general business or aviation related.

Whether your pursuit of these channels is local, regional, or national depends on the urgency, uniqueness, and scarcity of the labor required. Such a search, if extended into a large network, may become almost a full-time job. It's something that a business owner or even a full-time personnel director must accommodate despite other normal demands on his or her time.

Recruiters

Recruiters and executive search or "headhunter" agencies are usually national businesses that for a fee of 15 to 25 percent of the first year's salary will seek out qualified specialists, screen them by phone, in writing, and even (if you pay) in person. Out of dozens of possibilities, they present the employer with three to five people to interview over the phone and then see in person. While this is a costly process, a reputable recruiter will present only interested candidates who have met all of your criteria. All that is left for you to do is pick the person with whom the rapport is best. You pay the fee, any travel costs, and the cost of relocation, if necessary. Normally you would have about 30 days to change your mind and pay nothing if the person does not work out. In the interest of self-preservation and good business ethics, a good recruiter will not make the first move to recruit that person away from a placement he or she has made.

Employment Agencies

Employment agencies operate in somewhat the same manner as recruiters, except that the candidate, not the employer, may pay all or part of the fee. Their labor pool tends to be more local. Agencies tend to work in regional or metropolitan labor markets and deal with more general types of skills such as office workers, accountants, purchasing agents, and computer specialists who have reasonable transferability of skills from one industry to another. There is often intensive competition among agencies. When you let a need be known, numerous candidates may be sent for interviews, with only one or two that actually meet requirements. Employer-paid fees are growing more common, and it may be advantageous to work with just one person in one reputable agency in cases where the national, specialized labor pool of the recruiter is not necessary.

Colleges and Trade Schools

These facilities are often one of the best sources of personnel for specialized aviation positions. The school's curriculum and national standing are available to you as a guarantee of consistent quality before you even see a specific individual. The faculty will, in time, begin to know the type of person you like and the functions you need to staff. School schedules often facilitate student employment as well as part-time and seasonal hiring, which can accommodate an FBO's varying personnel needs. An advantage of hiring student labor is that a person can be tried out for a considerable period of time before a permanent commitment is made.

Cooperative education (usually referred to as co-ops) and internships are another excellent way to utilize college and university students. Co-op programs can be set up with an option for payment or non-payment. Oftentimes the student receives college credit from his or her institution and the benefits of working in an industry environment while earning college credit is excellent. Again, it gives the employer an opportunity to preview a prospective employee with little investment.

Advertising

Many employers consider advertising a last resort. Although it is not expensive when compared with some of the alternatives, its results can be very time-consuming. Typically, especially when e-mail responses are encouraged, many people respond that are not qualified. The advertisement may run a day or more after you have selected someone, yielding responses that cannot be used. Ways to get the best results from advertising follow:

1. Use only major newspapers, web sites or trade periodicals.
2. Use only a box number and do not totally describe the firm to the extent that a person can guess its name.
3. Ask all respondents to fill out an application form: Only the interested will do so.
4. Use a very specific job description and skill requirements to screen candidates prior to interviewing them in person.

Owing to the large number of immigrants seeking permanent residency in the US, widespread generic advertising searches, especially web-based, may result in many candidates who would require employer sponsorship in order to get the appropriate US visa. Web-based advertising also tends to generate candidates from a very large geographic area. The employer may need to write the ad specifying whether or no sponsorship is under consideration, and specifying relocation benefits (if any) should a non-local candidate be offered the job.

Selecting Employees

To a certain extent, the business manager is always looking for suitable talent whether there is a specific opening or not. Efficient handling of casual or unsolicited inquiries requires a selection process that existing employees must know about and can help to implement. However, all applicants, whether they come to the firm through a formal or informal process, need to be screened as to suitability.

Preliminary Screening

The preliminary screening or initial interview provides a ten-minute opportunity to determine whether the individual is a qualified prospect. Figure 5.5 is job description format.[15] If this preliminary process suggests that the person is suitable, he or she can be told about any available positions and asked to fill out an application form. If, on the other hand, the preliminary screening suggests the candidate is definitely unsuitable because of qualifications or attitude, the person can be told that the firm will contact him or her if a suitable situation arises. Figure 5.6 below offers a screening guide.

Figure 5.6 » Screening Guide to Help in Hiring

Date ______________________

Phone ______________________

Name ____

Address ____

No. Street City State Zip Code

Ask the following questions; but stop if the applicant gives a wrong answer.

1. How long have you lived at this address? ______________________
   (Must be at least a month.)
2. What experience have you had? ______________________
   (Not important unless you want an experienced person.)
3. What kinds of work have you done? ______________________
   (Is this what you need?)
4. How much pay do you expect? ______________________
   (Is this too much?)
5. Are you willing to work evenings? _____Yes _____ No; Saturdays? _____Yes _____ No;
   Sundays and holidays? _____Yes _____ No; Split hours? _____Yes _____ No.
   (Can you use this person?)
6. Do you want full-time work? _____ Full-time _____ Part-time _____ Hours per week
   (Can you use this person?)
   Are you willing to attend training programs conducted by our suppliers? ______________________
7. Are you over eighteen? _____If you are hired, you'll need to provide proof of your age and visa /nationality status. Will you be able to do that? _____Yes _____ No
8. Do you have a job now? _____Yes _____ No; (If no:) How long have you been out of work?
   (Must be less than 2 months unless reasonable reason.)
   How did that happen? ______________________
   (Reason must be very good—such as sickness, school, etc.)
9. What other experience have you had?______________________
   (Will this be helpful?)
10. What experience have you had with aircraft? ______________________
    (Will this be helpful?)
11. Can you drive a car [if needed for the job]? _____Yes _____ No; (if yes:) What kind of driver's license do you have? _____(OK?). May I see it? _____ Out-of-date, _____ Up-to-date; What notations are there on the license? ______________________
    (Is this person a safe driver?)
12. Can you fly [if needed/desirable for the job]? _____Yes _____ No; (If yes:) What kind of license do you have? ______________________(OK?)

If the applicant **won't do** because the answers to any of these questions means you can't use him or her or because you feel the person won't fit in with your organization, **say,** "I'm sorry but you don't seem to be the person we need right now. However, I have your name and phone number and I'll be glad to give you a call if we can use you some other time. Thanks a lot for talking with me."

If the applicant seems OK, say, "Fine, I'd like you to fill in an application. You can do it right here. Would that be OK?"

The Application Form

The primary value of an application form is its systematic and impersonal collection of data. It establishes a consistent database for all applicants and represents one step in equal opportunity. It also provides the means, through names of former employers and references, of conducting a more detailed investigation on a person before hiring them. It should be tailored to your own needs, carefully addressing current employment law, and will probably contain at least:

> Name, address and phone;
> Previous employer's address, immediate supervisor, supervisor phone, starting and ending salary, reason for leaving, dates of employment;
> Education, formal and informal;
> Social Security Number; and
> Height, weight, physical limitations, or disabilities, (only if applicable to job).

The application form provides a basis for interview questions and, on occasion, may be a further screening mechanism leading to a decision not to further interview the person. If the person is hired, the form becomes a useful background item in their personnel file. Figure 5.7 is an application blank based on one developed by Piper Aircraft in selecting flight instructors.

The Interview

A full interview may last an hour or more and should probably never last under 20 minutes if an offer is going to be made. Some experts strongly recommend that more than one interviewer be brought into the process, especially when the manager has a poor record of picking good staff, and/or where he or she has a tendency to pick people like him- or herself, regardless of the job. A number of studies in recent years suggest that philosophy, style, and values may be as critical as technical skills in causing an employee to fit well and be productive. It is important for the employer not to ask leading questions in such areas, nor in areas that could be interpreted as discriminatory, as the candidate may try to present only what he or she thinks is wanted. If certain skills, licenses, or education are prerequisites for the job, it may be appropriate to develop a checklist for use with every candidate. The interviewer should guard against forming such a liking for the candidate that he or she forgets to ask about all the key issues. It will not pay to hire a likable incompetent! The following principles should guide most interviews:

> Make a checklist of questions to ask, preferably including questions about how the person would handle problems and crises that typically appear in your business;
> If several candidates are being interviewed, use the same set of questions for each and keep interview notes on file;
> Set up a quiet atmosphere with no interruptions;
> Put the applicant at ease and give him or her your full attention;
> Keep the discussion at a level suitable to the applicant;
> Listen attentively;
> Never argue;
> Observe style and manner, for example, ability to answer directly and on the subject;
> Provide the applicant with pertinent information about the job;
> Note key replies and concerns; and
> Encourage candidate questions.

Note that the above factors are somewhat subjective and again, notes should be taken and kept regarding the employer's assessment of each.

Figure 5.8 provides twelve key factors to look for in interviewing or screening. Note that none of these factors relate to technical skill or training.

It is vital to avoid asking discriminatory questions. The only issues that are pertinent relate to the person's ability to do the job. For most pilot positions a current medical would be adequate, although temporary disabilities such as a broken limb or pregnancy could be pertinent. It is not illegal to let the candidate volunteer such information that would be illegal to request.

Some questions that may seem harmless enough can be interpreted as discriminatory. For example, asking a potential employee if he or she rents or own his/her own home, whether married or not, whether the candidate has any children, which organizations or societies he/she belongs to (other than professional organizations), or the person's age are all potentially risky discriminatory questions.

Figure 5.7 » Application for Instructor Position

Application for Instructor Position

(All information treated confidentially)

Date ______________________

Name (print) ______________________ Telephone number ______________ Is this in your name? ______

Present address ______________________________ How long have you lived there? ________
No. Street City State Zip

Previous address ______________________________ How long did you live there? ________
No. Street City State Zip

Business address ______________________________ Business Telephone number ________
No. Street City State Zip

Are you a citizen or legal worker of the U.S.? ☐ Yes ☐ No Soc. Sec. No. ______________

Why are you applying to this Company? ______________________________

1. What influenced you to enter general aviation? ______________________________

____

2. Do you plan a general aviation career? ☐ Yes ☐ No

Education								
Type of School	Name of School	Courses Majored In	Check Last Year Completed				Graduate? Degrees Received	Last Year Attended
College			1	2	3	4		19
Other			1	2	3	4		19

Jobs While in School and During Summer

Scholastic standing in H.S. ______________________ In College ______________________
(Designate top 25 percent, middle 50 percent, lowest 25 percent)

Awards and honors received ______________________________

Favorite subjects ______________________ Least liked ______________________

Extracurricular Activities (exclude racial, religious, or nationality groups)

In high school______________________ In college ______________________

______________________ ______________________

Offices held______________________ Offices held______________________

What scholarships or fellowships have you received? ______________________

What hobbies do you have? ______________________________

Service in U.S. Armed Forces

What is your current military service status? ______________________________

If exempt or rejected, what was the reason? ______________________________

Have you served in the U.S. Armed Forces ☐ No ☐ Yes; (if yes) Date active duty started ____________ xx

Which force? ☐ Army ☐ Air Force ☐ Navy ☐ Marines ☐ C.G.:

What branch of that force? ______________________ Starting rank ____________

Overseas: Date(s) ______________________ Location(s) ____________

Date of discharge ______________________ xx_____ Rank at discharge ____________

What citations and awards have you received? ______________________________

What special training did you receive? ______________________________

Figure 5.7 » Continued

Work History

Include (a) self-employment and (b) secondary or moonlighting jobs (mark the latter with an asterisk)

Beginning with the most recent, list below the names and addresses of all your employers: a. Company name b. Address and telephone number	Kind of Business	Time Employed				
		From		To		
		Mo.	Yr.	Mo.	Yr.	
1. a. / b.						
2. a. / b.						
3. a. / b.						
4. a. / b.						
5. a. / b.						

Indicate by number________________ any of the above employees whom you do not wish us to contact.

Have you had sales experience? ☐ Yes ☐ No

If "yes" please specify type sales: (Big ticket, over the counter, delivery sales, route sales to homes, technical sales, specialty sales-tangibles; books, etc.; intangibles: insurance or services)

List employer(s) for whom you sold:

Name	Address	Lines Sold	Year(s)

If necessary, are you willing to work nights? ________ Weekends? ________

Personal References (Not former employers or relatives)	Address	Phone Number
1.		
2.		
3.		

Date of last FAA physical exam, if applicable. ________________

Class ____

Restrictions ____________________________________

Figure 5.7 » Continued

Work History

Include (a) self-employment and (b) secondary or moonlighting jobs (mark the latter with an asterisk)

Nature of Work at Start	Earnings Per Month at Start	Nature of Work at Leaving	Earnings Per Month at Leaving	Reason for Leaving	Name of Immediate Supervisor
					Name Title
					Name Title
					Name Title
					Name Title
					Name Title

Flying Experience

Certificate and Ratings: (Give Date Each Acquired)

A. ____________ D. ____________ G. ____________

B. ____________ E. ____________ H. ____________

C. ____________ F. ____________ I. ____________

Flight Schools Attended	From	To	Course	Graduation

Pilot Experience (Other Than Instructor Time)

Pilot In Command ____________

Copilot Time ____________

Instrument Time ____________

Multi Engine Time ____________

Night ____________

____

Instructor Experience (Hours)

Total Instructor Time ____________

Private ____________

Commercial ____________

Night ____________

Instrument ____________

Multi Engine ____________

Aircraft Flown: (Give Approximate Hours In Each)

A. ____________ E. ____________ I. ____________

B. ____________ F. ____________ J. ____________

C. ____________ G. ____________ K. ____________

D. ____________ H. ____________ L. ____________

Figure 5.7 » Continued

Personal Instruction Activity:

		% Passed FAA Exam
A. Number of Pilots Instructed.	______	______
B. Number of Commercial Pilots Instructed.	______	______
C. Number of Instrument Pilots Instructed.	______	______
D. Number of Multi Engine Pilots Instructed.	______	______
E. Number of Instructors Instructed.	______	______
F. Number of ATR Pilots Instructed.	______	______
G. Number of Glider Pilots Instructed.	______	______
H. Number of Float Plane Pilots Instructed.	______	______

Accidents:

Date: ______

Circumstances: ______

______

Damage or Injury: ______

______

Forced Landings:

Date: ______

Reason: ______

Damage or Injury: ______

______

Has your pilot certificate ever been suspended or revoked? ______

______

Other Statements

Are there any experiences, skills, or qualifications that you feel would especially fit you for work with this Company?

______

______

What are your plans or aims for the future? ______

______

If your application is considered favorably, on what date will you be available for work? ______ xx ______

How much notice will you require? ______ Days

Signature ______

*Not to be asked unless job related.

Figure 5.8 » Twelve Steps to Assessing a Job Candidate's Suitability

1. Has applicant done some homework about the company?
2. Is applicant dressed appropriately for the interview (example: one degree more formal than the position's current employees)?
3. Did the person arrive alone for the interview?
4. Did he /she arrive on time or call ahead to explain any delay and ask if the interview can still occur?
5. How did he/she greet you?
6. Is she/ he assertive and confident?
7. Is he/ she argumentative?
8. Does the person present a positive attitude about the most recent employer?
9. Does the candidate have a positive attitude about this company?
10. Does the applicant seem to be observant and learning during the interview process?
11. Does the person project enthusiasm, confidence, energy and dependability?
12. Does the person project loyalty, honesty, pride in work, and a desire to offer work and service for pay received?

Source: Julie F. Rodwell, 2003

Testing and Investigation

In many cases testing for FBO jobs will not be necessary as long as checking is done to confirm that all claimed qualifications are current. For typing, a speed and accuracy test is appropriate. An actual document should be required such as a letter or memo, as the ability to lay out work attractively is part of the document production person's job. In other cases, the quality of technical skills should be assessed by discussion with former employers, clients, or teachers, if these parties are willing. An increasing number of employers no longer provide references, offering only confirmation of the person's dates of employment.

Background checks under pilot record and maintenance requirements are not mandated for Part 91 flight operations. Although not strictly required, many employers do find it prudent however, to require some checks as a matter of course including drug and alcohol testing. Insurance companies sometimes require these checks. They can include a check of the National Driver's Record in Washington, DC. If you have had a problem with alcohol or drugs as it relates to driving it would show up on this record. As the Transportation Security Administration focuses more on general aviation, owners and managers can expect more stringent background check requirements that are likely to vary with the type of position being sought.

Personality testing is another matter. People do not always know themselves very well; they may have picked a technical area of training that does not fit ideally with their basic temperament, or they may have personality and managerial skills well beyond the level they envisage for themselves. Various personality style-testing instruments are available. They generally group people loosely into four categories: leaders, influencers, detail workers, and supporting types.[16] Each of us has characteristics of each category but tend to be predominantly one type. We may also change as we mature. Someone who loves to manipulate numbers all day and is shy should not be put on the front desk to greet people. Someone friendly should be on the line or the desk so long as they are also results-oriented and can successfully juggle several clients. Technical skills are generally more teachable at any stage in life than personality traits. Personality traits can be improved but never radically changed. A person is happiest and most productive when both personality and technical skills are well used. A good manager needs strength in all the personality styles and the ability to "switch gears" from one style to another as needed to be able to interact most effectively with employees who operate in a different mode.

This type of styles testing requires money and time ($50.00 and up and several hours). If it is carefully used, it can lead to more successful screening and deployment of personnel. If existing personnel take the test, much will be learned that will be a longer-term guide to personality assessment and appropriate assignments. Excellent materials also exist for training the various types of person to work best with those having different styles.[17]

Background and References

Reference checking is critical prior to making a job offer. The most valuable contacts are generally those who have known the person in a business rather than personal context. Any personal references listed have probably been specifically selected by the candidate because of their likelihood of making pleasant remarks about him or her. Previous employers, business associates, and clients may be willing to give a candid appraisal of a person's strong and weak points (everyone has both) once they know the type of job and company for which a person is being considered. If a negative comment comes up that is unexpected or contradicts the candidate, it may be desirable to give him or her a chance to clarify.

Telephone reference checking is generally more reliable than written requests because it provides an opportunity to ensure that the person being asked really remembers the candidate and is not just looking up file information. It also allows questioning and prompting on the part of the reference checker. Figure 5.9 provides a form for use in telephone reference checking. As mentioned, many companies no longer allow their employees to provide references because of legal liability; however, they will verify employment. Despite this difficulty, references should always still be pursued prior to hiring.

Credit checks may also be a means of obtaining information on a prospective employee and are particularly appropriate for jobs involving money. In this, as in all hiring matters, it is crucial to use consistent procedures. The request for a credit report must be communicated to the applicant; it is desirable to seek the candidate's permission.

Rules are still evolving about providing a higher level of immigration, police, and other checks for candidates seeking sensitive jobs in aviation. The business manager must stay abreast of the new regulations as they come out of the Transportation Security Administration and act accordingly.

The Physical Examination

With the exception of pilot positions, where a current medical may be sufficient to ensure that the applicant can handle the job, a physical examination can be important in hiring. Physicals should especially be used when the job requires features such as:

> Strength;
> Good vision;
> Ability to stand continuously;
> Freedom from allergies;
> Unusual stamina; or
> Other qualities above the average.

However, asking health questions and conducting the company's own physical exam can put the firm at risk in relation to discrimination issues. Use legal advice in particular for this area.

The Job Offer

The job offer may be made in person, by letter, or by phone. It should include not only the position, but also the compensation, hours, fringe benefits, the supervision, and general working rules. Some firms use a job contract that both parties sign. Most people, when offered a job, ask for a few days to decide, and a deadline for a decision should be established. Do not send out regret letters to anyone else until your chosen candidate has accepted or even started work. The eventual "decline" letter is an important courtesy because later you may want to offer the other candidates jobs.

Orientation and Training

New Employees

New employees need orientation in order to develop a sense of belonging, as well as to know whom to turn for help in the early days. Some firms assign a colleague or "buddy" for the first few days until the newcomer knows the way around. Existing employees should be apprised that hiring is in process and informed of the newcomer's status and functions. The manager needs to be sensitive to fears that a new person will diminish someone else's importance.

Orientation will usually involve both written materials and person-to-person review of tasks. In larger companies, the personnel department usually plays a key role, for example, in telling about the history of the firm, its values and goals, the fringe benefits, and the company-wide activities and information systems. If this is how things are to be done, ideally new employees should report on the first day to the person that hired them, be taken to meet the senior managers, and then go for orientation with personnel. Then they will be ready to start work with their new colleagues and not be pulled off new assignments in order to

Figure 5.9 » Telephone Reference Check Guide

Telephone Reference Check on Applicant ____________________
Name of Applicant

____
Person Contacted   Position

____
Company   City and State   Telephone Number

QUESTIONS

1. I wish to verify some of the information given to us by Mr. or Ms. (name), who has applied for a position with our firm. Do you remember him or her? What were the dates of his or her employment with your Company? — From ______ 19 ___ To ______ 19 ___
   Do dates check?
2. What was he or she doing when she started? ____________________
   Did she exaggerate?
   When she left? ____________________
   Did she progress?
3. She says she was earning $ ____ per ____ when she left. Is that right? — ☐ Yes ☐ No; ____________________
   Did she falsify?
4. How much of this was salary? — $ ______ Commission? ______
5. How was her attendance? ____________________
   Conscientious? Health problems?
6. What type of instructing did she do? ____________________
   To whom?
7. How did her efforts compare with others? ____________________
   Industrious? Competitive?
8. Did she supervise anyone else? — ☐ No, ☐ Yes; How many? ______
   Does this check?
   (If yes) How well did she handle it? ____________________
   Is she a good leader?
9. How closely was she supervised? ____________________
   Was she hard to manage?
10. How hard did she work? ____________________
    Is she habitually industrious?
11. How well did she get along with other people? her students? ____________________
    Is she a troublemaker?
12. Did she have arguments with customers? ____________________
    Does she like selling? Can she control her temper?
13. What did you think of her? ____________________
    Did she get along with her superiors?
14. Why did she leave? ____________________
    Good reasons? Do they check?
15. Would you rehire her? — ☐ Yes, ☐ No; Why not? ______
    Does this affect her suitability with us?
16. What are her outstanding strong points? ____________________
17. What type of work do you feel she would do best? ____________________
18. What, if any, are her weak points? ____________________

HIRING MANAGER'S NOTES

From ______ xx ___ To ______ xx ___
Do dates check?______

Source: Dr. J. D. Richardson

attend to the administrative aspects of orientation. A checklist of possible administrative and cultural items to cover in orientation includes:

> Company history, policies, and practice;
> Company values and goals;
> Facilities;
> Organizational structure;
> Employee conduct and responsibilities to the company;
> Company responsibilities to employees;
> The compensation program, including any awards, contests and other benefits;
> The benefits program life insurance, medical, pension, profits, deferred compensation;
> The evaluation program and schedule;
> Promotion policy;
> A tour of premises and the employee's own department;
> Introduction to fellow employees;
> Safety and security program including any required trainings such as CPR;
> Overview of company's emergency plan;
> Training opportunities and aid;
> Hours and pay schedule; and
> Work assignments.

The process should also involve a check-back after about three days to answer any new questions that arise. On the first day, it makes settling in easier if someone is assigned to make sure that the new employee does not eat lunch alone.

Training

Training involves three areas: training in the job for which the person was hired, training for more advanced functions in the company, and training to address social and economic changes that affect the way the company must operate. All employees need training for one or more of these areas. There are four basic modes of providing training:

> On the job, by supervisors;
> Classroom activity at the workplace (e.g., during less busy periods of the week, with inside or outside instructors or vendors);
> Apprenticeship; and
> Special courses, seminars and classes off the premises, provided by specialists outside the firm.

Training may include both technical and human resource development areas.

On-the-Job Training

On-the-job training is the basic training system used by all aviation businesses to some degree. Its success is strongly related to its being a hands-on process. It generally requires that the immediate supervisor become an effective teacher. One effective program for this is the Job Instructor Training (JIT), which was developed during World War II. Its major elements are:

How to Get Ready to Instruct

Step 1: Have a Timetable

> How much skill do you expect the person to have?
> By what date?

Step 2: Break Down the Job

> List important steps.
> Pick out the key points.

Step 3: Have Everything Ready

> The right equipment, material, and supplies.
> Have the workplace properly arranged just as the worker will be expected to keep it.

How to Instruct

Step 1: Prepare the Worker

> Put him or her at ease.
> State the job and find out what the trainee already knows about it.
> Get him or her interested in learning the job.
> Place in correct position.

Step 2: Present the Operation

> Tell, show, and illustrate one important step at a time.
> Stress each key point.
> Instruct clearly, completely, and patiently, but no more than the student can master.

Step 3: Try Out Performance

> Have the trainee do the job; correct errors.
> Have the trainee explain each key point to you as he or she does the job again.

> Make sure he or she understands.
> Continue until you know the trainee knows.

Step 4: Follow up

> Put the trainee to work alone.
> Designate to whom he or she goes for help.
> Check frequently.
> Encourage questions.
> Taper off extra coaching and close follow-up.
> If the worker hasn't learned, the instructor hasn't taught.

Developing Supervisors and Managers

Some people are natural managers, some can acquire the necessary skills, and some would prefer to spend their careers without getting into management. Given the difficulty of attracting experienced talent and the value of seasoned personnel who know your business, it may often be advantageous to bring in entry-level people and train them for management after a period of evaluating their suitability for advancement. The selected management training process should foster self-development, be tailored to individual needs and educational gaps, and should be a long-range concept.

Virtually by definition, management training will involve more than on-the-job training. Although working with someone on selected tasks is one approach, it will probably need to be supplemented by seminars, courses, workshops, and conferences provided by such organizations as:

> Aircraft manufacturers;
> Aviation associations such as the National Air Transportation Association (NATA), the National Business Aircraft Association (NBAA), state associations of airport managers, and other aviation groups;
> Chambers of Commerce;
> Colleges and universities;
> Banks and other service organizations;
> Professional education groups such as the American Management Association;
> Small Business Administration; and
> Training consultants and vendors providing customized programs.

Who pays and whether or not the programs are undertaken on company time must be resolved, in advance. The management trainee can perhaps be encouraged to choose among several courses with any of them covering the needed material. Some firms retroactively pay a percentage of tuition costs for any relevant program completed by any employee. Other firms pay for tuition and time in exchange for having the trainee teach the new material to the other staff.

The concept of lifelong learning applies to virtually every profession in our society today. In an industry such as aviation, it is ever important to stay abreast of new technologies, revised regulations, and market trends. The term "lifelong learning" encompasses everything from attending college courses to professional workshops and conferences, to reading industry-related periodicals.

Training to Keep Abreast of Social and Economic Change

The world is changing at an ever-increasing pace and this can affect the marketplace for an aviation business. If it becomes harder to make a profit from the sale of fuel or aircraft, perhaps other products and service lines need to be emphasized. If so, different personnel may be involved and need guidance on merchandising and promoting the new items. If the airport operator is receiving a growing volume of noise complaints from certain areas in the flight pattern, then flight instructors need to be trained in more depth on noise issues and abatement procedures. Then they, in turn, can teach this in the air and in the classroom. If the business is investing in a new computer for accounting purposes, perhaps all the staff would benefit from a short presentation by the computer vendor about other functions that could be performed on the system. The manager must stay current with trends both within and beyond aviation, and the manager must determine how much of the staff's time to allot to briefings, reading of trade and general business publications, and formal classroom activities.

Evaluating the Training Program

Any training takes time away from revenue-producing work. Although theoretically it will pay off by reducing mistakes and increasing productivity and motivation, this consequence is not automatic. A training program must have before and after measurements. Depending on the specific training that was taken, measurable items in an aviation business include:

> Complaint rate;
> Appreciation rate;
> Invoice errors;
> Accident rate;
> Absenteeism rate;
> Personnel turnover;
> Rework rate on repairs;
> Time required to perform a task;
> Cost per task;
> Scores on formal written tests;
> Volume of sales; and
> New clients.

The measures selected for evaluation of the training program must be items readily collectable or already routinely being collected. It may be desirable to also survey employee job satisfaction and to review the individual evaluations turned in by employees at the end of a specific training.

Communicating

Basic Elements

Considerable successful communication has already occurred when a new member of a firm has been recruited, screened, selected, and hired. But even the strongest candidate has to learn to communicate in various ways about new tasks with new colleagues in order to be successful on the job. Communication skills are starting to be specifically taught in schools and business seminars. Their acquisition and continual improvement is a necessity for every employee.

Communication occurs whenever information is transferred from one person to another and understood so that it may be correctly acted upon. Information goes through five phases:

> Encoding—expressing the idea in written, oral or gesture form;
> Transmission—by sound waves, paper, light waves, and so on;
> Reception—by the correct party in a timely manner;
> Decoding—translation of the material into ideas; and
> Understanding—evaluation and analysis of meaning.

Figure 5.10 shows this process.

Communication can fail because of a problem with any one of these steps. If a supervisor fails to ascertain whether an employee, especially a new employee, has understood a message, then that supervisor has not communicated adequately. People new to an organization may require training in its vocabulary and style of communication. The amount of time it takes for them to pick this up depends not only on their intelligence, but also on their cultural background and the amount of their previous adaptation.

Barriers to Effective Communication

These problems in the communications process are often referred to as barriers to effective communication. The most common ones are:

1. We hear what we expect to hear.
2. We ignore information that conflicts with what we already "know."
3. We judge the value of information by its source.
4. We are influenced by our group bias.
5. Words mean different things to different people.
6. Groups may have their own jargon or insiders' vocabulary.
7. Our emotional state conditions what we hear.
8. We don't know how the other person perceives the situation.
9. We fail to listen.
10. We ignore body language.
11. We try to convey too much at once.
12. The receiver is not "tuned in."
13. Understanding is assumed rather than ascertained.
14. Intermediates involved in the transmission filter or amend information.

Verbal and Non-Verbal Communications

Verbal communication skills are the most commonly discussed in communications. However, non-verbal communications can be just as important in sending a message. In fact, if the non-verbal cues being given conflict with the verbal message, more often than not the non-verbal message will be the most powerful.

Figure 5.10» Model of the Communication Process

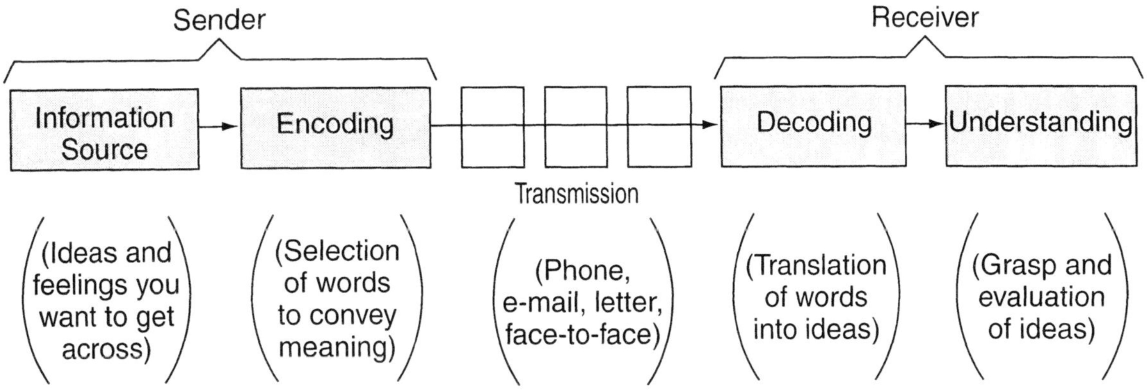

Source: Dr. J. D. Richardson

Good verbal communication skills include not only the words used to convey the message but other factors as well. For example, the tone of voice being used can imply a variety of messages. Using a matter of fact versus a sarcastic tone will certainly leave different images of what the sender is trying to say, even if the words are exactly the same. The rate of speech delivery, the volume of voice, and pitch all relate to how the message is received. And, silence sends a powerful message all its own, depending on how it is used.

Non-verbal communication includes everything from eye contact to gestures, from facial expressions to jingling of keys in the pocket to pacing. A person who stares at the ceiling while talking with someone is generally perceived to be untruthful. Good eye contact helps instill trust in the listener and implies honesty. Raising your eyebrows or rolling your eyes while shaking someone's hand and saying how pleased you are to meet them, sends the opposite message to the person you are meeting. A good manager should be aware of non-verbal cues, not only to ensure they are consistent with the verbal message sent, but also to watch for the non-verbal cues of others. A common managerial fault is to tell a visitor they have your attention, yet continue shuffling papers on the desk. The body language contradicts the words.

Improving Communications

One of the most useful texts in recent decades for improving communications in the workplace is The One-Minute Manager.[18] Its first recommendation is the joint development by manager and employee of a goal for that employee's work performance that can be written down and takes a minute or less to read. The manager gives "one minute praisings" for performances that shine and "one minute reprimands" ending with a reminder of the value of the person being reprimanded. Thus people know what they are supposed to be doing and know they will hear immediately when they do something well or poorly. The manager doesn't just save up grievances ("gunny sacking") or praise for annual review day.

A basic set of tools for improving communications includes:

> Utilizing feedback to make sure the message was not only received but also understood;
> Developing sensitivity to the receiver;
> Being aware of the symbolic meaning of words;
> Being aware of the meaning of words in other cultures;
> Timing messages carefully;
> Reinforcing words with action;
> Using simple, direct language; and
> Introducing the proper amount of redundancy.[19]

Utilizing feedback means constantly being on the alert for clues to whether or not one is being understood. Feedback from the recipient of the message may take the form of a "yes." It could be an understanding look, an attentive nod, or the desired action. Lacking any of these, the communicator should try again. Good supervisors actively encourage questions to make sure the instructions are clear, and instruct employees in the need to give clear feedback.

Sensitivity to the receiver means attempting to adjust to the receiver's needs, especially possible interpretations of the message. Cultural and emotional factors must be considered.

Awareness of symbolic meanings is important because words can have meanings in the mind of the receiver that distort and interrupt the communications effort. The communicator should avoid such words once they are identified.

Careful timing of messages is important because the receiver must be ready and able to handle the new input. Poor timing can include times when the receiver is already busy on a task, is overloaded with new input, is tired, or has become preoccupied with a distracting problem. It can also include times when prior events mean the person's mind is already made up on an issue. The message-sender should anticipate these situations and adjust accordingly.

Reinforcement of words by action will greatly increase the chance of a communication being accepted, as well as the expectation of action based on past events.

The use of simple, direct language will enhance good understanding. Don't use technical terms and long tangled statements.

The proper amount of redundancy is important. Good teachers know that their ability to convey a new idea often depends on their ability to rephrase the same thing in as many different ways as necessary until all the class members have discovered its meaning in their own terms. Sales people are often taught that it takes six different exposures to the product before people are generally ready to respond. This repetition of ideas, often in different forms, is needed until it is clear the message has been understood. However, pay attention to ensure that your audience is not tuning out due to the repetition. The message may be more effective if given on several occasions.

The use of communications training can be important. Many people do not know the ways they communicate until they see themselves in role-playing, on videotape, or hear a tape recording. Guided practice and feedback can almost always be part of a manager's personnel training program. Last but not least, it is the job of the message sender, NOT the recipient, to make sure the message has arrived.

Motivating

Array of Needs

Some three decades of thinking about motivation have been based on a hierarchy of needs first described by Maslow.[20] His theory (1) gave recognition to the fact that motivation comes from within and (2) depicted the driving forces as a hierarchy with simple physical needs for food, shelter and safety at the bottom. The typical individual's attention goes to social needs once the basic needs are met. Then their needs become more sophisticated, and esteem and self-respect become the primary motivators. Finally, at the top of the hierarchy—and attended to only if or when all preceding needs are met—is the motivator of self-actualization. This hierarchy or staircase of needs is depicted in Figure 5.11.

Other long-standing theories of what motivates workers are described as theories X, Y, and Z. A summary (in sexist language!) follows:[21]

> "Douglas McGregor in his book, "The Human Side of Enterprise" published in 1960 has examined theories on behavior of individuals at work, and he has formulated two models which he calls Theory X and Theory Y.
>
> "Theory X Assumes that the average human being has an inherent dislike of work and will avoid it if he can. Because of their dislike for work, most people must be controlled and threatened before they will work hard enough. The average human prefers to be directed, dislikes responsibility, is unambiguous, and desires security above everything. These assumptions lie behind most organizational principles today, and give rise both to "tough" management with punishments and tight controls, and "soft" management, which aims at harmony at work. Both these are "wrong" because man needs more than financial rewards at work; he also needs some deeper higher order motivation—the opportunity to fulfill himself. Theory X managers do not give their staff this opportunity so that the employees behave in the expected fashion.
>
> "Theory Y Assumes that the expenditure of physical and mental effort in work is as natural as play or rest. Control and punishment are not the

Figure 5.11 » Maslow's Hierarchy of Needs: Two Views

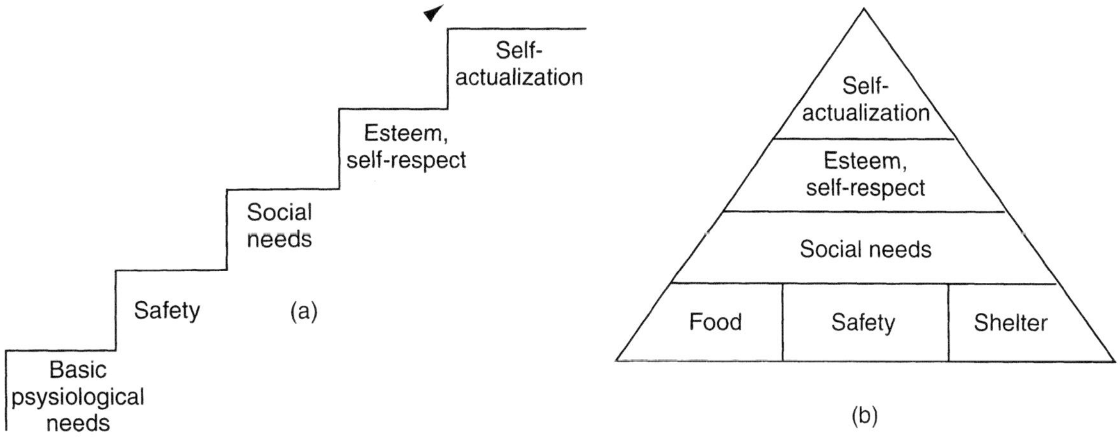

Source: Richardson/Rodwell derived from Abraham Maslow, 2003

only ways to make people work, man will direct himself if he is committed to the aims of the organization. If a job is satisfying, then the result will be commitment to the organization. The average man learns, under proper conditions, not only to accept but also to seek responsibility. Imagination, creativity, and ingenuity can be used to solve work problems by a large number of employees. Under the conditions of modern industrial life, the intellectual potentialities of the average man are only partially utilized.

"Comments on Theory X and Theory Y: Assumptions include that these assumptions are based on social science research which has been carried out, and demonstrate the potential which is present in man and which organizations should recognize in order to become more effective. McGregor sees these two theories as two quite separate attitudes. Theory Y is difficult to put into practice on the shop floor in large mass production operations, but it can be used initially in the managing of managers and professionals.

In "The Human Side of Enterprise" McGregor shows how Theory Y affects the management of promotions and salaries and the development of effective managers. McGregor also sees Theory Y as conducive to participative problem solving. It is part of the manager's job to exercise authority, and there are cases in which this is the only method of achieving the desired results because subordinates do not agree that the ends are desirable. However, in situations where it is possible to obtain commitment to objectives, it is better to explain the matter fully so that employees grasp the purpose of an action. They will then exert self-direction and control to do better work quite possibly by better methods than if they had simply been carrying out an order which they did not fully understand.

"The situation in which employees can be consulted is one where the individuals are emotionally mature, and positively motivated towards their work; where the work is sufficiently responsible to allow for flexibility and where the employee can see his own position in the management hierarchy. If these conditions are present, managers will find that the participative approach to problem solving leads to much improved results compared with the alternative approach of handing out authoritarian orders. Once management becomes persuaded that it is under-estimating the potential of its human resources, and accepts the knowledge given by social science researchers and displayed in Theory Y assumptions, then it can invest time, money and effort in developing improved applications of the theory.

"McGregor realizes that some of the theories he has put forward are unrealizable in practice, but wants managers to put into operation the basic assumption that staff will contribute more to the organization if they are treated as responsible and valued employees".

More recent analysis by several management experts suggests that what motivates people can be any and all of these factors at the same time. As society becomes more mobile and close-knit, family networks are harder to maintain and the workplace often becomes the primary social outlet. Everyone who works is motivated to a greater or lesser extent by money, or the need for more money; however, this is not usually the sole consideration for most people. Job satisfaction takes other forms.

Needs Satisfied by Working

Some companies appear to be arranged only to meet people's lower level needs. Executives and factory operators alike put most of their creative energy into diverse hobbies outside the workplace, requiring elaborate equipment and planning. However, research such as found in *In Search Of Excellence* found that the excellent companies were "organized to obtain extraordinary effort from ordinary human beings."[22] The same feature of motivating even mediocre employees to be the best they can be is a feature of the larger Japanese companies, which in years gone by have offered lifetime employment so that they must find ways of motivating all personnel.[23] Some of the needs that can be met in the workplace include: autonomy and a sense of control over one's situation, being part of a team or a sense of belonging, public recognition and rewards, and a sense of responsibility for vital functions.

Creating a Motivating Environment

If these are the non-monetary rewards that people seek from their work, how can managers arrange working conditions so that these rewards occur?

Autonomy and control mean training a person to know he or she is empowered in specific areas. An atmosphere of trust can be generated by such techniques as abolishing time clocks in favor of an honor system, using flextime, allowing as much freedom as possible over workspace arrangements, and, in general, treating people as adults.

Recognition in the best companies seems to involve several steps. First, clear and specific performance goals are set up. They are set deliberately quite low so that almost everyone can be a winner. Reaching the goal is praised publicly and with varying levels of celebration. Praise and rewards are instant, specific, consist of things important to the performer rather than the rewarder, and may be sporadic and unpredictable, the result of the manager wandering around and particularly looking for things people are doing right.

Money is only one of many factors contributing to job satisfaction. Other important factors include participation in decision-making, challenging assignments, positive feedback from one's superior, and the chance for advancement.

Most employees are highly motivated by recognition and acknowledgement. The precise mode of giving recognition will vary with the style and value system of the company. Some considerations to include in the design of the recognition system are:

1. The award must have meaning for the recipient (not just for the company).
2. The recipient must understand why the award is being given.
3. The presentation must be dignified, sincere, and conducted before peers and supervisors.
4. The award must have intrinsic value and uniqueness.

Being part of a team of winners in a corporate family is another technique deliberately fostered by some companies. The ways of achieving this can include making the effort to acquire knowledge about each employee's personal situation; company trips and outings; and acceptance of the individual's uniqueness. Some companies have a store of myths and stories about the business especially perhaps in its early days which help to perpetuate the sense of belonging to something special. A strong and often repeated corporate philosophy stated in simple ways, such as "product quality and customer service" can be a major contributor. Some firms shift their personnel among functions, and this can strengthen corporate pride because people learn to understand the whole, rather than just a part of the business, and to respect daily challenges handled by their peers in other departments. It gives the rotated employees a hands-on appreciation of the issues and problems facing many divisions of the company.

Finally, delegation means responsibility. If someone is put in charge of a task, then they must be allowed to carry it out in their own way without the boss constantly interfering. However, good delegation does mean that the supervisor is available to answer questions that will inevitably arise; good employees should be encouraged to ask these questions rather than just proceeding along a path that may not be what is wanted. Specific results by specific dates mean specific success or failure. These milestones allow the boss to re-delegate the task differently if all is not going well by using the opportunity to communicate in more detail some of the "how" as well as the "what." Judgment must be used in giving responsibility commensurate with ability; this is one of the key tasks of a manager, since one seldom has at hand exactly all the right talents embodied in one person. This is discussed in Chapter 2, Management Functions.

Leadership

Leadership is one of the major functions of a manager. In a small or new business, it may be almost without effort that the owner/manager conveys to the staff the excitement and drive that motivate him or her. In a bigger or older company, it may take more conscious effort. As mentioned, one author recommends first that people with appropriate values be the only ones hired. A possible set of values for all employees follows:[24]

1. Any and every company problem is your problem (Don't pass the buck or point the finger).
2. Glitter on your own time (Don't worry about status symbols or showing off on the job).
3. We price and sell service, not technology, or products.
4. Let the customer take advantage of you.
5. Finish, and put your name on, every task you start.
6. Bake the incentives into the work itself.
7. Pace company growth to staff growth.
8. Simplicity rules.
9. Know your customers' shoe size.

Such values, or minor variations on them, could probably fit almost any company. The same authors recommend that new employees be given at least eight hours of value orientation during their first three months on the job.

Evaluating Employees

The process of employee discipline and evaluation may be best accomplished primarily in the style of The One-Minute Manager, that is, by the one-minute reprimand about a specific thing done wrong, immediately, but including a reassurance to the employee about his or her worth. This is as an alternative to the "gunnysack" approach in which all the bad things, along with the good, are dumped out on the conference table once every six months or every year at performance evaluation time. The principle of tackling little errors promptly when they occur is aimed at ensuring that big errors do not have much chance to happen. Nevertheless, periodically the manager will need to sit down with each employee and review how things are going. This probably will be tied to periodic merit, cost-of-living, or other pay reviews.

An effective employee appraisal plan will:

> Achieve better communication between the manager and employee;
> Relate pay to work performance and results;
> Provide a standardized approach to evaluating performance over time and among employees; and
> Help employees better understand what is expected of them and how they can improve.

The appraisal process should consider the following and should be reviewed with all supervisors doing reviews so that there is a reasonably consistent approach to applying these factors:

> Results achieved;
> Quality of performance;
> Volume of work;
> Effectiveness in working with others in firm;
> Effectiveness in dealing with customers, suppliers, and so on;
> Initiative;
> Job knowledge;
> Dependability; and
> Enthusiasm.

A sample performance appraisal form utilized by Midcoast Aviation is shown in Figure 5.12.

Promoting Employees

Promoting employees from within is ideal if at all possible, because staff will develop greater loyalty to a company that clearly indicates it can use them as they mature and acquire more skills. By

Figure 5.12 » Sample Performance Appraisal

MIDCOAST AVIATION, INC.

NONEXEMPT
PERFORMANCE APPRAISAL / IMPROVEMENT PROFILE

Name: ______________________________

Job Title: ______________________________

Department: ______________________________

Date Assigned to Present Job: ______________________________

Date of This Review Period: From: ______________ To: ______________

Reviewed By: ______________________________

INSTRUCTIONS:

This form is to be completed for each salaried nonexempt employee:

- **Annually.**
- **On an interim basis, as necessary, to review the Employee's performance.**

This report covers all important aspects of the past performance of the employee, a summary of his/her current status, and a discussion of potential for growth and development. In addition, the report provides a vehicle for your personal discussion of the appraisal results with the employee. Carefully consider the employee's performance during the review period based on assigned duties and level of responsibility. Check the appropriate block in each category which best identifies the employee's current performance. Next, check the block indicating the change in performance since the last evaluation.

Source: Midcoast Aviation

contrast, an ambitious and capable employee that sees no internal career path will likely start looking for jobs outside the company. Promotions need to be done in an equitable way, however. If a new position is to be created, or if someone leaves or retires, then the manager will get best results by posting the opening and giving all interested parties a chance to be considered. In a small company this may mean interviewing everyone. In a large company some preliminary screening is necessary and appropriate. But if only a few applicants are going to be screened out, it may be

Figure 5.12 » Continued

Performance Factor	Current Evaluation					Since Last Evaluation		
	Unsatisfactory	Acceptable	Competent	Competent Plus	Outstanding	Reverse	Same	Improved
1. **ATTITUDE:** Consider the employee's work attitude including overall appropriateness of behavior towards the environment, fellow employees and supervision. Is the individual willing to accept new assignments, policies and procedures? Is he/she flexible in meeting changes, additional requirements, etc.								
2. **ORGANIZATION:** Consider the individual's ability to effectively organize his/her work load and establish priorities. Does the individual properly plan out work including coordinating with others as required?								
3. **PRODUCTIVITY – QUANTITY:** Consider the individual's overall productivity in terms of quantity of work produced in timely basis. Consider the individual's ability to meet or exceed job requirements.								
4. **PRODUCTIVITY – QUALITY:** Consider the individual's ability to produce neat, accurate work on a timely basis. Does the employee possess acute attention to detail when it is an essential factor?								
5. **INITIATIVE:** Consider the employee's ability to work without constant supervision and his or her ability to begin and/or follow through with assignments.								
6. **TECHNICAL OR JOB COMPETENCY:** Consider the individual's overall technical knowledge and job competency, and the employee's ability to put this knowledge into practical application.								
7. **ATTENDANCE:** Consider the individual's attendance record. Does the individual attempt to adhere to policies concerning lunch hours and work breaks? Does the individual notify his/her supervisor of absenteeism or tardiness?								

better for company morale to interview them all. An inexperienced employee who has little or no idea why she or he is not qualified for the opening can become a problem if their aspirations are not acknowledged. The interview can be an opportunity for the manger to hear directly from that person what their aspirations are, what they are doing now to prepare themselves, and it becomes an opportunity to steer that person on to the career path most likely to be best for them and the company.

Figure 5.12 » Continued

OVERALL PERFORMANCE SUMMARY

Indicate the performance level that most closely reflects how the employee's overall performance measured up to what should normally be expected from an employee with similar experience at this level.

☐ Unsatisfactory	☐ Acceptable	☐ Competent	☐ Competent Plus	☐ Outstanding
Doesn't meet objectives, falls short of required performance, consider trial (probationary period), transfer to a more suitable job or termination.	Usually meets objectives, areas for improvement noted in appraisal, level of performance is less than expected but acceptable.	Consistently meets objectives, full utilization of ability and experience to produce the desired results expected from a qualified employee.	Consistently meets objectives and actively contributes to achievement of overall company goals. Superior performance in some aspects of job. Performance above the competent level.	Consistently exceeds objectives, actively develops teamwork and cooperation, seeks new and better ways to accomplish tasks, extremely capable and versatile in adjusting priorities to current needs, an effective communicator.

PRINCIPAL JOB DUTIES DURING REVIEW PERIOD. Briefly describe the principal work assigned to the individual. List and number specific job objectives and goals established.

Signatures and Dates:

Appraised by:	Director, Human Resources
Department Head	Employee

Figure 5.12 » Continued

JOB PERFORMANCE STRENGTHS (Summarize the employee's most significant strengths.)

DEVELOPMENT PLANS (Summarize the activities such as special coaching, special assignments, off-the-job training, etc., that are planned to help this employee improve job performance during the next appraisal period.)

IMPROVEMENT NEEDS (Summarize the employee's most significant areas needing improvement.)

ADDITIONAL COMMENTS:

EMPLOYEE COMMENTS:

Compensation Systems

Job Evaluation

Using the task information described in the Comparable Worth section on page 118, and some criteria about responsibility levels, jobs under review now have to be evaluated in relation to one another. One method for doing this is simple ranking, which ranks and groups the jobs by their value to the firm. Then the groups of jobs are arranged in a series of pay levels.

Ranking the jobs in order of their value to the firm takes into account only the internal situation. The salary that people in these jobs can command elsewhere must now be investigated. Possible sources of such data include:

> Trade and professional groups such as NATA and Aviation Maintenance Technician (AMT), which conduct an annual salary survey;
> Chambers of Commerce;
> Major firms in the area;
> U.S. Bureau of Labor Statistics;
> American Management Association;
> Employment agencies; and
> Newspaper want ads.

In analyzing pay in your area and comparing it to your company's jobs, be sure to compare actual job descriptions and not just job titles. Based upon the average pay for each type of position developed from your market survey, a midpoint pay level for your own company can be constructed for each position. Commonly the low point in each range will be 85 percent of the mid-point and the high will be 115 percent. Such a range will enable employees to join your firm at the bottom of the pay range for that position and get 30 percent in raises without promotion to a higher job category. A more fine-grained breakdown of each pay range may also suit your purposes.

Fringe Benefits

Most full-time positions carry with them an array of non-salary benefits such as medical insurance, life insurance, pension plans, profit-sharing plans, and other supplementary compensation. The primary advantages of these are:

1. In the event of the employee's death or disability, the dependents are provided for in a planned manner.
2. Group purchasing enables the employer to buy more benefits for the same dollar than employees could alone, particularly in insurance.
3. Good fringe benefits are a major means of employee retention in tight labor markets.

Most companies offer certain items on a mandatory basis, such as a minimum level of life insurance, and then provide optional additional benefits such as disability insurance. There may be choices of medical plans with varying levels of coverage and varying levels of employee participation in payment. The trend in this area is the "cafeteria" approach in which the company determines a fixed dollar amount or percentage of salary to be used for fringe benefits, and each employee chooses precisely and only that package of services that he or she really wants.[25] As more and more households involve both a husband and wife working for different employers with different benefit options, this ability to custom-design one's benefits is a great advantage. Computerization of benefits processing is the technology that makes this approach possible.

For most businesses, the typical scale of fringe benefits is in the range of 30–37 percent of basic pay. Benefits have been rising faster than wages and salaries in the past three decades so that ways to control these costs, especially health care premiums, are clearly important. The flexible benefits approach can give employees more of what each really needs without increasing total costs to the company.

Administration of the Total Compensation Plan

Many employees are unaware of the total dollar value of their salary plus benefits. When hiring new staff, it is desirable to be able to cite lower and upper limits for the value of the total compensation package. Administration of the compensation plan will probably also involve periodic activity to stay current with what competing businesses are doing. It should involve a clear and consistent policy about raises, promotions, merit increases, bonuses, and the like. The plan needs to give the manager the flexibility to take quick steps to prevent the loss of a key employee without causing problems with the other staff. It must provide the freedom to bring in specialized talent at the going rate while not slighting long-standing, loyal employees. It must allow a visible career ladder within the firm so that staff can envisage their long-range futures. If pay levels and changes are soundly based on market competition, clearly set out, and fairly administered, it will go a long way toward minimizing trouble over what can otherwise be an ongoing source of employee discontent.

Disciplinary Problems

Conflict Resolution

Because most businesses involve operating under time pressure with a diverse group of personalities, job situations may lead periodically to disagreements on how something should be, or should have been done. An autocratic manager or boss who rules, "In the future we'll do it my way, and that's the end of the matter," is losing in several ways:

1. Resentful employees may consciously or unconsciously seek other ways to undercut their boss's authority. Morale will drop.
2. Good suggestions from employees on how to improve the company's methods will not be heard, and this will not only mean loss of a good solution today, but will tend to stifle future problem-solving ideas and activities.
3. Junior staff are not given either recognition or the ability to grow, thereby heightening the chance of future inadequacies.

If, instead of an autocratic approach to disagreements, the manager is willing to be more open-minded, the guidelines in Figure 5.13 can be helpful in achieving a satisfactory solution.

Figure 5.13 » 21 Steps to Fighting Fairly

A. *When Something Happens That Upsets You/Makes You Angry*
   1. Ask the person involved for a specific time to talk over something; tell him/her what you want to discuss.
   2. Set a mutually agreeable time and place.
   3. Prepare. Make notes or run through in your mind what seems to have happened and why you're angry about it.
   4. Do it soon. Don't put the other person in suspense overnight or over a weekend, unless it can't be helped.

B. *Holding the Discussion*
   5. Do it in private.
   6. Allow no interruptions.
   7. Finish it. Don't leave until both feel clear a resolution has been reached.
   8. Acknowledge the other may have had a good reason (to him/her) for doing what he/she did, regardless of how stupid it seems to you. Ask for clarification.
   9. Listen, interpret, and clarify.
   10. Stick to the issue. When discussing what A did, don't get sidetracked by discussions of the times B has done the same thing.
   11. Use "I" statements; be accountable for your own feelings.
   12. Allow your own anger.
   13. Expect and acknowledge the other's anger but don't take responsibility for it.
   14. Don't let the other person's anger make you angrier; you are not the target.
   15. Stick to one issue at a time. If necessary, set another time and place for other issues or agree to continue then and there.
   16. Don't gunnysack ("twice is always").
   17. Don't walk away.
   18. Don't interrupt.

C. *Concluding the Discussion*
   19. Completion and clarity on the issue; mutual understanding of how to deal with it.
   20. Reassurance and reaffirmation of the other person.
   21. Let it go. Don't bring it up again or blame others. What's done and resolved is over. Be friends again.

Source: Julie F. Rodwell, 2003

Administering Discipline

Positive discipline through motivation and self-control is what makes most companies work well most of the time. Negative discipline—punishment of some type—may only result in behavior adequate to avoid punishment, not in real correction of the problem. However, even under the best of conditions with trained and loyal employees and excellent leadership, someone is bound to violate the rules now and then so that there are serious negative consequences. When this happens, there is a need for some generally accepted principles to guide management. In administering discipline, two conflicting goals—protecting the rights of the individual to be disciplined, and preserving the interests of the organization as a whole—must be reconciled. Within this context the following guidelines are generally considered desirable:

1. Provide definite policies covering discipline.
2. Establish reasonable rules and standards.
3. Communicate rules to all concerned.
4. Investigate each case thoroughly.
5. Ensure consistency.
6. Provide a logical sequence of progressive penalties.
7. Establish a right of appeal.
8. Document all disciplinary matters in writing with dates and names.

The "Red-Hot-Stove" Rule

A practical approach to discipline is the "red-hot-stove" approach in which the consequences of a misdemeanor are immediate, consistent, and impersonal. The act and the discipline seem virtually like one event. This involves:

1. Having advance warning—knowledge of the rule and the consequences of breaking it.
2. Immediate and painful results from the violation.
3. The same results for everyone, no matter what their status.
4. The result is not because of who you are, but what you did.

This process may be difficult to apply in every case, but persistence will pay off at least in part because of its deterrent effect.

The Troubled Worker

Stress and fragmentation of our lives occur not just in the workplace, but also in the rest of life as well. The above descriptions of how to handle normal disagreements and infractions may not be applicable when the worker in question is in some kind of non-work trauma. This could be death, divorce, serious mental or physical illness of oneself or a loved one, problems with children or stepchildren, substance abuse, domestic violence, financial worries, or a number of other causes. While the truly professional worker will attempt not to bring these problems to the workplace, sometimes the situation is so severe that effects will show at work.

The supervisor or manager's role is very sensitive in such situations. Discussions with the employee must be restricted to the problem's effect on job performance. It is not the supervisor's business to become a diagnostician or a counselor. If the issue is not resolved satisfactorily through a supervisor and employee discussion, it may be necessary to seek outside help. Many companies are now contracting with "Employee Assistance Programs" or EAPs, where the troubled worker can obtain expert counsel and, if needed, referral to a detoxification program or other treatment facility. As in all cases of disciplinary action, careful documentation of the steps taken, the commitments made, and their schedule must be retained. This is vital if the employee must later be fired because it will provide the necessary documented evidence of failure to perform.

Particularly in the case of drug and alcohol abuse, the supervisor must carefully monitor behavior and deal with the deterioration in work performance before it poses a threat to the safety or productivity of other workers, or a risk to the company through poor work.

In 1988 the federal government adopted requirements for drug testing of certain personnel in aviation. Aviation employees with safety or security related responsibilities are subject to drug testing. Part 135 companies of any size are required to develop and submit a plan to FAA that includes random drug testing. It also requires pre-employment and post-accident testing. While employers are not required to offer rehabilitation, they are encouraged to consider such plans in establishing the total compensation plan. Employers must designate a physician as the Medical Review Officer for administration of the drug-testing plan.

Separation

Whether voluntary or involuntary, there should be some standard procedures for termination. The departing employee may become a vendor, a source of referrals to the business, or may even at some point be rehired. A person who does not fit the company's present needs may still have desirable skills in changed circumstances. In all cases, an exit interview is recommended to seek information from the outgoing employee about concerns and issues and to provide management with ideas for changes to benefit the remaining staff. A second purpose of an exit interview is to stimulate the maximum self-esteem and positive feeling about the company in the mind of the departing employee. A sample form for exit interviews is presented in Figure 5.14.

If a company makes the effort to be receptive even where the parting is not totally amicable, information received from departing employees can be very useful in analyzing problem areas and in providing for organizational improvement. The key to successful exit interviewing is to encourage the employee to talk as freely as possible. Establish yourself as a sympathetic listening post so that his true feelings and opinions may be obtained. The following questions covering basic areas should be used to set the interview pattern. Other topics, appropriate to individual cases should be explored as indicated. The interviewee should be provided with information regarding what will be done with the exit interview form afterwards—will it be kept of file for management actions in response, saved, kept in the employee's record?

Personnel Policy Manual

This chapter has touched on numerous aspects of personnel management, particularly as it affects the small FBO business. It assumes that the company has no personnel manager, and that the company manager and various supervisors must carry out personnel activities as part of their jobs. Since consistency is such a major feature of so many personnel issues, there is a need for a written manual. The manual will likely contain at least the following:

- Purpose;
- Authority of the manual;
- How to use the manual;
- Responsibilities of department heads, supervisors, and employees;
- Employee relations policy;
- Recruiting and selection policy;
- Training and development policy;
- Working schedules and hours;
- Compensation policies and procedures; pay and fringes;
- Promotions, transfers and layoffs;
- Attendance, punctuality and absenteeism;
- Safety and security programs;
- Operational rules;
- Profit awareness;
- Complaint and grievance procedures;
- Communications;
- Labor relations; and
- Personnel forms.

Manual Style

The manual can be anything from a formal, legalistic compendium of all current policies (perhaps in a loose-leaf binder), to a small, perhaps humorous brochure. Many companies are abolishing the old hard-copy three ring binder and replacing it with a company web site, employee-only, electronic version. In many companies it may be appropriate to have both—a reference site with all the detail, and something short for each employee. New employees should be required to study the book and ask questions. The owner/manager also needs to decide whether he/she alone will update the policies, or whether to seek advice from supervisors, or assign the full responsibility to someone else for recommending updates.

Personnel Records

A number of record sheets will accompany the personnel manual. A typical list of needed sheets is presented in Figure 5.15. Examples of some of these have been presented earlier in the chapter.

Figure 5.14 » Exit Interview Form to Be Used with the Departure of Each Employee

____
Interview Date

Employee's name ____

Job ____________________________ Employment date ________________

Department ____

Reason for Separation ____________________________________

Departure Date ____

____

Reason for termination? ____________________________________

Do you have another job? __________ Where? ________________ Pay? __________

Did you like the work you were doing? ______________________________

How were the working conditions? ________________________________

When you first started here was your job fully explained? ______________________

Were you introduced to co-workers? ________________________________

Did you enjoy pleasant relationships with co-workers? _______________________

____________________________ Exceptions? ____________________

Did you like your supervisor? ____________________________________

Did your supervisor seem to know his/her job? ___________________________

How well did your supervisor handle gripes or complaints? ______________________

____

Was it easy to communicate with him/her? _____________________________

____

Do you feel your pay was fair? ___________________________________

____

Were benefits satisfactory? _____________________________________

____

Was there sufficient opportunity for advancement? __________________________

____

Do you know how you stood as far as work performance was concerned? ________________

____

What suggestions do you have for improving policies, procedures, work situations, etc.? __________

____

____

What are your plans for the future? ________________________________

____

Others? ____

____

Explain benefits and future relationships with company. _______________________

Comments: ____

____

____

Interviewer ____________________

Source: Dr. J. D. Richardson and Julie F. Rodwell

Figure 5.15 » Personnel Forms and Records

Activity	Form
1. Researching or studying various jobs to obtain information necessary in developing the organization.	Job Analysis
2. Clearly describing a given job in terms of its contents and tasks involved.	Job Description
3. Describing the requirements of a job in terms of skill, effort, responsibility needed by the person on the job.	Job Specification
4. Advising the personnel office or the employment agency of the type person you are recruiting for a specific job.	Requisition
5. Recording biographical, training, experience and personal information about a job applicant.	Application Blank
6. Conducting an interview with a job applicant.	Oral Interview Guide
7. Checking job applicant's references and data to insure validity and gain additional information.	Reference Check (a) Telephone (b) Letter
8. Conducting a physical examination of applicant to insure ability to handle job and determine overall physical condition.	Physical Examination
9. Orienting or inducting new employees into the organization.	Orientation Check List
10. Recording all necessary data and activities on each employee.	Employee Personal Record or Folder
11. Recording attendance and results from various training programs.	Training Records
12. Evaluating and recording the performance of employees.	Performance Rating Form
13. Recording disciplinary situations and action taken.	Disciplinary Forms: (a) Warning (b) Layoff (c) Dismissal
14. Providing a means of handling employee complaints and grievances.	Grievance Forms
15. Providing a means of obtaining employee suggestions.	Suggestion Forms
16. Collecting information and data from all personnel leaving the company.	Exit Interview Form

Source: Dr. J. D. Richardson and Julie F. Rodwell

Employee Organizations

A significant percentage of American labor is unionized (about 20 percent). Although unionism is not as prevalent in general aviation operations as in the airlines, where it's around 40 percent, it ranges around 5 percent in most parts of the country. According to the BLS, almost one-half of all aircraft mechanics, including those employed by some major airlines, are covered by union agreements. The principal unions are the International Association of Machinists and Aerospace Workers and the Transport Workers Union of America.

The International Brotherhood of Teamsters represents some mechanics. The financing and power behind the nation's major unions means that if unionization begins, a single business owner might be unable to resist. In recent years some traditionally non-union areas such as office workers have become increasingly unionized. The usual reasons for unionization can often be addressed by fair and reasonable personnel policies. These reasons may include:

> Changes in management;
> Pay system problems;

> Elimination of promotional opportunities;
> Sudden work-force reductions;
> Unsatisfactory or more restrictive working conditions;
> Poor or inconsistent supervisory practices;
> Desire for greater voice;
> Desire for better income and working conditions; and
> Desire for control over benefits.

Impact on Management

The existence or introduction of a union has an impact on the entire organization. This impact can include:

> Competition for loyalty of employees;
> Possible challenge to management decisions;
> Use of time at work to discuss union issues;
> Stimulation of more careful personnel practices;
> More rigid working rules;
> Possible threats to flexibility and efficiency;
> Centralization of personnel decisions;
> Introduction of outsiders to the management-employee relationship; and
> Higher labor costs.

Every manager should consider very carefully the reasons that contribute to the formation of employee organizations, the impact that such an organization would have upon the business, and develop a managerial philosophy and action program accordingly.

Summary

The success of an aviation business can largely be attributed to its personnel. Human resource programs are instrumental in providing an environment that stimulates people to contribute their best effort. Programs are designed to provide and service a steady flow of personnel into the organization. This flow is like a pipeline with various control points along its length: identification of needs, recruiting, selecting, orientation, training, development, compensation, evaluation, discipline, promotion, and separation. The areas of communications and motivation are especially critical to the organization's success and should receive special managerial attention.

» DISCUSSION TOPICS

1. What is meant by the "pipeline concept"?
2. Identify and briefly discuss five "control points" instrumental to the success of human resource management programs.
3. Identify the key steps involved in the selection of employees.
4. What issues should be covered in an exit interview?
5. What are the key elements of orientation and why are they important?
6. What are some factors that could cause complaints about discrimination in the hiring and managing of personnel?
7. How does Maslow's hierarchy of needs relate to the ways a manager can choose to supervise his or her team?
8. What are three reasons for having a personnel policy manual?

Endnotes

1. Peters and Waterman. *In Search of Excellence—Lessons from America's Best-Run Companies.* New York: Warner Books, 1982.
2. See *http://stats.bls.gov/oco/ocos1011.htm.*
3. See *http://stats.bls.gov/oco/ocos107.htm.*
4. See *http://www.rea.com/careers/pilots.cfm,*see also *http://www.pama.org/tech/career.cfm.*
5. Note 3, op.cit.
6. See BLS at *http://stats.bls.gov/oco/ocos179.htm.*
7. See *http://www.nbaa.org/careers/.*
8. "Overview of The Aviation Maintenance Profession" *FAA Advisory Circular* No. 65-30, June 27, 2000.
9. See *http://www.amtonline.com/salary/2001.htm.*
10. See *http://college.hmco.com/adjuncts/news/news_microsoft.html.* "Microsoft Limits Temporary Workers."
11. Brandt, Steven C. *Entrepreneuring: The Ten Commandments for Building a Growth Company.* Chs. 5 and 6, New York: Mentor Executive Library, 1982.
12. See *http://www.law.cornell.edu.*
13. As above.
14. As above.
15. Cessna Pilot Training Manual, Wichita, KS, undated.
16. "Jackson Vocational Interest Survey," Sigma Assessment Systems, Port Huron, MI; "Performance Testing," Performance Systems International, Minneapolis, MN; "Strong Interest Inventory," Consulting Psychologists Press, Inc., Palo Alto, CA; "Myers-Briggs Type Indicator," Consulting Psychologists Press, Inc., Palo Alto, CA. These testing instruments are also generally available through the Web.
17. For additional information on a specific program for aiding the various styles of personality to work better together, contact the author at *julie.cfd@ccountry.net.*
18. Blanchard, Kenneth, PhD, and Johnson, Spencer, M.D. *The One Minute Manager.* New York: Berkeley Books, 1982.
19. Here is a classic, if perhaps apocryphal example: an old story tells about the problems that Chevrolet had in trying to market the Chevy Nova in Mexico. "No va" in Spanish means "won't go."
20. Maslow, Abraham. *Motivation and Personality, 2nd Edition.* New York: Harper Bros., 1970.
21. See *http://www.accel-team.com/human_relations/hrels_03_mcgregor.html* and also Ouchi, William G. *Theory Z: How American Business Can Meet the Japanese Challenge*. Avon Books, 1982.
22. Peters and Waterman, op. cit.
23. See 21, Ouchi, op. cit.
24. See 1, op. cit.
25. *Flexible Compensation—The Wyatt Approach.* Seattle, WA: The Wyatt Company.

6

Organization and Administration

OBJECTIVES

- Recognize the advantages and disadvantages of various business organizations: sole proprietorship, partnership, and corporation.
- Understand the difference between "line" and "staff" positions.
- Demonstrate the logic of organizing and its relationship to other managerial functions.
- Understand the organizational principles of specialization and decentralization.
- Recognize that the exact number of people a manager can effectively supervise depends on a number of underlying variables and situations.
- Draw a distinction between formal and informal organizations.

Introduction

Once the workload of an enterprise grows beyond what a single person can do, organization becomes necessary. Various tasks must be assigned to different people and their individual efforts must be coordinated. As the business expands, this process leads to departments and divisions with each having its own particular mission. One should consider the resulting organization as a complex machine. Each part performs a necessary function. The different parts are carefully balanced and fitted together in order to meet the stringent demands placed upon such a system. A change in any one of the parts will frequently call for an adjustment in several others.

The organization must be developed to accomplish the job, and a social structure must be built to meet the needs of the people doing the work. It is composed of several parts or elements that must be carefully balanced in order to achieve the desired goals. To accomplish tasks the manager must utilize both technical and social tools of organizing. The techniques of structure, procedures, and manuals must be appropriately used in a social setting that recognizes the influence of individuals and groups on the ultimate outcome of business efforts.

Goals and Objectives

Basically speaking, when the manager sets about organizing business efforts, there are two major initial considerations: (1) what are the goals and objectives? and (2) what resources are available to achieve these goals? With these two elements firmly in mind, the manager can prioritize and organize the efforts of the business to pursue the desired goals. The two constantly interact, since resources are always finite.

Care should be exercised, however, that the resources or apparent resources do not limit the potential of the business. Certain goals may warrant extending the present resources to a point not previously considered possible.

Determining available resources means simply identifying the financial means available, reviewing the personnel capabilities, and surveying the physical assets of the organization. The business must have the required resources available, find ways to get them, or else develop a structure more compatible with the ready resources.

Answering the following questions methodically and carefully should provide the manager with an idea of what resources are available:

General

1. Do you have a written plan for arranging and relating resources to meet planned objectives?
2. Do you have a firm estimate of the resources required?
3. Do you have an inventory of resources on hand?
4. Are additional resources available?
5. Do you have a plan for obtaining additional resources?

Financial Area

1. Do you have current, accurate financial statements?
2. Do you routinely compare your present financial status with your past record?
3. Do you project your financial needs into the future?

Personnel

1. Do you have a current list of your present personnel indicating qualifications, skills, history, and performance?
2. Do you have an ongoing training and development program for your present personnel?

Physical Assets

1. Do you maintain an accurate listing of buildings, equipment, vehicles, aircraft, and real estate?
2. Does your listing indicate value, physical state, needed improvements, their costs, and operational capabilities?

Having clearly identified the existing resources of the organization, the manager should determine the capacity for the business to acquire additional resources. Some insight into this capability can be gained by answering the following questions:

1. Is additional capital available either in the form of equity, loans, or credit?
2. Can the labor market provide additional personnel of the type required?
3. Can additional physical resources in the form of real estate, buildings, or operating areas be acquired?

The next step is to establish goals and objectives. The framework for this activity was presented under the managerial function of planning discussed in Chapter 2, Management Functions. Here it becomes the structure that guides the day-by-day organizing activity of the manager and the total business.

Organizational activity develops a structure that will facilitate and encourage the achievement of these goals.

Context in a World of Change

Human knowledge seems to be growing exponentially. Access to almost instantaneous information from around the world means that it is easy to be overwhelmed by issues and information. One definition of the "Renaissance Man" is a person who is familiar with, even highly steeped in, all areas of human knowledge. The Renaissance, ending five hundred years ago, is the last time that this was possible. Today the volume of information and its rate of change are just too great.

So the business owner and manager must somehow select what information to pursue in more depth, and what to ignore. Some of his or her employees may have a tendency to flit too superficially from one data set to another, thinking they know what it implies for the business, while other, more detail-oriented employees may tend to get stuck in what some call "analysis paralysis"—the desire to really know enough before making a recommendation or decision. The astute manager will be on the lookout for both these tendencies and provide some corrective direction.

Routine-ize the Routine

Given that so much always seems to be a state of flux, it is the more important that managers dispense with as many day-to-day items as possible through standard routines. Every worker's job should consist of some percentage of routine work following prescribed procedures, and some smaller percentage of non-routine work where non-standard ideas and solutions have to be created. Generally, the higher one is in the firm, the less routine and more non-standard the work will be, yet even top managers need routines, and if this is not their strong suit, need good subordinates such as administrative assistants and department heads who will keep them on track.

A World of Change

It used to be said that nothing is sure in life except death and taxes. The new truism might refer to death, taxes, and change. New technology is constantly being offered on the market, new computer software, new political issue face the airport, new people get involved or disappear, and new problems and issues arise that the business owner and his or her team must tackle.

For many workers, massive uncertainty and being faced with a new situation is very challenging. It is hard for them to believe that out of the current confusion, a road map and decisive actions will appear. A useful analogy for the manager to use at such times is this:

> "Imagine that a small group of people is trying to put together a big, complex jigsaw puzzle. At first, someone shakes all the pieces out of the box on to the table, and it's impossible to tell if in fact there are several puzzles in the heap, or just one.
>
> "Then, it gets sorted out into piles and one puzzle is separated off. The group begins to find corner pieces and put them in place, then side pieces, and then pretty soon a few middle pieces get placed. Before long, the picture begins to emerge, and after a while there are just a few pieces left that even a child could place correctly.[3]
>
> "But, remember the lesson of the puzzle—every time a new situation arises, it will probably feel overwhelming and confusing. Some people have a higher comfort level than others with that. Some people relish shaping order out of confusion; others are happier when the tasks are more cut and dried and the framework in place. Eventually every pile of loose pieces gets to that point if people persist."[4]

Legal Structure

The manager has several forms of business organizations available. By carefully selecting the appropriate form, he or she can increase profit, decrease taxes, protect business assets, provide for orderly growth of the business, and balance the resources against the challenges provided by the competitive world of business. The following basic types of business organizations are available:

> Sole proprietorship;
> Partnership; and
> Corporation.

A flying club might also qualify as a not-for-profit educational organization. There are variations in partnerships and corporations, but we will consider only these three major categories. No selected form of business organization needs to be the permanent choice; a new form can be developed to meet new needs while the business still operates under the original form. As the business grows, it will change in its operations and needs, and the financial and tax situations will more than likely also change. Likewise, statutory, legal, and tax developments may change the characteristics and advantages of the various business structures available. In view of the changing business world, the manager should re-examine at regular intervals the business framework most suitable for a certain situation.

Let's consider the major advantages and disadvantages of the three principal forms of legal structure.

Sole Proprietorship

The sole proprietorship is usually defined as a business owned and operated by one person. In community property states, the spouse may also have an ownership interest. To establish such a business, all that is required is any local and state business licenses.

Advantages include:

- Ease of formation and dissolution;
- Sole ownership of profits;
- Control and decision-making vested in one owner;
- Flexibility; and
- Relative freedom from regulation and special taxation.

Disadvantages include:

- Unlimited liability for business debts that may affect all the owner's personal assets; (Additional problems of liability such as physical loss or personal injury may be reduced by proper insurance.)
- An unstable business life, highly dependent on the health and welfare of the owner; potential lack of continuity;
- Less available capital in most cases; relative difficulty in obtaining long term financing;
- Relatively limited viewpoint and size, and a lack of "sounding boards"; and
- Difficulty in building equity in the company for sale or retirement purposes.

Partnership

A partnership is an association of two or more people for business purposes. Written articles of partnership are customarily executed, and one expert in this area suggests each prospective partner write out their desires and goals from participation in the enterprise before any formal negotiation.[1] This will clarify, for example, any conflicting ideas about time to be put in versus compensation taken out, about the level of company facilities such as office space, cars, furniture and so on to be acquired before profits are made; and about how long each party is willing to subsidize operations, and to what degree. Written articles normally address at least:

- Name, purpose, domicile;
- Duration of agreement;
- Nature of partners (general or limited, active or silent);
- Contributions by each (at inception, subsequently);
- Business expenses (how handled);
- Authority of each partner to make decisions;
- Chief Executive Officer and how appointed;
- Separate debts;
- Books, records and methods of accounting;
- Division of losses and profits;
- Draws or salaries;
- Rights of a continuing partner;
- Death of a partner (dissolution and winding up);
- Employee management;
- Release of debts;
- Sale or transfer of partnership interest;
- Arbitration;
- Additions, alterations, or modifications of agreement;
- Settlement of disputes;
- Required and prohibited acts; and
- Absence and disability.

It is recommended that partners be mutually subject to intensive background, credit, and character investigation because most new ventures that founder do so because of disagreements among partners.

Advantages of partnership include:

- Ease of organization;
- Automatic availability of a soundong board for business choices;
- Minimum capital required;
- More capital available than for a sole proprietorship; and
- Broader management base and provision for continuity.

Disadvantages include:

- Potential for conflicts among partners with divergent personalities, goals, values or other factors;
- Less flexibility for the individual owner owing to the need for consultation with partners;
- Unlimited liability, as with sole proprietorship, unless the form used is a Limited Liability Partnership or LLC;

> Potential size limitations;
> Capital restrictions; Firm may be inappropriately bound by actions of just one empowered partner; and
> Difficulty of transferring partnership interest.

Incorporation

The corporation, under Subchapter C, the basic form, or Subchapter S where the profits go directly to the owner, has a separate legal life from its members; it is "an artificial being, invisible, intangible, and existing only in contemplation of the law."[2] Corporations are usually formed under the authority of state governments. Multistate or out-of-state corporations are more complex because they must comply not only with various state laws, but also with the requirements of interstate commerce.

Other things being equal, the advantages of corporations include:

> Limitations of the stockholders' liability to the amount invested, with respect to business losses (though not with respect to damage suits, and so on);
> Ownership is readily transferable;
> Separate legal existence, even with the de mise of all current owners; can be inherited or sold;
> Relative ease of obtaining capital compared with other organizational forms;
> Tax advantages, including owner's fringe benefits and other considerations; some ability to take compensation as dividends instead of salaries—reduces social security tax liability;
> Permits larger size;
> Structure lends itself to easy expansion;
> Only incorporated companies can sell stock on the stock exchange ("go public");
> Delegated authority from the corporation to its employees and officers; and
> Potentially broader skill base as a potentially larger firm.

Disadvantages include:

> Closer governmental financial regulation;
> Relative cost and complexity to set up;
> Activities limited by charter;
> Business could be open to manipulation of minority stockholders; and
> Double taxation-on corporate net income and on individual salaries and dividends.

This last feature may be overcome by establishing Subchapter S status. The purpose of Subchapter S (IRC 1371 1379) is to permit a small business corporation to have its income taxed to the shareholders as if it were a partnership. One objective is to overcome the double taxation feature; another is to permit shareholders to offset business losses against their other income.

Some conditions for subchapter S are that the corporation have ten or fewer shareholders, all of whom are individuals or estates, that there be no nonresident alien shareholders, that there be only one class of outstanding stock, that all shareholders consent, and that a specific portion of the corporation's receipts be derived from active business rather than enumerated passive investments. No limit is placed on the size of the corporation's income and assets.

Given the choices of structure, many businesses may want to advance gradually to more complex forms as they grow. The benefits of incorporation may be particularly strong for family enterprises.

Organizational Principles for Internal Organization

No matter what the legal structure of the firm, that structure normally does not impact employees in their day-to-day tasks, and the firm has numerous choices of internal structure to get the daily work done. In the past decade or even the past five years, internal business organization seems to be undergoing some radical change. Most aviation businesses are quite small. Aviation Maintenance Technician Magazine reported in 2002 that the average business had 10 or fewer mechanics. This means that there may be little latitude for research and experimentation, or for choices of organizational structure within the company, and that learning from the industry at large may be an important means of staying current.

The Rational Model vs. Some New Approaches

Adam Smith, in his classic *The Wealth of Nations*, set the stage for the success of the industrial revolution by addressing the issue of division of labor, and therefore, specialization.[5] A twentieth-century prophet in the same vein was Frederick Taylor, who pioneered the idea of motion study; namely, each task has only one best way to do it, and finding this best way will lead to efficiency and profit.[6] The advancement of statistical tools of analysis, together with the ability to process large amounts of quantitative information using computers, seems to be a continuation of this school of thought. However, Taylor's approach completely removes human factors from the discussion and seeks to make each worker as machine-like and quantitatively productive as possible.

Several studies of Japanese productivity and of highly successful US firms seem to lead to a new view of business organization as requiring not only technical and analytical tools but also human qualities.[7] The talents required for custodianship of an existing corporate leviathan may now include creativity, innovation, adaptation to change, and high quality. One of the "new" leaders in this area includes Jack Welch (now retired) when he was CEO of GE.[8]

Explicit Corporate Philosophy

Corporate values help shape the corporate culture. One tool of management and organization that seems to be gaining ground is the statement of corporate values and goals. Examples include Nordstrom's generous return policy, Frito-Lay's 99.5 percent reliability of daily calls to all stores, McDonald's stress on hygiene, Hewlett-Packard's emphasis on sufficient profit to finance company growth and provide the resources needed for other corporate objectives, and many others. A company statement, visible to all employees, telling how the corporation wants to handle service, can provide the backdrop and value system for everything that goes on in the company, and it can help to explain the nuances of structure and provide guidance where the structure does not state anything specific.

Organizational Culture

The effectiveness of an organization is also influenced by the organization's "culture," which affects the way the managerial functions of planning, organizing, staffing, leading, and controlling are carried out. Culture includes many facets, such as how people at various levels dress, how often they come to work early or stay late; how much after-hours socializing there is within the rank and file, to what degree communications flow freely from junior staff to top management (or must be only through approved channels); how open the company is to trying employee suggestions—these are but a few aspects of a composite that adds up to corporate culture.

As it relates to organizations, culture is the general pattern of behavior, shared beliefs, and values that members have in common. Culture can be inferred from what people say, do, and think within an organizational setting. It involves the learning and transmitting of knowledge, beliefs, and patterns of behavior over a period of time, which means that an organizational culture is fairly stable and does not change fast. It often sets the tone for the company and establishes implied rules for the way people should behave.

Many slogans give a general idea of what a particular company stands for. Here are some examples:

Delta describes its internal climate with the slogan "the Delta family feeling."

The Disney Corporation refers to its customers as "guests" and its employees as "characters" (implying they are all considered to be on stage while working).

In similar ways Maytag wants to be known for its reliability, Ford for quality, and so on.

Managers, especially top managers and owners, create the climate for the enterprise. Their values influence the direction of the organization. Changing a culture may take a long time, even 5 to 10 years. It demands changing values, symbols, myths, and behavior. This is important for a new manager or business owner to keep in mind.

Specialization and Job Rotation

A general overview of U.S. history suggests that great strides were made in producing larger quantities of goods at lower cost partly because of specialization—the application of Adam Smith's ideas. As the number of an employee's duties became more limited, he or she became an expert in a narrow area.

Evidence from Japan and elsewhere suggests that there may be limits to this approach. Some problems include:

- Monotony and boredom;
- Lack of ability to see or understand the whole enterprise;
- Lack of pride in products, as a person only carries out one small task on each item;
- High absenteeism; and
- High turnover.

By contrast, where entry-level managers are rotated to every key part of the firm and have to learn every job, they relate well to the big picture and to the problems of other departments. When senior management has been through this apprenticeship there is more contact with the technical realities of the job. Likewise, when employees on the line are organized so that they see the total fruits of their labors, quality and satisfaction go up. When line employees are asked for help on improving the processes (e.g., quality circles), they often contribute enthusiastically and constructively.

Decentralization and Decisions by Consensus

The rational model indicated that the owner/manager should reserve all major decisions. The new approach is more oriented toward making all decisions at as low a level as possible; that is, as close as possible to the people who will be putting them into effect. The availability of e-mail and the Internet on almost every employee's desk means that no longer is top management the only level of a company that knows detailed information about the firm and other firms. People have access to more information and many will use it, often almost unaware, to bring more expertise to their jobs. In consequence they may want more say.

Decentralization does not refer to specialization of the work itself, but to the division of the managerial work and assignment of specific duties to various department heads or executive levels. The key issue becomes: how much of the managerial work, the planning, organizing, directing, and controlling shall be done by the president, or manager, and how much should be assigned to other personnel? This allocation of managerial work is one of the most critical and most sensitive aspects of the organizing process. The amount of decentralization reflects many considerations such as importance of work, individual capabilities, and managerial desire to decentralize. In many situations the executive finds a need to decentralize out of sheer necessity in order to lighten the workload. Often it is found that such action results in improved morale, better local coordination, and faster action on important matters.

A manager should look closely at the workload in deciding what part or parts of his total job should be transferred to executives at lower levels. As discussed in Chapter 2, he or she should remember that delegating authority is:

- Assigning duties;
- Granting authority and creating an obligation on the part of the subordinate; and then
- Getting out of the way so the assigned work can get done.

These three elements have been compared to the legs of a three-legged stool. All three are required for the whole to exist effectively. Assigning duties without the necessary authority over resources to accomplish the duty illustrates the need for all three elements if the manager is to successfully decentralize.

In deciding how much decentralization to attempt, or where to place authority and obligation in an organizational structure, the manager might consider the following guides:

1. Who knows the facts, has the technical ability, and can get them together most readily?
2. Who has the capacity to make sound decisions?
3. Is it necessary that speedy, on-the-spot decisions be made?
4. Is it required that local activity be carefully coordinated with other units?
5. How significant are the decisions in the area under consideration?
6. What is the existing workload for managers?
7. Will morale and initiative be significantly improved by decentralization?

When the manager decentralizes the operation in the process of developing an organizational structure, he or she should recognize the importance of this action and the change that will be required in his or her manner of personal operation. Decentralization needs to happen in an equitable way so that, for example, all department heads have about the same authority and none is seen as being the boss' favorite.

Experience has shown that planning is the most critical of the managerial functions if decentralization is to be effective. The process of identifying problems and deciding the correct action to take, is something the manager is loath to release to others; it is something he or she is prone to supervise closely. The functions of organizing, directing, and controlling are very important, but they tend to depend upon how the planning duties have been allocated.

Management by Walking Around

A phrase apparently coined by Hewlett-Packard, this means the owner/manager gives himself a direct, unscheduled view of what is going on, including stopping to ask junior staff what they are doing and what the obstacles are to doing it better. Great tact, of course, is required in order not to undermine the authority of the immediate supervisors or cause them unwarranted anxiety about how their department is perceived to be run. The chief executive should take up any observed problems privately with supervisors and managers and be sure to give them a chance to explain why they took their chosen course. In a sizable tight line/staff organization, management by walking around is the only way the owner/manager can keep in touch with what's happening on the floor. Rather than relying only on reports from the five to ten department heads and aides who report directly, he or she makes personal, direct observations as well.

Management by Results

The ultimate result of any business is profit, and the intermediate results are quality and customer satisfaction. Management by results is a variation of management by objectives that explicitly gives the people responsible the necessary latitude to decide for themselves what techniques to use to obtain desired results (within the ethics and quality standards of the firm).

Span of Control

Span of control is a concept used in organizational activity that is based largely on a theory of human limitations. Ideally a particular manager in a specific situation can directly and effectively supervise a limited number of subordinates. There is considerable controversy over the nature and implications of the span-of-control concept. There has to be some limit to how many people a manager can supervise directly, but the exact figure varies, and the figures cited in various studies vary widely.

A practical approach may be to realize that the correct span of control is affected by a number of factors and to try to organize the business structure with these factors in mind. In following this practice one would consider:

- The complexity of the work being controlled;
- The degree of similarity to other work;
- The degree of interdependency with other work;
- The stability of the organization and situation;
- The degree of standardization;
- The caliber of the manager, including the span of attention, energy, and personality;
- The availability of the CEO, including demands for outside appearances and public affairs activities, and any other business ventures using up his or her time; and
- The caliber of the subordinates and their motivation.

The "correct" span for one manager in one situation at a particular time may vary widely from that of another manager, situation, and/or time. Ralph Davis, in his classic 1951 study, suggested that if a manager is supervising subordinate managers and the work is difficult, then the span should be limited to approximately three to nine.[9] If one is supervising operative employees, acceptable spans are from ten to thirty.

The specific determination of the span of control must be decided on an individual basis by remembering that the outcome determines the supervisory relationship between superior and subordinate and the shape of the organizational structure. The manager must remember, too, the basic human needs and the primary needs of the organization for an effectively coordinated and controlled effort.

In this day and age of e-mail and the Internet, employees have access to more information as quickly as management does, and the old concepts of "need to know" sharing of information are fast disappearing. This consideration influences span of control.

Another consideration for a small FBO business is that if the organization chart is a many-leveled pyramid, then there will be some layers of positions that are purely overhead, the Assistant vice president type positions. Most smaller companies cannot afford too many of such positions, meaning the operating managers such as chief pilot, maintenance manager, probably report directly to the owner/manager.

Effective Work Groups

Just as there are individual personalities and differences, there are also group personalities and differences. Organizational activities tend to create and influence the development of work groups. By knowing something about groups, their characteristics, and their behavior, the manager can improve his or her management. She can develop more effective work groups. He must accept the work group as an integral component of the total organization.

Rensis Likert has said, "An organization will function best when its personnel function not as individuals but as members of highly effective work groups with high performance goals."[10] Because of the group's importance to the organization, we will attempt to understand how it works, how its structures and procedures can influence business results, and how it can be used, as well as misused, in advancing the organization's interests. A starting point is the determination of the characteristics of the group. By considering these characteristics, a manager can plan the organizational activity to achieve goals or measure progress from the past. The key characteristics of a group and some important concepts or guidelines from the manager's point of view are shown in Figure 6.1. The manager needs to recognize these characteristics of a group and utilize the pertinent concepts to his or her advantage in order to develop the organizational structure.

Staff Support

In designing an organizational structure, most managers utilize some sort of staff. The staff function is normally separated from the primary chain of command and from the line functions, to produce economy and effectiveness of operation.

Figure 6.1 » Key Characteristics of a Group

Characteristics	Concepts
Group Goals	Group members are more dedicated to goals they help establish than to those imposed upon them by others.
Structure	There is both formal and informal structure in small groups.
Size	Should be large enough to obtain sufficient ideas yet small enough not to hamper free communication or inhibit participation.
Leadership	Indications are that every group requires some "central focus."
Participation	Group size, power and status structure and style leadership are determinants of the nature and extent of participation.
Cohesiveness	Determined largely by the degree to which group goals help satisfy individual needs. If cohesiveness is obtained for official, task-oriented groups, the organization stands to gain through increased cooperation and motivation.
Norms	There is a tendency for the behavior of group members to coincide with group norms.
Agreement	Pressures toward group norms tend to produce agreement. Most business groups prefer to work toward a consensus, meaning acceptance without necessarily fully approving personally.

Source: Dr. J. D. Richardson

The concept of *staff* refers to a supportive unit not directly involved in the end product or salable items of the organization, that is, the support functions. The CEO him or herself is fulfilling a staff function. Serving in the normal fashion, staff units typically:

1. Give advice—the personnel office may offer advice to the manager of the maintenance department on the interpretation of selection screening devices used by the company.
2. Perform services—the accounting department in developing an analysis of the costs involved in conducting flight instruction is providing a service for the flight department.
3. Provide information—in many instances the staff provide information on personnel, on employment data, on tax questions, and on many areas in the technical competence of the specialist.

It should be recognized that the distinction between the two terms line and staff represents an oversimplification. For one thing, the real relationship in terms of authority, influence, and control is much more complicated. For another, in small organizations most managers may fulfill both line and staff functions. Instead of the departmentalization that is seemingly emphasized by the concept, the real focus should be on the high degree of interdependence required if the major systems in the organization are to function at maximum effectiveness.

Without cooperation and coordination in the pursuit of joint goals, conflict can emerge in line-staff relationships. Line functions may believe they make money for the organization by themselves; staff functions may feel under-recognized and know that they are essential to the bottom line too. Lack of resolution of these innate differences may lead to many operational problems and ultimately to the need for managerial corrective decisions. Astute managers are aware of the inbuilt differences in the two functions and seek to keep the two working harmoniously together.

Human Factors

A major element in organizing a business is the recognition of the human aspects of organization. A good starting point is the realization that people work to satisfy needs and that the design of the organizational structure makes a tremendous impact on the achievement of these needs. The typical hierarchy of needs met from working is discussed more fully in Chapter 5, Human Resources.

Our primary concern at this point is meeting human needs through the organization, since the structure of a company defines an environment of formal rules, job descriptions, and communication networks during working hours. This environment can satisfy needs or block them. It can help develop good attitudes or bad attitudes, and it can partly determine what people think and learn. Company structure becomes a highly important element in getting results. It can contribute to or detract from the satisfaction of human needs. The following are a number of ways that organization design can contribute to human needs:

Small units. By assigning workers to small groups of three to ten, social satisfactions are greater.

Non-isolated jobs. One should not break down work into such extremely specialized and independent parts that a person lacks the opportunity to interact with fellow workers.

Job enlargement. A closely related issue, narrow specialization, or division of the work into extremely small components may diminish worker satisfaction and affect the employee's opportunity for growth. By enlarging the job many companies have realized benefits, including increased worker satisfaction.

Broad responsibilities. A very narrow area of responsibility tends to create a situation of always giving and never receiving. To satisfy social needs, a person's relationships with others should be reciprocal.

Place or status. The place or status of the individual in the organization may create pride in the position and even in the title itself.

Decentralization. Increasing the freedom of action of the subordinate and the opportunity to satisfy the need for self-expression are two benefits of decentralization.

New Approaches to Organization

Organization is a management tool—a most powerful tool—designed to fulfill specific needs. As the needs change, new ways are required to satisfy the changing conditions. There is an interaction between the manager's knowledge and skill level, the organization's existing situation, and the impact of the environment and its changing demands. The combination of these elements results in the identification of an existing organizational situation.

As we have discussed, change is ever more inevitable in the business world, so the manager has a real concern for the application of new approaches to organization that will make it easier to meet the demands of change. In one situation, it may mean simply the introduction of a formal organizational chart and structure in order to achieve a degree of stability. In another, it may mean identifying the need to relate more strongly to the customer. In still another way, it may require being aware of the special needs resulting from complex problems, special environmental issues, or technological changes. Each of these situations suggests the need for a new approach to organizational design. Some of the new directions that have been suggested include:

1. Hiring "idea" people to promote innovative ways of approaching and developing answers to problems.
2. Hiring individuals who are manifestly "different" from those normally hired in order to ensure fresh ideas.
3. Focusing management control on the outcome of work rather than the way work is done.
4. Increasing rotation among jobs.
5. Increasing employee participation in decision-making.
6. Encouraging professional association involvement so that people identify with a group outside the organization.
7. Using project teams whenever feasible.
8. Including formal consumer representation.
9. Decreasing the number of supervisory levels or eliminating the superior and subordinate relationship.
10. Implementing individual profit centers.
11. Providing compensation based upon results achieved.
12. Allowing much greater freedom of access to information.
13. Encouraging mobility of individuals.
14. Increasing individual rights.
15. Supporting continued education.

A prototype organization for the business of the future has been suggested. It may not be completely realistic, but it should stimulate additional thought and action in developing the new form needed for the business of tomorrow. This proposal has four major features:

1. Hierarchical and bureaucratic structure are reduced to an absolute minimum.
2. Most middle-level jobs are conceived of as temporary.
3. Individual employees are assigned to competence centers or profit centers.
4. Career development is emphasized by the introduction of many varied programs.

New Communications Technology for Internal Organization

For some years, forward looking companies have been shifting to telephone conference calls, increasingly more sophisticated phone systems, palm pilots and other tools to enable internal communications to be more effective. Today what is known as "real-time meetings" use a combination of web, audio, and video tools to enable work groups to "meet" and do business without having to be in the same location. Larger companies with more than one outlet are turning to this approach to save money and time and to meet the needs of their clients. While this topic is covered here, it is also highly pertinent to marketing and may provide new means of meeting customer needs also. Various vendors are evolving in a market place that is thought to be growing at 30–40 percent per year.[11,12] Face to face contact is still need to build the relationship and work out any difficulties, and the air travel may not be affected as much as FBOs may fear, because like all new technologies this enables people to do more, not just do better what they were already doing. The software systems also allow for real-time shared editing of documents and drawings as well as "archiving" real time speeches, presentations and discussions for later use in training.

Internal Structure Design

In developing an organizational structure in a certain business, the manager should consider such factors as departmentalization, decentralization, delegation, specialization, managerial resources, staff capabilities, and the specific types of business activity involved. Managers need to use each of these concepts in developing an effective total organizational structure. The determination of the overall structure is based upon four major considerations:

1. What balance and emphasis should be given to the various departments?
2. How can the span of control or supervision of each manager be effectively utilized?
3. How can dynamic change be provided for?
4. How can this organization be integrated into the other phases of planning, directing, and controlling?

The answers to these questions provide direct assistance in identifying the desired organizational structure.

Formal Internal Structure

In developing the formal structure of the organization, the manager has three basic formats to consider: functional, line, and line and staff. Since many aviation businesses need to utilize elements of all three business structures, it is recommended that the manager understand the terms and be able to use all three concepts in organizing a business.

Functional or Matrix Management

Fashions come and go regarding the value of the functional or matrix form of organization. An example of how it works is shown in Figure 6.2. The functional organization has a supervisor in charge of each function rather than in charge of specific employees. Each of these supervisors is a specialist and makes decisions for that functional area. The suitability of the matrix or functional organization form to an aviation service business is limited because many of the line personnel must be specialized and certified e.g. as pilots or a maintenance technicians, thus they cannot do another's job without dual certification. However, like the manager of a small business, many employees wear many hats, and in that sense, an FBO may be operating with a functional organizational structure. Thus, although the functional structure has difficulties, the small aviation business may to some extent find itself operating on a functional basis. As the owner/manager hires an assistant or supervisor, this person is normally placed in charge of a specific function and all employees receive guidance from him or her in that one area. As additional supervisors are added with functional specialties, the employee must move from supervisor to supervisor (function to function) as he or she performs different physical tasks.

Figure 6.2 » Functional or Matrix Organization

EMPLOYEE	FUNCTIONAL AREA 1 Led by Matt	FUNCTIONAL AREA 2 Led by Judy	FUNCTIONAL AREA 3 Led by Jack	FUNCTIONAL AREA 4 Led by Jean
Mary	O		O	O
Jose		O	O	
John	O			O
June	O		O	
Spike	O		O	O

O = assists as needed, reports to that functional supervisor for assigned tasks

Source: Julie F. Rodwell, 2003

This is one source of difficulty with the functional organization; employees can become confused, conflicts can develop, supervisors battle for employees' availability, and problems arise in evaluating quality of work and performance on the job. On the other hand, *temporary* functional assignments into special purpose task forces, which have a leader, a mission, and, a set amount of time to do the task and disband, can have great value.

Line Organization

The second type of formal organization structure is the pure line organization. In this type of structure, the supervisor is in charge of a specific operational unit and of the time of all people assigned to work in that unit. This is frequently thought of as the military form of organization. The line organization has one person in charge of another person, who in turn is in charge of other persons. although the number of layers can be minimized. (See Figure 6.3)

Line and Staff Organization

For companies that have grown beyond the direct supervision stage, the line and staff organization becomes the most feasible form of structure. It differs from the straight line because a staff element has been added to the structure. With regard to actual operations, the structure operates similarly to the line structure. However, the staff element is there to advise the line manager and the CEO on the technical features of that staff specialty, thus assisting that manager in getting the job done. The staff unit is normally designed to provide advice, information, and services to line managers and the CEO. Figure 6.4 suggests a line and staff structure for an aviation business. In this type of structure, the supervisors in sales, instruction, service, and flight have the responsibility for getting the job done in their individual areas, and the staff personnel in administration and finance have the task of advising and assisting in their areas of specialty. For example, accounting might advise on the necessary records and budget guidelines, or administration might advise on OSHA requirements and coordinate report deadlines.

The aviation manager should be aware of all three types of organizational structures and recognize that there are elements of each in every business. The most likely pattern is that when a business starts, it will be functional, then become a line structure, and then, with size, assume the characteristics of a line and staff structure.

Informal Internal Structures

The formal organization consists of the official, authorized relationships prescribed by management, usually as depicted by company and depart-

Figure 6.3 » Line Organization

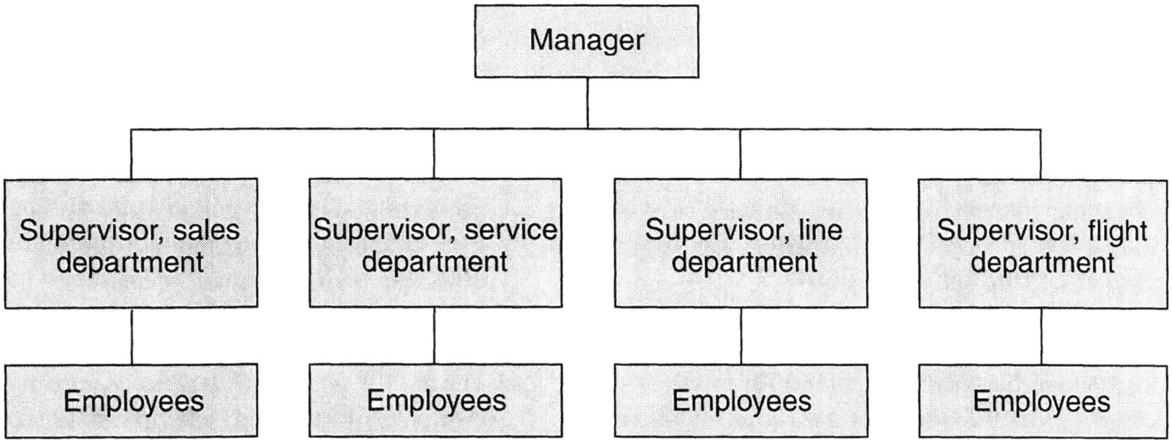

Figure 6.4 » Line-Staff Organization

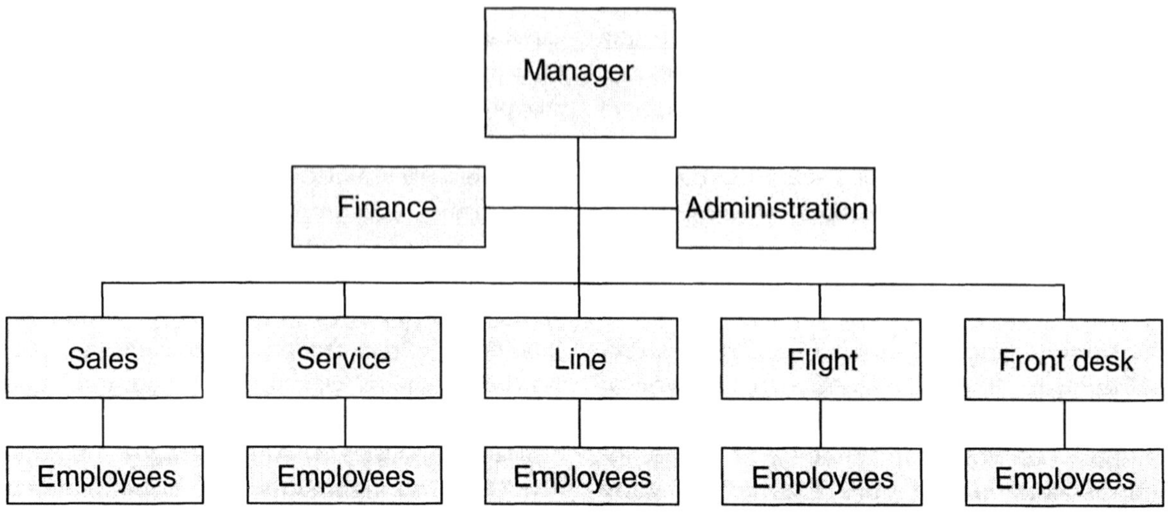

ment organization charts. Informal organization consists of the myriad relationships, unofficial and unauthorized, created by the many individual personalities and groups within the formal structure. These relationships, both good and bad, spring up spontaneously, inevitably, and continually. There is no choice whether to have an informal organization; it is a fact of organizational life. Since it exists regardless of the manager's approval, it is advantageous to examine its advantages and disadvantages. More likely, there will be many pockets of separate organization. A healthy company will, however, seek to encourage inclusiveness rather than cliques.

Informal work groups are an inevitable fact of life in any organization. Managers who do not understand group behavior and attempt to break up groups are frequently frustrated when new alignments form and present continuing problems. The successful manager is one who understands the nature of group forces, who is perceptive to group needs, understands why employees need to talk together about various aspects of work, and who can successfully blend the informal groups' goals with those of the formal organization. A perceptive yet light touch is needed.

The informal structure is the source of many positive values that can contribute to the organization. Management's chief concern in this area is to achieve positive feelings and identification, which will provide a maximum benefit to the organization's efforts. Although this goal may depend strongly on the individual manager's skillful use of organizational tools (including the ability to direct and control), it also includes the ability to achieve a high level of harmony without eliminating the value of individual freedom and dissent.

Advantages

1. It fills in gaps and deficiencies in the formal structure.
2. It facilitates the majority of the organization's work.
3. It lengthens the effective managerial span of control.
4. It compensates for the violation of formal organizational principles.
5. It provides an additional channel of communications.
6. It stimulates better management.

Disadvantages

1. Informal activities may appear to work counter to organizational goals (for example if a subgroup of employees decides to become more vocal about working conditions—nevertheless, the informal structure is important way for management to learn early about worker concerns and desires).
2. There is less ability to predict and control outcome of informal group activity (for example an employee suggestion committee

may create a great deal of work for department heads who then have to investigate its proposals and report back on what may be feasible to implement; such a committee may feels strongly about certain suggestions even if department heads don't feel they will work).
3. Since virtually by definition, individuals self-appoint to particular informal groups, there is less interchangeability of individuals within groups, thus reducing managerial alternatives and influence.
4. There can be high costs (for example, in terms of employee time) of maintaining a positive, informal set of relationships.
5. If management is unaware of informal relationships, negative or positive, then assignments may be made that have potential problems, either that the assignees get along too well, or don't get along at all, meaning the assigned task may not get done on time.

The informal organization can be identified and charted using sociometric techniques. The most common applications of this procedure develop: (1) a chart depicting actual contacts between particular people, (2) a chart reflecting the feelings of people toward each other, or (3) the influence-of-power chart, which depicts the level of influence of each member in the group. Each of these techniques provides the means for gaining some insight into the informal structure and provides additional information to supplement the organizational efforts of the formal structure. Keep in mind, however, that if the effort is made to explore informal structure to this degree, first, such exploration may cause resentment, and second, relationships are constantly changing so the outcome may not be very useful.

The informal group selects a leader who reflects the views of the group toward the formal structure. Even if this leader is removed as a troublemaker or malcontent, the difficulty is not solved because the group will most likely simply select another representative who, in turn, will present the same views, perhaps even less helpfully. The manager can work with the group leader to obtain full cooperation from the group. This does not mean that he or she should channel orders through the leader or attempt to make him a member of the management team. When this is attempted the usual result is the identification of a new informal leader. The manager can, however, devote a little extra attention to winning the support and approval of the group leader when the need arises, or perhaps on a continuing basis.

The informal organization can be used to supplement the formal channel of communications. The informal structure has been recognized as being fast to form, but at the same time, prone to being full of distortions. It can, however, be utilized to gain input on group discontent or pending problems and be of tremendous help to managers. In most instances it is considered wise to utilize the informal communications network and to deal with the informal leader in a delicate and discreet manner.

In a large organization where rapid change is occurring, many rumors may develop and circulate through the informal networks of the business. Rumors have a way of being based on only partial information in the first place, and becoming more distorted as they pass around. One technique that management can apply in this situation is a "rumor board." An erasable board is placed in a convenient yet non-customer area such as the lunchroom, and employees are invited to write rumors they have heard on the left side of the board. Management checks the board daily and writes either answers, or that no answer is available yet and a date when it will be, and initials this input. A clerical person is assigned to copying down both rumors and answers as the board gets full, and they can be put on the company's employee web site. Alternatively, an electronic rumor board can be set up on the employee web site.

Quality Circles

Quality circles are another feature borrowed from the Japanese, although it was an American who introduced the Japanese to quality planning.[13] A circle of workers is jointly responsible for a finite, complete product and—in addition to being on the production team together—meets regularly to iron out problems and make improvements. Various circles doing the same thing may become quite competitive. Posting weekly performance can be an incentive toward high results.

Task Forces

As mentioned above, task forces may be short-lived and interdepartmental. Many companies use them to brainstorm a problem on an intensive basis, and some firms use an annual weekend retreat to do much the same thing.

Social Structures

Some firms deliberately encourage and even subsidize sports teams and other clubs with the intent of mixing all types of employees together in informal settings. A superior's usual aloofness can be set aside for a period. Parties and picnics can do some of the same things, depending on how they are run. Management needs to gauge whether employees really enjoy these functions, or are just attending for fear of not being thought a team player if they stay away. Some companies have started polling employees as to what they would rather do. Public celebration of work achievements is sometimes part of these functions, or the public recognition "hoopla" may be reserved for other times.

Other Networks

Special-interest professional groups of all types can give senior staff members the exposure that they might not otherwise get to junior staff members. They also help to convey directly the corporate values and culture to all levels of employment. Remoteness of senior officials is not necessarily an advantage to the company.

External Pressures on Choices of Structure

In designing the structure of an aviation business, consideration is given, consciously or unconsciously, to the pressures of external elements-pressures that suggest or dictate certain patterns to your organizational structure.

Industry Norms

The overall aviation industry, as the major environmental element of small aviation businesses, creates a pressure toward an organizational design somewhat common throughout the industry. Hangar design, ramp location, services requested by the customer, and competitor activity all tend to pressure the manager to conform to the general industry organizational structure.

The companies supplying the major aircraft product lines (The New Piper, Raytheon, Beech, Cessna, Gulfstream and so on) provide a degree of pressure through franchises or other agreements, which results in the development of a structure suggested by the company and similar to others in the organization. These standard structures have generally been found to be successful and have been promoted in order to achieve standardized operations and successful businesses.

Geography

Geographic influences have had a definite impact on organizational structures and managers should recognize them. Environmental features influence the type of aviation activities, the type of structures erected, and the physical layout. Each of these, in turn, directly influences the shape of the organization required to meet customer needs.

Government and Regulatory Influences on Organizational Structure

Governmental activity at all levels plays an important part in structuring aviation businesses. By requiring reports, manuals, and procedures and by offering financial support, federal, state, and local regulations cause the manager to structure the organization in a certain fashion. For example, OSHA requirements have caused many managers to write procedures, appoint safety directors, and in some instances reorganize the business. For those managers involved with Part 135 operations, this type of business activity requires a certain organizational structure as well as operating manuals and routine periodic checks that create certain organizational structures. FAA, VA, and state educational agencies have created requirements for flight schools that literally determined organizational structure for aviation businesses engaged in instruction. Aviation maintenance as stipulated by the FAA and equipment manufacturers very effectively contributes to the structure of aviation maintenance activities.

Practical Applications

Guidelines

Thus far the primary focus has been on basic concepts and principles and planning the organizational effort. Now the focus is on the practical task of dividing the business into functional areas and assigning these separate functions to specific individuals. Another three-legged stool analogy that the manager should keep in mind is the three legs that support a successful business of any type:

1. Delivering outstanding services and products; producing what you are in business to produce.
2. Marketing and sales to make sure people know you have great products and services.
3. Managing the finances and administration, and the paper trails.

Most business owners start their companies because they love what they do and believe they can do it better than others. Their problems arise when they discover they are not very good at, or don't enjoy, the other two legs of the stool. Usually neglect of marketing and /or finance are what cause businesses to fail even when products and services are great.

In organizing, the manager is constantly balancing two factors: the desired structure and the available personnel. Does he or she design the structure and then attempt to find or train personnel to do the work, or does he or she utilize the available human resources and work with the resulting organization? He or she will undoubtedly work with a combination of these two approaches, although the successful manager apparently sets his organizational goals and then works to build the structure that will achieve these objectives. This topic was considered in Chapter 5, Human Resources.

In a practical sense organizing is the basic process a manager uses to unite the efforts of different people to achieve company goals. There are two elements present in the process of organizing: (1) dividing work into separate jobs, and (2) ensuring the separate areas of work are combined into a total team effort. Let's now consider the various steps that become part of this practical organizing activity.

First, identify the basic or recurring pattern of work that takes place in the business. The best approach is to group work on the basis of geographical areas, products, customers, or functions. Many aviation organizations can and do utilize all four groupings. This is evidenced by companies who have regional salespeople, who distinguish employees working on Piper aircraft from those working on Beech aircraft, who classify customers by income level and assign salespeople to each major category, and who group work on a functional basis such as service, sales, or charter. This first step becomes an effort in understanding the activities that will take place within the business.

The second step is describing the relationships that will exist between the various groups within the business. This can be done through a chart on paper, a written description of the working relationships that exist, or both. Typically this is achieved through an organization chart and organization manual.

Define precisely what each unit will do as a portion of the overall organization. In identifying units, the basic principles of specialization, decentralization, span of control, work groups, staff activity and human factors should be kept in mind.

Assign business activities to specific individuals and units of the organization. This may be done casually in conversation or formally by charts, job descriptions, operations manuals, meetings, or joint understanding.

Provide for the means of tying the organization together and for developing integrated, cooperative action in the day-by-day transaction of business. Normally this is accomplished through communications, procedures, rules, and controls.

In summary, the organizing process involves:

> Identifying the kinds of work that take place;
> Describing the relationships among work groups;
> Defining precisely what each group will do;
> Assigning activities to specific individuals or groups; and
> Developing integrative action among work groups.

Problems

The practical activity as just outlined represents the minimum that should be included in the organizational process. It is actually an oversimplification of the procedure. Realistically, the manager should recognize that there are many problems inherent in the process and should try to avoid these difficulties. Some of the problems frequently experienced are:

> Lack of clearly defined duties and resulting friction;
> Expansion of activities beyond assigned areas by overzealous managers;
> Desire to create a situation in which the unit reports high up the administration chain;
> Failure to adapt to necessary changes; and
> Failure to integrate with the other functions of planning, directing, and controlling.

The Organization Manual

As mentioned earlier, one of the most effective tools for developing a business structure is the organization manual, management manual, or handbook. This particular manual does not follow a specific format or content outline, but provides a flexible technique for meeting individual organizational needs. As usually visualized, this document is a centralized source for policies, organizational structure, relationships, responsibilities, rules, and procedures. Properly designed, implemented, and maintained, it becomes an extremely valuable tool in organizing the business. It becomes a source for individuals in the organization in order to guide them in day-to-day operations and a source for training new employees. Primarily, it is a means for creating and maintaining the desired organizational structure and activity.

Manual Outline

Although the contents of an organization manual should vary in order to meet the needs of each organization, usually one finds the following subjects covered:

1. Introduction, philosophy.
2. Organization structure.
   a. Authority.
   b. Responsibility.
3. Departmental organization.
   a. Activities.
4. Staff activities.
   a. Personnel.
   b. Financial.

Summary

Organizing the business is a continuing challenge for the aviation manager. Both the external legal structure and the internal practical structure must be established to support the goals and activities of the company. The choice of ownership structure should be made consciously and reviewed periodically. Internal organization should recognize the needs of the various company de-

» DISCUSSION TOPICS

1. How should a manager use the organizational structure to address a) change and b) routine tasks?
2. What are the key advantages and disadvantages of the three legal structures? In starting a new FBO, which one would you choose, and why?
3. Describe the formal and informal organizations. How can they work in harmony?
4. Discuss the organizational principles of specialization and decentralization.
5. What is span of control and how can the business choose appropriate spans?
6. Why is an organizational manual useful? Name three elements in it.

partments as well as the informal structures that help a company function. External pressures and industry norms may need to be considered.

Endnotes

1. Brown, Deaver. *The Entrepreneur's Guide.* New York: Ballantine, 1980.
2. Op. cit.
3. Many children are much better at puzzles than adults and there can be great value in inviting children's opinions and advice at times of business confusion. Children tend to have more open and agile minds.
4. Community Facilitation & Development, Ashland, OR.
5. Smith, Adam. *An Enquiry Into the Nature and Causes of the Wealth of Nations.* Collier Books, 1901.
6. Taylor, Frederick Winslow. *The Principles of Scientific Management.* Norton, 1967.
7. The reader is recommended to several new "classic" texts of the past few decades, such as Ouchi, William G. *Theory Z: How American Business Can Meet the Japanese Challenge.* Avon Books, 1981; Pascale, Richard and Athos, Anthony G. *The Art of Japanese Management: Applications for American Executives.* New York: Warner Books, 1981; Weiss, Andrew. *Simple Truths of Japanese Manufacturing.* Harvard Business Review, July-August 1984; Peters and Waterman. *In Search of Excellence—Lessons from America's Best-Run Companies.* New York: Warner Books, 1982.
8. For example: 1. Bryne, John A., and Welch, Jack. *Jack: Straight From the Gut.* 2. Slater, Robert. *Jack Welch & The G.E. Way: Management Insights and Leadership Secrets of the Legendary CEO.* 3. Welch, Jack, et al. *Jack: Straight From the Gut* (Unabridged) Audio Cassette.

See also Johnson, C. Ray. *CEO Logic: How to Think and Act Like a Chief Executive.* Also McCoy, Charles W. Jr. *Why Didn't I Think of That? Think the Unthinkable and Achieve Creative Greatness.*

9. See *http://www.ucl.ac.uk/Library/special-coll/rdavis.htm.*
10. Likert, Rensis. *New Patterns of Management.* New York: McGraw-Hill, 1961.
11. Special Advertising Section, Hemispheres Magazine, May 2002.
12. See for example: Review Video at *http://www.reviewvideo.com;* SPL Integrated Solutions at *http://www.splis.com;* Meeting Place at *http://www.meetingplace.net;* and Captaris at *http://www.captaris.com.*
13. See W. Edwards Deming web site at *http://www.deming.org/.*

7

Management Information Systems

OBJECTIVES

- Understand the necessity of a business information system.
- Understand how effective financial management and profitability monitoring are accomplished through the use of ratios and financial reports.
- Relate the requirements of an effective business information system to an aviation business.
- Recognize the problems in maintaining an effective records system in an aviation business.
- Demonstrate the origins, pathways, and use of key elements for an aviation business.
- Describe the factors to consider in designing a system and upgrading computers for a business operation.

Introduction

A management information system is one that supports managerial decision-making by supplying relevant information when required. This chapter discusses the types of data needed in the typical fixed base operator business, the formats and flows involved, the analysis and use of performance data for keeping the company on the right track, and the choices of tools for data processing. Finally the chapter looks at information collection in relation to what the books indicate about the business.

Industry Changes—Franchises and Computerization

In the 21st century, significant factors affecting FBO management information systems include the following:

1. The availability of special-purpose computer hardware and software designed to keep track of every aspect of an FBO's business means that the competitive company will be computerized in virtually every respect. Leading vendors of industry software are

Main screen from FBO Manager Front Desk (using touch screen interface). Courtesy of FBO Manager.

FBO Manager, and TotalFBO; generic systems suitable for any business are QuickBooks, Manage Your Own Business, and Peachtree.

2. Computers not only enable traditional tasks to be routinized and done in more automated fashion, they enable more and different tasks to be done. Expectations for quantity and quality of work increase and so the advent of the computer system to an office does not necessarily mean labor is saved; more likely, people do more work, both as they get skilled on the new system and in using all the new applications that are available.
3. Despite the availability of more sophisticated information management systems, "garbage in" still produces "garbage out." A muddled or haphazard approach to management information produces muddled results even if one obtains a state of the art computer system, the best-designed forms, and the most expert advice.
4. The increased numbers of FBO franchises and FBOs with multiple locations (chains) means that aviation businesses are sharing a centralized approach to information procedures, including standardized forms and customized computers systems. Franchises are expensive investments. As a result, it is less easy than in the past for other operators to access and mimic the forms and business methods of the leading aviation service companies, meaning they will need to either design their own or have them custom created through use of one of the above-mentioned specialty software companies.

System Purposes

There are a number of reasons for keeping good records on a regular basis for any small business. These include to:

> Ensure financial survival;
> Enable performance improvement;
> Create special reports;
> Comply with taxes and legal obligations; and
> To provide a check on reality.

Financial Survival

Knowing how much is being sold, whether it has yet been paid for, the cash on hand, the cost of opening the doors each day, and the break-even level of activity are basics for the survival of any business. Even a small business will involve more than the manager can carry in his head. It is particularly easy to overlook upcoming expenses. Any plans for expansion will also require knowledge of unit costs, potential profits, and the market picture. Most important, a small or new business cannot wait until the end of its fiscal year to find out how it is doing. Monthly status reports are essential, and in some cases, weekly or daily posting of results may be appropriate.

It is recommended that the operator have available a Profit and Loss (P&L) statement for each section of the business i.e. maintenance, flight school, pilot shop, charter, concierge services, inventory etc. The operator will also need to have a P&L for each human or equipment "asset" within each profit center of the business. For example, what are the gross and net of each aircraft on the flightline, each instructor, each mechanic? An operator needs this information to fully identify the profit centers and money-losers within the company, so that corrective actions can be taken. Additionally, if cash flow becomes a problem, the operator should know which equipment assets can be sold quickly to generate capital. Although the cost of accounting/management software may seem high, it is necessary for the operator to have access to information in order to operate in a profitable manner.

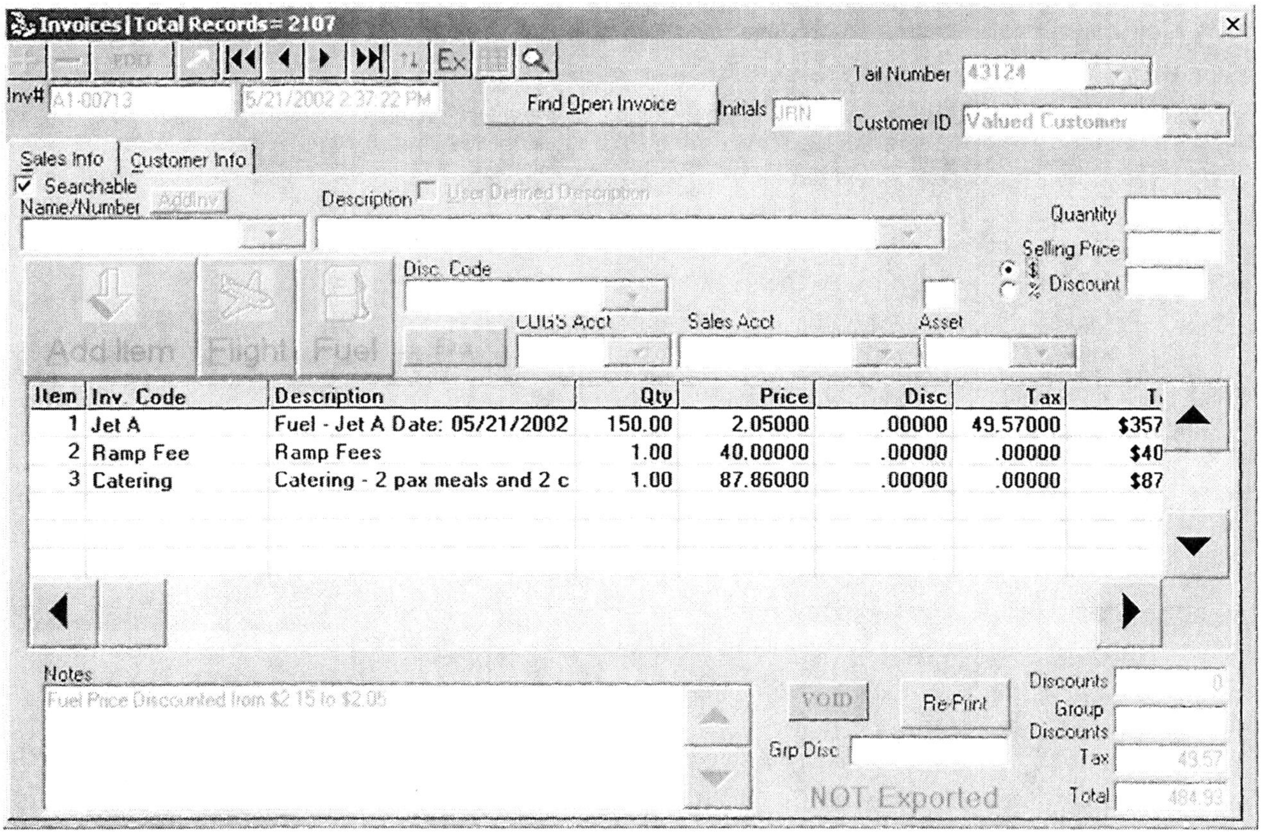

Invoice screen shown in FBO Manager. Courtesy of FBO Manager.

Performance Monitoring and Improvement

Good information systems permit the examination of the whole business and also subareas such as projects, sales territories, individual employees, profit centers, and cost centers. Such data can then permit the manager to initiate actions to correct any problems. Accurate comparative data on employee performance, such as productivity, hours worked, and absences can be important in establishing a clear and fair case for promotion or termination. The earlier that it is reported that a certain area is "off-course," the sooner and easier it is to make "course corrections." Good management entails almost constant course corrections in all areas of the business.

Special Reports

Apart from monthly postings of a regular nature, good records can permit special reports on specific subjects as the need arises. These might include five-year trends in parts costs compared with maintenance labor costs in order to determine a policy on sale of parts to self-repairers. The analysis would examine whether the profit is greater on sale of parts or on labor and how the two are likely to relate in the future, based on past trends. Or a special analysis might look at the allocation of time of a certain group of employees among tasks. Jobs might be reorganized to use less costly personnel for less profitable areas of activity. A look at seasonal and daily peaks might change marketing and work shift strategies, and so on. The manager's ability to have special reports prepared depends on knowledge of the readily available data in the firm and what those data can reveal if used intelligently. Much more can be found from data kept for accounting purposes than is generally intended, and computerization makes it relatively easy to create such reports. For example, Figure 7.1 shows fuel sales ranked by customer volume over a three-year period.

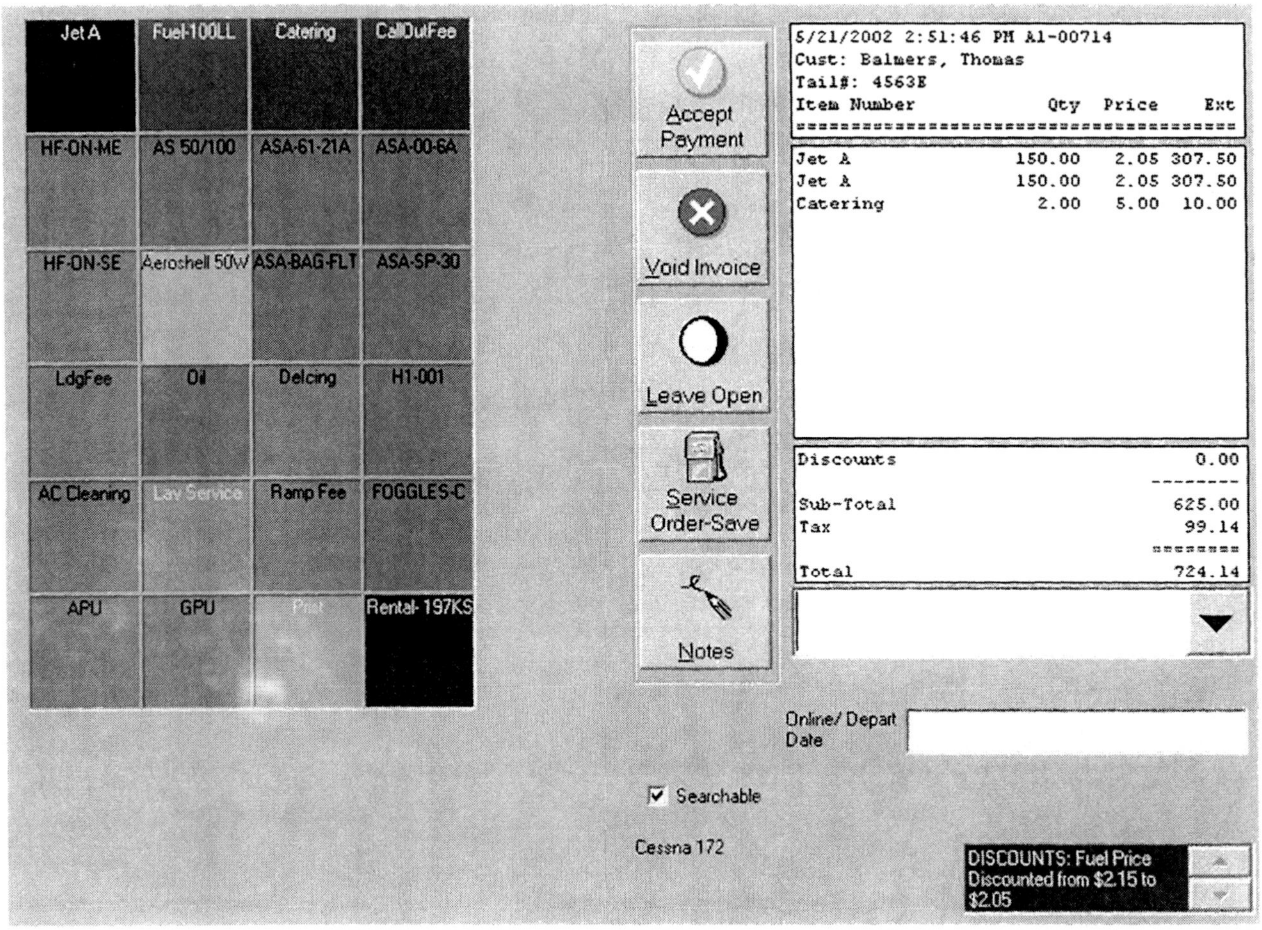

Sales screen providing for user defined layout of items and colors. Courtesy of FBO Manager.

Figure 7.1 » Fuel Sales by Type by Customer

Fuel Sales by Type by Customer for 11/01/1998 to 12/31/2001

Jet A

Customer	Quantity	Taxes	Sub-Total	Total	Eff Price
Moodyman, James	34600.00	$13,072.28	$74,390.00	$87,462.28	$2.53
Mattingly, Robert W	10703.40	$2,572.29	$22,542.71	$25,115.00	$2.35
Boyd gaming	6806.70	$671.27	$14,549.31	$15,220.58	$2.24
Valued Customer	6777.90	$1,079.50	$14,557.54	$15,637.04	$2.31
Balmers, Thomas	6181.50	$773.46	$12,934.62	$13,708.08	$2.22
Beaudoines, Jay	3200.10	$54.39	$6,424.17	$6,478.56	$2.02
7331	3070.00	$0.00	$6,166.75	$6,166.75	$2.01
McAlister, Stuart	2969.80	$809.81	$6,988.07	$7,797.88	$2.63
Williamson, John	2268.90	$826.74	$4,748.45	$5,575.19	$2.46
McClures, Steve	2019.00	$578.28	$4,290.85	$4,869.13	$2.41
Stevens, Samantha	1720.00	$410.78	$3,626.00	$4,036.78	$2.35
A.VFuel Test	1599.20	$416.80	$3,398.28	$3,815.08	$2.39
Stuart-Macdonald	1548.00	$517.27	$3,328.20	$3,845.47	$2.48
Baltzer, Jacob	1520.00	$533.33	$3,268.00	$3,801.33	$2.50
Allens, David	1241.80	$364.27	$2,300.77	$2,665.04	$2.15
Del Monte Aviation	1103.00	$395.40	$2,261.15	$2,656.55	$2.41
Claus, Santa	1074.60	$75.80	$2,270.34	$2,346.14	$2.18
Winkler, Henry	500.00	$75.78	$1,075.00	$1,150.78	$2.30
Mouse, Mickey	350.00	$56.83	$752.50	$809.33	$2.31
Miller, Lee L	310.00	$117.48	$666.50	$783.98	$2.53
AvFuel	300.00	$0.00	$645.00	$645.00	$2.15
Bees, Wade	300.00	$37.90	$645.00	$682.90	$2.28
Executive Jet	252.00	$0.00	$541.80	$541.80	$2.15
Pedro	250.00	$94.73	$537.50	$632.23	$2.53
Dawsonest, Ken	200.00	$75.78	$430.00	$505.78	$2.53
415WM	200.00	$0.00	$430.00	$430.00	$2.15
Rowers, Dan	150.20	$0.00	$322.93	$322.93	$2.15
Calverts, Dennis	150.00	$0.00	$322.50	$322.50	$2.15
Mullen, Sandi	136.60	$51.76	$293.69	$345.45	$2.53
Nelson, John	122.00	$0.00	$262.30	$262.30	$2.15
Gilligan, Jim	116.00	$0.00	$249.40	$249.40	$2.15
Deerport Aviation	100.00	$0.00	$155.00	$155.00	$1.55
Whitman, Chip A	100.00	$37.90	$215.00	$252.90	$2.53
Chambers, Art	74.00	$0.00	$159.10	$159.10	$2.15
Haspels, Ralph O	60.00	$22.74	$129.00	$151.74	$2.53
Gibbsons, David	49.66	$0.00	$106.77	$106.77	$2.15
Taylorama, Greg	49.00	$0.00	$105.35	$105.35	$2.15
Saelzle, Peter	5.00	$0.00	$10.75	$10.75	$2.15
Kellam, David S	-6546.00	$85.64	($14,073.90)	($13,988.26)	$2.14
TOTAL	85632.36	$23,808.21	$182,026.40	$205,834.61	

Courtesy of FBO Manager.

Taxes and Legal Obligations

A good data system can not only assure that required reports and payments are made on time, but it can also flag upcoming events so they can be anticipated.

Checks on Reality

Good paper records of inventory, cash in hand, receivables, and volume sold can check against employee laxness or actual theft. A company where the boss regularly checks records against what is observable in the stockroom and elsewhere will establish an atmosphere in which pilfering or fixing the books is less likely. If an employee or customer is stealing, good records are essential both for prosecution and for insurance claims.

System Processes

Integrated Flow

Data systems all begin with the recording manually or on a computer of all data at its point of origin. The flow from that point on should be virtually automatic. The data should flow freely from user to user, with repetitive work and human intervention minimized. This means the initial data should be collected in a format that suits the needs of its final users and perhaps with more detail being recorded than is needed for intermediate purposes.

Requirements of an Effective System

In all the diverse areas where information should be collected, there are a number of common requirements. The management information systems set up to address these requirements must be timely, must aid in the allocation of resources and must improve decision making by assisting in the selection of alternatives. They should be adequate to fit the needs of the particular business without being over-designed and should address the total operation of the company, not just accounting and financial records. They should be understandable and operational and adhere to the existing organizational structure but also be flexible. Most importantly, they should flag problems or deviations from the norm and indicate corrective action.

First Steps

In developing the information systems, the manager should develop a master plan that covers the basic requirements and stands in readiness when additional needs are identified. To develop a master plan means starting with the desired end product and working backwards. First steps include:

1. Establish long-range objectives for the data system.
2. Establish the required reports and data.
3. Define the information currently being collected and its adequacy, using chronological or input-output flow and, if appropriate, relating information flows to floor layouts.
4. Make short-range improvements that are consistent with long-range plans.
5. Establish the schedule and responsibility for the long-range plan.
6. Implement the plan.

The long-range objectives for the data system may be drawn from the overall company business plan (see Chapter 2, Management Functions). Specific data requirements will need to consider:

- Data source;
- Frequency of occurrence;
- Batching versus transmitting as data comes in;
- Time period for complete information cycle;
- Lags between event and its report to manager in meaningful form;
- Format of data after tabulation or analysis; and
- Adequacy of existing data: is enough data being collected in a useful form to actually provide guidance to management?

Aviation Management Information Systems

Human Resources

Many personnel issues arise not on a regular basis, but in relation to changes in personnel and personnel requirements. A few, however, occur on a regular basis. These include time sheets or cards, punctuality records, sick time, and leave taken. These records will likely be kept by the employee on a daily basis and submitted on a weekly or biweekly basis for payroll processing. For employees wearing more than one hat or belonging to more than one profit center, time records will report not just time on the job but time by project. It can be useful to break down the manager's own time between such activities as marketing, public relations, administration, other overhead, and direct revenue-generating time, if it exists in any area.

Figure 7.2 shows the complete array of probable human resource data requirements, sources, and controls.

Financial

The cash data needs of the organization are shown in Figure 7.3.

Material

"Material" covers all the tangible assets of the business such as buildings, aircraft, vehicles, inventory, shop, flight school, and office equipment. Information is needed on the condition, contribution, and replacement of these assets, as well as flags for scheduled preventive maintenance. Figure 7.4 summarizes these assets and their information sources and controls, and Figure 7.5 shows a sample physical inventory worksheet for monitoring the parts and supplies in the maintenance shop.

Figure 7.2 » Human Resource Data Needs

Activity	Source of Information	Control Measure
1. Identifying human resource requirements	Inventory of company's human resources Job requirements	Company goals, objectives Organization requirements
2. Recruiting	Examination of practices Review of results	Turnover goals Stability desired Training needed
3. Selection	Personnel records Performance results	Organization requirements Position requirements
4. Training	Training records	Training requirements Individual needs Defective rate
5. Using human resources	Personnel records Time cards Job orders	Turnover rate Tardiness rate Labor productivity Organization requirements

Figure 7.3 » Cash Data Needs of an Organization

Activity	Source of Information	Control Measure
1. Obtaining adequate funds	Organization requirements Financial statement analysis	Goals Comparative data
2. Accounting for funds	Accounting record Routine reports	Accounting standards Comparative data
3. Utilizing funds	Financial analysis	Organization goals Historical data Industry data

Figure 7.4 » Summary of Business Assets

Activity	Source of Information	Control Measure
1. Aircraft	Physical inspection Profit records Customer indications	Organization goals Historical records Industry data
2. Inventory	Routine inventory records Profit records Customer indications	Goals Historical records Industry data
3. Physical plant	Physical inspection Preventive maintenance records Engineer reports Customer indications	Company goals Historical records Comparative data
4. Equipment	Physical inspections Preventive maintenance records Customer indications	Company goals Historical data Manufacturer requirements

Figure 7.5 » Sample Physical Inventory Worksheet

George's Test Data

Physical Inventory Worksheet

Type	Part Number	Description	Unit Cost	Bin/Location	Dept	Current Stock	Actual Count
SP	066-1046-00	NavCom	200.00	AV3		0.0	
SP	066-1046-00	NavCom	364.00	AV3		0.0	
RP	099001-041	EXHUST SYST ASSY	998.00	SH-B4	SP	2.0	
SP	10-600	GPS - Hand Held	499.00	AV7		0.0	
RP	102280-1	CANOPY FAIRING AFT	87.50	SH-B3	FS	1.0	
RP	102344-19	MOLDING WINDO LH	68.00	SH-B11	SP	1.0	
RP	102428-1	BEARING RETAINER	9.00	SH-C4	SP	9.0	
RP	1182-B3	SPARK PLUG	0.65	SH-C18	SP	18.0	
RP	1182J3	SPARK PLUG	0.72	SH-C18	SP	24.0	
RP	118P60592S4	CAPACITOR	85.00	AV-1		10.0	
RP	12345-67890	Widget	0.00			0.0	
RP	123456789ABC	FILTER, ELECTRONIC	37.50	SH-F11	SP	4.0	
SP	127-15952	Intercom	179.59	AV6		1.0	
SP	135-32202	Altitude Alerter	459.00	AV4		0.0	
SP	135-32202	Altitude Alerter	459.00	AV6		0.0	
SP	135-32202	Altitude Alerter	459.00	AV4		0.0	
SP	135-32601	GPS	1,114.50	AV8		0.0	
RP	152 SPINNER	SENSENICH PROP MOD	185.00	SH-D19	SP	2.0	
RP	1C172BTM7359	PROPELLER ALUM SPACER	1,477.00	SH-D19	SP	1.0	
RP	202033-1	WEIGHT	36.00	SH-D18	SP	4.0	
RP	2231	Carb Spring	0.34	SH-C22	SP	49.0	
RP	223311	Condenser	0.02	AV2		144.0	
RP	23450	Gumout Carb Cleaner	0.15	PL2	SP	144.0	
RP	301025-501	STABILIZER R/H	649.00	SH-B4	SP	2.0	
RP	401121-706	LINE	37.49	SH-Z11	SP	1.0	

Figure 7.5 » Continued

George's Test Data
Physical Inventory Worksheet

Type	Part Number	Description	Unit Cost	Bin/Location	Dept	Current Stock	Actual Count
RP	406006-501	AIRBOX	22.00	SH-B1	SP	19.0	
RP	453331	Rotor	0.31	SH-B15	SP	144.0	
RP	456678	Cessna Door Lock	6.00	SH-D19	SP	10.0	
RP	479729	FILTER NYLON	30.00	SH-Z11	SP	9.0	
RP	503006-2	THERMOID TUBE	9.95	AV4		4.0	
RP	5102270-3	SPACER	0.25	SH-C12	SP	14.0	
RP	5102329-3	SEAT ATTACH BRKT LH OUTBO	37.00	SH-B2	SP	1.0	
RP	5102361-501	RETAINER	37.00	SH-C11	SP	2.0	
RP	5201174-5	FAIRING	864.00	SH-B5	SP	1.0	
RP	5302039-1	BRACKET	17.00	SH-B3	SP	10.0	
RP	5406001-1	DUCT	15.00	SH-B1	SP	2.0	
RP	5503006-502	BUTTERFLY	19.00	SH-C16	SP	10.0	
RP	5607003-502	ACTUATOR ASSY	14.00	SH-C16	SP	2.0	
RP	5803007-108	PLACARD FLASHING BEACON W	0.99	SH-C19	SP	10.0	
RP	5804018-2	SPACER	13.75	SH-C22	SP	10.0	
RP	600X6 TUBE G/Y	TUBE. GOODYEAR	17.95	SH-D2	SP	2.0	
RP	607004-4	COLLAR OUTBOARD	8.65	SH-A3	SP	3.0	
RP	641431	RING, FOURTH GROOVE	3.33	SH-A3	SP	3.0	
RP	7-6412	PTT Switch	1.27	FRONT		5.0	
RP	701063-2	BRACKET	277.00	SH-A4	SP	1.0	
RP	72CKS6	Sensensich Prop Bolt Kit	14.79	SH-A5	SP	1.0	
RP	78-23444	Sandpaper, Wet/dry	0.08	SH-Z9	SP	50.0	
RP	78A110	LOCK CLIP	0.25	SH-A5	SP	10.0	
RP	7CS10425-5	BRACKET ASSY	79.00	SH-A3	SP	2.0	
RP	7F10401-13	COVER	169.00	SH-B9	SP	1.0	
RP	7L10238-13	NUT	3.35	SH-Z19	SP	1.0	
RP	7P10616-17	BRACKET	10.00	SH-Z11	SP	0.0	
RP	7SCF012-1	TRANSDUCER	0.00	AV2		0.0	
RP	803007-13	PLACARD,CANOPY LOCK	0.00	SH-C19	SP	0.0	
RP	804019-509	FAIRING	0.00	SH-B3	SP	0.0	
RP	8357672	Hubbell Surge Fitting	0.16	SH-A11	SP	52.0	
RP	85-43-201-38	SEAL- WASHER	0.00	SH-D22	SP	-1.0	
RP	93	Bulb	0.37	AV3		8.0	
RP	A3236SS012-27	DIMPLE WASHER	0.00	SH-Z14	SP	0.0	
RP	ABC123	Pilot Book	11.23			7.0	
RP	AES1300-1	BOLT	0.00	SH-Z14	SP	-4.0	
RP	AN175-14	BOLT	0.00	SH-Z15	SP	0.0	
RP	AN500-416-6	SCREW	0.00	SH-Z15	SP	0.0	
RP	AN7-34A	BOLT	0.00	SH-Z16	SP	0.0	
RP	AN960-516L	WASHER	0.00	SH-Z16	SP	0.0	
RP	BCT-414	Facts Of Twin-Engine Flying	9.95	FRONT		2.0	
RP	C21-9159	COMPASS FWD GASKET	0.00	SH-D23	SP	0.0	
RP	CH27-1477	Fuel Filter	17.00	SH-F11	SP	17.0	
RP	CH48109	Oil Filter, Spin On	8.78	SH-F11	SP	12.0	
RP	CH48110	Oil Filter, Spin On	9.11	SH-F11	SP	12.0	
RP	CHART-1100	Sectional -Dallas	1.25	FRONT		18.0	
RP	CHART-1200	Sectional-Kansas City	1.25	FRONT		22.0	

Figure 7.5 » Continued

George's Test Data
Physical Inventory Worksheet

Type	Part Number	Description	Unit Cost	Bin/Location	Dept	Current Stock	Actual Count
RP	DC12053OZ	GLASS PRIMER,RTV732	0.00	PL2	SP	0.0	
RP	GAES1022Z8-10	SCREW	0.00	SH-Z17	SP	0.0	
RP	GX147-2153	Ground Cable	0.00	SH-C22	SP	0.0	
RP	HP1010	Laserjet Toner	129.00	Closet		10.0	
RP	IN-1001	Instrument Pilot Test Manual	9.00	FRONT		29.0	
RP	KCP2 1/2	FIRE EXT	41.00	SH-E10	SP	1.0	
RP	KL9954	Signal Test Kit	0.00	AV1		0.0	
RP	LW16511	CAMSHAFT 0320-H2AD	0.00	SH-R15	SP	0.0	
RP	M647	SPARK PLUG GASKET	0.00	SH-C17	SP	0.0	
RP	MS20364-832C	NUT	0.00	SH-Z18	SP	0.0	
RP	MS24665-360	COTTER PIN	0.19	SH-Z20	SP	-4.0	
RP	MS35333-38	WASHER LOCK	0.00	SH-Z21	SP	0.0	
RP	NAS451-56	7/8^ STEEL HOLE PLUG	0.00	SH-Z22	SP	0.0	
RP	PA1912	Brake Line - 19x1/2"	7.00	SH-C19	SP	13.0	
RP	PAPER-LETTER	Copier Paper	26.25	Closet		40.0	
RP	PR-1001	Private Pilot Test Manual	9.00	FRONT		49.0	
RP	PTS-1700	Pilot Requirements-Private	2.35	FRONT		5.0	
RP	PX145-19	Tire	17.00	SH-R5	SP	-1.0	
RP	REM-40	SPARK PLUG	0.00	SH-C17	SP	0.0	
RP	REM38	SPARK PLUG	0.00	SH-C17	SP	0.0	
RP	REM40E	SPARK PLUG	0.00	SH-C17	SP	0.0	
RP	S-220	PLASTIC REPAIR KIT	0.00	PL3	SP	0.0	
RP	SH-117 WHITE	White Paint	7.00	PL1	PS	26.0	
RP	SH-118 BLUE	Blue Paint	6.48	PL1	PS	25.0	
RP	SK130-1	THROTTLE CABLE CLAMP MOD	0.00	SH-Z22	SP	0.0	
RP	ST-43189	C-172 Strut	0.00	SH-B1	SP	0.0	
RP	SW411	SWITCH	0.00	AV3		0.0	
RP	T17-50	Cessna Tire-10"	59.00	SH-R5	SP	30.0	
RP	Z1974126	Battery, 12 Volt	15.00	SH-A13	SP	10.0	

Courtesy of TotalFBO Accounting and Business Management Software by Horizon Business Concepts, Inc.

Aviation Operations

This topic is crucial because it represents the areas where the business makes its money. Some of the information needed in these areas originates elsewhere in the system and must be converted or transferred for managerial decisions about operations. Figure 7.6 summarizes these aviation operations data areas.

Legal and Tax Information

The accounting system yields data on the various taxes due and the schedules for payment. Legal information may be more sporadically generated and is vitally important. It must be well organized and complete.

Market Information

Information about industry trends and about what the competition is doing comes from many sources, as discussed in Chapter 3, Marketing. The manager must decide how to monitor and assemble this information so that it is readily accessible.

Figure 7.6 » Aviation Operations Data

Activity	Source of Information	Control Measure
1. Line operations	Gas/oil sales records Related sales Customer indications Personnel reports Profit records	Volume goals Profit objectives Historical data
2. Maintenance	Volume of work Customer indications Work redone Labor allocation FAA inspection	Volume goals Project objectives Historical data Industry data
3. Instruction	Volume of work Customer indications Profitability Instructor and aircraft utilization records FAA inspection	Volume goals Project objectives Historical data Industry data
4. Flight services	Work volume records Customer reports FAA inspections Profit records Utilization	Volume goals Profit objectives Historical data Industry data
5. Aircraft parts sales	Sales volume records Profitability Customer indication Sales reports	Unit goals Historical data Industry data
6. Miscellaneous (Rental, parking, and so on)	Specific activity reports Profit analysis	Predetermined goals Historical data

Technological Information

Aviation technology is constantly changing, and decisions have to be made about whether to try new manufacturers, product lines, and methods. The success or failure of each test should be documented, as should requests from customers for something new.

Analyzing Business Activity

Sometimes described as financial analysis, this task is a combination of checking over the accounting data and critically reviewing the operating procedures and accomplishments. Accounting data provide the measures of actual activity and management expertise, as expressed through the business plan. These must be used to set up performance standards to measure the actual results.

General Procedure

Sources of performance standards to apply to the business can come from:

- Results from a previous operating period;
- Contrasting two previous operating periods;
- Industry averages, from National Air Transportation Association (NATA) or other national sources;
- Competing businesses, as obtainable; and
- Similar businesses, as reported in trade press articles or in advertising.

Analyzing the Business as a Whole

The purpose of this activity is threefold—to determine whether goals and objectives are being met, to identify areas with potential for improvement, and to suggest possible corrective actions.

Specific tasks will include:

> Comparison of financial statements with budget and financial projections;
> Comparison of current financial statement with previous years' statements; and
> Comparison of financial statement with those of similar businesses, if possible.

Specific measures should include:

> Net income;
> Return on equity;
> Qualitative considerations;
> Community considerations; and
> Balance of different departments within the firm.

After an examination of the financial statement/balance sheet as a whole, it is appropriate to examine the individual items on it. They should also be compared with expectations, previous results, industry, and even general business norms. The help of an accountant or banker may be appropriate.

Secondly, the income statement should be examined in the same way. It is particularly useful to express income in each department as a percentage of the total. Gross and net profit by department should be calculated, and profit centers ranked.

The final step in the analysis of the overall business through financial statements involves the use of ratios. Ratios are developed to show the relationship of key areas identified on the statements. They may be classified according to their source data as balance sheet, income, and mixed ratios. They may also be classified according to the purpose of the ratio comparison:

> Liquidity measures;
> Managerial efficiency;
> Leverage measures; and
> Profitability measures.

Prior to examining key ratios in each of these areas, certain basics regarding the use of this technique should be considered. A ratio is most useful when compared to previous ratios, to industry ratio averages, and to generally accepted standards. Ratios based upon poorly prepared statements are practically worthless and may be misleading to the unsuspecting analyst. Finally, ratios indicate business situations in a general sense; they indicate positions that may require further investigation in order to analyze and understand the situation adequately.

Liquidity ratios. These ratios describing liquid assets are helpful in analyzing the ability of a business to meet its debts and liabilities and to move rapidly in meeting unexpected business opportunities.

Current assets: current liabilities. Figures are taken from the balance sheet for this calculation. A ratio of 2 is desirable. The value of for sale aircraft in inventory will greatly influence this ratio.

Fixed assets: tangible net worth. Figures are taken from the balance sheet. Tangible net worth excludes "goodwill" or similar accounts. Dunn and Bradstreet suggests that a desirable figure is under 75 percent. Figures over 75 percent suggest the operation has too much invested in fixed assets and may be weak in operating assets or may not be flexible or liquid enough to meet changing business conditions.

Inventory: net working capital. Net working capital is considered as current assets less current liabilities. Once again, Dunn & Bradstreet has suggested that a desirable ratio is something less than 80 percent. A business with a higher figure is felt to have too much in inventory. The organization is not considered "liquid" enough to meet the rapidly changing conditions of the business world.

Ratios of managerial efficiency. Ratios in this category are designed to analyze the efficiency with which managers handle the assets of the organization. Specific ratios cover the various assets of the business.

Receivables: sales per day. The accounts receivable collection period measures management's efficiency in handling the assets tied up in outstanding accounts. The soundness of the accounts receivable and the credit policies of the company are indicated by this relationship. It is generally felt that a collection period of between 30 and 45 days is optimal. If collections take longer than 45 days, it may be that customers are "using" the funds of the organization or, in other words, credit policies are too lenient.

Cost of sales: average inventory. Inventory turnover reflects the efficiency of management's use of the assets represented by the inventory. The desirable turnover must be identified through experience, nature of the product, industry averages, and other factors such as shortages. Desirable turnover of inventory is 3-4 times per year if this activity is to be profitable.

Leverage ratios. Ratios in this area reflect the balance of borrowed funds and ownership funds. They provide an indication of management's ability to "lever" funds into additional assets by way of increased borrowing. The existing leverage provides a measure of the support and faith lenders have in the organization and the existing management.

Total debt: tangible net worth. If the relationship is over 100 percent, the equity of the creditor exceeds that of the owner. It has been suggested that if this relationship is over 80 percent, the organization is facing possible difficulty. Of course, higher leverage allows a greater return on ownership. It also, however, becomes a weakness when there is a decline in earnings.

Current debt: tangible net worth. This ratio reflects leverage through the amount of current debt that can be acquired with respect to the existing net worth of the organization. It reflects the trust that creditors place in the management of the organization as well as the management philosophy.

Total debt: total assets. This ratio reflects again the leverage that exists in the value of the assets and in the management of those assets.

Profitability ratios. Ratios in this area are designed to provide a measure of the profitability of operations. Earnings or profits are compared with key indicators of ownership to reflect the profitability of such activity.

Earnings before taxes: total assets. This ratio, normally referred to as return on assets, reflects the relationship between annual profits and the investment in assets committed to this profit. Indications are that with the aviation business community this return should be around 5-10 percent.

Net profits: net worth. With this ratio, the owners are provided with a measure of the earning power of their investment. The desirable return will depend upon the alternatives available, the risk tolerance of the investor, and industry averages. Considering the risk element in the aviation business and relatively secure alternatives, the owner's return should be approximately 15-30 percent.

Net profit: sales. The profit for a period as related to the sales for that period offers an indication of profitability as well as a measure of the efficiency of the business.

Special-purpose ratios. There are a large number of items in the financial statements that can be evaluated through ratio analysis. Individual expense items can be related to sales. Income categories can be compared with total sales. Ratios of this type are useful in period-to-period comparative analysis, for comparison with industry averages, and for budgetary control work.

Management Audit

The management audit is the second procedure that may be used by the manager in analyzing the overall business. This process uses a number of the same tools and techniques employed in financial analysis, but the general concept is different. What is a management audit? By definition, it is a systematic checklist approach to the analysis of a business, its functions, operations and decisions. By carefully reviewing each of the functional and operational areas of a business, and comparing existing conditions with previously identified goals and required or desired standards, some measure can be obtained of strengths and weaknesses and corrective action suggested. By examining the entire business in this manner, an auditor is really examining management, hence the name "management audit."

Appendix V contains an Aviation Management Audit. It is designed as a self-audit, one that can be conducted by the management team. To do this as it should be done requires a thoughtful, objective point of view. Of course, the audit can be expanded and made much more beneficial when administered by an impartial third party such as an aviation management consultant. By having such an outsider conduct the audit, a higher degree of objectivity and more penetrating questions can be developed. The participants can also use the audit in a seminar setting to achieve a higher level of management awareness and an exchange of information. A typical seminar has a small group of 18 to 25 aviation managers in attendance. Each has received an audit manual and has been requested to complete the self-audit prior to arrival. The seminar reviews the audit manual with individual replies, group comparison, and leader comments and analysis of each of the items. Further benefit could be received by the tabulation of accumulated audit responses and perhaps even the preparation of nationwide norms and standards.

The management audit is not an accounting or financial audit, but a review of the overall business as well as the individual departments. A thorough audit provides management with invaluable information and advice regarding the organization; consequently, it is considered a valuable supplement to the regular information system portrayed throughout this chapter. Conducted at regular intervals, one audit can serve as a benchmark for successive audit reviews and promote successful change.

Analyzing Departmental Activity

Introduction

The normal tools used in analyzing departmental activity are:

> Plans and objectives;
> The budget;
> Operating controls; and
> Financial records.

Although each is a separate technique, they combine as a sequence that forms a method of analyzing department activity. The process is described so that the manager may consider the major elements of each step.

Plans and objectives. Identifying plans and objectives represents the first step in conducting a thorough review of departments or profit centers. Without a definite business objective, it becomes difficult to determine whether the activity of that portion of the business is successful. To paraphrase the Cheshire cat from *Alice in Wonderland*, "If you don't know where you're going it doesn't matter which way you go, and you won't know if you get there." The following are questions that should be asked in this first step:

1. What are the objectives of the department? List.
2. Are the objectives definite, clear-cut, and, most importantly, measurable?
3. Are they attainable?
4. Are the objectives understood and accepted by those involved in their attainment?
5. Are the department objectives compatible with and supportive of overall company objectives?

By using these questions, a manager should be able to develop an initial set of standards to measure business success or failure.

Budget. Practically speaking, a budget is a quantitative expression of the plan or objectives of the department. As such, it becomes an aid in coordination and implementation. It is indispensable in grappling with uncertainties. Its benefits exceed its costs. Budgets should be positive vehicles for progress and improvement.

Operating controls. These controls are used as guidelines to prevent excessive spending, to provide ample supplies, to monitor personnel and aircraft utilization, etc. For the parts department, the control may be inventory limits; for aircraft sales there may be a unit dollar limit; for service there may be a desired level of billed mechanic time; for credit, a total outstanding accounts receivable in each of 30, 60, 90 and 120 days; for flight instruction, a desired level of flight hours per instructor; and for passenger activity, a mandatory procedure for briefing and debriefing with each flight.

A series of general questions should help in the examination of a department's operations:

1. What is the true worth of departmental assets? List them.
2. What is the extent and character of departmental liabilities? List them.
3. Is there the ability to earn a fair return?
4. What is the capacity to withstand setbacks?
5. What is departmental labor efficiency?
6. How efficient is the utilization of equipment?
7. Is departmental and company-wide space utilized properly?
8. Are the departmental records maintained accurately?
9. Do the activity indicators reflect constant action (e.g., sales calls; inactive student follow-up)?
10. Are salaries adequate? Too high? Too low?
11. Do expenses appear in line? Do they match budgeted figures?
12. Is the department inventory maintained accurately? Is it adequate? Excessive?
13. Are the department-generated receivables too high? Too low? What is the bad debt experience?
14. Prepare an analysis of departmental income by key categories.
15. Develop a break-even analysis for the department. Determine key indicators.

Financial records. The financial records for this purpose are the income statement and various supplements used to amplify or explain indications of the statement. Figure 7.7 illustrates the general ledger departmental income and expense report provided by TotalFBO. Using this report as a guide, a manager may conduct a review of a department's activity. The manager should examine each subject category on the statement line by line to determine whether departmental objectives have been achieved, operations are efficient, and problems exist.

As an illustration, suppose a review is made of several of the lines on the income statement. The following analysis shows possible comparisons to make:

Total sales. Compare with budgeted figure on a monthly and year-to-date basis. Analyze the various components of the total sales figure (new, used, geographic, demographic) to determine relationship of previous marketing action and to suggest possible future activity.

Cost of sales. Consider efficiency of buying practices. Identify possible weaknesses and means for improving methods.

Consider expenses associated with creating this revenue. Compare salaries/wage expense with budget projections, historical data, and other businesses. Examine job requirements and consider impact on incumbents in the job. Ensure compliance with federal and state regulations.

Gross profit. Compare with budgeted figure and with data for similar periods of operation. A large difference would suggest further examination and analysis.

Last Section—Net Income for the Period—Profit or Loss

In like manner, the manager should first determine the general situation and then identify problems that may exist within each line. In conducting this type of analysis, he or she must remember that the income statement is:

> The result of facts;
> The result of accounting conventions; and also
> The result of personal judgments and evaluations.

Analysis supplements. Special supplements to the financial statement are tremendously valuable in examining the various operational activities and developing insight into possible cause-and-effect relationships.

Tables, charts, graphs, and worksheets can be prepared for a variety of departmental activities and will present specific, detailed data for the desired business activity. The supplements may be practically applied to the activities of service, sales, parts, flight, passengers, line, or other departmental activities. Typical supplements of interest to managers include:

> Accumulated aircraft sales per salesperson;
> Monthly parts sales compared to projections;
> Aircraft utilization by aircraft and by type flight;

Figure 7.7 » General Ledger Standard Income Report

George's Test Data
General Ledger Standard Income Report
For The Period: 1/ 1/2002 Through: 5/31/2002
All Departments Consolidated

Income

	Month-To-Date		Quarter-To-Date		Year-To-Date	
4000.00 Parts Sales	0.00	0%	28.13	0%	28.13	0%
4010.00 Fuel Sales	6,427.60	50%	6,747.20	50%	6,747.20	48%
4015.00 Into-Plane Fees	0.00	0%	0.00	0%	500.00	3%
4060.00 Solo Aircraft Rental Revenue	572.40	4%	572.40	4%	572.40	4%
4070.00 Dual Aircraft Rental Revenue	96.00	0%	186.00	1%	186.00	1%
4080.00 Charter Revenue	5,520.00	42%	5,520.00	41%	5,520.00	39%
4081.00 Charter Income - Aircraft Standby	20.00	0%	20.00	0%	20.00	0%
4082.00 Charter Revenue - Pilot Standby	10.00	0%	10.00	0%	10.00	0%
4100.00 Flight Store Revenue	134.60	1%	134.60	1%	134.60	1%
4140.00 Instruction - Primary Revenue	22.40	0%	22.40	0%	22.40	0%
4160.00 Ground School Revenue	25.20	0%	25.20	0%	25.20	0%
4930.00 Miscellaneous Revenue	40.00	0%	90.00	0%	90.00	0%
Total Income:	**12,868.20**	**100%**	**13,355.93**	**100%**	**13,855.93**	**100%**

Cost Of Sales

	Month-To-Date		Quarter-To-Date		Year-To-Date	
5000.00 Parts Cost Of Goods Sold	87.50	0%	96.50	0%	96.50	0%
5010.00 Fuel Cost Of Goods Sold	3,940.96	30%	4,134.31	31%	4,134.31	29%
Total Cost Of Sales:	**4,028.46**	**31%**	**4,230.81**	**31%**	**4,230.81**	**30%**
Gross Profit:	**8,839.74**	**68%**	**9,125.12**	**68%**	**9,625.12**	**69%**

Expense

	Month-To-Date		Quarter-To-Date		Year-To-Date	
7010.00 Lost Fuel Inventory	95,859.13	744%	95,859.13	717%	95,859.13	691%
7110.00 Salaries/Wages Expense	658.00	5%	658.00	4%	1,581.08	11%
7140.00 Taxes-FICA	0.00	0%	0.00	0%	57.23	0%
7150.00 Taxes-Medicare	0.00	0%	0.00	0%	13.38	0%
7160.00 Taxes-FUTA	0.00	0%	0.00	0%	57.23	0%
7190.00 Taxes-Worker's Comp	0.00	0%	0.00	0%	9.23	0%
Total Expense:	**96,517.13**	**750%**	**96,517.13**	**722%**	**97,577.28**	**704%**
Profit Before Other:	**(87,677.39)**	**-681%**	**(87,392.01)**	**-654%**	**(87,952.16)**	**-634%**

Other Income

	Month-To-Date		Quarter-To-Date		Year-To-Date	
Total Other Income:	**0.00**	**0%**	**0.00**	**0%**	**0.00**	**0%**

Other Expense

	Month-To-Date		Quarter-To-Date		Year-To-Date	
Total Other Expense:	**0.00**	**0%**	**0.00**	**0%**	**0.00**	**0%**
Net Income:	**(87,677.39)**	**-681%**	**(87,392.01)**	**-654%**	**(87,952.16)**	**-634%**

Notes: Report Period: 1/ 1/2002 - 5/31/2002
All Departments Consolidated.

Courtesy of TotalFBO Accounting and Business Management Software by Horizon Business Concepts, Inc.

> Charter sales by month;
> Student completion rates;
> Instruction hours per month;
> Daily, weekly, and monthly fuel sales;
> Fuel inventory records;
> Transient aircraft count;
> Passenger analysis; and
> Employee training records.

Post analysis action. Such action may be corrective, reinforcing, or perhaps even innovative. The general objective is to improve the efficiency and profitability of departmental operations and ensure that they contribute to the achievement of overall organization objectives.

Figure 7.8 » Management Analysis and Action

Analysis	Action Taken
Instruction hours low	Promote additional students by telephone
Low fuel sales	Revise target volume of sales
Maintenance profits low	Reduce overhead
Parts sales low	Direct mail advertising campaign
Accounts receivable high	Special collection letter
Weak liquidity position	Obtain additional credit reserves

Taking Action

The analysis of information-system data should point toward some selected action. Normally there are two alternatives: (1) to revise or adjust the basic plan of the organization for the specific area under consideration, or (2) to adjust the business activity that is taking place. Of course, there is a third alternative available—do nothing and hope things will improve. Chances are that they will worsen if ignored, so this alternative is not realistic. Typically, the action taken is to make some adjustment in the current business activity.

Selling might be accelerated, hours changed, layout altered, personnel added, or a similar activity undertaken to help meet an objective of the organization. In some situations the objective or plan of business must be revised in order to meet new circumstances, but normally the manager makes some change in the business activity to achieve the selected goals. Figure 7.8 might well be typical of actions taken by an aviation manager after completing the analysis and finding that:

1. Analysis of aircraft revenue passenger seats indicates 50 percent utilization.
2. Gross profits as a percent of sales is found to be 30 percent.
3. The return on investment (before taxes) is reported at 6 percent.

In each of the areas a careful analysis must be made and then a decision reached on the appropriate action. A later section of this chapter is devoted to specific techniques used in analyzing the overall business as well as the individual departments. Special attention should be given to the material because it is an important expansion of this section on information-system utilization.

The entire cycle of events involved in the use of the information system by a manager is depicted in Figure 7.9.

Controlling the information flow in an aviation activity is no easy task. It implies much more than just having information. The manager controls both the availability of information and the action taken as a result.

Records and Record Keeping

Although records and record keeping are obviously important, many aviation firms fail to do an adequate job. Record keeping is almost a nuisance, and hiring personnel to do it generates expensive overhead. For the manager who yearns to experience the thrill of flying, record keeping becomes an unpleasant task, especially for the individual who lacks appreciation of its benefits and the legal and tax reasons for keeping immaculate records, and who has an inadequate background in some of its fundamental concepts.

Good records are essential. Bankrupt aviation businesses typically have failed to record adequate information. Conversely, successful businesses have been found to have effective record systems. Good records, as identified in the earlier section on the components of an overall management information system, are necessary in achieving bet-

Figure 7.9 » Information Cycle

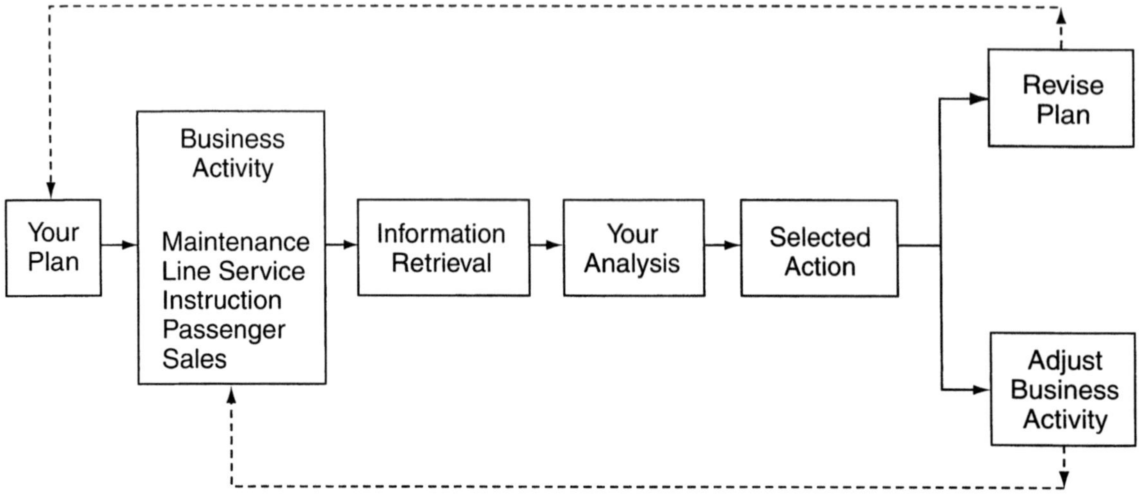

ter control over operating results. They are also desirable in supporting credit applications to bankers and other creditors and are necessary in filing tax returns and making reports to regulatory agencies. Internally, a good record system makes possible the detection of employee frauds, material waste, errors, spoilage, and other losses requiring prompt correction. It may also pinpoint employee skill deficiencies as well as internal organization problems.

Records Design

The amateur seldom does the design of records and record keeping systems very well. In setting up a system, careful attention must be given to the achievement of the objectives mentioned earlier in the chapter. System requirements associated with the three areas of managerial concern—people, money, and material—should be identified and included in the design of the system. The design of efficient, economical forms is very important. They should be prepared so that completion time is minimized while necessary information is provided. Each form should clearly state its purpose in its heading. The form size should be suitable for both filing and entering into posting and bookkeeping systems. Forms should be kept simple and capable of being completed by hand or by computer. Recurring information should be preprinted on the form. All prospective users should check any proposed new forms to ensure that they contain the desired data.

Most if not all forms for use by today's aviation businesses are computer forms—either generated on the screen or preprinted and completed on the computer printer. In addition to material, software vendors can frequently provide valuable assistance in analyzing a system and its needs. They can adapt and work up special forms to fit individual company needs. Many of these forms are the practical source documents that guide personnel in correct operational procedures as well as provide financial data.

Correspondence

Correspondence or letter writing used to be the most prevalent form of office paperwork. It is being replaced for many purposes by e-mail. E-mail has the advantage of being quick and enabling the correspondent to communicate with several people at one time. However, e-mail can be subpoenaed even when the computers involved have deleted the message, can be inappropriately forwarded to other parties, and is in general less professional and more casual than a letter. Letters are still an important way of conducting business and over the last few decades correspondence, including fax communication, has increased quite dramatically in volume and diversity. This expansion has led to the need to improve and control correspondence procedures as well as develop new techniques. Given the average cost of a letter—reading, drafting, typing, editing, and mailing, it is apparent that correspondence should be a great economic concern to the aviation manager.

Two basic approaches may be taken to improve the correspondence handled by a front office: (1) training the letter writers and (2) lowering correspondence costs. Letter writing, like other skills, can be improved by training and practice. Training can increase the readability of correspondence, reduce the length of letters, reduce the number of rewrites, and increase the number of letters per writer. There are many sources for this kind of training.

Reducing the costs of correspondence primarily involves improving the rate of production. These improvements can be achieved by the following methods:

Reducing planning time. Planning the correspondence frequently takes more time than writing the letter itself. Writing letters that are short and easy to read and using form letters, guide letters, and other prepared kinds of correspondence can substantially reduce the planning time.

Reduce reading time. Correspondence that is poorly conceived and written is frequently difficult to understand and takes longer to read. By improving the readability of letters, the reading time of recipients and the subsequent time devoted to clarifying telephone calls and correspondence is reduced.

Reducing writing time. The time taken to prepare a 175-word letter will vary depending upon its manner of preparation. The average time for a handwritten letter is 59 minutes, for a dictated letter 30 minutes, and for a form letter 3.5 minutes. To reduce the writing time for correspondence, the following guidelines are useful:

> Greater use of form and guide letters;
> Greater use of dictation and voice recognition computer software equipment;
> Fewer rewrites and fewer levels of approval;
> More judicious use of telephones including effective use of voicemail to impart information;
> Greater use of the informal reply;
> Greater use of routing slips; and
> Complete elimination of hand-drafted letters; all employees should do computer drafts even if a support person sets out and finalizes the letter.

Reducing reviewing time. The average letter receives three reviews prior to being mailed. More care in preparation or the use of form or guide letters may reduce or even eliminate the review completely. Reviews for inspection by the author or approval by top officials can be reduced in this manner. Delegating signature authority, routing courtesy copies, and eliminating perfunctory approvals will all reduce reviewing time.

Reducing word processing time. By writing shorter letters, using form and guide letters, following a simplified format, and using window envelopes, word processing time can be noticeably reduced.

Reducing delivery time. The time from preparation to delivery can be reduced by cutting the number of reviews, lowering the signature level, improving accuracy in addressing and in using priority and express mail services where appropriate and cost-effective.

Reducing filing time. Filing time can be cut substantially by using good judgment as to what should and should not be filed. For those items that require filing, only the necessary copies should be prepared and filed. The use of a subject line or filing key by the author will greatly reduce the filing time of the clerk or office manager. Another quick way to file is to keep one set of correspondence in a chronological file and another set in a subject file. Files should be purged at least annually and only key legal and financial records saved.

Using supplies and equipment effectively. Office productivity can be improved by the efficient use of computers, scanners, fax machines, dictating equipment, and printing and mailing supplies such as self-mailers, postcards, brief printed messages, and continuous stationery. Information available by computer can be stored on the computer e.g. through website bookmarking and does not always need to be printed and filed.

It should be recognized that most business activity is accomplished through words, and many of them are written or typed. The better the manager writes, the better the job is done and the more successful the organization. The goal of correspondence management is the achievement of these objectives.

Records Management

Records have been described as the working tools of management, the memory of the organization, and the source of many kinds of valuable information that's needed in the process of making business decisions. The tremendous increase in the volume of business records in the past few years has created a challenge to the organization—a challenge that grows with each passing year and with organizational growth. The reason for this growth is clear. Rapidly developing technology, a changing economy, the use of photocopying and scanning, and the increasingly complex aviation business all contribute to the growth of records and to the problems identified through the terms "red tape," "information explosion," "flood of forms," and the "paper-words jungle." The challenge to management is to bring the tidal wave of records under control and to create a system that serves the needs of the company as efficiently and economically as possible.

Record identification. For most aviation businesses the following records are normally part of the business routine:

> Correspondence, including letters and memos;
> Business forms;
> Reports and summaries;
> Maintenance records for your own and customers' aircraft—perhaps the most crucial records required of an FBO;
> Standard organizational instructions and procedures; and
> Handbooks and manuals.

One can also divide records into administrative and operational records. The administrative records, which make up 10 to 15 percent of the total, include rules and regulations, policy and procedures manuals, financial and planning records, articles and by-laws, and agendas and minutes. The operational records, which make up the remaining 85 to 90 percent, are made up of purchase orders and requisitions, claims, bills of lading, personnel records, construction records, invoices, cancelled checks, and maps and blueprints.

All records follow a similar path or cycle in their existence. They are (1) created, (2) classified, (3) stored, (4) retrieved when needed, and (5) returned to storage or destroyed. Each of these steps must be understood and controlled as part of an active records management programs.

Records management program. There are many approaches that could be taken in the identification of the various components of records management. On a practical basis, records management encompasses all those activities dealing with the creation, maintenance, and disposition of records. The following are parts of a well-rounded records-management program:

> Control of reports;
> Control of administrative directives;
> Control of paper forms;
> Control of paperwork procedures;
> Records protection;
> Microfilming or CDs;
> Mail service controls;
> Files control;
> Records retirement or disposition by shredding or recycling;
> Records storage/archiving; and
> Reviewing requests for space and equipment for records.

The control of reports becomes a major concern to the manager when he or she views the number of internal and external reports required in the operation of an aviation business. The necessity for a reports-control system to monitor important areas and to ensure that all external report commitments are met on schedule can become critical to the success of a business. Internal reports should also be monitored and controlled with the same concern, since the organization originates many of these reports. It is necessary to avoid duplication and overlapping of data and to cull unnecessary reports.

The length that records must be kept varies with the content. Land acquisition records should be kept permanently as should legal documents establishing the company. Tax records should be disposed of after the statute of limitations on audits. Annual reports should be kept permanently, as should items of potential historic interest about the company. The Tort Reform Act now provides for an 18-year limit on product liability suits since 1994; however, the period for which product, aircraft purchased and aircraft maintenance records need to be kept is still a "cradle to grave" record for each item.

The control of administrative procedures and directives is another internal problem that increases as the organization grows and is stimulated by the complexity of the typical aviation business. In order to control this area effectively, it is necessary that directives and guidelines be developed for the organization and that their implementation be administered consistently. The content of this framework will vary depending upon the needs of the organization's size, diversity of activity, number of personnel, geographic locations, and management pattern. It may range from a simple system of working procedures and informal memoranda to a more complicated structure with a formal manual that specifies the complete system of procedures and directives and their administration.

The control of forms used in an aviation business becomes an extremely important part of a records management program because of the many requirements for information and records pertaining to passenger statistics, student activity, maintenance progress, and fuel allocations as well as internal departmental activities and analysis. They are necessary to transmit information and instructions and to record data. Forms are carefully designed papers that perform, simplify, and standardize office work. They accumulate and transmit information for reference or decision-making purposes. They may be classified in various ways, but a typical system classifies them according to their business functions such as purchase forms, sales forms, correspondence forms, and accounting forms. There are three objectives in forms control: (1) to eliminate as much unneeded information and as many business forms and records as feasible, (2) to combine as many of the business forms as possible, and (3) to simplify the forms in content, arrangement, and method of preparation. With these objectives in mind, the manager can utilize the following three principles in the standardization and control of forms:

1. A form should exist only when there is a need for it.
2. The size, quality, and color of paper used in all forms should be standardized to reduce costs and confusion.
3. The design, use, and replacement of business forms should be centrally controlled.

One effective method of attaining the desired objectives and achieving efficient and economical forms is through the use of a design checklist. Such a checklist can be used in reviewing existing forms or in developing new forms.

The control of paperwork procedures is another key element in a complete management program. With rising costs in every portion of the business, the manager must control the use of personnel involved in handling paperwork. Clear-cut procedures allowing maximum productivity of the personnel will result in the best possible results. A logical flow diagram of the various steps involved in the use of paperwork will help the manager visualize the complete procedure and control the process. For larger organizations with many personnel engaged in paperwork, work standards can be utilized successfully. In some aviation businesses a program of work measurement is beneficial.

With the relatively low cost of today's personal computers and the myriad of software programs available to assist business and accounting functions standardization of forms is easily performed via computer. Computers actually reduce the amount of paperwork generated through the utilization of E-mail and other electronic communication means.

Mail-service control should be reflected through a system that is tailored to meet the particular needs of each organization. Accuracy, speed, and economy are the three key criteria. Mail-service procedures will be quite different in various organizations, depending upon size and type of business activities. Since mail is one of the communication links of an aviation business with its customers and suppliers, the mail office should be equipped, organized, staffed, and supervised to do the job effectively. Management should provide for practical organization, up-to-date equipment, written procedures, planned layout, informed personnel, and controlled costs. Each of these areas needs to be carefully reviewed by management, and action taken to ensure that the desired level of mail service is being achieved. The responsibility for mail service must be assigned and fixed. The proper equipment to expedite the handling of mail should be identified and obtained. The procedures for handling internal, as well as external communications, should be planned and written for reference purposes, for compliance and update information. The layout or arrangement of a mailroom varies depending upon the size of the activity, but the primary emphasis is on efficiency. Mail service personnel should be trained to understand and handle their mail service for the company. They should be knowledgeable about company policies, mail procedures, and postal regulations, as well as dependable, accurate and thorough. The costs of mail service must constantly be reviewed. There are many specific ways to cut costs without reducing service. Alert and trained personnel using the proper equipment in an efficient layout can identify these opportunities and take advantage of them. In today's world of high-speed communications, virtually all aviation businesses find a facsimile machine (fax) indispensable, and it is wise to have a separate phone line unless the business is very small. There are many choices of product.

File control includes the identification and development of an appropriate filing system, the acquisition of supplies and equipment, the training of personnel, and the development of working procedures that will result in the filing activity needed by the organization. A most crucial step is to ensure protection of active files through a daily process of duplication or storage. The operational adequacy of the filing system can be examined through the use of a file audit like the following one. This audit is a systematic examination of day-to-day internal operations in a particular filing operation. The following checklist illustrates the technique of auditing the filing system and the records-management activity:

1. Are files under central control?
2. Is there a records manual? Is it up to date and adequate?
3. Are files neatly maintained?
4. Is filing kept up to date?
5. Are personnel adequately trained?
6. Are all records marked with a retention period?
7. Are obsolete records destroyed?
8. Are records adequately protected?
9. Has provision been made for expansion?
10. Do different files duplicate records? Is this necessary?
11. Is employee handwriting of records legible?
12. Has microfilming been examined to determine its feasibility?
13. Is provision made for the transfer or removal of inactive records?
14. Is there an inventory of all records?
15. Have records been classified in terms of being vital, required, routine, and so on?
16. Are control reports required and submitted?
17. Is there an on-going program of evaluation and follow-up?
18. How much is records maintenance costing?

Through this kind of critical examination and its implied follow-up activities, the files of an organization can be developed and maintained at the desired level of capability. As with other administrative or support functions, the level of sophistication will vary with the size and complexity of the business. The full file audit can be of tremendous value to any organization.

Records retirement or retention is another extremely important element of administration. The number of records required to manage an aviation activity today has reached gargantuan proportions. This has resulted in stuffed files and the necessity for a planned program for record retirement. Various records are kept or disposed of according to different requirements such as the Statutes of Limitation and the stipulations of different regulatory agencies. To assist in evaluating records for retirement, the manager might consider the following:

> Value for administrative use;
> Value for legal use;
> Value for policy use;
> Value for fiscal use;
> Value for operating use;
> Value for research;

- > Value for historical use;
- > Supporting value; (Is the record necessary to support other records of importance?)
- > Physical duplication; (How many copies are available?)
- > Duplication in content; (Is the content duplicated in some other record?) and
- > Volume of file. (The value of all records should be weighed against the volume of the file in terms of equipment, floor space, and resultant maintenance cost.)

The National Fire Protection Association has developed a record classification system that should be helpful to aviation businesses in developing a retirement/retention program.[1]

Vital. Those records that underlie the organization and give direct evidence of legal status, ownership, assets, and liabilities. The loss of them would seriously affect continuing a business.

Important. Those records that are essential to the business and could be reproduced from original sources only at great expense.

Useful. Those records that have routine significance. The loss of them would cause temporary inconvenience but they are not essential to continuing a business.

Nonessential. Those records of no present or future value that should be destroyed. As a guide to everyday activity, many organizations have developed a schedule covering the retention period of their records. This schedule should be adjusted to meet the needs of individual businesses and the changing requirements of federal, state, and local laws. When records have served their purpose, tearing, shredding, or burning may dispose them of. These techniques are useful when the contents are confidential and mutilation is necessary. It is good management to account for the destruction of all important papers and to have a system that provides for the retirement of the others. As mentioned earlier, microfilming can possibly play an important part in the records retirement and retention program. Although the emphasis is normally placed upon the immediate dollar savings resulting from reduced storage requirements, the importance of preserving business experiences and history should not be overlooked. Information regarding motives and reasons for making decisions can become useful in later years.

Records storage can be considered in two forms: operational storage and inactive storage. The key governing factors in maintaining a proper balance in storage are availability, cost, and organization. Operational storage, as mentioned earlier under files control, is concerned primarily with material being used daily, weekly, or on some regular basis. Of course, records that are not valuable should be destroyed before they reach the files for storage. A retention guide will greatly assist an organization in identifying what to retain in storage and for how long. Most organizations retain far more paperwork than is necessary. The National Records Management Council has estimated that 95 percent of all corporate paperwork over a year old is never used as a reference. Carefully screening records according to a retention list and transferring only those necessary valuable records to a low-cost storage location can realize considerable savings. Storage facility requirements vary considerably. Generally they should offer protection from theft, fire, dust, dirt, moisture, and vermin, and should provide reasonable accessibility. A classification and retrieval system is essential—there is no value if having records stored if the right ones can't be found when needed.

A dynamic organization will undoubtedly experience a continuous need for additional filing space and equipment. Requests for such additional capability should be considered carefully. When the file cabinet overflows, it may be time to get rid of some records through archiving and elimination, rather than buying another file cabinet.

Communications

Success in an aviation business depends increasingly upon communications. Managers need to study the techniques and devices that make communications as successful as possible. Communication problems are troublesome and businesses should consequently give them careful attention.

The first step in developing a satisfactory communication plan for an aviation business is to analyze and identify both the internal and external needs of the organization. Careful consideration should be given to such factors as types of communications, internal layout, types of employees, workflow, customer distribution, and economic concerns. Such an analysis will consider the following areas:

> The number and kinds of communications that are transacted internally and externally;
> Frequency, duration, and timing of internal and external communications;
> The relationship between cost and service level;
> The importance of speed;
> Whether the responsibility for communication is fixed;
> The importance of exact understanding and accuracy for some or all communications;
> Whether there is a need for direct communication hookups to branches, suppliers, or customers;
> What the key internal communication system needs are; and, last but not least,
> The communications ability of the organization's personnel.

The second step is acquiring and installing the desired communications equipment and techniques to meet the internal and external needs of the organization. Electronic and regular company bulletin boards, correspondence, newsletters, booklets, meetings, suggestion systems, attitude surveys, e-mail systems, intercom systems, messenger systems, pagers, walkie-talkies and closed-circuit TVs are examples of primary internal communications equipment. The external methods of communication include electronic and regular mail service, telecopiers, facsimile machines, and telephones. Each of these areas contains a wide variety of possibilities and each should be considered carefully to ensure that organizational needs are being met as completely and economically as possible. Communications equipment sales personnel or service representatives can greatly assist in identifying needs and matching these needs with available equipment.

The third step in creating an adequate communication network is training personnel in the communication process and in how to use available communication equipment. Training in communication is a continuous effort that should include all personnel and should focus on eliminating problems that plague oral and written communications. A great deal can be accomplished through the use of lectures, training sessions, practice, demonstrations, bulletins, illustrative literature, and instruction sheets.

Duplicating Information

Office copying machines have improved so much in recent years, and the price has decreased so much that other office copying systems, such as carbon paper, stencils and mimeograph, are completely things of the past. Considerations in regard to photocopying equipment include:

> Whether to rent or buy;
> Automatic feed or hand feed; and
> Collate manually or automatically.

There are machines of every level of power and capacity. For the best quality, and to save staff time, when several hundred copies or color are required, offset printing may be less expensive.

Aviation Accounting

Accounting is simply maintaining a record of business activities. It is the systematic recording of the financial transactions and facts of a business so that periodically the status of the business and the results of its operations can be presented correctly and understandably in statement form. A businessperson needs to know almost on a daily basis about whether the business is profitable. Which lines of aviation activity are the most or least profitable? What are the cash needs? What are the working capital requirements? The business owner can get reliable information like this only if there is a good accounting system, which is a key component of the Management Information System (MIS). The manager or owner of an aviation business is normally very knowledgeable about the technical aspects of the business. However, frequently he or she does not have a background in accounting, but is an aviation enthusiast first and a businessperson second. As a result, the typical manager avoids accounting and continually delegates it to others. Ultimately, he or she becomes unable to use it as a managerial tool. Because of this tendency, the following material points out the relative simplicity of aviation accounting, which can lead toward a more successful business.

Accounting Flow

The manager accounts for business activities with financial statements such as balance sheets and income statements. Essentially, a balance sheet shows what the business owns (assets), what it owes (liabilities), and the investment of the owners in the business (net equity) at a certain point in time. The income statement, on the other hand, is a summary of business operations for a certain period, usually between two balance sheet dates. It indicates the financial results of the company's operations for the selected period of time. In very general terms, the balance sheet tells where you are, and the income statement tells how you got there. Accounting includes the "systematic recording of financial transactions and facts of business." The first step in this process is the completion of the source documents—a record of individual business transactions. These transactions include sales, purchases, payroll, and obligations such as depreciation, insurance, and taxes. From the source documents the accounting information flows through the system and becomes input to the financial statements. Figure 7.10 graphically depicts this flow of information through the accounting system. The manager should be familiar with this flow of information and the various records involved. In order to more fully understand the flow of accounting information, each step in the process is examined.

Figure 7.10 » Information System Activity Flow Chart

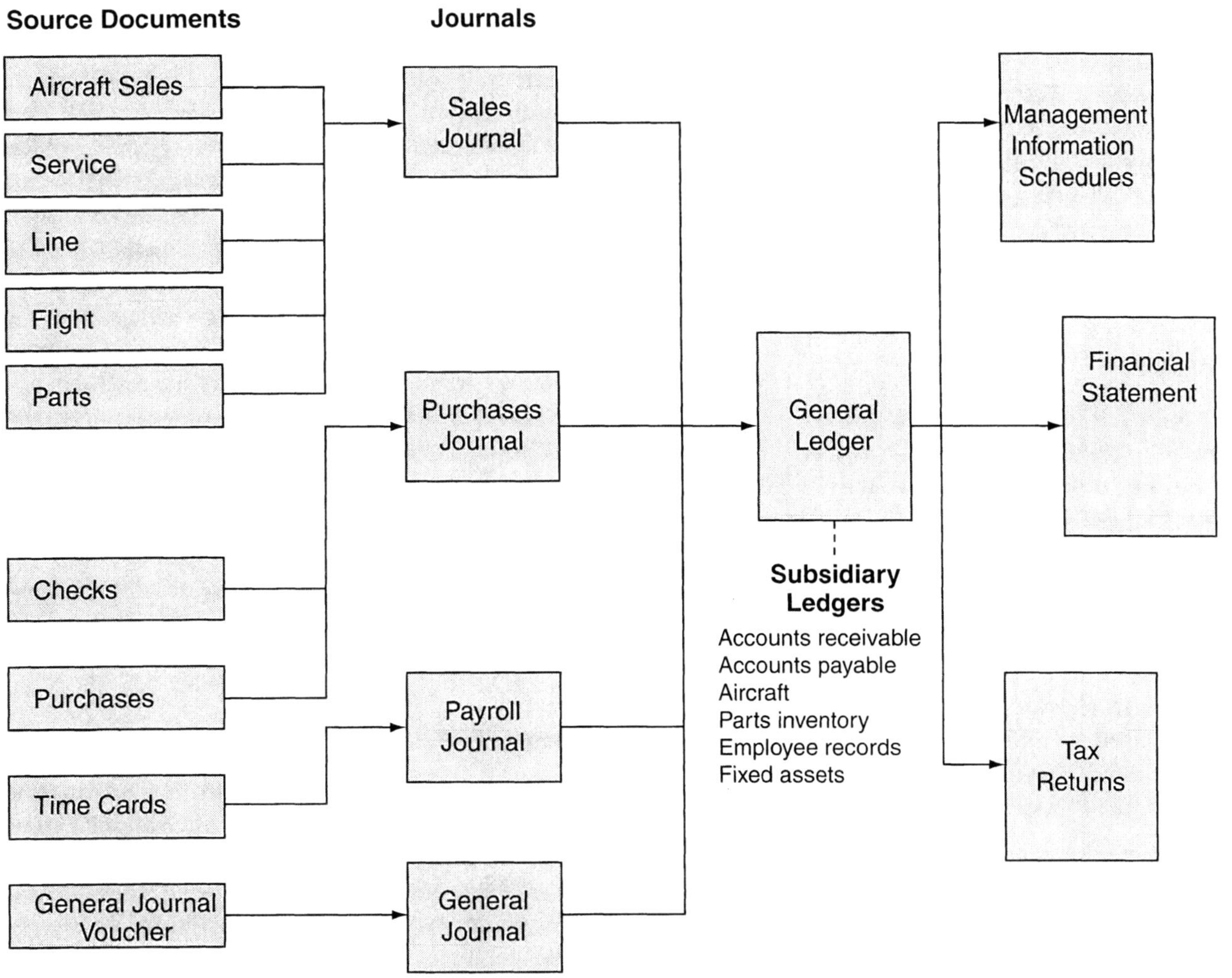

Source Documents

For the typical aviation activity, the normal source documents are sales invoices, journals, general ledger, and financial statements.

Sales Invoices will be from the following areas:

> Aircraft;
> Charter;
> Passenger;
> Flight Instructions;
> Service;
> Line activity;
> Parts;
> Rental;
> Cash receipts;
> Checks;
> Vendor invoices;
> Time cards; and
> General journal vouchers.

Figure 7.11 shows a sample computerized invoice.

Appendix VI to this book illustrates typical forms used as source documents for these kinds of business activities. Today these will all be computer-generated. The development of individual forms to meet specific business requirements should be done with great care. Forms control is an important responsibility of the central office.

Journals

Information from the individual source documents is entered into the journals—the first accounting record of the transaction. These books are frequently called the "books of original entry" and they represent a chronological record of all transactions conducted by the business. A journal is simply a financial diary. A typical aviation accounting system has the following journals:

> Cash receipts and sales journal;
> Purchase and cash disbursements journal;
> General journal; and
> Payroll journal.

In order to ensure the flow of accounting information, administrative procedures must be established that ensure the accurate completion of all forms and the timely submission of all completed forms to the accounting office. At the end of an accounting period, the column totals of all journals are balanced and posted to the general ledger. The use of a computer is essential to automatically and rapidly take care of this flow.

General Ledger

The ledger is a computer file made up of the accounts identified in the business. A separate account is maintained for each type of asset, each type of liability, and each element of equity. The data transferred from the journals is entered into the appropriate ledger account. The balances in the ledger accounts are then reflected in the financial statement when it is prepared. Any transactions during the operating period result in increase or decrease in assets, liabilities, and owner's equity.

Financial Statements

As previously mentioned, business activity is summarized and presented in the two financial statements—balance sheet and income statement. Figures 4.4 and 4.5 in Chapter 4, Profits, Cash Flow and Financing illustrated these two reports. A more detailed version of aviation statements will be utilized later in this chapter to illustrate the process of analyzing business activities. Accounting records and books of a business are not directly involved in decision-making; however, they are used by the finance manager or outside accountant to prepare financial statements and special supporting documents that are used by the owner/manager in decision-making. Since the preparation and handling of data, documents, and records has a tremendous influence on the outcome as represented by the financial statements, it is essential that the owner/manager have a thorough working knowledge of the system and be involved in some of the decisions in designing and administering it.

Accounting Activity Flow Chart

The complete flow of accounting information from the source documents to the financial statements was depicted in Figure 7.10 and is broken down into individual areas in Appendix VI. This illustration suggests the basic outline of an aviation business accounting system and is not intended to be all-inclusive. Source documents can

Figure 7.11 » Sample Computerized Invoice

George's Test Data
"Where Your Dreams Take Flight"
address
city, ST 99999
phone numbers, etc
and another line

Sales Person: George

Invoice: TU-01059 5/14/2002
9:35PM

Sold To: Rebecca Allen
1134 S. Broadway
Skiatook, OK 74070

Ship To: Allen, Rebecca

Line#	Type	Item/Description	Cr?	Aircraft	Quantity	Units	List Price	Disc	Unit Price	Extended
1	Rntl	4060.00		N2519	4.4	Hour	50.00	10	45.00	198.00
		Solo Aircraft Rental Revenue			Hobbs Out: 8054.0 In: 8058.4					
		Taxes Included in Subtotal:					Subtotal			198.00
		State Sales Tax: 15.84					Sales Taxes/Fees			15.84
							Total Due			213.84
							Added To Account			213.84

Thank you for your business, or whatever trailer message you'd like at the end of each invoice.

Courtesy of Total FBO Accounting and Business Management Software by Horizon Business Concepts, Inc.

be expanded or contracted, journals realigned, or ledgers developed to meet specific business needs. Although the balance sheet and the income statement are considered the two major products of the accounting system, other system products are extremely valuable to the manager, such as the material for income tax returns and the various information schedules used by the manager in making operational decisions on a continuing basis.

A major managerial function is organizing. This normally includes the development of an organizational structure and the allocation of functions and duties to organizational units and to individuals. The manager's primary objective is to establish work teams that can function efficiently and profitably. As a part of this effort, it is necessary to develop a flow of information pertaining to each work team or activity center in order to ascertain the actual business results. This information flow is needed to measure progress and provide direction for future management activity. A clear picture of how records are processed (Who does what? And when?) is necessary for training personnel in the process. Variations undoubtedly exist from business to business, but the general framework should be like the one presented in Appendix VI. Management must ensure a logical, efficient flow of information, provide for necessary personnel training in the use of the system, and maintain a system of checks and controls to guard against a loss of resources through inefficiencies or theft.

Accounting System

Each account is given a number that serves as its identifier and as the means of guiding and controlling the flow of information through the accounting system. At a minimum, the accounting records should provide information on:

> Assets, including real estate, equipment, inventory, receivables, and cash;

- > Liabilities to banks, suppliers, employees and others, including income taxes due;
- > Owner's equity in the firm; and
- > Sales, expenses and profit for the accounting period.

In developing a system to meet these requirements and the needs of his organization, the aviation manager can take one of several approaches. With the help of a local accounting firm and appropriate software support, he or she can (1) develop his or her own system, (2) turn to one of the many large accounting firms that have an aviation accounting system available, (3) solicit the help of large printing houses that have developed complete systems, or (4) obtain assistance from one of the aircraft manufacturers or specialty vendors that has developed complete systems for its dealers.

In view of the unique issues encountered, it would be better as soon as affordable, to acquire a system designed specifically for an aviation business and to avoid the problems of developing one from the very beginning. There are now several primary vendors of aviation software; however, this is a rapidly changing service. As already discussed, you must be careful to select the appropriate vendor.

The system developed by is an excellent example of a financial information system designed specifically for the aviation business community. The total system is made up of the following components:

- > Financial statements;
- > Chart of accounts;
- > Source documents;
- > Accounting system;
- > Accounts receivable portion;
- > Accounts payable portion;
- > Payroll section; and
- > General ledger.

All the components are fully integrated, with each keyed to the chart of accounts. The statements, source documents, and the accounting system are preprinted with the appropriate account numbers to facilitate efficient operations. It is a compact structure with the capacity for flexibility and growth. Source documents comprise an integral part of the accounting system. They are designed specifically for aviation businesses and are coded with account numbers to facilitate their use and reduce transfer errors.

Profit Center Accounting

The typical aviation business is engaged in many types of activities: selling aircraft, providing service, giving flight instruction, providing air transportation, selling parts, pumping fuel, renting aircraft, leasing space, as well as other related enterprises such as car rentals. In order to properly operate each of these activities, the manager needs to have current information on the profitability of each. He/she needs an accounting system that will properly allocate the income and expenses of each business activity to that activity so that the worth of each as a profit center can be judged. The system will also allocate company-wide overhead on a percentage basis to each profit center.

In order to develop and administer a profit center accounting systems, it is necessary to understand and implement the following.

Responsibility accounting recognizes various activities in an organization and traces costs, revenues, assets, and liabilities to the individual managers who are primarily responsible for making decisions for that activity. Ideally, revenues and costs are recorded and traced to the one individual in the organization who shoulders primary responsibility for the area.

Controllable costs are critical to responsibility accounting. These costs are directly influenced by a manager within a given time span. Thus, we must identify the manager of a specific activity and delineate the time span under consideration.

It is hard, however, to determine whether an item is controllable or uncontrollable, or what degree of control is available. There is the additional problem of trying to assign clearly the sole responsibility to one person. Perhaps several individuals exert influence over a cost center. The question is: "Who is the one person in the organization with the most decision-making power over the item in question?"

A selected manager generally excludes uncontrollable costs from his performance report. However, the opposite point of view suggests that each manager should be assigned some of these costs to become more aware of the operational problems of the total organization.

Cost allocation is an inescapable problem in nearly every organization. How should the costs of an aviation business be split among the flight department, line department, service department, and so on? How should staff costs, computer, advertising, and equipment be allocated? These are tough questions and the answers are not always clear. We need to gain insight into these problems to do a more acceptable job of dealing with profit centers and to increase the overall business profit.

Three major aspects of cost allocation include:

1. Delineating the cost center; that is, the department, product, or process.
2. Choosing and accumulating the costs that relate to the cost center: material, labor, and overhead.
3. Choosing a method for specifically relating costs to cost centers. This normally means selecting an allocation base for the individual costs.

The cost centers of primary concern are those departments or work areas that have been identified by the accounting system.

Choosing and accumulating the costs to be analyzed are basic concerns of the manager and of the information system. The system should identify the key costs and provide the mechanism for accumulating and transporting them to the manager in usable form. The actual method of relating costs to business areas will vary, depending upon the criteria selected for making decisions. Possible criteria include:

> Physical identification;
> Services used;
> Facilities provided;
> Benefits received;
> Ability to bear costs; and
> Fairness or equity.

Allocation bases for overhead. There is a tendency to aggregate overhead costs in pools and use one allocation base for each pool. The following bases are widely used:

> Physical units produced;
> Direct labor hours;
> Machine hours;
> Direct labor costs; and
> Direct materials.

The major problem in choosing a proper base is relating overhead to its most closely related cause. At the same time, the base factor that is easiest and cheapest to apply should be selected.

In allocating costs to properly develop an organization for achieving objectives, the administration must select an allocation system that influences employees and managers to take the correct action. The best system measures cause-and-effect relationships of business activity. The fully allocated versus partially allocated cost question can never be answered with one solution for all situations. There are many variables that influence the decision to fully allocate all costs. Among those frequently considered are:

> The size of the line organization;
> The sophistication of the information system;
> The relative cost of the allocation;
> The importance of cause-and-effect relationships;
> Managerial awareness of the concept; and
> Anticipated personnel reactions.

Existing cost allocation systems in many businesses are crude. However, tremendous improvement can be realized through the intelligent use of averages, the development of the "best possible" system, and the tendency toward full allocation of costs.

A suggested procedure for allocating costs is contained in the following steps:

1. Use the income statement for the business as the starting point.
2. Determine initial policy on allocation, that is, full or selective.
3. Review each item in the total income and expense columns.
4. Determine allocation unit and method of allocation.
5. Extend the selected allocations for several financial periods.
6. Analyze and compare the consequences.
7. Ask the question: Does this system provide me with the necessary profit-center evaluative data?
8. Consult with managers of the individual departments on the appropriateness of the selected system.
9. Identify additional requirements.

10. Resolve any difficulties.
11. Implement the allocation system.
12. Communicate and educate.
13. Evaluate the system after a period of operation.
14. Modify as required.

Contribution concept. The term contribution or contribution margin is an expression used in accounting but frequently not understood by managers. It is important to the successful application of the profit-center concept and ultimately to an analysis of departmental and overall business activity.

The contribution margin is considered the excess of income over the variable expenses. It can be expressed as a total, as an amount per unit, or as a percentage. To more easily present the concept, let us develop a graphical presentation of contribution margin. The three components used in the graph are variable expenses, fixed expenses, and income. These elements are used in a graph where the horizontal axis represents the number of units handled or the volume of services delivered. The vertical axis is graduated in dollars and will be used for dollars of expense or income. The first step is to add the variable expenses, those costs that increase with increasing volume. Next, add the fixed expenses, those costs that remain constant over the volume range being considered in the chart. Finally, add the income or revenue as reflected by varying sales volume. The combination provides the cost/volume/profit chart—better known as the break-even chart. Figure 7.12 is an expanded version of the chart. It identifies the components just described as well as the contribution margin. This is the same chart used in Chapter 4, Profit, Cash Flow and Financing (see Figure 4.3).

Figure 7.12 » Contribution Margin as Graphically Illustrated in a Break-Even Chart

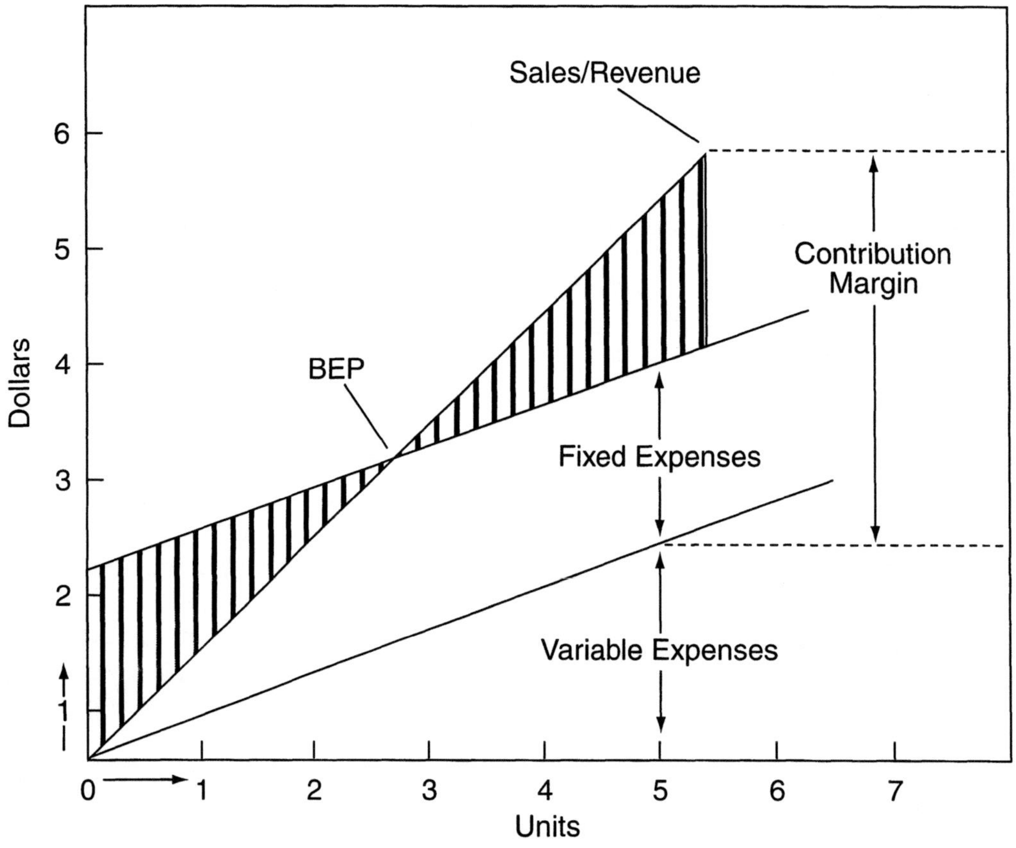

By using the definition of contribution margin as the excess of income over variable expenses, we can see from the graph that below the break-even point (BEP) that we still have a contribution (to the organization) of dollars toward the fixed costs incurred by that department or activity. The manager's goal is to sell enough units so that each department or activity realizes a profit. But in the event a profit is not realized, he or she should recognize the "sunk cost" aspects of fixed expenses and appreciate that some portion of those costs are being offset by that business income. More importantly, in the event that this component of business income is eliminated, the remainder of the business activity has to shoulder those expenses.

Information System Tools

Introduction

No small business of the 21st century is complete without a computer system, most likely a desktop networked small computer system.

Computers are to manual accounting systems as the horse is to the automobile. The norm today is to expect to upgrade every few years as hardware and software improve; the need is for the staff to be computer-literate and for change to be expected.

Computer upgrades, like the first time a computer came into the business, mean you can get there faster so you save time. But you find different ways to spend that saved time by going places you never could before. That is to say, a manager should not expect to reduce personnel or other administrative costs with a computer upgrade. He or she will find however, that after the start-up or upgrade phase, existing functions can be accomplished more efficiently and that all kinds of new information storage, tabulation, and analysis are possible. This opens up new horizons for better managerial control and faster reaction to problems.

In the 21st century the typical office is buying desktop computers for word processing and these lend themselves to other more sophisticated functions. At present the only typing jobs a computer cannot easily do is fill out someone else's (PDF) forms. Given the current pace of technological innovation, this will no doubt soon be resolved.

There are many choices of computer system, and these are discussed below.

Desktop Computers

Handling all functions in-house through networked desktop computers is becoming much more common as the capabilities of these systems increase. Advantages include:

1. It's yours, which means a greater degree of confidentiality is possible.
2. It can be a multi-user system—everyone in the office who needs one can hook in through a terminal.
3. Because of this feature, every part of the business using a terminal can feed into the same data bank. For example, the repair shop and front desk can simultaneously use it for a cash register/inventory control program, and daily reports on receipts and inventory can be tabulated.

On the other hand, if a computer network is down, it's down.

A desktop computer can conduct all the accounting functions that might be done manually by the bookkeeper or sent out to a service bureau. In addition, the following can be done with ease and speed:

1. Form letters, individually typed, with salutation and as many references to the individual as you may want in the text.
2. Sorting, for example of mailing lists by zip code, date of last purchase, aircraft owner or not, and any number of other criteria.
3. Alphabetizing lists.
4. Printing invoices.
5. Printing shipping documents.
6. Retrieval and display of a customer's account and credit status.
7. Contracts or leases with standard text plus one-time insertions.
8. Conditional printing, causing a paragraph to go in a document only if certain conditions are met.
9. Cash register functions.
10. Automatic inventory tally and reorder reminders.
11. Budget projections including any number of "what-ifs."
12. Break-even analysis.
13. Special reports on any data collected on the computer, for example, productivity, allocation, and cost trends.

14. Forecasts using linear regression.
15. Spelling checkers.
16. Tracking of projects and programs.

Selecting the Right Functionality

It is important that the operator choose a software package that has three main functions. The first is that the software will produce complete financial statements, including but not limited to, profit and loss, cash flow analysis, accounts receivable, general ledger, flight and charter accounts receivable, payroll, inventory analysis, checkbook, aircraft leaseback reports, fuel consumption reports. Before choosing a software package, the operator should list the requirements for each type of statement needed, as well as the frequency needed. One should verify that the system can generate each financial statement currently required, and be expandable as the business grows. An operator does not want to spend thousands on a system and still need an outside bookkeeper to generate financial statements. That would be duplication in time and energy, as well as extra costs.

The second area the operator should be aware of is the hardware requirements and the cost of the software. The operator must consider the cost of networking the terminals, the cost of the computers, as well as the cost of the software. The dedicated software packages determine the cost of the software by the number of terminals. The cost of the hardware will usually average about $1,000 to $2,000 per computer. The cost of networking is dependent on the company's physical layout. The cost of the software is also dependent upon the number of computers networked together.

The third area the operator must consider is customer technical support and software updates. Customer technical support has a yearly fee. The operator should consider the hours available for technical support, the length of time the software developer has supplied customer support, and the frequency of software updates. Software updates should be included in the customer support contract. Purchasing software is not a one-time purchase.

Additional computer system selection considerations:

1. Compare the degree of "user friendliness" of your system with the degree of computer literacy of your personnel. Some systems have easy to use software because of prompts and questions on the screen, but manuals that are almost unintelligible to a beginner.
2. Establish the degree of training and support the vendor will provide.
3. Clarify the warranty and repair arrangements; including what happens if the system is "down."
4. Select a vendor with a track record. How long have they been in business? Do they offer revised software? As users, do they make suggestions?

Pros and Cons of the Software Choices

Generic Business Software. When an FBO is beginning operation, many use QuickBooks, or similar generic software such as Peachtree or Manage Your Own Business (MYOB). The FBO will hire a person to customize the software for their particular needs. For example they use QuickBooks to calculate running balances on customers' flight accounts and maintenance accounts. Usually, the FBO hires a computer "techie" who is somewhat familiar with their limited operations. This can be a difficult process because it is difficult to find someone who is intricately familiar with QuickBooks and similar programs, as well as FBO accounting.

There are several downsides to using this generic software. First, as the FBO grows, the software applications become more complex and intertwine within the company. Second, customer service must be available during normal business operations. If the "techie" is employed full-time elsewhere, it is difficult to get customer service on demand. Another problem occurs when the "techie" has moved away or on to other projects. It is difficult to find another person to expand the software and interpret the customizing that has been completed. Another problem is the tracking of inventory. The problem occurs when inventory is received. It only takes a few missed invoiced parts to lose one month's profit. As the FBO grows, it usually will move on to a more complex software package.

TotalFBO. A powerful software package system available is TotalFBO by Horizon Systems. The system is complete to include flight school, maintenance, inventory, scheduling, charter, fuel, payroll, etc. The company has full-time customer support available for a yearly fee. It can generate almost any report needed by the operator, and the user has the capability to design macros for custom fit. The advantage is a complete, networked system throughout the company. The main disadvantage is initial setup time for the entire company. However, the operator can set up sections of the company, for example, the flight school, instruction and payroll in a timely but spread out manner. This system can generate general ledgers, profit and loss statements, cash flow analysis, bank deposits, payroll, etc. Horizon Systems has been in business for many years, so the customer support personnel are usually knowledgeable about the system and how to use if effectively. The company specifies:

> "Since TotalFBO™ is so broadly based, almost any type of aviation business can make use of its features. Included are features for Flight Schools, Repair Stations, Airport Managers, Engine/Accessory Overhaulers, Charter Operators, as well as FBOs. The program is modular so that users don't get overburdened with items that are not needed for a particular operation.
>
> "Features available in the various modules include:
>
> - Total Integration for Speed & Accuracy
> - Full GAAP Accounting functions
> - Accurate Invoice Pricing by Customer
> - Schedule-Flights, Maintenance, Anything!
> - Charter Quotes Adjusted for Winds & Performance
> - Hundreds of Reports
> - Customer/Employee Pilot Currency
> - Full Part 135 Crewmember Duty Log Tracking
> - Aircraft Maintenance Projections
> - Prints FAA forms: 337, 8130-3, 8710
> - Weight & Balance Tracking
> - Bar Code Input & Printing
> - Track Cores
> - Integrated Employee Timeclock
> - Front Counter Super Screen
> - Mechanics' Currency
> - Customizable Instruction Syllabus
> - Complete Flight Manifest
> - Full Departmental Accounting
> - Fuel Truck Interface
> - Automatic Credit Card Processing
> - TouchScreen Invoicing
> - Enterprise-Wide Data
> - Email Printouts in PDF format."

FBO Manager by Cornerstone Logic is similar to TotalFBO in terms of capability and support, and is an excellent software system providing packages for flight school management, charter flight scheduling, fuel sales, and tracking. The main distinction is that it ties with the customer's own choice of accounting software to create the financial and activity reports. Because of this it takes less time to set up and install than TotalFBO, yet will possibly require the additional services of a bookkeeper as well as set-up time for the installation of the accounting software. Here are some points that the company makes:

> "We have the ONLY software for aviation that can swipe credit cards, thereby eliminating your POS machine.
>
> "We have our 'FrontDesk' interface, a touch screen version of the software that speeds transactions and reduces training time.
>
> "Fuel automation is definitely our area of expertise. Not only do we have PocketFuel—our handheld fueling system for the ramp, but we connect to the Fuel Master track mounted system too.
>
> "Lastly, we give you a choice when it comes to accounting. FBO Manager is integrated with popular accounting packages QuickBooks, PeachTree, MAS90, and BusinessWorks. Many people ask why we did not develop our own general ledger program. The reason is simple—we want you to use the BEST front desk package (FBO Manager) with the best accounting package you choose. Some companies write their own accounting, but as you and I both know, they don't work."[2]

The main disadvantage to either package is that they are designed for a very specialized, complex market. Costs are high, and due to a lack of growth in the FBO industry, will probably continue to be high. There is not a mass market for such software. The advantage is that the software packets are highly tailored to the industry and are being offered by vendors that understand the nature of an aviation business and that improvements are continually being made as customers make suggestions and develop new needs.

Computer selection. This chapter cannot provide a detailed review of all the issues surrounding the purchase of your upgraded computer, but these are the key considerations:

1. Decide what things you want to automate and pick the software that can do it.
2. Select the hardware compatible with initial and future software. If you have identified special aviation or other software, make sure your system can run it.
3. Consider the expansion possibilities of your system; for example, in the future would it be useful to do graphics? If so, can your system be upgraded? Can more memory be added? How much?
4. Consider other software compatible with your system.

Computer Service Bureaus

Service Bureaus are shrinking in scope as businesses have shifted to more powerful in-house computer systems. They commonly now just do payroll and perhaps benefits. Depending on the areas you chose to contract out, they take your raw data such as:

- Checks;
- Sales slips;
- Receipts;
- Journal entries; and
- Payroll data—names, hourly rates, hours worked, withholdings.

Then they use their own computer, staff, and time to contract and produce reports and other products such as:

- Paychecks;
- Cash receipts journals;
- Check registers;
- Payroll registers;
- Sales journals;
- General journals;
- General ledgers;
- Receivables ledgers;
- Payables ledgers;
- Property ledgers;
- Balance sheets;
- Income statements;
- Aged accounts-receivable listings, with customers' statements;
- Inventory status reports;
- Payroll reports, including those to be filed with government agencies;
- Budget reports; and
- Operating ratios.

The bureau will work with you to establish a virtually seamless process, so that it's difficult to tell where the company computer work left off and the outside bureau stepped in, for the contracted functions.

If your computer service bureau is also your bank—an option—then they will even pay your bills, issue checks, and deduct the funds from your account. Your company's personnel do not need to know anything about computers, though they will still have to know something about accounting to check things over. Of course, sending everything out can be expensive. Also, the necessary turnaround time means that you cannot get instant answers and must plan ahead.

Other Devices

Other electronic devices available to managers today include fax machines (although most minicomputers, including notebook and laptop versions, come installed with fax/modem capability), cellular telephones, portable electronic appointment schedulers, and beepers. All of these devices are great time savers and help managers stay organized.

Business Security

Confidentiality and Control of Information

Even the smallest business will probably need to keep some information for the manager's use only. Locked file cabinets or keeping key information in a safe or at home are possibilities. With a computer there are controls on the system. For classified information, the user must provide a proper user code or password before the file is made available. Computer "hackers" are forever finding ways to beat such systems and computer manufacturers are forever making them more elaborate. If the company contains a computer hobbyist or fanatic, some monitoring may be advisable. Other personnel probably lack the means or persistence to bother with trying to beat the system.

There is concern about losing records through computer or operator failure. Financial records such as monthly statements should be printed on paper. All computer work should have a back-up file, which is created automatically by some systems. For really important data, a duplicate disk should be stored somewhere. No computer should cause the manager to abandon previous good habits of saving all basic records—such as register receipts—for at least three years. Power aberrations should be guarded against with a surge protector ($25 and up). Using these precautions, the risk of losing computer data is no more likely than it is for other kinds of office records. One risk from computerization is the computer "virus." This is most likely to be "caught" when one's computer system is connected to other systems. New "virus" problems occur, however, as fast as they are fixed, and this phenomenon must be taken into account.

Types of Losses

Every employer needs to watch for the possibilities of employee theft (as opposed to simple curiosity). Embezzlement is the fraudulent appropriation of property by a person to whom it has been entrusted. Theft can include many levels of sophistication and value including:

> Taking home office supplies;
> Giving unofficial "discounts" to friends and relatives;
> Making personal toll calls;
> Using company time for personal business;
> Receiving cash for sales and keeping it;
> Lapping—the temporary withholding of receipts, with progressively larger amounts being taken from subsequent payments;
> Check-kiting—depositing business funds in a personal account and covering the checks before the bank clears them;
> Payroll fraud;
> Dummy suppliers and fictitious purchases;
> Kickbacks from vendors—purchase of goods at inflated prices with employee and vendor splitting the profit;
> Padding of expense accounts;
> Charging personal items to the company;
> False vouchers for use of petty cash;
> False overtime claims; and
> Use of company postage and photocopiers for personal business.

Methods of Combatting Losses

No system where delegated authority exists is foolproof. By definition, other people are in positions of trust. Criminal and credit records can be checked before hiring but that will not identify the potential thief. What employers can do includes:

1. Set a scrupulous example.
2. Establish a climate of accountability.
3. Design an accounting system with sufficient internal controls.
4. Separate the duties of employees so that the same person does not handle incoming checks and cash as well as enter them into the accounts receivable record.
5. Obtain operating statements at least monthly, compare them with previous months, and clarify satisfactorily any anomalies.
6. Look for clues—an employee who scarcely ever leaves the desk and does not take vacations, increases in returned goods, unusual bad-debt write-offs, declines in cash sales, inventory shortages, profit declines, increases in expenses, and slow collections. These items are not necessarily indications of theft, but could be. The manager's close scrutiny of all these areas will act as a deterrent.

Summary

The information system in an aviation business, as in any business, plays a key role in helping management determine whether the business is developing according to plan. As the business grows, information systems will likely need updating. Information should be kept on four subject areas: (1) human resources, (2) financial, (3) material, and (4) aviation operations. Records and record keeping are necessary components of the information system, and they should be tailored to the needs of the individual business. Appendix IV illustrates the forms and source documents likely to be needed. Many computer vendors are now offering systems that can serve all aspects of FBO operations; before embarking on computerization, some analysis of choices and the readiness of the existing system should be considered. Many forms can be produced by computer and potentially save storage space.

DISCUSSION TOPICS

1. Name three reasons why a business information system is needed. Which is the most important reason, and why?
2. Outline the principal requirements of an effective business information system for an aviation business.
3. What are the major problems in maintaining an effective records system in an aviation business?
4. Outline in a flow diagram the origins, pathways and use of the four key elements of aviation business information.
5. Identify the purpose of each of the following ratios: (a) liquidity, (b) efficiency, (c) leverage, and (d) profitability.
6. Describe at least two examples of the ratios discussed in the preceding question.
7. What is a management audit? Give some reasons why it is not more widely used.

The task of analyzing business activity to measure progress should be undertaken regularly. Both financial analysis and a management audit (shown in Appendix III) are useful tools for this; they should be applied to individual profit centers or departments as well as to the business as a whole.

Endnotes

1. See http://www.nfpa.org/Home/Search/search_site.asp? *query=records+retention*.

2. Given the rapid pace of change in the software industry, new providers may come online at any time.

8

Operations: Flight Line and Front Desk

OBJECTIVES

- Distinguish differences and similarities in the flight line and the front desk.
- Describe the various functions of the flight line operation.
- Give examples and explain the difference between internal and external customers of a fixed base operation.
- Recognize the areas, issues, and functions aided by a procedures manual.
- Recognize the factors inherent in making the flight line a profit center for itself and other parts of the operation.

Introduction

The two operational activities, flight line and front desk, are extremely important in establishing the desired image of the business and in contributing to the efficient flow of business activity. The flight line is that portion of the organization that deals with the customer in or around the aircraft. The front desk is the visible nerve center of the business that deals with the customer who comes into the organization by aircraft, as well as those who drive or walk to the business. The flight line and the front desk are both show windows and nerve centers for the organization. Operating the two efficiently will contribute tremendously to the success of the business. Efficient and safe operation comes from a clear identification of the functions, positive organization of the resources, and thorough training of assigned personnel.

The physical location of the front desk is normally in the lobby or reception area of the business and close to the administrative offices.

The two activities, flight line and front desk, are considered as separate entities in this chapter. In many businesses they are clearly separate, while in others one can find a variety of mergers and combinations. To management, it is important that the two be organized according to the physical layout and the overall objectives of the business. In addition to the material in this chapter, job descriptions and necessary skills are described in Chapter 5, Human Resources.

Customer Service

As the first points of contact for all customers, be they pilots or other visitors such as vendors, the flight line, and front desk are the places where customers get their impressions of the company. First and foremost are the employees and how they treat all visitors. Do they have side conversations on the phone or with another employee when someone is waiting to be helped? Or, do they go out of their way to see what help is needed by someone who seems a bit lost? A recent article emphasizes that even one negative contact can destroy all the positives:

> ". . . superior personal contact from every employee at the airport is a must. . . . every encounter must be positive. If only one employee fails to greet, smile and provide sterling service, the whole evolution can prove faulty. . . . Statistics indicate that (the customer experiencing poor service) will tell at least 10 people of this incident."[1]

Staying Up to Date

Technological Change

Technology affecting ordinary office procedures continues to improve and change. Fax machines, copiers, pagers, cell phones, scanners, intercoms, laptop computers, palm pilots and other office gadgets have made a huge difference over recent decades in how business is conducted. Customers get a good impression from seeing a business that uses modern tools, and the manager must be aware of developments, see new applications of these technologies as they emerge, and budget for their acquisition and the necessary training.

Facility Appearance

The general appearance and upkeep of the facility and its surroundings can say a lot about the business. A lobby or lounge that is not kept clean and in a general state of disorder does not give a good first impression. Maintenance shops where spare parts litter the floor and tools are left out in the open in a haphazard manner do not instill confidence in aircraft owners as to the type of work done in that shop. A prospective new student pilot who is met by individuals in the office who are indifferent, and who notes that the aircraft on the ramp look as if they have not been washed in months, may be reluctant to learn to fly at this operation.

Thus, poor appearance can and does have tremendously detrimental effects on potential business. Appearance, signage, uniforms or dress code, all contribute to an image of brisk professionalism and should not be treated lightly or dismissed.

A negative example: Students from an aviation management class at a university in Atlanta, Georgia were asked to select an FBO in the metropolitan Atlanta area and critique it. In submitting their written and oral reports to the class, the majority of students were amazed at the poor customer service attitudes and the general condition of the facilities they visited. One student saw incidents of unsafe fueling, lack of pre-flight inspections, a dissatisfied aircraft owner returning an aircraft radio he had brought in earlier for repair that still did not work, and a student whose lesson had just been cancelled because the flight instructor had elected to take a charter flight instead. All of this occurred in a one-hour visit!

Flight Line

The flight line is that part of the business that greets, services, and sends off transient aircraft traffic; services local tenant customers; and supports other departments of the organization. It normally provides temporary parking for transients, fuel and oil, minor maintenance, and flight servicing for larger aircraft. In the process of performing these duties, the line department may operate fuel trucks, ground power units, tugs, "follow-me" vehicles, pre-heaters, aircraft tow bars, vacuum sweepers, pressure washers, snow removal or ramp sweeper equipment, and lavatory service equipment. It may provide gas and oil trucks, high pressure air, air conditioning (heating and cooling), oxygen recharging, passenger and cargo access ladders, baggage vehicles, lavatory service equipment, water- and food-servicing equipment, deicing equipment, servicing ladders, meals and coffee, and block heaters for aircraft engines.

For local customers, aircraft parking services are generally purchased on a monthly or annual lease. Fuel, oil, and other services are much the same for both transient and based aircraft. In a fully departmentalized organization, the line department may

A neat and orderly area makes a good impression on visitors. Courtesy of Executive Beechcraft, Inc.

also provide services to the company's own flight department and the maintenance department by parking, fueling, and washing aircraft, as well as providing similar services. Even in smaller organizations, where departmentalization is not complete, it is beneficial to identify any other parts of the business receiving line services, so that appropriate costs are allocated to the right department.

It is important to recognize at the onset that line operations are primarily a service. The activity is not a product sales business, but a service business. With some exceptions, the price of fuel, oil, etc. is much the same at any airport; the courtesy and flexibility of the service received is the main selling point and the primary reason for repeat sales. There is a wide variation in the size of line operations at the various airports around the country, the number of aircraft passing through or based at the facility, and the volume of fuel pumped. Indeed, in some businesses the flight line activities are the predominant source of income. Regardless of its size and the contribution of the flight line to total company sales, it should be operated as a profit center. This is accomplished through the application to the flight line of managerial functions of planning, organizing, directing, and controlling.

Aviation businesses must be concerned first with the pilot and passengers as customers. The customer views your line operation as the entrance to the airport and your business. The image created by the initial contact with the business is likely to be lasting and will be extrapolated to the entire operation. Since the flight line is such a critical part of the business, we will consider the key elements that contribute to the initial image: line layout, line operations, training of personnel, record keeping, and profitability.

Line Layout

To the transient pilot (or local customer) taxiing into an aviation operation, the line location and layout will contribute to that important "first" impression. Is the ramp visible and easy to identify? Is the flight line operational and easily accessible? Are signs legible? Do ramp markings stand out adequately? What is the general appearance of the line? Is it neat and orderly or does it look like a graveyard for relics of World War II? Does it appear modern and up-to-date, or does it sprout faded advertisements on the side of aged buildings, misspelled signs, and disorder? Is grass growing in the cracks of the pavement? Are tiedown anchors and lines in good condition?

The simple process of reviewing the operation "through the eyes of a visitor" may answer these questions. The next time you taxi into your ramp, review it critically to see if the layout meets the criteria of being:

> Operational;
> Easy to understand, visualize and pass through by a transient or complete newcomer;
> Positive in image; and
> Practical to support.

Naturally, the size of the ramp layout varies depending upon the volume of business and the services offered. Regardless of size, there is a great deal that can be done to develop and maintain a line that is efficient for the volume of business and that presents a neat, clean, attractive image. The physical layout of the flight line or ramp varies drastically with the number and size of aircraft involved. A small airport that's concerned primarily with light training aircraft will probably provide fixed fuel pumps, a hard surface upon which to taxi for service, and tiedown points for the aircraft. A larger facility may have a parking spot adjacent to the main terminal for discharging passengers and improved hard surfaced tiedown areas for the aircraft. Service is usually provided to the aircraft in either location by fuel trucks. There are three basic considerations that govern the size and configuration of the ramp:

1. The size of the loading area required for each type of aircraft.
2. Aircraft parking configuration; nose in, angled nose in, nose out, angled nose out.
3. Mix of based and transient aircraft.

Within these ramp requirements, aircraft can be grouped adjacent to the terminal in four basic parking systems:

1. Frontal or linear system. Aircraft are parked in a line immediately adjacent to the terminal building.
2. Open-ramp or transporter system. Aircraft are parked in groups away from the terminal building.
3. Finger or pier system. Fingers or protrusions extend out from the terminal building into the ramp area, allowing additional aircraft to be parked using the frontal system.
4. Satellite system. Small buildings are located on the ramp and connected to the terminal by means of a tunnel. Aircraft are parked around each satellite building.

At larger airports, aircraft need to be serviced at their respective gate positions. Fueling may be accomplished by trucks, fuel pits, or hydrant systems. Other servicing may be accomplished through fixed installations; mobile equipment is also widely used. Lighting, ramp marking, blast protection, passenger comfort, security, communications, and safety are concerns at all flight lines, and they become even greater concerns with larger aircraft, larger numbers of aircraft, and more passengers.

Line Operations

The operation of a flight line differs according to the size of the airport. The same functions of greeting arriving aircraft, directing, and servicing, however, will be accomplished at any location. As an example of the sequence of events in a line operation, consider what typically happens at a medium-sized airport.

A visitor's initial contact with an organization could be via the UNICOM, a direct radio link between the aircraft and the service organization. This could be via either frequency 122.7 or 122.8 Megahertz (MHz) when there is no tower or on 123.0 MHz when there is a tower in operation. Through the UNICOM the incoming aircraft, while still airborne or on the taxiway, can request fueling assistance, parking directions, inquire about ground transportation facilities and service and obtain other assistance. In general, early communications can greatly facilitate the service stop of an aircraft at a given location.

The ground usage of radio can do much to create an initial favorable impression on the visiting travelers and provide the organization with the information needed to do a superior service job.

The second point of contact with the line may be a vehicle marked "Follow Me" for the larger operations or the line service representative for the smaller ramps. The "Follow-Me" vehicle enables ramp personnel to cover a larger area. The vehicle may have the capacity to provide for immediate transportation of personnel, luggage, or supplies to the hangar or terminal. After assisting in parking the aircraft, the line representative creates a favorable impression by greeting the potential customer, inquiring about needs, and doing as much as possible to facilitate requests. Of course, the basic function of line service personnel is taking orders for fuel, oil, service, and other business needs. This is the primary reason for his or her presence. Delivering these services in a friendly, helpful manner as well as making sure that the front desk is made aware of any other needs (such as provision of a rental car) is the ultimate measure of their success.

The layout, construction, and facilities of the flight line deserve the special attention of the manager. The following considerations should be reviewed periodically from an operations standpoint to see if the needs of the organization and the customers are being met.

1. Is the line layout operational and safe from the incoming pilot's point of view?
2. Is the design and construction of the line itself adequate in regards to size, parking areas, safety in access and egress, pavement markings, weight-bearing capacity of ground or hard surface?
3. Is the designated traffic flow evident to all users?
4. Are the facilities of the line adequate for the level of activity being serviced; is there an adequate number of available and proper size chocks, and adequate tie-down facilities?
5. Are there adequate service facilities to meet expected customer needs?
6. Is the operational safety of the flight line given special emphasis? Are safe parking areas for fuel trucks identified and utilized? Are adequate fire extinguishers available, and required grounding facilities present and in use?
7. Is the flight line secure, with access restricted to authorized persons, so that transient pilots can conduct their business elsewhere with assurance?
8. Are line personnel receiving adequate ongoing training in customer service, security, and safety?

Transportation arrangements for passengers, luggage, and cargo will naturally vary, dependent upon the size of operation, the volume of each, and the ramp parking system. Passengers cross the ramp by foot or by vehicle. Smaller airports tend to rely completely on foot passage from the airport to the terminal or hangar. A red carpet is provided at many FBOs. This is especially important for outbound passengers because its function as a doormat helps keep the aircraft clean.

Baggage and cargo handling facilities will likewise vary from motorized ramps, trains, or carts to wheeled luggage racks that the pilot or passenger uses to push luggage to the parking lot. Some of the smaller airports have golf cart-type luggage and personnel carriers or a van or bus to carry passengers and luggage from the distant aircraft—particularly in inclement weather. Many passengers handle their own luggage.

The actual handling and servicing of aircraft by flight line personnel is important to the customer and to the aviation manager. These activities must be accomplished to the customer's satisfaction as well as efficiently and safely. Aircraft handling and servicing can be viewed as several distinct operations. Each requires an organizational structure, personnel training, and a high level of safety. The major flight line activities are:

- Directing the movement of aircraft;
- Parking aircraft;
- Tying down aircraft;
- Towing aircraft;
- Taxiing aircraft;
- Fueling aircraft; and
- Servicing aircraft systems (oxygen, food, coffee, water, toilet, and so on).

Procedures are needed in order to prevent injuries to personnel and damage to aircraft as well as to create and maintain an efficient and profitable activity that meets the customers' needs. Federal Aviation Administration Advisory Circular NO: 00- 34A on Aircraft Ground Handling and Servicing contains useful data with generally accepted information and safety practices for many of the flight line activities listed above.[2]

Line Administration

The administration of the flight line becomes a critical element in the eyes of the customer and in the ultimate success of the operation. The term administration is used here to embrace both the internal administration of the flight line operation and the overall coordination of the flight line with the total organization. The overall coordination is frequently the responsibility of the "front desk." This important function will be covered in detail in a later portion of this chapter.

The administration of the flight line is examined here. The most critical element when a plane arrives at the airport is the impression created by the actions and attitudes of the line personnel. The visual and mental image created by these individuals can do much for the company. The desired image is a friendly, courteous, efficient, and concerned individual that's interested in the welfare of the customer.

During the customer's stay, one way of enhancing efficiency and accomplishing successful servicing of the customer's aircraft is through the use of a simple order form. Figure 8.1 depicts a typical line service request form, generated from the TotalFBO software system. This form serves as a reminder to the service personnel, provides specific written instructions, and may be used to obtain additional information about customers and their needs.

The order form becomes a method of ensuring that the desired service has been performed and provides a basic record of what was accomplished. The internal paperwork to record and charge the customer for all services rendered will vary depending upon the method of payment. Cash, charge, or credit card may be used to settle the bill.

One method of handling this transaction is through the use of a Line Invoice Form as illustrated in Figures 8.2 and 8.3. On these computer-generated forms is space for a custom or periodic greeting or message to customers.

Figure 8.1 » Sample Line Service Request Form

George's Test Data
Client Request Report

Customer Service Request

Carry, Cachin — Arriving: 5/21/2002 8:30 AM — Entered By: George
907 E Bluefield — Departing: 5/21/2002 7:45 PM — On: 5/ 1/2002
Tucson, AZ 90302

Aircraft Services Requested

Aircraft: N1234 — Type: — Home FBO:
Pilot:
Co-Pilot: — Home Airport:
Quick Turn? No — Remain Overnight? No — Hangar Requested? No
Fuel? Top Off — Fuel Type: Jet-A — Include Prist? No
Quoted Price: 0.000
Oil? Check — Oil Type:
Wash Aircraft? No — Wax Aircraft? No — Clean Interior? No — Clean WindScreen? No
Clean Lavatory? Yes — Power Cart? Yes — Oxygen? No — Nitrogen? No
Water? No — Tug Service? Yes — Departure De-Ice? No

Passenger Transportation

Brand: Hertz — Size: Compact — Status: Confirmed
Driver: — Confirmation #: 12345432323 — By: gel
Cancellation #: — By:

D/L #: — State: — Expires: / / — DOB:

Courtesy of TotalFBO Accounting and Business Management Software by Horizon Business Concepts, Inc.

Figure 8.2 » Sample Line Invoice Form

Cornerstone Logic Inc.: INVOICE/RECEIPT

Remit to:	Cornerstone Logic, Inc. P.O. Box 1744 New Smyrna Beach, FL 32170 USA Ph: +1 904 427 4222 Fax: +1 904 427 1159

Bill to:	Valued Customer	Ship to:	Valued Customer

Invoice Date	*PO Number*	*Terms*	*Tail Number*	*Type*	*Invoice Number*
05/21/2002			43124	INVO JRN	A1-00713

Item Number	*Inv. Item*	*Description*	*Quantity*	*Unit Price*	*Discount*	*Tax*	*Total*
1	Jet A	Fuel - Jet A Date: 05/21/2002 14:37:34 Equip: Jet 1 Meter: WAC1-Front Tail=43124	150.000	2.050	.000	$49.57	$357.07
2	Ramp Fee	Ramp Fees	1.000	40.000	.000	$0.00	$40.00
3	Catering	Catering - 2 pax meals and 2 crew meals	1.000	87.860	.000	$0.00	$87.86

Notes: Fuel Price Discounted from $2.15 to $2.05

These are test notes that you can put on your invoice! Just choose [File]/[Configure Business]/[Configure Business] and click on the invoice notes tab.

Use this space for payment terms information, liability disclaimers or to put a message of the month

Good luck with your FBO Manager or Flight School Manager demo!

Customer Signature:______________________

Discounts	$0.00
Group Disc	
Sub-Total	$435.36
Tax-FET	$31.50
Tax-Flowage Fee	$3.00
Tax-Misc Fuel Tax	$3.00
Tax-Misc Tax	$3.07
Tax-SET	$9.00
Total	$484.93
Credit_Card	$484.93
	AMEXXXXX
Change Due	**$0.00**

Courtesy of FBO Manager.

Figure 8.3 » Sample Line Invoice Form

George's Test Data
"Where Your Dreams Take Flight"
address
city, ST 99999
phone numbers, etc
and another line

Sales Person: George

Invoice: TU-01053 5/ 1/200; 9.23PM

Sold To: Ronald R Adams
5710 S. Union
Tulsa, OK 74107

Ship To: Adams, Ronald R

Line#	Type	Item/Description	Cr?	Aircraft	Quantity	Units	List Price	Disc	Unit Price	Extended
1	Fuel	100LL			200.0	Gallon	2.000	2	1.950	390.00
		Avgas			Meter Start: 4579.5		Stop: 4779.5			
		Taxes Included in Subtotal:					Subtotal			390.00
		Fuel FET: 38.80					Sales Taxes/Fees			26.98
		Local Flowage Fee: 14.00					Total Due			416.98
		State Sales Tax: 26.98					Added To Account			416.98

Thank you for your business, or whatever trailer message you'd like at the end of each invoice.

Courtesy of TotalFBO Accounting and Business Management Software by Horizon Business Concepts, Inc.

The third phase of handling a flight line customer is the "send-off." The departure of a customer, although frequently not recognized as it should be, is as important as the other phases of the visit and should be specifically recognized by the organization and by the line personnel.

Every effort should be made to ease and facilitate the departure. Rolling out the red carpet, baggage help, last minute check on the adequacy of the service, help with chocks and tie-downs, start up, taxi assistance, and a cheery wave will all influence the customer to return for future business.

Training Line Personnel

The flight line is often the place where entry level personnel and part-timers are employed, because young people tend to seek these jobs in order to be around aircraft, and are prepared to handle the menial nature of some of the work—washing aircraft and pumping fuel. However, this is not unskilled work. Washing aircraft involves a gentle hand so that paintwork and fixtures are not damaged, as well as knowledge of properly addressing the runoff. Fueling requires special safety training. All activities require a customer orientation. Because it is generally the customer's first contact with the FBO, it is critically important that these junior-level staff are trained to be skilled, professional service providers.

Three key areas of training are needed—safety, security, and customer service. Additionally, line service personnel need training in dealing with unexpected contingencies and obtaining more senior help as necessary. A number of fuel companies and other organizations offer detailed training manuals for the safety purpose.[3] An individual FBO should consider its level of training needs and select accordingly from such sources.

Customer Service Training. As already emphasized, everyone within the organization must realize that they play a part in customer service. Whether it is the lineperson fueling the airplanes, the receptionist, or the FBO owner-customer service must be first and foremost in everyone's mind.

One important concept of customer training is defining the customer. Too often we think only of the individual coming through the door, or taxiing up to the ramp to utilize our business, as the customer. Customers can also include vendors, visitors, and other employees. Other employees are usually considered the "internal" customers.

Example: If the chief mechanic has procrastinated in completing the paperwork on an aircraft repair, thereby delaying the airplane's return to the line, this can impact the flight instructor and student pilot who intended to use it for a flight lesson. Not only is the student pilot, usually considered a typical or "external" customer, affected, but the flight instructor who works for the same company has been impacted as well. Thus an employee that the external customer may not even see was responsible for the company delivering poor service.

Employees who are rude to each other or who do not honor each other's deadlines and time schedules, impact the entire operation.

Whether general aviation is in a down period, with few people actively engaged in flight activity, or the industry is blooming and business is brisk, excellent customer service can be the one element ensuring customer satisfaction, which means repeat business.

Service Array and Profitability

The ability of a flight line to generate profits for the organization varies depending upon many factors, such as size, volume of aircraft traffic, competition, management, operative personnel and the general economy. Regardless of these factors, the flight line should, as already mentioned, be operated as a profit center. On the smallest field, the records should reflect the income-cost profit picture for the line operation. During past periods of economic depression, experience has proved that for the large majority of general aviation businesses around the country, the fueling operations of the flight line provided the "bread and butter" income that enabled them to survive. Large metropolitan airports have found that it is difficult to operate a general aviation activity without a fuel concession. Where the airport authority or city retained the fueling rights the airport has frequently been plagued by a turnover of general aviation businesses.

Line operations and fuel service can be profitable if properly managed. The area is becoming more competitive in terms of self-service fuel. Customer courtesies, such as coffee, restrooms, flight planning area and magazines help keep customers coming back for full service; thus the flight line and front desk always work together to ensure happy customers. Quality service seems likely to continue as the most important consideration. This means that good administration, good layout, and good employees will assure consumer satisfaction.

Fueling

The fueling activities perceived by the aviation customer are only the tip of the iceberg when the whole process of supplying safe fuel in a safe manner is considered. Owing to a number of recent changes in the fuel situation, this topic requires special attention. Numerous publications by the National Fire Protection Association, the American Petroleum Institute, and the Federal Aviation Administration address guidelines on the safe handling and storage of fuel at airports.[4] At air carrier airports, Federal Aviation Administration requirements under the FAR Part 139 mean that FBO line employees must undergo specific training. The supervisors must go through an approved fuel service course and must then, in turn, train other line employees. Certain economic aspects are summarized here.

Trends in Autogas Use

The FAA has gradually approved the use through Supplemental Type Certificates (STCs) of cheaper autogas in more and more reciprocating engines to replace 80-octane avgas. A recent article reviews the performance and safety issues involved.[5] Some aircraft, such as ultralights, were designed from the outset to use auto gas or "mogas."

The trend toward mogas is good news for aircraft owners because of cost savings. But it has been bad news both for FBOs and for government agencies collecting flowage fees or fuel taxes.

Fuel service can be profitable if properly managed. Courtesy of Executive Beechcraft, Inc.

The declining demand for 80 octane fuel (caused by many factors) means that many airports have the greatest difficulty in obtaining fuel suitable for light aircraft, thus strengthening the market for alternatives such as auto gas.

If the number of auto gas users goes up, there will be an increasing economic effect unless procedures change at airports. The volume of auto gas being brought by car or truck to airplanes and the increasing numbers of pilots transferring it by diverse means from car to plane represent a growing safety hazard at airports. Some FBO owners are now providing auto gas as a customer alternative.

Self-Fueling

The trend towards self-fueling is not just represented by ultralight operators bringing five gallons at a time to the airport in their cars. More and more corporations with based aircraft are starting to supply their own fuel. The Federal Aviation Administration's guidelines and individual public airport requirements in regard to airport minimum standards can be used to ensure that these operations are safely run. But the FAA's requirements with respect to competition at federally funded airports means that as long as standards are met, corporate or other self-fueling must be permitted.

Many FBOs when polled identify self-fueling operations at their airports. Self-fueling is to some extent inevitable, yet constitutes losses of revenues and profits, so that FBOs should be vigilant to observe what trends are occurring in self-fueling and whether with service changes, any of those customers could be attracted back to the FBO.

Some years ago, an NATA Task Force polled 112 corporate self-fuelers asking their reasons for the change and found reasons that likely still hold true although proportions may have changed:

- Better price—87%;
- More control, avoid mis-fueling, invoice errors, lack of detail—65%;
- Lack of timely service—49%;
- Better aircraft security—43%;
- No turbine fuel, had to install own—19%.

Only 42 of the 112 consulted with the FBOs at the field before deciding on self-fueling. Clearly, FBOs need to present a better customer service image to their corporate clients and find out more about their frustrations and plans.

The FBO seeking to persuade an airport-owner landlord not to permit self-fueling may be able to present the best case by demonstrating the company's high level of expertise and quality facilities. Early discussions with each corporate-based aircraft owner—staying close to the customer on needs—are very important.

Front Desk

The front desk is the nerve center of the aviation organization. As such, it represents the organization to the customer, to the public, and to the employees. It deals with the individual who comes into the organization by aircraft as well as the person who drives or walks into the business. As the hub for all business conducted by the company, it is the reception desk and the public relations center for the company. It coordinates business transactions with all the departments and strives to see that the customer receives the most efficient and courteous service possible. Its secondary goal is to ensure that all company procedures and guidelines are followed in achieving a successful front-desk operation.

As with many other aspects of the aviation business, the functions of a front desk must be provided for by every organization. The very small "mom-and-pop" operation may not have a formal reception desk, but individuals find that they serve the same function. The majority of middle-sized airports and most general aviation businesses of any size have a front desk. The very large airport will have a passenger terminal and then each fixed

The front desk is the nerve center of the aviation organization. Courtesy of Executive Beechcraft, Inc.

base operation will have its own front desk. Some FBOs operate without a staffed front desk at all, but this approach is likely to harm the business.

Procedures

As the hub of the business operation, one goal of the front desk is to ensure adherence to all company procedures and guidelines. Developing and providing a front desk procedures manual can achieve this very efficiently. In Appendix VII, the outline of such a manual is shown. Telephone skills are an important element in front desk customer service training. Being polite, friendly, and professional on the telephone requires a certain amount of practice, and the benefits can be tremendous. Knowing how and when to put people on hold, how to take a good message, how to tactfully deal with an angry or upset customer, are all-important skills to know. Companies that choose to use a voicemail menu instead of a live person on the reception phone may also be harming their business. A 2002 article in Aviation Maintenance technician asks:

> "How much business are you losing because people give up (on your voicemail menu system) and call your competitor who uses a real, live receptionist that is geared to get the callers connected with the folks that can help them?"[6]

Transient Traffic

From time to time an aviation service business should conduct formal or informal customer surveys. These may relate to satisfaction and performance, to new products or services and how they are viewed, or to problems such as noise-sensitive areas. By being conducted regularly and by addressing the contribution of this flight to the local economy as well as asking about customer needs, a transient survey could help create information to assist in ensuring the very survival of the airport. This is discussed more fully in Chapter 12, Physical Facilities. The FBO might seek to identify key users of the airport as a first step in assessing its contribution to the local or regional economy. Whatever the purpose, based aircraft owners and other local customers, such as regular charter customers, are usually easy to identify from tie-down lists, etc. But transient operators may not be so easily identified. For this reason it is strongly recommended that a detailed transient log or guest book be kept specifying:

- Company, if applicable;
- Phone number, address of pilot in command;
- Number of people in flight;
- Where from today;
- Where to when leaving;
- Trip purpose at this airport; and
- Comments on service quality.

The logbook or guest book should be placed prominently at the front desk, and personnel should be trained to ask all transient pilots to complete it. If many pilots do not enter the building, then the line staff should have a similar log for them to fill out at the same time as fuel orders. The log can also provide the manager with day-to-day information on activity and possible problems, allowing a quick follow-up with appropriate staff or customers.

Related Services

Many FBOs make part of their revenue from activities other than direct aviation services. If this is the case, the front desk staff will likely be the information-givers, schedulers, and coordinators of these services. Predominant non-aviation activities include rental cars and auto parking, followed by small stores and restaurants. More FBOs are entering the hotel/motel business; a hotel near the Teterboro, N.J. airport caters specifically to aviation and offers such items as weather information at the hotel.

FBOs who do offer only aviation services will still find themselves being asked for help on how to find ground transportation and places to stay, to eat, and places to be entertained. Many merchants give discount coupons and display materials for visitor use; coordination with the local Chamber of Commerce can supply these, and the front desk is an excellent place to offer them.

Flight Planning and Services

Pilot Services. As front desk services become more competitive, some FBOs are extending their range of accommodations for pilots and passen-

Increasingly, FBOs are offering more flight planning equipment to pilots. Courtesy of Executive Beechcraft, Inc.

gers. Traditionally, an area with chairs for flight-planning purposes is offered. A telephone link to the Flight Service Station will generally be provided. It is becoming more commonplace to also offer computerized weather information.

Flight Service Stations

Pilots are able to avail themselves of flight conditions on various radio stations especially catering to aeronautical and nautical weather, and they may also receive in-person briefings from FAA Flight Service Stations (FSS). Pilots not within reach of the nation's FSSs may get weather briefings and file flight plans by phone or computer by contacting an FSS.

The ground support systems for weather and flight planning is changing as part of the National Airspace System Plan (NAS). A consolidation of flight service stations into just 61 automated stations has occurred. Many of the new stations will not be at the same locations. Most pilots using the FSS system will do so not on a walk-in basis but through remote terminals or by phone. This increases the need for FBOs to provide comfortable courtesy phone areas, although it is likely that most pilots today also carry a cell phone.

Weather Information Systems

This planned substitution of indirect contact for direct contact under the FAA program is already being supplemented by the private sector. Advances in this sector are substantially altering the FBO role in flight planning and preflight weather information. A number of private vendors have developed weather-automated systems for private clients, and increasing numbers of FBOs are offering these services.

Other Pilot and Passenger Services

Some FBOs are now offering additional attractions such as exercise rooms, sleeping rooms, meeting and conference rooms, and clerical support services. As business/corporate/private aircraft travel increases, growth in specialized high quality front-desk services will continue, although careful monitoring is needed of these more luxurious facilities to determine if they are really used and valued.

Summary

The flight line and front desk are the first points of contact for aviation customers arriving by air and by ground. The impression created by each is strongly influenced by the physical layout, the level of upkeep, and the knowledge and friendliness of the personnel. Three factors generally create a strong impression: (1) the initial reception, (2) the provision of service, and (3) the sendoff. These characteristics affect the ultimate profitability of the whole business, since the flight line and front desk not only serve customers directly but also refer prospective clients to other parts of the business such as the repair shop.

In many aviation service businesses the true "hub" or nerve center of the operation is the front desk. The individuals serving here coordinate many customer-related activities as well as other aspects of the total business. The functions of the front desk should be based on a procedures manual that ensures a consistent level of quality regardless of who is on duty, and that contains rapid reference to key company policies on how to deal with various customer and other transactions.

Some FBOs offer amenities such as a pilot lounge. Courtesy of Executive Beechcraft, Inc.

DISCUSSION TOPICS

1. Distinguish between the flight line and the front desk. What do they have in common?
2. Name six functions of the flight line. Discuss the importance of each to the customer.
3. What should be the principal objectives of a flight line training program? Why?
4. What kinds of employees are typically assigned to the flight line and what problems does this create?
5. What factors will enable the flight line to generate profits for itself and other parts of the business?
6. What areas, issues, and functions can be aided by a procedures manual? By operations checklists?
7. What is meant by saying that the reception desk is the nerve center of the aviation business?

Endnotes

1. Morton, Dave. "A Philosophy of Airport Customer Service," *Airport Magazine,* March 4, 2002.
2. "Aircraft Ground Handling and Servicing," *Advisory Circular* #00-34A, Washington, D.C.: Federal Aviation Administration.
3. For example the American Petroleum Institute *http://www.api.org*.
4. See API at http://api-ep.api.org/search/; also NFPA 407 "Standards for Aircraft Fuel Servicing," at *http://www.nfpa.org/Codes/nfpa_codes_and_standards/list_of_nfpa_documents/nfpa_407.asp*; "Aircraft Fuel Storage, Handling, and Dispensing on Airports," *Federal Aviation Administration Advisory Circular* 150/5230-4; and "Aircraft Ground Handling and Servicing," *Federal Aviation Administration Advisory Circular* 00-34A.
5. Szymanski, John. "Autogas vs. Avgas," *Aviation Maintenance Technician,* March 2002.
6. de Decker, Bill. "First Impressions Count!" *AMT Online,* October 2001.

9

Flight Operations

OBJECTIVES

- Understand the requirements necessary for an air taxi operator to be approved for Part 135 operations.
- Recognize the differences between air taxi and commuter operations.
- Discuss the problems and opportunities inherent in a flight instruction program.
- Describe several opportunities involving actual flight operations to ensure a profitable business.
- Explain the role flight simulators play in a flight instruction program, including benefits to both the business and the student.

Introduction

Flight operations refer to the provision of aircraft and/or personnel for flight services and the monitoring of these activities to ensure profitability.

Types of Flights

The reader should refer to the "Taxonomy of General Aviation" shown in Chapter 1, Figure 1.4. The following types of flight service may occur:

Air Transportation

- Charter;
- Air taxi;
- Aircraft rental;
- Aircraft leasing;
- Aircrew and ferry services;
- Air cargo; and
- Air ambulance.

Use of Aircraft for an Activity While Airborne

- Flight instruction;
- Aerial patrol-power line, pipeline, forest, fire, highway, border, and so on;
- Aerial advertising-banner towing;
- Aerial application such as crop dusting, seeding, fertilizing;
- Sightseeing services;
- Helicopter operations;
- Gliding and sailplaning;
- Ballooning;

> Parachuting;
> Ultralights;
> Aircraft demonstrations;
> Medical evacuation;
> Search and rescue;
> Fish spotting; and
> Aerial photography.

These lists show only some of the types of flight service that may be offered. Each must be considered in terms of what types of client are involved—business and executive, other commercial clients, flight students, or sport and recreational flyers.

Market Trends

Flight operations constitute a key profit center for many FBOs. Numerous services can be offered, some highly compatible with one another and others perhaps less so.

In the late 1970s and 1980s, the U.S. general aviation industry saw a massive reduction in aircraft shipments and a decline in active aircraft. Some causes were discussed in Chapter 1. Even though aircraft output has been rising in the past decade, the GA industry continues to be volatile and unpredictable, and seems, as a result of 9/11/01 and other factors, to be more than previously subject to regulations, procedures and restrictions that make business-as-usual difficult. As a result, the profit-seeking FBO must constantly be alert for new flight operation market opportunities. In recent years FBOs around the country have become involved in such diverse areas as:

> Air ambulance;
> Airline aircraft servicing;
> Aerobatics;
> Aircraft management;
> Aerial fire fighting;
> Air taxi service;
> and many others.

System Issues Affecting Flight Operations

Seven main issues affect general aviation flight operations:

1. Loss of access to certain airports and airspace due to the terrorism of 9/11/01.
2. Loss of airports and restricted access to airports, before 9/11/01.
3. Loss of access to air carrier airports in key locations.
4. Changes in airspace usage.
5. Lack of understanding of the economic benefits of aviation both as a form of transportation and as a means of performing various functions while airborne.
6. Increasing levels of complaint, from airports all around the country, about aircraft and airport-area noise levels.
7. A volatile customer base meaning that business planning, and planning for time and money to spend on the above issues, are difficult to budget.

Many of these issues are discussed in further depth in Chapter 12, Physical Facilities.

Terrorism and After. General aviation flight operations may never be quite the same again after the terrorist attacks of 9/11/01. Flight schools were shut down; a considerable amount of the national airspace was closed to low level flights. For example, a lead article on NBAA's web site dated April 25, 2002 complains that "America's businesses still do not have access to DCA"—Reagan National Airport (DCA) prior to 9/11/01 handled 60,000 GA operations per year of which 90 percent were business aviation; these flights were still not permitted to land almost 9 months later.[1]

Access to Major Airports. The nation's busiest airports and airspace were becoming more congested in the 1990s, and the impacts of 9/11/01 seem likely to be only temporary—the twelve-year growth projection is about the same. Congestion is due to airline traffic growth, fewer air traffic controllers, airline schedules focused on peak periods, and hub-and-spoke airline service development that causes more landings and takeoffs per passenger trip. The terrorist attacks of 9/11/01 have reduced airline enplanements and put a temporary hold on aviation growth; however, as the public becomes more assured about flying again, it seems likely that the upward growth trend, and congestion at major airports, will continue. As a result of growth pressures, various pricing and management strategies have evolved to reduce the access of general aviation aircraft to certain airports and airspace areas in order to reserve space for airline aircraft.

This trend particularly affects business aviation, where passengers often seek the same major city destinations as the airlines. Rural and recreational general aviation is less severely impacted. The general aviation industry and flight operators such as FBOs need to be cognizant of this trend and vocal through the various aviation lobby groups, in order to ensure that general aviation continues to have access to the aviation system. While all airports with public funds are intended to be open to all users, the reality of the situation is a little different, particularly at the nation's most crowded airports. The airport "slot" system whereby airlines compete for available landing slots, leaves little room for non-scheduled flights. NBAA describes how one such problem unfolded:[2]

> "The most important battle for airport access, however, would be over the right to operate at Boston's Logan International Airport. In March 1988, the Massport airport authority unveiled its Program for Airport Capacity Efficiency (PACE), which used high fees to discourage use of the airport by smaller aircraft. Within a month, NBAA, and other interested parties filed suit in federal court to block the PACE plan but were unsuccessful. However, by the end of the year, the US Department of Transportation (DOT) ruled that PACE was inconsistent with national transportation policy, and in August 1989, an appeals court found that pace was contrary to federal law. Fees that had been collected at Logan while the PACE plan was in effect during 1988 were refunded."

Changes in Airspace Usage. A number of other issues, developing before 9/11/01, are affecting general aviation access to airports. For example, increased globalization and international GA flying mean integration with airspace procedures in other parts of the world. For example, the DRVSM program is in the planning stages. The following summary was created by NBAA:[3]

> **"Don't Delay Your DRVSM Preparations!**
>
> "With Reduced Vertical Separation Minima (RVSM) one of the many solutions being applied around the globe to safely increase capacity in airspace that is becoming progressively more congested, NBAA Members should be aware that Domestic RVSM (DRVSM) soon will be coming to the United States. It is vital that Members start preparing now for its implementation.
>
> "RVSM started in the North Atlantic (NAT) a few years ago and has since spread to European, Northern Pacific (NOPAC) and Western Atlantic Region (WATRS) airspace. RVSM is exclusionary in all of these regions from FL 290 to FL 410 inclusive. To fly in RVSM airspace, older aircraft must go through an equipment upgrade, and all aircraft must go through monitoring requirements to be certified. According to the FAA, at least some level of implementation of DRVSM will take place in the United States by December 2004. An FAA Notice of Proposed Rulemaking officially defining requirements and procedures for DRVSM will be published in April 2002 (sic) with a Final Rule expected by June 2003. The FAA is actively working with the NBAA on specifics, such as the flight levels affected and a final implementation date. A DRVSM Letter of Authorization (LOA) will be necessary for operations within DRVSM airspace, requiring not only selected hardware and software upgrades but also crew and staff training.
>
> ". . . NBAA Staff members anticipate that the downtime to equip aircraft will vary from airframe to airframe; it also will vary depending on the backlog at the time the aircraft enters the shop. One large OEM has estimated that it may take three to five years to have their fleet equipped and certified. In addition, NBAA staff members estimate that the cost to equip aircraft will vary widely, from \$35,000 to \$200,000 depending upon airframe and present state of equipage.
>
> "NBAA urges Members not to put off preparations for DRVSM, such as scheduling installations and arranging height-monitoring flights. Those operators that do not meet DRVSM requirements will not be permitted to fly in RVSM airspace. Instead, those operators will be forced to fly at altitudes higher than the RVSM airspace, if the aircraft is capable, or below it, which is inefficient, dictating possible refueling stops for flights that might otherwise be conducted non-stop.
>
> "Preparation for DRVSM will follow the FAA 91-RVSM document and approval process, which could take from 90 days to six months depending on solution and service center capacity. Operators holding LOAs will be in compliance when DRVSM is implemented.
>
> "NBAA Staff members have worked to ensure that DRVSM implementation is performed in such a way as to cause the least inconvenience and expense to the Association Membership and have the least possible impact on the small number of

Member aircraft that cannot be equipped (due to equipment or cost limitations) for RVSM operations. Association Members with aircraft that cannot be equipped for RVSM operations are encouraged to contact the aircraft manufacturer or product support organization and communicate their desires for a DRVSM solution.

"The FAA hosts a well-documented RVSM Web site at www.faa.gov/ats/ato/rvsm1.htm and a new DRVSM site at www.tc.faa.gov/act-500/niaab/drvsm/Default.asp. NBAA provides RVSM information at www.nbaa.org/member/rvsm. NBAA Members should visit these Web sites to familiarize themselves with RVSM and DRVSM news and requirements as they develop."

In addition, as a result of 9/11/01, TSA is proposing new security rules including new fingerprint criminal history checks in some cases for charter flights in aircraft over 12,500 pounds. Industry organizations have commented that this proposed rule making is ambiguous and problematic, thus it may take some time to get finalized, although the Transportation Security Administration (TSA) is seeking an implementation date by late 2002.[4]

Economic Benefits of Aviation. NBAA and GAMA recently commissioned some work by the accounting firm Arthur Andersen to examine the likely effects of owning a corporate aircraft on the profits of the company involved. They found very significant benefits.[5] These will only increase as the difficulties of airline transportation continue, with 20 percent fewer flights, long lines, and tiresome security inspections at airline airports. The huge growth in fractional aircraft ownership will be enhanced by these factors too.

Airport Noise. No FBO flight department can succeed over the long haul without a good understanding of airport noise. Three components of noise all have the same effect on airport neighbors. These three are:

> Noisy aircraft engines;
> Noisy flight operations techniques; and
> Proximity to the flight path of unsuitable and noise-sensitive land uses.

The issue of airport noise is by no means new, and it has not been solved. Noise control can come from three techniques—quieter aircraft engines (addressed through FAR Part 36), different flight techniques, and removal of land uses that are noise sensitive. Aircraft engines are now much quieter than in the past and this topic is not addressed in this book. Some state aviation agencies (e.g. Oregon, Massachusetts) had active noise abatement assistance programs for smaller airports as early as the 1970s. FAA through elimination of noisier Stage 2 aircraft has helped to remove the noisiest portion of the noise source. The primary conflict is institutional, in the sense that while FAA controls aircraft in the air—and holds firmly to the need for an interstate airport system that does not have a patchwork quilt of operational restrictions such as night curfews—it is local jurisdictions that control land use around airports.

Most metropolitan airports fifty years ago were well outside the urban boundary, and homes and other noise-sensitive uses have simply encroached on airports as the built-up area has grown. At the same time, annual operations have grown from a few score to in many case, hundreds of thousands of flights in and out, and people who bought homes when the airport had negligible activity levels feel justifiably frustrated that their environment has changed so much.

Local jurisdictions may put the needs of housing expansion and economic development higher in their priorities than airport protection. Pilots and airport business owners tend not to live in the jurisdiction right around the airport but further afield; airports don't generally contribute much—and are perceived as contributing nothing—to the local economy—and thus conflict situations continue to be permitted and even encouraged.

No longer can FBOs stand aside and view this as the airport manager's or other operators' problem. The FBO owner manager must budget some of his time each week to networking with the Chamber of Commerce, with elected officials, and with community members, to convey more fully what their airport does, and for whom, and to identify and fix and problems caused by his or her business. These are necessary activities for airport survival. This topic is addressed more in Chapter 12, Physical Facilities.

In terms of flight operations, the FBO both in a flight school operation and in operating the flight department has a tremendous opportunity for applying good noise abatement flying techniques.

Like justice, these not only need to be done, but seen to be done. Noise abatement techniques are important for the individual business at a given airport even if no procedures have been adopted by the airport as a whole. If all students, pilots, tenants and customers are encouraged by seeing signs, receiving verbal instructions and being provided with handouts about the need for quiet flight, then when there are noise complaints and the FBO owner has to respond to them, he or she will be able to describe the detailed efforts that the business is making to keep noise to a minimum over sensitive areas. Then, if noise complaints are made about that particular FBO, the manager will be able to demonstrate that all customers and employees follow written posted procedures for flap settings, thrust settings, areas to avoid flying over and so on. These procedures can be tailored to the individual airport in consultation with the airport manager, tenants groups and tower, if the latter exist, and should draw on published materials made available to members by AOPA, NATA, NBAA, and other industry groups.

This chapter addresses flight operations. Effort may need making too to ensure that airport management does what is needed. The photo shows a noise abatement sign that clearly is not high on anybody's radar—the paint is peeling and the print is likely too small in any case for taxiing pilots to be able to see it and really relate to its meaning.

AOPA, NBAA and others offer fly-friendly techniques involving steeper departure paths, quieter flap settings, use of minimum thrust (safely, of course) to depart the area before going to full throttle, and so on. Many airports have adopted such procedures and can share them with airports that have not yet developed their own.[6]

How effective is this sign to taxiing pilots?

Operational controls can include such steps as:

1. Use of a preferential runway system—a runway whose flight path lies over the least noise-sensitive areas, used in as many wind conditions as possible.
2. Displaced landing thresholds so that arriving planes are at higher altitude over noise sensitive areas and land farther along the runway.
3. Longer runways so that departing aircraft can start their take-off roll further back and achieve greater altitude before being over sensitive areas.
4. Turning away early out of the flight pattern; adoption of a unique flight pattern for that airport to avoid sensitive areas after departure.
5. Cutting back the throttle after a certain altitude or when airspeed has been reached after departure.
6. Limitations on certain types of activity during certain hours of the week.
7. Limitations on take-off or landing noise levels above a certain decibel level (set with guidance from FAA and applied consistently).
8. Reversal of the landing pattern to avoid sensitive areas.

While such operating restrictions may be frustrating to pilots, in some places they may be essential to the continued availability of that airport, and cooperation must be required by the aviation businesses in relation to aircraft they rent and lease out. This can be done by such actions as:

1. Teaching noise-abatement techniques in ground school and flying lessons.
2. Requiring renters to sign a promise to follow the FBO's operating procedures.
3. Maintaining a clear and responsive process for receiving and dealing with complaints, even if the problem was not caused by the FBO's aircraft.
4. Close coordination with the airport owner/landlord on what is happening on the rest of the field in terms of noise abatement and complaints.

NBAA is one industry organization that has been addressing airport noise since the 1960s. Figure 9.1 shows their recommended approach and departure techniques to minimize noise. More details are available in their full noise abatement document.[7]

AOPA also has noise abatement techniques available, as shown in Figure 9.2.[8]

Volatile Customer Base. The number of pilots has fluctuated over the past few decades, as has the number of aircraft. Without steady growth trends, most industries have problems planning for the future and identifying the strong markets to focus on and weak markets to avoid. Aviation is very much this way and although there are promising trends, they may prove to be just more fluctuations. The FBO may be best able to address this problem by having reasonably diverse services, by staying very close to the underlying causes of apparent trends, and by acting quickly when analysis shows that a new market can in fact be relied on the make a profit for the company. Some flight operations activities may be tried and dropped. Document what happened and why the project did not continue!

Choosing What Services to Offer

Certain types of flight operation will be in heavy demand at a certain airport. For example, an island or resort community may have a strong demand for air taxi and sightseeing trips. A metropolitan airport may have a high level of business charters and rentals, whereas a rural airport may be extensively involved in aerial patrol and agricultural application. Because of the varied types of aircraft required for many of the more specialized functions, the FBO will have to be selective about what services to offer. Where several FBOs are on the same field, they may each specialize in specific areas and avoid direct competition. Also, on many fields small specialized operators handle just one type of activity, such as a parachute center, glider service, aerial photography, agricultural application, etc. Whether these single-service operators can be defined as FBOs is debatable. FAA guidelines do not specify a minimum amount of services in order to justify the title, but some individual airport minimum standards do.[9] The choice of what to offer depends on the clients' needs, the services offered elsewhere on the field or in the region, the owners' preferences, and the expected profit from each area. Chapter 3, Marketing discussed the development of forecasts for various types of activity, and should be referred to here as the Flight Operations business plan is developed.

Figure 9.1 » NBAA Noise Abatement Techniques

NBAA Standard Departure Procedure

Figure 1—Diagram of Standard Departure Procedure

1. Climb at maximum practical rate at V2+20 Knots indicated airspeed (KIAS) to 1,000 feet above field level (AFL) with takeoff flap setting.
2. At 1,000 feet AFL, accelerate to final segment speed (Vfs) and retract flaps. Reduce to a quiet climb power setting while maintaining 1,000 FPM maximum climb rate and airspeed not to exceed 190 KIAS until reaching 3,000 feet AFL. If ATC requires level off prior to reaching 3,000 feet AFL, power must be reduced so as not to exceed 190 KIAS until at or above 3,000 feet AFL. (See note below)
3. At 3,000 feet AFL and above, resume normal climb schedule with gradual application of climb power.
4. Observe all airspeed limitations and ATC instructions.

NOTE: It is recognized that aircraft performance will differ with aircraft type and takeoff conditions; therefore, the business aircraft operator must have the latitude to determine whether takeoff thrust should be reduced prior to, during, or after flap retraction.

NBAA Close-In Departure Procedure

Figure 2—Close-In Departure Procedure

1. Climb at maximum practical rate at V2+20 KIAS to 500 feet AFL with takeoff flap setting.
2. At 500 feet AFL, reduce to a quiet climb power setting while maintaining 1,000 FPM maximum climb rate and V2+20 KIAS until reaching 1,000 feet AFL.
3. At 1,000 feet AFL, accelerate to final segment speed (Vfs) and retract flaps. Maintain quiet climb power, 1,000 FPM climb rate, and airspeed not to exceed 190 KIAS until reaching 3,000 feet AFL. If ATC requires level off prior to reaching 3,000 feet AFL, power must be reduced so as not to exceed 190 KIAS. (See note below)
4. At 3,000 feet AFL and above, resume normal climb schedule with gradual application of climb power.
5. Observe all airspeed limitations and ATC instructions.

NOTE: It is recognized that aircraft performance will differ with aircraft type and takeoff conditions; therefore, the business aircraft operator must have the latitude to determine whether takeoff thrust should be reduced prior to, during, or after flap retraction. Also, aircraft in excess of 75,000 lbs. GTOW operating under FAR, Part 121, Part 125, or Part 135 may not be permitted to comply with this procedure.

NBAA Approach and Landing Procedure VFR & IFR

Figure 3—Approach & Landing Procedure VFR & IFR

1. Inbound flight path should not require more than a 20 degree bank angle to follow noise abatement track.
2. Observe all airspeed limitations and ATC instructions.
3. Initial inbound altitude for noise abatement areas will be a descending path from 2,500 feet AGL or higher. Maintain minimum airspeed (1 .3Vs+20 KIAS) with gear retracted and minimum approach flap setting.
4. At the final approach fix (FAF) or not more than 4 miles from runway threshold, extend landing gear. Final landing flap configuration should be delayed at pilot's discretion to enhance noise abatement.
5. During landing, use minimum reverse thrust consistent with safety for runway conditions and available length.

Source: National Business Aircraft Association

Figure 9.2 » AOPA Guidelines for Noise Abatement

Airport Noise: We can make a difference

Through a concerted effort, and by demonstrating your sensitivity to the concerns expressed by the community as it relates to airport noise, your relationship with those affected by airport noise can be significantly improved. But we must be willing to VOLUNTARILY take the steps necessary to be thoughtful to our fellow community members. Should voluntary efforts not be considered important to the airport, you may find your airport facing local legislation to fix the problem, and this solution isn't always in the best interest of the airport or its users.

Here are some ideas that might be applied voluntarily to improve the noise impact at your local airport:

Pilots—

> Be aware of noise sensitive areas, particularly residential areas near airports you use, and avoid low flight over these areas.

> Fly traffic patterns tight and high, keeping your airplane in as close to the field as possible.

> In constant-speed-propeller aircraft, do not use high rpm settings in the pattern. Prop noise from high-performance singles and twins increases drastically at high rpm settings.

> On takeoff, reduce to climb power as soon as safe and practical.

> Climb after liftoff at best-angle-of-climb speed until crossing the airport boundary, then climb at best rate.

> Depart from the start of the runway, rather than intersections, for the highest possible altitude when leaving the airport vicinity.

> Climb out straight ahead to 1,000 feet or so (unless that path crosses a noise-sensitive area). Turns rob an aircraft of climb ability.

> Avoid prolonged runups, and do them inside the airport area, rather than at its perimeter.

> Try low-power approaches, and always avoid the low, dragged-in approach.

> If you want to practice night landings, stay away from residential airports. Do your practice at major fields where a smaller airplane's sound is less obtrusive.

Instructors—

> Teach noise abatement procedures to all students, including pilots you take up for a biennial flight review. Treat noise abatement as you would any other element of instruction.

> Know noise-sensitive areas, and point them out as you come and go with students.

> Assure that your students fly at or above the recommended pattern altitude.

> Practice maneuvers over unpopulated areas, and vary your practice areas so that the same locale is not constantly subjected to aircraft operations.

> During practice of ground-reference maneuvers, be particularly aware of houses or businesses in your flight path.

> Stress that high rpm prop settings are reserved for takeoff and for short final but not for flying the pattern. Pushing the prop to high rpm results in significantly higher levels of noise.

> If your field is noise sensitive, endorse your students' logbooks for landing at a more remote field, if available within a 25-nm range, to reduce touch-and-go activity at our airport.

Figure 9.2 » Continued

Fixed-Base Operators—

> Identify noise-sensitive areas near your airport, and work with your instructors and customers to create voluntary noise abatement procedures.

> Post any noise abatement procedures in a prominently visible area, and remind pilots who rent your aircraft or fly from your airport of the importance of adhering to them.

> Mail copies of noise abatement procedures with monthly hangar and tiedown bills. Make copies available on counter space for transient pilots.

> Assure that your instructors are teaching safe noise abatement techniques.

> Call for use of the least noise sensitive runway whenever wind conditions permit.

> Try to minimize night touch-and-go training at your airport if it is in a residential area. Encourage the use of nonresidential airports for this type of training operation.

> Initiate pilot education programs to teach and explain the rationale for noise abatement procedures and positive community relations.

And For The Surrounding Community—

> Send a copy of the noise abatement pattern established for your airport, along with a brief explanation of its purpose, to the local newspaper. Let the public know PILOTS ARE CONCERNED.

> See that the pattern, approach, and departure paths are designated on official ZONING AND PLANNING MAPS so real estate activity is conducted in full awareness of such areas.

> Lobby for land use zoning and building codes in these areas that are compatible with airport activity and will protect neighboring residents.

> Stress, publicize, and communicate the value of the airport to the community and how its operation adds to the safety, economy, and overall worth of the area.

> Sponsor "airport days" at the airport to involve nonfliers with the business and fun of aviation and possibly attract potential new pilots.

> Encourage beautification projects at the airport. Trees and bushes around the runup and departure areas have proven effective in absorbing ground noise from airplanes.

Source: Aircraft Owners & Pilots Association

Organization

Organizing the aviation business for safe, profitable flight operations is one of the most important aspects of the entire company. Goals and objectives must be identified, structure formulated, responsibilities assigned, duties outlined and understood, rules, regulations and procedures established, and controls provided in order to ensure that flight operations goals are achieved safely and profitably.

For each of the major flight categories listed above, this chapter reviews the nature of the operation and its requirements.

Air Transportation

Benefits

The use of private business aircraft as a means of transportation is increasing faster than many other segments of general aviation. Since the Airline Deregulation Act of 1978, scheduled passenger service, while increasing in quantity, has diminished in terms of available non-stop flights. One reason for this is the adoption by major and national airlines of a "hub-and-spoke" system of operation, and another is the desire, vastly increased since 9/11/01, of operations for the heightened security, private work environment and reduced trip times that use of a corporate aircraft can facilitate.

While some airlines such as Delta have been using the hub-and-spoke concept for over 50 years, for many others deregulation triggered the growth of this concept. At the time of deregulation, the major carriers had less than 50 percent of their total domestic capacity devoted to hub flying. By the late 1980s these same carriers allocated over 80 percent of their domestic seat miles to hub-and-spoke flying, and this pattern has continued into the 21st century.

Reasons from the airline point of view for hub development include:

1. Scheduling efficiency—fewer aircraft to serve the same points.
2. New market synergy—one new spoke added to a hub adds many new markets.
3. Market control—connections more easily made on the same carrier through the same hub point.
4. Market fragmentation—less service available for small points and greater number of connections to complete the trip.

In addition to hub and spoke implications, the initial reduction in airline fares after deregulation has generally been replaced by substantial fare increases. The cost is especially greater when the ticket is booked without much advance notice, as many business trips are.

These factors: hub development, higher airfares, and security concerns; combine to make private air transportation comparatively more appealing to the busy executive.

Many feature articles have been written in the past few years that address the benefits of business flying. These benefits include:

1. Increasing the executive's effective time by as much as 100 percent.
2. Elimination of tiresome and slow airline processing since 9/11/01.
3. Permitting en route business conferences to be held in privacy.
4. Reducing overnight hotel and meal costs by eliminating awkward airline connections and circuitous routing.
5. Ability to access over 10,000 small communities compared with a between four and five

Different services require different types of aircraft. This Super Cub has tundra tires for agricultural use.

hundred by airline and far fewer with nonstop flights.

6. Ability to increase contact between managers through ease of travel between branches.
7. Ability to run an enterprise with fewer corporate staff because of mobility to all divisions.
8. No lost baggage or missed flights.

For many corporations, the gradual increase in use of private business aircraft follows this progression:

1. Airline trip is made involving multiple connections, take-off delays, and overnight stops to accomplish business.
2. Urgently needed business trip is required and business traveler cannot get there in time and back using airlines.
3. Charter flight is booked through local FBO.

For several years, a leading aviation magazine reported studies of aviation use by the nation's top companies—the Fortune 1000. Year after year, the aircraft-using companies, which now number about half the group, had about 80 to 90 percent of the gross sales, the profit, and the return on investment and about twice the labor productivity. The non-aircraft operating half of the group had only 10 to 15 percent of the performance. More recently, there appears to be a causal connection as identified by the recent GAMA/NBAA study performed by Arthur Andersen. To the aviation business, capturing the local demand for business air travel can be a rewarding and profitable activity.

Charter and Air Taxi

Charter operations are the nonscheduled flights that carry passengers or cargo when the party receives the exclusive use of the aircraft. Certificated air carriers may negotiate charter agreements, as they often are for tourist flights, or by general aviation businesses.

Air-taxi flight activity describes the semi scheduled and nonscheduled commercial flights of general aviation businesses. Individuals purchase air transportation as they would a taxicab. Light-to-medium weight aircraft are used to carry passengers and cargo to and from the small communities that do not have enough traffic for scheduled airline service and where scheduled airlines cannot serve the needs of the customer.

Aircraft. The aircraft utilized for charter work varies from a large jet transporting a group on an intercontinental trip to a light, single-engine aircraft carrying two business people from one community to another. Air taxi flying is normally accomplished with light-to-medium general aviation aircraft, normally twin-engine types.

Rules and regulations. The Federal Aviation Administration regulates basic operating procedures for charter and air taxi flights. General aviation businesses conduct charter and air taxi flights as a form of commercial flying regulated primarily by Part 135 of the Federal Aviation Regulations (see Appendix VIII, sample, Air Taxi Operations Manual). However, the rules for Part 135 Operations have become much closer to the Part 121 requirements, and this trend is expected to continue.

In charter operations, the manager is selling air transportation to meet a customer's specific need. The aircraft and pilot are provided to the customer according to agreement for his exclusive use. For example, Allied Petro-Chemical may call to charter a helicopter to carry and return two of its sales executives on a vendor call. In complying with Part 135 and other pertinent regulations, the manager must ensure the following:

1. The receipt of an air taxi/commercial operator (ATCO) operating certificate.
2. A current manual for the use and guidance of flight, ground operations, and maintenance personnel in conducting operations.
3. Procedures for locating each flight for which an FAA flight plan is not filed.
4. Exclusive use of at least one aircraft that meets the requirements of the operations specifications.
5. Qualified aircrew personnel with appropriate and current certificates and the necessary recency experience.
6. Maintenance of required records and submission of mechanical reliability reports.
7. Compliance with the operating rules prescribed in FAR Part) 91 and 135, including:
   > Airworthiness check;
   > Area limitations on operations;

> Available operating information for pilots;
> Passenger briefing;
> Oxygen requirements;
> Icing limitations;
> Night operations;
> Fuel requirements, VFR and IFR;
> VFR operations; and
> IFR operations.

These requirements reflect only a summary of the pertinent sections of Part 135. The reader is referred to the Federal Aviation Regulations (FARs) for complete details of the requirements.[10]

Aircraft Rental

In this kind of flight operation, the manager is engaged in renting aircraft to the customers who provide their own pilot for the flight. All types of planes may be rented, although most businesses utilize light- and medium-weight general aviation aircraft. In providing and controlling rental activity, the manager is primarily concerned with:

1. Establishing rental rates that will cover all costs and provide a planned profit.
2. Clear and adequate hull and liability insurance.
3. Providing administrative procedures for handling rental activity.
4. Positive renter-pilot identification.
5. Evidence of renter-pilot qualification and competence:
   > Past experience and proficiency;
   > Valid pilot certificate;
   > Current medical certificate; and
   > Flight checkout.
6. Accounting procedures to control income and expenses.

Fractional Aircraft

The most common way today for a company to have partial use of an aircraft is the fractional ownership arrangement. A number of companies, starting with NetJets, initiated this concept in the latter part of the 20th century. It operates more or less like a vacation condo timeshare, with each of say, 8 owners having the right to a certain number of flight hours per year.[11] NetJets says:

> "With NetJets fractional aircraft ownership, you gain all the convenience, access and time advantages of owning a jet aircraft . . . at a fraction of the cost. You maintain control by deciding when and where to fly in order to meet your individual business or personal objectives. Yet, you have no day-to-day aircraft management concerns, scheduling issues, maintenance worries, payroll responsibilities, unproductive downtime, or unexpected costs.
>
> "We tailor a NetJets solution to meet your needs. For example, in the United States a 1/16 interest entitles you to 50 occupied hours per year, and a 1/8 interest is equivalent to 100 occupied hours per year. Select as little as a 1/16 interest, or larger interest sizes depending upon the number of flight hours you require. In fact, NetJets has tailored fractional solutions to meet the needs of some Owners who fly more than 3,000 occupied hours per year."

Clearly, businesses can fly their fractional aircraft for a much lower cost than owning a corporate aircraft. It appears that it is cost-effective to be a fractional owner rather than continue chartering, when hours flown reach about 250–300 per year. The typical FBO could have its charter market harmed by fractional aircraft providers, and aviation service businesses need to explore how they too can benefit from the fractional ownership trend. For example, if they can meet fractional company standards, they may be able to contract to provide "supplemental lift" when the fractional company is fully booked and one of their owners needs a flight. While the competitive threat of fractional companies is real because this new segment of aviation is growing so fast, the FBO should keep in mind that fractionally—owned aircraft number only about 600 so far, out of about 20,000 turbojet and turboprop aircraft in the nation. Given that fractional companies maintain rigid and rigorous standards, they will impose such standards on any firms they contract with, which may ultimately be to the benefit of the charter industry.

Aircrew and Ferry Services

Providing aircrew services to the customer may take various forms. They range from an occasional trip with a non-instrument-rated pilot customer who needs instrument capability for a specific trip, to the corporate customer who has a large twin (but no pilots) and contracts for full crew (pilot, co-pilot and flight attendant) to meet his or her schedule. In providing this kind of service, the aviation manager should regard it as a specific business opportunity to be approached on a sound economic basis.

Operational guidelines and procedures should be developed, as well as administrative methods and controls, adequate insurance coverage, and a provision made for the routine flow of information on income and costs that can be examined regularly to ensure its profitability.

In addition to providing pilot services, the business may offer to completely maintain and operate an aircraft for the customer. For the non-pilot businessperson, this may offer an economical way of operating his aircraft while at the same time enabling the aviation business to obtain greater utilization of its personnel and facilities. To assure a smoothly working arrangement, the manager should develop a contractual relationship that will clearly delineate the responsibilities of both parties.

Air Cargo

Air cargo (freight and mail) is important to all levels of air transportation providers, and there are a number of all-cargo scheduled airlines, with overnight and other delivery options using hubs where packages from throughout their systems are gathered, sorted and redistributed. General aviation also plays a key role in the air cargo area with activities such as transporting cancelled checks, shipping urgently needed factory parts to keep a production line going, express small package delivery, and so on. The size of aircraft may range from the single-engine prop to a plane able to accommodate containers. Very often small amounts of freight or mail will accompany passengers in the same compartment.

The market is likely to continue to be strong for any cargo that is high-value/low-bulk or any cargo that is time-sensitive, such as documents, and perishables such as blood, human organs awaiting transplant, and flowers. An air taxi operator may coordinate with a metropolitan courier service to provide door-to-door small package service in markets that are already covered for passenger service.

Air Ambulance/Medical Evacuation

This area has been growing rapidly due in part to the disparity in quality of medical care between rural facilities and metropolitan hospitals, some of which are unique in the nation for their specialized research and equipment. Custom-remodeled aircraft

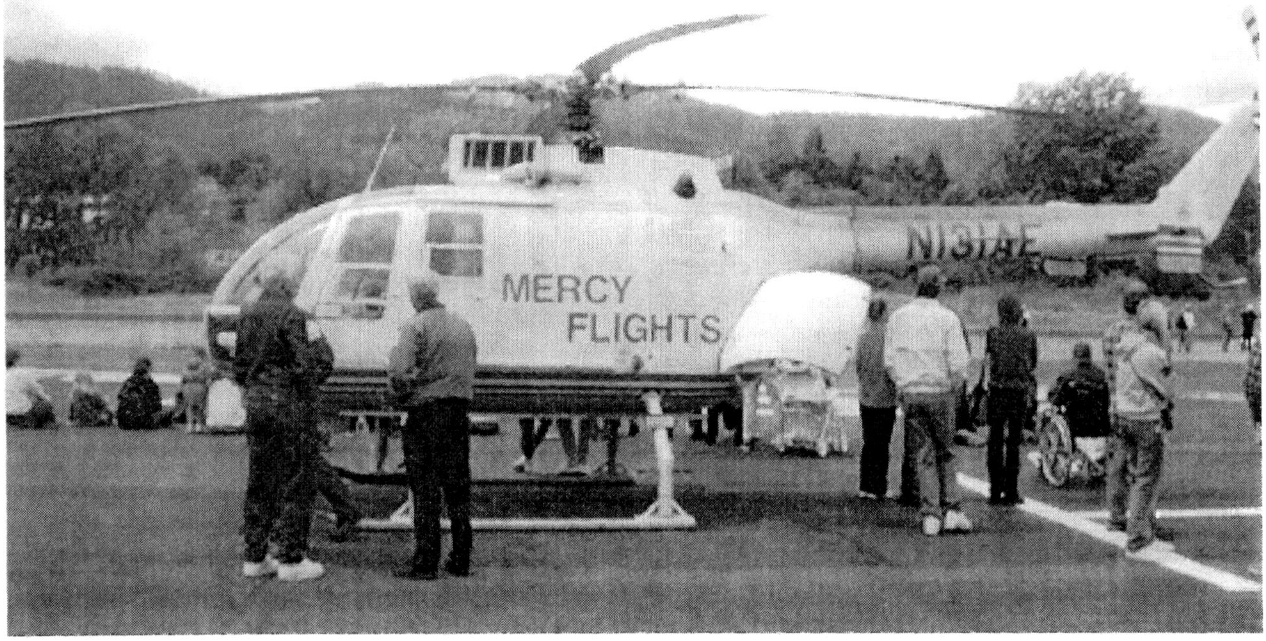

Custom remodeled aircraft is required for in-flight medical care.

that can take stretchers and supply in-flight medical care are required. This type of operation is becoming subject to increasing scrutiny and regulation.

As medical care becomes increasingly sophisticated and specialized, and as hospital competition grows, services are a growing market area for the FBO. Not every FBO will want to enter this market as it is also dependent on volatile insurance reimbursement policies.

Other Commercial Flight Operations

Aerial Patrol

Flight operations for the purpose of pipeline, power line, forest, highway, and border patrol are fairly widely used, although the actual flight activity is normally restricted geographically and seasonally. Forest patrols cover specific wooded areas and are most active in a dry season. Power and pipeline patrols cover designated lines and may be most active following heavy rainfalls and inclement weather. Highway and border patrol flights are assigned specific sectors and normally have missions related to traffic, construction, illegal entry, and so forth. Uniformed police or border patrol personnel in aircraft owned by a federal or state agency fly many of these flights. There is, however, an opportunity for general aviation businesses to provide maintenance services under a contractual arrangement with enforcement agencies for the support of these aircraft.

One opportunity for conducting flight activities that many aviation businesses consider is the Aerial Fire Detection Services for the United States Department of Agriculture (USDA) Forest Service. The various national forests throughout the United States develop air detection plans for their areas of responsibility. These plans establish the procedures covering air operations, including the base of operations, pilot and aircraft requirements, required flight patterns, flight frequency, the fire season, and general flight operating procedures.

The contracting officer for the particular area advertises the Aerial Fire Detection Requirements and the detailed specifications are identified. A typical contract covers the following items:

- Scope of contract;
- Descriptions of operation base;
- Flight paths;
- Flight speed;
- Observer personnel;
- Governmental furnished equipment;
- Aircraft specifications;
- Pilot qualifications;
- Flight duty limitations (pilot);
- Flight time requirements;
- Inspection and approval of aircraft and pilots;
- Safety requirements;
- Flight time measurement; and
- Method of payment.

A regional air officer of the Forest Service must inspect and approve the successful bidder's aircraft and pilots. The contracting officer or his or her representative will authorize and regulate the standby and flight time schedule. Actual flight time will be entered on Forest Service Form 6500-122, Daily Flight Report and Invoice, and submitted by the contractor. The typical contract will contain a minimum guarantee per year in dollars, an hourly bid rate for flight time, and the rate allowed for standby time.

Power line and pipeline patrol activity are normally conducted under contractual arrangements similar to those used by forest patrols. They are typically low-level flights providing visual inspection of cross-country pipelines or electric power lines. Patrol activity of this type is normally accomplished in high-wing aircraft with good visual capability. Relatively slow speeds are desirable with adequate power for emergency needs. Frequently the Super Cub, Cessna 182, and the Helio Courier are used for this type of work, although other model aircraft are being used, including helicopters.

The aviation manager in this situation is concerned with equipment selection, pilot selection and training; procedures for scheduling, conducting, and controlling flights, insurance requirements, administrative paperwork, and the profitability of the operation.

In many cases of aerial patrol, the helicopter can be an asset because of its ability to safely handle low-altitude flight, hovering, and landing in restricted areas. The decision to invest in helicopter rental or charter equipment is a major one because of the substantially higher cost of the aircraft and the high level of skill needed to operate it.

Aerial Application

Agricultural flying is a term used to describe the use of aircraft in the interest of agriculture, forestry, fishery, and public health, where its use is primarily a tool for making observations or applying product. Most agricultural flying is aerial application: the distribution from an aircraft of agricultural chemicals or seeds. The aerial applicator is one of the most versatile and highly trained specialists. He or she must be a businessperson as well as a top-flight pilot who is knowledgeable in chemistry, physics, agronomy, entomology, farming, engineering, meteorology, and cost accounting. A great deal of agricultural application work is done at a height of 5 to 10 feet above the target, with concern for the following factors:

1. Accurate marking for successive straight swath runs.
2. Application rate, or the total quantity of material applied per acre, depending on the:
   - output of each nozzle;
   - number of nozzles;
   - width of swath; and
   - ground speed.
3. Distribution of the spray liquid on the target, determined by:
   - droplet size;
   - number of nozzles;
   - flying height and speed;
   - swath width; and
   - meteorological conditions.
4. Operational influence of wind, rain, temperature, and humidity on the aircraft procedures and the distribution of material.

Aerial application is used for spraying chemicals such as insecticides, fungicides, herbicides, defoliants, and desiccators; and for spreading solid materials such as seeds, fertilizer, and lime. Other activities, such as minnow seeding, are also undertaken by aerial applicators.

Aircraft characteristics. Aircraft used in early agricultural application work were designed for other purposes and then converted for this use. Currently most aircraft doing aerial application work are specifically designed for their job. Those qualities desired in an agricultural aircraft include:

1. Good performance from small, unprepared strips.
2. Safe operating speed of 60 to 100 m.p.h.
3. Maneuverability.
4. Docile handling characteristics.
5. Good field view from cockpit.
6. Protection and comfort for pilot (in a crash).
7. Fire protection: fuel tanks away from pilot.
8. Simplicity in construction and maintenance.
9. Resistance to corrosion by agricultural chemicals.

The size and power required of the aircraft varies according to the type of operation and the working conditions. Most aircraft are single engine with 150 to 600 horsepower and a capacity to carry 600 to 3,000 pounds of material.

Rules and regulations. Agricultural application by aircraft is one of the most thoroughly and tightly controlled aviation activities in the United States. The Federal Aviation Agency, the United States Department of Agriculture, the United States Food and Drug Administration, the Environmental Protection Agency, and state departments of aviation, agriculture, and public health have established rules, regulations, and codes. Feed-processing companies, as well as chemical and food industry groups, provide additional regulations.

Primary aviation control is provided through Federal Aviation Regulations, Part 137-Agricultural Aircraft Operations. This regulation covers the following:

- Definition of terms involved in agricultural aircraft operation;
- Certification rules for an operator's certificate;
- Operating regulations;
- Aircraft requirements;
- Personnel requirements; and
- Required records and reports.

In addition to demonstrating a knowledge of the performance capabilities and operating limitations of the aircraft, the applicant for an agricultural aircraft operator's certificate will be tested on:

1. Steps to be taken before starting operations, including survey of the area to be worked.
2. Safe storage and handling of poisons and the proper disposal of used containers and rinsate for those poisons.

3. General effects of poisons and agricultural chemicals on plants, animals, and people, and the precautions to be observed in using poisons and chemicals.
4. Primary symptoms of poisoning, the appropriate emergency measures to be taken, and the location of poison control centers.
5. Safe flight and application procedures and a demonstration of:
   - Short-field and soft-field takeoffs;
   - Approaches to working area;
   - Flare-outs;
   - Swath runs; and
   - Pull-ups and turnarounds.

Profitability. As with other flight activities, the aerial applicator is concerned with the profitability of the operation. Assuming the existence of adequate financial, accounting, and operational information, the manager must carefully determine all costs, both fixed and variable, add the desired amount of profit, and market the service to ensure a successful level of operation. The following is a detailed list of the typical expenses incurred in an aerial agricultural operation:

- Pilot wages;
- Other wages, for example, flagger;
- Officer wages and salaries;
- Radio repairs;
- Equipment repairs;
- Aircraft repairs;
- Shop and equipment supplies;
- Truck and automobile rent supplies;
- Airport and office rent;
- Room rent;
- Dues and subscriptions;
- Donations;
- Travel;
- Advertising;
- Flags;
- Aircraft insurance;
- Employee insurance;
- Other insurance;
- Aircraft depreciation;
- Truck and auto depreciation;
- Radio and equipment depreciation;
- Other equipment depreciation;
- Interest (loans);
- All utilities;
- Aircraft gas and oil;
- Vehicle gas and oil;
- Office and administrative;
- Property taxes;
- Unemployment taxes;
- Individual insurance; and
- Licenses and taxes.

The manager normally groups these individual expense items into categories for regular review and analysis.

The major concern to the manager is ensuring a positive margin of profit between the earnings of the aircraft and the total cost of operating. Two basic alternatives are available—to raise the price for aerial application services or to improve the efficiency of the business. The latter can be achieved through the reduction of those items that constitute the direct and indirect costs of operation and through increased aircraft utilization. Still another target of the manager is the improvement of the work rate capability of the operating aircraft. The key factors are ferry distance, payload, swath run, speed of flight, turning time, and loading time. These elements strongly influence the work rate or the number of acres serviced per hour. By improving the efficiency of operation, the work rate can be increased and the actual cost per hour reduced. Profit will be improved by the increased acres per productive flight hour.

Aerial Advertising

Another profit potential in flight activity and another way to extend the utilization of existing aircraft is through banner towing. By making this unique advertising medium available to a wide range of businesses, additional flight-service revenue can be generated.

With a maximum recommended top speed of 80 mph (banner drag and wear increase rapidly above this speed), the aircraft used must have adequate engine cooling and positive flight control at low speeds. Be sure all spelling is correct on the banner!

Fish Spotting

The use of small aircraft to spot fish shoals is of great importance to commercial fishing operations in certain areas and in some cases to those involved in recreational fishing. Fish spotting is particularly used in locations such as the Alaska coast, where the salmon season is controlled to the minute, and good timing is important. The aircraft pilot uses a radio to direct fishing boats. Although highly seasonal, this activity can be lucrative for an FBO because of the high value of the potential catch and the fact that no special equipment is needed for the aircraft.

Aerial Photography

Aerial photography has at least five important applications:

1. High level vertical photos for photogrammetry and mapping.
2. Low-level photos for advertising, site planning, and development.
3. Low-level infrared pictures for heat-loss study.
4. Plant disease study.
5. Demographic study.

Few general aviation businesses are involved in the sophisticated areas of aerial photography because of the equipment and skills required. High-level vertical photos, for example, require a camera mounting in the floor of the plane as well as oxygen, since heights may be 20,000 feet or more. Infrared photography also requires special cameras. The likely level of involvement for most general aviation businesses will be in conducting occasional flights for realtors, land developers, news reporters, city and state planners, and engineers and commissioners who usually make their own observations and take their own pictures.

Flight Instruction

The Changing Market

The cost of flying has risen rapidly in the last few years so that now an hour in a Cessna 150 with an instructor costs more than $70.00. However, the BE A PILOT program is offering an introductory rate of $49 for the first flight hour.[12] More flight students are learning to fly for career reasons and others are learning just for fun. Those learning just for fun and are probably also in the market for skiing, scuba, recreational vehicles, and tropical vacations. Thus, these activities all compete for financing with the same discretionary dollars.

Training Programs

Some flight programs involve an integrated program of ground school and in-flight instruction. This method of learning to fly is valuable for the student who wants to have some theoretical understanding of aerodynamics, navigation, and safe procedures before taking the controls. Others are best able to learn by doing, and may attend formal ground school later. There are many self-study courses available to help such students prepare for the FAA written exams. In view of different needs, an FBO may offer in-flight instruction on demand, but only periodically offer ground school. It may be best to run each service as a separate profit center for this reason.

Ground school instruction comes in a myriad of forms today, including not only the traditional classroom style taught at the airport or a local college or university, but also situations where technology is playing more of a part. Videotape series can be purchased to help prepare individuals for the written and flight tests for virtually any flight rating or certificate.

Computer based training is another alternative, with various programs available, for almost any personal computer. With the introduction of computerized testing, computerized ground school has become much more attractive. Use of simulators and computer training devices can increase skill while requiring no fuel or instructor, and thus, a much lower hourly cost to the student. The use of true simulators is very valuable in enabling the student to practice dangerous scenarios such as an engine-out, in a safe environment.

Instructional flight operations include the formal training that leads to private, commercial, instrument, multiengine, airline transport pilot rating (ATP), instructor, glider, and balloon licenses and ratings. They also include instruction that leads to type ratings, such as specific aircraft checkout, aerobatics, and agricultural aircraft operation.

In establishing flight-training programs, the manager is normally concerned with the requirements expected of graduates of the program, an effective and efficient syllabus, competent instructors and the profitability of the instruction. The major source of guidance in determining pilot requirements for various certificates and ratings is the Federal Aviation Administration. The requirements for the following certificates and ratings are contained in the indicated sources:

- Student Pilots FAR 61, Subpart C
- Recreational Pilots FAR 61, Subpart D
- Private Pilots FAR 61, Subpart E
- Commercial Pilots FAR 61, Subpart F
- Airline Transport Pilots FAR 61, Subpart G
- Flight Instructors FAR 61, Subpart H
- Ground Instructors FAR 61, Subpart I
- Instrument Rating FAR 61.65
- Note: Other ratings (multiengine, helicopter, gyroplane, powered-lift, glider, airship, and balloon) are within each subpart as appropriate.

The proposed new recreational license was discussed in Chapter 3, Marketing and will make it much easier for pilots to enter the system. Given the dramatic rise in sport and experimental aircraft both in the past decade and predicted in the future, this seems likely to be a growth area that FBOs should consider.[13]

Part 61 of the Federal Air Regulations is very important to all pilots because it deals with pilot qualifications, privileges and limitations. It is equally im-portant to the manager who is responsible for ensuring that qualified personnel are handling his aircraft.

To ensure that the student pilot achieves the level of proficiency stipulated by the FAA or other sources, the manager should ensure the adequacy of the training program for the certificate or rating involved. The private pilot flight-training program is the most prevalent in the United States. There is an abundance of training programs. They range from the most fundamental topical ground and flight outline to sophisticated syllabi with audiovisual materials. Learning programs that the manager can consider acquiring and installing at the business include such programs as the Cessna Pilot Center "Integrated Flight Training System" and the various Jeppesen/Sanderson programs.[14,15]

Other programs are available from various developers and publishers. In addition to complete flight and ground school programs, there are numerous manuals published to help student pilots master private pilot subjects, instrument topics, and multiengine concepts. These manuals can be obtained from a number of aviation publishers and suppliers.

There are many flight-training organizations throughout the United States that have developed their individual program and syllabi for the various ratings. These schools may be of some assistance to the manager intent upon opening a training center. Of course any aviation business that plans to open a flight school should study FAR Part 141-Pilot Schools very carefully. This regulation prescribes the requirements for becoming a certificated pilot school and provides for the approval of pilot training courses offered by certificated schools. Federal Aviation Administration Advisory Circular 1411-Pilot School Certification sets forth guidelines to assist persons in obtaining a pilot school certificate and associated ratings under the Federal Aviation Regulations, Part 141. Advisory Circular No. 140-2J-List of Certificated Pilot Flight and Ground Schools contains a list of those schools that have been recognized as approved by the Federal Aviation Administration.

Instruction Administration

The administration of a flight instructional program presents many challenges to the manager. There are procedures to develop, rules to establish and follow, schedules to make and carry out, personnel to manage, progress checks to administer, and controls to monitor. The training program may become large enough to become an independent department with the full organizational structure of a school. The administrative procedures established should provide for:

- Registration of students;
- Curriculum identification and improvement;
- Scheduling the utilization of aircraft, instructors and students;
- Identifying and coordinating aircraft maintenance;
- Student progress checks;
- FAA and state approval of flight school;
- School operational guidelines;
- Procedures including visa checks for foreign students;
- Maintenance of flight training records;
- Accounting system; and
- Flow of information and economic analysis of school activity.

Several organizations have recognized the need to develop a complete package for the management of a flight school, and quite a few are available today. One of the most thorough and complete is the Cessna Pilot Center System developed by Cessna Aircraft Company.[16] This system was developed to provide "a total package with which to conduct a profitable flight training business." The management manual for the Cessna integrated flight training system provides a well structured and comprehensive approach to flight training through the identification and application of the following system components:

> Integrated flight training curriculum;
> Management system for operating a flight school;
> Management training;
> Instructor curriculum training; and
> Consultation services by Center specialists.

A review of these components clearly indicates the Cessna approach to be well structured and comprehensive. The operational elements in the management system include:

> Flight counter procedures;
> Student enrollment forms;
> Flight training agreement;
> Appointment cards;
> Student record folders;
> Flight scheduling forms;
> Aircraft maintenance schedule;
> Instructors' work schedule;
> Instructors' scheduling cards;
> Aircraft rental agreement;
> Flight line procedures;
> Facility appearance guidelines;
> Equipment utilization;
> Accounting system;
> Financial analysis;
> Tax considerations;
> Human resources programs; and
> Reports and controls.

The total package from the Cessna Pilot Center System is designed as an integrated program with coordinated supplies, records and procedures. The core of the system is the integrated flight and ground curriculum. Other companies have approached the development of flight instruction along the same lines. These companies include Beech, with its Aero Club and the various flight instruction programs of Aero Products Research, Inc. FBO Manager from Cornerstone Logic also offers a complete flight school management package. Figure 9.3 shows a sample "Hobbs Report" from FBO Manager.

Flight Instructors

Flight instructors are perhaps the most critical element in the development of successful flight instruction activity. The desired image of an instructor is professionalism. He or she should be well qualified technically, possess the desired teaching skills and motivation, and demonstrate the ability to implement these skills. In many real-life aviation businesses, there are several problems associated with flight instructor selection and utilization that create difficulties for the flight department manager:

> Poor selection procedures;
> No company orientation program;
> Lack of training;
> Rapid turnover and/or lack of reliability of instructor personnel;
> Low salary scale;
> Lack of a career orientation;
> Fluctuating seasonal demands for labor;
> Lack of marketing orientation; and
> A weak identification with the organization.

It has been observed that many aviation businesses do a poor or indifferent job of selecting their flight instructors. Many managers have fallen into the practice of having their office call the next name on the availability list when another instructor is needed. Too much emphasis is often placed on the possession of an "instructor's ticket," and little attention is given to other qualifications that the organization should find desirable in its instructors. This approach appears to be caused by the lack of management's ability, either in time or knowledge, to engage in careful identification of personnel needs and then to exercise care in the selection of new instructors.

As discussed in Chapter 5, Human Resources, many aviation organizations as small businesses lack time or interest in developing adequate personnel structures. The first and obvious step is the development of a position description of an

Figure 9.3 » Sample "Hobbs Report"

Cornerstone Logic Inc.

Aircraft Detailed Hours_Flown
from 01-Jan-00 to 30-Apr-02

Tail Number	Name	Ref #	INV Number	Date Out	Date In	Hobbs Out	Hobbs In	Tach Out	Tach In	Hours Flown	Rental Rate	Revenue	Type	Method
197KS	Winkler, Henry	102	97-0610	04/17/00 15:16	04/17/00 15:16	219.00	220.00	12.00	13.00	1.00	$41.00	$41.00	Reg	Hobbs
197KS	Winkler, Henry	103	97-0611	04/17/00 15:17	04/17/00 15:17	220.00	221.00	13.00	14.00	1.00	$41.00	$41.00	Reg	Hobbs
197KS	Winkler, Henry	104	97-0613	04/17/00 15:19	04/17/00 15:20	221.00	222.00	14.00	15.00	1.00	$41.00	$41.00	Reg	Hobbs
197KS	Baltzer, Jacob	105	97-0622	04/25/00 23:04	04/25/00 23:04	222.00	223.00	15.00	16.00	1.00	$41.00	$41.00	Reg	Hobbs
197KS	Albert, Fat	106	97-0638	04/26/00 00:17	04/26/00 00:17	223.00	224.50	16.00	17.50	1.50	$41.00	$61.50	Reg	Hobbs
197KS	Baltzer, Jacob	107	97-0664	04/26/00 21:26	04/26/00 21:26	224.50	226.00	17.50	19.00	1.50	$41.00	$61.50	Reg	Hobbs
197KS	Wilson, Scott	108	97-0668	04/28/00 02:58	04/28/00 02:58	226.00	227.00	19.00	20.00	1.00	$41.00	$41.00	Reg	Hobbs
197KS	Wilson, Scott	109	97-0668	04/28/00 02:58	04/28/00 02:58	227.00	228.00	20.00	21.00	1.00	$41.00	$41.00	Reg	Hobbs
197KS	Wilson, Scott	110	97-0668	04/28/00 02:59	04/28/00 02:59	228.00	229.00	21.00	22.00	1.00	$41.00	$41.00	Reg	Hobbs
197KS	Wilson, Scott	111	97-0670	04/28/00 03:12	04/28/00 03:12	229.00	229.20	22.00	23.00	0.20	$41.00	$8.20	Reg	Hobbs
197KS	Wilson, Scott	113	97-0670	04/28/00 03:13	04/28/00 03:13	229.20	230.00	23.00	24.30	0.80	$41.00	$32.80	Reg	Hobbs
197KS	Wilson, Scott	112	97-0670	04/28/00 03:13	04/28/00 03:13	230.00	231.00	24.30	25.00	1.00	$41.00	$41.00	Reg	Hobbs
197KS	Beaudoines, Jay	114	97-0828	05/09/00 15:04	05/09/00 15:04	231.00	233.50	25.00	27.00	2.50	$41.00	$102.50	Reg	Hobbs
197KS	Bees, Wade	115	97-0866	05/10/00 11:37	05/10/00 11:38	233.50	235.00	27.00	29.00	1.50	$41.00	$61.50	Reg	Hobbs
197KS	Balmers, Thomas	116	97-0902	05/11/00 11:41	05/11/00 11:41	235.00	237.00	29.00	31.00	2.00	$41.00	$82.00	Reg	Hobbs
197KS	Allens, David	117		06/08/00 15:53	06/08/00 15:53	237.00	238.00	31.00	32.00	1.00	$41.00	$41.00	Reg	Hobbs

Courtesy of FBO Manager.

instructor job as needed in that organization. From this description, a job specification can then be developed that identifies the qualifications the prospective employee must possess. Chapter 5 contains information on the functions and skills needed for the position of a flight instructor.

After an active recruiting program to ensure an adequate number of candidates for job openings, the next step can be the utilization of an application blank for all potential flight instructors. Such a form can be very effective in screening candidates and identifying those pilots best suited to the needs of the organization. Figure 5.6 in Chapter 5, Human Resources depicts a form that is very comprehensive, provides a great deal of information on the applicant, and should be extremely useful in selecting new flight instructors.

At some point in time, it will become necessary to interview the stronger candidates in order to verify or amplify the data contained in the application blank and at the same time provide the candidate with information about the position and the organization. An interview form is very useful to busy managers. Such a form is somewhat like a pre-takeoff checklist in that it serves as a reminder to the interviewer and helps evaluate the candidate. An example is shown in Chapter 5, Figure 5.7.

Instructor Training

Training of flight instructors should include those elements that will enable the person to perform the total job more effectively. This means training in:

> Flying;
> Instructional skills;
> Marketing;
> Administrative duties; and
> Organizational responsibilities.

Historically, primary emphasis has been placed on flying skills, and minimal emphasis has been placed on instructional and educational skills. Frequently, due to wages being based upon the number of hours flown at an hourly rate, other responsibilities were minimized or not included, and skills or talents in other areas were never developed. More and more organizations have realized the advantage of hiring instructors on a full-time basis, providing training in broader organizational responsibilities, and realizing additional benefits from airborne and ground activities of instructor personnel. There must be an adequate student load and related business activity to economically justify the individual instructor.

Freelance Instructors

Just as some FBOs must contend with "tailgate mechanics" and so-called "gypsy" operators, so too the *freelance* instructor is another possible source of unfair competition. Any pilot with a Certified Flight Instructor (CFI) rating can give lessons legally as far as the FAA is concerned. However, the owner of a based aircraft who gives lessons at someone else's airport is probably in business without a lease or operating permit. Since he presumably pays only his own hangar or tiedown rent and has little or no other overhead, such an operator can invariably undercut the FBO's prices. But he or she does not offer the student the guarantees of high-quality instruction, the use of facilities for classroom time, or backup aircraft. Because of low-budget maintenance and lack of regulation on the field, such operators can also be a safety hazard that could also make the FBO liable despite his or her not being directly responsible.

Simulator Usage

Simulators have been designed for use in flight training to assist in training for basic flight, for instrument work, and for specific aircraft and equipment checkouts. It has been said that the worst possible place to give flight instruction is in the air because of the noise, the distractions of many physical sensations, and the inability to stop the machine and talk about a mistake. To help overcome these problems, a wide variety of simulators and training devices have been developed.

When a ground trainer or simulator is being used as part of a training course, the extent of its use should be clearly stated in the syllabus. FAR Section 141.41(a) prescribes the requirements used to obtain the maximum flight training credit allowed for ground trainers in approved courses. FAR 141.41(b) provides for the use of ground trainers that do not meet the requirements of Section 141.41(a). The training course must clearly show that the simulator being used meets the stated goals of the syllabus and adheres to the guidelines of 141.41(a) or (b).

The simulator can be a valuable adjunct to a flight-training program by accomplishing the following:

1. Reducing the calendar time required for a given training program.
2. Providing additional utilization of flight instructors.
3. Providing a means for sustaining student interest and proficiency during periods of inclement weather.
4. Providing an improved training environment.
5. Facilitating the scheduling process of the organization and the student.
6. Providing a less expensive training opportunity for the student and for the organization.
7. Providing a means for the student to overcome specific learning obstacles.
8. Saving fuel.
9. Eliminating touch-and-go and other noise.

The Federal Aviation Administration has recognized the usefulness and effectiveness of the simulator in instrument training by allowing credit for instrument rating experience to be completed in an acceptable instrument ground trainer. Other ratings also recognize and accept simulator time. Most airframe manufacturers have recognized the advantages of simulators for instructing and qualifying pilots in the more sophisticated aircraft. Here the emphasis may be on the operation of complicated systems and emergency procedures as well as on the actual operation of the aircraft.

Simulators used to be expensive for a small FBO, though their comparative cost-effectiveness has improved as fuel costs have increased. Today's microcomputers have opened up a whole new ground trainer technology. A student with most brands of personal computer can now purchase training device software to use at home as well as at the flight school.

Sport and Recreational Flyers

Gliders and Sailplanes

Where terrain and climate provide good thermal currents, this is often a popular activity. It may go well with business-oriented FBO services because it is largely a weekend activity. However, the mix of slow unpowered aircraft in the traffic pattern can be a hazard. Some fields are dedicated to just this type of activity. The main revenue to an FBO will come from fuel sales to the tow plane and from glider pilot tow fees. Many glider owners transport their aircraft to and from the field in special containers, so the potential for tie-down income is limited. This aspect of general aviation continues to experience modest growth in suitable locations however; it is a very small contributor to national FBO income.

Parachuting

Like gliding, parachuting can present problems at a field with a heavy traffic pattern. The jump-landing zone needs to be isolated; departing pilots in other aircraft need to watch for the drop. However, owing to slow speed and high visibility, descending parachuters do not present a major hazard. This too tends to be a weekend activity. It can generate important revenue from bystanders, for example, at an outdoor airport restaurant, as well as from participants.

Ultralights

The first ultralight fly-in was in Florida in 1974; thus, ultralights have now been around for three decades. But the rest of the general aviation industry still seems very uncertain about how to handle them. Ultralights require only a few hundred feet of landing area, go at very slow speeds, and so far the pilots are not required to be licensed or pass any course of instruction. Since they use autogas and mostly do their own repairs, they do not appear to generally offer a source of profit to FBOs and are often viewed as a hindrance to the regular customers. Whether they use separate landing areas within existing airports or completely separate fields, they may in certain locations present a new opportunity for FBO services.

The FBO owner/manage who is able to harness the enthusiasm and dedication of these avid flyers, may find them an asset rather than a liability. Some of these pilots may be interested in obtain-

Ultralights require little landing area, fly at slow speeds, and their pilots are not required to be licensed.

ing their pilot certificate at some point and/or renting or purchasing a more traditional aircraft.

Experimental and Home-Built Aircraft

This facet of the general aviation industry appears to be growing more vigorously than personal flying in conventional aircraft. A major reason is the substantially lower cost to both operate and own such aircraft. Almost one million people, with close to 12,000 aircraft from all around the world, attend the annual fly-in of the Experimental Aircraft Association in Oshkosh, Wisconsin. The organization also boasts a network of over 800 local chapters.

The number of experimental aircraft completed in the early part of the 1990s was almost as great as the number of general aviation factory-built aircraft in the U.S. As was indicated in Figure 1.2, the total number of experimental, and "other" i.e. homebuilt aircraft, balloons, gliders etc was 19,900 in 1995, 27,100 in 2001 and is predicted to rise to 28,300 by 2013.

Balloons

Ballooning is very popular in some areas, but it does not need an area the size of an airport or an FBO to function, although it can add to the glamour and excitement of an air show. Conflicts with other recreational uses frequently cause ballooning to be sited at airports rather than parks.

Rotorcraft

Helicopter ratings have become more attractive as we move into the 21st century. This is due, at least in part, to the availability of such machines as the new Robinson R-22 helicopter and the

Helicopter flight training can occur at an airport offering fixed wing flight training without undue burden to either operation. Courtesy of Timberland.

Schweizer 300-CB. The R-22 was designed primarily as a training helicopter, much like the Cessna 150 for fixed-wing flight training. A lightweight, two passenger aircraft, the Robinson is also a more affordable helicopter, although still more expensive than learning to fly in a small two seat aircraft.

Helicopter flight training can occur at an airport offering fixed wing flight training without undue burden to either operation. Typically, the helicopters fly at a pattern of 500 feet above ground level, versus 800–1,000 feet for aircraft. And, because helicopters are not restricted to taking off and landing on runway surfaces, they can initiate their own traffic pattern, parallel to or away from the fixed wing traffic. Most airports with rotorcraft activity do have a marked H for the helipad area.

Sight-Seeing

Flying customers around the city, over sensitive scenic areas such as the Grand Canyon, or along the oceanfront so that they can view the panorama has long been a popular part of aviation. In general, it requires something scenic to view and normally is seasonal work, peaking in summers, vacation periods, or even on sunny, pleasant weekends. With few exceptions, this type of business is conducted with existing, standard aircraft almost on a pick-up basis. Aside from the usual aircraft and pilot insurance requirements, there are some special concerns for the manager, such as safety on the ground and in the air, pilot training, and passenger briefing, noise minimization, and specific flight time and route controls. With care, this type of flying can improve aircraft utilization, provide additional income, and stimulate interest in aviation that may lead to business in flight instruction and aircraft sales. The notion of whether or not aircraft should be allowed to fly over national parks was up for discussion in the 1990s. The proposed final ruling by the FAA, not yet adopted by mid-2002, restricts procedures and hours flights over many national parks.

For most FBOs recreational aviation of various types is not an important element of their business. At some airports such activity is discouraged because of conflicts with faster, heavier traffic. The more innovative types of recreational aviation such as ultralights tend to be volatile, with many operators and manufacturers leaving the industry each year. Insurance for some aspects of sport and recreational aviation is either unavailable or a prohibitive expense. Nevertheless, for the right FBO in the right location, this industry segment may provide a previously overlooked market.

Aircraft Sales

New Aircraft

Aircraft sales are the largest item of business for some FBOs, while for others it is not significant. NATA surveys showed that in the 1990s, the percent of members in the aircraft sales business was shrinking. This was particularly true for the sale of new aircraft. Selling aircraft requires the financial ability to carry an expensive inventory for unpredictable amounts of time. It also requires substantial showroom space. The average time in inventory is generally longer for new aircraft than for used, according to studies conducted by NATA.

The percentage of FBOs who were franchised aircraft dealers rose steadily in the early 1980s, from 57 percent in 1981 to 84 percent in 1984. However, it took a dive in the late 80s and 1990s as so few aircraft were being made and sold nationwide due to the insurance cost element of the finished new aircraft. This began to improve again the mid-1990s.

A significant change in terms of aircraft sales relates to the number of foreign aircraft being sold in the U.S. Many companies such as the French-based EADS, Canadian-based Dimona, and Swiss-owned companies are doing good business in the U.S.

Used Aircraft

As with auto sales, used aircraft may be taken as trade-ins. Usually the FBO refurbishes and checks out the aircraft before resale, which involves some costs that must be included in calculating the selling price. Inventory times are typically shorter for used aircraft.

Brokerage

Selling aircraft as a broker means that one does not have to carry the inventory or finance the sale, but simply act as a matchmaker between buyers

Various flight activities require specific aircraft and flying skills. Courtesy of Timberland.

and sellers. The commission on this activity can be worthwhile. Some FBOs also sell aircraft on consignment; that is, they do not pay the seller until the aircraft has a new buyer.

Demonstration Flights

Although not usually time-consuming, these flights are key to a successful sales operation, and the personnel best suited to presenting the aircraft's features and benefits should make them.

Flight Operations Manual

A flight operations manual has various meanings in different organizations. In many small businesses, it refers to a general guide for conducting flight operations that attempts to set the tone for the overall business and its related activities. Such a manual contains both policy and specific rules and regulations. In an effort to indoctrinate all employees in the philosophy and procedures selected by the organization, the manual becomes required reading. It also provides specific guidance to key operating personnel, including those at the front desk, on the flight line, instructors, and pilots.

In some aviation organizations the term "operations manual" refers specifically to the publication that is required in order to operate air taxi aircraft under the authority of FAR Part 135-Air Taxi Operations and Commercial Operation of Small Aircraft.

Summary

Flight operations form the core of the aviation business. The other activities such as maintenance, aircraft storage, parts supply, and administration develop from the need to keep aircraft in flightworthy condition. Flight activities may be grouped into those involved simply in transporting people or products between two points, such as charters, air taxi, business aircraft operation and air ambulance; and those activities involving conducting a business operation as an intrinsic part of being airborne. The second group consists of flight instruction, agricultural applications, aerial photography, fish spotting, survey, and patrol work, construction, and many others, all specialized and some requiring special aircraft equipment. Each of the various activities requires specific aircraft and flying skills. Each possesses characteristics that must be identified and understood by the FBO if they are to become profitable elements of

DISCUSSION TOPICS

1. What requirements must an air taxi operator meet for Part 135 operations?
2. What are the differences between air taxi and commuter operations?
3. What are some of the built-in problems and opportunities of flight instruction?
4. What five flight operations techniques can be used to reduce noise and when should each be applied?
5. How does climate affect the market for flight operations?
6. What are some of the technical requirements facing the agricultural operator?
7. What procedures should be used to ensure the profitable operation of such activities as aerial photography, sightseeing and banner-towing?
8. Identify five FBOs within a 100-mile radius and determine (1) what percentage of their revenues comes from flight operations, and (2) how the flight operations revenue is divided among the various flight operations areas. Which flight operations areas have they chosen and why?
9. Assume you are entering the aircraft rental business. What questions must be addressed for each rental transaction?

the business. An understanding of the key elements involved in each activity, identification of the type of aircraft and other equipment needed, knowledge of the rules and regulations governing that type of flying, and awareness of the primary economic considerations are all part of the aviation manager's job. Finally, the use of internal operating procedures and guidelines to assist in achieving established goals facilitates a consistent and streamlined operation in the flight department.

Endnotes

1. See http://*www.nbaa.org,* April 25, 2002 and "Airports in Focus."
2. Searles, Robert A., and Parke, Robert B. *NBAA's Tribute to Business Aviation.* Fiftieth Anniversary Publication, 1997.
3. See http://*www.nbaa.org,* op. cit., February 25, 2002.
4. See http://*www.nbaa.org,* April 25, 2002.
5. Anderson, Arthur Inc. "Business Aviation in Today's Economy, A Guide to the Analysis of Business Aircraft Use, Benefits and Effects on Shareholder Value," *White Paper Series* Number 9, Summer 2001.
6. See for example the "fly friendly" procedures adopted at Renton Municipal Airport, WA at *http://www.ci.renton.wa.us/pw/airport/abatement.htm.*
7. See *http://www.nbaa.org/noise/index.htm.*
8. See *http://www.aopa.org/members/files/airport/apsup04.html.*
9. "Minimum Standards for Commercial Aeronautical Activities on Public Airports," *FAA Advisory Circular* 150/5190-1A.
10. See Appendix II for a list of Federal Air Regulations. FAR Part 135, Air Taxi Operators and Commercial Operators, is to be found in Code of Federal Regulations 14, Parts 60-139, available from United States Government Printing Office, Washington, D.C. 20402 or from FAA's web site.
11. See NetJets web site http://*www.netjets.com* and their publication The Buyer's Guide to Fractional Aircraft Ownership.
12. BE A PILOT is an industry program. See *http://www.beapilot.com.*
13. See *http://www.faa.gov/avr/afs/sportpilot/.*
14. See *http://learntofly.com/cessna/index.chtml.*
15. See *http://www.jeppesenpcpilot.com/* (desktop simulation software) and also *http://www.jeppesen.com/wlcs/index.jsp.* Jeppesen Sanderson is now owned by Boeing.
16. For example, *http://www.angelfire.com/sd/GreatPlanesAviation/LTF5.htm.*

10

Aviation Maintenance

OBJECTIVES

- Identify and describe the four subdivisions usually found in the organizational structure of a maintenance department.
- Explain the certification process necessary to earn an FAA airframe and powerplant certificate.
- Describe the facilities and equipment necessary to open and operate an aviation maintenance shop.
- Understand the implications of product liability on an aviation maintenance operation.
- Recognize the advantages and disadvantages of subcontracting out all maintenance work.
- Understand the concept of flat-rate pricing.

Introduction

Goals of the Maintenance Shop

The maintenance field must be viewed from the standpoint of four factors that don't always work in the same direction:

- FAA requirements;
- Customer satisfaction;
- Profitability; and
- The ability to recognize and address changing market and technological situations.

The repair and maintenance jobs must be done right, not only from FAA's standpoint, but from the customer's standpoint. The customer wants all FAA compliance to be done and documented correctly and also wants good communication, friendly managers and technicians and a sense of trust that derives from feeling quality work is being done at a reasonable price and that the customer's wishes and specifications are being listened to very closely. Profitability of the maintenance shop as an individual profit center is necessary and helps to make the overall business profitable. The challenge is to cover costs, make a profit, and still price repair and maintenance services competitively with other nearby operators. The ability to recognize and address changing market conditions is essential and may even result in a decision to downsize or close the maintenance facility.

To achieve these four objectives, the issues of approvals, personnel, shop facilities and equipment, parts and supplies, quality control, subcontracting, product liability, marketing, administration, pricing and profitability must all be addressed. In this chapter we will review all of these aspects of maintenance, emphasizing the manager's role in guiding the activity toward established objectives. The chapter addresses both the mandatory elements and the areas where the maintenance manager has more discretion.

Changing Issues

Fractional Aircraft Ownership. One of the biggest industry changes is the shift toward fractional aircraft ownership. It appears that most of the sales of new aircraft are now to fractional aircraft operators. Typically, the repair of these aircraft is provided on contract with the manufacturer. Running repairs are still required in the field. Thus the typical airport maintenance shop operator may encounter a major new source of competition. Since maintenance and repair shops require being a certain size in order to achieve economies of scale, if a portion of the business disappears as former air taxi and charter customers become fractional owners, then the shop may not longer be large enough to maintain the diversity of skills and functions needed for a full-service operation.

There appear still to be many unknowns in the fractional aircraft arena, perhaps more in relation to aircraft maintenance than in any other area. In an article in Aviation Maintenance Technician, attorney Stephen Prentice raises some of the questions that were current toward the end of the 20th century:[1]

> "You probably have heard about fractional interests in aircraft ownership by now. It seems like they have bought out all corporate jet production for years to come. Sales are booming, but have you thought anything about the status of employees of the management arms of such companies or what the impact will be in maintenance field? These companies now employ hundreds of technicians and pilots and have a significant impact in the commercial corporate flight environment. Are they here to stay? Will their structure change? Will they be regulated?
>
> "Fractional owners don't retain their own technicians, but maybe they should. Current arrangements call for the management company to supply all maintenance. Many companies are closing their (corporate) flight departments and moving to a fractional arrangement because of the perceived dollar savings. In addition, individual aircraft manufacturers have set out on a plan to provide inhouse maintenance services for most of the routine inspection process. This is the area that is of concern to some. Will these arrangements impact the average technician?"

In reality, it seems likely that FBOs willing to meet the high standards of fractional companies will be able to become contract fractional maintenance facilities for these operators.

FAA is developing fractional aircraft rules that are discussed in Chapter 3, Marketing. However, it seems too soon to predict what the effect will be of more fractionally owned aircraft on FBO maintenance shops.

Technology. In some industries the use of laptop computers for tracking repair orders, ordering parts, tracking hours of repairmen labor, and doing diagnostics on the equipment itself is state of the art.[2] An efficient maintenance shop will need to explore installing such modernizations in the coming decade in order to stay competitive. This means not only outlays for new hardware and software, but also training of maintenance technicians in computer usage. For the younger employees this is not an obstacle since computers are now in common use in the classrooms of kindergarteners. Many older workers are self-taught or company-trained and develop a quick facility with computers. But many others have a low comfort level with the new technologies. Once an FBO computerizes the maintenance shop, all employees will need to use the same system, so the noncomputer literate employee will need special support and training. Two major software companies, FBO Manager and TotalFBO provide full-service aviation maintenance management packages.

RSVM/DRVSM. Domestic and overseas Reduced Vertical Separation Minima are being developed in order to accommodate more aircraft at high altitudes. Instead of the current 2,000 foot vertical separation, the plan is to go to 1,000 feet.[3] To be certified for RVSM flight, an aircraft has to be able to demonstrate improved measurement systems, to insure accurate altimeter reading, so that it can fly safely within a very precise altitude envelope. From a maintenance standpoint, therefore, RVSM will mean upgrade work to aircraft wishing to make RVSM flights. The requirements are complex and the procedures and fines stringent, meaning that FBOs in the repair business will need to be fully conversant with all details. The above-cited article expands as follows:

> "Ongoing maintenance is an issue all in itself. Should an unfamiliar aircraft arrive at a service center, one of the most important questions asked should be about RVSM qualification. For example, if altimeter certification is due per airworthiness requirements, the air data computers are to be removed and sent out and replacement units are to be installed. Research needs to be conducted to determine RVSM acceptable part numbers. Installation of one part number may be valid for the basic aircraft, but not for RVSM flight."

Tort Reform Bill. Since 1994, the time period that a maintenance shop could be sued for faulty aircraft repairs goes back (only) 18 years. This might be assumed to mean that excellent records must be kept for only 18 years on each aircraft that passes through the shop. However, the Tort Reform Act did not alter FAA's requirement for "cradle to grave" tracking of every part with a serial number and every action performed in aircraft repair and maintenance. The customer should have copies of everything too.

Alternative Maintenance Approaches. FAA sets inspection and maintenance requirements, and because having that equipment out of service means the cost of backup equipment to maintain flight schedules, the airlines have been leaders in looking for ways to reduce down time while still meeting and exceeding safety standards. Three approaches are discussed in a recent edition of AMT Online—Continuous Airworthiness Maintenance Programs, On-Condition Engine Maintenance, and the MSG-3 Maintenance Concept.[4] The forward-looking maintenance manager must constantly be reviewing the state of the art and making determinations as to what can fit in his or her particular operation or for particular clients.

Maintenance Activity

Overview

Maintenance activities are not undertaken by all airport service businesses; where they are part of the service, they are basic to its success. Good maintenance provides reliable aircraft, ensures customer satisfaction and aircraft utilization, increases the stature of the business in particular and of aviation in general, in the public's eye, and leads to further development of the industry. Without the support of good maintenance, the reverse happens; business dries up and the industry stagnates, regardless of the products manufactured.

Maintenance activity at a general aviation business started when the flyer/manager found that he had to maintain his or her own aircraft in an airworthy status in order to stay in business. With the arrival of privately owned aircraft on the field, the manager found that she was performing maintenance on these additional aircraft. This represented a mixed blessing, for although she now spread her costs over a wider base; she is also in the maintenance business and must comply with a host of FAA requirements for commercial repair shops.

With most aviation businesses today, maintenance work is done for company aircraft as well as for external customers. In some larger full service operations, where maintenance is a separate profit center, the shift has been so complete that internal company requests for maintenance must compete with external customer requests for available shop time and are also billed at standard rates.

The aviation manager entering the maintenance business needs to understand the structure of this complex field, to understand the rules and regulations and to know the equipment and personnel needed for the various levels of maintenance activity. The Federal Aviation Regulations provide the major guidance and control for the operation of aviation maintenance facilities.[5]

This guidance is contained primarily in:

1. Part 43—Maintenance, Preventive Maintenance, Rebuilding and Repair.

With most aviation businesses today, maintenance work is done for company aircraft as well as for external customers. Courtesy of Executive Beechcraft, Inc.

2. Part 65—Certification: Airmen Other Than Flight Crew Members.
3. Part 145—Repair Stations.
4. Part 147—Aviation Maintenance Technician Schools.
5. Related Advisory Circulars covering many aspects of aviation maintenance.

Maintenance activity at an aviation business can be described in terms of the various levels of work accomplished. The following definitions of the key service or maintenance activities outlined by the Federal Aviation Administration:

1. "Maintenance" means the inspection, overhaul, repair, preservation and replacement of parts, but excludes any preventive maintenance.
2. "Preventive maintenance" means simple or minor preservation operations and the replacement of small standard parts not involving complex assembly operations.
3. "Major repair" means repair (a) that if improperly done might appreciably affect weight, balance, structural strength, performance, power plant operation, flight characteristics, or other qualities affecting airworthiness; or (b) that is not done according to accepted practices or cannot be done by elementary operations.
4. "Major alteration" means an alteration not listed in the aircraft, aircraft engine, or propeller specifications that might appreciably affect weight, balance, structural strength, performance, power plant operation, flight characteristics or other qualities affecting airworthiness; or an alteration that is not done according to accepted practices or cannot be done by elementary operations.

Part 43-Maintenance, Preventive Maintenance, Rebuilding, and Alteration prescribes rules governing the maintenance, preventive maintenance, rebuilding and alteration of aircraft having a U.S. airworthiness certificate and the airframe, aircraft engine, propeller or appliances of such aircraft. These rules identify the persons authorized to perform maintenance, preventive maintenance, rebuilding and alterations, or to return an aircraft or component to service; the form of maintenance records; the guidelines for performing maintenance work (methods, techniques and practices); and the identification of specific operations classed as major alterations, major repairs, and preventive maintenance.

The persons who may perform maintenance, preventive maintenance, rebuilding and alteration are:

1. The holder of a mechanic certificate, as provided in Part 65.
2. The holder of a repairman certificate, as provided in Part 65.
3. Individuals working under the supervision of a mechanic or repairman.
4. The holder of a repair station certificate, as provided in Part 145.
5. An air carrier, as provided in Parts 121, 127 or 135.
6. The holder of a commercial operator certificate as provided in Part 42.
7. The holder of a pilot certificate issued under Part 61 who may perform preventive maintenance on any aircraft owned or operated by him that is not used in commercial air service.
8. A manufacturer operating under a type of production certificate.

Organization

Maintenance activity by an aviation business is generally accomplished in accordance with the Federal Aviation Regulations. To assist in achieving the business's objectives, most concerns are organized specifically for this purpose. The typical organizational structure of a maintenance or service department would look like that in Figure 10.1. Even if the organization is small and the personnel are few, the functions represented by this organizational chart are accomplished when the business provides service support for aircraft, power plants and electronic equipment. The chart enables the business manager to identify the various functions provided and the relationships between them and a framework for future growth of the maintenance activity. The components of the structure are responsible for the following:

1. Manager, maintenance department: Responsible for the overall operation of the department including profitability of service,

Figure 10.1 » Typical Organization of a Maintenance Department

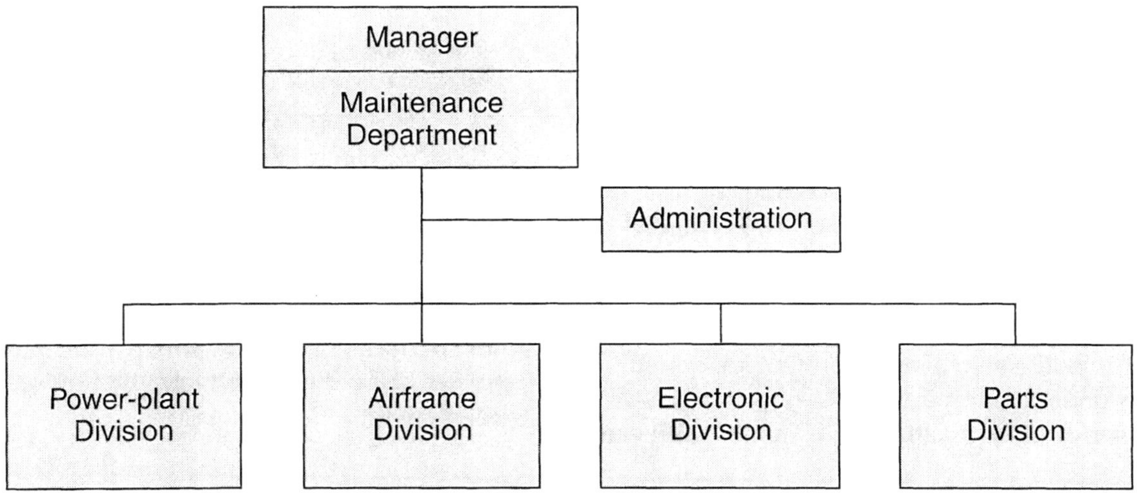

coordination, technical competence, compliance with rules and regulations, quality of product and highest possible safety standards, and hiring and training.

2. Administration: Provides administrative support to the department by maintaining department records, maintenance manuals, Airworthiness Directives (ADs), shop orders, and required reports.
3. Power-plant division: Responsible specifically for service activity dealing with power plants, propellers, fuel systems, and related engine accessories. This includes trouble-shooting, repair and replacement of the equipment authorized by the FAA.
4. Airframe division: Provides support for the authorized maintenance of composite and all-metal construction aircraft as contained in the FAA authorization.
5. Electronics division: Responsible for maintenance activities dealing with communication equipment, navigational equipment, radar, and instruments. Frequently this includes accessories such as starters, magnetos, and electronic systems. The approved activities are identified in the FAA certificate.
6. Parts division: Provides the parts, material, and logistics support for the department. Procures, stores, and maintains the inventory necessary to maintain the best economic balance for the business.

Certification

Aviation businesses must be identified as facilities qualified to conduct aircraft maintenance. Part 145-Repair Stations prescribes the requirements for obtaining a certificate as a repair station that authorizes aircraft maintenance work. This part prescribes the requirements for such a certificate, the procedure for obtaining the permit, general operating rules, and the various ratings issued. An applicant for a certificate applies on a form and in a manner prescribed by the FAA and forwards its inspection procedures manual, a list of any maintenance functions to be performed by others under contract, and a list of propellers and accessories to be maintained, if those ratings are requested. FAA is in the process of updating and revising Part 145. Figure 10.2 illustrates the application form used for a repair station certificate. The domestic repair stations may seek the following ratings:

Airframe ratings:

- Class 1: Composite construction of small aircraft;
- Class 2: Composite construction of large aircraft;
- Class 3: All-metal construction of small aircraft; and
- Class 4: All-metal construction of large aircraft.

Power plant ratings:

- Class 1: Reciprocating engines of 400 horsepower or less;
- Class 2: Reciprocating engines of more than 400 horsepower; and
- Class 3: Turbine engines.

Propeller ratings:

- Class 1: All fixed-pitch and ground-adjustable propellers of wood, metal or composite construction;
- Class 2: All other propellers by make.

Radio ratings:

- Class 1: Communication equipment;
- Class 2: Navigational equipment; and
- Class 3: Radar equipment.

Instrument ratings:

- Class 1: Mechanical instruments;
- Class 2: Electrical instruments;
- Class 3: Gyroscopic instruments; and
- Class 4: Electronic instruments.

Accessory ratings:

- Class 1: Mechanical accessories;
- Class 2: Electrical accessories; and
- Class 3: Electronic accessories.

The specific requirements for each of the ratings and the included classes are established in Part 145. The applicant is expected to provide the equipment and materials necessary for efficiently performing the identified job functions. Appendix VIII contains the job function required for each rating.

Figure 10.2 » Federal Aviation Administration Application for Repair Station Certificate

If additional space is required for any item, attach additional sheets of paper. OMB Approved 2120-0010

U.S. Department of Transportation
Federal Aviation Administration

Application for
Repair Station Certificate and/or Rating

1. Repair Station Name, Number, Location and Address

a. Official Name of Station — Number

b. Location where business conducted

c. Official Mailing Address of Repair Station *(Number, Street, City, State & ZIP)*

d. Doing Business As:

2. Reasons for Submission

- ☐ Original Application for Certificate and Rating
- ☐ Change in Rating
- ☐ Change in Location or Housing and Facilities
- ☐ Change in Ownership
- ☐ Other *(Specify)*

3. Ratings Applied for:

☐ Airframe	☐ Powerplant	☐ Propeller	☐ Radio	☐ Instrument
☐ Class 1	☐ Class 1	☐ Class 1	☐ Class 1	☐ Class 1
☐ Class 2	☐ Class 2	☐ Class 2	☐ Class 2	☐ Class 2
☐ Class 3	☐ Class 3		☐ Class 3	☐ Class 3
☐ Class 4				☐ Class 4

☐ Accessories	☐ Limited			
☐ Class 1	☐ Airframe	☐ Accessories	☐ Rotor Blades	☐ Specialized Services *(specify)*
☐ Class 2	☐ Engine	☐ Landing Gear	☐ Fabric	
☐ Class 3	☐ Propeller	☐ Floats	☐ Emergency Equip.	
	☐ Instrument	☐ Radio	☐ Non-Dest. Test	

4. List of Maintenance Functions Contracted to Outside Agencies:

5. Applicant's Certification

Name of Owner *(Include name(s) of individual owner, all partners, or corporation name giving state and date of incorporation)*

I hereby certify that I have been authorize by the repair station identified in Item 1 above to make this application and that statements and attachments hereto are true and correct to the best of my knowledge.

Date	Authorized Signature	Printed Name of Authorized Signer	Title

Agency Display of Estimated Burden: The FAA estimates that the average burden for this report form is 15 minutes per response. You may submit any comments regarding the accuracy of this burden estimate or any suggestions for reducing the burden to the Office of Management and Budget. You may also send comments to the Federal Aviation Administration, Aircraft Maintenance Division, AFS-300, 800 Independence Avenue, SW, Washington, DC 20591, Attention: OMB number 2120-0010.

FAA Form 8310-3 (6-95) Supersedes Previous Edition — AFS Electronic Forms System - JetForm FormFlow - 12/1998 — NSN: 0052-00-686-1002

Figure 10.2 » Continued

Record of Action
Repair Station Inspection

For FAA Use Only | **For FAA Use Only**

6. Remarks ***(Identify by item number. Include deficiencies found, ratings denied.)***

7. Findings - Recommendations	**8. Date of Inspection**
☐ A. Station was found to comply with requirements of FAR 145.	
☐ B. Station was found to comply with requirements of FAR 145 except for deficiencies listed in Item 6.	
☐ C. Recommend certificate with rating applied for on application be issued.	
☐ D. Recommend Certificate with rating applied for on application *(EXCEPT those listed in item 6)* be issued.	

9. Office	**Signature(s) of Inspector(s)**	**Printed Name(s) of Inspector(s)**

10. Supervising or Assigned Inspector

ACTION TAKEN	**CERTIFICATE ISSUED**	
☐ APPROVED as shown on certificate issued on date shown.	Number	Inspector's Signature
☐ DISAPPROVED	Date	Inspector's Printed Name — Title

FAA Form 8310-3 (6-95) Supersedes Previous Edition — AFS Electronic Forms System - JetForm FormFlow - 12/1998 — NSN: 0052-00-686-1002

Personnel

Maintenance personnel are the key to success in the aviation maintenance business. In order to ensure that the maintenance department is successful and contributes to the profitability of the overall business, the manager should be as knowledgeable as possible about the qualifications required of maintenance personnel, the training procedures, the process of certification, and the capabilities and limitations of maintenance personnel. Growing shortages of qualified aircraft maintenance personnel mean all possible steps should be taken to recruit and train people who will stay.

Qualifications

The Federal Aviation Regulations, Part 66, prescribe the requirements for an aviation mechanic and associated ratings and set forth the general operating rules for holders of the certificate. Subpart D of Part 66 specifies the eligibility requirements for a certified mechanic as follows:

1. At least 18 years of age.
2. Able to read, write, speak and understand the English language.
3. Has passed all the prescribed tests within a period of 24 months.
4. Meets the requirements for the specific rating requested.

A mechanic certificate can be obtained with an airframe or power-plant rating or both, if the applicant meets all the requirements. These requirements include knowledge as demonstrated in a written test, practical experience in the rating area sought, and skill demonstrated in an oral and practical test. The knowledge requirement calls for the applicant to pass a written test covering the construction and maintenance of aircraft appropriate to the rating he or she seeks and the regulations as contained in Parts 43, 65 and 91. The experience requirements may be met through completion of a certificated aviation maintenance technician school; or satisfactory evidence of eighteen months of practical experience in constructing, maintaining, or altering airframes or power plants, or thirty months of practical experience concurrently performing duties appropriate to both ratings. The oral and practical tests cover the applicant's basic skill in performing practical projects on the subjects covered by the written test for the rating.

Federal Aviation Regulation Part 147 was modified dramatically, effective in 1994. Of significance was a reduction in the number of hours required for learning about radial engines, fabric covering of aircraft, and woodworking. However, the substantial new requirements added to the curriculum include information about composite materials manufacturing and repair, avionics and electronics, as well as turbine and jet knowledge.

Training

Completing of a certificated aviation maintenance technician program usually fulfills the training or experience requirements of an aviation mechanic. A review of the requirements for such a program will provide some insight into the training given an aviation mechanic. The following are the major elements of the curriculum required by the FAA:

- Airframe—1,150 hours (400 general plus 750 airframe);
- Power plant—1,150 hours (400 general plus 750 power plant); and
- Combined airframe and power plant—1,900 hours (400 general plus 750 airframe and 750 power plant).

Coverage of the following subject areas is included:

- General curriculum;
- Basic electricity;
- Aircraft drawings;
- Weight and balance;
- Fluid lines and fittings;
- Materials and processes;
- Ground operations and servicing;
- Cleaning and corrosion control;
- Mathematics;
- Maintenance forms and records;
- Basic physics;
- Maintenance publications;
- Mechanic privileges and limitations;
- Airframe curriculum;
- Structures;
- Wood structures;

- Aircraft covering;
- Aircraft finishes;
- Sheet metal structures;
- Welding;
- Assembly and rigging;
- Airframe inspection;
- Airframe systems and components;
- Aircraft landing gear systems;
- Hydraulic and pneumatic power systems;
- Cabin atmosphere control systems;
- Aircraft instrument systems;
- Communication and navigation systems;
- Aircraft fuel systems;
- Aircraft electrical systems;
- Position and warning systems;
- Ice and rain control systems;
- Fire protection systems;
- Power plant curriculum;
- Power-plant theory and maintenance;
- Reciprocating engines;
- Turbine engines;
- Engine inspection;
- Power plant systems and components;
- Engine instrument systems;
- Engine fire protection systems;
- Engine electrical systems;
- Lubrication systems;
- Ignition systems;
- Fuel metering systems;
- Engine fuel systems;
- Induction systems;
- Engine cooling systems; and
- Engine exhaust systems.

Propellers

The curriculum must:

- Include practical projects;
- Balance theory and other instruction;
- Show a schedule of required tests; and
- Provide at least 50 percent of the total curriculum time should be in shop and laboratory instruction.

The majority of maintenance technician training is accomplished in FAA certificated schools using the recommended and approved curriculum of study. The FAA maintains a directory of all certificated schools that can be used in locating and selecting a school. This directory is published as Advisory Circular 147-2.2.

Training in specific aircraft, power plants, parts, and accessories is available from manufacturers or distributors of the various products as well as from various specialty commercial providers such as FlightSafety International and CAE Simuflite.[6] This training is most beneficial in enabling the maintenance technician to meet the FAA requirements and to understand the requirements of the manufacturer and the maintenance manuals for the equipment concerned. The maintenance manager must contact the manufacturer or his representative for a schedule of schools and programs and arrange attendance at the sessions needed by his personnel. The variety is too great and the schedule changes too numerous to attempt a listing here.

Certification

A candidate for an aviation mechanic's certificate must apply for the certificate and associated rating on a form prescribed by the Federal Aviation Administration. After review of the application and the supplementary documents indicating successful completion of the requirements in the knowledge, experience and skill areas, a certificate, and the appropriate ratings will be issued by the FAA.

Capabilities and Limitations

A certified mechanic is authorized by the FAA to perform certain functions, so long as he or she meets specified requirements. He or she may perform or supervise the maintenance or alteration of an aircraft or appliance, or part thereof, for which he or she is rated. If he has an airframe rating, he may approve and return to service any airframe, or any related part of appliance, after he has performed, supervised, or inspected its maintenance or alteration—excluding major repairs and major alterations, or after he has completed the 100-hour inspection required by Part 91. If he or she holds a power-plant rating, he or she may accomplish the same for a power plant, propeller, or any related part or appliance. To exercise these privileges, the mechanic must meet the following requirements:

1. He or she must have satisfactorily performed the work concerned at an earlier

An inspection authorization allows its holder to inspect and approve aircraft for return to service. Courtesy of Executive Beechcraft, Inc.

date, showed the FAA his/her ability to do it, or accomplished the work under the supervision of a certified mechanic who has had previous experience.

2. He or she must understand the current instructions of the manufacturer and the maintenance manuals for the specific operation concerned in order to exercise the privileges of his/her certificate and rating.
3. He or she must have had recent experience in his/her field. The FAA must have found within the preceding 24 months that he or she is able to do the work or that for at least six months he or she has served as a mechanic, technically supervised other mechanics, or supervised in an executive capacity the maintenance or alteration of aircraft.

Inspection Authorization

The next level of experience and responsibility for aviation mechanics is obtaining an inspection authorization. The holder of this authorization may inspect and approve for return to service any aircraft or related part or appliance (except those under a Part 121 or 127 continuous airworthiness program) after a major repair or major alteration. The holder of this authorization may also perform an annual inspection and perform or supervise a progressive inspection.

The candidate for an inspection authorization must meet additional requirements to qualify for this position. He or she must have been a certified mechanic for at least three years. For the last two years he or she must have been actively engaged in maintaining aircraft; have a fixed base of operations; have available the equipment, facilities and inspection data necessary to properly inspect aircraft; and pass a written test on his ability to inspect according to safety standards for returning aircraft to service after major repairs, major alterations, and annual and progressive inspections. The inspection authorization expires on March 31 of each year. To be renewed, the holder must show evidence that he or she (1) performed at least one annual inspection for each ninety days that he held the authority, (2) performed inspections of at least two major repairs or major alterations for each 90 days that he or she held the authority, or (3) performed or supervised and approved at least one progressive inspection in accordance with prescribed standards. Continuing education is also required.

Repairmen

A repairman certificate may be issued to personnel employed by a certified repair station, a certified commercial operator, or a certified air carrier that is required by its operating certificate or approved operations specification to provide a continuous airworthiness maintenance program according to its maintenance manuals. These personnel must be specially qualified to perform maintenance, be employed for a specific job requiring those special qualifications, and be recommended for certification by the employer. Additional requirements include 18 months of practical experience and English language qualifications.

A certified repairman may perform or supervise the maintenance of an aircraft or its components for the job that he or she was employed and certified, but only for his/her employer. He or she must perform these duties in accordance with the current instructions of his employer, the manufacturer of the article being maintained, and appropriate maintenance manuals.

Facilities and Equipment

Overview

A manager with the desire to operate a maintenance department must meet specific FAA requirements for facilities and equipment in order to qualify for a repair station certificate and rating. The facilities requirements include the following:

1. Housing for necessary equipment and material.
2. Space for the work to be accomplished under the rating.
3. Facilities for properly storing, segregating, and protecting materials, parts and supplies.
4. Facilities for properly protecting parts and subassemblies during disassembly, cleaning, inspection, repair, alteration, and assembly.
5. Suitable shop space where machine tools and equipment are kept and where the largest amount of bench work is done.
6. Suitable assembly space in an enclosed structure where the largest amount of assembly work is done. The space must be adequate for the work on the largest item covered by the rating requested.
7. Suitable storage facilities used exclusively for storing standard parts, spare parts, and raw materials. This area must be separated from the shop and working space, organized so that only acceptable parts and supplies will be issued for any job, and follow standard good practices for properly protecting stored materials.
8. Adequate storage and protection for parts being assembled or disassembled or awaiting work in order to eliminate the possibility of damage.
9. Suitable ventilation for the shop, assembly area, and storage area so that the physical efficiency of workers is not impaired.
10. Adequate lighting for all work being done so that the quality of the work is not impaired.
11. Temperature and humidity of the shop and assembly area must be controlled so that the quality of the work is not impaired.
12. For an airframe rating, there must be suitable permanent housing for at least one of the heaviest aircraft within the weight class of the rating.
13. For a power-plant or accessory rating there must be suitable trays, racks, or stands for segregating complete assemblies during assembly and disassembly.
14. A station with a propeller rating must provide suitable stands, racks, or other fixtures for proper storage of propellers.

15. For a radio rating there must be suitable storage facilities to assure protection of parts and units from dampness or moisture.
16. An instrument shop must be reasonably dust free, preferably air-conditioned.

The equipment requirements specified by the Federal Aviation Regulations for a repair station include the following:

1. The equipment and materials necessary to efficiently perform the functions of the ratings held (see Appendix VIII for a listing of these functions).
2. The equipment and materials required must be those that can efficiently and competently do the work. All inspection and test equipment shall be tested at regular intervals to ensure correct calibration.
3. Equipment and materials required for the various job functions must be located on the premises and under the full control of the station unless related to an authorized contract.

Managerial Concerns

The manager of a maintenance facility must be concerned with additional requirements in developing and operating the business. Included are:

> A concern for the economic efficiency of the facilities and equipment;
> The working environment for all employees concerned;
> The image presented by the facility to the customers and the general public;
> Fire, safety and construction laws promulgated by city, state and federal agencies;
> Requirements of manufacturers and distributors, if operating under a franchise arrangement; and
> Special requirements that may be generated by the manager or other source.

The equipment needed to furnish a maintenance shop for business represents a large capital investment and is a major concern, especially in view of the industry's rapidly changing technology and the resulting changes in aircraft construction, components and systems. Practical problems in this area include

> Determining the acquisition and inventory of test and repair equipment;
> Control of equipment and tools;
> Replacement and repair of facilities and equipment;
> Maintenance capability and capacity;
> The utilization of facilities; and
> Whether to make the necessary investments to establish an avionics shop or whether to refer or contract these needs to other FBOs.

Parts and Supplies

The inventory of maintenance supplies and parts provides another challenge to the manager, the maintenance department, and the entire organization. The goal is to maintain the proper balance between capital invested in supplies and parts, utilization of the mechanic's labor time, and customer satisfaction. An unlimited inventory of parts and supplies enables the manager to efficiently utilize maintenance labor and provide maximum customer satisfaction through rapid repair work. Such an investment level in inventory is prohibitive to any business. The cost of maintaining such an inventory far outweighs the advantages and results in a financial drain on the organization. Figure 10.3 shows a parts sales summary from FBO Manager.

On the other hand, a minimum inventory results in an inefficient utilization of shop personnel and sharp customer dissatisfaction. A minimum inventory results in needed items not being available locally. Consequently, shop personnel experience shortages, frequent waiting, and poor utilization of shop space. Customers find themselves waiting for parts to be located, ordered, and delivered. The longer they wait, the greater the dissatisfaction. All these elements would strongly influence the profitability of the overall maintenance activity.

The manager, as part of his responsibility, must consider all these factors and take the appropriate action. He must establish guidelines to be used in the operation of the parts department, identify the criteria to be used in evaluating the operation, and establish controls to be utilized in maintaining direction.

Figure 10.3 » Parts Sales Summary

Cornerstone Logic Inc.

Sales by Part Name for 11/01/1998 to 12/31/2001

Name	Description	Qty Sold	Taxes	Total (No Tax)
00-10-009	Narco ELT Battery	66.00	$82.94	$7,115.24
0050505725007	Paper Clips	248.16	$7.20	$1,017.64
13836	Bearing Race	88.80	$16.80	$749.65
13889CP RLR B	Timkin Tapered Roller Bearing	53.20	$27.74	$1,261.45
150-SR	Cessna 150 Seat Rails	44.00	$152.97	$3,957.80
1815179171001	Austria Book	19.00	$0.00	$246,399.33
250	250	570.00	$0.27	$33,094.00
251	251	6.00	$0.00	$0.00
252	252	4.00	$0.00	$17.00
52382	Baron Exhaust Stack	4.00	$128.99	$2,457.00
631544	Exhaust Gasket	39.00	$3.18	$72.82
631832	Upper Bracket	14.00	$3.00	$2,937.18
642917-1	642917-1 Intake Hose	38.00	$7.46	$358.19
649290	Spacers	110.00	$97.72	$2,042.23
649959	Gasket	4.00	$0.06	$1.60
652314	Lower Bracket	5.00	$6.00	$149.75
9781560273554	ASA Airframe Test Guide	15.00	$0.00	$579.15
AC Cleaning	Aircraft Cleaning	1.00	$0.00	$75.00
Aeroshell 50W	Aeroshell 50W	291.92	$47.60	$848.79
AN 4-5 A Bolt	AN 4-5 Hex Head Bolt	228.00	$0.00	$134.52
AN822-4D	90 Degree Fitting	318.00	$11.28	$18,291.36
Annual 36	Annual Inspection 36 Hours	2.00	$0.00	$3,200.00
APU	APU	1.00	$0.00	$150.00
AS 50/100	Aeroshell 50/100W	30.00	$7.02	$117.00
ASA-00-6A	Aviation Weather	21.00	$0.00	$252.00
ASA-61-21A	Flight Training Handbook	15.00	$0.00	$150.53
ASA-61-27C	Instrument Flying Handbook	17.00	$2.73	$146.00
ASA-97-FR-AM	1997 FAR/AIM	-51.00	$29.53	$3,303.54
ASA-BAG-FLT	Flight Bag	70.00	$0.00	$4,055.66
ASA-SP-30	Pilot Log Book - Black	25.00	$0.70	$173.75
CallOutFee	Call Out Fee 0-50 Gallons	3.00	$0.00	$200.00
Car Rental	Rental Car	1.00	$0.00	$78.00
Catering	Catering	7.00	$0.00	$1,010.87
CH48109	Champion Oil Filter	21.00	$0.17	$387.66
Charter Ops	Charter Operations	300.00	$0.00	$897.00
CreditCardFee	Credit Card Fees	20.00	$0.00	$5,839.41
CreditTransAc	Credit Card Transition Account	726.45	$0.00	$726.45
DeIcing	De-Icing	1.00	$0.00	$50.00

Courtesy of FBO Manager by Cornerstone Logic, Inc.

Inventory Control

A good system of control for parts and supplies will greatly improve the buying and selling activity and result in a more efficient service activity. A good system will provide information on the following:

1. The right quantities to buy;
2. Items no longer popular;
3. The amount of a given item sold;
4. The season or time a given item sells;
5. The time to stop buying seasonable goods;
6. The kind of goods customers want;
7. The time to display and promote certain items;
8. Articles that are slow movers;
9. Particular items for which demand is declining;
10. Best buying sources;
11. Best buying prices;
12. Price preferences of customers;
13. Possibilities for new lines or kinds of goods; and
14. Whether stock is in proper balance.

A system that provides this kind of information to the manager will eliminate many inventory problems and contribute to the success of the maintenance shop. Efficient and profitable control of the inventory of parts and supplies does not have to be difficult, complex, or expensive. Many manufacturers, agencies, and associations can furnish good inventory systems to aviation businesses. Most of these systems are economical, simple, and easy to operate. They are easy to install, can be expanded or contracted to fit the business need, and can be handled in a few minutes each day by personnel with little special training. Typical of the systems available to aviation businesses is the inventory control system made available by The New Piper Aircraft Corporation to the organizations providing service to Piper aircraft. Figure 10.4 illustrates the preprinted inventory card that is part of the basic system.

There are three common methods of securing the information needed for inventory control in an aviation activity: observation, physical check, and perpetual inventory. Observation is used by the smaller aviation businesses and may be sufficient where the number of items is not large, the flow of sales is fairly constant, and the manager is in close daily contact with all the suppliers. The physical check of the inventory does become desirable, or even necessary, when the rate of sales

Figure 10.4 » Piper Aircraft Inventory Card

PART NO. ______ ITEM ______ MIN. ______ LOCATION ______

MFGR ______ STD. PAGE ______ MAX. ______ LIST PRICE ______

DATE	ORDERED	RECEIVED	SOLD	BALANCE	DATE	ORDERED	RECEIVED	SOLD	BALANCE	

PART NO. ITEM

varies on some basis or when there are some higher-valued items included in the inventory. This kind of periodic stock-taking is basically a physical count of the parts and supplies at a given time, which can then be compared to the number received and sold in the past in order to arrive at an estimate of the amount needed to replenish the stock. The perpetual inventory record, as illustrated in Figure 10.4, enables the manager to know at all times the amount of goods that should be on hand.

Economic Ordering Quantity. (EOQ) In maintaining a sound inventory control, a manager must determine the most economical ordering quantity for the various materials in the aviation parts department. The most economical amount of material to purchase at one time and at a given price is that quantity where the total cost per unit is at a minimum. This low point occurs when the unit cost of preparing the purchase order for that quantity is equal to the unit cost of carrying the material in the supply room. In other words, the costs of inventory acquisition (ordering) must be balanced against inventory possession (storing). Figure 10.5 graphically presents the basic EOQ formula. The fundamental cost relationships may be expressed by the following formula:

$$Q = \sqrt{\frac{2RA}{P}}$$

Q = Quantity
R = Annual Requirements
A = Acquisition costs per order
P = Possession costs of holding one unit of inventory for one year

When maintaining good inventory control, it is important that the manager know when to order the material as well as the correct quantity to or-

Figure 10.5 » Basic EOQ Graph

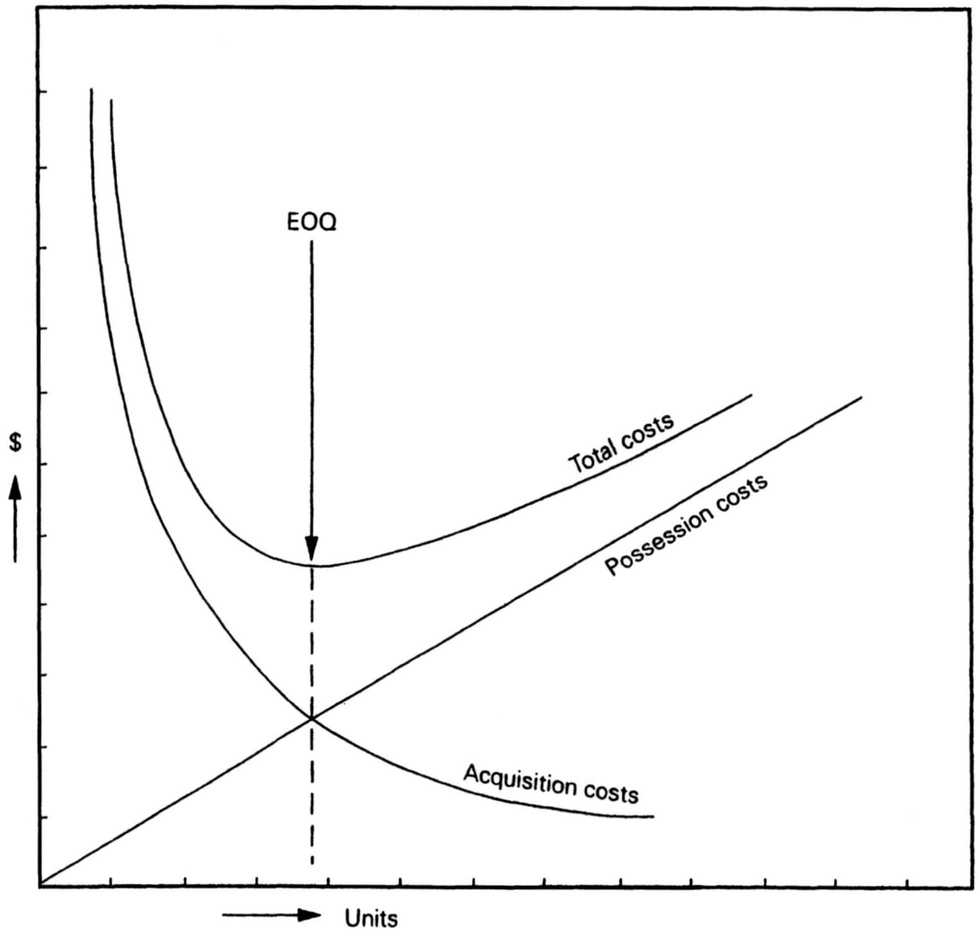

Source: Dr. J. D. Richardson

der. In determining the correct reorder point it is necessary that two factors be considered: (1) the consumption rate in units; and (2) the time required for procurement. Normally, since an out-of-stock situation is costly, the manager adds a buffer of a minimum safe inventory level to the theoretical ordering point in order to arrive at the actual reordering point. The following example illustrates this procedure with spark plugs of a particular type:

1200	Spark plugs used annually
2	Weeks reorder time
46	Theoretical reorder point (1200 ÷ 26)
25	Average one-week safety level
46 + 24 = 71	Actual reordering point

More and more businesses are using Just-In-Time (JIT) ordering of inventory, where less is maintained in stock because required items can be obtained very fast and often overnight by air express. The items touched upon in this section represent the major elements of inventory control—the inventory records and a replenishment system. To realize the benefits listed at the beginning of this section, the manager must install the system and utilize the data represented by the records. Careful analysis of accumulated inventory data leads to decisions that keep inventory within bounds.

Quality Control

Producing good maintenance is desired primarily in order to secure customer satisfaction. Quality control is a key method for ensuring that a maintenance department consistently produces a product that results in high customer satisfaction. Although the term quality control may produce

A great deal of aviation maintenance work includes lengthy procedures with many safety checks and requirements. Courtesy of Executive Beechcraft, Inc.

an unpleasant image in some minds—akin to that of police officer or monitor—the concept actually should be much more agreeable and supportive. The best quality control is achieved when the work environment lets individual employees know that good work is desired and expected, and they strive to achieve this as a personal as well as an organizational goal. Fortunately, there are some specific steps a manager can take to develop this attitude throughout the maintenance organization:

1. Provide training in the specific procedures to be followed and requirements to be met for each maintenance operation.
2. Provide checklists and guidelines to facilitate quality work.
3. Provide for the inspection of finished work by a person other than the one doing the work, and create an environment in which this procedure is totally accepted as desirable.
4. Ensure the recognition of quality work and of the individuals responsible for its accomplishment.

Training

Aviation mechanics that graduate from certified technical schools have a sound educational basis for their job. Throughout their training the need for quality work is emphasized. There is a need for continued training in the specific procedures to be followed and in the requirements of quality maintenance, repair, and alteration. This continued training is necessary for new procedures; new materials such as composites, new equipment, new requirements; and as a refresher course. Some of this training can be accomplished on-site in the local shop, while other training must be accomplished at plants, schools, or in training seminars. The organization's emphasis on quality will develop the desired attitude toward a quality product.

Checklists

A great deal of aviation maintenance work includes lengthy procedures with many safety checks and requirements. To ensure that all the required work is accomplished in the proper sequence with the desired safety checks and with the proper level of quality, checklists and guidelines have been developed. Figure 10.6 illustrates a typical list developed to ensure that all necessary items were checked on the inspection of a new aircraft after its first 50 hours. Operating and maintenance manuals frequently use checklists and procedure guides to ensure that disassembly, repair, and assembly are accomplished in proper sequence. One problem in the use of checklists is the tendency for some individuals to work from memory, and then later sign off the checklist as having been completed. Unfortunately, since this practice can lead to items being overlooked and subsequent difficulties, it is highly desirable that individuals and the organization strive to develop work patterns that utilize checklists and guides as a standard procedure.

Inspection

In the regulations dealing with maintenance personnel and maintenance procedures, the Federal Aviation Administration has provided for inspectors and inspection procedures. Quality of work and safety of flight are of primary importance, and one way to ensure them is to provide for the inspection of work by a person other than the one doing the work. It is hoped that this procedure will provide a degree of objectivity and an alternative viewpoint that will catch items overlooked or not completed correctly. Of course, the success of an inspection procedure will depend largely upon the qualifications and thoroughness of the inspecting personnel. The attitude of employees and the working environment must be such that the inspection procedure be universally accepted.

Recognition

One important aspect of obtaining quality work by a maintenance unit is the prompt recognition of high-quality work and of the individuals who have produced that work. This recognition can take many forms, ranging from personal praise, unit recognition, and publicity to financial incentives. Of course, the recognition must be sincere. Acknowledgement of low-quality work must also ensure that it does not become the accepted standard. Verbal reminders, corrective action, discipline, and even firing may be used to point out that low quality is not acceptable.

Figure 10.6 » Aircraft Maintenance Inspection Checklist

PIPER AIRCRAFT CORPORATION

INSPECTION REPORT

THIS FORM MEETS REQUIREMENTS OF FAR PART 43

MAKE	MODEL	Serial No.	Registration No.
PIPER CHEROKEE	PA-28R-180 PA-28R-200		

Circle Type of Inspection (See Note)

50 100 500 1000 Annual

Perform inspection or operation at each of the inspection intervals as indicated by a circle (O).

DESCRIPTION	50	100	500	1000	Inspector
A. PROPELLER GROUP					
1. Inspect spinner and back plate (See Note 5)	O	O	O	O	
2. Inspect blades for nicks and cracks	O	O	O	O	
3. Check for grease and oil leaks	O	O	O	O	
4. Lubricate propeller per lubrication chart	O	O	O	O	
5. Check spinner mounting brackets		O	O	O	
6. Check propeller mounting bolts and safety (Check torque if safety is broken.)		O	O	O	
7. Inspect hub parts for cracks and corrosion		O	O	O	
8. Rotate blades of constant speed propeller and check for tightness in hub pilot tube		O	O	O	
9. Remove constant speed propeller, remove sludge from propeller and crankshaft			O	O	
10. Inspect complete propeller and spinner assembly for security, chafing, cracks, deterioration, wear, and correct installation		O	O	O	
11. Overhaul propeller				O	
B. ENGINE GROUP					
CAUTION: Ground Magneto Primary Circuit before working on engine.					
1. Remove engine cowl	O	O	O	O	
2. Clean and check cowling for cracks, distortion and loose or missing fasteners		O	O	O	
3. Drain oil sump (See Note 2)	O	O	O	O	
4. Clean suction oil strainer at oil change (Check strainer for foreign particles.)	O	O	O	O	
5. Clean pressure oil strainer or change full flow (cartridge type) oil filter element (Check strainer or element for foreign particles)	O	O	O	O	
6. Check oil temperature sender unit for leaks and security		O	O	O	
7. Check oil lines and fitting for leaks, security, chafing, dents and cracks (See Note 4)	O	O	O	O	
8. Clean and check oil radiator cooling fins		O	O	O	
9. Remove and flush oil radiator	O	O	O	O	
10. Fill engine with oil per lubrication chart	O	O	O	O	
11. Clean engine		O	O	O	
CAUTION: Do not contaminate the vacuum pump with cleaning fluid. Ref: Lycoming Service Letter 1221A.					
12. Check condition of spark plugs (Clean and adjust gap as required, adjust per Lycoming Service Instruction No. 1042.)		O	O	O	
13. Check cylinder compression ref: AC43. 13-1		O	O	O	
14. Check ignition harness and insulators (High tension leakage and continuity.)		O	O	O	
15. Check magneto points for proper clearance (Maintain clearance at 0.016.)		O	O	O	
16. Check magneto for oil leakage		O	O	O	
17. Check breaker felts for proper lubrication		O	O	O	
18. Check distributor block for cracks, burned areas or corrosion, and height of contact springs			O	O	
19. Check magnetos to engine timing		O	O	O	
20. Overhaul or replace magnetos (See Note 3)				O	
21. Remove air filter and tap gently to remove dirt particles (Replace as required.)	O	O	O	O	
22. Clean fuel injector inlet line screen (Clean injector nozzles as required.) (Clean with acetone only)	O	O	O	O	
23. Check condition of injector alternate air door and box	O	O	O	O	
24. Check intake seals for leaks and clamps for tightness		O	O	O	
25. Inspect all air inlet duct hoses (Replace as required.)		O	O	O	
26. Inspect condition of flexible fuel lines		O	O	O	
27. Replace flexible fuel lines (See Note 3)				O	
28. Check fuel system for leaks		O	O	O	
29. Check fuel pumps for operation (Engine driven and electric.)		O	O	O	
30. Overhaul or replace fuel pumps (Engine driven and electric (See Note 3)				O	
31. Check vacuum pump and lines		O	O	O	
32. Overhaul or replace vacuum pump (See Note 3).				O	
33. Check throttle, alternate air, mixture and propeller governor controls for travel and operating condition		O	O	O	
34. Inspect exhaust stacks, connections and gaskets (Refer to PA-28 Service Manual, Section III. Replace gaskets as required.)		O	O	O	
35. Inspect muffler, heat exchange and baffles (Refer to PA-28 Service Manual, Section III.)		O	O	O	
36. Check breather tube for obstructions and security.		O	O	O	
37. Check crankcase for cracks, leaks and security of seam bolts		O	O	O	
38. Check engine mounts for cracks and loose mountings		O	O	O	
39. Check all engine baffles		O	O	O	
40. Check rubber engine mount bushings for deterioration (Replace as required.)		O	O	O	
41. Check firewall seals		O	O	O	
42. Check condition and tension of alternator drive belt (Refer to PA-28 Service Manual.)		O	O	O	
43. Check condition of alternator and starter		O	O	O	
44. Check fluid in brake reservoir (Fill as required.)	O	O	O	O	
45. Lubricate all controls		O	O	O	
46. Overhaul or replace propeller governor (See Note 3)				O	
47. Complete overhaul of engine or replace with factory rebuilt (See Note 3)				O	
48. Reinstall engine cowl	O	O	O	O	

Owner 508

230 259 710111

Figure 10.6 » Continued

Circle Type of Inspection (See Note)
50 100 500 1000 Annual

Perform inspection or operation at each of the inspection intervals as indicated by a circle (◯).

DESCRIPTION	50	100	500	1000	Inspector
C. CABIN GROUP					
1. Inspect cabin entrance, doors and windows for damage and operation		O	O	O	
2. Check upholstery for tears		O	O	O	
3. Checks seats, seat belts, security brackets and bolts		O	O	O	
4. Check trim operation		O	O	O	
5. Check rudder pedals		O	O	O	
6. Check parking brake and brake handle for operation and cylinder leaks		O	O	O	
7. Check control wheels, column, pulleys and cables		O	O	O	
8. Check landing, navigation, cabin and instrument lights	O	O	O	O	
9. Check instruments, lines and attachments		O	O	O	
10. Check gyro operated instruments and electric turn and bank (Overhaul or replace as required.)		O	O	O	
11. Replace filters on gyro horizon and directional gyro or replace central air filter		O	O	O	
12. Clean or replace vacuum regulator filter		O	O	O	
13. Check altimeter (Calibrate altimeter system in accordance with FAR 91.170, if appropriate.)		O	O	O	
14. Check operation of fuel selector valve		O	O	O	
15. Check condition of heater controls and ducts		O	O	O	
16. Check condition and operaton of air vents		O	O	O	
D. FUSELAGE AND EMPENNAGE GROUP					
1. Remove inspection plates and panels		O	O	O	
2. Check baggage door, latch and hinges		O	O	O	
3. Check battery, box and cables (Check at least every 30 days. Flush box as required and fill battery per instructions on box.)	O	O	O	O	
4. Check electronic installation		O	O	O	
5. Check bulkheads and stringers for damage		O	O	O	
6. Check antenna mounts and electric wiring		O	O	O	
7. Check hydraulic pump fluid level (Fill as required.)	O	O	O	O	
8. Check hydraulic pump lines for damage and leaks		O	O	O	
9. Check for obstructions and contamination in inlet of back-up landing gear extender actuator inlet head	O	O	O	O	
10. Check fuel lines, valves and gauges for damage and operation		O	O	O	
11. Check security of all lines		O	O	O	
12. Check vertical fin and rudder surfaces for damage		O	O	O	
13. Check rudder hinges, horn and attachments for damage and operation		O	O	O	
14. Check vertical fin attachments		O	O	O	
15. Check rudder hinge bolts for excess wear (Replace as required.)		O	O	O	
16. Check stabilator surfaces for damage		O	O	O	
17. Check stabilator, tab hinges, horn and attachments for damage and operation		O	O	O	
18. Check stabilator attachments		O	O	O	
19. Check stabilator and tab hinge bolts and bearings for excess wear (Replace as required.)		O	O	O	
20. Check stabilator trim mechanism		O	O	O	
21. Check aileron, rudder, stabilator, stabilator trim cables, turnbuckles, guides and pulleys for safety, damage and operation		O	O	O	
22. Clean and lubricate stabilator trim drum screw			O	O	
23. Clean and lubricate all exterior needle bearings				O	
24. Lubricate per lubrication chart	O	O	O	O	
25. Check rotating beacon for security and operation		O	O	O	
26. Check security of AutoPilot bridle cable clamps		O	O	O	
27. Inspect all control cables, air ducts, electrical leads, lines, radio antenna leads and attaching parts for security, routing, chafing, deterioration, wear, and correct installation		O	O	O	
28. Reinstall inspection plates and panels		O	O	O	
E. WING GROUP					
1. Remove inspection plates and fairings		O	O	O	
2. Check surfaces and tips for damage, loose rivets, and condition of walk-way		O	O	O	
3. Check aileron hinges and attachments		O	O	O	
4. Check aileron cables, pulleys and bellcranks for damage and operation		O	O	O	
5. Check flaps and attachments for damage and operation		O	O	O	
6. Check condition of bolts used with hinges (Replace as required.)				O	
7. Lubricate per lubrication chart	O	O	O	O	
8. Check wing attachment bolts and brackets		O	O	O	
9. Check fuel tanks and lines for leaks and water		O	O	O	
10. Fuel tanks marked for capacity		O	O	O	
11. Fuel tanks marked for minimum octane rating.					
12. Check fuel cell vents		O	O	O	
13. Inspect all control cables, air ducts, electrical leads, lines and attaching parts of security, routing, chafing, deterioration, wear, and correct installation		O	O	O	
14. Reinstall ispection plates and fairings		O	O	O	
F. LANDING GEAR GROUP					
1. Check oleo struts for proper extension (N-2,75 in. /M-2.0in.) (Check fluid level as required.)	O	O	O	O	
2. Check nose gear steering control and travel		O	O	O	
3. Check wheels for alignment		O	O	O	
4. Put airplane on jacks		O	O	O	
5. Check tires for cuts, uneven or excessive wear and slippage		O	O	O	
6. Remove wheels, clean, check and repack bearings		O	O	O	
7. Check wheels for cracks, corrosion and broken bolts		O	O	O	
8. Check tire pressure (N-30 psi/M-27 psi)	O	O	O	O	
9. Check brake lining and disc		O	O	O	
10. Check brake backing plates		O	O	O	
11. Check brake and hydraulic lines		O	O	O	
12. Check shimmy dampener		O	O	O	
13. Check gear forks for damage		O	O	O	
14. Check oleo struts for fluid leaks and scoring		O	O	O	

Figure 10.6 » Continued

Circle Type of Inspection (See Note)

50 100 500 1000 Annual

DESCRIPTION	50	100	500	1000	Inspector
15. Check gear struts, attachments, torque links, retraction links and bolts for condition and security		O	O	O	
16. Check downlock for operation and adjustment.		O	O	O	
17. Check torque link bolts and bushings (Rebush as required.)			O	O	
18. Check drag and side brace link bolts (Replace as required.)				O	
19. Check gear doors and attachments		O	O	O	
20. Check warning horn and light for operation		O	O	O	
21. Retract gear – check operation		O	O	O	
22. Retract gear – check doors for clearance and operation		O	O	O	
23. Check anti-retraction system		O	O	O	
24. Check actuating cylinders for leaks and security		O	O	O	
25. Inspect all hydraulic lines, electrical leads, and attaching parts for security, routing, chafing, deterioration, wear, and correct installation		O	O	O	
26. Check position indicator switch and electrical leads for security		O	O	O	
27 Lubricate per lubrication chart	O	O	O	O	
28 Remove airplane from jacks		O	O	O	

Perform inspection or operation at each of the inspection intervals as indicated by a circle (O).

DESCRIPTION	50	100	500	1000	Inspector
G. OPERATIONAL INSPECTION					
1. Check fuel pump and fuel tank selector	O	O	O	O	
2. Check fuel quantity, pressure and flow readings	O	O	O	O	
3. Check oil pressure and temperature	O	O	O	O	
4. Check alternator output	O	O	O	O	
5. Check manifold pressure	O	O	O	O	
6. Check alternate air	O	O	O	O	
7. Check parking brake	O	O	O	O	
8. Check vacuum gauge	O	O	O	O	
9. Check gyros for noise and roughness	O	O	O	O	
10. Check cabin heater operation	O	O	O	O	
11. Check magneto switch operation	O	O	O	O	
12. Check magneto RPM variation	O	O	O	O	
13. Check throttle and mixture operation	O	O	O	O	
14. Check propeller smoothness	O	O	O	O	
15. Check propeller governor action	O	O	O	O	
16. Check engine idle	O	O	O	O	
17. Check electronic equipment operation	O	O	O	O	
H. GENERAL					
1. Aircraft conforms to FAA Specification	O	O	O	O	
2. All FAA Airworthiness Directives complied with	O	O	O	O	
3. All Manufacturers Service Bulletins and Letters complied with	O	O	O	O	
4. Check for proper Flight Manual	O	O	O	O	
5. Aircraft papers in proper order	O	O	O	O	

NOTES:

1. Both the annual and 100 hour inspections are complete inspections of the airplane – identical in scope. Inspections must be accomplished by persons authorized by FAA.
2. Intervals between oil changes can be increased as much as 100% on engines equipped with full flow (cartridge type) oil filters – provided the element is replaced each 50 hours of operation.
3. Replace or overhaul as required or at engine overhaul. (For engine overhaul, refer to Lycoming Service Instructions No. 1009.)
4. Replace flexible oil lines as required, but no later than 1,000 hours of service.
5. Inspect in accordance with Piper Service Bulletin 309.

REMARKS:

Signature of Mechanic or Inspector	Certificate No.	Date	Total Time on Airplane

230 290

Courtesy Piper Aircraft Corp.

Balance

Quality control, like other business activities, is costly. Additional quality can be obtained with additional training, more checklists and guidelines, more inspectors, and lavish recognition programs. At some point the question must be asked: "How much quality is desired—and how much can we afford?" The manager must obviously determine the desirable balance between the costs involved and the acceptable level of quality, and then strive to maintain that balance.

Competition

Nonexclusive Rights

Airports that have been federally funded or that hope to be are obligated to permit all aeronautical operators who can be accommodated to use the field, provided they meet certain standards. Thus existing FBOs are constantly under the threat of new competition at federally funded airports. While this in some ways is in the public interest, at small fields it makes it difficult to achieve a reasonable profit.

Referrals

As a result of the competitive environment facing many FBOs, some prefer to refer their maintenance and repair work out to other operators on the field or elsewhere. This referral process will probably work well in both directions until there is a change in the performance of the other business. In this case not only does the FBO have very little control over his clients' maintenance needs, but also the poor service from the maintenance operator may drive them to another field for all their needs.

Subcontracting

Aviation managers frequently find themselves considering the feasibility of subcontracting some, or all, of their maintenance or avionics work. It may be that the light maintenance workload does not warrant having a shop or that it is not adequate to support the purchase of some special and expensive test equipment. Also it may not be sufficient to acquire and utilize the necessary skilled maintenance technicians. Any of these concerns might cause the manager to subcontract maintenance work. The decision of when to subcontract is normally based upon a consideration of the points just identified.

The use of financial comparisons may also be valuable in arriving at a decision on subcontracting. In each situation it becomes necessary to accumulate all the cost and income data related to the decision while being as objective as possible. There may be a number of factors that cannot be easily quantified but still must be considered, such as available human resources, management capability, space utilization, time to accomplish maintenance, control over quality, and customer reaction. All these elements should be considered in a rational decision-making process as described in Chapter 2, Management Functions.

When maintenance work is subcontracted, the amount should be recorded, and periodically the volume of work and the overall situation should be analyzed in order to verify the decision to continue subcontracting. This analysis should be done to identify the point when it becomes economically or strategically feasible to acquire the people, equipment, and space and financing needed to accomplish the maintenance work within the organization.

Problems. There are several problem areas that are related to subcontracting that should be identified by the manager, considered in the decision-making process, and monitored on a day-by-day basis. Included are:

1. Negotiating an equitable contract and monitoring its operation.
2. Handling warranty questions to the satisfaction of the customer and the contractor.
3. Dealing with liability situations in the legal environment.
4. Providing for customer satisfaction and customer identification with the primary business as well as the subcontractor.
5. Ensuring that the subcontracting operation is profitable on a direct job-basis and on a long-range basis.

Recognizing these problem areas and striving to overcome their potential difficulties becomes the responsibility of the manager and a challenge to administrative skills.

"Through-the-Fence" Operations

This type of activity refers to FBOs who are not airport tenants but own or lease adjacent land and access the airport through a real or imaginary fence at the property line. They can siphon off business from the FBO(s) on the field who are paying for the operation of the airfield, taxiways and other public areas. Where a new through-the-fence proposal is made, there are some safeguards recommended by FAA for protecting existing tenants. But where the situation has existed for many years, as often seems to be the case, it can periodically become very troublesome. The airport owner has no real control over such an operator, except denying access until acceptable financial and performance arrangements are established. In a case where a through-the-fence operator has an existing access easement with the airport owner, it may be difficult to negate or tighten its terms. Ideally an access fee should be charged for use of the airport.

As available land on public airports becomes scarcer, the public airport system seems likely to receive more requests for through-the-fence rights, and the semi-active through-the-fence operator may become more of a challenge also. FBOs whose airports have potential or actual sites for through-the-fence activity need to make their own interests and concerns clearly known to the public airport operator.

Tailgate, Shade Tree, and Gypsy Mechanics

As costs of repairs go up, more people are repairing their own aircraft. As long as they comply with the required inspections, this is a legitimate activity. However, commercial repair services unofficially operating in individual hangars or other locations are not legitimate. All aeronautical operators providing services for sale on a public airport must have permission and an appropriate lease. Illegal operators may be doing poor work that the legitimate FBOs may later have to correct, even to the point of liability for aircraft originally sold but never maintained by them. The "gypsy" operator conveniently disappears when trouble starts. Thus, as with through-the-fence operators, the FBO must be ever diligent in reporting such activities and insisting on enforcement of the same minimum standards for all.

Corporate and Other Self-Maintenance

Like self-fueling, this is a growing trend for economic and other reasons and is permitted under the nonexclusive rights provisions at federally funded airports. The FBO may still be able to capture some of these repair dollars for specialized work, FAA inspections, and the sale of parts.

Administration

The administration of a maintenance department and its associated paperwork is another area requiring specific attention by the manager. These functions can and should consume a fair amount of time. It cannot be over-emphasized that appropriate record keeping in accordance with FAA requirements is essential to the long-term health of the business. The following activities are included in the term "maintenance administration":

1. Developing, understanding, and administering the overall maintenance organization and system.
2. Developing and maintaining the necessary maintenance procedures, records, and library.
3. Complying with the necessary records and entries required in accomplishing maintenance repair or alteration.
4. Maintaining the necessary internal records associated with accounting, budgeting, job or work orders, and time cards.
5. Dealing with FAA regulations, procedures, and inspections.

These major activities will vary in content and meaning from business to business. Normally, they are included in the package known as administration. The first area is primarily the job of efficiently organizing the department and then developing the administrative structure and procedures for effective operation. The second activity deals with the need to develop, maintain, and administer:

1. The operating procedures and guidelines to be followed in effecting maintenance, repair and alteration.
2. The necessary technical records that must be maintained.
3. The manuals and data that must be available in the department library.

The third activity area includes compliance with regulations and the completion of various FAA and manufacturer records required when doing maintenance work. The final activity area for shop administration deals with the completion of the necessary internal business records. Included are the records dealing with accounting, budgeting, personnel, processing shop orders, employee time cards, purchase orders, and safety reports.

Figure 10.7 shows a shop order sample from FBO Manager, and Figure 10.8 shows an example of the computer screen shop order from TotalFBO. Figure 10.9 shows an internal aircraft shop order form from TotalFBO.

Flat-Rate Pricing

Pricing determinations for the products of the maintenance department normally include all the considerations mentioned in Chapter 3, Marketing. These considerations must recognize the three cost components: material, labor, and overhead.

In many instances the traditional methods of determining prices for aviation maintenance work, assigning workloads to mechanics, and compensating individual employees have not resulted in an efficient operation. The organization might find itself with a poor utilization of maintenance labor and a departmental profit center that is not profitable! One suggested solution to this problem has been the development and application of a flat-rate price structure to aircraft maintenance. The technique is not new; it has been used in the automobile industry for years. Use of a flat-rate manual in the aviation industry is growing. Its procedures, advantages, and problems are included here. The operating procedure when using a flat-rate billing structure is as follows:

1. A flat-rate manual covering the type of maintenance service to be offered is acquired or developed.
2. The job to be accomplished is positively identified.
3. The manual is used to obtain the standard time suggested for accomplishing the job.
4. The work is accomplished by assigned personnel.
5. The individual completing the job is compensated according to the time schedule in the flat-rate manual, not how long it takes to actually complete the work.
6. If the job is returned for rework or correction, it is accomplished by the person doing the initial work, on his or her time, and without additional compensation.

When an aviation business begins operating under a flat-rate manual procedure, the following advantages are normally experienced:

1. Maintenance employees become work-oriented and time conscious.
2. The maintenance department experiences increased productivity and efficiency.
3. The quality of maintenance work improves and produces better customer satisfaction.
4. The flat-rate process tends to up-grade the level of employees with the marginal or less motivated leaving voluntarily.
5. The maintenance employees operating under a flat-rate manual experience a 10 to 20 percent increase in compensation.

The most frequent concerns regarding operating a maintenance facility under a flat-rate procedure have been:

- "My mechanics will never go for that procedure!"
- "Quality of work will go down, and we cannot tolerate that in aviation!"
- "I have no flat-rate manual for aircraft in my geographic area."

The first concern regarding mechanic reaction is best handled by a knowledgeable and determined manager who convinces his employees of the advantages of the procedure. As for the second concern, experience in several operations suggests that poor quality does not result from the system itself. Once the work force has stabilized under a flat-rate system, the quality seems to improve; perhaps the workers with higher qualifications are striving to do a better job and prevent rework and correction. Of course, the normal quality-control procedures and inspections continue in order to maintain the desired level of work.

The final problem is obtaining a flat-rate manual that adequately covers the type of aircraft serviced by a particular business in its unique geographic location. Since the various aircraft makes

Figure 10.7 » Shop Order

WORK ORDER TU-1076

Remit to:	

Bill to:			Shop Order #: TU-1076 Date Printed: 05/21/2002 Date Opened: 03/01/2002 Date Closed: 03/01/2001 Phone Number

Aircraft Information
Number:

Item: 1	ACCOMPLISH INCOMING INSP. DEPARTURE INSP. LOG BOOK ENTRY AND ALL ASSOCIATED PAPERWORK. (INSP USE ONLY).				
Corrective Action:	ACCOMPLISH INCOMING INSP. OF EXTERIOR AND INTERIOR A/C.				
	Labor Charges -	2.50 @	$62.00	+$0.00=	$155.00
				Labor SubTotal	$155.00
				Item SubTotal	$155.00

Item: 2	ACCOMPLISH LT AND RRT ENGINE 150 HR INSPECTIONS.				
Corrective Action:	COMPLIED WITH 150 HR ENGINE INSPECTION ON R/H AND L/H ENGINES AS REQUIRED. OIL FILTER REQUIRES ENGINE RUN FOR LEAK CHK. LEAK CHK GOOD - NO DISCREPANCIES NOTED AT THIS TIME.				
	Labor Charges -	10.50 @	$62.00	+$0.00=	$651.00
				Labor SubTotal	$651.00
				Item SubTotal	$651.00

Item: 3	ACCOMPLISH LT AND RT 150 THRUST REVERSER INSPECTIONS.				
Corrective Action:	PERFORMED A 150 HR THRUST REVERSER INSP. PER LEAK JET MM ON L&R THRUST REVERSER.				
	Labor Charges -	7.50 @	$62.00	+$0.00=	$465.00
				Labor SubTotal	$465.00
				Item SubTotal	$465.00

Item: 4	REMOVE AND REPLACE ENGINE FIRE BOTTLE.				
Corrective Action:	PULLED L/H FIRE EXT & REMOVED L/H FIRE EXTINGUISHER BOTTLE INSTALLED FIRE BOTTLE PER MM 26-20-01. (SAFETIED SWIVEL FITTINGS & SQUIBS, NO DISCREPANCIES NOTED AT THIS TIME.				
	Labor Charges -	8.00 @	$62.00	+$0.00=	$496.00
Part #	Description	Quantity	Price	Tax	Total
30402102-1	FIRE BOTTLE	1	$1,488.00	$0.00	$1,488.00
				Shop Order #:	**TU-1076**
				Labor SubTotal	$496.00
				Parts SubTotal	$1,488.00
				Item SubTotal	$1,984.00

Outside Labor	$0.00
Outside Parts	$0.00
Total Parts	$1,488.00
Labor Hours	28.5
Total Labor	$1,767.00
Tax	$0.00
Total	$1,550.00

Notes: Invoice Number: TUL-0002

Courtesy of FBO Manager.

Figure 10.8 » Shop Order Screen

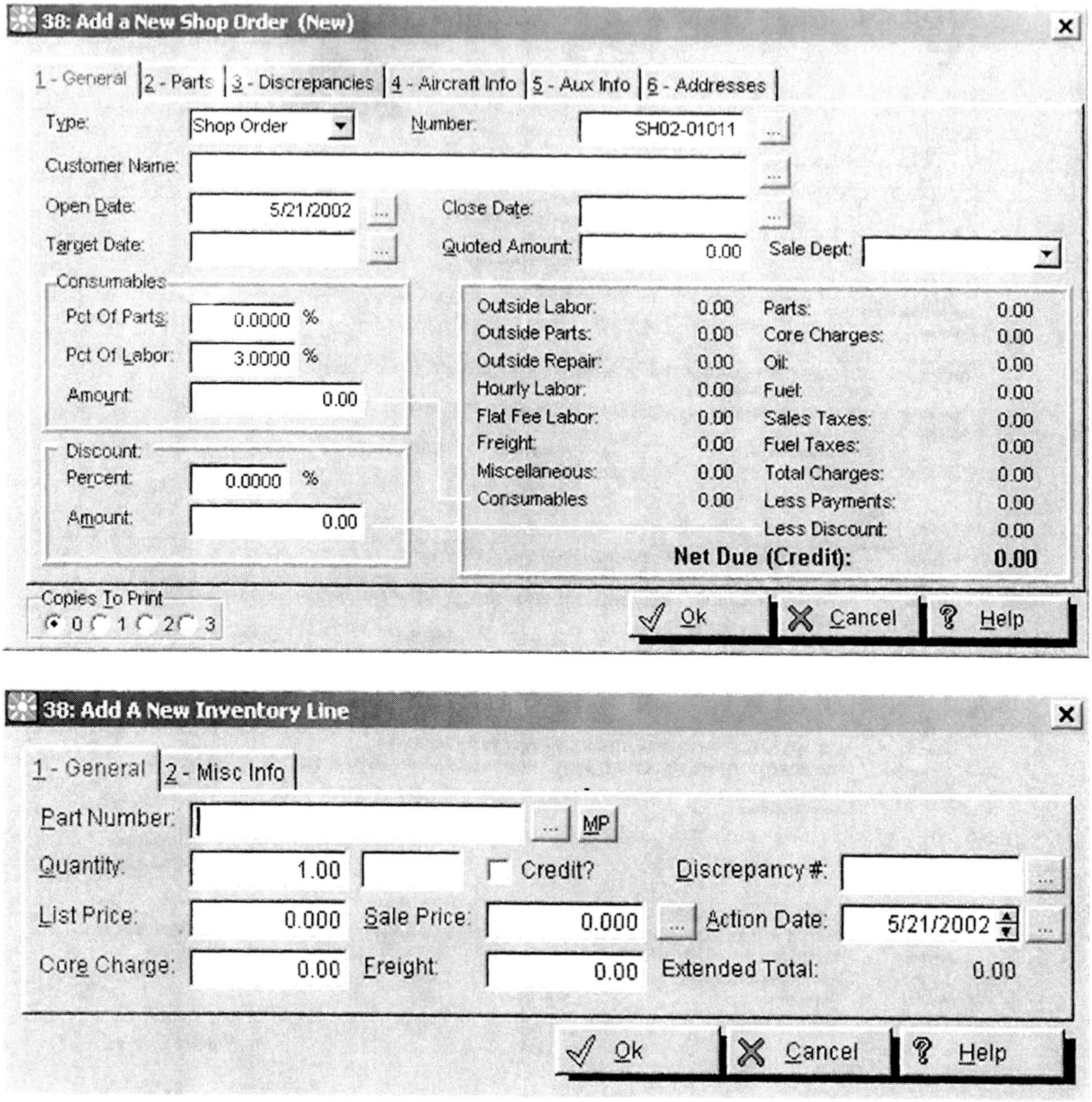

Figure 10.8 » Continued

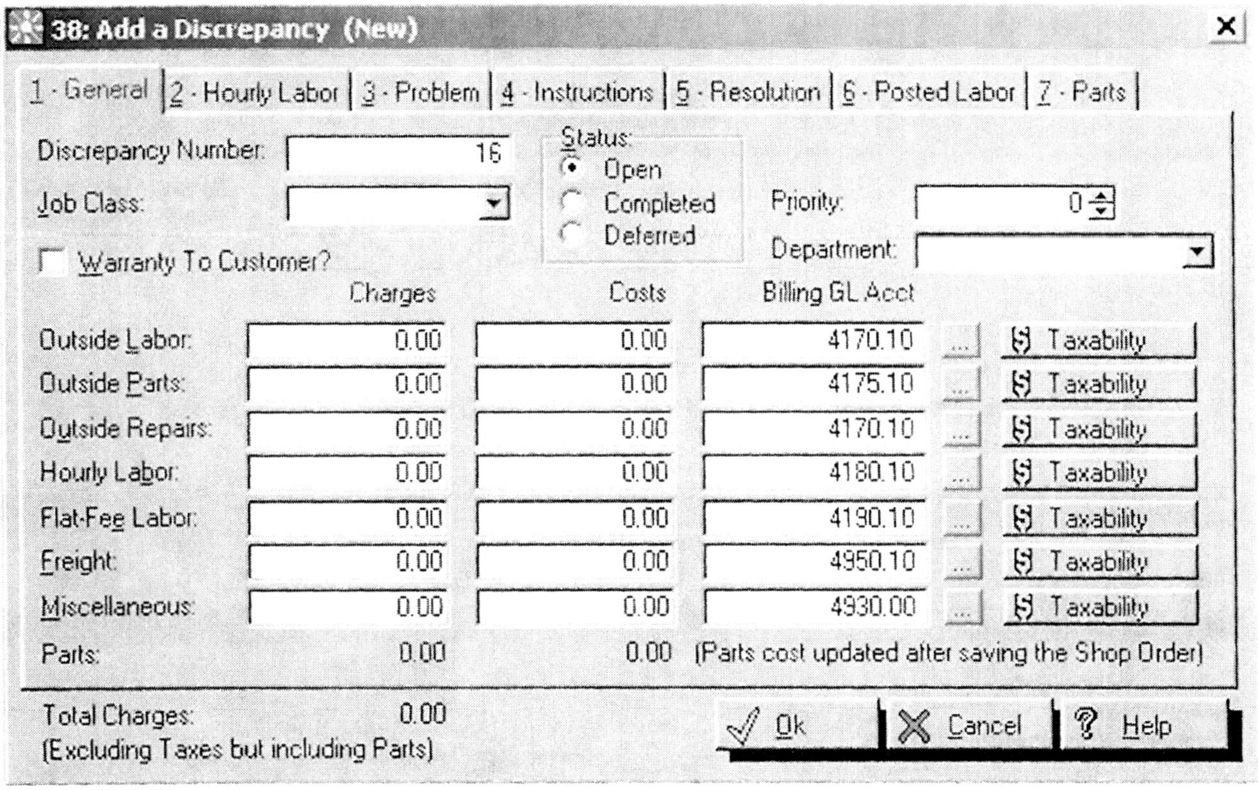

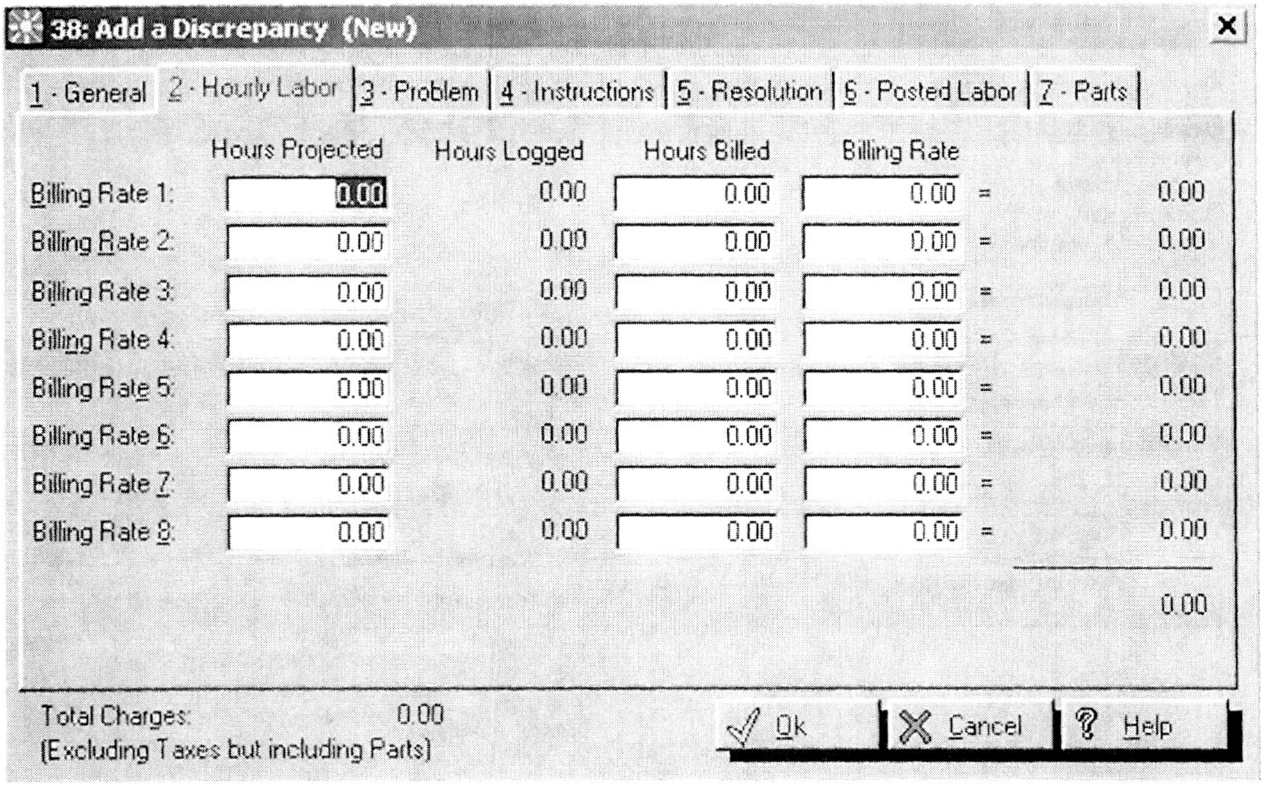

Source: Horizon Business Concepts, Inc.

Figure 10.9 » Internal Shop Order Form

George's Test Data
"Where Your Dreams Take Flight"
Street Address
City, ST 99999
Phone numbers and
1 more line available

Shop Order: 10007

Opened: 5/19/1999
Closed: 5/21/1999

Sold To: Internal-Flight S Maintenance

Aircraft Number: N2519 **Type:C-150** **S/N: 15069123**

Total Time: 8,012.1 Hobbs Time: 8,012.1 Tach Time: 7,237.4

Eng#	Type	S/N	Time	Cycles	Prop Type	Prop S/N	Prop Time
1	CONTINENTAL	123456456	7,237.4				

Discrepancy: 1

Problem:
Fix squaw ks on lights
Action Taken:
replaced w ingtip position lightbulbs

	Projected	Billed		Cost	Charges
Charges This Item:	0.0	2.75 Hours (	55.0		151.25
		Cost Of Labo		46.28	

Part Number	Description	Credit	Quantity	Units	Unit Cost	Mkup	Unit Price	Extended
93	Bulb		2.00	Each			0.370	0.74
	PO #:	Rcvd:		From:				

Discrepancy: 2

Problem:
needs oil change
Action Taken:
drained and replaced oil

	Projected	Billed		Cost	Charges
Charges This Item:	0.0	1.25 Hours (	15.0		18.75
		Cost Of Labo		11.88	

Part Number	Description	Credit	Quantity	Units	Unit Cost	Mkup	Unit Price	Extended
AS15W50	Oil		6.00	Liter			0.280	1.68
	PO #:	Rcvd:		From:				

Miscellaneous Charges:

Consumables	5.10

Summary:

Total Parts:	0.74	Total Oil:	1.68
Consumables:	5.10	Total Labor - 4.00 Hours:	170.00
Projected Labor - 0.00 Hours:	0.00		

Totals:

SubTotal:	**177.52**
Sales Taxes:	**0.60**
Total Due:	**178.12**
Added To Account:	**178.12**

Parts and Labor Costs:

Printed: 5/21/2002 Shop Order: 10007 Page: 1 of 2

Figure 10.9 » Continued

George's Test Data
"Where Your Dreams Take Flight"
Street Address
City, ST 99999
Phone numbers and
1 more line available

Total Inventory Cost:	0.00
Total Outside Parts Cost:	0.00
Total Outside Repair Cost:	0.00
Total Freight Cost:	0.00
Total Miscellaneous Cost:	0.00
Total Labor Cost:	58.16
Total Outside Labor Cost:	0.00
Total Flat Fee Cost:	0.00
Total Costs:	58.16

Thank you for your business. Fly Safe!

Printed: 5/21/2002 Shop Order: 10007 Page: 2 of 2

Courtesy of TotalFBO Accounting and Business Management Software by Horizon Business Concepts, Inc.

(The New Piper, Cessna, Beech, Bellanca, and so on) are constructed differently, it is necessary to have a manual for each plane. The climatic differences around the country with varying ranges in temperature and working conditions influence the time involved in accomplishing repair operations. These differences must be recognized when establishing a manual for a location.

One illustration of a successful application of the flat-rate procedure to aviation maintenance work is Southwest Air Rangers of El Paso, Texas. There, a flat-rate manual was developed for use primarily on Piper aircraft. The manual was prepared initially from the analysis of a large amount of accumulated historical data on maintenance activity. Several revisions to the manual have been made as additional experience and data have been acquired. Figure 10.10 illustrates a page from the Southwest Air Rangers flat-rate manual. Additional information on the operation of the system and copies of the complete manual may be purchased from the management in El Paso.

Computer-Assisted Maintenance

As aircraft have grown larger and become more and more sophisticated, it has become increasingly difficult for the manager to keep up with the myriad of details associated with keeping modern aircraft operational on a tight schedule. Many businesses have turned to the computer for assistance in ensuring that maintenance is scheduled and completed efficiently.

A number of organizations have developed complete computerized aircraft maintenance programs that they provide as a service to aircraft operators. These programs include a recommended maintenance schedule that can be adapted to individual needs. Figure 10.11 shows a computerized maintenance warning report for the individual customer's aircraft. After the required data has been entered into the computer, the following reports are printed for the customer:

- Monthly aircraft status report;
- Monthly maintenance due list;
- Monthly aircraft history report;
- Annual budget performance and reliability summary; and
- Inspection and services summary.

Part of the system includes maintenance requirement cards that contain the latest acceptable maintenance procedures.

Figure 10.10 » Sample Page From an Aviation Flat-Rate Manual

Job Description	18	23-4	23-250	23-AT	23-LT	24	24-T	25	28-4	28-6	28-R	30+39	30+39-T	31	31-P	31-T	32-260	32-300	34	36
Absolute pressure controller (cowl off)				1																
Actuator—brake	1	1	1	1	1	1	1	1	1	1	1	1	1	1			1	1	1	
Actuator—flap (hydraulic)		3	3	3	3															
Actuator—gear door (hydraulic)		1	1	1	1									1						
Actuator—landing gear (hydraulic)		3	3	3	3						1			4						
Actuator—waste gate (cowl off)				2																
Adapter—oil filter														4						
Adjust electric trim solenoid									1½	1½	1½						1½	1½		
Aileron	1	1½	1½	1½	1½	1½	1½	1	1½	1½	1½	1½	1½	1½			1½	1½	1½	
Aileron hinge or bearing (1 aileron)		2	2	2	2	2	2		2	2	2	2	2	2			2	2	2	
Aileron hinge doubler (1 aileron)									4	4	4						4	4	4	
Air box—carburetor (cowl off)	¾	1	1	1					1	1							1			
Air filter—central (during insp)		¼	¼	¼	¼	½	½		¼	¼	¼	¼	¼				¼	¼		
Air pressure pump		1¾	1¾	1¾	1¾									1¼						
Air—propeller (service ea)		¼	¼	¼	¼							¼	¼	¼						
Align wheels (on jacks)		¾	¾	¾	¾	¾	¾					¾	¾	¾						
Alternate air cable (complete)			10	10	10	2	2		2	2	2	10	10					3	10	
Alternate air cable (core)			2	2	2	1	1		1	1	1	2	2					1	2	
Alternator (cowl on)			2¼	2¼	2¼	1½	1½	1½	1½	1½	1½	2	2	1½			1¾	1¾	3	
Alternator (cowl off)			1	1	1	1	1	1	1	1	1	1	1	1			1	1	1	
Alternator or generator belt (prop off)	¼	¼	¼	¼	¼	¼	¼	¼	¼	¼	¼	¼	¼	¼			¼	¼	¼	

By permission, Southwest Air Rangers, El Paso, Texas, 1985.

In addition to being valuable to many aircraft operators, the system is indicative of the part that the computer can play in maintenance work.

Profitability

As mentioned earlier, the focus of an aviation business should be on generating the desired level of profits. The goal of the maintenance department should be to contribute its share to the overall business profitability. All of the material presented in this chapter should assist in the managing of the department and in achieving the desired profits. Additional assistance can be obtained through the development and use of an information system, the analysis of all relevant data, and finally the application of control techniques to assure the accomplishment of goals.

Chapter 7, Information Systems is devoted to an in-depth examination of the development and use of information systems. Since this section is designed only to illustrate some aspects of maintenance profitability, the one area that should be clearly identified is the charge for service labor. It is important the charge made to the customer cover all of the costs incurred by the organization plus a component of profit.

Figure 10.11 » Maintenance Warning Report

George's Test Data
Maintenance Warning Report
Includes All Maintenance Reminders

Aircraft: N1234 | Make: | Model: | Type: KING AIR | S/N: 44557-97864

	Eng Time	Last MOH	Prop Time	Last POH1	Last POHD	Tach Time	H/S Time	H/S MOHT	H/S Cycles	H/S MOHC	Hobbs Time
1 -	923	0	251	0		950	461	850	83	1,200	1,048
2 -	950	0	950	0		977	461	850	83	1,200	0

Total Time Tracks:	Tach 1	Total Time Offset	1,250
Total Time:	2,200		
Landing Cycles:	814		

Maintenance Description (Type):	Due {Past Due} Hours	Days	Cycles
Engine 1 Runout	76.9		
Engine 2 Runout	49.9		
Prop 1 Runout	548.9	(720)	
Prop 2 Runout	(150.1)	(720)	
Hot Section 1 Runout	888.9		1,317
Hot Section 2 Runout	888.9		1,317
Annual Inspection			0
100-Hr Inspection		(73,558)	
Altimeter Certification	(1,048.7)		
Transponder Certification	(1,048.7)		
Static System Certification	(1,048.7)		
ELT Battery Expiration	(1,048.7)		
Encoder Certification	(1,048.7)		

Courtesy of TotalFBO Accounting and Business Management Software by Horizon Business Concepts, Inc.

Information

It is imperative that a service manager receive operational information on the various aspects of the department and that this information be received in a timely manner. Data and costs on income are needed in great enough detail to cover jobs, aircraft, individuals, and so on. Data must be provided as fast as possible in order to analyze and take corrective action immediately.

Analysis

The analysis of reported service data can be accomplished using several techniques. Included here are:

> Comparison with established goals;
> Comparison with previous operating periods;
> Comparison with other similar businesses; and
> Comparison with generally accepted measures of efficiency.

The typical maintenance data subjected to this type of analysis would include:

> Total maintenance revenue generated;
> Revenue generated by each major working area;
> Labor utilization;
> Volume of rework;
> Net profit as a percentage of sales; and
> Indirect expenses.

Control

Control is a continuation of the analysis. It is the final stage of the comparison process that identifies the desired corrective activity and then implements that activity. For the maintenance manager, it may mean reducing personnel, increasing inventory, establishing a new inspection procedure, or engaging in a concentrated effort to promote annual inspections. The activity will be specifically related to the suggestions that resulted from the analysis and might be adjusted later in order to achieve desired goals.

Techniques

There are numerous procedures and techniques that utilize information, analysis and control that can be useful in gaining and maintaining the desired level of profitability for the maintenance department. Several practical illustrations follow.

Budgeting. There are various applications of budgeting that may be utilized in achieving the desired level of operating profits. Sales are first estimated for the 12 monthly periods. Then, using the historically developed and desirable percentages for cost of sales, gross profit, expenses, and operating margin, the anticipated dollar values for each of these items is calculated for the monthly sales projections. As the operating months are completed, the actual cost of sales, expenses, gross profit, and operating margin are entered in the second line for each month, and the actual percentages for each are calculated. In this manner the budget assists in monitoring sales and maintaining the desired relationship of cost of sales, gross profit, expense and operating margin. Trends can be identified and corrective action can be taken on a monthly basis to ensure the desired operating margin.

Productivity. A second practical technique for measuring the efficiency of a shop is through the examination of its productivity. Figure 10.12 illustrates the calculation of individual and shop productivity measures. The goal is to bill out as many of the mechanics' working hours as possible. Realistically, this can seldom be 100 percent because there is administrative, training, vacation and other overhead time that should not be directly billed to the customer. In this illustration, the manager should investigate the low productivity of number 4 mechanic (64 percent) and the high productivity of number 10 (100 percent).

Figure 10.13 illustrates a technique for reviewing and controlling the overall shop productivity. This chart shows that the break-even point for this shop at 100 percent productivity is three mechanics. The relationship of number of personnel, their productivity, and maximum income are illustrated. By applying the shop productivity average of 89 percent for the ten employees in Figure 10.12, one can tell at a glance how the department is doing. This concept can be very valuable in analyzing the overall situation and considering the need to reduce or increase the number of employees, develop additional business, or improve internal efficiency.

Figure 10.12 » Individual and Shop Productivity

Mechanic	Hours Paid	Hours Billed	Percent
1	184.7	160.6	87
2	176.0	171.3	97
3	169.2	164.3	97
4	193.0	123.6	64
5	169.9	145.0	85
6	198.4	165.2	83
7	175.6	157.4	90
8	184.9	175.2	95
9	160.0	152.8	96
10	160.0	160.0	100
	1,771.7	1,575.4	89

Ratios. Another very practical technique to use in monitoring the progress of a shop and its financial success is through ratios in monitoring the income statement. Financial ratios, or the relationship of one element of the income statement to another element, can provide a means of measuring the progress of the maintenance department and determining its degree of success or failure. A ratio can be used in comparison with an earlier ratio for the same department, in comparison with departments in other businesses, in comparison or with standards generally considered acceptable. Some of the key ratios in use and the normally accepted standards are shown in Figure 10.14.

These techniques—budgeting, productivity review, and ratio analysis—are only a few of the many techniques available to the manager in maintaining the profitability of the department. However, constant surveillance of maintenance activity and decisive action are the two managerial functions most necessary to ensure a successful maintenance department.

Professional Maintenance Organizations

There are three primary maintenance-related aviation organizations. They include the Aircraft Electronics Association (AEA), Aviation Technical Education Council (ATEC), and the Professional Aviation Maintenance Association (PAMA). AEA represents over 900 FAA Part 145 Certified Repair

Figure 10.13 » Break-Even Chart Used for Controlling Overall Service Shop Productivity

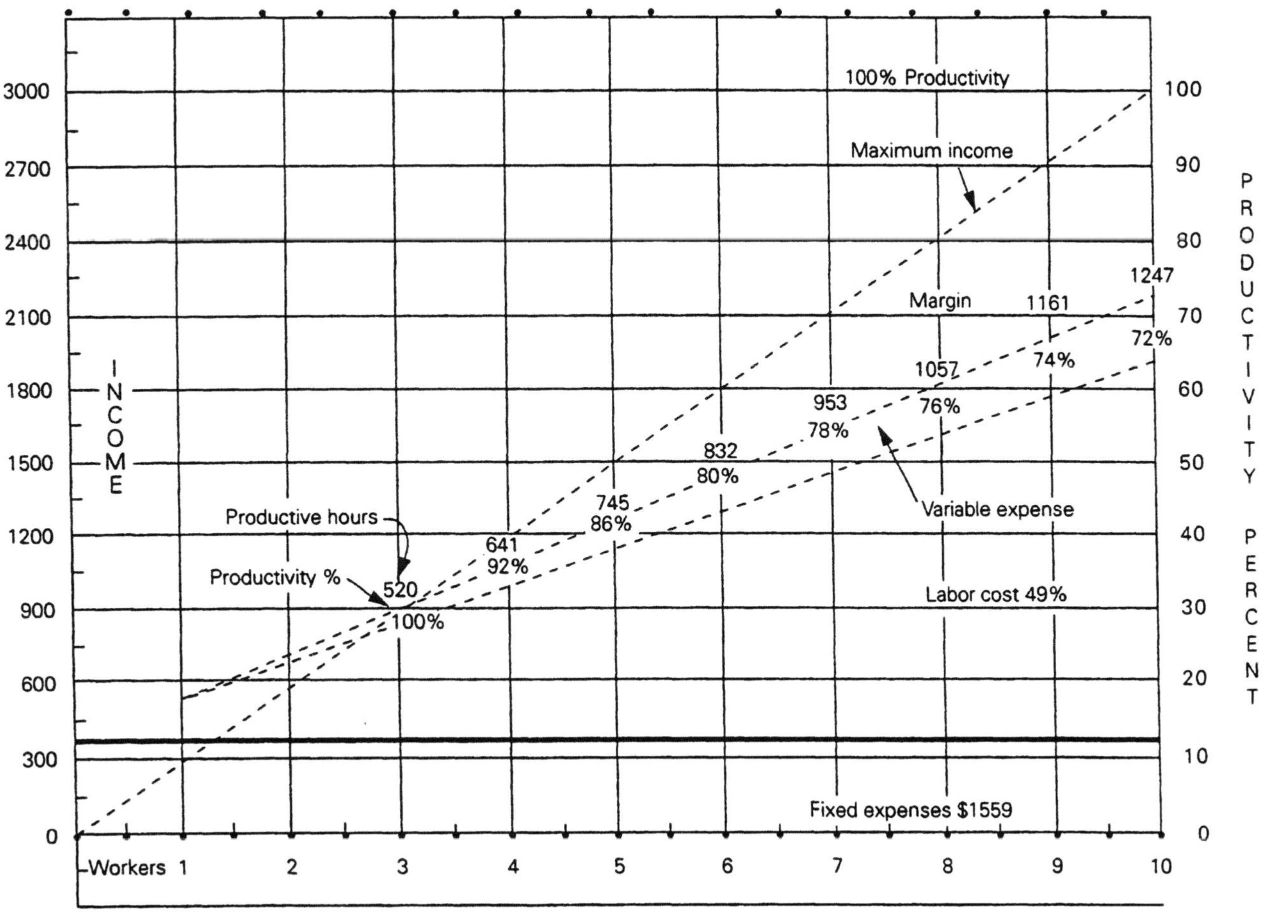

Courtesy of Robert Varner, Lane Aviation, Columbus, Ohio

Figure 10.14 » Key Ratios and Normally Accepted Standards for Maintenance Departments

	Type	Acceptable Range
Ratio:	Gross profit as a percent of sales	
	Service	45 to 47 percent
	Parts	18 to 22 percent
	Electronics	28 to 30 percent
Ratio:	Expenses as a percent of sales	
	Service	44 to 46 percent
	Parts	13 to 17 percent
	Electronics	26 to 28 percent
Ratio:	Operating profit as a percent of sales	
	Service	1 to 3 percent
	Parts	5 to 9 percent
	Electronics	2 to 4 percent

Source: Dr. J. D. Richardson

DISCUSSION TOPICS

1. Identify four subdivisions frequently encountered in the organizational structure of a maintenance department and discuss their responsibilities.
2. How would an interested person become a certificated aircraft maintenance technician with an airframe and power-plant rating?
3. What facilities and equipment are needed to open and operate an aviation maintenance shop?
4. How would one set about identifying a practical inventory level for a new aviation service shop? For a shop that has been in business for some time?
5. "Quality control expenditures must be carefully weighed against the benefits thereby obtained." Discuss.
6. What are three implications of product liability for an aviation maintenance facility?
7. What considerations weigh in favor of subcontracting out all maintenance work? Against?
8. "The manager must be involved in setting and maintaining an adequate profit level for a shop." Identify and discuss these managerial activities.
9. Discuss the advantages and disadvantages of flat-rate pricing.

Stations as well as most manufacturers of general aviation avionics equipment and airframes. ATEC represents aviation educators and professionals. PAMA is a national professional association of aviation maintenance technicians, with some 4,000 individual members and 250 affiliated company members.

Avionics Repair Stations

Avionics repair stations located at fixed-base operations may operate independently or as an integrated part of an existing maintenance operation. As aircraft become more sophisticated and avionics becomes a part of the operating system, there will be a greater need for integrated shops and people who are competent to do both kinds of jobs.

Summary

Managing an aircraft maintenance facility is a separate business or profit center requiring the same business management tools as other segments of the company. A comprehensive organizational structure is key, as is the quality of personnel. Careful attention must be paid to the selection, training, certification, and utilization of mechanics, inspectors, and repair people. Many aspects of repair shop facilities and procedures are controlled by FAA. Identification and compliance with requirements must be done carefully.

Whether as a section of the maintenance department or as a separate unit, the parts and supplies department contributes directly to the success of the maintenance shop. Keeping the optimum parts inventory on hand is a key concern to the service manager.

Quality control depends on the individual mechanic and on the entire organization. It may be achieved through training, procedures, inspection, and recognition. Other areas of concern for the service manager are subcontracting, liability, marketing, administration, and pricing. The key activity is the surveillance of departmental profitability and the use of information, analysis, and controls to assure the attainment of desired profit goals.

Endnotes

1. Prentice, Stephen P. "Fractional Technicians? What's At Stake?" *AMT Online,* April 1999.

2. de Decker, Bill. "Is There a Laptop in Your Future?" *AMT Online*, May-June 1998.

3. Sparks, Jim. "RVSM—Doubling the Number of Aircraft Will Affect Us All," *AMT Online,* February 2002.

4. de Decker, Bill. "Value for Money: Choosing the Right Maintenance Program for Your Operation," *AMT Online*, September 2000.

5. Code of Federal Regulations, 14, Parts 1-200, published by the Office of the Federal Register National Archives and Records Service, General Services Administration, Washington, D.C., 20402. Outline shown in Appendix II.

6. See *http://www.flightsafety.com/ and http://www.simuflite.com/.*

11

Safety, Security and Liability

OBJECTIVES

- Explain the difference between "risk management" and "risk transfer."
- Describe the "deep-pocket" theory.
- Recognize the advantages and disadvantages of self-insurance.
- Discuss the specialized areas of insurance typically found when dealing with aviation.
- Explain how the General Aviation Revitalization Act of 1994 changed the outlook on aircraft sales for the aviation business owner/manager.
- Describe the differing roles of the Federal Aviation Administration and the National Transportation Safety Board in relation to aircraft accidents.
- What is the mandate of the TSA and why?

Introduction

All types of business enterprise are exposed to some degree of risk. Our system of business and government, our very way of life, relies heavily on honest individuals, be they customers, employees, or visitors. When a person has a nefarious intention, be this an act of terrorism, or merely theft, the aviation system, like most other parts of the economy, is a relatively leaky sieve. The terrorist attacks of 9/11/01 and the intense concern with aviation security and safety that arose as a result, did not, for example, prevent a 15-year old student pilot in January 2002 from stealing a plane and crashing it into a building. This chapter discusses normal business risks, the special risks of an aviation business, and the process of risk management through risk reduction and risk transfer. Finally, it discusses what must be done when something goes wrong, and it focuses on the new and rapidly evolving activities and requirements relating to aviation security in an environment where aircraft have been used as weapons of mass destruction.

The Need for Risk Management Procedures

Risk management consists of two related areas: risk reduction, which is accomplished through careful conduct of each aspect of the business, and risk transfer, whereby the business owner passes some of the risk to another entity through the purchase of insurance. The more effective the risk reduction, the less expensive the risk transfer. Risk reduction consists of the application of good management techniques by leaving only unforeseeable occurrences to be insured against. Insurance premiums tend to be lower with good risk reduction techniques.

An aviation business needs to address the risk management area with great care partially because of the numerous other factors involved in airport services and facilities. There may be a lack of clarity in airport leases and operating agreements as to who is responsible for which functions and areas. This can blur the distinction between aviation business liability and airport management operating liability. Reasons for this include: (1) FBOs frequently have contract responsibility to provide airport management functions, and (2) airports themselves frequently provide the same or similar functions as FBOs, and this overlap can lead to shared blame.

An adjunct to this mixed responsibility is the "deep-pockets" approach. This means litigants generally sue the wealthiest party, regardless of whether they're believed to be negligent. Some parties involved in aviation, including private airport owners, pilots, aircraft owners, and others may not carry sufficient (or any) insurance, so the aviation business must consider being adequately covered against the deficiencies of others.

Interaction of Safety, Security, and Liability

Steps to run a safe, secure airport operation with adequately trained staff are a top priority in risk management. Negligence in an area quite unrelated to a particular claim may be cited as evidence of overall poor attention to detail. A well-run airport operation not only reduces the risk of accidents, but also assists in achieving favorable insurance rates. In some areas the safety requirements are common sense; in others FAA sets them forth, and now, in the security areas, the Transportation Security Administration, formed in the fall of 2001, sets them forth.

Risk Exposure

Normal Business Exposure

The typical business is exposed to at least these risks:

> Fire;
> Theft by employees and others;
> Vandalism, problems arising from unauthorized access;
> Severe weather and "acts of God";
> Inadequate security of personnel, facilities and equipment;
> Product liability;
> Third party or non-employee liability;
> Employer's liability and workers' compensation;
> Automobile liability;
> Loss of key person or persons; and finally,
> Business interruption due to any of these events.

Aviation Risk Exposure

In an FBO operation, additional risk occurs because of the nature of the goods and services involved and the high degree of skill required for many of the operations. In addition, several highly incompatible products may be found in different parts of the operation. These include running engines, moving propeller blades, a mixture of automobiles and aircraft moving around on ramps, the presence of fuel and oil, oxygen, welding materials, electrical equipment, and paint. Areas of traditional concern to an aviation business include:

> Aircraft hull damage;
> Bodily injury and property damage to third parties resulting from travel in the company's aircraft;
> Non-ownership liability-for occurrences in aircraft flown by other than company personnel;
> Premises and product liability, including aircraft and parts;
> Fueling safety;
> Hangar keeper's liability;
> Underground fuel-storage tanks: potential leakage and contamination;
> Agricultural chemicals used by crop-dusters: their storage and disposal;

> Other hazardous and toxic wastes such as used motor oil;
> New rules and more stringent inspections and security requirements post-9/11/01 for Part 135 charter flight operations imposed by the TSA;
> Emergency crash, fire and rescue (CFR) response capability at air carrier airports;
> Employee exposure to hazardous products on the job; and
> Security and crime prevention.

In short, the regulatory context and insurance needs of the typical aviation business are increasing, and this trend seems likely to continue as the TSA refines its proposals, and as other federal agencies such as the FBI, INS and Department of Justice become more involved in scrutiny of aviation personnel.

Risk Reduction

Normal Risk Reduction

Risk management involves active risk reduction as well as risk transference through insurance. It is not simply the purchase of insurance for protection in case of loss. An adequate insurance program is only a part, and not the ultimate goal, of risk management. Actions taken by management before insurance is negotiated, during the life of a policy, and after a loss occurs, are all part of risk management. They influence the premium costs to the business as well as the total loss experienced. In each risk area, specific organizational actions are available to reduce the risk and the ultimate costs involved. Additionally, in today's insurance marketplace where deductible amounts tend to be much higher than in previous decades, risk management is vital to cost control.

Fire Risk. Much can be done to reduce the risk of fire, including the use of fire resistant materials and protective devices such as automatic sprinklers and fire extinguishers, and training personnel in housekeeping practices, fire prevention, and fire fighting. Figure 11.1 illustrates typical fire-risk reduction procedures. If premises are remodeled to the extent that a local building permit is required, they will need to be brought up to modern standards in regard to fire risk e.g. the installation of sprinklers. However the aviation manager may want to perform a fire risk audit even where not required by the local building department.

Crime Risk. One of the most serious threats to business property today is the crime threat—acts of terrorism, burglary, vandalism, robbery, and theft. Managing these threats becomes an important aspect of risk management. Insurance is only one part of managing this risk; reduction and prevention are also extremely important. As small businesses, many aviation operations are prime targets for the burglar and robber. However, many things can be done to reduce this risk by using protective devices, sound operating procedures, and employee training. Protective devices include silent central station burglar alarm systems, burglar resistant locks and equipment, and indoor and outdoor security lighting. Effective operating procedures may include minimizing cash receipts through switching to credit only transactions.

New technology is available, and constantly being improved, to assist in the area of airport security. Electronic devices may be installed in aircraft that transmit a signal when unauthorized tampering occurs. Sophisticated computerized monitoring and alarm systems are available for the premises. Lock systems for airport and premises access can be computer controlled and codes changed frequently. Better quality locks can be installed on aircraft and hangar doors. Additional precautions, such as removing the distributor cap, may be advised when the aircraft stops at an unknown field. Local police do not always realize the value of aircraft and aviation business equipment, and it's useful to actively keep them informed so that their speedy assistance is available.

A businessperson must deal with an occasional dishonest employee and dishonest customer. In the case of the dishonest employee, the manager's first problem is identifying the amount of the loss. Fidelity bonds can be obtained on those employees who have access to large amounts of money. Inventory shrinkage resulting from employee pilferage and other dishonest acts is substantial for many organizations. Risk management in this area includes the reduction or prevention of losses by the careful screening and selection of personnel, an

Figure 11.1 » Fire Inspection Checklist

Emergency Preparation

- ☐ Fire organization posted
- ☐ Fire drill held regularly
- ☐ Fire exits well marked and unobstructed
- ☐ Fire alarms well marked and unobstructed
- ☐ Aisles and stairs clear
- ☐ Evacuation procedures posted
- ☐ Procedures for handling fuel spills posted
- ☐ Emergency equipment well marked, in place, and ready for use

Hangars and Buildings

- ☐ Hydrants and water supply checked and serviceable
- ☐ Sprinkler system, checked and serviceable
- ☐ Foam and CO_2 systems checked and serviceable
- ☐ Fire doors checked and serviceable
- ☐ Fire extinguishers well marked, in place, checked and tagged
- ☐ Hose stations, checked and serviceable
- ☐ Electrical circuits identified, enclosed, and provided with proper overload protection
- ☐ Gas systems, checked and serviceable
- ☐ Fuel pumping equipment, in good condition and free of leaks (extinguishing equipment adequate and available)

Maintenance Equipment

- ☐ Spray booths, clean and properly ventilated and sprinkler heads protected from overspray
- ☐ Power tools and accessories, wiring in good condition
- ☐ Pressurized bottles, properly connected and secured
- ☐ Mobile equipment extinguishers well marked, in place, and serviceable
- ☐ Powered equipment, properly grounded
- ☐ Test equipment, free of leaks, wiring in good condition

Management

- ☐ General housekeeping, adequate
- ☐ Changes (alterations, processes, methods, and procedures) first cleared with Fire Marshal
- ☐ Floors, clean and free of flammable fluid spills
- ☐ Storage of material, orderly and in accordance with regulations*
- ☐ Aircraft fueling, in accordance with regulations*
- ☐ Spray painting, in accordance with regulations*
- ☐ Welding and other open-flame operations in accordance with regulations*
- ☐ Ramp and grounds, clean and free of debris
- ☐ Proper disposal of soiled shop towels and rags

*Separate checklists should be made for these operations.

From "Aviation Ground Operation Safety Handbook," copyright 2000 by National Safety Council, Chicago, IL 60611. Used with permission.

effective accounting system, and varied control methods. Safeguards to be considered include

> The use of outside auditors;
> Countersignatures on all checks;
> Immediate deposit and duplication of all incoming checks;
> Bank statement reconciliation by an employee other than the one who makes the deposits;
> Joint access to safe deposit boxes;
> "Professional shopper" checks on cash register operating procedures; and
> Ensuring that all employees handling money take regular vacations.

In addition, if company morale is high, petty theft tends to be minimal, but where morale is low and management is felt not to care about employees, some develop a sense of entitlement in regard to using company phones for personal calls, taking home office supplies and the like. Thus, a prevention program relating to morale and motivation may be the most effective tool, as well as benefiting the company in other ways such as higher productivity.

The dishonest customer represents to the manager the additional perils of shoplifting and bad check passing. Retail operations expect to lose a percentage of their merchandise through shoplifting. Although most FBO operations do not include retail functions, office supplies, maintenance supplies, and inventory can be at risk. This kind of loss can be reduced by constant vigilance, special equipment, and sound operating procedures. Equipment such as two-way and convex mirrors and closed-circuit television, coupled with wide aisles, clear vision, and alert employees will help prevent the loss of merchandise. Prominently displayed warnings against shoplifting and rules that provide customer guidance will deter the would-be offender in many instances.

Today's color copiers are of such high quality that a more significant risk from customers is the passing of counterfeit money, the creation of blank checks using someone else's account, and the passing of fake ID. These white-collar crimes may be a greater threat than the traditional areas and employees need training in how to spot them.

Bad check losses pose a problem that can be minimized through sound procedures and well-trained employees. Proper identification should be requested before accepting checks, and then only for the amount of the purchase. The identification procedure should include a photograph along with a sample signature; or, in lieu of this, two forms of identification may be required. Postdated, illegibly written, or two-party checks should not be accepted. Employees should be trained in following the procedures selected and in identifying potential bad-check passers. An on-line check authorization service is an essential precautionary service.

General Emergency Risk. Not only fire and theft but also earthquakes, acts of terrorism, tornados, and similar drastic and sudden events may affect airports that call for a more broad-based emergency response plan. The airport administration should be working with other units of local, state and federal government to prepare emergency response plans, and do table-top planning exercise and drills. The aviation business may be asked to participate and should do so if possible. If not asked, the FBO manager should ascertain the status of these plans and encourage full readiness. The National Safety Council is one organization that offers a guide to emergency planning.[1]

Aviation Risk Reduction

Risk reduction comes from the application of sound management practices, as described in previous chapters. As evidenced by the many types of aviation insurance and liability suits, there are many exposure or risk elements in the aviation operating areas. Poor maintenance, bad housekeeping, nonexistent or vague guidelines and procedures, inadequately trained personnel, low quality standards, lack of emphasis on safety, and poor supervision all can lead to accidents and costly legal conflicts. The aviation business is faced with potential threats from a wide variety of consumers who feel that they have been injured by a variety of "products." Risks in this area also include careless selection of parts for installation on an aircraft, in appropriate "signing off" work as having been completed, or premature returning of an aircraft to flight status when it requires maintenance. These and other similar actions should be considered carefully and steps should be taken to avoid unnecessary exposure or risk.

Because of concerns with the scale of claims for general aviation related accidents and injuries, product liability legislation that provides some relief was lobbied for and achieved in 1994, as discussed in Chapter 1. The General Aviation Revitalization Act (GARA) provides for an 18-year statute of limitation on product liability claims where previously no limit was in place—a "statute of repose" for aviation manufacturers. The 18-year liability limit provides some relief from potential legal action and appears to be helping revitalize general aviation. FBOs still have additional risk exposure because of repairing a part of an aircraft engine or airframe; they, too, may be part of a lawsuit when an accident occurs, and need to keep a good paper trail going back 18 years in case of being included in a legal action.

Good operational risk management will:

1. Select and train qualified aviation personnel.
2. Provide adequate operational guidelines and procedures.
3. Insist on good housekeeping practices.
4. Place a high emphasis on safety.
5. Require consistently high quality standards for services and products.
6. Provide the supervision and maintenance necessary to ensure that these elements routinely take place.

Insurance companies recognize the relationship that exists between an efficient, well managed, safe aviation organization and a low accident rate and minimum risk exposure. Prior to insuring against some of the aviation risks, many companies will survey the organization carefully, checking all the key operational areas and developing some concept of the premium rate structure. Although overall insurance rates are more controlled by the purchaser's clout in the marketplace than by good practices, other things being equal, lower premiums should be awarded to those aviation businesses that can demonstrate good organizational practices and procedures, and higher premiums will be assigned to the others. The practices, procedures, and recommendations of this book should assist the manager in identifying and correcting some of the operational risk exposures and should result in lower insurance premiums. The Operational Procedure Guide and the Operational Manual that appear as Appendices to this book should be especially useful as starting points when dealing with some of the flight operation areas, along with some evidence that employees are required to adhere by the company's manuals. The chapters dealing with human resources and maintenance will also provide assistance in those areas.

Aviation Safety and Security Regulations and Guidelines

There are a number of FAA Advisory Circulars about safe aviation operations in such areas as fueling, aircraft handling, and the condition of premises.[2] Along with airport certification requirements and the regulations for FAA-approved maintenance, instruction, and other FBO operations, these provide a very detailed set of requirements and suggestions on how to run a sound operation.[3]

As mentioned, as of fall 2001, the Transportation Security Agency has taken over FAA's responsibilities regarding security and is in the process of expanding them. It is not yet clear what will be the new security requirements for smaller airports, as the dominant issue thus far has been air carrier airports and the need for better passenger screening. However, many general aviation businesses fly charter and air taxi flights that bring passengers to and from scheduled flights, and are thus likely to be required to enact similar security procedures. This is discussed later in the chapter.

Additionally, aviation businesses must also deal with the State and federal Environmental Protection Agency (EPA) regulations and Occupational Health and Safety Administration (OSHA) requirements regarding various hazards, including federal and state requirements about hazardous products handling and disposal. In addition, such organizations as the National Safety Council and the National Fire Protection Association provide a number of aviation and other booklets.[4] Individual airport minimum standards may provide another set of requirements for safe FBO operations in various areas. In the words of an aviation lawyer, this is how to regard the FAA documents:

> "Rest assured that a plaintiff's attorney will acquire the Advisory Circulars and that the lawyer (and probably a jury) will fault an airport for any area in which its facility is deficient according to the Advisory Circular recommendations, even though these are not mandatory."

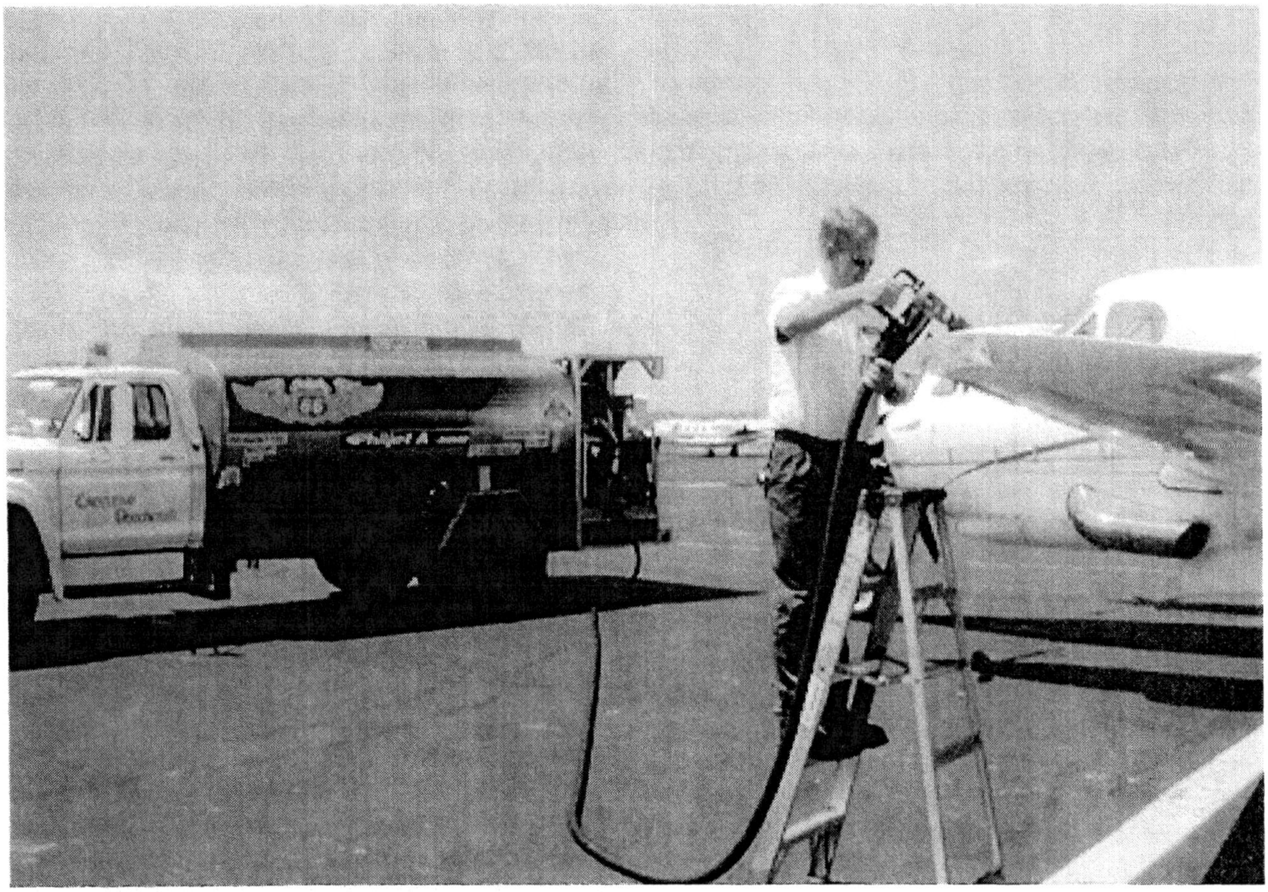

There are a number of FAA Advisory Circulars about safe aviation operations in such areas as fueling. Courtesy of Executive Beechcraft, Inc.

Airport Risk Audit

This lawyer recommends a self-applied risk audit where the airport operator, or in this case the FBO, goes over every area of activity to see if it is up to FAA and other standards. The Management Audit shown in Appendix V is a good starting point.

Procedures Manual

The safety procedures applied by the aviation business should be written and reference appropriate Advisory Circulars and other standards. This document should be used for training and for recording the dates of risk audits and corrective actions.

Documentation

If a suit is ever brought against an FBO, then clear and dated documentation of standards, training, corrective action, and follow-up will be an asset in presenting evidence of a risk-preventing attitude. Lack of documentation may permit the plaintiff to go unchallenged.

Inclement Weather

Weather exerts a tremendous influence on aviation operations. The level of activity and safety of personnel, equipment, and facilities are influenced by inclement weather, and they are a major management concern. Of course, the primary concern is for the welfare of personnel, equipment, and facilities. The secondary concern is for the reduction or curtailment of aviation operations. High winds, torrential rains, heavy snows, dust storms, or floods can all injure people, damage aircraft, disable equipment, and ruin physical facilities.

A well-developed weather response plan includes evacuation schedules (aircraft, vehicles and personnel), protection of inventory, supplies, and records, security of utilities, and procedures for getting the facility back into operation. As with other inclement weather situations, the primary concerns are: knowing the situation, obtaining early warning, having a plan to follow, making the decision to act, and then following through as needed.

Risk Transfer

Principles of Insurance

The principle of insurance is to pool risk with others in similar situations so that in the event of a problem some protection is obtained—an approach that assumes, sometimes incorrectly, that not all in the risk pool will be hard hit at the same time. Taking out insurance does not eliminate risk; there will still be some risks covered only by the operator (deductibles or ineligible areas); and some high-risk situations may call for such high premiums that the aviation business chooses to buy only partial coverage or to be self-insured. In some cases the owner has such a large internal risk pool that it is less expensive (or at least it is thought to be less expensive) to self-insure. This situation occurs, for example, in some agencies that own several airports, as it does with some large corporations. However, in the case of self-insurance, funds need setting aside to address claims. Moreover, it may be a challenge for an aviation firm to successfully self-insure for all categories of risk.

Insurance Regulations

Some insurance is optional; some is mandatory. Workmen's Compensation falls into the latter category and, in most cases, airport owners require some level of insurance for operators on their airport. This should be spelled out in the airport's minimum standards and also in the lease.

The U.S. Insurance Market

Industry as a whole. Since the general aviation insurance market is highly specialized and quite small compared, say, with the auto insurance market, the complaint over the years seems to be that there are too few providers and that rates are too high. The industry tends to be very volatile, with new providers entering the market at times when high earnings can be achieved through the funds collected. This occurred in the early 1980s. Then in the 1990s rates were somewhat flat or even falling in some cases. In the 21st century, small operators in particular are again having problems getting coverage as some major providers left the market.[5]

Much of the insurance written in the United States is reinsured. By passing on part or most of the exposure to other insurers, a company can reduce its overall risk of being insufficiently covered for a major claim from one source. The ultimate reinsurer is Lloyds of London. The same economic forces were affecting the reinsurance market over this period. Companies that enter the reinsurance business because of lucrative investment opportunities get out again when claims become too onerous.

Aviation insurance. Aviation insurance is almost totally a reinsurance business, so that the sources of insurance have decreased even more than for most types of coverage. There are only about a dozen companies offering aviation coverage, and not all of these offer all types of coverage. There may be only one offer or for a particular need. In addition to these, there are others who have been unable to complete their treaty agreements with Lloyds, and may not reappear in the aviation marketplace.

Within aviation, the most buying power is held by the airlines. General aviation is both perceived to have higher risks and has less marketplace buying power. Within general aviation the highest risk areas are:

> Old aircraft;
> Homebuilts;
> Ultralights and other experimentals; and
> General aviation after-market modifications.

With the decline of aviation insurance availability, the lowest risks tend to be the only ones able to get coverage. This applies to new policies as well as renewals.

The effects are as follows:

> For small FBOs, coverage is almost non-existent;

- > Publicly owned airports can still get coverage, but at rising cost;
- > Underwriters are seeking limits of $100,000 per seat-virtually useless for a fatal or severe accident, given court settlement levels, which in the United States are the highest in the world and often over a million dollars.

Everyone remotely involved in a claim resulting from an accident may be sued under "joint and several liability" considerations—the aircraft manufacturer, the most recent FBO that worked on the plane, the maker of parts, the airport, and so on.

One effect of the insurance and claims situation has been the cost of product liability insurance. This is due to the value of many liability suit settlements of the past decades, as well as to other trends in the insurance industry. For example, Bob Martin, general counsel of Beech Aircraft, estimated that product liability claims against Beech, Cessna, and Piper before 1994 exceeded $1 billion. This was approximately twice the net worth of these three companies combined.

The costs of product liability insurance are a part of the cost of each year's production of general aviation aircraft. Liability costs have also raised FBO prices for repair and maintenance of aircraft.

It would appear that aviation insurance will continue to have a negative effect on general aviation growth although GARA's liability limit should help level off some insurance costs in the near future.

Normal Business Insurance

In general, the following types of insurance are available to the aviation manager:

1. Fire and general property insurance—covering fire losses, vandalism, hail, and wind damage.
2. Public liability insurance—covering injury to the public, such as a customer falling on the property.
3. Product liability insurance—covering injury to the customer arising from the use of materials or service bought at the business.
4. Burglary insurance—covering forced entry and theft of merchandise, equipment, or cash.
5. Consequential loss insurance—covering loss of earnings or extra expenses in case of suspension of business due to fire or other catastrophe.
6. Fidelity bond—covering theft by an employee.
7. Fraud insurance—covering counterfeit money, bad checks, and larceny.
8. Workmen's compensation insurance—covering injury to employees at work.
9. Life insurance—covering the life of the owners, key employees, and other personnel.
10. Plate glass insurance—covering window breakage.
11. Boiler insurance—covering damage to the premises caused by boiler explosion.

These specific types of insurance can be classified into four general categories:

1. Loss or damage to property owned by the business.
2. Bodily injury and owners property damage and liability.
3. Business interruptions and losses resulting from fire and other damages to the premises.
4. Death or disability of key executives.

The aviation business is concerned with these basic risk areas and the insurance that will serve to protect it. The list just described includes the typical operations, facilities, and resulting exposures of any business. A second area includes those exposures associated primarily with aviation businesses and their unique needs.

Loss or damage of property. The average aviation business has a considerable investment in buildings, furnishings, and inventory. These investments should be protected against fire and other perils such as smoke, windstorms and hail, riot, civil commotion, explosion, and damage by aircraft or motor vehicles. The latter form of risk insurance, or extended coverage, can be added to the basic fire insurance policy at little additional cost. Vandalism, malicious mischief, earthquake, and boiler explosion can also be added to the policy. In the beginning, the manager is concerned with the determination of insurable value and the approach to be taken. There are two basic measures: actual cash value and replacement cost value.

Replacement cost means that the cost of replacing the facility with a similar structure of a like kind and quality at present-day prices. Actual cash value is based on replacement cost and is generally considered to be replacement cost minus depreciation. In planning for property insurance, the manager should consider accepting a coinsurance clause, as it may result in a substantial reduction in premiums. Under the provisions of a coinsurance clause, the manager agrees to maintain insurance equal to some specified percentage of the value of the property (80, 90, or 100 percent) in return for a lower premium rate. Payment is made under the coinsurance provision on the basis of the following formula:

$$\frac{\text{amount of insurance carried}}{\text{amount of insurance agreed to carry}}$$
$$2 \times \text{amount of loss} = \text{amount paid}$$

If, at the time of loss, the insured organization has failed to maintain the specified percentage, it cannot collect the full amount of its loss, even if the loss is small. It is important to note that the coinsurance clause is applied at the time of loss and that the insured has the responsibility for maintaining the proper amount of insurance.

Under recent inflationary trends, and due also to more stringent building codes, building costs have increased rapidly, generally much faster than the overall rate of inflation. Thus, premises replacement costs are much higher and have resulted in a tendency for older buildings to be underinsured. The manager should check frequently to see that facilities are adequately insured. Insurance companies frequently offer assistance in determining replacement value by means of an "appraisal kit," which includes multipliers to apply to the original cost, based on the age and location of the facility.

Legal liability. Legal liability is potentially the greatest risk that a general aviation manager faces. The loss associated with business property is limited to the value of the property. However, in liability exposure there is no fixed loss limit, and a judgment against the business in a personal injury or property damage suit may be a far higher amount. The size of damage suit awards has risen sharply in recent years, and today liability coverage of $1 million or more is not considered high or unreasonable. "Wrongful death" settlements, for example, range from $1,000,000.00 and up in recent U.S. aviation cases. Without liability insurance, a single judgment might strip an organization or put it out of business completely. Consequently, liability insurance is considered essential.

There are four types of liability exposure:

- Employer's liability and workmen's compensation;
- Liability to non-employees;
- Automobile liability; and
- Professional liability.

Employer's liability and workmen's compensation. Under common law as well as under workmen's compensation laws, an employer is liable for injury to employees at work caused by failure to:

- Provide safe tools and working conditions;
- Hire competent fellow workers; or
- Warn employees of an existing danger.

Employee coverage and the extent of employer liability vary from state to state.

Non-employee liability. Non-employee liability, general liability or third-party liability is insurance for any kind of bodily injury to non-employees except that caused by automobiles and professional malpractice. This includes customers, pedestrians, delivery people, and the public at large. It may even extend to trespassers or other outsiders even when the manager exercised "reasonable care."

Automobile liability. Cars and trucks are a serious source of liability. Such liability is encountered primarily in vehicles owned by the business, but can be experienced under the doctrine of agency when the employee is operating his or her own or someone else's car in the course of employment. In this instance, the business could be held vicariously liable for injuries and property damage caused by the employee. If it is customary or convenient for an employee to operate his or her own car while on company business, the business is well advised to acquire non-ownership automobile liability insurance.

Professional liability. This is insurance for errors and omissions by the business in its advisory capacity and is very costly, such that many companies may seek to do without this element of coverage.

Business interruptions and losses. Although losses resulting from property damage may be covered by insurance, there are other losses that may be the consequence of property damage or that are indirect. For example, a fire may force the business to move to another location or to actually cease operations temporarily. Business interruption insurance can be purchased to cover the fixed costs that would continue if the business were forced to cease operations temporarily, extra expenses incurred in moving, and estimated profits lost during the period.

Death or disability of key people. The death or disability of a "key person" in the organization can cause serious loss to the business. If one person is critical to the success of the company, his or her death or disablement may result in the demise of the company. Even if the key person is a non-owner employee, his or her disability can be extremely serious to the company, for the person's services may be lost, yet the obligation to pay that person's salary may continue. These risks can be minimized by acquiring life and disability insurance on the key person(s) payable to the company in amounts that will permit the business to operate and survive.

SMP-Special Multiperil Policy. The commercial risk insurance field has a comprehensive policy similar to the homeowner's policy. It is called the Special Multiperil Policy. Under this policy, the manager can purchase one insurance policy to cover most of the risks that normally would require separate underwriting agreements. The only ones not included in the package are workmen's compensation and automobile. By combining the policies into one package, policy writing and handling costs are reduced by creating savings reflected in reduced premium rates. This procedure can result in as much as a 25 percent savings in insurance costs and can cause the manager to consider his risk and insurance problem as one, rather than several individual difficulties. The likely end result is avoiding overlapping coverage and developing a program that covers the important risk exposures.

Special Aviation Coverages

Aviation is a very specialized area of insurance; general aviation, in particular, lacks buying power in the insurance market place. Therefore, it is vital to choose a knowledgeable agent. The following is a guide.

The aviation organization, in addition to the normal exposures of business, is faced with the special exposures and problems of the aviation world. These risks must be recognized and handled in a manner similar to other risks. Because of the magnitude of the risks, the premium costs involved, and the potential impact on the business if adequate protection is not provided, special emphasis and attention should be given this area by the manager. The major insurance coverages in aviation include:

- Aircraft hull;
- Aircraft liability;
- Airport liability;
- Workman's compensation;
- Aviation product liability;
- Underground tank coverage; and
- Hazardous waste.

Aircraft hull coverage may normally be written to cover two basic types of coverage: "all risks" and "all risks, vehicle not in flight." The "all risks" coverage is a broader form of insurance and protects the owner against damage to, or physical loss of, his or her aircraft while on the ground or in flight. It is frequently written with a deductible clause that applies to all losses except fire, lightning, explosion, vandalism, transportation, and theft. This deductible is frequently varied for the "not in motion" exposure and the "aircraft in motion" risks. The size of the deductible has a direct bearing on the premium and is one of the factors considered by the manager in planning his insurance coverage and risk management. The "all risks, vehicle not in flight" is a coverage that protects the physical aircraft against loss or damage while on the ground. Deductibles follow the same pattern as for "all risks" coverage.

Aircraft liability insurance covers the insured's legal liability that results from ownership, maintenance, or use of the aircraft. There are many exposures that must be considered in this area, including:

> Passenger bodily injury;
> Bodily injury excluding passengers;
> Property damage;
> Medical payments-passenger and crew;
> Voluntary settlement coverage; and
> Non-ownership liability.

In general, the liability of aircraft owners and operators for injury or damage to persons or property conforms to the state laws applicable to damage suits stemming from accidents that occurred on the land or water. The basic legal principles applied are the common law rules of negligence—that is, the burden is upon the person who has been damaged to prove fault as a proximate cause of the accident. This has been expressed as a failure to exercise the requisite degree of legal care owed to the damaged plaintiff. The coverages included in bodily injury, property damage, and medical payments are self-evident from the terms. The limits of the coverage, especially because of the catastrophic nature of aviation hazards, are a primary concern. It is extremely difficult to select adequate limits in these three areas for the exposure involved. The trend over the last few years has been toward higher and higher limits because of larger court settlements.

Voluntary settlement or admitted liability insurance is available in conjunction with passenger legal liability. It is written on a limit-per-seat basis. Regardless of the legal liability, it offers to pay on behalf of the insured the prearranged sums for loss of life, limbs, or sight suffered by passengers in the aircraft. When voluntary settlement payment is offered a passenger, a release of liability against the insured must be obtained. In the event the claimant refuses to sign a release, the offered payment is withdrawn and the passenger liability coverage applies.

Non-ownership liability arises when the individual or corporation utilizes rented, borrowed, or chartered aircraft. Generally the owner's policy does not protect the user, so additional coverage is obtained through non-ownership policies or policy clauses that covers the use of other aircraft or substitute aircraft.

Airport liability insurance is designed to protect the owner and/or operator of a private, municipal, or commercial airport against claims resulting from an injury to any member of the public or damage to property suffered while on the airport. Owners and operators are liable for all such damage caused by their failure to exercise reasonable care. This liability extends to lessees, airplane owners, passengers, and persons using the facilities of the airport as well as to spectators, visitors, and other members of the general public who may be on or about the premises. Airport operators owe a duty to a wide range of people, and litigation may arise from a wide variety of events occurring on and off the airport. The principal areas where litigation might take place can be summarized under the following headings:

> Aircraft operations (liability to bailees, tenants and invitees):
> Aircraft accidents;
> Fueling;
> Hangar-keeping;
> Loading services;
> Maintenance and service; and
> Search and rescue.

Premises operations (liability to tenants and invitees) is the same as for other industries:

> Automobile parking lots;
> Elevators and escalators;
> Police and security;
> Slips and falls;
> Special events;
> Tenants and contractors; and
> Vehicles.

This list is neither inclusive nor complete. It does, however, suggest the variety of occurrences where the airport manager has a legal duty. The hangar-keeper's legal liability endorsement provides coverage for another exposure of concern to airport owners or operators. Damage to aircraft in the care, custody, or control, but not owned by the facility operator is normally not covered in the standard airport liability policy. Many claims have been directed against airport management for aircraft loading-stand accidents, although the majority have been against air carriers and ramp-service companies. Rescue operations, if conducted negligently, may lead to legal liability for damage to persons or property. Aircraft maintenance contracts can also be the source of claims for liability and damages.

Activities on the airport premises include a number of occasions and events that have led to legal action and judgments. Among these are automobile parking lots, stairs, elevators and escalators, police and security actions, airport special events, airport tenants and contractors, and vehicle operations. These areas are similar risk areas for many business activities and are not peculiar to aviation. The law follows the general rule that the operator has a legal duty to keep the premises in a reasonably safe condition for those persons who either expressly, or by implication, come to the facility by invitation.

Workman's compensation under common law, as well as the laws of the various states, considers an aviation employer liable for injury to employees at work caused by his failure to:

> Provide safe tools and working conditions;
> Hire competent fellow employees; or
> Warn employees of an existing danger.

Although employee coverage and the extent of the employer's liability varies from state to state, most states require employers to pay insurance premiums either to a state fund or to private insurance companies. The funds generated in this manner are used to compensate the victims of industrial accidents or occupational illness. Premiums are based on rates that reflect the hazards involved and safety program effectiveness.

Aviation product liability coverage is another area of great concern to aviation managers. The rapidly increasing number of products liability claims and the substantial costs incurred in defending these suits, as well as paying for adverse judgments, have dramatized the need for sound insurance protection in this area. Typical claims have arisen from incorrect fueling, poor maintenance, and deficient design or construction of airframe, engine, or components.

Product liability law works in curious ways and has created a growing problem for the aviation business. The airplane manufacturer, as a larger corporation, has been a frequent target for product liability suits. In these suits, where the product is alleged to be defective, it has been easy under our judicial system to find the jury applying present-day standards in judging the safety of a product built many years ago. Coupling this with the humanitarian impulse—the feeling that someone has been hurt and should therefore be helped—juries are inclined to provide recovery from those best able to pay, rather than those responsible for causing the damage. An illustration of this is a suit brought by a widow against an airframe manufacturer. She claimed the aircraft in which her husband crashed was defective. He was a VFR pilot who, after an evening on the town, loaded his plane above gross takeoff weight, flew into a raging snowstorm without checking the weather, iced up, and subsequently crashed. The jury awarded $1,000,000, which was paid by the aircraft company's product liability insurance policy. When a juror was later asked why the jury made the award when the fault was clearly the pilot's, he responded: "Well someone was hurt, so we felt someone had to pay." This trend is further illustrated by a California jury who awarded punitive damages of $17.5 million against Beech Aircraft Company—an amount that was about 40 percent of Beech's net worth at that time. The rising cost of product liability has been reflected in the price tag placed on new aircraft. Today, the price of a new single engine aircraft includes several thousand dollars to cover the cost of product liability insurance. The consumer ultimately absorbs this cost, just as though it were an item listed on the bill of sale. The insurance cost varies with the size of the plane and the price.

Aviation businesses engaged in maintenance, fueling, sales, or similar activities have been engaged in product liability suits. One aircraft service company, which had contracted to perform a 100-hour inspection, was sued because a broken valve stem was the cause of an accident. The company was alleged to be negligent in failing to discover the defect that caused the accident.

In another case, the underlying cause of an accident was determined to be the installation of bolts and bearings that did not meet specifications and an inadequate inspection that failed to reveal this condition. Damages in this case were awarded at $1.4 million.

Manufacturers and installers of aircraft components can be subject to legal action. There have been court cases involving fuel pumps, nose gear actuating cylinders, cylinder barrels, and propeller controls. Both the manufacturers and the aviation business using the products are involved in legal actions of this type.

The sale of used aircraft is also subject to this type of legal action, as evidenced by a case where the court held the seller liable for latent defects affecting the airworthiness of the aircraft.

Fueling activities have led to several accidents and resulting products liability suits for aviation businesses. Using de-icing fluid instead of ADI fluid, and jet fuel instead of aviation gasoline are two actions that have led to many aircraft crashes and resulting court cases.

Underground storage tanks. A key area for aviation business concern is underground fuel storage tanks. Many older tanks have corroded and begun to leak, risking contamination of water supplies and other hazards. The EPA has issued stringent requirements for inspection and, if necessary, removal of tanks. One aspect of the new rule is that aviation businesses and others with underground tanks must provide a $1 million or more bond as assurance of their ability to handle any tank problem. For most aviation businesses this results in a need for new insurance coverage.

Hazardous wastes. EPA regulations regarding the handling, storage, disposal and disclosure of hazardous wastes have several effects for aviation businesses with maintenance shops and the more specialized agricultural operator.

Aviation Tenant-Landlord Agreement

When an FBO is a tenant, it is best to obtain a written agreement with the airport owner/landlord regarding responsibilities on the airport. This should relate to area, functions, and information flows between the two. As much risk as possible should be shifted to the airport owner. This document should be reviewed, if not prepared, by a lawyer.

Selection of Aviation Insurance

Knowing what kind of insurance to carry and how much to purchase are important aspects of good risk management. Here are some guidelines of risk management and insurance selection.

1. Consider carefully:
   - The size of the potential loss;
   - Probability of loss occurring; and
   - Resources to replace the loss should it occur.
2. How much the business can afford to lose:
   - If the loss is likely to produce serious financial impairment or bankruptcy, then the risk should not be assumed.
3. Consider the scale of the risk in relation to insurance costs:
   - A large loss may be protected by a small premium.
4. Consider the probability and the size as potential losses:
   - Repeated losses are predictable and typically small; and
   - Small losses can be assumed and budgeted as a cost of business.
5. The following risks can be covered by insurance:
   - Loss or damage of property;
   - Personal injury to customers, employees, and the general public;
   - Loss of income resulting from interruption of business because of damage to the firm's operating assets; and
   - Loss to the business from the death or disability of key employees or the owner.

Selection of Aviation Insurer

Care is needed in selecting a knowledgeable, reliable, and resourceful aviation insurance broker. One aviation group recommends asking these questions about the insurance provider:

1. Will the person responsible for my policy be an aviation expert with authority to bind coverage on behalf of his/her company?
2. Will I see my representative on a regular basis?
3. Will all coverages be handled in one simple policy?
4. Can I have an itemized monthly billing showing the cost of each aircraft plus other endorsements and coverages?
5. Will premiums cover only the actual number of days I own an aircraft with no short-rate penalty or finance charge?

6. Is my policy continuous, eliminating the annual problem of filing certificates to lien holders and others?
7. Is my policy flexible enough to handle special needs the business may become involved in, such as banner towing, pipeline patrol, and so on?
8. In the event of a loss, will an outside adjuster be called, or does my representative have authority to settle claims?
9. If an aircraft is damaged or a total loss, will I have to wait weeks or months to receive payment?
10. Is my policy tailored to my exact needs and usage?

Accident Policy and Procedures

In the event that an accident does occur on the FBO's property, to one of his passengers or to his aircraft, there are not only insurance claims to be filed, but also a number of other regulatory agencies with which to coordinate. Moreover, the following of proper procedures in handling accidents can reduce risk at the time and maintain a higher level of confidence on the part of your insurer for the next time.

Federal Reporting Requirements

Both the National Transportation Safety Board (NTSB) and the FAA are required to be involved in aviation accident investigations, depending on the nature and severity of the accident. A description of each agency's role and requirements follow. If an act of terrorism or vandalism is suspected, the TSA, FBI and Justice Department may also have roles.

The National Transportation Safety Board (NTSB) is the federal agency responsible for determining the probable cause of all U. S. civil transportation accidents. This responsibility is vested solely in the Safety Board and cannot be delegated to any other agency. If during the course of its investigation of accidents, the Board discovers facts, conditions, and circumstances that in the interest of public safety require corrective action, it may issue safety recommendations calling for remedial changes in any phase of civil aviation. The knowledge gained from accident investigation is used to prevent additional accidents. The Board also generates safety recommendations from the findings of special studies.

In carrying out its responsibility to determine the cause of all U. S. civil aviation accidents, the Board has issued United States Safety Investigation Regulations (SIR). Part 830 of the Regulations specifies rules pertaining to aircraft accidents, incidents, overdue aircraft, and safety investigations. It is important for managers and pilots to be familiar with and comply with the provisions of this regulation. Important sections of Part 830 follow.

> "An accident. The National Transportation Safety Board has defined an "aircraft accident" as an occurrence associated with the operation of an aircraft that takes place between the time any person boards the aircraft with the intention of flight until such time as all such persons have disembarked, in which any person suffers death or serious injury as a result of being in or upon the aircraft or by direct contact with the aircraft or anything attached thereto, or the aircraft receives substantial damage."

Serious injury means any injury that:

1. Requires hospitalization for more than 48 hours, commencing within seven days from the date the injury was received.
2. Results in a fracture of any bone (except simple fractures of fingers, toes, or nose).
3. Involves lacerations that cause severe hemorrhages, nerve, muscle, or tendon damage.
4. Involves injury to any internal organ.
5. Involves second- or third-degree burns or any burns affecting more than 5 percent of the body surface."

NTSB rules involving accident notification responsibilities include that the definition of a "fatal injury" includes any injury that results in death within 30 days of an accident. The definition "incident," is an "occurrence other than an accident, associated with the operation of an aircraft that affects or could affect the safety of operations."

Substantial damage means damage or structural failure that adversely affects the structural strength, performance, or flight characteristics of the aircraft and that would normally require major repair or replacement of the affected component. The following describes the NTSB's requirements pertaining to accidents, overdue aircraft and safety investigations.

Immediate Notification. The operator of an aircraft shall immediately, and by the most expeditious means available, notify the nearest National Transportation Safety Board, Bureau of Aviation Safety Field Office when:

1. An aircraft accident or any of the following listed incidents occur:
   > Flight control system malfunction or failure;
   > Any required flight crewmember is unable to perform his normal flight duties as a result of injury or illness;
   > Turbine engine rotor failures occur;
   > In-flight fire occurs; or
   > Aircraft collide in flight.
2. An aircraft is overdue and is believed to have been involved in an accident.

The notification shall contain the following information, if available:

1. Type, nationality, and registration marks of the aircraft.
2. Name of owner and operator of the aircraft.
3. Name of the pilot-in-command.
4. Date and time of the accident.
5. Last point of departure and point of intended landing of the aircraft.
6. Position of the aircraft with reference to some easily defined geographical point.
7. Number of persons aboard, number killed, and number seriously injured.
8. Nature of the accident, the weather and the extent of damage to the aircraft, so far as is known.
9. A description of any explosives, radioactive materials, or other dangerous articles carried.

Manner of notification. The most expeditious method of notification to the National Transportation Safety Board by the operator will be determined by the circumstances existing at that time. The National Transportation Safety Board has advised that any of the following are considered examples of acceptable notification.

> Direct telephone notification;
> Notification to the Federal Aviation Administration, who would, in turn, notify the NTSB by direct communication—that is, dispatch or telephone.

Reports. The operator must file a report on NTSB Form 6120.1 or 6120.2, available from the National Transportation Safety Board Field Offices, or the National Transportation Safety Board, Washington, D.C.:

> Within ten days after an occurrence for which notification is required;
> When, after seven days, an overdue aircraft is still missing; or
> Upon request of an authorized representative of the National Transportation Safety Board.

If physically able at the time the report is submitted, each crewmember shall attach thereto a statement setting forth the facts, conditions, and circumstances relating to the accident or occurrence as they appear to him or her to the best of his or her knowledge and belief. If the crewmember is incapacitated, he or she shall submit the statement as soon as physically able.

Where to File the Reports. The operator of an aircraft must file with the Field Office of the National Transportation Safety Board nearest the accident or incident any report required by this section.

The Safety Board is a relatively small organization and has delegated to the Federal Aviation Administration the task of investigating nonfatal minor crashes involving light aircraft grossing less than 12,500 pounds, with the exception of air-taxi aircraft and helicopters. The Safety Board still determines the probable cause of these minor crashes after evaluating the FAA's investigation findings.

The Federal Aviation Administration has the investigative role mentioned, as well as other related safety concerns. A statement of the FAA's investigative role has been given as follows:

> "FAA's responsibility in accident investigation is of a two-fold purpose: to assist the National Transportation Safety Board in carrying out its prime investigative task and to determine whether there may have been a breakdown in any of the following areas of responsibility charged to the FAA under the Federal Aviation Act of 1958:

> Violations of the Federal Aviation Regulations;
> Operation and performance of air navigational facilities;
> Airworthiness/crashworthiness of FAA-certified aircraft; and
> Competency of FAA-certified airmen, air agencies (such as repair stations and flight schools), commercial operators or air carriers."

If no-one were hurt in a small (less than 12,500 pounds) plane accident and the damage was minor, the FAA investigation consists of little more than calling for a written report from the pilot in command at the time of the accident.

State and Local Reporting Requirements

State roles in accident investigation vary. Some states have staff that work with FAA (and NTSB, when applicable) to locate downed aircraft, keep onlookers away, and assemble evidence. Some states issue their own reports of probable cause, generally much faster than NTSB. Local police and municipal chief executives may also be required by law to be informed, or this may be just a courtesy in the interest of good airport public relations. The FBO should be apprised of all local requirements.

Crash, Fire and Rescue (CFR) Procedures

Airports operating under FAR Part 139 are required to have CFR equipment and procedures. Some extensive debate and study has taken place in the last few years about how small an airport needs to be to be exempt from CFR rules. General aviation airports do not have any federal requirements, but good management suggests that the FBOs and the airport owner should have a joint plan and periodic drills. There has been some debate about whether smaller airports should also have specific CFR procedures and FBOs at smaller airports should monitor this issue.

Airports other than certificated airports that maintain fire fighting and rescue services will find the guidelines contained in FAR Part 139 and AC 139.49-1 very useful. Airports that do not maintain fire-fighting services might benefit from these sources as well as from the bibliography contained in the appendix of this circular. In addition, Advisory Circular 150.5200-15 is a valuable document. Availability of the International Fire Service Training Association's (IFSTA) Aircraft Fire Protection and Rescue Procedures Manual and the Advisory Circular 150/5200-16, Announcement of Report AS 71-1 "Minimum Needs for Airport Fire Fighting and Rescue Services" should be of value and interest to the aviation manager concerned with providing adequate facilities. Fire fighting training is now required for FBO employees.

Search and Rescue

Some states handle this one way, others another. The state police, National Guard, or aeronautics agency may each be the lead agency, and these are not the only possibilities. The FBO may be actively involved by taking steps such as loaning aircraft, coordinating Civil Air Patrol (CAP) spotters, providing a communications base, or may choose to limit his or her company's involvement.

Aviation Security

Flight Security

Risk management and risk transfer through insurance may apply to other risk areas such as aircraft theft, drug trafficking, hijacking, and so on. Perhaps unlikely events for the typical FBO to witness, these could be very serious threats to life if they occur.

Widespread criminal and terrorist activities directed against the aviation community have increased in occurrence and in intensity in recent years, and the aviation community's focus on this issue was heightened by the terrorism attacks of 9/11/01. As a result, all FAA security functions were transferred on 2/17/2002, to the new Transportation Security Administration.

The main impact of airport and aircraft security regulations so far has occurred at air carrier airports. However, some of this impact is felt at feeder airports where scheduled air-taxi operators have customers who are "through" passengers, connecting with Part 121 carriers. In order for the ATCOs (Air Taxi Commercial Operator) to discharge their passengers into secure concourses, they are required to develop and maintain approved security programs that meet the minimum acceptable standards. At the present time the new procedures

Figure 11.2 » Sample Security Mission Statement

ABC AVIATION
SECURITY MISSION STATEMENT

ABC Aviation is committed to the safety and security of our customers, co-workers, and community.

To ensure the highest level of protection for you and your aircraft, and in support of national efforts to increase aviation security across the country, please adhere to the following procedures:

— Positive ID required for ramp access. Please see the front desk.

— All baggage must remain under your control prior to boarding aircraft.

— Maintenance hangars are limited to employees only.

— Flight crew must identify all passengers and baggage prior to boarding aircraft as a group.

— Immediately report any suspicious activities or individuals to the front desk.

Thank you for your patience and cooperation.

Provided As a Member Service of
NATA
The Voice of Aviation Business

Source: National Air Transportation Association

are unclear; the TSA is acting rapidly to conform with mandates set by Congress, but the industry has many concerns about whether the proposed rules, such as the "twelve-five rule" affecting aircraft over 12,500 pounds, are actually implementable.[6]

Another set of rules seeks to address the fact that several of the 9/11/01 terrorists were in the US on expired or inappropriate visas and were learning to fly at FBOs that might have noticed suspicious aspects if they had been alert, for example that a student did not want to fly in a small plane but wanted large jet simulator experience. TSA legislation requires flight schools to advise the Attorney General of any foreign applicants for flight instruction, and to provide specific information on them. The Department of Justice, INS, and FBI are working on exact procedures at the time of this edition.

Other elements of the TSA legislation include a GA security study, and improved perimeter access security.[7]

Thus several new federal agency involvements are required of FBOs, adding to the regulatory burden and complexity of running this type of business.

NATA suggests the following sample mission statement on security to its members:

Summary

Aviation safety, security and liability issues are similar in many cases to those arising in any business. The four general categories of insurance:

1. Loss or damage to property.
2. Bodily injury and property damage liability.
3. Business interruptions and losses resulting from fire and other damage to the premises.
4. Death or disability of key executives are as much applicable to an aviation business as any other.

Because of the nature of operations, there are also other insurance needs stemming from the specific risks faced in aviation. The discussion is divided into three sections: risk exposure and how to minimize it; risk transfer in an aviation business, and accident policy and procedures to follow if needed.

DISCUSSION TOPICS

1. Distinguish between risk management and risk transfer. What would be the drawbacks of a risk management plan that had only the first of these elements? Only the second?
2. Explain the "deep-pocket" theory.
3. What are the pros and cons of self-insurance?
4. What are the problems associated with reducing insurance costs by using a high deductible?
5. What are the four main types of risk exposure and which is the hardest to obtain adequate coverage against?
6. What are five types of insurance coverage particular to aviation?
7. Discuss trends in product liability suits and their effect on the typical FBO.
8. Discuss the top three aviation security needs of an aviation service business and of a general aviation airport and how they can best be met.

Endnotes

1. About $80 from *http://www.nsc.org/*.

2. "Aircraft Fuel Storage, Handling, and Dispensing on Airports," *Federal Aviation Administration Advisory Circular* 150/5230-4 and "Aircraft Ground Handling and Servicing," *Federal Aviation Administration Advisory Circular* 00-34A.

3. Federal Air Regulations, see Appendix II.

4. For example *General Aviation Ground Operation Safety Handbook*, Chicago, IL: National Safety Council; *Fire Inspection Checklist*, from Aviation Ground Operations Safety Handbook, Chicago, IL: National Safety Council; *Fueling, Rescue, Hangars, Oxygen, Painting, Welding, Vehicles, Terminals, Sprinklers*, booklets by the National Fire Protection Association-Aviation Series 400, Quincy, MA.

5. See for example NATA Special Report, "The Realities of the Aviation Insurance Market," by Paul Seidenman and David Sapanovich. *www.nata-online/2Govwatch*.

6. See for example NATA article "TSA Requires Security Program for Select On-Demand Air Charter Operators; Small Air Carriers," dated March 13, 2002. See also *http://www.house.gov/transportation_democrats/Of_Interest/010912_JLOTerrorist.htm*.

7. See AOPA Issue Brief "Key GA Provisions of Aviation Security Law" *www.aopa.org/whatsnew/1a-security.html*.

12

Physical Facilities

OBJECTIVES

- Convey the role of the airport business owner/manager in using, protecting, and promoting the airport.
- Describe the major parts of an airport master plan.
- Recognize some of the issues to address when negotiating financing for developments on leased airport land.
- Discuss major environmental issues relevant to airport properties and businesses.
- Understand techniques used to help reduce noise levels around airports, including the possible impact on the FBO operator.
- Understand the degree to which GA airports are threatened, the reasons, and the ways an FBO can help address this situation.

Introduction

The closing of domestic airports in the US is widely acknowledged in the industry to be the biggest threat facing FBOs during the next decade. Airport losses are mainly at the mid-size general aviation airports where FBOs make a good deal of their income, as well as among the private fields that in the past have been absorbed into the public use system. This chapter addresses physical facilities starting with the national airport system, moving to the local airport's environment in its community, the airport itself, and the FBO facilities on that airport. Each of these four areas is first described, and then two final sections discuss problems and opportunities. Obviously, problems and opportunities that face the national system can very quickly occur at the individual local airport, so even if an airport business is not currently facing a problem, this chapter should help identify what may occur in the future and what can be done about it.

The Four Levels of Airport Service Business Involvement in Physical Facilities

Airport businesses are dependent, for the operation of their companies, on the provision of a national airport and airway system and on continued availability and maintenance of the particular airport(s) where they are located. Few other businesses are so dependent on facilities over which they have so little control. In recent years, the national airport system has been losing one airport per week, and replacing this inventory is extremely difficult to replace. Debates about siting new airports, extending existing ones, and preventing noise-related and other operating restrictions can go on for years before being resolved, and far from all are resolved favorably from the aviation standpoint. Thus businesses operating on airports need to be concerned with four levels of airport physical facilities. These are:

1. The national and international airport and airway systems.
2. The community affected economically and environmentally by the operation of the FBO's local airport.
3. The airport itself: runways, taxiways, ramps, terminal buildings, parking lots, and so on.
4. The FBO's own facilities.

Each of these four levels must be well planned and safely operated for the individual FBO to run an efficient, profitable business. Yet only the last, the airport businesses or FBO's own facilities, are under FBO control. At publicly owned airports, even the use of premises is subject to many obligations and restrictions. An important part of running a successful airport business involves monitoring and interacting with the other entities responsible for operating the four levels of the physical facility.

The National Airport Hierarchy

The Airport System

Chapter 1 discusses the national airport hierarchy and its operation. Figure 12.1 shows the numbers and types of airports in the US. There are approximately 18,345 airports in the United States.[1] Of those, 12,988 are generally privately owned and restricted to private use. Another 5,357 are open to public use, including 1,191 that are privately owned but made available. Some 3,344 of the public use airports are included in the 1998 National Plan of Integrated Airport System (NPIAS), including 185 privately owned airports.

All 3,344 NPIAS airports are eligible for federal grants for planning and construction. Of the 1,191 privately owned public use airports not in the NPIAS, some are run by their owners and some are run by FBOs on contract. Figure 12.2 shows the activity levels in the system.

Publicly owned airports have government funding opportunities not always available to privately owned fields—with some exceptions since 1982. The private fields usually compete for the same aviation market as public airports and need to have an understanding of their position in the marketplace. Among the nation's NPIAS airports, facility planning includes the use of federal Airport Improvement Program (AIP) funds collected from passenger ticket taxes, fuel taxes, and a variety of GA taxes. In addition, passenger service airports over a certain volume are eligible to apply Passenger Facility Charges (PFCs), the revenue from which does not go into a national fund but directly back to the airport levying the PFC.

FAA classifies passenger service airports in the United States into four categories: large hub airport, medium hub airport, small hub airport, and small non-hub airport. The classification is based on the amount of civilian air traffic generated by the aviation community. A large hub contains 1.0 percent of total enplaned passengers, a medium hub 0.25 to 0.99, a small hub 0.05 to 0.24, and a non-hub has less than 0.05 of the nation's total. Other airports are general aviation airports and general aviation reliever airports.

Reliever airports are some of the most important in the system; their purpose is to allow the smaller aircraft to operate safely and decongest the scheduled airline airports. The following excerpt sums up their role:[3]

> "General aviation, basically everything other than scheduled passenger transportation, does not always fit cohesively at large commercial airports. Even though large corporate aircraft fit easily into the commercial carrier environment, their flexible schedules may cause perturbations to commercial airport operations. Add in the full range of general aviation aircraft, single and multi-engine piston aircraft, single and multi-engine turbo-prop aircraft, corporate aircraft, and rotorcraft, and the scene becomes more complicated and far more difficult to manage effectively. When further consideration is given to the myriad of

Figure 12.1 » National Hierarchy of Airports

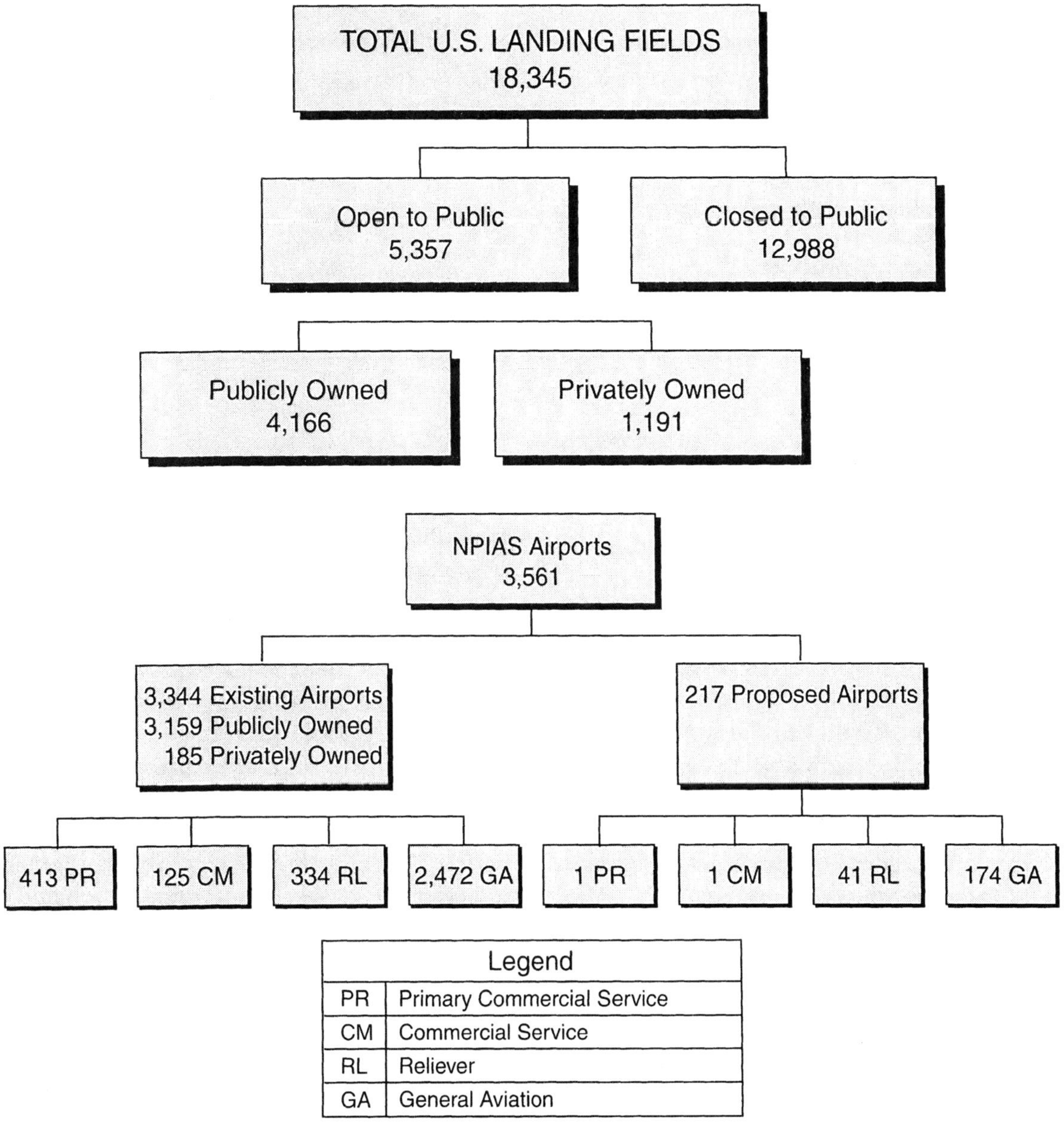

Source: FAA

services afforded by general aviation operators, including flight instruction; banner towing; aerial photography; sky diving; air evacuation; corporate/executive transportation; air taxi; and charter, the need to separate commercial carriers and general aviation is clear. Reliever airports were intended to resolve this incompatible mix of aircraft and operations. The United States Congress defines a Reliever Airport as an airport that relieves congestion at a commercial airport and provides general aviation access to the community."

The Airspace System

The national airspace system was described briefly in Chapters 1 and 9 of course is also a vital element to the airport business. General aviation activity was severely restricted in the aftermath of the 9/11/01 terrorist attacks and access has not been fully restored. The FAA has made many changes to how it operates the airway system, including a great increase in the past two decades

Figure 12.2 » Distribution of Activity

Number Airports	Airport Type	Percentage of All Enplanements	Percentage of Active GA Aircraft[2]
29	Large-Hub Primary	67.3	1.3
42	Medium-Hub Primary	22.2	3.8
70	Small-Hub Primary	7.1	4.7
272	Nonhub Primary	3.3	11.4
125	Other Commercial Service	0.1	2.1
334	Relievers	0.0	31.5
2,472	General Aviation	0.0	37.3
3,344	Existing NPIAS Airports	100.0	92.1
15,000	Low Activity Landing Areas (Non-NPIAS)	0.0	7.9

Source: FAA

in the number of FAA air traffic control towers operated under contract instead of directly.

Public Airport Organizational Structure

An airport's organizational structure can vary greatly depending on its size and ownership. In a large metropolitan area served by several airports, one authority may have jurisdiction over all aviation operations or even an entire transportation system. For example, the Massachusetts Port Authority operates both Logan International Airport and Hanscom Field, a suburban airport. Some airports have small port authorities that govern them and may also run ports and marinas. Other airports are run by cities, as a separate city department or within a department of public works, parks, or public utilities. Many airports are county-run, and this may give them a degree of separation from their elected officials, both because the jurisdiction may be larger and because county functions are quite diverse. When the airport has little direct governance by an elected body devoted just to this function, the public authority frequently sets up an airport advisory committee with considerable power of recommendation. If such an arrangement exists, airport tenants need to make sure that they are fully represented on it.

The Airport's Wider Environment

Overview

Airports are but one component of the national and local transportation system. According to FAA, most of the country's population lies within 20 miles of a NPIAS airport. The wider environment consists of the airspace around an airport, the approach zones, the flight pattern, the noise impacted areas and the airport users, be they recreational or business flyers.

There is very little that can be said about this wider environment that is not about problems. As has been said elsewhere in this book, airport businesses and pilots often do not live in the local community, and local voters are often more vocal to elected officials about their problems with the airport than the users are about their satisfaction with it. The biggest problem is noise that impacts the community for three reasons that have grown over the past five decades:

1. Residential and other development has been allowed to get closer and closer to existing airports.
2. Air traffic at what used to be "puddle-jumper" airports fifty years ago now has increased from just a few operations a year to 200,000 or more.
3. The fleet mix now includes jets, helicopters, intensive touch and go training at the smaller number of towered airports in the system, as well as the relatively unobtrusive single engine or twin aircraft cross-country flight.

How FAA Handles Aviation Noise

As was mentioned in Chapter 9, Flight Operations, aircraft noise lends itself to three types of abatement and control: source control, operating controls, and land use controls.

Source control means quieter aircraft technology by controlling and reducing the amount of noise emitted. Major steps have been taken in this direction; however, it is largely outside the control of FBOs. In recent decades, much was done to develop quieter "Stage 2" and "Stage 3" aircraft. As of December 31, 2000 all Stage 2 and noisier aircraft over 75,000 pounds were banned for domestic travel. Stage 3 aircraft may be new, re-engined, or hush-kitted. In Europe there is considerable debate about whether re-engining and hushkits are acceptable, and further joint efforts seem likely to set standards for aircraft making international flights.[4]

For some years the conventional wisdom was that a Stage 4 (even quieter) aircraft was not possible, because of the noise the aircraft body makes in motion, but more recently steps are being taken toward developing a Stage 4 design.

Operational controls mean various flight techniques to reduce noise around airports. These were discussed more fully in Chapter 9, Flight Operations.

Land use controls consist of various mechanisms to reduce or stabilize the number of noise-sensitive activities around the airport. In fully developed areas this approach has sometimes involved the purchase of homes and schools and their relocation or demolition.[5]

Other tools include soundproofing existing buildings and the construction of berms, noise walls, hush-houses, and run-up pits to contain noise on the airport. The largest soundproofing program to date is at Minneapolis-St Paul airport with almost 5,600 homes and also 11 schools retrofitted, at a cost of $130m in the 1990s. In some cases it is possible to purchase an avigation easement to the title of a house so that the owners and their successors forgo their right to complain about noise in exchange for a fee.[6]

The fleet mix at many airports includes single engine or twin aircraft, helicopters, and other aircraft.

The cost of installing adequately designed fuel tanks is a key consideration for an FBO.

Where land is not yet developed there is more opportunity to prevent problems. However, this is often accompanied by less urgency, until one day someone realizes that a new nursing home or elementary school is under construction off the main runway. Available land use controls for undeveloped areas include:

1. Transfer or sale of development rights to the airport owner.
2. Avigation easements.
3. Soundproofing as part of the airport area building code.
4. Zoning restrictions, for example, in an "overlay" airport zone that adds more stringent conditions to existing zoning, or a complete rezone that eliminates incompatible land uses entirely from the airport area zoning. However, where this is perceived as "downzoning" to a less commercially desirable use, there can be a question of "taking" private property.
5. Full disclosure of the airport's proximity in leases of new buildings.

The noise report of the Oregon Aeronautics Division provides sample legal language for these and other techniques and several FAA publications are also available.[7]

FAR Parts 150 and 161

This portion of the Federal Aviation Regulations deals with aviation noise. It provides for a percentage of each year's Airport Improvement Program to be allocated to noise studies and to land acquisition for noise-abatement purposes.

The noise study requirements include the preparation of a noise map showing present or future noise sensitive areas. Once this map is accepted, the next step of a Part 150 study is an abatement plan that, working through a participatory process, evaluates all possible operational and land use strategies and presents a plan that will achieve the most effective results for that particular airport area. If appropriate, federal grant funds are available to purchase land for noise-abatement purposes. Smaller airports may not be able to get funding for noise activities, even though they may have noise-sensitive neighbors, because hitherto their noise contours of DNL 65 dB and above have fallen within the airport property line. However, a more flexible recent approach by FAA may improve this situation.

FAA has for many years funded the removal of homes in highly noise sensitive areas such as under the flight path of a major jet airport. In other locations, considerable funding has been made available for soundproofing of residences—at a cost of over $20,000 per home. FAA now is addressing schools and multi-family housing. In addition, it has funded noise and land use studies to help local policy-makers.

Facilities on the Airport

Introduction

Some FBOs are owners of the airport and control all the facilities. Others may manage a private or public airport on contract or may simply be one of several tenants. The state of facilities on the field requires constant monitoring and feedback, especially in those functions where the FBO does not have direct control.

Facilities on the airport affecting the FBO's operations may include the following:

- Runways and taxiways;
- Air traffic control tower;
- Terminal buildings;
- Lights, radio, and so on;
- Navigational aids such as NDB, ILS, Glide slope, and VASI;
- Utilities;
- Maintenance;
- Auto access and parking; and
- Space leased to other FBOs.

The Airport Master Plan and ALP

Airports in the National Airport System Plan are eligible for federal planning and construction grants under the Airport Improvement Program (AIP). Eligible airports are encouraged to prepare a full Master Plan about every five years and to keep track of intermittent changes to facilities and activities. Smaller airports may not do a full Master Plan but rather an Airport Layout Plan (ALP) that shows the ultimate layout of the airport as it expands over the next 20 years. The ALP is also a key end product of the full Master Planning process, but it is supported by more analytical detail explaining how the chosen ALP was selected. Smaller airports with fewer complexities may not need all this documentation.

A full Master Plan involves the following steps:

1. Inventory—of facilities, of activity and of financial performance.
2. Forecasts of demand—usually over 5-, 10-, and 20-year timeframes. Forecasts are generally prepared for based aircraft, operations and passengers, by aircraft type (for noise analysis), and by year, peak day (for noise), and peak hour.
3. Demand/Capacity analysis—looking at the difference between existing facilities and what will be needed in the future, based on peak-hour demands. Traditionally this topic has been examined mainly in terms of runway capacity, but at many general aviation airports, the limits of aircraft-basing capacity will be reached long before runway saturation, so that basing capacity may become a key variable.
4. Development alternatives—different layouts and changes to accommodate the forecasted demand. These can include land acquisition and runway expansion, though not necessarily so.
5. Financial plan—an examination of capital and operating accounts and revenue sources to examine how to pay for the needed capital improvements. Increasingly, too, this task will examine how the operating account can be improved, for example, by new revenue sources.
6. Noise and environmental analysis—to see whether any growth and expansion will be within acceptable environmental limits. Certain topics may require a full Environmental Impact Statement (EIS) at federal and/or state level.
7. Implementation program—how to stage the desired improvements, usually including a phased capital improvement program for the 5-, 10-, and 20-year periods.

8. Public participation program—usually at two levels, a technical committee that will receive advance copies of the study reports and review them, and a public process. Certain proposals, such as runway extensions, also require a formal public hearing with legal notice periods, a transcript, and a formal schedule. In today's world, no such formal end to a study should take place without all interested parties having input into draft concepts. There should be no surprises on either side at a public hearing.

Participation by Airport Businesses in Airport Policy and Planning

The FBO, air-taxi operator, commuter, or other aeronautical provider at a public airport should actively seek participation in the technical level process of a master plan. What is done to the public portions of the airport and the decisions that are made about how to allocate still-vacant land at the airport can vastly affect the FBO's prosperity. An FBO may have prospective clients who are being held back by lack of another 500 feet of runway, by lack of the right fuel, or other deficiencies that the federally supported planning and construction process could remedy. There may be inadequacies in the condition of existing facilities—the runway needs a crack seal job, the taxiway needs widening, snow plowing is getting done too slowly, or a host of other possibilities for which the master plan will set budgets and priorities. The master plan will address what role the airport is to play. Will it serve primarily single engine trainers? Does the airport owner see a major corporate twin and jet market? Are capacity limits looming up that will inhibit growth for the FBO's business?

The FBO should seek a full role in the study. Airports are unique in the national transportation system because now they rely on teamwork between public and private sectors to keep them viable. The master plan is a key opportunity to audit and alter this symbiosis.

Figure 12.3 » NPIAS Cost by Airport Type

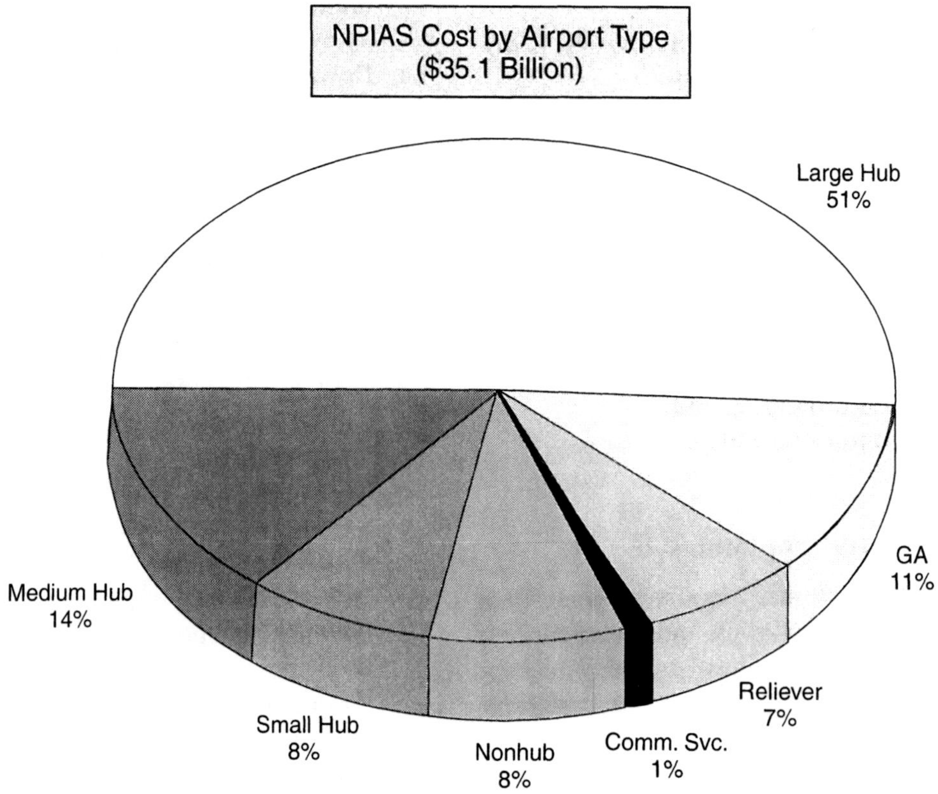

Source: FAA

Figure 12.4 » NPIAS Cost by Type of Development

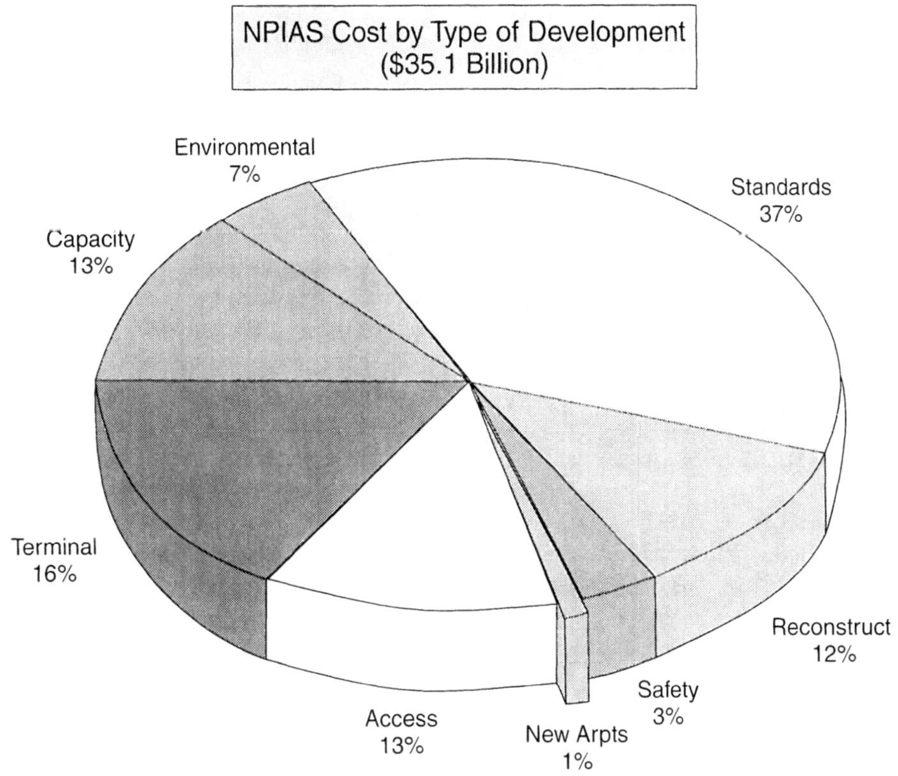

Source: FAA

Private Airports

Since the AIP legislation of 1982, certain private airports have become eligible for AIP funding. They must fit the following criteria:

1. Any privately owned reliever airport, OR
2. Any privately owned airport, which is determined by the Secretary of Transportation to enplane annually 2,500 or more passengers and receive, scheduled passenger service of aircraft, which is used or to be used for public purposes.

The following conditions also apply:

1. The airport must continue to function as a public-use airport during the economic life of the federally funded facilities (at least ten years).
2. The airport must comply with the other grant conditions made to all sponsors, summarized here in Figure 12.5.

Airport Revenue Planning

One component of the airport master plan is a financial plan. It typically examines needed construction costs compared with available federal, state, and local revenue sources. It also examines future operating revenues and rates to see if reserves can be set aside to cover the construction plan. Some airports have general funds or bonding powers available. Funds are often sought directly from the airport—the FBO leases and concession fees. The FBO, therefore, needs to be very close to policy-making in this area and be prepared to explain the costs and revenues of the business, especially if he or she believes that higher rates will be self-defeating because of lost demand.

On the other hand, as discussed in Chapter 3, Marketing, the FBO and airport owner may overlook many profitable areas for new aviation and non-aviation business. The FBO's knowledge of these areas and their break-even levels may help

Figure 12.5 » Grant Conditions Under Airport Improvement Program

1. The airport will be available for public use on fair and reasonable terms and without unjust discrimination (all like users shall have like rates and terms).
2. No exclusive right shall be granted for the use of the airport by any person providing aeronautical services to the public (the providing of services by a single FBO is not considered as an exclusive right if it should be unreasonably costly, burdensome or impractical for more than one FBO to provide such services, and if allowing more than one FBO would require reduction of space leased to an existing FBO.
3. The airport shall be suitably operated and maintained, with due regard to climatic and flood conditions.
4. Aerial approaches to the airport must be adequately cleared and protected.
5. Appropriate action, including the adoption of zoning laws, has been or will be taken, to the extent reasonable, to restrict the use of land adjacent to or in the immediate vicinity of the airport to activities and purposes compatible with normal airport operations.
6. Facilities will be available for the use of United States aircraft.
7. The airport owner will furnish to the government, without cost, any land needed for air traffic control, air navigation, or weather services.
8. Project accounts and records will be kept in accordance with prescribed systems.
9. The fee structure will permit the airport to be as self-sustaining as possible.
10. The airport owner will submit financial reports as requested.
11. The airport and its records will be available for inspection.
12. Revenues at public airports will go to aviation purposes.
13. Land acquired for noise control with federal funds will, when resold, retain restrictions making development on the land compatible with the airport.

Source: Public Law 97-248, September 3, 1982, paraphrase of Section 511. For precise conditions see P.L. 97-248 itself.

to refocus the search for more money away from raising rates and toward provision of new services.

The FBO's Own Facilities

An FBO on a public airport is not only a tenant renting certain physical space, but is also involved in an operating agreement that provides certain rights and obligations relating to how the business is run. FBO facility management and lease development is thus somewhat more complex than the usual commercial lease.

The FBO in a full-service operation normally leases or owns the following:

> Aircraft parking;
> Tie-down areas;
> Hangars;
> Fueling facilities;
> Administrative space, front desk and waiting area;
> Maintenance shop; and
> Aircraft showroom.

Data Collection

The FBO will have considerable data on hand about current facilities and activities and should keep this in a current and usable format. Data on market trends, new opportunities, and the likely growth in demand for existing services are discussed in Chapter 3, Marketing. Data on existing activities should include:

> Number of based aircraft, by corporate and personal ownership, by equipment type and amount of use;
> Identity of frequent transients (see Chapter 8, Flightline and Front Desk, for a discussion of a useful transient log);
> Seasonality and time-of-day peaking;
> Noise complaints and responses given;
> Revenue by area;
> Profit by area; and
> Activity of any concessions or ancillary operators such as car rental, restaurant, vending machines, industrial parks.

Data on existing facilities should include maps, plans and condition of:

> Navigational Aids under FBO control;
> Buildings;
> Ramps;
> Tie-downs; and
> Hangars.

The FBO may find it useful to review his database with the airport owner to see if other information would assist in the overall airport planning process.

Planning a New Airport

A study done in the late 1970s suggests that the newest airports entering the system are airports on private land. Such facilities may be as simple as a farmer rotating which field he uses for crop-dusting flights, or they may from the outset be planned as public use facilities. Any new landing area requires FAA approval and in most cases either approval or at least registration with the state aviation agency. In addition, since airports are often not permitted uses under municipal or county zoning, there may have to be zoning approvals or variances. There could also be requirements for compliance with state and/or local environmental regulations.

Facility Expansion

The decision to build a second maintenance hangar will depend on break-even analysis as discussed in Chapter 4, Profits and Cash Flow. In addition, it will almost certainly require approval from the landlord even if the site has already been leased.

Facility replacement may likewise require approvals. Design control may be involved, and certainly compliance with all FAA requirements on obstructions and setbacks will be necessary, as will compliance with local building codes and possibly airport requirements beyond the municipal code. Building codes have become much more stringent over the last thee decades, meaning that expansion will cost more and even a modest remodel may require the presumed unaffected parts of the premise to be brought up to code e.g. by addition of sprinklers. Many states also have regulations affecting airports that will need to be considered. For his own purposes, the FBO will, of course, have to develop a staging plan for continuation of business during construction in order to minimize disruption.

Preventive Maintenance

Preventive maintenance—repairing and maintaining physical facilities before they collapse—is a key to good facility planning. Prevention versus after-the-fact repairs is a trade-off between forestalling unnecessarily frequent crises that disrupt service and the cost of a 100 percent prevention program. One aviation expert suggests a split of the maintenance budget into 70 percent preventive maintenance and 30 percent crisis troubleshooting. The 70 percent may have a proportionally larger labor element because it involves such things as a planned schedule for replacing light bulbs, while the 30 percent may involve the sudden purchase of major equipment to replace that which has unexpectedly collapsed, such as the furnace or the air-conditioning system.

Scheduled Replacement of Plant and Equipment

The expected life of all well-maintained equipment provides the basis for a planned replacement schedule that may extend over as much as 20 years. Each year various major items are replaced. This must be part of the facilities budget. The replacement schedule will only be adjusted when the unexpected premature collapse of a major item occurs. Even then, the preventive maintenance budget should ideally be able to handle such needs, rather than the long-range equipment budget. The deferral of major replacement tasks is to be avoided, if possible, because every delay increases the risk of several major collapses close in time that could seriously disrupt the smooth operation of the business. Regular inspection of facilities will help make any appropriate changes in priorities as the years go by.

As with many other areas of the economy, there is an increasing interest at airports in encouraging the private sector to provide facilities that were previously built by the public airport authority. For example, as mentioned, there are a growing number of air traffic control towers run on contract under FAA regulation by private companies. As discussed in Chapter 9, Flight Operations, the reduction in flight service stations has triggered a new service area: private weather systems provided by FBOs. Potential profits for FBOs and/or other private investors are in such areas as the development of business offices on the airfield, restaurants, and hangars. Hangars have often been built by public airport operators, but recent years have seen increasing questioning of why scarce public funds should be used to build facilities that (1) benefit only certain airport users; and (2) can be profitable for the private sector. Certain types of portable hangars and "clamshells" can be particularly profitable as well as flexible.

FBOs who wish to expand their base of operations should be constantly aware that the lines between public sector and private sector investment at airports are shifting and that this shift may present new opportunities for profit.

Zoning and Other Local Controls

Zoning regulations are varied and may not necessarily be aimed at fostering compatible uses around the airport. Where existing zoning restricts something an FBO would like to do, he or she has the choice of either seeking a variance for the one special case, or of seeking a rezoning of all pertinent parcels. The latter is usually a more major undertaking than an FBO might want to attempt, but if a rezone has already been initiated, he or she may want to have input into the process. He or she may also want to have input to any zoning changes in the immediate airport neighborhood, since approval of some types of land use will simply favor the climate for new noise complaints.

In addition to zoning, developments the FBO may want to undertake will be restricted by local fire and building codes as well as any state requirements, FAA setback, and runway protection zone considerations.

Environmental Compliance

Environmental compliance is another area where codes and requirements have become much more stringent in the last 30 years. Aircraft wash pads, deicing areas, fueling areas, paint shops and other basic facilities come under intense scrutiny and often require corrective actions and expensive remediation. Some airports, for example Dayton International in Ohio, have completely banned the use of ethylene glycol for deicing, and others are catching and recycling it on-airport.[8] Underground storage tanks must usually be removed and replaced above ground.[9]

There is a strong push for airports, like all other parts of the economy, to be more conscious of sustainability through recycling, re-use and more frugal consumption of everything from oil to paper. In 1999 then-President Clinton adopted an Executive Order *Greening the Government Through Efficient Energy Management,* which puts a fairly forceful approach to environmental consciousness on the radar of federal agencies.[10]

Leases

The right to operate an aviation business at a particular airport may be obtained through ownership of the land, that is, where the FBO is also the airport owner, or, more commonly, through a lease arrangement with a public or private airport owner. As the instrument that provides the basic parameters of the business and establishes a framework for success or failure, it is absolutely necessary that the manager understand the process and is able to obtain as favorable an arrangement as possible. Of course, from the onset the manager should recognize that it is necessary to obtain the services of an attorney to assist in molding the contractual arrangement, and it is also best to find one familiar with the aviation business or be prepared to spend time acquainting him or her with the technical implications and operational difficulties of the problems involved.

Initial considerations. Prior to dealing with the contents of a lease and the typical framework of the contract, one should clearly identify the following considerations:

1. The aviation lease is a composite agreement, a combination of a real estate lease as it is normally understood by lawyers and nonprofessionals, and an operating agreement that sets forth the obligations, duties, and restrictions that apply to the manner in which the aviation business shall be conducted on the leased premises. Some special-

ists recommend, and many public agencies require making the operating agreement a separate document, incorporated into the lease by reference.

2. The pre-lease situation is normally one in which the lessor and lessee (land owner and aviation manager) are in a bargaining situation. It is not a precast, fixed situation. Guidelines are available, but each lease is different, representing the local situation and various local and state laws.
3. The contractual relationship between the base operator and the owners of the airport has an enormous impact upon both parties and more importantly, upon the community they both serve. Because of the economic impact upon the community, the lease should attract a competent aviation organization and provide the opportunity for an adequate margin of profit on the required investment of time, money, and experience. It should cover a long enough period of time to sustain the financing required to establish and operate the business.
4. Developing a lease is not a one-time or periodic activity. A lease is a living instrument that controls a constantly changing relationship and as such should be under constant review. This is reflected in the comment "start working on your second lease the day after signing your first one."
5. Developing a lease is in reality developing a plan. As such, the plan should include those elements that will ensure success for both parties. A basic concern in creating the plan is the need to set the terms and length of the lease with full consideration of the requirements of the potential lenders, who will supply the large financing required of the proposed investment. In the eyes of the lender, the amount loaned will be limited to an amount that can be adequately amortized from the funds expected to be generated by the business during the term of the lease. Therefore, a 25-year or longer lease will be needed for many financing purposes.
6. To meet the requirements of business flexibility and frequently the lending institution's needs, there is a basic interest in the assignability provisions of the lease. Normally the lessee should be empowered to assign or sell the lease for financing purposes upon written notice to the lessor, with approval thereof not unreasonably withheld. The lessee should typically have the right to sublease part of the space covered by the lease, provided the sublessee is subject to the same conditions and obligations as those in the basic lease. Furthermore, it is desirable that the lease state the lessee has the right to sell without restriction to any corporation formed by it, consolidated, or merged with it, provided, however, that the purpose of the surviving organization is to perform under the lease.
7. An understanding of local and national economic aviation trends is important in projecting FBO sales over the life of the lease as well as anticipating increases in lease payments.

Preliminary Planning. Prior to any actual negotiations over the terms of the lease, considerable planning needs to be accomplished. Achieving a successful lease and ultimately a profitable business will depend to a major degree on the thoroughness of the planning efforts. In this plan you should:

1. Become acquainted and on social terms with the airport board and airport manager.
2. Review and study the lessor's previous agreements with parties operating similar businesses.
3. Review and study lessor's agreements with any airlines serving the airport; such contracts may have direct and indirect influences upon proposed general aviation businesses.
4. Develop a prospectus for the business and make financial projections for the future. This information is vitally necessary to the lessee for making decisions on the lease costs that can be accepted without compromising legitimate profit objectives. The airport board, in acting on the bid for a lease, has the right to probe into many personal and business financial issues to satisfy itself of the FBO's ability to perform.
5. Determine exactly what lease terms will be acceptable to the specific lending institutions expected to provide financing.

6. Obtain the advice of the intended fuel supplier on the lease agreements dealing with fuel-storage facilities, fuel handling, and the related fee structure such as the fuel flowage fees.
7. Determine through a title search that the lessor has clear title to the property being considered and is empowered to lease it to you.
8. Determine that the individuals negotiating the lease as lessors have the legal capacity and authority to represent the community or agency having actual title to the property.
9. Review the master plan for the airport and determine whether the future projections are in harmony with the proposed lease and the included business and financial projections of the aviation business. Be sure that the areas you plan to lease will not be harmed by future facility developments elsewhere on the field.
10. In a new lease, review such issues as the underground storage tank conditions on the leased property; the airport noise situation and community relations; and whether the airport is in compliance with FAA requirements, OSHA requirements, local fire codes and other pertinent regulations and what is needed to maintain this compliance.
11. Review existing and future liability and insurance needs for the leased property, and examine coverage held by the airport operator to determine that there are no nebulous areas of liability between lessor and lessee.

Procedural steps. The normal procedural steps followed in negotiating and awarding a lease are:

1. The development and release of an invitation to bid by the lessor. The invitation is aimed at soliciting responses from all interested and qualified parties and contains the basic information necessary to identify the property, the desired services, and the basic leasing arrangement. In order to ensure coverage of desired items and an element of standardization among prospective lessees, a sample lease bid is usually included in the bid announcement, along with any applicable airport minimum standards that serve to screen out unqualified bidders. Bonding capability is a likely requirement.
2. The interested lessees then prepare and submit lease bids to the lessor. These are usually closed bids with simultaneous bid opening for all respondents.
3. All proposals received by the owners are evaluated fully through a detailed analysis of the major elements in each proposal. An airport board may establish a lease committee for this purpose.
4. Negotiations are conducted with the bid respondents submitting the most acceptable proposals in order to assure complete understanding of the proposals submitted and to reach any modifications deemed necessary.
5. The bidder offering the most acceptable final proposal is identified.
6. The detailed lease and operating agreement will be completed and agreed upon.
7. The final lease proposal is agreed upon and the unsuccessful bidders advised and released from their offers.

Appendix IX provides guidelines to its members from NATA for lease negotiations including sample leases. Appendix X is FAA's similar document "Guidelines for Leases or Agreements Granting Commercial Franchise Privileges for Aeronautical/Non-aeronautical Activities at Public Airports Affected by Federal Agreements" which is useful to the FBO in knowing the constraints under which his/her landlord must operate.

It may provide a basis for a final lease document to address a specific situation.

Major lease components. Most aviation leases follow a format similar to the ones contained in Appendix IX, and since there are certain basic concerns, they cover common elements. The major components in a lease are:

> Site location;
> Terms of the lease;
> Options;
> Termination before expiration;
> Rights after termination (reversion);
> Lease release;
> Lease disputes and how they will be handled;

> Rights and obligations; and
> Rent and conditions under which it will be increased.

We will examine these components, identify each, and consider elements of primary concern.

Site location. The premises being considered should be described clearly, fully, and accurately with the official plot plan and survey drawing of the properties attached and incorporated by text reference.

First right of refusal for adjacent areas to the site should be accorded to the lessee.

The privilege to use all general public airport facilities and improvements such as landing areas, runways, taxiways, parking areas, aprons, ramps, navigation facilities, and terminal facilities should be identified.

Term of the lease. The lease term should be established by setting the dates for the beginning and end of the lease period.

Provisions should be included for the extension of the term of the lease.

Term of the basic lease should be long enough to permit the amortization of loans made for physical improvements on the property and the erection of hangars and other installations. Financiers will be reluctant to make loans for longer periods than the basic lease even if renewals are available.

Options. Provision for extending the lease for an additional term should specify the length of the term, the maximum amounts by which rents, fees, and payments can be increased during the option period; and the basis on which those increases are to be calculated, as with, for example, a local cost of living index.

Allowance should be included for appropriate extension of the term of the lease in the event of interruptions due to causes beyond the control of the lessee. In lieu of such extension, the lease should provide for a moratorium on rent payments under such circumstances.

Termination before expiration. The rights of both parties must be clearly set forth in the lease to cover the contingency that the lease may be terminated before its stated expiration date.

The lessor can usually terminate for one or more of the following reasons:

1. Substantial non-performance or breach of contract.
2. Failure of the lessee to observe and conform to the terms of the lease and his or her continuing failure to bring his operations into compliance within 30 days after receiving notice from lessor to do so.
3. Failure of the lessee to pay the rent when it is due. The lease should set a period of time (usually 30–60 days) during which the lessee may remedy the fault.
4. If the lessee becomes bankrupt.
5. If the lessee makes a general assignment of the lease for the benefit of creditors.
6. If the lessee abandons the premises. Under this circumstance the lessor generally has the right to remove the lessee's abandoned effects without being liable for damages.

The lessee may terminate the lease prematurely for the following reasons:

1. If the lessor fails to perform substantially under the terms of the lease. Termination may require written notice to the lessor and the lapse of a stated period of time (usually 30 to 60 days) before the actual termination.
2. If the lessor commits any act or engages in any activity that prevents the lessee from doing business for a period of time (normally specified in the lease).
3. The lease might provide that the lessee can terminate the lease in event of civil commotion, acts of the military, acts of God, damage to runways, court orders restraining the use of the airport, or similar events that may interrupt normal business for a specified period of time. In lieu of premature termination of the lease, there may be a provision for a moratorium on rent payments during such interruptions and/or the extension of the primary term of the lease during such time period.
4. If the lessee is hindered by the lessor or unreasonably prevented from doing business in accordance with the terms of the lease, he or she has recourse to the courts and may receive compensatory damages.

Rights after termination. The lease should contain provisions covering the rights of both parties after termination. Many leases call for reversion of title of the lessee's premises to the lessor at the end of 30 years or after some period of lease renewal. The lessee may or may not have first rights of renewal of the lease.

Some leases provide that the lessor has a purchase option on improvements to the real estate at a depreciated value.

Depreciation schedules should be spelled out in the lease and provisions included for handling property under early termination conditions.

Reversion. When an airport tenant builds facilities on public airport land, the most common form of agreement is that after an amortization period of 25 or 30 years, the facilities' title will revert to the airport owner. The reversion issue used originally to be in leases because the typical airport building was not designed to last more than 30 years and usually needed to be torn down at the end of the lease period. In the past few decades, building codes have gradually become more stringent so that premises may have a much longer life and owners often seek lease extensions to reflect that life.

Usually the tenant will have rights of first refusal to become the renter of the facilities and at a rate to be negotiated. If the FBO in question has not been maintaining a quality operation, the airport operator may, not unreasonably, seek to use the end of the lease period as a means of getting a better operator into the premises. Affected FBOs must address whether (1) they are operating in such a way as to ensure their rights of first refusal are in good standing and (2) what is a reasonable rent for the 25- or 30-year-old buildings that they now must start to lease? The monthly cost may be higher than the mortgage, given original construction prices and interest rates. Some FBOs have torn down their hangars rather than rent them from the airport, and the reversion issue is often contentious.

One innovative solution that has tax benefits is for the building to revert to the airport as soon as it is completed. The FBO then becomes a tenant from the outset. Instead of paying property taxes on the full value of the premises, he or she pays an occupancy or leasehold tax related only to the value of that year's lease payments. Over a 25 or 30-year period, this cuts taxes by a factor of ten or more. The landlord and tenant must provide in the leases for maintenance, repairs, utilities, and insurance on the premises.

Lease release. The lease may also be terminated before the date of expiration in a mutually acceptable release.

By a subsequent written agreement, both parties can agree to terminate the original agreement. For example, both parties may agree to terminate the lease if performance becomes impossible or impractical due to causes beyond the control of either party.

The lease can be written so that all obligations shall be held in abeyance during the period of interruption, and when operations under the lease are resumed, the term of the lease is extended for a period equal to the period of interruption.

Lease disputes. Even the most thoroughly prepared lease may not cover all potential problems, and disputes may arise. The lease should include a means for settling such disputes. One method provides for a three-person arbitration committee, with one arbitrator picked by each of the parties to the lease and the two selected arbitrators picking a third disinterested party. The selected means of dispute resolution should be agreed to and specified in the lease.

Rights and obligations. Both parties to the lease must clearly understand their respective rights and obligations. A "right" is what the lease says *may* be done; an "obligation" or "duty" is what *must* be done. This section of the lease is actually the basic operating contract because it specifies what the lessee shall do and the functions to be performed in order to satisfy the requirements of the lessor. Likewise, the rights and obligations of the lessor should be identified. It is extremely important that the terms of the lease be designed to give the lessee sufficient latitude to operate the business profitably. The rights and obligations of each party, if the other fails to perform, should also be spelled out. The following items are frequently included in an aviation lease under rights and obligations:

Covenant not to compete. Assuming the lease covers a business operation, there should be a provision that the lessor will not compete with the lessee; or if there is competition, its extent and character should be specifically identified. An example of this (and something to avoid) would be the airport manager (lessor) employed by the city and also engaged in a general aviation business in competition with the lessee. Another example would be both the lessor and the FBO having the right to sell fuel.

Operation. The lease must give the lessees and their customers the right to ingress, egress, and have free access to the premises, as well as "peaceful possession and quiet enjoyment" thereof. There should also be an assurance that the lessor will continue to operate the airport as a public airport for the duration of the lease, consistent with government regulations and that there will be no restrictions to normal operations or contingent restrictions that might apply to the proposed leasehold operation during the term of the lease.

It is usual for a lessor to require indemnity insurance holding the public airport harmless from all claims, risks, accidents, or injuries caused by lessees or their employees acting in the airport's behalf in the operation of the leasehold business. The amount of such insurance coverage should be negotiated after competent consideration of all factors.

Duty to make improvements. The lease frequently requires the lessee to provide physical improvements and installations on the premises. Examples of this requirement could include the erection of hangars, shop facilities, office facilities, landscaping, paving, parking areas for motor vehicles and aircraft, creating and paving taxi strips, ramps, aprons, and erecting advertising displays and signs. The lessee might also be required to install fixtures, decorations, and equipment as well as to construct specific facilities for the use of the public. The lessee should know the requirements of the lease before negotiating or awarding any construction contracts.

Right of prior approval. A lease gives the lessor the right to approve or disapprove all architectural plans and designs for required improvements and require the lessor's prior approval of the contractor selected to perform the improvements. For this obligation, it is recommended that the lessee take every precaution to prevent the development of arbitrary or capricious demands or restrictions by the lessor. It is far better to set forth clearly and carefully the required improvements in the proposed plan and specifically consider the design or implementation requirements during the negotiations.

Minimum criteria. Many leases specify that the lessee comply with certain minimum criteria in meeting the requirements for improvements. Some specify a minimum fiscal expenditure, some describe the requirements in terms of space (for example, 200,000 square feet for a hangar), and others identify that the lessee must abide by the regulations promulgated by the authorized officials of federal, state, county, city, and airport officials. The lessee should carefully review the implications of these types of requirements and ensure his or her capability and interests. As in other areas, the advice of an attorney is beneficial, if not essential.

Deadlines. Deadlines for required improvements should be clear and feasible. There is a possibility that the lessor will want a deadline for any construction and improvements required in the leasehold. Clauses requiring completion "within 120 days of signing the lease" or stating that "construction must be complete within six months of design approval" are typical of this type of provision. They may be extremely difficult for the lessee, especially when non-completion penalties are involved. In negotiating these kinds of lease clauses, it is desirable that the lessee obtain as much flexibility as possible in schedules for completing hangars, buildings, and other physical improvements. It is also desirable that the lessee be protected where there are delays caused by such events as fire, earthquake, flood, military action, civil strife, strikes, picketing, or other intervening causes beyond the control of the lessee.

Equipment and fixtures. It is desirable that the lessee have the right to install (at his or her own expense) the equipment and fixtures required to perform the functions of the business and the right to remove them at any time (also at his or her own expense). In some instances the lessor's prior approval is required before removal of equipment; in these cases, provision should be made to ensure that it will not be unreasonably withheld. Under removal circumstances, the lessee is normally expected to restore the premises to a condition satisfactory to the lessor.

Maintenance and repair. The lease should clearly specify which party is to be responsible for repair and maintenance of the leased facilities. Where the tenant got financing and built a building, they would be fully responsible for its maintenance. At issue may be determining who is responsible, landlord or tenant, for maintaining the leased apron area of the leased premises. Where the building has reverted to the landlord and is being rented back, then the lessor normally pays for structural repairs and specific major items, and the lessee pays for maintenance needed because of ordinary wear and tear. Under these circumstances, if the lessee does not perform the necessary maintenance and repair, the lessor is normally given the right (after a specified time delay) to enter the premises and perform the necessary work at the lessee's expense.

Fire loss. Most leases require the lessee to replace buildings or facilities destroyed by fire and to return them to the pre-damaged condition so that the replacement is equivalent in value to the original facilities. The following provisions are normally made in this area:

1. Seventy-five to 80 percent fire and extended coverage and hangar-keeper's liability coverage is usually required with the lessor approving the insurance company.
2. The lessor and any mortgage holders are normally named on insurance policies as additional insured.
3. The abatement of rent should be sought while facilities are not in use due to the fire.

Ownership after termination. The normal provision for ownership after termination of the lease indicates that title to the improvement shall remain with the lessee during the term of the lease, but passes to the lessor at the end of the lease. This would allow the lessee to have depreciated the property and liquidated the debt incurred with any financial supporters. The lease, and both parties, should ascertain the rights of lenders in the event the lease is prematurely terminated.

Some leases provide that the property title must pass to the lessor as soon as construction of the improvements agreed to in the lease are completed. These arrangements have advantages and disadvantages that should be considered when developing the lease.

Removal at termination. Lease negotiations should cover the question of removing tenant improvements, fixtures, or equipment from the site at the termination of the lease. Normally a "reasonable" time is given to the lessee to exercise his or her option to remain. If the option to renew is not exercised and the lease is thereby terminated, the lessee should be given the authority to remove certain clearly defined fixtures or equipment within a stated time (for example, sixty days) or otherwise title of these will revert to the lessor.

Relocation of site. In some situations, lessors determine that they need the leased premises for the expansion or further development of the airport. The lease should include provisions for this contingency. One possible arrangement indicates that the lessor has the right on six month's notice to relocate or replace at lessor's expense the lessee's facilities in substantially similar form at another generally comparable location on the airport. If this is done, the lessee's loss of income during the transition period must be considered, and all contingencies covered such as abating the rent and/or extending the period of the lease. If not covered in the lease, it should be remembered that the public authority owning the airport has the right of eminent domain and has the inherent right to condemn the leasehold and improvements for appropriate compensation in the usual manner provided by law.

Performance bonds. The lease frequently includes the provision requiring the lessee to furnish bonds for the "full performance" under the terms of the lease for such items as facility construction, guarantee of wages, and payment of contracts.

Rent. The remaining lease component of rent will be covered fully in a later section of this chapter dealing with lease payments.

The operating agreement. A major portion of the lease constitutes an operating agreement between the lessor and the lessee. The earlier portions of this material are common to most real estate leases, but this area is unique to the lease dealing with aviation businesses. Since people outside the aviation industry may not understand many of the following topics, care should be exercised in selecting legal advice and in negotiating items in this portion of the lease. The typical aviation business lease provides coverage of the following topics in the operating agreement:

> Permitted sales;
> Permitted flight operations;
> Permitted line service;
> Signs and advertising;
> Service charges;
> Lessor inspection;
> Security;
> Snow removal;
> Uniforms;
> Fuel sales and charges;
> New functions;
> Collection of any fees on behalf of the lessor;
> Motor vehicle parking;
> Vending machines;
> Maintenance, repair, and overhaul;
> Subleases;
> Taxes or payments in lieu;
> Towing disabled aircraft;
> Business practices;
> Exclusive rights;
> Collection of landing and parking fees;
> Subleases; and
> Vending and game machines.

A review of each of these operating topics with special emphasis on its application to the aviation business is desirable.

Insurance. Because of the complexity, cost, and increased deductibles in the ever-changing and volatile aviation insurance market, an important consideration in the FBO's operating agreement with the airport owner is, who is responsible for what liability in the event of a problem. This requires the attention of an expert in aviation insurance, as does the premises insurance.

Sales. The lease should specifically permit the lessee to sell (retail and wholesale) new and used aircraft, new and used radio and electronic equipment, aircraft parts, navigation equipment, and pilot supplies and equipment. In addition to the sale of aircraft, equipment, parts, and accessories, the lessee should have the right to finance such equipment, to insure aircraft and contents, or to act as agent for another party for these purposes.

Flight operations. The lessee should be specifically given the right to engage in flight operations that may include:

> Demonstration of aircraft for sale;
> Charter flights;
> Air taxi activity;
> Commuter airline operations;
> Flight training (primary and advanced);
> Aircraft leasing;
> Aircraft rental;
> Test flights;
> Sight-seeing flights and other miscellaneous flight activities; and
> Aerial application.

In some instances the lessor may feel that certain flight activities, such as primary flight training, should not be conducted at the airport. Here the lessee should not be prohibited from conducting such flight activity away from the airport. For example, the lessee should not be prohibited from transporting the primary student by air to an outlying airport or practice area. Normally it should be acceptable for the lessee to have the right to conduct advance, recurrent or periodic flight training of licensed pilots at the airport. Some activities such as aerial application will entail special requirements on the part of the lessor.

Maintenance, repair and overhaul. The lessee in an aviation business should have the right to maintain, repair and overhaul all types of aircraft, engines, instruments, radio and electronic gear and to remove, install or re-install such equipment in aircraft in his or her care, custody, and control. Depending upon the circumstances, it may be desirable to indicate in the lease that the lessee also has the right to maintain, repair, and overhaul motor vehicles used in his business.

Line service. It is highly desirable that the lessee have the right to conduct aircraft fueling and line-service activities. In many instances this should include the right to service the large aircraft operated by scheduled carriers who do not maintain their own servicing equipment on the airport and the servicing of military aircraft under government contracts. The location of fueling and line service operations should be clearly defined in the terms of the lease. The lessee should have the right to load and unload passengers and cargo and to transport passengers from transient aircraft parking areas to the terminal and other areas of the airport.

Service charges. The lessee on an airport must have the right to assess charges and fees to customers for services rendered. The lessor may periodically be given the right to review the schedule of fees and charges. Some leases provide that the lessee must set charges at levels that are reasonably competitive with those in the surrounding area.

Towing disabled aircraft. The lessee should be given the *right* to tow disabled aircraft from or about the airport. The stipulation that this also be an *obligation* of the lessee should be considered carefully due to equipment requirements. If the obligation is necessary, perhaps it would be wise to limit the size of the aircraft to less than 12,500 pounds.

Security. The lease will probably require the lessee to prevent unauthorized persons from transiting the facilities or entering into restricted flight or loading areas. This probably will mean that the lessee has the additional responsibility of providing fencing of a size and quality acceptable to the lessor and personnel practices and procedures, which will ensure control of visitors and customers. The terrorism attacks of 9/11/01 and their aftermath have increased the awareness of the need for greater security even at small airports. Lessors may ask lessees to commit as part of the lease language to the security requirements such as employee background checks that are emanating from the Transportation Security Administration as new rules.

Snow removal. The lease should be clear regarding the duties and obligations of both parties to remove snow (and like hazards) and should include a specific description of the various areas of responsibility. An FBO tenant may have the opportunity to contract with the airport to remove the snow for the airport agency.

Uniforms. Some leases stipulate that the lessee's employees are to wear uniforms at the lessee's expense, and that this sometimes requires the prior approval of the lessor regarding design.

Motor vehicle parking. The lease must also provide for the identification of adequate space for the parking of motor vehicles. Provisions must be made for vehicles operated by lessee, lessor, customers, employees and the public at large. This should include vehicles operated on the normal vehicle roadway as well as the airport ramps and taxiways.

Vending and game machines. The lessee should be given the right to operate vending and game machines on leased premises. If the lessee does not own such machines, their installation may be subject to the approval of the lessor and, if the lease is on a proportional rental basis [i.e. lessee pays a percentage of the gross revenue in rent] their income may be included in the calculation of the rent for the facilities.

Signs and advertising. The lease should specifically provide the lessee with the right to install signs and advertisements promoting the business name and the brand names of any aircraft, fuel, and other products or services. If the lease provides that the lessor's consent be required prior to sign installation, it should also specify that such consent will not be unreasonably withheld or that unreasonable criteria will not be established. Municipalities usually have local signs codes [ordinances] that may be applicable to the airport, and this must be taken into consideration. Procedures should be established that provide for the removal of signs after the termination of the lease or affiliation with the manufacturer or supplier of products or supplies.

Subleases. When desirable, the lease should authorize the lessee to operate ancillary businesses on the leased premises, such as rental car agencies, gift shops, restaurants, barbershops, newsstands, and so on. It should also authorize the subleasing of space to provide under-one-roof services such as electronic repair-related businesses, corporate office, or aircrew spaces.

Taxes/payments in lieu. The income tax burden of a lessee is the responsibility of the business, not the responsibility of the lessor. In many states, leaseholds are exempt from property tax per se but are taxed instead under a leasehold tax that operates in lieu of property tax. The potential lessor should make sure to be clear about the requirements of the specific jurisdiction and budget for the necessary taxes.

Lessor inspection. The lessor may desire provisions in the lease that provide rights to inspect the leased premises and to review and audit the records and accounts of the lessee's business. If these rights are included in the lease, it is recommended that the lease specify that such rights be exercised reasonably, that they not be used improperly to harass the lessee, and that the expenses of such reviews, inspections, and audits be borne by the lessor. Sometimes this is written up to say that if all is found to be in order, the costs will be borne by the lessor, but if not, then the lessee must pay. Extreme caution should be taken in this area to ensure that lessor rights are not created that will result in an unfavorable business situation for the lessee. If the lessor or a subsidiary business is in competition with the lessee, the lease should be designed to prevent an unfair advantage through intimate knowledge of the lessee's day-by-day operation of the company's books and records.

Business practices. The lease should provide the lessee with broad latitude in exercising his own judgment in areas of normal business activity. Lease terms requiring lessor's approval of price and discounts should be avoided. The lessee should have broad latitude in establishing charges and in the inventory to be maintained and sold. He or she should avoid lease terminology that forces an investment in slow-moving items of merchandise, including some grades of aviation fuel. The lease should also provide that the lessee may engage in other aviation—or aviation related businesses—not specifically covered in the lease by making a request in writing to the lessor, and that approval will not be unreasonably withheld. It w ill be important to know whether such approvals can be made administratively, or must be made by a decision of the elected body.

Exclusive rights. An airport is a limited geographical area, and investors providing funds for a business in this space would normally like protection to limit the chance of cutthroat competition. Frequently, a clause is requested for the lease that would prevent additional aviation businesses from entering the airport for a specified period of time. Such clauses will not normally be permitted at airports that have received federal funds, as indicated in FAA's Advisory Circular on Non-Exclusive Rights. However, the FAA's Advisory Circular on Minimum Standards can help an FBO combat competition from unqualified operators such as "tailgate mechanics" and free-lance flight instructors.

Minimum standards. Any FBO on the field may have to comply with minimum standards set by the airport owner. FAA provides guidelines on these. High minimum standards may help to keep out under-financed operators who would likely "skim the cream" of aviation business for a short time and then perhaps move on. The FBO already on the field can encourage stringent standards for his/her own protection but must, of course, be prepared to comply with them also.

Collection of landing and parking fees. Leases vary, and frequently the lessee is required to collect landing and parking fees as an agent for the lessor. Naturally it would be desirable if the lessee were compensated for this service. The question of parking fees for aircraft awaiting or undergoing maintenance should be anticipated and normal business latitude be provided the lessee in such matters.

Lease payments. In exchange for the privilege of operating an aviation business and receiving the benefits of such activity, the lessee normally agrees to some form of lease payment to the lessor. The calculation of this payment and the rate of payment vary widely from lease to lease primarily according to local conditions, the value of the lease, and the bargaining power of the two parties. The typical aviation operation is potentially a complex, multi-business operating in a volatile and sometimes erratic environment. The goal of airport owners, developers, and managers is to achieve the best possible aviation facilities. The economic balance of a lease is very delicate with a need to consider two major factors: (1) adequate economic incentive to support and motivate the lessee in providing satisfactory aviation services and (2) minimum cost to the lessor in meeting the obligation to provide these services. Because of wide differences in the economic potential of airports, there have been some leases that paid the lessee to manage the airport while others have provided substantial returns to the lessor. It is important to recognize the existing situation and develop a lease that has the correct balance. The lessee must be able to operate at a reasonable profit level and not be forced out of business. The lessor (normally a public agency) has to meet the need for providing adequate public aviation services and for doing this as economically as possible.

Lease payments may be made in three different ways or in a combination of them:

> Rent on real estate by cents-per-square foot;
> Fees based on the lessee's unit sales, such as cents-per-gallon of gas sold; and
> Percentage of gross sales.

Frequently the lease provides for all three sources, rents, fees, and revenue percentage payment. Rents and fees are fairly straightforward, whereas the percentage of gross may result in an excessive burden to the lessee if not kept within prudent bounds. The areas of concession fees and revenue percentages are full of pitfalls for both landlord and tenant and should be explored carefully. The tendency of the lessor to extract heavy payment from the lessee must be guarded against in order to have a dynamic business that meets the needs of the growing aviation public. All three forms of payment may be combined into one rate per square foot, which then allows comparison with FBO rates on similar fields.[11]

Real estate rent. Rent is the fee charged for the use of real property where the business operates. Real property is normally identified in the lease as unimproved property, improved property, buildings, office space, terminal building space, aprons, and ramps. Establishment of the rental rates is a bargaining process, and the lessee must determine whether the proposed rates are competitive and within the business potential for the location. Rates are constantly changing because of the economic pressures being exerted upon the airport operators. The trend of the last few years is toward higher rentals. This trend has continued, as would be expected. Since rentals are competitive, there is considerable variation among airports. The figures at least provide some guidance and a departing point in calculating the existing competitive situation.

Comparable figures should be obtained from other airports, as well as from other leases on the lessor airport. Also, when examining a given rate structure, a lessee should consider the entire lease because it is possible that a low rate in one area will be offset by a high rate in another area. Individual rates can be raised by the lessor using different lessees to achieve a higher overall rate. Frequently, a sliding scale of rentals is developed for the benefit of a new aviation business. In the early years of operation the rate is low, and it increases over time as the business grows. This arrangement encourages the growth of a stable business that can provide necessary services rather than maximizing the immediate cash flow for the lessor. It is realistic for both parties to anticipate that as the business grows, the lease may include provisions for increases in future rentals.

Percentage of the gross. Many aviation business leases provide for rent schedules based upon a "percentage of the gross," usually with fixed minimum rental payments. This manner of rental payment calculation can be beneficial to an aviation business because if sales go down, rent goes down. On the other hand, it makes it much harder to budget expenses as rent is now a variable cost instead of a fixed cost. Also, using a percentage of the gross rather than net income means that if there are some high costs involved in the business, the tenant will be paying unduly high rent that isn't due to high income but to high costs. If the percentage is set too high, it may establish a basis for rent payments so high that the lessee cannot operate at a profit.

If the lessor insists upon using gross sales revenues as the selected formula for establishing rents, the lessee may maintain some predictability and fairness by striving for a reduced schedule for the fixed real estate rental and for the use of an "adjusted gross formula," which is defined as the gross income, less taxes, less bad debts, less fuel flowage fees, and less aircraft sales.

Aircraft sales. Some lessors strive to obtain payments on a percentage of the gross or net revenue from aircraft sales. For the typical aviation business, however, it is felt that aircraft sales should be encouraged by not taking a direct percentage on any sales (wholesale or retail), presuming that a long-range benefit will result from more aircraft operating hours, more maintenance, storage, fuel, and other related businesses. Some states apply a sales tax that is returned in part to the local jurisdiction where the sale took place.

Fuel sales. Payments on the sale of fuel through the imposition of flowage fees should receive careful consideration by both parties to the lease. Fuel is part of the line service, which is expected and provided in the support of transient aircraft. The income from fuel sales often provides the revenue base that contributes to the development of a stable organization. It tends to support a business when sales or other revenues may not be forthcoming. Where the public body (for example: city, county, airport authority) retains fueling rights without providing other services, transients are frequently discouraged by the arrangement, service is not as responsive, and the aviation businesses tend to be weak with higher failure rates. Fuel flowage fees range from one-half cent to a few cents per gallon on fuel pumped by the lessee. Flowage rates above this level create a heavy economic burden on the lessee and may cause additional burdens as fuel prices increase, controls become heavier, and customer reaction becomes stronger.

If fuel flowage fees are included in the lease, it is desirable that the following practical guidelines be followed:

1. The lessee has the right to fuel the business's own aircraft without flowage charges.
2. The lessee has the right to fuel aircraft operated by the local, state, or federal government without charge.

Fuel is part of the line service, which is expected and provided in the support of transient aircraft.

3. Air carrier aircraft with "turn-around" fuel contracts should not reflect a charge.
4. Fuel fees should be based upon fuel sold and not on volume delivered into the storage facilities.
5. The fuel fee should be based upon a specified sum (for example, two cents a gallon) only for fuel sold at retail to transient aircraft.
6. The lessee should have the absolute right to select the fuel supplier.
7. Clear provisions should be included in the lease to cover bulk fuel storage agreements so as not to restrict the lessee or to proliferate the number of storage units.

Landing and parking fees. The lease may have a requirement that the lessor collect airport landing fees from its customers and transient visitors on behalf of the airport administration. Landing fees have long been a problem at airports, especially those open to the public. Many operators have found that the administrative costs of collecting landing fees for small aircraft and small airports exceed the revenues. In addition, these funds are so small that they contribute very little income to the public agency. Many operators have found that landing fees act as a deterrent to itinerant pilots, especially to general aviation aircraft with alternative landing options. In going elsewhere, the aircraft take their additional and perhaps major business activity with them. If landing fees are required, it is suggested that they aren't collected from non-commercial aircraft. Those aircraft involved in commercial passenger or freight operations such as certificated carriers, commuter airlines, charter, and air taxi are normally charged landing fees.

A partnership. The lease for the operation of an aviation business is more than a simple contractual agreement. Both the lessor and the lessee are partners who work for the benefit of the entire community. The agreement is more than a lease; it is a lease, an operating agreement, a partnership agreement, and a community service plan that establishes a mutually beneficial relationship among the two parties, and the public that they serve. This kind of relationship is necessary if the airport's service and support facilities in a given community are to grow and to provide a stimulus to the growth of the aviation sector and the overall economy of that community. For aircraft to be really useful in business and personal transportation throughout the network of approximately 15,000 landing facilities in the United States, there must be a sustained growth in the quality of the aircraft-support facilities across the country. The number of aircraft is growing, and more and more individuals and organizations are using aircraft for personal as well as business transportation. The partnership element of the aviation business lease will do a great deal to promote the necessary growth of aircraft support activities. This agreement cannot be one-sided, but must be equitable and represent the interests of both parties.

Competition with Other FBOs

FAA non-exclusive rights policy. Any airport that has received federal funds from the Aviation Trust Fund must by law be available to all users. This includes being available to all FBOs who are interested and can meet required standards. This means that even airports that hope to be funded must comply with the FAA regulations. Yet the rules also recognize that if new competition would mean neither the old nor the new FBO would have enough business to be viable, there can be some protection for the existing FBO. In many cases the airport minimum standards permit self-fueling and self-maintenance by qualified operators. In cases where the airport standard prevents a certain type of newcomer (such as one offering too few services or too small an area, or one that is undercapitalized), then the FBO needs to be vigilant that the standards are being enforced and applied fairly.

Since an existing FBO at a publicly funded field has limited protection against the granting of leases to new competitors, the best protection may be to provide a full-service, quality operation so that no outside entrepreneur can find any unmet needs.

Through the fence. A "through-the-fence" operation is one on land not owned by the airport owner but with legal or long-standing rights of access through an actual gateway or across an imaginary property line onto the airport. Some airports actively encourage such through-the-fence activities as, for example, corporate aircraft hangars connected in surrounding airport industrial parks. In other cases the through the fence situation may involve only one operator who may have an established aviation business. The problem for the airport operator is that there may not be very much control or revenue (if any) from operations off an airport.

The problem for other FBOs is that the through-the-fence operator may not be paying the true cost of airport facilities. Businesses on the field may be subsidizing the through-the-fence operator. FBOs already on an airport will generally find that it isn't in their favor if through-the-fence activities are permitted. However, FBOs seeking to enter operations at a busy field may find that there is no available airport land and that a through-the-fence easement to adjacent land may be their best alternative. FAA discourages it, but local airport administrations may be persuaded to permit it, as may private airport owners. As existing airports use up their available land, this type of situation may become more common, and FBOs need to fully understand both sides of the question.

Threats to the General Aviation Physical System

Lack of Appreciation of GA's Role

The role of the national general aviation airport system is little understood except by those directly involved. While most people have at some time flown on an airline or expect to do so and appreciate its availability, most do not hold the same expectation for general aviation. General aviation's negative or frivolous image derives from barnstormers, the silk-scarf and goggles set, jet set playboys buzzing around on weekends, and so forth. The GA airport is seen as "a marina for planes" at best, or at worst, simply a public nuisance. Despite the many important functions that general aviation fulfils both in providing a major element of the national transportation system, and in enabling many revenue-generating and protective activities to be performed from the air, the average member of the public has very little knowledge or understanding of the GA industry's contribution, and if impacted, is much more likely to be vocal about the problems than the benefits.

As was discussed in Chapter 9, Flight Operations, corporations find GA to be of increasing value to their efficient operations. Yet, on the whole they tend to exacerbate GA's poor image in several ways:

- Business flight and business or corporate aircraft are seen as overly luxurious;
- Some companies allow employees use of their aircraft for private purposes, and are perceived as taking the tax write-offs but without appropriate employee reimbursement, reinforcing the idea that GA is a perk or luxury; and
- Corporations are secretive about their reliance on GA travel, not only for fear of offending stockholders but also of the potential security risk to senior executives of making their aircraft readily recognizable.

Airspace Restrictions

The lack of favorable image for GA will tend to mean that it gets less favorably treated when priorities must be set, such as the use of the national airspace system, despite the fact that as Figure 12.2 showed, GA reliever and other GA airports do handle almost 70 percent of GA flights and thus substantially decongest the larger airports of small aircraft traffic.

Noise and Operating Restrictions

Many small airports were sensibly built outside of towns. But the towns have spread in all directions and now often surround the airport. At the same time the airport traffic has often grown heavier and more frequent; and if jets or frequent touch-and-go training flights are involved, it's often significantly noisier.

The early phase of airport master and system planning in the 1970s often led to confusion in the public mind. For example, the term "reliever airport" (defined by legislation as general aviation airports relieving general aviation traffic from airline airports) is still often misconstrued by the public to mean that their little suburban airport may start serving jumbo jets. It doesn't matter that there is not room for the necessary runways and that airline logistics preclude split operations except at the biggest hubs. Such misinterpretation over the years has led to substantial community fears about airport growth, noise, and safety. However, residents' fears about increased airport noise are not a myth but a reality, and must be tackled by all involved with the airport if it is to survive and thrive. This presents many problems.

Before 1990, many airport communities acted independently to introduce night curfews, restrictions on particular classes of aircraft and types of aircraft operations. In 1990, Congress enacted the Aircraft Noise and Capacity Act (ANCA), which seeks to protect the entire national airport system by not allowing operating restrictions unless it can be proven, through a very onerous process, that the economic benefits outweigh the costs. This is now codified as FAR Part 161. Since the benefits are to the noise-impacted community and the costs are to the aviation operators, it is virtually impossible to prove the case and get the restriction. In the more than decade since this legislation no community has been successful although a few have proceeded anyway with local restrictions. For example, Naples, FL has been strenuous about pursuit of operating restrictions and given other preoccupations, the industry appears not to be battling this particular case at present.

In general however, the Part 161 rules were written so stringently that it is virtually impossible to get a Part 161-based airport operating restriction in place. The irony of this situation is that a community's only recourse is then to close the airport down completely, which can happen all too easily.

Airport Closures

Public airports are at risk for closure. In theory the fact that a public airport has accepted federal funds commits it, through the grant assurances, to stay open another 20 years. A landmark case that reached legal resolution in 2002 suggests otherwise. Kansas City, Missouri wanted to give up the runway portion of Richards-Gebaur airport and use the area instead for a freight rail/truck cargo transfer point. AOPA filed suit to prevent FAA from releasing the city from its grant obligations. A second suit by friends of the airport was joined with the AOPA suit, but the 8th Circuit Court ruled in favor of FAA in 2000 and in 2002 the US Supreme Court declined to hear the appeal. So the airport is closed, leaving a very unfortunate legal precedent.[11]

NATA created a list of the nation's 100 "most needed" airports, which are in fact the 100 most vulnerable airports. Many key airports in the system are on this list, for it is the busier fields that generate the most resident concern.[12]

Disappearance of Private Airports and Backcountry Strips

A study in the late 1970s showed that the private airport system is the main source of new airport facilities. While there have been some results in recent years in the effort to expand publicly owned airports, it is still true that the pipeline of new fields into the system depends heavily on private actions. A private restricted field may open, may eventually become a public-use field, and eventually offer a full array of aviation services and facilities. Yet the privately owned airports, this historic source of airport system growth, are some of the most threatened airports in the system for such reasons as:

1. There is no guaranteed succession when the founder/owner dies or retires. Today, World War II, Korean era and Vietnam War era pilots who became Fixed Base Operators are retiring (or dying) and the next generation may see much greater value from selling the land for development, and less reward in taking over a stressful business.
2. As private facilities, such airports are often required to pay property taxes from which their publicly owned counterparts are exempt, making it harder to compete financially. They may be taxed at highest and best use, rather than actual use, which can be financially punitive and often force development.
3. They must finance all capital improvements—even those for which fees cannot be directly charged—from internal funds. Public airports, on the other hand, can be 90 percent subsidized. Since 1982, private airports in the NPIAS can apply for federal funding, but those who have tried have founds many

hoops to jump through and strings attached, that make it almost not worthwhile.

4. As private businesses, these airports may not get the support of local decision makers for needed land use and airspace obstruction controls.

In 2001, GAMA and others were active in supporting a bill to protect general aviation access to airstrips on federal land and the airspace over it.[13] The bill was aimed at ensuring that the state aviation agency and FAA would have an opportunity to determine the necessity of an airstrip before other government agencies are allowed to take action to restrict access or permanently close it. It is ironic to note that while a major concern of FAA is to maintain and promote the nation's airport system, other federal agencies may be operating counter to this.

Siting New and Expanded Facilities

At the same time that the privately owned airports are coming under such pressure, the public system has its own problems. Because of fears about noise, safety, and unlimited expansionism, it is becoming increasingly difficult to obtain (in full) all the necessary approvals for a new publicly owned airport. As Figure 12.1 indicated, the NPIAS anticipates building only 217 new GA airports in the next decade. From inception to ribbon cutting, a new public airport can take 10 to 15 years and cost millions of dollars, thus it is unlikely they will all get built. It can be very difficult to site a new airport or expand an existing one. Encroachment by housing and commercial development may make it costly to acquire needed land for larger runway protection zones and runway lengthening. The site requirements of even a modest new airport are extremely challenging because in metropolitan areas, conveniently-located flat land, suitable for a runway, is the first to be developed for other purposes since this is cheaper than building on a slope. While new GA airports do not require vast acreage, new air carrier airports have been getting larger and larger—Dallas-Fort Worth has over 17,000 acres (Seattle-Tacoma has just over 3,000, as a comparison); the new Peotone airport outside Chicago is seeking to obtain 27,000 acres.

For a period after the new international airport at Denver was opened, experts were heard to comment that this might be the last new airport of any reasonable size to be created in the US. In 2001 and early 2002 action began regarding the new Chicago area "South Suburban" airport at Peotone to serve as a relief valve to O'Hare International (still the US's busiest airport). Even though the first land has been bought, opponents are still raising questions about whether the need could be handled in another way.[14] Similarly, plans to expand Fort Lauderdale's airport, in development for more than a decade, have run into heavy community opposition. A public meeting in 2002 to review runway extension proposals drew 650 opponents.[15]

Lack of Suitable Land Use Controls

Poor land use planning and zoning to protect small airports are still a problem. Incompatible developments, such as housing, are still often permitted adjacent to airports. Some of the most avidly anti-airport organizations are in communities still permitting incompatible developments next to the runway or under the flight path. Communities and local elected officials seem unwilling to protect airports from encroachment through land use controls. This is partly because in the face of the numerous competing local priorities, the value of the airport does not seem high enough to take special steps that may be at odds with housing and economic development policies city-wide. In addition, voters tend to complain to elected officials about noise more than airport users and proponents talk to them about airport benefits. A typical example is reported in the Atlanta Citizen: a land area just south of Falcon Field, one of Atlanta's airports, is zoned for industry but unbeknownst to the airport authority, the land-owner and the city have entered conversations about rezoning it for a 121-unit subdivision right under the flight path.[16]

FAA's own procedures help to create the problems. FAA deals only with aircraft in the air but leaves it to local communities to address land use, development, and zoning. Yet FAA has operated until very recently from a strictly interpreted guideline that airport noise is only a community impact if the annualized nose contour is above DNL 65 dB. This noise metric has a long history; one of its rationales is that in urban areas, below DNL 65 dB it is difficult to distinguish airport noise from ambient urban noise due to traffic etc. Suffice it to say, however, that EPA suggests new housing should not be built on sites exposed to above DNL 55 dB. FAA does appear to be getting more flexible about enabling a lower noise metric to set the standard.

Even FAA itself is not succeeding in restricting encroachment by unsuitable uses—for example a recent news article reported that FAA was changing its regulations from banning landfills within 6 miles of any airport (because of bird strike risks) to only banning them if they have airline service.[17] Yet the airport system is virtually finite; therefore, it needs preserving. Even a small new airport requires at least one mile of flat land with road and utility access as well as unobstructed approaches. Such prime real estate, if it can be found, cannot serve major metropolitan and urban centers unless it lies close to the developed areas. An inherent conflict exists between airports and communities.

Bird Strike Threat

Bird strike is a serous aviation safety problem. Yet, in another example of inadequate land use controls, local officials allow such incompatible facilities as land fills near airports. A protected waterway may encourage wildfowl too near the airport. Bird control is anathema to animal rights activists. Airport administrators use falcons, firework-type explosions, shotguns, and the planting of unappealing grass as ways to minimize the presence of birds on and around the airport. But it is an uphill battle.

Revenue Diversion

In the past fifteen years or so, revenue diversion has become a major aviation issue. Communities with profitable airports have sought to use—and actually used—the surplus to benefit other community programs. FAA and the USDOT Inspector General have been assiduous in seeking to ensure that these funds are retained for aviation use, since national airport and airway system funding needs are much greater than available resources. The FAA Authorization Acts of 1982, 1987, 1994, and 1996 provided progressively more stringent and clearer guidelines regarding what is and is not revenue diversion.

This is not an area that an FBO can do much about unless he or she is also the publicly owned airport operator—in which case she or he will be provided with detailed guidelines about how to proceed. Despite the publicity that the issue has received, it seems likely that as communities face heavier demand on other revenue sources, they will continue to look to profitable airports as a source of local government finance.

Inadequate Funding

The Aviation Trust Fund was established in 1970. It provides the funds for airport planning and construction. From the beginning, the larger airports through passenger ticket taxes have generated most of the revenue. They have also been allocated most of the grants. The current legislative program provides most of the funds to primary airports, those enplaning 0.01 percent or more of national passenger enplanements (about 30,000).

Small airports, even though key to the national airport system, must compete against one another for very limited funding compared with the primary airport system, which is entitled to a certain amount of funding based upon its passenger enplanements level, and to all its PFC funds if charged.

During the 1980s and 1990s, the available funds for airport improvements have accumulated much faster in the Aviation Trust Fund than expended. Pressure is mounting for a higher level of funding, especially for larger airports. If this does not occur, the passenger ticket tax will be cut back to reduce the balance in the trust fund, even though national airport needs far exceed available funds. Tenants and operators at small and large airports alike need to ensure that these airport improvement funds continue to be available at appropriate levels.

The airport system nationwide can demonstrate a much greater need for capital improvements than revenue projections would appear to support. Continued growth in passenger travel and in flight operations mean that existing airports all around the country are approaching capacity in their airspace, their terminals, their aircraft parking and storage areas, and their runway capacity.

The problem has been greatly exacerbated by the fact that Congress has been unwilling even to appropriate all the funds accruing in the national Aviation Trust Fund. At GA airports the total available is relatively small in any case, due to the formulas of the Airport Improvement Program (AIP). An FBO desiring to identify funds slated for his or her NPIAS airport may find the data on the web; Figures 12.3 and 12.4 (see p. 314–315) show how the $35.1 billion of the national plan is proposed to be allocated by type of airport and purpose.[18] Only 18 percent of the total is assigned to general aviation airports, of which 7 percentage points is for relievers.

New Initiatives and Opportunities

The above list of issues means it is becoming increasingly important to the health of the general aviation system—and that means to FBOs—to preserve and enhance the viability of the airport system that already exists. To accomplish this requires an intensive two-pronged nationwide strategy, addressing noise and economic benefits.

Noise Abatement Programs

It appears that FAA is becoming more flexible about measuring and addressing airport noise; more willing to adapt national noise metrics to local conditions. In a strongly worded article in Airport Magazine, it is suggested that airports adopt their own measures for incompatibility—if an airport is surrounded by hills for example, the higher homes will experience much more noise than if the land were flat, even though the FAA Integrated Noise Model may not generate noise contours above DNL 65 dB. Thus, if people are being disturbed, DNL 65 dB is too low a measurement for this community.[19]

According to this article:

> "Minneapolis and Cleveland have recently taken steps to formally establish DNL 60 dB as their local threshold for compatible land use. Both announced programs to expand their Part 150 residential sound insulation programs to the DNL 60 dB contour line. But will the FAA approve the use of Federal funds for sound insulation programs outside of DNL 65 dB noise contours? Cleveland's Part 150 update contains a measure to sound insulate residences within or contiguous to the 60 DNL band of the . . . noise contours. FAA approved the measure in August, 2000 on the basis that the airport operator has adopted the DNL 60 dB noise contour as the designation of non-compatible land use, thus making the measure fully eligible for AIP or PFC funding."

In FAA's noise policy update draft published for comment in 2000, it promised to support efforts to establish local noise standards and that FAA will recognize those standards in Part 150 noise compatibility programs. However, NATA in an October 2000 statement to FAA about its noise policy, opposed the lowering of the 65 DNL contour. This is an ironic move, since this is a tool that could help communities do more about appropriate land use around airports, especially if it made them eligible for federal funds to soundproof homes in a broader area. If implemented, it would to some extent reduce the pressure for operating restrictions.[20]

Continuous Noise Abatement Strategy

A noise study will not, in one step, eliminate noise and the threat it can pose to an airport's future. Indeed, in many cases the opportunity to be heard encourages airport neighbors to mobilize in opposition to the airport. Prevention, rather than cure, is the best strategy. Prevention means setting up good operational techniques before they are demanded. It means making sure that chronic complainers are invited to see the positive side of the airport in every way possible. It means keeping the business community and town leaders aware of the corporations the FBO serves and the way they depend on these services to do business in the community.

Economic Benefits Studies

The two prongs of an approach to airport preservation and enhancement are (1) noise abatement and (2) convincing the neutral or hostile airport neighbor of the economic importance of that local airport to his or her community. This section discusses communicating the economic benefits of the airport. It is a difficult challenge that requires continuous effort.

In the past, there have been two basic approaches to documenting the economic benefits of general aviation airports. One is heavily statistical and seeks to quantify every component of impact generated directly or indirectly by the airport. This includes airport operator, FBO and airline salaries, taxes paid, income from airport users, spending in the community by air travelers, and "multiplier" effects as direct income generated by the airport is re-spent in the local or regional economy.

The other approach is more qualitative or journalistic and presents profiles of key airport users and what they produce, showing descriptively how the airport is vital to their business.

The former approach can become immersed in data so it is hard to "see the forest for the trees." The latter approach may not contain enough hard facts to convince the skeptics. Therefore, a middle ground may be the best. Regardless of the airport owner's activities in pursuing such studies, it is advantageous for marketing and public relations if the FBO makes its own ongoing effort in this regard. The FBO should know who its aircraft tenants are, why and how much they use the airport, and how their businesses are evolving. Employment and payroll figures should be readily available for the FBO itself and for its customers. The FBO should keep a good transient log and, periodically, when a new company signs in, should call to find out if there will be regular visits, and whom they are coming to see. The FBO should be active in at least one local business group such as Kiwanis, Lions, Jaycees, Rotary, or Chamber of Commerce so that the facts about the FBO operation—and the role of the airport—reach ears other than those in the aviation community. FBOs should become involved in airport economic studies sponsored by others in order to maximize their own favorable publicity.

Some airports do much more than this. For example, Cheyenne, Wyoming's airport conducts a full economic impact study every 2 years, and publishes 2,500 bound copies for media, legislators, business groups and others. The airport manager is frequently found providing presentations to these groups about the merits of the airport. By repeating the study methodology over time, the airport has been able to demonstrate its increasing contribution to the economy.[21] The same article describes how many other airports are undertaking similar research and communications efforts. Airport business owners can press for such studies where they are not being done, contribute to them when they are, and work with the airport administration to help spread the word about the airport's benefits to the community and region.

NATA offers a Community Relations Toolkit that is shown as Appendix XI, and AOPA also has a kit.[22]

Airport Privatization Program

Worldwide, there is a growing trend toward selling off public airports and having them run by a private company. This privatization trend took hold also in railroads and a number of other infrastructure areas. In the US it is still a fledgling program, but may grow as early issues are resolved. For the fixed base operator, working at a publicly owned airport could suddenly change to having a private company as landlord and possibly even as competitor. The FAA's Reauthorization Act of 1997 first recognized this possibility as a Pilot Program was authorized in that bill.[23] It sought to try privatization at five locations and invited participants. At first not much happened because the revenue diversion issue, already mentioned, becomes a major obstacle when a private company wants to take some of the airport revenue as profit for the risk of running the operation. Indianapolis International Airport, even before the Pilot Program, had handed over its operation to BAA on a long-term lease, and Stewart International Airport was an early Pilot Program applicant.[24] Various other airports were exploring the possibilities. By 2000, it appeared that Stewart was to be joined by Brown Field in San Diego; Rafael Hernandez Airport, Puerto Rico; New Orleans Lakefront Airport, and Niagara Falls International Airport. However, no plans have yet materialized from these other airports and they appear to be withdrawing from the program.

How this program will affect airport tenants remains to unfold. It does not seem likely to grow fast, if only because the airport manager who would be assigned to investigate its merits would him or herself be out of a job if a private company took over, thus motivation may not be high. In addition, at air service airports a stumbling block is the program's provision that airlines at that field may have veto power over airport projects and related fee increases. Such a restriction would be a major deterrent to most potential operators.[25]

NASA Small Aircraft Program

NASA in recent years has become very active in general aviation. It has introduced the concept of a Small Aircraft Transportation System (SATS) involving a fleet of automobile-sized, high tech, on demand jet powered aerial taxis and various aerospace enhancements. There are many small airports nationwide from which these aircraft could operate. If this program were to take off, it could encourage aviation-dependent business development at many smaller communities nationwide that have smaller, less congested airports.[26]

Airport and Aviation System Planning

The single airport has no value; it must be part of a system. The FBO who recognizes this and is aware of the changing roles of competing airports, changing markets, and demographics is positioned to take advantage of new opportunities. Periodically state and regional planning agencies undertake regional and system wide aviation studies. The FBO should be aware of the opportunities these present to express opinions on aviation concerns beyond the individual airport's boundaries.

Summary

When it is a matter of upkeep and improvement of the physical facilities that make his or her business possible, most FBOs—unless they own the airport—find that they have relatively little direct control. In addition, the health of their business depends on having access to a viable national and international airport network. The attitudes and concerns of airport neighbors can also have a major impact. Sound physical facility planning, therefore, takes into account the airport's wider environment and community attitudes. Airport physical facilities may be grouped into two categories: (1) the public use facilities, such as runways, taxiways, terminals and auto parking, which may be shared by other FBOs, and (2) the private-use facilities that the FBO has the use of through an operating agreement and lease. These facilities may include hangars, ramps, maintenance and of-

DISCUSSION TOPICS

1. How is an FBO affected by the operation of those parts of the airport not covered in his or her lease?
2. Why should an FBO be concerned with promoting the airport to the business community and airport neighbors?
3. What are six steps involved in an airport master plan?
4. What might be some of the considerations to be resolved when an FBO seeks financing for developments on leased airport land?
5. What is the most significant environmental issue at most airports and why? What can an FBO do about mitigating it?
6. What is the value of preventive maintenance and how would you set about developing such a program for a combination of repair hangar and office?
7. Identify five operational techniques that can be used to reduce noise around airports. What are their pros and cons from (1) the community's viewpoint; (2) the FBO's viewpoint?

fice facilities. Public planning for an airport usually starts with a master plan following FAA guidelines. Funding may come from several public sources for the public portions of the airport; the FBO will have to raise private funding. FBOs can benefit greatly—as well as be adversely affected—by the planning and publicity created by an airport's public sponsors. Therefore, it is advisable to stay closely involved with all public actions affecting the field, to understand the planning and funding processes, and to communicate the economic value of the individual FBO operation.

Endnotes

1. Cook, Barbara. "The Evolution of FBOs—Seeking the Perfect Mix," *Airport Magazine,* March 4, 1997. Quoting James Coyne, Executive Director of NATA.

2. See *http://www.faas.gov/arp/pdf/narrat.pdf.*

3. NewMeyer, D.A., Hamman, J.A., Worrells, D.S. and Zimmer, J. R. "Needs Assessment of a Major Metropolitan Reliever Airport," *Journal of Air Transportation World Wide* 1998, 3(2), 49-63.

4. Atwood, Mark. "Noise Wars: The EU-US Dispute Over Hushkits and Re-engined Aircraft," at *www.faa.gov/region/aca/noise1a.htm.*

5. For example, Boston-Logan International Airport, Boston, MA; also, Sea-Tac Communities Plan, Seattle-Tacoma International Airport, Seattle, WA.

6. For an excellent summary of noise control efforts around the country see Bremer, Karl. "Aircraft Noise: Cooperation Not Confrontation," *Airport Magazine,* July 8, 1999.

7. See for example the latest editions of the following: *Airport Compatibility Guidelines,* Oregon Aviation System Plan, Volume VI, Salem, OR: Oregon Department of Transportation, Aeronautics Division; "Airport Landscaping for Noise Control Purposes," *Federal Aviation Administration Advisory Circular* 150/5320-14; "Noise Control and Compatibility Planning for Airports," *Federal Aviation Administration Advisory Circular* 150/5020-1; Federal Aviation Administration Part 150-Airport Noise and Part 161; "Airport Master Plans," *Federal Aviation Administration Advisory Circular* 150/5070-6; "Minimum Standards for Commercial Aeronautical Activities on Public Airports," *Federal Aviation Administration Advisory Circular* 150/5190-1, August 23, 1966; "Potential Closure of Airports," United States Department of Transportation/Federal Aviation Administration, January 1978; "A Model Zoning Ordinance to Limit Height of Objects Around Airports," *Federal Aviation Administration Advisory Circular* 150/5190-4, August 23, 1977.

8. See for example Bremer, Karl. "The Three R's: Reduce, Recycle, Recover," *Airport Magazine*, March 4, 1998.

9. Johnson, David. "In Case You Haven't Started Yet: A Primer on 1998 UST Requirements," *Airport Magazine*, July 8, 1996; see also *http://www.epa.gov/swerust1/index.htm* and *http://www.epa.gov/swerust1/1998/index.htm.*

10. See *http://ceq.eh.doe.gov/nepa/regs/eos/eo13123.html.*

11. See *http://www.aopa.org/whatsnew/newsitems/2002/02-1-148x.html.*

12. See *http://www.nata-online.org/Govwatch/Archive/S.20010105.100Arpts.htm.*

13. GAMA Press Release, June 14, 2001.

14. See Suburban Chicago News, April 16, 2002.

15. South Florida Sun Sentinel Report, April 16, 2002.

16. The Atlanta Citizen News, April 14, 2002.

17. This situation in Lander, Wyoming is described at *http://www.trib.com/HOMENEWS/WYO* April 16, 2002.

18. At *http://www.faa.gov/arp/pdf/appenda.pdf.*

19. Albee, William. "The Compatible Land Use—Noise Challenge," *Airport Magazine,* March 4, 2001.

20. See *www.nata-online.org/2Govwatch/Archive/S.20001020.AbatementPol.htm.*

21. Cook, Barbara. "Small Airports—Front Door or Doormat?" *Airport Magazine,* December 1995.

22. See *http://www.aopa.org/asn/apsup04.html.*

23. 1997 Reauthorization Act—Public Law 104-264.

24. Arthur, Holly. "Airport Privatization—A Reality Check," *Airport Magazine*, October 1998.

25. Arthur, Holly. "FAA's Airport Privatization Pilot Program—Are We There Yet?" *Airport Magazine,* November 2000.

26. Croft, John. "Small Airports: To Be or Not To Be?" *Aviation Week and Space Technology,* April 15, 2002.

13

The Future

OBJECTIVES

- To describe and explain the global and national trends that appear to be affecting businesses and individuals in the 21st century, with a focus on those most impacting general aviation.
- To provide the reader with resources and tools to take this analysis farther, as his or her needs for understanding may require, by providing references and analytical processes that can help the student to help him or herself.
- To help the FBO practitioner or student understand the problems inherent with change in any business environment.
- By doing these things, to provide a road map for the future, marking both the opportunities and the potential pitfalls.

Trying to predict the future by looking at the past
is like trying to drive a car using only the rear-view mirror.
(Author Unknown)

Introduction

For the aviation manager, the expectation of change, and the continual re-definition of what business one should be in as change occurs, are essential skills for facing the future.

Why do we need to know about the future? For the aviation business owner, a limited view into the future may be sufficient for some purposes. However, for other purposes, the long range must be evaluated. For example, construction of new facilities may involve 20- to 30-year financing. What will the market for such facilities be like in the next few decades?

Are there reasons right now to get involved in the lease or purchase of a large new aircraft to serve a particular charter market? Can a five-year lease be justified? —will the need for this airplane still be there two or three years from now?

Chapter 1 reviewed the decline in new US general aviation aircraft production that had taken place since the late 1970s, and the turnaround since the mid-1990s. The causes of this decline and turnaround were also discussed, as were future projections. Some factors have abated and may no longer have significant impact in the future. Others still prevail and most likely will affect future general aviation trends. Since FBOs service both the general aviation industry, with some also servicing major airline accounts, the future of all aviation and the future of airport service businesses will tend to go hand in hand.

Kitty Hawk—100 Years Later

December 17, 2003 represents one hundred years of powered flight. This comparatively recent technology has completely changed the world in numerous ways. It has enabled people to travel from continent to continent in just hours. It is hard to remember that in pre-air days of the 19th century, it took 3–4 days to cross the United States by rail, and before the advent of the railroad, it took many months using canoes and covered wagons. Not only has air transportation enabled easier travel, but also it has already generated a whole new industry of aerial construction, servicing and inspection relating to crops, pipelines, industrial installations, oil rigs and the like as well as aerial photography and aerial advertising.

The centennial celebrations of powered flight are an occasion not just for looking back but also for looking forward. The general aviation industry in particular has been volatile since its beginnings. This up and down behavior of the industry is not just related to cyclical business cycles, for its does not always mirror them; aviation has been subject to its own growth and decline periods for reasons that have not much affected the general economy. So what does the future hold? Will the general aviation industry begin to stabilize and develop long-term predictable growth patterns in the coming century, or will it continue to fluctuate? And likewise, will FBO businesses be able to stabilize and grow?

The various general aviation lobby and interests groups recognize that general aviation is not well understood outside the industry. They put a lot of resources into communicating, but are not reaching and educating the public at large. The post 9/11/01 situation, where many people for the first time are realizing that GA can meet a need that they formerly thought only the airlines could meet, creates an opportunity for the industry. Perhaps linking the 100th anniversary of powered flight to the potential in air travel services could raise the awareness of a broader segment of the public. The aviation groups would do well to combine their efforts more in education about the value of general aviation.

Purpose of Education

Since this is a college textbook, its primary purpose is as an educational tool. The purpose of education is not to impart a body of knowledge, although knowledge and information will be imparted. Rather, its purpose is to teach the student how to think about information, how to research, reason, analyze, develop alternatives and formulate choices. As has been stressed in this book, information is changing rapidly and moreover, now reaching the average American within hours from all over the world. So one book with a multi-year shelf life cannot provide all the needed information. What it can aim to do is provide the tools for gathering up to date information and deriving meaning from it. This chapter cannot discuss in-depth all the available "futures" studies and their meaning for aviation. Rather, it seeks to identify some major considerations and their possible implications for the aviation service business of the future.

Need to Understand the Causes Behind Trends

When the cause behind a trend is identified and understood, then it is much easier to predict the likely direction of that trend, and to relate it to similar trends that may converge on the same issue.

Forecasting

Predicting the future of general aviation as a whole, and FBOs in particular, is a very uncertain business even for the relatively short range. In the 1970s, the Federal Aviation Administration's forecasting branch expended considerable effort developing a "General Aviation Dynamics" model that sought to calculate the effects on aviation activity from changes in a number of factors. These included the price of avgas, student pilot starts, and many other variables. However, the conclusion seems to be that the "drivers'" of aviation activity levels, the equations in this econometric model, are difficult to pin down and don't behave consistently over time. Subsequently, FAA's forecasting for general aviation activity has become cautious, and, while still more than trend-based, does not claim to have isolated all the factors that make this industry grow or shrink. The FBO manager should keep an eye on national forecasts, but season them well with local trends and with common sense, because a unique factor may drive a regional or local market without being apparent at the national level. An example is the series of extreme forest fire situations in the west over the past few summers, greatly increasing the demand for aerial fire spotting and fighting.

Scope of Chapter

This chapter addresses the questions that affect an aviation service business' future. It builds on the trends of recent times discussed in Chapter 1 and seeks to identify factors and their underlying causes that will likely affect general aviation in the next few years. As in Chapter 1, the discussion follows a format that first examines broad economic trends, and then reviews how these trends might specifically affect aviation. The trends reviewed include: sustainability, the changing role of the US in the wider world, the new focus on business ethics, environmental trends, world and US demographic trends, business trends, regulatory trends, and new technological developments. With all this as context, the chapter then examines the key strategic threats and opportunities facing aviation service businesses.

External Trends and How They Affect Aviation

Paradigm Shifts

Sustainability—What it is and Why the World Needs It. The term *sustainability* will increasingly be heard not just in environmental but in governmental and business circles. The US has a little over 4 percent of the world's population and currently consumes 25 percent or more of the world's natural non-renewable resources such as petroleum products and many minerals and other raw materials. Given the almost world-wide availability of US TV shows, the rest of the world for the most part aspires to enjoy a US standard of living. With over 6 billion people in the world, rapidly climbing toward ten billion, this simply is not possible. Non-renewable resources will not stretch that far. US residents also consume far more per capita of local resources such as water, and this too may be a trend that cannot continue. Sustainability means farming and creating cities and lifestyles where no more is taken out of the system than is put back.

This is a very great challenge and will not happen even within a generation, but if it does not at least start to happen, then western life as we know it will begin to come to an end, perhaps abruptly or in a series of steep declines. Since the US economy and the health of individual companies have always been postulated on growth, the idea of a *steady state* being healthy and acceptable is in itself a difficult one. This is a new paradigm requiring new thinking. A whole book could be written on the sustainability issue, and the student or practitioner is commended to the many web sites on the subject for more information.[1]

Role of US in Wider World. The terrorism acts of 9/11/01 and the applause they generated in certain parts of the world made many Americans wonder why they are so hated. The statistics in the above section are themselves a hint. Much is produced world-wide for import to the US in conditions that are no longer tolerated of producers in this country, for example clothing and shoes produced in sweatshop factories by small children, and non-organic bananas which are sprayed with chemicals that make the children of the workers very sick. At one level is the individual American's choice to not buy such items, and increasing amounts of information about which products are being generated in harmful ways to their producers. At another level is the fact that individual changes have not yet brought about major national or business policy shifts.

Growing Focus On Business Ethics And Personal Accountability. Chapter 2, Management Functions, discussed the need for business ethics, not only to keep a company out of legal and media trouble but also to be able to motivate and assure its workers. This trend of public focus on ethical practices seems likely to continue and the typical FBO may want to spend some time on the issue and perhaps adopt an ethics statement. If this step were taken, it would be well to consult employees in its development.

Environmental Trends

Resource Depletion. The sustainability topic above touched upon the resource depletion issue. Depletion first affects cost, and then affects availability. Commodities that may be relied on for aircraft manufacturing or repair may no longer be as readily available. Recycling will become more emphasized.

Fuel Supply and Price. Aviation is one of the most dependent modes when it comes to fossil fuels. While the new hybrid cars are running partly on electricity, it's not currently feasible to plug an aircraft into a power outlet or use batteries to power it. Predictions about the duration of the world's fossil fuel supplies keep changing. A great deal depends on the rate of increase in consumption. If the US held consumption at stable levels then supplies would last much longer than at say, a 5 per cent per annum increase.[2] Cost and then availability will be problems in the current century.

Global Warming. Global warming due to greenhouse gases is not a phenomenon accepted by all, as is evidenced by the George W. Bush Jr. Administration's refusal hitherto to sign the Kyoto Agreement. However, reputable organizations such as the Environmental Protection Agency and the Pew Charitable Trust have concluded that the phenomenon is real and that actions of humans are contributing.[3, 4] One result of global warming is sea level rise. According to one prediction, for example, a 90 centimeter rise (about a yard), which is possible within 100 years or less, would put 1/3 of the city of Shanghai under water.[5] Since most of the world's major cities are on the coast, similar implications exist worldwide. For aviation, this could lead in time to a focus on new cities inland, building on existing often-smaller airports. This would tie in well with NASA's SATS program, as discussed below.

Noise/Encroachment. Contrary to what some have said, airport area noise is the single biggest reason why communities oppose airports and want to see them restricted or closed.[6] While some states have specifically recognized that airports are unique and must be protected, few have taken the necessary steps to impose a higher level of control than local zoning. One exception is Washington State, where under the Growth Management Act, airports are recognized as Essential Public Facilities (EPFs) that the local jurisdiction cannot remove in its Comprehensive Plan but must accommodate and sustain. In addition, Washington State has separate legislation that requires municipalities to protect the approaches to airports and not build unsuitable projects such as homes, retirement communities, schools, daycares and the like. The purpose of this second piece of legislation is safety, to minimize the population in approach zones, but it also has benefits for noise. But even where such legislation exists, the local elected officials may be more concerned with the noise complaints of their voters than with the larger regional need for air transportation access and airport protection. The encroachment of airports by unsuitable land uses, and the ensuing noise complaints, will continue into the 21st century and needs tackling beyond the local level.

Airport Usage Restrictions and Closures. Closely related is the concern about airport closures. The flow of new airports into the system has come from private and military fields becoming public use and then publicly owned. Very few municipal airports have been started from scratch. Yet private fields are being sold for other development when the founder retires or dies, and the next generation does not want to take over but would rather pocket the gain that comes from rising land values. Municipal and other publicly owned airports are threatened by noise complaints, exacerbated by the fact that those enjoying the airport often live in other communities, while those suffering the impacts live in the jurisdiction that manages the field. The system needs more and better airports, not loss of facilities. Yet this trend will likely continue.

Contamination and Toxics. A national trend toward less economic regulation (at least of the nation's transportation industries) appears to be accompanied by a trend toward greater regulation in areas relating to safety and environmental quality. One of the most significant recent regulations affecting FBOs is undoubtedly the introduction of requirements for existing and new underground fuel storage tanks. Most FBOs will have to obtain insurance to demonstrate their financial ability to handle any seepage and cleanup problems. The cost of installing adequately designed tanks is a key factor for any FBO planning expansion or updating of a fuel farm. Airports must continue to address cleaning up underground storage tanks and establishing wash and de-icing pads that treat the runoff appropriately. These are but two of the contamination concerns that airports must deal with in more stringent ways as general awareness of contamination and of its effects on fish and wildlife become more pervasive. Much historic contamination shows up when studies are done for new construction or for lease changes, and the aviation tenant must be braced for these considerations. In time, as new developments and operations are run correctly, this issue should diminish, but at least the first two or three decades of the 21st century seem likely to have to deal with contamination that may not have been caused by current tenants and operators.

Other regulations relate to the training of FBO personnel in safe fueling and fire fighting at airline airports. Several approved programs are now available. FBOs involved in the disposal of any kind of hazardous waste such as used oil and crop-spraying chemicals must meet more stringent standards that will also be costly.

Demographic Trends

World Population Growth. World population growth is likely to continue at a rapid rate because many of the people who will have those new children are themselves already born. Furthermore, many poor couples in other parts of the world aim for large families in order to have someone to provide for them in their old age. In many parts of the world this is between 30 and 40 years of age (in the US around 1900, life expectancy was only about 50).

For services to continue, more and better airports are needed.

Greater Immigration Pressures. The US has had a relatively generous immigration policy and pressure to continue this despite any difficulties of rapid absorption will continue because immediate family members are allowed to join those already here, because world population growth and refugee situations will keep up the demand, and there will likely be low-end jobs available for such immigrants. Not all immigrants are in minimum wage employment however; there is a high degree of entrepreneurship and also many immigrants arriving with, for example, excellent software and other technical skills.

Changing Ethnic Mix. The US dominant component of the workforce has been visualized as the white male. In fact the white male worker is in the minority, and in some states Hispanics and other immigrant groups are increasingly dominating the employment scene, as are women throughout the country. Since aviation is one of last bastions of white male employment, the aviation community should anticipate a more radical change in coming decades than many other areas of society, where ethnic and gender integration has already been occurring.

Aviation Labor Shortages. Labor shortages can be expected in aviation, especially for entry-level labor positions. Many military-trained pilots and technicians who were the primary labor supply for the aviation industry are no longer in the pipeline for future replacements; at least not at the levels needed. Shortages can be expected for all aspects of aviation labor, and general aviation, particularly FBOs, tend to get hit hardest because they train people who then move up the system for higher pay, benefits and better working conditions. FBOs need to consider pay levels and charge customers in a business-like way at rates that cover realistic costs, because there is a cost to high turnover in labor as well as a cost to paying people a competitive wage and benefits. The FBO will bear the additional burden of continuing to be the training and proving ground for employees who, once trained, will move on to better jobs at small airlines and corporate flight departments. The more successful FBOs will adjust their hiring, compensation, and training policies to retain good staff as long as possible.

Changing Labor Force Profile. As has been mentioned, the overall profile of the US labor force is changing. For aviation, especially general aviation, the national profile is still one of white males as the dominant element in the work force. General aviation will need to start hiring more broadly if only to find enough people. Hiring alone does not create a diversified work force. Cultural norms have to change. Language differences will need to be addressed, and a climate of acceptance of many different types of people from many countries and cultures must be created. This means offering respect, opportunities for advancement, and changes in company expectations to embrace cultural diversity.

Increase in Personal Wealth in US During 1990s. The vast increase in personal wealth during the past decade has already been mentioned. While the dot-com boom and its instant millionaires may not be repeated, it seems likely that there will be a continuing trend for a select group of people to make major fortunes while still young. Many are turning to general aviation and becoming pilots, for both business and pleasure.

Business Trends

Globalization. Above we discussed the globalization of manufacturing and food production as it affects the individual. At another level is the World Trade Organization and a growing control of the world economy by "transnational" corporations, many of whose gross sales are greater than the national income of a number of small countries. Trade rules are made through WTO with very little input by the US legislature and executive, let alone the common voter. Other organizations such as NAFTA involve congressional approvals so there are more checks and balances. The US is a dominant world economy and thus has greater leverage in world trade, leverage that can be expressed in a variety of directions. Tracking the role our government and businesses are playing as it relates to the aviation business owner is just one more external task that such businesses must tackle, at least to some degree, if they are not to be blind-sided by events from this realm. Globalization of the marketplace will continue to expand. Foreign companies will open more offices and manufacturing bases in the United States. U.S. companies will continue their trend of doing more business overseas.

Overseas Manufacturing. Today the United States makes much less of the world's manufactured goods. The aircraft manufacturing industry is following this trend. Boeing aircraft on order for Japan Airlines, for example, were partially made in Japan. In addition, their quality is very high. The People's Republic of China, now a dominant manufacturing country selling much of its output to the US, has entered the aircraft manufacturing industry. We can expect to see continued U.S. innovation, but a gradual transfer of actual production to other countries with cheaper labor. The extremely high degree of customization in much aircraft assembly may be the saving grace of the U.S. small aircraft industry. For avionics and other parts, the trend may grow towards overseas production. This trend has implications for the FBO maintenance shop's warranty and spare parts situation, as well as for the lucrative aircraft refurbishing and remodeling market.

On the other hand, companies such as EADS (formerly Aerospatiale) whose corporate headquarters are in France have opened up manufacturing facilities in the United States. Mooney Holding Corporation in France now owns even traditional U.S. manufacturers such as Mooney Aircraft Company, and Learjet, Inc., owned by Bombardier, Inc. in Montreal, Canada.

A Service Economy. As we continue into the twenty-first century, major structural shifts are occurring in many areas of the economy, including the aviation sector. Some of the key trends are:

1. Growth in the service sector, especially "high-tech" such as computers and medical/bio-engineering. Within all types of business, including manufacturing, there is growing emphasis on service rather than one-time sales.
2. Shifts in manufacturing, including the transfer of some U.S. jobs to overseas locations including Mexico, Pacific Rim nations, and Europe. Recent worldwide trade agreements will only serve to increase this trend.
3. Transportation's role in the context of growing electronic communications.
4. U.S. business ownership appears to be becoming more decentralized. Some companies specifically select small communities for plant expansion because of the quality of life offered to their employees. Along with the effects this has on local schools and the housing market, it often has implications in terms of airport and aviation growth. Many businesses are acquiring aircraft with the range for both international and transcontinental flights. FBOs can service these aircraft and meet their special need for constant availability.
5. Mergers and acquisitions are likely to continue both among the airlines, meaning a continued quest by passengers for service and quality, and among FBOs, meaning new corporate cultures and approaches have to be learned by the company that is absorbed.

Communications Considerations

The Demand for Transportation is a Derived Demand. Other than sport aviation and aerial functions such as pipeline patrol, firefighting and aerial application, aviation, like any other form of transportation is what economists describe as a derived demand, that is, the market for it exists because people want to get from A to B, and the real demand is for whatever they are planning to do at A and B. So the market for air transportation will always be driven by changes in A and B as well as by new choices with the transportation arena such as a new type of aircraft.

The benefits of the transaction affect what people buy. When they choose general aviation over other means of accomplishing their purpose, the benefits are generally these:

1. Speed;
2. Privacy;
3. Control over itinerary;
4. Cost advantages; and
5. Access to a larger number of airports compared with airlines.

The FBO manager must address the future by constantly considering two things. First, he or she must consider what business they are in. This is not in the business of aircraft provision, repair, and instruction so much as in the business of facilitating people's access to their ultimate (rather than derived) demands or interests. Second, he or she must consider that as a result of this definition of the business, the competition is not necessarily other providers of transportation, or even other providers of support services for air transportation. The competition is any other technology or business that facilitates people's access to their ultimate interests.

What kinds of access do people want, and to what kinds of places and things? In a rapidly changing world, there is no easy answer to these questions, but they are the right questions. As a consequence, the FBO manager of the future must be very aware of economic and social change going on outside as well as within the aviation industry. By the time some other aviation business has started to offer a new service or process, it may be too late for other FBOs to catch up. The FBO manager will need to anticipate, rather than react to, changes in the marketplace.

Communications Technology. The next wave of communications changes seems to be the combining of phone and computer technology to create inexpensive, desktop telecommunications technology. This will mean that companies with several branches can communicate more easily within the company; that businesses can talk more easily with clients, and that real-time problem solving can occur. This coupled with the high costs of travel and the delays and cuts in service since fall 2001 may mean that more businesses turn to teleconferencing and use face to face travel less.

In future decades, particularly if energy shortages constrain aviation before alternative fuels are feasible, the true competition for FBOs may be telecommunications. The telecommunications industry can sell instant electronic access to people and places at less cost than aviation. While direct contact is still likely to be necessary at certain stages of business relationships, telecommunications technology may be able to help lay the groundwork by screening out alternatives that previously would have taken a personal visit to resolve. Some realtors, for example, are using video to show properties to prospects and only taking them to actually visit those that look most promising. Such an approach is being applied to many other industries and areas of business.

Applying this approach to the FBO's own business suggests such activities as video for brokering aircraft, presenting marketing packages to prospective customers, presenting public relations material about the FBO, accessing information at the parent company or aircraft manufacturer on a real-time basis, accessing real-time weather information, selling how-to manuals for computer or video use, and providing home study flight training floppy disks, CDs and audio or videotapes.

Another affected area is the task of helping a company decide whether it needs a corporate or fractional aircraft. The consulting skills of the FBO may need to be tailored to address wider issues such as whether certain telecommunications technology can replace direct travel for some of the company's current or expected access needs. An immediate and inexpensive opportunity is the installation of a computer on-line service for use by charter customers delayed or cancelled by weather.

The availability of more sophisticated computers, and access to the world wide web, mean that the average person can now locate a great deal of data very quickly and convey information very quickly to a large number of contacts. This means that if a particular airport suddenly becomes threatened by, say, an adverse city council decision, the news of this is passed around the country virtually overnight, and aviation groups that were not aware can rapidly rally support and information to counter the situation. Years ago the writer John Naisbitt in *Megatrends* talked about the need to counter-balance this high tech approach with a "high touch" contact meaning, face time with the affected parties. However, assuming that all-important contacts seeking persuasion and negotiation can be done electronically would be a mistake. The electronic communication can serve as a heads-up and provide background material, but the real communication needs to be face to face so that body language can be ascertained and concerns nipped in the bud before they escalate. The effective airport businessperson will use both methods to promote the needs of his or her company and airport.

Instant Information. Events are communicated around the world almost as readily as they occur. Lifestyles of other countries, especially the US—clothing, music, icons, are pursued particularly by youth. It is relatively easy through the Internet to participate in international chat rooms and get international information, much of which is in English. This flow alters expectations.

Computers. Computers in aviation are as commonplace as in most other American businesses. To be competitive, FBOs will need to use computers for the financial and administrative aspects of the business, especially as companies become larger and more complex. Being able to pull up the customer's record on a screen is not just efficient; it tends to convince the customer that the entire operation is efficient. "Computer-literate" employees are needed in aviation businesses across the board, as they are in any other business. There are implications for training older employees and those with "computer phobia."

Because of access to computer data banks as well as traditional print media, more information about things within and beyond the FBO business will become more and more readily available. The FBO manager will have to make more decisions about how much time to allocate to sifting through this material to see what its meaning for the business may be. To be competitive, the FBO will almost certainly have to computerize information processes within the business. Care will need to be given to deciding what to collect about performance and how often results should be tabulated. In all this flow of published data, the manager may need to remember once in a while that there is no substitute for going and looking, or "management by walking around."

Chapter 7, Management Information Systems, discusses the application of computers to the running of an FBO business, and this book refers in almost every other chapter to how computers are coming into use in the rest of the aviation system, for instance:

1. Improved weather services, private and public.
2. Computer diagnostics for aircraft repair.
3. ELT location calculations.
4. Computer disks and videos for training.
5. Computer brokerage for aircraft.
6. Computer-controlled parts suppliers.
7. Simulation and flight training on computers.
8. Access to national data bases such as the stock market.
9. Personal computers, raising the typical FBO customer's and employee's "computer literacy" and offering at-home access to programs such as flight simulation.
10. Computers in education at all levels.
11. Cockpit computers for increasing numbers of functions.
12. FAA-required computerized exams for pilots and maintenance technicians.

Regulatory and Legislative Trends

Tougher Labor Laws. Labor laws have grown increasingly stringent, and employees increasingly inclined to raise the problem of workplace harassment since the courts have supported such concerns. There does not seem likely to be any softening of such laws and thus a good employer must address them as a normal part of being in business, and be more sensitive to such issues, as more diverse hiring occurs.

US Congress and Other Decision-Makers' Awareness of GA. There are few US Senators who can run their statewide election campaigns without using general aviation to get around during campaign season. Many candidates for the House of Representatives also depend on GA during the campaign season. Thus, many legislators have a good grasp of the contribution of general aviation because they would be unable to conduct their election campaigns without the speed and access to small communities provided by private aircraft. This means that the general aviation industry has unique access to congress and a relatively well-educated audience about the value of general aviation as a means of transportation. This foundation could be built upon more strongly. As more people turn to general aviation instead of airline travel, the benefits will become more widely understood and the influence of the industry much greater. Increasingly, this awareness will spread to business decision makers. The result will hopefully be a better understanding of why general aviation should have continued access to the nation's airspace and top airports—an understanding that has not been apparent in recent years. The growth in demand for business aircraft travel creates an opportunity for FBOs to educate key decision makers about the importance of the industry. Every FBO must develop this role.

Fractional Aircraft Rule. The Notice of Proposed Rulemaking expected to be finalized by the end of 2002 will greatly clarify the regulatory context for fractional ownership and likely provide another spur to the growth of this segment of general aviation.

Post 9/11/01 Security Focus. Society as a whole, and aviation in particular, are forever changed by the terrorism acts of 9/11/01. The US will continue to spend resources and keep its focus on protection against weapons of mass destruction and acts of terrorism.

Security and TSA. The need for aviation security is likely to continue to dominate all parts of the industry. As the new security standards for airlines begin to fall into place, the TSA will focus its attention more on general aviation. This will include a number of considerations, including screening of personnel and flight school students to ensure that visas are in order (if applicable) and that police checks are carried out for any positions that could put the company, an aircraft, or the aviation system at risk. Security facilities on airports will be increased, despite their implications for customer service.

There will be some confusion along the way as evidenced by this article in AvWeb News Wire service.[7]

> "The Aviation and Transportation Security Act enacted last November included a provision that "each air carrier and foreign air carrier operating a passenger flight in foreign air transportation to the United States shall provide to the Commissioner of Customs by electronic transmission a passenger and crew manifest." Part 135 operators are included among those who must meet these new requirements, which went into effect February 18 (2002). Problem is, unlike the airlines, the charter operators didn't receive the technology—called the Advance Passenger Information System (APIS)—enabling them to do so. Customs made a stab at providing an alternate means of compliance—on February 20, two days late—but it proved cumbersome and impractical, according to the National Air Transportation Association (NATA). Nonetheless, Customs began fining Part 135 operators for noncompliance."

This article in the same issue discussed the problematic "12-5" rule:

> "Meanwhile, after a careful study of the Transportation Security Administration's (TSA) so-called "twelve-five" rule requiring aircraft of 12,500 pounds or more to implement a security program, including criminal history background checks on the flight crew, NATA has determined that it too applies to Part 135 operators. Among other concerns is whether the TSA even has the manpower necessary to achieve compliance by the December 6, 2002, deadline."[8]

AvWeb continues:

> "Regardless, NATA, through Vice President for Government and Industry Affairs Joseph E. (Jeb) Burnside, is pledging their fullest cooperation to achieve compliance with both rules . . . just as soon as the many unanswered questions raised are resolved. Basically, there is a logistical and bureaucratic barrier that prevents the operators—who are otherwise willing—from complying with the new rules. Ultimately, answers will be found, but the episode highlights the framework and infrastructure that must be built to support every new law or regulation . . . in even the amiable adoption of the simplest of new procedures."[9]

Tort Reform and Aviation Insurance. In 1994 President Bill Clinton enacted the General Aviation Aircraft Product Liability Bill into legislation. A nine-year struggle by the aviation community was finally put to rest with an eighteen-year statute of repose bill. How much this will affect the insurance rates has yet to be determined. The expectation is that it will, at the least, curb the substantial increases incurred over the past few years, and the possibility of a leveling of current rates in the near future. Aircraft manufacturers continue to carry a high amount of product liability insurance and to pass the costs of this along to customers. However, the Tort Reform legislation of 1994 is likely to be a one of a kind event, not to be repeated in the 21st century. Other factors than product liability reform will help keep the industry growing. Continued variation and high cost in the insurance industry, can however, be expected in the future.

Sport Pilot License. The new sport pilot license will assist in continuing a strong trend that's already in place—the growth in sport, recre-

Flying clubs and organizations can become strong clients for an FBO interested in their aircraft maintenance work. Courtesy of Executive Beechcraft, Inc.

ational, experimental and homebuilt aircraft flying. This small aircraft end of the industry, and its growth triggers and trends, should not be ignored by FBOs because it is growing fast, and has become the way that many pilots learn about aviation. While most of the sport flyers will remain just that, some will want to continue to more advanced ratings and to careers, not just hobbies, in aviation. In addition, flying clubs and organizations can become strong clients for an FBO interested in their aircraft maintenance work.

GA User Fees. The possibility of a partially or fully privatized air traffic control system will grossly affect the general aviation industry in terms of fee assessments. The future of the Aviation Trust Fund may be in question. Whether it will continue to be used to offset the federal deficit or whether the fund will be abolished completely in light of the proposed privatized corporation and fee assessment structure is to be determined. Thus the federal funding that has been relied upon by general aviation airports for years may change in amount and application, and GA operators may be called onto contribute more to funding the system at a time when many of them can barely survive because of the hardships resulting from 9/11/01.

New Technological Developments

Electronics and Avionics. The 21st century is likely to see a continuation of technological innovation and miniaturization of electronics that will affect aviation as well as many other areas.

Airspace

A good summary of recent evolutions and changes of direction regarding US airspace is provided in NBAA's 50th anniversary publication:[10]

> ". . . major changes in the ATC system were underway (in the 1990s). In 1988, FAA had completed the transition to a new computer system, as the last of 20 air route traffic control centers (ARTCCs) received the so-called 'host computer'. The agency also was planning to replace all instrument landing systems (ILS) with Microwave Landing Systems (MLS) by 1998.
>
> "However, technical problems with MLS, the growing popularity of Loran C and the emergence

of a new, even more-promising technology—satellite navigation (satnav)—caused the FAA to rethink its plans. After considering the possibilities of using the US military's Navstar Global Positioning System (GPS), the FAA announced it would support a multi-phase transition to satellite navigation. By 1995, the International Civil Aviation Organization (ICAO) had cleared the way for worldwide acceptance of satellite navigation by modifying its policy that all international airports be outfitted with MLS.

"The transition to GPS moved rapidly and is expected to be complete by 2010, after which all conventional ground-based navigation aids are to be decommissioned. However, NBAA and other general aviation groups have urged continued funding and upgrade of the Loran C network as a backup for GPS at least through 2010.

"When fully implemented, GPS is expected to permit 'free flight'—a system in which pilots can choose their own routes and altitudes. Theoretically, air traffic controllers would only intervene when traffic conflicts might occur."

Airframe and Avionics. New aircraft design and manufacturing processes continue to enter the market. Development of new aircraft designs generates new aircraft certification regulations. Composite aircraft designs will continue to increase as will the development of new technology, especially in the area of avionics.

Composites are an increasingly important component of higher-end aircraft, and this is leading to new equipment requirements for testing and repair, that may be beyond the cost of most FBOs and result in more specialization.[11]

The increase in the average age of the general aviation fleet (as people have held on to old aircraft because new ones became so expensive) means that increased maintenance and flight checks will add to the work of FBO maintenance shops.

NASA Concept. As mentioned in Chapter 12, Physical Facilities, NASA is working on designing a small aircraft for use at smaller airports. Most of the US population is within 20 miles of such airports. If this program were to take off, it could encourage aviation-dependent business development at many smaller communities nationwide that have smaller, less congested airports.

Small Airports in Small Communities. U.S. business ownership appears to be becoming more decentralized. Some companies specifically select small communities for plant expansion because of the quality of life offered to their employees. Along with the effects this has on local schools and the housing market, it often has implications in terms of airport and aviation growth. For the FBO, the decentralizing pressures that seem to be

Is this the aircraft of the future? Courtesy CarbonAero, Adam Aircraft Industries, Englewood, Colorado, 80112. Photography by James A. Sugar.

appearing suggest new market opportunities in the nation's smaller communities that are seeking to attract high technology and growth industries. There should be growth opportunities for both business and personal aviation, including air-taxi feeder service to the nation's hub airports. The presence of an airport with an innovative and well-run FBO can be an important factor in attracting new companies.

Aviation Industry Trends

Airline Deregulation. The Airline Deregulation Act of 1978 continues to affect the entire aviation industry. Within the airline industry there has been a tremendous growth in the number of passengers, varied fares, types of frequent flyer benefits, mergers, failures and consolidations among airlines, and perhaps most significantly for the FBO, increased hub-and-spoke patterns of airline route systems. Except between major cities that have direct flights, air trips generally take longer because of the likelihood of one hub stopover. In addition, owing to the declining role of Essential Air Service and shrinking subsidies, many smaller communities no longer have scheduled air service. Both these deficits in the airline system represent market opportunities for the FBO.

With the advent of low cost, no frills airline operators such as Southwest Airlines, United's Shuttle, and Continental Lite, the competition among airlines has become more fierce. Some of the amenities of airline travel such as meal service and prearranged seating are being eliminated. Although this is helping the airlines to offer fares at lower costs to stay competitive, it is concurrently making the benefits of airline travel less attractive, especially to the business traveler. Hence, another opportunity exists for the FBO to advance the benefits of flying a general aviation aircraft.

Airline deregulation's continuing effects in fare wars, mergers, bankruptcies, and consolidation of flight service to a small number of increasingly congested hubs will continue to make general aviation look more cost-effective and appealing to a growing segment of the business travel market. Many service companies are purchasing fractional or complete aircraft or chartering aircraft more often for business purposes. Some of the faster growth areas of the economy are in the service sector and these service companies have a high degree of need for fast flexible travel. FBOs need to monitor the changes in their local economy and consider approaching new and growing businesses that may not be familiar with the benefits of general aviation.

The National Business Aircraft Association and the General Aviation Manufacturers Association have been promoting nationally the use of private aircraft to business owners and FBO owners and managers should help promote the concept in their local areas.

Fractional Aircraft Trends. The fractional aircraft business will continue to grow rapidly, with more providers entering the field, and likely more providers using used aircraft and smaller aircraft. Not all fractional companies will perform all functions in-house; there likely will be an increase in contracted services such as aircraft maintenance. Such clients will be excellent clients for FBOs, although they will be very demanding in terms of performance quality and punctuality.

Experimentals and Homebuilts

Homebuilt aircraft are still on the increase, and some companies once selling homebuilt "kits" are now selling completed aircraft. This trend may continue. As was shown in Chapter 1, the growth rate for this segment of general aviation is predicted to be quite high, and FBOs should not assume, just because the aircraft are small and the operators paying all costs rather than having them picked up by a business, that this is not a lucrative market niche. All high growth segments of the industry should be considered as targets.

Single and Twin Markets

This segment of the industry is less lucrative, especially the recreational as opposed to business portion of the market. Many operators in this segment of the market may often be (humorously) characterized as choosing every week whether to feed their children or put gas in the aircraft, and struggling to somehow pay the hangar rent rather than having to switch to a tie-down and have their precious plane stored out in the elements. They stay involved because of their love of aviation, which many of them are also involved in professionally.

Strategic FBO Threats and Opportunities

Introduction

A common acronym for business strategic planning is SWOT—Strengths, Weaknesses, Opportunities and Threats. Each should be analyzed and brainstormed. The last two are discussed here, taking the negative first.

Threats

Chapter 12, Physical Facilities, reviewed the many threats facing the physical airport system: lack of appreciation of GA's role; airspace restrictions; noise and operating restrictions; airport closures; disappearance of private airports and backcountry strips; siting new and expanded facilities; lack of suitable land use controls; bird strike threat; revenue diversion, and inadequate funding. While the threats to the physical airport system may be the greatest are of concern, other problems include the fragmentation, diffusion, and common lack of professionalism among business owners and managers, the all too apparent frequency of FBO closures, labor shortages exacerbated by low pay and a perceived or real sexism and racism in this industry, combined with an inability to react to changing market conditions.

FBO Opportunities

For the creative and market-oriented FBO, there will be many new business opportunities in the changing future. Chapter 1, the Role of the General Aviation Service Center or "Fixed Base Operator" in the National Aviation System reviewed the main trends affecting the industry in the past few decades: airline deregulation, the general aviation revitalization act of 1994 (GARA); airport improvement funding; fractional aircraft ownership; NASA's involvement in general aviation; the new Transportation Security Administration, and the revolution in avionics technology. These create the market context for future FBO activity.

FBO opportunities will be discovered and quantified not by considering what the FBO likes to do best, but by close contact with existing and potential customers to find out more about their high growth areas, likely change, and new needs. Each unmet need must then be subjected to a rigorous analysis of whether the competition is pursuing this market and whether it can be a profitable line of service for the FBO, given start-up costs and probable sales, using the break-even analysis shown in Chapter 4, Profits and Cash Flow.

The past decades have seen the elimination of many of the "mom-and-pop" aviation businesses through merger, bankruptcy, and retirement, especially at smaller airports. As aircraft range increases, services may be needed at less frequent intervals. In order to remain competitive, more capital is needed to sustain an FBO. Therefore, it seems likely that the trend towards larger FBOs, franchises, and chains will continue.

Airport administrators are feeling the pressure to be more self-supporting. Many airports have done little to tap the potential opportunities in this area, partly because it was not necessary. Some airports have good potential for greater revenues from non-aviation activities such as car rentals, restaurants and motels. Another possible service at smaller airports is meeting rooms and small conference centers, so that business people can fly in, conduct business, and leave without arranging ground transportation and spending extra time. Computer, copying, typing, and other services on demand would be an extension of this concept.

The opportunity exists to create a high degree of professionalism, coupled with a well-managed labor force that is therefore stable and loyal. Market share growth should focus on growth areas (e.g. sport aviation, fractionals), and be realistic about the limited growth prospects and tight budgets of many single and twin aircraft recreational flyers.

On the plus side, the early 20th century pioneering spirit of general aviation continues and is shown in a sense of excitement, camaraderie, enthusiasm for innovation and a desire to share a love of aviation with one's friends and neighbors. What remains is to generate some of that enthusiasm among residents of airport areas who so far have viewed it as a source of annoyance rather than of pleasure.

One way that any FBO can achieve this is through "Good Neighbor Coupons." An FBO could work with the airport owner to identify the noise-impacted area, and through direct mail, offer a discounted flying lesson such as the BE A PILOT $49 rate, or even a free lesson for anyone say, under 25 or over 60. In this way, some young airport area residents may embark on an aviation career, and some older residents may become airport volunteers.

Conclusion

"Business as Usual" is the least likely future for the FBO. In 1980, there were some 10,000 fixed-base operators in the U.S., but today there are fewer than 4,000 and the number is still shrinking.

There are a number of reasons for this decline, according to the study. For one, there has been no increase in the average aircraft flight hours, and FBOs are caught in a price and volume squeeze. They are unable to raise the fuel prices to increase their profit margins because of competitive pressures, and they are unable to expand their market because of the flat or declining flying activity. Another factor causing problems for both FBOs and airport operators is the continued growth in governmental regulations, particularly those promulgated by the Environmental Protection Agency. The most expensive of these EPA regulations are the ones concerning underground tanks, spill prevention, and storm water runoff.

Those FBOs that remain will find many new needs to meet and will require an understanding of the major underlying trends in the economy and society in order to seize new opportunities. Qualified staff may be in short supply, and a competitive salary, fringe benefits, and challenges will attract those that are available. The FBO manager will be a true professional by managing, by delegating, and by watching quality at all times while keeping an eye on the bottom line.

In addition, he or she will budget only about 70 percent of the work week to the internal managing of the business, allowing 30 percent for the key role of representing both the business and the airport in a positive light to airport noise complainers, elected officials and the local business community.

Summary

Continued change in the wider economy will likely mean continued change for FBOs. This can

The early 20th century pioneering spirit of aviation continues today. Courtesy of Executive Beechcraft, Inc.

DISCUSSION TOPICS

1. How and why has the general aviation industry evolved in a different direction than the airlines?
2. Why is general aviation a key element of the US transportation system? Why is this less true in Europe?
3. Name three problem areas likely to face general aviation managers in the future. How can they be constructively addressed?
4. What is a contingency plan and how can an aviation manager employ contingency planning techniques to help overcome uncertainty about the future?
5. Can good management be learned, or is it inborn? Explain your point of view.
6. What type of continuing education program might best serve the needs of senior managers in a medium sized FBO?
7. What are three problems associated with change in a business organization? How can they be handled?
8. Why would an FBO manager spend 30 percent of his or her time on activities other than running the business? What activities would you suggest?

either be decline or growth, depending on whether an astute grasp of new opportunities is seized. The strongest growth area seems most likely in the business and executive travel area, particularly if airline travel continues to be more costly and difficult. FBOs need to make a constant effort in several areas:

> Maintaining professional business techniques and personnel practices in order to stay competitive;
> Tuning in to national and local economic trends in order to spot strategic opportunities and threats; and
> Improving the image and understanding of the general aviation industry as a whole so that it gets its share of resources and support.

Finally, the successful aviation service business of the 21st century must remain flexible to face unknown issues in this fast-changing industry.

Endnotes

1. *http://www.garynull.com/Documents/erf/The_Meaning_of_Sustainability-Part2.htm.*
2. See *http://www.mtn.org/iasa/mirage.html.*
3. See *http://www.epa.gov/globalwarming/climate/index.html.*
4. See *http://www.pewclimate.org/.*
5. Gaffin, Stuart R. "High Water Blues—Impacts of Sea Level Rise on Selected Coasts and Islands," *Environmental Defense Fund,* 1997.
6. NATA: "Trends Affecting Aviation Service Providers," Prepared by Northwestern University, March 2002.
7. See *http://www.avweb.com/newswire/news0209a.html.*
8. See above, op. cit.
9. See above, op. cit.
10. Searles, Robert A. and Parke, Robert B. "NBAA's Tribute to Business Aviation," NBAA Washington D.C. 1997.
11. See 6, op. cit.

APPENDIX

I

Selected Aviation Websites

Note: Some (in quotes) descriptions are extracted verbatim from each organization's web site. Web site addresses change from time to time and not all that follows may be current; however, the reader can use a search engine such as Google.com or Yahoo.com to find any web site no longer current here. The library at Daniel Webster College generously provided some of these web sites; web searches located most of them. You can link directly to these web sites by going to www.kendallhunt.com and search by author Rodwell. The web sites are listed on the book's description page and linked directly to each site.

1. Overview Sites

These sites contain many links to other sites.

Aviation Reference Desk

http://www.aviationreferencedesk.com/: This is a huge web site of many aviation related links including the following major heading areas: commercial transport, aviation industry news, other world news, business aviation, general aviation, key aviation organizations, weather and travel, aerospace suppliers, defense and space, engineering, and last but not least, aviation enthusiast. It also has an aviation calendar.

Flightcom directory

http://flight.com/dir/: "This is the page where you will find categorized links to a wide variety of aviation resources. There are sites here about manufactures, retailers, personal pages, software, events, and more! Make sure to log onto Flight.com daily to check for new additions to the already vast number of links. If it's about aviation on the web, it should be in here. If you would like to add your site, simply login or register for a FREE." Categories include:

- Aircraft Manufacturers
- GPS Sites and Manufacturers
- Aviation Software
- Classified Advertising Sites
- College Training Programs
- Simulator Training Programs
- Fixed Base Operator Flight Schools
- Government Web Sites
- Airlines
- Avionics
- Arts
- Employment
- A/V Aviation Galleries
- National Air Forces
- Aviation History
- General Space
- Space Agencies

> Gliders and Soaring
> Ballooning
> Radio Controlled Aircraft
> Flight Simulators (Combat)
> Flight Simulators (Non-Combat)
> Aerial Photography
> Stories and Narratives
> Aviation Museums
> Safety and Accidents
> Weather
> Helicopters
> Skydiving
> Air Traffic Control

Airweb

www.airweb.faa.gov: This site contains a complete list of all regulatory materials from FAA.

2. FBO Related Sites

Professional Aviation Maintenance

http://www.pama.org/org/mission.cfm: Aviation maintenance technicians. "Our Mission: To enhance professionalism and recognition of the Aviation Maintenance Technician through communication, education, representation and support—for continuous improvement in aviation safety."

Aircraft Electronics Association

http://www.aea.net/. Its publication, *Avionics News,* may be found at **http://www.aea.net/AvionicsNews/default.asp?Category=3** its mission is "to be a worldwide self-sustaining organization committed to enhancing the profitability of its members by:

> Providing effective leadership to its members;
> Facilitating the communications between members and with their various constituent groups;
> Encouraging members to establish quality processes;
> Furthering the education of members and their various constituent groups; and
> Influencing the applicable legislative and regulatory processes."

Aviation Technician Education Council

http://www.atec-amt.org and **info@atec-amt.org.** It is an organization of Federal Aviation Administration approved Aviation Maintenance Technician schools and supporting industries. ATEC was founded in 1961 to further the standing of FAA approved schools with education and industry, and to promote mutually beneficial relations with all industry and government agencies. Contact: Aviation Technician Education Council, Dr. Richard Dumaresq, 2090 Wexford Court, Harrisburg, PA 17112 (717) 540-7121.

3. FBO Services

http://www.fboweb.com/21/default.asp: This site fboweb.com is an Internet-based tool for anyone interested in aviation. Pilots can access the web site to obtain information and plan their flights, and FBOs can use the site to track flights, attract aircraft to their facilities, and help manage their operations. Charter outfits can use the site to manage their fleet.

National Aircraft Appraisers Association (NAAA)

http://www.plane-values.com/: "This organization is the Trade Association for professional aircraft appraisers. Since 1980 the NAAA has been the Certification entity and has established the standards and Code of Ethics for professional aircraft appraisers in the United States and abroad . . . The NAAA's service is unique. The primary mission of NAAA members is to provide you with a prompt, accurate aircraft appraisal at a reasonable price. The Association's computer software application, extensive database, and standardized method of evaluation, enable our members to appraise your aircraft at its current market value, not the historical value."

Employment Law

http://www.law.cornell.edu/topics/employment.html: This non-commercial web site covers all aspects of employment law including links to relevant statutes and case law.

4. Government Agencies—Executive Branch

Federal Aviation Administration

http://www.faa.gov/: The Federal Aviation Administration (FAA) is part of the United States Department of Transportation (US DOT) and supervises the operation of the nation's airports and airways, pilot licensing as well as certifying new aircraft production and aircraft maintenance. The site covers information on Aviation Rules and Regulations, Federal Air Regulations (FARs), Advisory Circulars, Notice of Proposed Rulemakings (NPRMs). It provides information on aviation safety, FAA organizations, and aviation careers.

http://www.api.faa.gov/pubs.asp: FAA publications including forecasts.

FAA Administrators Factbook

http://www.atctraining.faa.gov/factbook: Current statistics on safety, air traffic, airports, airmen, and industry trends.

Federal Aviation Regulations (Title 14 of the Code of Federal Regulations (CFR))

http://www.faa.gov/avr/AFS/FARS/far_idx.htm: Full text of the Federal Air Regulations.

Transportation Security Administration (TSA)

http://www.tsa.gov/: "On November 19, 2001, the President signed into law the Aviation and Transportation Security Act (ATSA), which among other things established a new Transportation Security Administration (TSA) within the Department of Transportation. This Act established a series of challenging but critically important milestones toward achieving a secure air travel system. More broadly however, the ATSA fundamentally changed the way transportation security will be performed and managed in the United States. The continued growth of commercial transportation, tourism, and the world economy depends upon effective transportation security measures being efficiently applied. However, the threat to transportation is not restricted solely to those motivated by political or social concerns. In addition to terrorism, TSA will also work to prevent other criminal acts, regardless of motivation.

"The ATSA recognized the importance of security for all forms of transportation and related infrastructure elements. This cannot be accomplished by the TSA in isolation and requires strengthened partnerships among Federal, State, and local government officials, and the private sector to reduce vulnerabilities and adopt the best practices in use today. Infrastructure protection of critical assets such as pipelines and more than 10,000 FAA facilities is another key mission of the TSA. Along with rail and highway bridges, many other national assets are critical to our economic and national security and vital for the free and seamless movement of passengers and goods throughout the country."

U.S. Department of Transportation

http://www.dot.gov/: "As stewards of America's transportation system, the U.S. Department of Transportation (USDOT) must remain vigilant in the face of change, and visionary in planning for the future. As Secretary Coleman said, "our national transportation system is too inextricably linked to external developments and too pervasive in our society to enable us to build for the future without fully evaluating the potential consequences of the decisions we make today." We recognize that the transportation system is about more than concrete, asphalt, and steel; it is about people and their daily lives. It is about their dreams and aspirations, their connection to the economy and to each other—transportation is the tie that binds. And we know that to be effective, it must be international in reach, intermodal in form, intelligent in character, and inclusive in service. As we take stock of the challenges we face, USDOT has embraced a decision making process that ensures the public's interests are served, and that the public is involved in the process. How is this process different than others before it? The key is a tenacious focus on outcomes—beyond inputs, activities, and outputs—and a commitment to measure our performance against the outcome goals we set."

National Aeronautics and Space Administration (NASA)

http://www.nasa.gov/ and **http://aerospace.nasa.gov/programs/ga.htm:** General aviation revolutionized the latent market for personal and travel early in the 21st century. The goal of Advanced General Aviation Transport Experiments (AGATE) project is to support the revitalization of U.S. general aviation, by developing technologies to improve the utility, safety, ease-of-use, reliability, environmental compatibility, and affordability of the next generation of general aviation. The primary focus is single-pilot, light, fixed-wing personal transportation aircraft, business and commuter aircraft, and rotorcraft.

Through partnerships with industry and the states, the Small Aircraft Transportation System (SATS) project builds on the success of the AGATE and GAP projects, by developing technology that allows small aircraft unlimited access to the 18,000 total landing facilities that serve the vast numbers of communities in the U.S.

National Oceanographic and Atmospheric Administration

http://www.noaa.gov/ and **http://www.strategic.noaa.gov/strategic.pdf:** NOAA provides data of value to pilots about weather, climate, and related matters.

Bureau of Labor Statistics

http://www.bls.gov/iag/iaghome.htm: Provides national statistics and reports on labor, wage scale, accident and other employment data by industry.

Government Printing Office

http://www.access.gpo.gov/; http://www.access.gpo.gov/su_docs/aces/aces140.html: The Government Printing Office (GPO) keeps America informed. For nearly 140 years, GPO has produced and distributed Federal Government information products. Whether providing public access to Government information online, or producing and procuring printed publications, GPO combines conventional technology with state-of-the-art methods for supporting nearly all the information needs of the Congress, Federal agencies, and the American public.

Bureau of Transportation Statistics

http://www.bts.gov/: "The 1991 Intermodal Surface Transportation Efficiency Act (ISTEA) established the Bureau of Transportation Statistics (BTS) for data collection, analysis, and reporting and to ensure the most cost-effective use of transportation-monitoring resources. We strive to increase public awareness of the nation's transportation system and its implications and improve the transportation knowledge base of decision makers.

> "BTS supplements the data collection programs of other agencies and serves as the lead agency in developing and coordinating intermodal transportation statistics. We are unique in that we are the only federal agency to combine statistical analysis, mapping, and transportation analysis under one roof. We are committed to quality, accessibility, usability, and objectivity in transportation statistics and to respect for your privacy."

National Transportation Library: Aviation

http://ntl.bts.gov/ntl/subjects/aviation.html: Full-text government documents from the U.S. Department of Transportation organized into the following topics: Air Traffic Control, Airports and Facilities, Aviation Economics and Finance, Aviation Energy and Environment, Aviation Planning and Policy, Aviation Safety / Airworthiness, Aviation Laws and Regulations, Aviation Human Factors, Newsletters & Journals.

National Association of State Aviation Officials

http://www.nasao.org/: Founded in 1931, the National Association of State Aviation Officials (NASAO) is one of the most senior aviation organizations in the United States, predating even the Federal Aviation Administration's predecessor, the Civil Aeronautics Authority. The states first established NASAO to ensure uniformity of safety measures, to standardize airport regulations and develop a truly national air transportation system responsive to local, state, and regional needs. Since 1931, NASAO has been unique among aviation advocates. Unlike special interest groups, which speak for a single type of aeronautical activity or a narrow band of the rich spectrum of the American aviation community, NASAO represents the men and women, in state government aviation agencies, who serve the public interest in all 50 states, Guam and Puerto Rico. These highly skilled professionals are full partners with the federal government in the development and maintenance of the safest and most efficient aviation system in the world.

NASAO members organize, promote, and fund a wide variety of aviation programs across the nation. All states develop statewide aviation system plans and airport capital improvement plans. The states invest about $450 million annually in planning, operations, infrastructure development, maintenance, and navigational aids at 5,000 airports across the country. Many states also build, own, and operate their own airports. Each year, state aviation officials conduct safety inspections at thousands of public-use airports. Countless aviation activities including statewide meetings, airport symposiums, pilot safety seminars, and aviation education forums are also organized annually by the states.

The role of state programs and the responsibilities of the state aviation agencies are expanding. In 1996, Congress made the state block grant program permanent. As a result, nine states are already fully responsible for directly administering federal Airport Improvement Program funds. In an era of declining federal budgets and downsized government programs, the states' involvement in aviation is growing.

Contains selected links to other sites.

International Civil Aviation Organization

http://www.icao.int/: ICAO, focused on the airlines, has the following aims:

> Standardization of CNS/ATM
> Regional planning
> Facilitation
> Economics
> Technical co-operation for development
> Law
> Making your airline flight safer

IATA/ICAO Airport Codes Index Page

http://www.house747.freeserve.co.uk/aptcodes.htm: Alphabetical listings of the International Air Transport Association (IATA) three-letter airport codes and the International Civil Aviation Organization (ICAO) four-letter airport codes and two-letter nationality codes. Listings are by code only, not by city or area, but include many small and less known airports. For each three-letter code the location and country code are listed, and sometimes the full name of the airport.

5. Government Agencies—Legislative Branch

General Accounting Office

http://www.gao.gov/: The General Accounting Office is the investigative arm of Congress. GAO exists to support the Congress in meeting its Constitutional responsibilities and to help improve the performance and accountability of the federal government for the American people. GAO examines the use of public funds, evaluates federal programs and activities, and provides analyses, options, recommendations, and other assistance to help the Congress make effective oversight, policy, and funding decisions.

In this context, GAO works to continuously improve the economy, efficiency, and effectiveness of the federal government through financial audits, program reviews and evaluations, analyses, legal opinions, investigations, and other services. GAO's activities are designed to ensure the executive branch's accountability to the Congress under the Constitution and the government's accountability to the American people. GAO is dedicated to good government through its commitment to the core values of accountability, integrity, and reliability.

National Transportation Safety Board

http://www.ntsb.gov/aviation/aviation.htm and **http://www.ntsb.gov/aviation/Stats.htm:** The National Transportation Safety Board oversees safety in all modes of transportation and investigates serious accidents, including all with fatalities. It makes reports of *probable cause* directly to Congress, issues advisory bulletins about prevention of future such accidents, and publishes accident statistics. See also:

National Transportation Safety Board Aviation Accident Database

http://www.ntsb.gov/NTSB/Query.htm: Searchable database of NTSB aviation accident report summaries.

Congressional Committees

http://www.house.gov/transportation/ctisub: The Congressional transportation committees oversee policy and also work with the congressional appropriations committees (see below) to fund the aviation system. See also **http://www.house.gov/transportation/** and **http://www.senate.gov/~appropriations/transportation/index.htm**

Funding for the following Federal departments, agencies and programs is under the jurisdiction of the Subcommittee on Transportation. If a Federal department, agency or program you're looking for isn't listed here, check the complete list to see which subcommittee has jurisdiction.

> Amtrak
> Architectural and Transportation Barriers Compliance Board
> Bureau of Transportation Statistics
> Federal Aviation Administration (Transportation)
> Federal Highway Administration (Transportation)
> Federal Railroad Administration (Transportation)
> Federal Transit Administration (Transportation)
> Interstate Commerce Commission
> National Transportation Safety Board
> Office of Commercial Space Transportation (Transportation)
> Panama Canal Commission
> Research and Special Programs Administration (Transportation)
> St. Lawrence Seaway Development Corporation (Transportation)
> Transportation, Department of (except Maritime Administration)
> U.S. Coast Guard (Transportation)
> Washington Metropolitan Transit Authority

6. Industry Groups

Ag-Pilot International

http://www.agpilot.com/: 10 N.E. Sixth, Milton-Freewater, OR 97862.

National Air Transportation Association

http://www.nata-online.org/: NATA is the national association of aviation business service providers. Its members provide on-demand air charter, fuel and ground services, aircraft maintenance and pilot training.

General Aviation Manufacturers' Association

http://generalaviation.org/mainNs.shtml: This is the web site of GAMA, representing aircraft makers and lobbying for their interests.

National Business Aviation Association, Inc.

http://www.nbaa.org/index.htm and **http://www.nbaa.org/aboutnbaa/:** The NBAA, based in Washington, DC, is a not-for-profit, nonpartisan 501(c) 6 corporation dedicated to the success of the business aviation community. For almost 55 years, NBAA has served this community through its leadership efforts at all levels of government and business, both in the United States and worldwide.

The Association represents the aviation interests of nearly 7,000 companies that own or operate general aviation aircraft as an aid to the conduct of their business, or are involved with some other aspect of business aviation. NBAA Member Companies earn annual revenues approaching $5 trillion dollars—a number that is about half the U.S. gross domestic product—and employ more than 19 million people worldwide.

Helicopter Association International

http://www.rotor.com/: The not-for-profit trade association for the civil helicopter industry. Its mission is "To provide our membership with services that directly benefit their operations and to advance the civil helicopter industry by providing programs to enhance safety, encourage professionalism, and promote the unique societal contributions made by the rotary flight industry.

American Association of Airport Executives

http://www.airportnet.org/: AAAE is the largest professional organization for airport executives in the world, representing thousands of airport management personnel at public use airports nationwide. The American Association of Airport Executives' primary goal is to assist airport executives in fulfilling their responsibilities to the airports and the communities they serve.

AAAE membership is truly representative of airport management throughout the country. It places equal emphasis on large and small airport concerns, reflecting a membership comprised of executives from large and medium size airports, as well as hundreds of managers from smaller airports used exclusively by general aviation or commuter airlines.

AAAE was founded in 1928 to represent airport management throughout the United States. Each year since its founding, AAAE has held an annual meeting to bring airport managers together to discuss the latest problems and issues facing the industry. In 1954, the annual conference expanded to include exhibitors of airport services, products, and equipment.

The most important event for AAAE, however, was the formal adoption of a professional standards accreditation program in 1954. Since that time, no one has been awarded Accredited Airport Executive (A.A.E.) status without meeting the requirements established by the Board of Directors. Since 1954, AAAE has sponsored a professional Accreditation Program for airport executives, who are affiliate members of AAAE. The professional membership requirements consist of an original management paper on some phase of airport management, a comprehensive written test, and an oral examination on a level comparable to other professional certifications. Upon successful completion of these requirements, the Accredited Airport Executive is admitted to the membership as an executive member and may use the initials A.A.E. after his/her name.

AAAE has members at primary air carrier airports, which enplane 99% of the airline passengers across the nation, as well as at many of the smaller commercial service, reliever and general aviation airports.

National Agricultural Aviation Association

http://www.agaviation.org/: "As the voice of the aerial application industry, NAAA works to preserve aerial application's place in the protection and production of America's food and fiber supply. Aerial application is one of the safest, fastest, most efficient and economical ways to apply pesticides. It is also the most environmentally friendly tool of modern agriculture. In addition to controlling insects, weeds and diseases that threaten crops, aerial applicators protect human health and our natural resources.

Aerial applicators are highly trained professionals. Like all Americans, they are concerned with human health, the environment, and performing their job in a responsible manner. NAAA promotes high standards for the industry through flight safety and drift minimization. The Washington DC based National Agricultural Aviation Association, organized in 1967, has more than 1,250 members in the United States and internationally. Membership includes owners of aerial application businesses, pilots, manufacturers of airplanes, engines and equipment, and those in related businesses."

7. Pilot and Aircraft Owner Groups

Aircraft Owners' and Pilots' Association

http://news.aopa.org/: "With a membership base of more than 375,000, or half of all pilots in the United States, AOPA is the largest, most influential aviation association in the world. AOPA has achieved its prominent position through effective advocacy, enlightened leadership, technical competence, and hard work. Providing member services that range from representation at the federal, state, and local levels to legal services, advice, and other assistance, AOPA has built a service organization that far exceeds any other in the aviation community."

Experimental Aircraft Association

http://acro.harvard.edu/EAA/eaa_homepg.html and **http://www.eaa.org/benefits/sportaviation/index.html:** The Experimental Aircraft Association is one of the largest aviation groups, representing innovative and homebuilt aircraft owners and organizing a national fly-in in Wisconsin as well as regional events at many other airports. **http://www.sportpilot.org/:** is the EAA's Sport pilot and light aircraft web page.

Be a Pilot

http://www.beapilot.com/indexfl.html: BE A PILOT is a GA industry sponsored program to increase understanding and knowledge about general aviation and to encourage people to learn to fly. Participating BE A PILOT flight schools offer introductory flights for $49 and BE A PILOT runs TV commercials, print ads and a media campaign to let people know about the flights and the reasons to learn to fly.

The Ninety-Nines (Women Pilots)

http://www.ninety-nines.org: This international organization of women pilots was founded in 1929 by 99 charter members for "the mutual support and advancement of aviation." Their focus is on all aspects of the role of women in aviation: history, biographies of yesterday's and today's aviators, future prospects, flight instruction, grants and awards, events worldwide. Their Learn to Fly section lists the complete requirements for obtaining a private pilot's license, along with links to further resources. Some features require Adobe Acrobat Reader.

Federation Aeronautiqe Internationale / World Air Sports Federation

http://www.fai.org/: FAI, formed in 1905, organizes international record setting and competitions in aviation.

8. Other

Airliners.Net

http://www.airliners.net: This site claims to have the largest aviation photo database on the Internet. There are over 9000 photos of commercial airliners, military aircraft, classic and historic airplanes, helicopters, accidents, airplane interiors, and airports. It is searchable by aircraft name, category, airline, and keyword. The site also has aviation statistics, history, and humor.

Air Traffic Control System Command Center (ATCSCC)

http://www.fly.faa.gov: Displays major airport delays in real time. General departure and arrival delays are displayed as well as delays by destination. Severe weather delays and ground delays are included in this site. There is also a glossary of air traffic management terms and a tour of the offices of the Air Traffic Control System Command Center. Some pages require routing and airport codes to navigate.

AirDisaster.Com

http://airdisaster.com: This site provides information on aircraft accidents and safety. Included are photos, videos, chronologies, and eyewitness reports of air disasters, with links to official reports, a glossary of terms, and a search interface for the Aviation Accident Database of the National Transportation Safety Board (NTSB).

Airliners.Net

http://www.airliners.net: This site claims to have the largest aviation photo database on the Internet. There are over 9000 photos of commercial airliners, military aircraft, classic and historic airplanes, helicopters, accidents, airplane interiors, and airports. It is searchable by aircraft name, category, airline, and keyword. The site also has aviation statistics, history, and humor.

Airlines of the Web

http://www.itn.net/cgi/get?itn/cb/aow/airlines/index2:7BbBHSD5GJ6*,itn/cb/aow: Site for the professional pilot or traveler. Links to the passenger carriers from North and South America, Europe, Caribbean, Africa, Asia, Australia and the Middle East. Covers information on services available, fares, reservations, weather, etc.

AirNav

http://www.airnav.com: This site provides free, detailed, regularly updated aeronautical flight planning information for the pilot. It includes airport locations (public, private, and military) in the U.S., detailed runway information, technical and operational information about radio navigation aids and communication frequencies, aviation fuel prices, and a fuel stop planner.

The Aviation Home Page

http://www.avhome.com: Site has a comprehensive index covering topics such as clubs and organizations, companies and businesses, and classified ads. There is a wealth of information for the aviation enthusiast. The links to art, photography, and poetry are a nice feature. The career and pilot training resources should be especially helpful for the student pilot.

Homebuilt Homepage

http://www.homebuilt.org: Website for the hobbyist or sport aviator. Gives leads for plans, kits, vendors, and clubs.

Landings

http://www.landings.com: This site offers everything for the aviation buff, including government links, supplies, services, career assistance, organizations, and companies, etc. Features include a directory for easy use.

NewsDirectory: Magazines: Aviation

http://www.newsdirectory.com/news/magazine/science/aviation: This is a linked list of aviation journals available online.

U.S. Air Force Factsheets

http://www.af.mil/news/indexpages/fs_index.shtml: Detailed fact sheets on individual U.S. Air Force aircraft, weapons, space programs, sub-organizations, and special topics. From the U.S. Air Force News Service.

United States Air Force Museum

http://www.wpafb.af.mil/museum: A large searchable collection of historic information and photos about aircraft and missile from aviation's early years; World War II; Korean war; modern and space flight; presidential aircraft; engines; weapons; equipment; uniforms; and more. There are special archives and galleries; an index of manufacturers; related links; and trivia quizzes.

WASP: Women Airforce Service Pilots

http://www.wasp-wwii.org/wasp/home.htm: This site provides information about the 1,074 women who flew military planes during WWII. There are official documents, records, and statistics, along with audio clips of speeches and many photographs. A special focus on Jacqueline Cochran, Nancy Harkness Love, and General Hap Arnold are included. Links to other sites and a bibliography of printed sources will help further research. Lesson plans, interactive quizzes, and an opportunity to e-mail or chat with a retired WASP make this site unique. Search engine included. Sponsored by Wings Across America.

Women in Aviation International

http://www.wiai.org: The organization's official site devoted to the advancement of women in the field of aviation.

Women In Aviation Resource Center (WIASC)

http://www.women-in-aviation.com: This site provides "Educational, historical, and networking resources to empower women involved in all aspects of aviation." However, there are numerous gender-free links to information about weather, air museums, publications, employment, and NASA; live transmissions from the Air Traffic Controls of New York's JFK Airport and Chicago's O'Hare Airport (RealAudio is required); and Hubble Space Telescope's aviation and cyberspace images. The site's author is an aviation historian and writer.

9. Publications

Aircraft Maintenance Technology Magazine
1233 Janesville Ave., Fort Atkinson, WI 53538.
http://www.amtonline.com/

The Aviation Consumer
P.O. Box 972, Farmingdale, NY 11737.
http://www.aviationconsumer.com

Aviation Career
PO Box 550070, Fort Lauderdale, FL 33355.
http://www.aviationcareer.net/

Aviation Safety
1111 East Putnam Avenue, Riverside, CT 06878.
http://www.aviationsafetymagazine.com

Aviation Week & Space Technology
http://www.aviationnow.com
Daily updates of the latest in civil and military aviation and space industry news and analysis. Includes selected full-text articles from the print version, plus headlines and links to news from Aviation Daily and Aerospace Daily magazines and a nice list of the Web aviation resources. Aviation Week and Space Technology, McGraw-Hill, 1221 Avenue of the Americas, NY, NY 10020. See also **http://aviationnow.com/avnow/news/channel_awst.jsp?view=top** and **p02cs@mcgraw-hill.com**

AvWeb (online only)
Publisher Tim Cole.
http://www.avweb.com/contact.html

Flight International
Business Press International, Quadrant House, The Quadrant, Sutton, Surrey, England SM2 5AS.
http://www.flightinternational.com

Flight Training Magazine
405 Main St., Parkville, MO 64152.
http://www.aopaflighttraining.org/

General Aviation News & Flyer
5611 76th St., W., Tacoma, WA 98467.
http://www.generalaviationnews.com

In Flight USA
PO Box 620447, Woodside, CA 94062.
editor@inflightusa.com

Pilot's Web
Pilot's Web editorial (631) 736-6643.
http://www.pilotsweb.com

Plane and Pilot
Werner & Werner Corp., Ventura Boulevard, Suite 201, Encino, CA 91436.
http://planeandpilotmag.com

Private Pilot
Macro-Comm Corp., P.O. Box 2432, Boulder, CO 80322.
http://www.privatepilotmag.com

Professional Pilot
West Building, Washington National Airport, Washington D.C. 20001.
http://www.propilotmag.com

Customer Service for the following publications can be reached via Email at the addresses below:

Business and Commercial Aviation
p02cs@mcgraw-hill.com

Overhaul and Maintenance
p18cs@mcgraw-hill.com

World Aviation Directory
p92cs@mcgraw-hill.com

A/C Flyer
p93cs@mcgraw-hill.com

Aviation Week Newsletters
awgnews@mcgraw-hill.com

The following website has access to many publications on aviation:
http://www.aviationnow.com/

APPENDIX

II

Summary of Federal Air Regulations

Code of Federal Regulations 14 Parts 1 to 200, Aeronautics and Space

Introduction

Fixed base operators and their customers are generally very familiar with certain federal air regulations (FARs), such as Part 61, which deals with pilot licensing, and Part 135, which covers air taxi operations. However, some of those in aviation are unaware of the details of some of the other FARs, which number 200 in all. The code of federal regulations is republished each year to reflect any updates and revisions. What follows here is a list of the FARs by title and number.

Subchapter A—Definitions

Part

1 Definitions and abbreviations

Subchapter B—Procedural Rules

11 General rule-making procedures
13 Investigative and enforcement procedures

Subchapter C—Aircraft

21 Certification procedures for products and parts

Part

23 Airworthiness standards: normal, utility, and acrobatic category airplanes
25 Airworthiness standards: transport category airplanes
27 Airworthiness standards: normal category rotorcraft
29 Airworthiness standards: transport category rotorcraft
31 Airworthiness standards: manned free balloons
33 Airworthiness standards: aircraft engines
35 Airworthiness standards: propellers
36 Noise standards: aircraft type and airworthiness certification
39 Airworthiness directives
43 Maintenance, preventive maintenance, rebuilding, and alteration
45 Identification and registration marking
47 Aircraft registration
49 Recording of aircraft titles and security documents
50–59 [Reserved]

Subchapter D—Airmen

60 [Reserved]
61 Certification: Pilots and flight instructors
63 Certification: Flight crew members other than pilots

Part

65 Certification: Airmen other than flight crew members
67 Medical standards and certification

Subchapter E—Airspace

71 Designation of Federal airways, area low routes, controlled airspace, and reporting points
73 Special use airspace
75 Establishment of jet routes and area high routes
77 Objects affecting navigable airspace

Chapter F—Air Traffic and General Operating Rules

91 General operating and flight rules
93 Special air traffic rules and airport traffic patterns
95 IFR altitudes
97 Standard instrument approach procedures
99 Security control of air traffic
101 Moored balloons, kites, unmanned rockets and unmanned free balloons
103 Ultralight vehicles
105 Parachute jumping
107 Airport security
108 Airplane operator security
109 Indirect air carrier security

Subchapter G—Air Carriers, Air Travel Clubs and Operators for Compensation or Hire: Certification and Operations

121 Certification and operations: Domestic, flag, and supplemental air carriers and commercial operators of large aircraft
125 Certification and operations: Airplanes having a seating capacity of 20 or more passengers or a maximum payload capacity of 6,000 pounds or more
127 Certification and operations of scheduled air carriers with helicopters
129 Operations of foreign air carriers
133 Rotorcraft external-load operations
135 Air taxi operators and commercial operators

Part

137 Agricultural aircraft operations
139 Certification and operations: Land airports serving CAB—certificated air carriers

Subchapter H—Schools and Other Certificated Agencies

141 Pilot schools
143 Ground instructors
145 Repair stations
147 Aviation maintenance technician schools
149 Parachute lofts

Subchapter I—Airports

150 Airport noise compatibility planning
151 Federal aid to airports
152 Airport aid program
153 Acquisition of U.S. land for public airports
154 Acquisition of U.S. land for public airports under the Airport and Airway Development Act of 1970
155 Release of airport property from surplus property disposal restrictions
157 Notice of construction, alteration, activation, and deactivation of airports
159 National capital airports
169 Expenditure of Federal funds for non-military airports or air navigation facilities thereon

Subchapter J—Navigational Facilities

171 Non-Federal navigation facilities

Subchapter K—Administrative Regulations

183 Representatives of the Administrator
185 Testimony by employees and production of records in legal proceedings, and service of legal process and pleadings
187 Fees
189 Use of Federal Aviation Administration communications system

Part
191 Withholding security information from disclosure under the Air Transportation Security Act of 1974

Subchapter L—M [Reserved]

Subchapter N—War Risk Insurance

Part
198 War risk insurance

Subchapter O—Aircraft Loan Guarantee Program

199 Aircraft loan guarantee program

APPENDIX

III

FAA Advisory Circulars

See also www1.faa.gov/aba/html_policies/ac00_2html for up to date list.

6/15/00

SECTION A
ADVISORY CIRCULAR NUMBERING SYSTEM

The Circular Numbering System

1. General. The advisory circular numbers relate to the FAR subchapter titles and correspond to the Parts, and when appropriate, to the specific sectionsof the Federal Aviation Regulations.

2. General and specific subject numbers. The subject numbers and related subject areas are as follows:

General Subject Number(1)	Specific Subject Number(2)	Subject
00		**GENERAL**
	1	Definitions and Abbreviations
10		**PROCEDURAL RULES**
	11	General Rule-Making Procedures
	13	Investigation and Enforcement Pro cedures
20		**AIRCRAFT**
	21	Certification Procedures for Products and Parts
	23	Airworthiness Standards: Normal, Utility, and Acrobatic Category Airplanes
	25	Airworthiness Standards: Transport Category Airplanes
	27	Airworthiness Standards: Normal Category Rotorcraft
	29	Airworthiness Standards: Transport Category Rotorcraft
	31	Airworthiness Standards: Manned Free Balloons
	33	Airworthiness Standards: Aircraft Engines
	34	Fuel Venting and Exhaust Emission Requirements for Turbine Engine Powered Airplaness
	35	Airworthiness Standards: Propellers
	36	Noise Standards: Aircraft Type and Airworthiness Certification
	39	Airworthiness Directives
	43	Maintenance, Preventive Mainte-nance, Rebuilding and Alteration
	45	Identification and Registration Marking
	47	Aircraft Registration
	49	Recording of Aircraft Titles and Security Documents

General Subject Number(1)	Specific Subject Number(2)	Subject
60		**AIRMEN**
	61	Certification: Pilots and Flight Instructors
	63	Certification: Flight Crewmembers Other Than Pilots
	65	Certification: Airmen Other Than Flight Crewmembers
	67	Medical Standards and Certification
70		**AIRSPACE**
	71	Designation of Federal Airways, Area Low Routes, Controlled Airspace,and Reporting Points
	73	Special Use Airspace
	75	Establishment of Jet Routes and Area High Routes
	77	Objects Affecting Navigable Air-space
90		**AIR TRAFFIC AND GENERAL OPERATING RULES**
	91	General Operating and Flight Rules
	93	Special Air Traffic Rules and Airport Traffic Patterns
	95	IFR Altitudes
	97	Standard Instrument Approach Pro-cedures
	99	Security Control of Air Traffic
	101	Moored Balloons, Kites, Unmanned Rockets and Unmanned Free Balloons
	103	Ultralight Vehicles
	105	Parachute Jumping
	107	Airport Security
	108	Airplane Operators Security

	109	Indirect Air Carrier Security
119		**CERTIFICATION:AIR CARRIERS AND COMMERCIAL OPERATORS**
120		**AIR CARRIERS, AIR TRAVEL CLUBS, AND OPERATORS FOR COMPENSATION OR**

General Subject Number(1)	Specific Subject Number(2)	Subject
	125	Certification and Operations: Airplanes Having a Seating Capacity of 20 or More Passengers or a Maximum Payload Capacity of 6,000 Pounds or More
	127	Certification and Operations of Scheduled Air Carriers with Helicopters
	129	Operations of Foreign Air Carriers
	133	Rotorcraft External-Load Operations
	135	Air Taxi Operators and Commercial Operators
	137	Agricultural Aircraft Operations
	139	Certification and Operations: Land Airports Serving CAB-Certificated Air Carriers
140		**SCHOOLS AND OTHER CERTIFICATED AGENCIES**
	141	Pilot Schools
	143	Ground Instructors
	145	Repair Stations
	147	Aviation Maintenance Technician Schools
150		**AIRPORT NOISE COMPATI– BILITY PLANNING**
	151	Federal Aid to Airports
	152	Airport Aid Program
	155	Release of Airport Property from Surplus Property Disposal Restrictions
	156	State Block Grant Pilot Program
	157	Notice of Construction, Alteration, Activation, and Deactivation of Airports
	158	Passenger Facilities Charges

		HIRE: CERTIFICATION AND OPERATIONS
	121	Certification and Operations: Domestic, Flag, and Supplemental Air Carriers and Commercial Operators of Large Aircraft
	159	National Capital Airports
	159/10	Washington National Airport
	159/20	Dulles International Airport
	161	Notice and Approval of Airport Noise and Access Restrictionsn
	169	Expenditures of Federal Funds for Nonmilitary Airports or Air Navigational Facilities Thereon
170		**NAVIGATIONAL FACILITIES**
	170	Establishment and Discontinuance Criteria for Airport Traffic ControlTower Facilities

General Subject Number(1)	Specific Subject Number(2)	Subject
	171	Non-Federal Navigation Facilities
180		**ADMINISTRATIVE REGULATIONS**
	183	Representatives of the Administrator
	185	Testimony by Employees and Production of Records in Legal Proceedings
	187	Fees
	189	Use of Federal Aviation Administration Communication System.
190		**WITHHOLDING SECURITY INFORMATION**
	191	Withholding Security Information from Disclosure Under the Air Transportation Security Act of 1974
	198	Aviation Insurance Program
210		**FLIGHT INFORMATION**
	211	Aeronautical Charts and Flight Information Publications

	212	Publication Specification: Charts and Publications
400		**COMMERCIAL SPACE TRANSPORTATION**
	440	Financial Responsibility

1—Based on FAR Subchapter Titles (Excluding the 210 series).
2—Based on FAR Part Titles (Excluding the 210 series).

3. Within the General Subject Number Areas, specific selectivity in advisory circular mail lists is available corresponding to the applicable FAR Parts. For example: under the 60 general subject area, separate mail lists for advisory circulars issued in the 61, 63, 65, or 67 series are available. An AC numbered "60" goes to all numbers in the 60 series: 61, 63, 65, 67. Breakdown of subject numbers. When the volume of circulars in a series warrants a subsubject breakdown, the general number is followed by a slash and a subsubject number. Material in the 150 series, Airports, is issued under the following subsubjects:

150/5000	Airport Planning.
150/5020	Noise Control and Compatibility Planning for Airports.
150/5100	Federal-aid Airport Program.
150/5150	Surplus Airport Property Conveyance Programs.
150/5190	Airport Compliance Program.
150/5200	Airport Safety–General.
150/5210	Airport Safety Operations (Recommended Training, Standards, Manning).
150/5220	Airport Safety Equipment and Facilities.
150/5230	Airport Ground Safety System.
150/5240	Civil Airports Emergency Preparedness.
150/5325	Influence of Aircraft Performance on Aircraft Design.
150/5335	Runway, Taxiway, and Apron Characteristics.
150/5340	Airport Visual Aids.
150/5345	Airport Lighting Equipment.
150/5360	Airport Buildings.
150/5370	Airport Construction.
150/5380	Airport Maintenance.
150/5390	Heliports.

4. Individual circular identification numbers. Each circular has a subject number followed either by a dash and a consecutive number (135-15) or a period with a specific FAR section number, followed by a dash and a consecutive number (135.169-2) identifying the individual circular. This consecutive number is not used again in the same subject series. Revised circulars have a letter A, B, C, etc., after the consecutive number to show complete revisions. Changes to circulars have Chg. 1, Chg. 2, Chg. 3, etc., after the identification number on pages that have been changed. The date on a revised page is changed to the date of the Change transmittal.

6/15/00

SECTION B

CANCELLATIONS

Cancellations are listed below. The suffix following an AC number indicates a revision to that AC and cancels the previous edition. For example, AC 00-6A replaces and cancels AC 00-6; AC 00-7D replaces and cancels AC 00-7C. ACs may also be canceled without replacement by the issuing office or by other ACs or publications.

20-5G Plane Sense (1998; AFS-630) by FAA-H-8083-19 Plane Sense—General Aviation Information (8/23/99; AFS-630)
21-39 Aircraft Certification Systems Evaluation Program (8/31/94; AIR-230) by AIR-230, 6/7/00

The following 5 ACs are canceled by AC 23-16, Powerplant Guide for Certification of Part 23 Airplanes (9/21/99; ACE-111)
23.909-1 Installation of Turbochargers in Small Airplanes with Reciprocating Engines, 2/3/86
23.955-1 Substantiating Flow Rates and Pressures in Fuel Systems of Small Airplanes, 6/10/85
23.959-1 Unusable Fuel Test Procedures for Small Airplanes, 1/14/85
23.961-1 Procedures for Conducting Fuel System Hot Weather Operation Tests, 1/14/87
23.1011-1 Procedures for Determining Acceptable Fuel/Oil Ratio as Required by FAR 23.1011(b). 11/14/83

The following 10 ACs are canceled by AC 23-17, Systems and Equipment Guide for Certification of Part 23 Airplanes (4/25/00; ACE-111)
23.679-1 Control System Locks, 7/25/85
23.683-1 Control System Operations Test, 9/25/84
23.701-1 Flap Interconnection in Part 23 Airplanes, 11/13/92
23.729-1 Landing Gear Doors and Retraction Mechanism, 3/26/84
23.733-1 Tundra Tires, 10/10/96
23.807-2 Doors Between Pilot's Compartment and Passenger Cabin in Small Airplanes, 9/22/83
23.807-3 Emergency Exits Openable From Outside for Small Airplanes, 12/30/86
23.841-1 Cabin Pressurization Systems in Small Airplanes, 12/30/86
23.1305-1 Installation of Fuel Flowmeters in Small Airplanes with Continuous-Flow, Fuel-Injection, Reciprocating Engines, 12/21/84
23.1329-2 Automatic Pilot System Installation in Part 23 Airplanes, 3/4/91

25-14 High Lift and Drag Devices (5/4/88; ANM-112) by 25-22 Certification of Transport Category Airplane Mechanical Systems (3/14/00, ANM-112)
60-14 Aviation Instructor's Handbook (7/7/76; AFS-630) by FAA-H-8083-9 Aviation Instructor's Handbook (11/99; AFS-630)
60-23 Conversion to the Computer Based Airmen Knowledge Testing Program (6/17/94; AFS-630) by AFS-1, 2/8/00
60-25C Reference Materials and Subject Matter Knowledge Codes for Airman Knowledge Testing (8/23/99; AFS-630) by 60-25D, Reference Materials and Subject Matter Knowledge Codes for for Airman Knowledge Testing (6/9/00; AFS-630)
60-26A Announcement of Availability: Flight Standards Service Airman Testing and Training Information (2/26/97; AFS-630) by 60-26B, Announcement of Availability: Flight Standards Service Training and Testing Information (6/8/00; AFS-630)
60-27 Announcement of Availability: Changes to Practical Test Standards (11/18/96; AFS-630) by 60-26B, Announcement of Availability: Flight Standards Service Airman Training and Testing Information (6/8/00; AFS-630)
61-12M Student Pilot Guide (7/27/94; AFS-630) by FAA-H-8083-27 Student Pilot Guide (6/15/99; AFS-630)

6/15/00

61-13B Basic Helicopter Handbook (1978; AFS-630) by FAA-H-8083-21 Rotorcraft Flying Handbook (2/10/00; AFS-630)
61-21A Flight Training Handbook (1980; AFS-630) by FAA-H-8083-3 Airplane Flying Handbook (8/23/99; AFS-630)
61-47A Use of Approach Slope Indicators for Pilot Training (3/26/79; AFS-840) by AFS-1, 11/17/98
61-101 Presolo Written Test (4/21/89; AFS-630) by FAA-H-8083-9 Aviation Instructor's Handbook (11/99; AFS-630)
61-103 Announcement of Availability: Industry-Developed Transition Training Guidelines for High Performance Aircraft (5/23/89; AFS-840) by AFS-1, 9/24/99
61-112 Flight and Ground Instructor Knowledge Test Guide (12/1/94; AFS-630) by FAA-G-8082-7 Flight and Ground Instructor Knowledge Test Guide (6/1/99; AFS-630)
61-113 Airline Transport Pilot, Aircraft Dispatcher, and Flight Navigator Knowledge Test Guide (2/9/94; AFS-630) by FAA-G-8082-1 Airline Transport Pilot, Aircraft Dispatcher, and Flight Navigator Knowledge Test Guide (6/1/99; AFS-630)
61-114 Commercial Pilot Knowledge Test Guide (2/9/95; AFS-630) by FAA-G-8082-5 Commercial Pilot Knowledge Test Guide (6/1/99; AFS-630)
61-115 Positive Exchange of Flight Controls (3/10/95; AFS-630) by FAA-H-8083-9 Aviation Instructor's Handbook (11/99; AFS-630)
61-116A Announcement of Cancellation: FAA-S-8081-11, Flight Instructor-Lighter-Than-Air (Balloon/Airship) Practical Test Standards (1/27/97; AFS-630) by AFS-1, 2/8/00
61-117 Recreational Pilot and Private Pilot Knowledge Test Guide (5/3/95; AFS-630) by FAA-G-8082-17 Recreational Pilot and Private Pilot Knowledge Test Guide (6/1/99; AFS-630)
61-119 Instrument Rating Knowledge Test Guide (5/3/95; AFS-630) by FAA-G- 8082-13 Instrument Rating Knowledge Test Guide (6/1/99; AFS-630)
63-1 Flight Engineer Knowledge Test Guide (6/8/95) by FAA-G-8082-9 Flight Engineer Knowledge Test Guide (6/1/99; AFS-630)
65-19G Inspection Authorization Knowledge Test Guide (8/14/96; AFS-630) by FAA-G-8082-11 Inspection Authorization Knowledge Test Guide (7/13/99; AFS-630)
65-27 Parachute Rigger Knowledge Test Guide (6/16/95; AFS-630) by FAA-G-8082-15 Parachute Rigger Knowledge Test Guide (7/28/99; AFS-630)
65-28 Aviation Mechanic General, Powerplant, and Airframe Knowledge Test Guide (8/3/95; AFS-630) by FAA-G-8082-3 Aviation Mechanic General, Airframe, and Powerplant Knowledge Test Guide (8/23/99; AFS-630)
65-29 Conversion of the Inspection Authorization Knowledge Tests to the Computer Based Airmen Knowledge Testing Program (10/29/96; AFS-630) by AFS-1, 2/8/00
67-1 Medical Information for Air Ambulance Operators (3/4/74; AAM-620) by AAM-1, 9/3/99
91-23A Pilot's Weight and Balance Handbook (6/9/77; AFS-630) by FAA-H-8083-1 Aircraft Weight and Balance Handbook (8/23/99; AFS-630)
150/5000-3T Address List for Regional Airports Divisions and Airports District/Field Offices (9/12/97; ARP-10) by ARP-10 10,22/99 (Internet access)
150/5000-4B Announcement of Availability: Airport Research and Technical Reports (2/11/85; AAS-100) by AAS-100, 7/15/99

Additions

Additions to this checklist appear in Section C. The airplane symbol preceding an AC number identifies new or revised ACs issued since the last edition of this checklist. Revised ACs are identified by a letter of the alphabet following the AC number.

6/15/00

SECTION C

NUMERICAL LIST OF ADVISORY CIRCULARS

Important Notice

This Advisory Circular Checklist, AC 00-2, is no longer sent automatically to addresses on free advisory circular mailing lists. Persons not now receiving AC 00-2 but who wish to receive it must specifically request to be placed on the AC 00-2 mailing list (see par. 5 for ordering information). Up to ten copies may be sent to any one address. Persons receiving this edition of AC 00-2 need not request AC 00-2 mailing list service as they have already been transferred to the new list.

General

Subject No. 00

00-1.1
Government Aircraft Operations
(4/19/95) (AFS-220)
Provides guidance on whether particular government aircraft operations are public aircraft or civil aircraft operations under the new statutory definition of "public aircraft." This AC contains FAA's intended application of key terms in the new statutory definition . For operations that have lost public aircraft status under the new law, information is provided on bringing those operations into compliance with FAA safety regulations for civil aircraft and provides information on applying for an exemption.

✈ 00-2.13
Advisory Circular Checklist
(6/15/00) (APF-100)
Transmits the revised checklist of current FAA advisory circulars as of June 15, 2000.

00-6A
Aviation Weather
(3/3/75) (AFS-400)
Provides an up-to-date and expanded text for pilots and other flight operations personnel whose interest in meteorology is primarily in its application to flying.
SN 050- 007-00283-1.
$8.50 Supt. Docs.

✈ 00-7D
State and Regional Disaster Airlift (SARDA) Planning
(9/15/98) (ADA-20)
Provides officials with guidance to access and utilize a broad range of aviation resources within the state, when needed to support civil emergency operations.

00-24B
Thunderstorms
(1/20/83) (AFS-400)
Describes the hazards of thunderstorms to aviation and offers guidance to help prevent accidents caused by thunderstorms.

00-25
Forming and Operating a Flying Club
(3/24/69) (AFS-800)
Provides preliminary information that will assist anyone or any group of people interested in forming and operating a flying club.

00-30B
Atmospheric Turbulence Avoidance
9/9/97 (AFS-400)
Describes to pilots, aircrew members, dispatchers, and other operations personnel the various types of clear air turbulence (CAT) and some of the weather patterns associated with it. Also included are "Rules of Thumb" for avoiding or minimizing CAT encounters.

00-31A
United States (US). National Aviation Standard for the VOR/DME/TAC Systems
(9/20/82) (ANN-130)
Informs the aviation community of the establishment and content of the United States (US). National Aviation Standard for the Very High Frequency Omnidirectional Radio Range (VOR)/Distance Measuring Equipment(DME)/Tactical Air Navigation (TACAN) Systems.

00-33B
Nickel-Cadmium Battery Operational, Maintenance, and Overhaul Practices
(7/9/97) (AFS-400)
Provides guidelines for more reliable nickel-cadmium battery operation through proper operational and maintenance practices, and has been reissued to include reconditioning information.

00-34A
Aircraft Ground Handling and Servicing
(7/29/74) (AFS-340)
Contains information and guidance for the servicing and ground handling of aircraft.

00-41B
FAA Quality Control System Certification Program
(10/10/89) (ASU-430)
Describes the Federal Aviation Administration (FAA) Quality Control System Certification Program and the mechanics of implementation. It is intended for guidance and information only.

00-44II
Status of the Federal Aviation Regulations
(4/97) (AGC-200)

This circular sets forth the current publication status of Federal Aviation Regulations (FARs), any Changes issued to date, and provides a price list, and ordering instructions.

00-45D
Aviation Weather Services
(2/7/95) (AFS-400)
Supplements AC 00-6A, Aviation Weather, in that it explains the weather service in general and the use and interpretation of reports, forecasts, weather maps, and prognostic charts in detail.
SN 050-007-01082-6
$12.00 Supt. Docs.

00-46D
Aviation Safety Reporting Program
(2/26/97) (ASY-300)
Describes the Federal Aviation Administration's Aviation Safety Reporting program which utilizes the National Aeronautics and Space Administration (NASA) as a third party to receive and analyze Aviation Safety Reports. This cooperative safety reporting program invites users of the National Aviation System to report to NASA actual or potential discrepancies and deficiencies involving the safety of aviation operations.

00-54
Pilot Windshear Guide
(11/25/88) (AFS-200)
Communicates key windshear information relevant to flightcrews. Appendix 1 of this advisory circular is the Pilot Windshear Guide, which is only one section of the two-volume Windshear Training Aid.

00-55
Announcement of availability: FAA Order 8130.21A, Procedures for Completion and Use of FAA Form 8130, Airworthiness Approval Tag
(1/19/94) (AIR-200)
Announces availability of subject order.

00-56
Voluntary Industry Distributor Accreditation Program
(9/5/96) (AFS-350)
Describes a system for the voluntary accreditation of civil aircraft parts distributors on the basis of voluntary industry oversight and provides information that may be used for developing accreditation programs. The FAA believes such programs will assist in alleviating lack of documentation and will improve traceability.

00-57
Hazardous Mountain Winds and Their Visual Indicators (9/10/97) (AND-720)
Assists pilots involved in aviation operations to diagnose the potential for severe wind events in the vicinity of mountainous areas. It provides information on preflight planning techniques and on in-flight evaluation strategies for avoiding destructive turbulence and loss of aircraft control. Pilots, dispatchers, air traffic controllers, and other who must deal with weather phenomena and the routing of aircraft will benefit from the information contained in this advisory circular.

00-58
Voluntary Disclosure Reporting Program (5/4/98) (AFS-350)
Replaces AC 120-56. Provides information and guidance that may be used by certificate holders, production approval holders, indirect air carriers, and foreign air carriers disclosing apparent violations to the FAA of regulations in 14 CFR parts 21, 107, 108, 109, 121, 125, 129 (security program violations only), 133, 135, 137, 141, 142, 145, & 147 under the self-disclosure program. The procedures outlined in this AC can be applied to all of the above. The procedures and practices outlined in this AC cannot be applied to those who are required to report failures, malfunctions and defects under 14 CFR part 21.3 and do not make those reports in the timeframe required by the regulation.

✈ 00-59
Integrating Helicopter and Tiltrotor Assets Into Disaster Relief Planning
(11/98) (AND-710)
Provides guidance to state and local emergency relief planners on integrating helicopters and tiltrotor aircraft into disaster relief planning efforts.

✈ 00-60
North American Free Trade Agreement and Specialty AIR Services Operations
(11/9/99) AFS-805)
Provides information for aircraft operators from the United States who plan to conduct specialty air services (SAS) operations in Canada or Mexico in accordance with the North American Free Trade Agreement. It also provides information for aircraft operators from Canada or Mexico who plan to conduct SAS operations in the U.S.
SN 050-007-01281-1
$2.50 Supt. Docs.

Procedural

Subject No. 10

11-2A
Notice of Proposed Rulemaking Distribution System
(7/26/84) (ABC-100)
Provides the public with information relative to participation in the FAA rulemaking process and explains the availability of the Notices.

13-1
Aviation Safety Inspector Work Site Access
(12/28/95) (AFS-120/AFS-300)
Explains the requirement and use of FAA Form 8000-39, Aviation Safety Inspector Identification Card, and its relation to the Aviation Safety Credential, FAA Form 110A. This AC is issued primarily to acquaint airport authorities and the airport security personnel with the FAA Form 8000-39 and the aviation safety inspector's need to be in restricted areas of the airport to perform official FAA business.

Aircraft

Subject No. 20

20-18A

Qualification Testing of Turbo-jet Engine Thrust Reversers
(3/16/66) (ANE- 100)
Discusses the requirements for the qualification of thrust reversers and sets forth an acceptable means of compliance with the tests prescribed in Federal Aviation Regulations, Part 33, then run under nonstandard ambient air conditions.

20-24B
Qualification of Fuels, Lubricants, and Additives
(12/20/85) (ANE-110)
Provides acceptable procedures for approving the qualification of fuels, lubricants, and additives for use in certificated aircraft engines.

20-27D
Certification and Operation of Amateur-Built Aircraft
(6/22/90) (AIR-230)
Provides guidance and information relative to the airworthiness certification and operation of amateur-built aircraft.

20-29B
Use of Aircraft Fuel Anti-icing Additives
(1/18/72) (ANE-100)
Provides information on the use of anti-icing additives PFA-55MB and Mil-I-27686 as an acceptable means of compliance with the FARs that require assurance of continuous fuel flow under conditions where ice may occur in turbine aircraft fuel systems.

20-30B
Aircraft Position Light and Anticollision Light Installation
(7/20/81) (AIR- 120)
Sets forth acceptable means, but not the only means, of showing compliance with the Federal Aviation Regulations (FAR) applicable to installed position lights and anticollision lights.

20-32B
Carbon Monoxide (CO) Contamination in Aircraft--Detection and Prevention
(11/24/72) (ACE-110)
Provides information on the potential dangers of carbon monoxide contamination from faulty engine exhaust systems or cabin heaters of the exhaust gas heat exchanger type.

20-33B
Technical Information Regarding Civil Aeronautics Manuals 1, 3, 4a,4b, 5, 6, 7, 8, 9, 13 and 14
(5/1/75) (AIR-100)
Advises the public that policy information contained in the subject Civil Aeronautics Manuals may be used in conjunction with specific sections of the Federal Aviation Regulations.

20-34D
Prevention of Retractable Landing Gear Failures
(8/8/80) (AFS-340)
Updates statistical information related to landing accidents involving aircraft with retractable landing gear and suggests procedures to minimize those accidents.

20-35C
Tie-Down Sense
(7/12/83) (AFS-340)
Provides updated information of general use on aircraft tiedown techniques and procedures.

20-36S
Index of Articles (Materials, Parts, Processes and Appliances) Certified Under the Technical Standard Order System (AFS-610)
AC canceled 11/99. Available in Access database as TSOA listing at **http://av-info.faa.gov**

20-37D
Aircraft Metal Propeller Maintenance
(8/15/89) (AFS-340)
Provides information and suggested procedures to increase service life and to minimize blade failures of metal propellers.

20-38A
Measurement of Cabin Interior Emergency Illumination in Transport Airplanes
(2/8/66) (ANM- 100)
Outlines acceptable methods, but not the only methods, for measuring cabin interior emergency illumination on transport airplanes, and provides information as to suitable measuring instruments.

20-40
Placards for Battery-Excited Alternators Installed in Light Aircraft
(8/11/65) (ACE-100)
Sets forth an acceptable means of complying with placarding rules in Federal Aviation Regulations 23 and 27 with respect to battery excited alternator installations.

20-41A
Substitute Technical Standard Order (TSO) Aircraft Equipment
(4/5/77) (AIR- 120)
Sets forth an acceptable means for complying with rules governing aircraft equipment installations in cases involving the substitution of technical standard order equipment for functionally similar TSO approved equipment.

20-42C
Hand Fire Extinguishers for use in Aircraft
(3/7/84) (ACE-110)
Provides methods acceptable to the Administrator for showing compliance with the hand fire extinguisher provisions in Parts 25, 29, 91, 121, 125, 127, and 135 of the FAR and provides updated general information.

20-43C
Aircraft Fuel Control
(10/20/76) (AFS-340)
Alerts the aviation community to the potential hazards of inadvertent mixing or contamination of turbine and piston fuels, and provides recommended fuel control and servicing procedures.

20-44
Glass Fiber Fabric for Aircraft Covering
(9/3/65) (ACE-100)
Provides a means, but not the sole means, for acceptance of glass fiber fabric for external covering of aircraft structure.

20-45
Safetying of Turnbuckles on Civil Aircraft
(9/17/65) (ACE-100)
Provides information on turnbuckle safetying methods that have been found acceptable by the FAA during past aircraft type certification programs.

20-47
Exterior Colored Band Around Exits on Transport Airplanes
(2/8/66) (ANM-100)
Sets forth an acceptable means, but not the only means, of complying with the requirement for a 2-inch colored band outlining exits required to be openable from the outside on transport airplanes.

20-48
Practice Guide for Decontaminating Aircraft
(5/5/66) (AFS-330)
The title is self-explanatory.

20-52
Maintenance Inspection Notes for Douglas DC-6/7 Series Aircraft (Consolidated Reprint. Includes Change 1).
(8/24/67) (AFS-310)
Describes maintenance inspection notes which can be used for the maintenance support of certain structural parts of DC-6/7 series aircraft.

20-53A
Protection of Aircraft Fuel Systems Against Fuel Vapor Ignition Due to Lightning
(4/12/85) (ACE-111)
Provides information and guidance concerning an acceptable means, but not the only means, of compliance with Parts 23 or 25 of the Federal Aviation Regulations (FAR) applicable to preventing ignition of fuel vapors due to lightning.

20-56A
Marking of TSO-C72b Individual Flotation Devices
(4/1/75) (AIR-120)
Outlines acceptable methods for marking individual flotation devices which also serve as seat cushions.

20-57A
Automatic Landing Systems (ALS)
(1/12/71) (ANM-110)
Sets forth an acceptable means of compliance, but not the only means, for the installation approval of automatic landing systems in transport category aircraft which may be used initially in Category II operations. Approval of these aircraft for use under such conditions will permit the accumulation of data for systems which may be approved for Category IIIa in the future.

20-59
Maintenance Inspection Notes for Convair 240, 340/440, 240T, and 340T Series Aircraft
(2/19/69) (AFS-330)
Describes maintenance inspection notes which can be used for the maintenance support of certain structural parts of Convair 240, 340/440, 240T, and 340T series aircraft.

20-59, Chg. 1
(8/24/72)
Provides additional material for Convair Models 240 and 600/240D; Models 340/440 and 640/340D/440D series aircraft maintenance inspection programs.

20-60
Accessibility to Excess Emergency Exits
(7/18/68) (ANM-110A)
Sets forth acceptable means of compliance with the "readily accessible" revisions in the Federal Aviation Regulations dealing with excess emergency exits.

20-62D
Eligibility, Quality, and Identification of Aeronautical Replacement Parts
(5/24/96) (AFS-340)
Provides information and guidance for use in determining the quality, eligibility and traceability of aeronautical parts and materials intended for installation on U.S. type-certificated products and to enable compliance with the applicable regulations.

20-64
Maintenance Inspection Notes for Lockheed L-188 Series Aircraft
(8/1/69) (AIR-3)
Describes maintenance inspection notes which can be used for the maintenance support of certain structural parts of Lockheed L-188 series aircraft.

20-64, Chg. 1
(10/26/73)

20-65
U.S. Airworthiness Certificates and Authorizations for Operation of Domestic and Foreign Aircraft
(8/11/69) (AIR-200)
Provides general information and guidance concerning issuance of airworthiness certificates for U.S. registered aircraft, and issuance of special flight authorizations for operation in the United States of foreign aircraft not having standard airworthines certificates issued by the country of registry.

20-66
Vibration Evaluation of Aircraft Propellers
(1/29/70) (ANE-100)
Outlines acceptable means, but not the sole means, for showing compliance with the requirements of the FARs concerning propeller vibration.

20-67B
Airborne VHF Communications Equipment Installations
(1/16/86) (AIR-120)
Sets forth one means, but not the only means, of demonstrating compliance with the airworthiness rules governing the functioning of airborne VHF communications equipment.

20-68B
Recommended Radiation Safety Precautions for Ground Operation of Airborne Weather Radar
(8/8/80) (AFS-600)
Sets forth recommended radiation safety precautions for ground operation of airborne weather radar.

20-69
Conspicuity of Aircraft Instrument Malfunction Indicators
(5/14/70) (AIR-120)
Provides design guidance information on methods of improving conspicuity of malfunction indication devices.

20-71
Dual Locking Devices on Fasteners
(12/8/70) (AIR-120)
Provides guidance and acceptable means, not the sole means, by which compliance may be shown with the requirements for dual locking devices on removable fasteners installed in rotorcraft and transport category airplanes.

20-73
Aircraft Ice Protection
(4/21/71) (AIR-120)
Provides information relating to the substantiation of ice protection systems on aircraft.

20-74
Aircraft Position and Anticollision Light Measurements
(7/29/71) (AIR-120)
Contains useful information concerning measurements for intensity, covering, and color of aircraft position and anti-collision lights.

20-76
Maintenance Inspection Notes for Boeing B-707/720 Series Aircraft
(10/21/71) (AFS-330)
Provides maintenance inspection notes which can be used for the maintenance support program for certain structural parts of the B-707/720 series aircraft.

20-77
Use of Manufacturers' Maintenance Manuals
(3/22/72) (AFS-340)
Informs owners and operators about the usefulness of manufacturers' maintenance manuals for servicing, repairing, and maintaining aircraft, engines and propellers.

20-78
Maintenance Inspection Notes for McDonnell Douglas DC-8 Series Aircraft
(7/11/72) (AFS-330)
Provides maintenance inspection notes which can be used for the maintenance support program for certain structural parts of the DC-8 series aircraft.

20-82
Maintenance Inspection Notes for Fairchild Hiller F-27/FH-227 Series aircraft (Includes Change 1)
(12/5/72) (AFS-230)
Provides maintenance inspection notes which can be used for the maintenance support program for certain structural parts of Fairchild Hiller F-27/FH-227 series aircraft.

20-83
Maintenance Inspection Notes for Boeing B-737 Series Aircraft (Includes Changes 1 and 2)
(1/17/73) (AFS - 330)
Provides maintenance inspection notes which can be used for the maintenance support program for certain structural parts of the B-737 series aircraft.

20-84
Maintenance Inspection Notes for Boeing B-727 Series Aircraft.
(1/22/73) (AFS-300)
Provides inspection notes which can be used for the maintenance support program for certain structural parts of the B-727 series aircraft.

20-84, Chg. 1
(8/8/74)
Updates material for the B-727 series aircraft maintenance inspection program. Inspection of selected areas of the wing, fuselage, empennage and landing gear of the B-727 series aircraft are presented supplementing information currently available in AC 20-84.

20-84, Chg. 2
(1/31/75)

20-88A
Guidelines on the Marking of Aircraft Powerplant Instruments (Displays),
(9/30/85) (ANM- 112)
Provides revised guidelines on the marking of aircraft powerplant instruments and electronic displays (cathode ray tubes, etc.). These guidelines offer acceptable, but not exclusive, methods of compliance with the powerplant instrument color marking requirements.
SN 050- 007-00683-7.
$1.50 Supt. Docs.

20-94
Digital Clock Installation in Aircraft
(3/4/76) (AFS-350)
Provides guidelines for operating and installing digital clocks in aircraft.

20-95
Fatigue Evaluation of Rotorcraft Structure
(5/18/76) (ASW-100)
Sets forth acceptable means, not the only means, of compliance with the provisions of FAR sections 27.571 and 29.571 dealing with the fatigue evaluation of rotorcraft structure.

20-96
Surplus Military Aircraft: A Briefing for Prospective Buyers
(12/2/76) (AIR- 200)
Provides many answers to questions regarding the purchasing of surplus military aircraft (type certification, is the aircraft flyable, is it sold for spare parts, scrap?).

20-97A
High-Speed Tire Maintenance and Operational Practices
(5/13/87) (AFS-340)
Provides information and guidance for maintaining aircraft tires to ensure their continued airworthiness.

20-99
Anti-skid and Associated Systems
(5/27/77) (ANM-100)
Provides an acceptable means, but not the only means, of complying with the requirement that anti-skid and associated systems must be designed so that no probable malfunction will result in a

hazardous loss of braking or directional control of an airplane.

20-100
General Guidelines for Measuring Fire-Extinguishing Agent Concentrations in Powerplant Compartments
(9/21/77) (AIR-120)
Describes the installation and use of a model GA-2A fire extinguisher agent concentration recorder in determining the distribution and concentration of fire-extinguishing agents when discharged in an aircraft powerplant compartment.

20-101C
Airworthiness Approval of Omega/VLF Navigation Systems for Use in the United States NAS and Alaska
(9/12/88) (ACE-130W/AIR-120)
Presents an acceptable means of compliance, but not the only means, for the approval of Omega and Omega/Very Low Frequency (VLF) Navigation Airborne Equipment as a means of Visual Flight Rules (VFR)/Instrument Flight Rules (IFR)/Area Navigation (RNAV) en route navigation within the conterminous United States and Alaska.
SN 050-007-00887-2.
$1.50 Supt. Docs.

20-103
Aircraft Engine Crankshaft Failure
(3/7/78) (AFS-340)
Provides information and suggests procedures to increase crankshaft service life and to minimize failures.

20-104
Revised Powerplant Engineering Report No. 3, Standard Fire Test Apparatus and Procedure (for Flexible Hose Assemblies)
(4/12/78) (AIR-120)
Announces the availability of the subject report.

20-105B
Reciprocating Engine Power-loss Accident Prevention and Trend Monitoring
(6/15/98) (AFS-340)
Updates statistical information and brings to the attention of aircraft owners, operators, manufacturers, and maintenance personnel the circumstances surrounding engine power-loss accidents with recommendations on how those accidents can be prevented.

20-106
Aircraft Inspection for the General Aviation Aircraft Owner
(4/1/78) (AFS-340)
Describes techniques used in aircraft inspections. Designed to familiarize owner, pilots, student mechanics, and others with inspection procedures, it does NOT qualify an individual to make airworthiness determinations.
SN 050-007-00449-4.
$5.00 Supt. Docs.

20-107A
Composite Aircraft Structure
(4/25/84) (AIR-103)
Sets forth an acceptable, but not the only, means of showing compliance with the provisions of FAR Parts 23, 25, 27, and 29 regarding airworthiness type certification requirements of composite aircraft structures involving fiber reinforced materials, e.g., carbon (graphite), boron, aramid (kevlar), and glass reinforced plastics. Guidance information is also presented on associated quality control and repair aspects.

20-109A
Service Difficulty Program (General Aviation)
(4/8/93) (AFS-620)
Describes the Service Difficulty Program as it applies to general aviation activities. Instructions for completion of the revised FAA Form 8010-4 (10-92), Malfunction or Defect Report, are provided.

✈20-110K
Index of Aviation Technical Standard Orders
(9/22/99) (AIR-120)
Describes the public procedure the Federal Aviation Administration (FAA) will use to develop and issue Technical Standard Orders (TSOs) for aeronautical articles to be used on civil aircraft. Presents an index of the FAA TSOs which contain minimum performance standards for specific materials, parts processes, and appliances used in civil aircraft.

20-111
Communication Caused By Unintentional Keyed Microphones
(10/10/80) (AFS-350)
Alerts the aviation community to the potential hazards created by unintentional keying of microphones resulting in radio transmissions from airborne, mobile, and ground based radio transmitters and gives guidance on alleviating ensuing hazards.

20-112
Airworthiness and Operational Approval of Airborne Systems to be Used In Lieu of Ground Proximity Warning System (GWPS)
(2/19/81) (AIR-120)
Provides information and guidance regarding airworthiness and operational approval of airborne equipment/systems in accordance with FAR 135.153(b) and (c).

20-113
Pilot Precautions and Procedures to be taken in Preventing Aircraft Reciprocating Engine Induction System & Fuel System Icing Problems
(10/22/81) (ACE-100)
Provides information pertaining to aircraft engine induction system icing and the use of fuel additives to reduce the hazards of aircraft operation that may result from the presence of water and ice in aviation gasoline and aircraft fuel systems.

20-114
Manufacturers' Service Documents
(10/22/81) (AIR-100)
Suggests acceptable methods by which product manufacturers may indicate FAA approval of recommended actions prescribed in manufacturers' service documents.

20-115B

6/15/00

Radio Technical Commission for Aeronautics, Inc. Document RTCA/DO-178B
(1/11/93) (AIR-130)
Calls attention to RTCA, Inc., (formerly the Radio Technical Commission for Aeronautics) Document RTCA/DO- 178B, "Software Considerations in Airborne Systems and Equipment Certification," issued December 1992. It discusses how the document may be applied with FAA technical standard order (TSO), authorizations, type certification (TC), or supplemental type certification authorization (STC).

20-116
Marking Aircraft Fuel Filler Openings With Color Coded Decals
(9/17/82) (ACE- 100)
Discusses the conditions under which color coded decals may be used to comply with the requirements in FAR Parts 23, 25, 27, and 29 for marking fuel filler openings.

20-117
Hazards Following Ground Deicing and Ground Operations in Conditions Conducive to Aircraft Icing
(12/17/82) (AFS-200)
Provides information on the identified hazards associated with ground deicing and ground operations in conditions conducive to aircraft icing.

20-117, Chg. 1
(4/15/83)
Corrects an error in Figure 3-2, Appendix 3, regarding the values of "TIME TO CRYSTALLIZATION (MIN)."

20-118A
Emergency Evacuation Demonstration
(3/9/87) (ACE-100)
Sets forth acceptable means, but not the only means, of showing compliance with the Federal Aviation Regulations (FAR) applicable to required emergency evacuation demonstrations from airplanes certified to the requirements of SFAR 23, SFAR 41, Appendix A of Part 135, or Part 23, commuter category.

20-119
Fuel Drain Valves
(2/7/83) (AIR-120)
Provides an acceptable means, but not the only means, of compliance with the requirements of the FARs for positive locking of fuel drain valves in the closed position.

20-120
Nondirectional Beacon Frequency Congestion
(6/18/84) (ASM-500)
Recommends several actions that the user can take to alleviate problems of frequency congestion in the 190-535 kHz frequency range.

20-121A
Airworthiness Approval of Airborne Loran-C Navigation Systems for Use in the U.S. National Airspace System (NAS)
(8/24/88) (AIR-120)
Establishes an acceptable means, but not the only means, of obtaining airworthiness approval of airborne Loran-C navigation systems for use under VFR (visual flight rules) and IFR (instrument flight rules) within the conterminous United States, Alaska, and surrounding U.S. waters.

20-122A
Anti-misfueling Devices: Their Availability and Use
(1/29/91) (AFS-340)
Includes information relating to the Society of Automotive Engineers (SAE) standard dimensions for fueling ports now being incorporated during new aircraft production by all General Aviation Manufacturer's Association member companies. It also makes recommendations to the fuel suppliers and Fixed Base Operators to change their fuel dispensing nozzles to meet the dimensions referenced in the SAE standard.

20-123
Avoiding Or Minimizing Encounters With Aircraft Equipped With Depleted Uranium Balance Weights During Accident Investigations
(12/20/84) (AFS-330)
Provides information and guidance to individuals who come in contact with depleted uranium contained in aircraft control surfaces during accident investigations.

20-124
Water Ingestion Testing for Turbine Powered Airplanes
(9/30/85) (ANM-112)
Describes a method of demonstrating compliance with the requirements of the FAR concerning the ingestion of water from the runway/taxiway surface into the airspeed system, the engine, and essential auxiliary power unit air inlet ducts of turbine engine power unit air inlet ducts of turbine engine powered airplanes.

20-125
Water in Aviation Fuels
(12/10/85) (AFS-340)
Alerts the aviation community to the potential hazards of water in aviation fuels. Additionally, it outlines recommended procedures to prevent, detect, and eliminate water in the fuel systems of aircraft.

✈ 20-126G
Aircraft Certification Service Field Office Listing
(11/30/99) (AFS-610)
Provides the nearest points of contact for information regarding issuance of type and supplemental type certificates and changes, as well as issuances of production and/or airworthiness approvals.

20-127
Use of Society of Automotive Engineers (SAE) Class H11 bolts
(7/8/87) (ANM- 110B)
Provides guidance on the use of SAE Class H11 bolts in primary structure on all aircraft, including gliders and manned free balloons, and on aircraft engines and propellers.

20-128A
Design Considerations for Minimizing Hazards Caused by Uncontained Turbine Engine and Auxiliary Power Unit Rotor and Fan Blade Failures
(3/25/97) (ANM-114)

Sets forth a method of compliance with the requirements of Sections 23.903(b)(1), 25.901(d) and 25.903(d)(1) of the FAR pertaining to design precautions taken to minimize the hazards to an airplane in the event of uncontained engine or auxiliary power unit rotor (compressor and turbine) failure and engine fan blade failures. It is for guidance and to provide a method of compliance that has been found acceptable.

20-129
Airworthiness Approval of Vertical Navigation (VNAV) Systems for use in the U.S. NAS and Alaska
(9/12/88) (AIR-120)
Establishes an acceptable means, but not the only means, of obtaining airworthiness approval of an airborne vertical navigation system for use under visual flight rules (VFR) and instrument flight rules (IFR) within the conterminous United States, Alaska and surrounding U.S. waters.

20-130A
Airworthiness Approval of Navigation or Flight Management Systems Integrating Multiple Navigation Sensors
(6/14/95) (AIR-130)
Establishes an acceptable means, but not the only means, of obtaining airworthiness approval of a multi-sensor navigation or flight management systems integrating data from multiple navigation sensors for use as a navigation system for oceanic and remote, domestic enroute, terminal, and non-precision instrument approach (except localizer, localizer directional aid (LDA) and simplified directional facility operations. This document does not address systems incorporating differential GPS capability.

20-131A
Airworthiness and Operational Approval of Traffic Alert and Collision Avoidance Systems (TCAS II) and Mode S Transponders
(3/29/93) (ANM-111)
Provides guidance material for the airworthiness and operational approval of Traffic Alert and Collision Avoidance Systems (TCAS II) and Mode S transponders. Like all AC material, this AC is not mandatory and does not constitute a regulation. Issued for guidance purpose and to outline a method of compliance with the rules.

20-132
Public Aircraft
(12/21/88) (AIR-200)
Provides guidance that public aircraft status does not exist outside the territorial limits of the United States.

20-133
Cockpit Noise and Speech Interference Between Crewmembers
(3/22/89) (AIR-121)
Provides information about the relationship between flight crew members cockpit voice communication and cockpit noise levels. Guidance, on speech interference levels, noise measurement and measurement systems, and methods to improve cockpit communication, is provided for those manufacturers, owners or operators who believe cockpit noise may be a problem on their aircraft. This guidance material is relevant to the operation of all types of civil aircraft.

20-134
Test Procedures for Maximum Allowable Airspeed Indicators
(2/16/90) (AIR-120)
Provides guidance concerning test procedures which may be used in showing compliance with the standards in technical standards orders C 46a.

20-135
Powerplant Installation and Propulsion System Component Fire Protection Test Methods, Standards and Criteria
(2/15/90) (ANM-112)
Provides guidance for use in demonstrating compliance with the powerplant fire protection requirements of the Federal Aviation Regulations (FAR). Included in this document are methods for fire testing of materials and components used in the propulsion engines and APU installations, and in areas adjacent to designated fire zones, as well as the rationale for these methods.

20-136
Protection of Aircraft Electrical/Electronic Systems Against the Indirect Effects of Lightning
(3/5/90) (ANM-111)
Provides information and guidance concerning an acceptable means, but not the only means, of compliance with Parts 23, 25, 27, and 29 of the FAR as applicable for preventing hazardous effects, due to lightning, from occurring to electrical/electronic systems performing critical essential functions. This material is neither mandatory nor regulatory in nature and does not constitute a regulation. The applicant may elect to establish an alternative method of compliance that is acceptable to the FAA.

20-137
Dynamic Evaluation of Seat Restraint Systems & Occupant Restraint for Rotocraft (Normal and Transport)
(3/30/92) (ASW-111)
Provides guidance regarding acceptable means but not the only means of compliance with Parts 27 and 29 of the Federal Aviation Regulations (FAR) applicable to dynamic testing of seats intended for use in Normal and Transport Category.

20-138
Airworthiness Approval of Global Positioning System (GPS) Navigation Equipment for Use as a VFR and IFR Supplemental Navigation System
(5/25/94) (AIR-130)
Establishes an acceptable means, but not the only means, of obtaining airworthiness approval of Global Positioning System (GPS) equipment for use as a supplemental navigation system for oceanic and remote domestic en route, terminal, and non-precision instrument approach (except localizer directional aid (LDA) and simplified directional facility (SDF) operations.

20-139
Commercial Assistance During Construction of Amateur-Built Aircraft
(4/3/96) (AIR-230)

6/15/00

Explains Federal Aviation Regulations and Federal Aviation Administration policy for the fabrication and assembly of amateur-built aircraft. Provides information and guidance in the construction of amateur-built aircraft, the manufacture of kits designed to be assembled into aircraft by amateur-builders, and aircraft fabricated from plans for certification as amateur-built.

✈20-140
Guidelines for Design Approval of Aircraft Data Communications Systems
(8/16/99) (AIR-130)
Provides guidelines for design approval of aircraft data communications systems and applications primarily used for air traffic services.

✈ 20-141
Airworthiness and Operational Approval of Digital Flight Data Recorder Systems
(10/5/99) (AIR-130)
Provides guidance on design, installation, and continued airworthiness of Digital Flight Data Recorder Systems. It outlines one method of compliance with Title 14 of the Code of Federal Regulations. This AC is not mandatory nor is it a regulation.

✈20-142
Eligibility and Evaluation of U.S. Military Surplus Flight Safety Aircraft Parts, Engines, and Propellers
(2/25/00) (AFS-307)
Provides information and guidance for use in evaluating and determining the eligibility of U.S. military surplus flight safety critical aircraft parts (FSCAP), engines, and propellers for installation on FAA type-certificated products.

21-1B
Production Certificates
(5/10/76) (AIR-200)
Provides information concerning Subpart G of Federal Aviation Regulations (FAR) Part 21, and sets forth acceptable means of compliance with its requirements.

21-2H
Export Airworthiness Approval Procedures
(9/6/95) (AIR-210/AFS-610)
Contains guidance and information on procedures for exporting aeronautical products and related special requirements submitted to the Federal Aviation Administration by other governments.

21-4B
Special Flight Permits for Operation of Overweight Aircraft
(7/30/69) (AIR- 200)
Furnishes guidance concerning special flight permits necessary to operate an aircraft in excess of its usual maximum certificated takeoff weight.

21-5N
Announcement of Availability of Summary of Supplemental Type Certificates, (Paper)
January 1998 (AFS-610)
Announces the availability to the public of a revised paper edition of the Summary of Supplemental Type Certificates, dated January 1998. Also available at internet site **http://av-info.faa.gov.**

21-6A
Production Under Type Certificate Only
(7/1/82) (AIR-200)
Provides information concerning Subpart F of FAR Part 21, and sets forth an acceptable means, not the sole means, of compliance with its requirements.
SN 050-007-00636-5.
$1.75 Supt. Docs.

21-9A
Manufacturers Reporting Failures, Malfunctions, or Defects
(5/26/82) (AIR-200)
Provides information to assist manufacturers of aeronautical products (aircraft, aircraft engines, propellers, appliances, and parts) in notifying the Federal Aviation Administration of certain failures, malfunctions, or defects, resulting from design or quality control problems, in the products which they manufacture.

21-10A
Flight Recorder and Cockpit Voice Recorder Underwater Locating Devices
(4/19/83) (ANM-110)
This AC provides an acceptable means of showing compliance with the underwater locating device (ULD) requirements of the Federal Aviation Regulations for recorder ULD's.

21-12A
Application for U.S. Airworthiness Certificate, FAA Form 8130-6 (OMB 2120-0018)
(3/26/87) (AIR-220)
Provides instructions on the preparation and submittal of subject form.

21-13
Standard Airworthiness Certification of Surplus Military Aircraft and Aircraft Built from Spare and Surplus Parts
(4/5/73) (AIR-200)
Provides guidance and instruction on establishing eligibility and submitting application for civil airworthiness certification of surplus military aircraft and aircraft assembled from spare and surplus parts, under FAR 21. (d) when an FAA Type Certificate has been issued under FAR 21.21. or FAR 21.27.

✈21-15L
Announcement of Availability: Aircraft, Aircraft Engines and Propeller Type Certificate Data Sheets and Specifications
(4/12/99) (AFS-610)
Provides information concerning the availability of the 1999 edition of the subject publication.

21-16D
RTCA Document DO-160C
(7/21/98) (AIR-130)
Calls attention to RTCA, Inc. (formerly Radio Technical Commission for Aeronautics) Document No. DO-160D, "Environmental Conditions and Test Procedures for Airborne Equipment," dated July 29, 1997, and discusses how the document may be used in showing compliance with airworthiness reqquirements.

21-17

Carriage of Cargo in Restricted Category Aircraft and Other Special Purpose Operations
(3/15/82) (AIR-200)
Advises that the carriage of cargo in a restricted category aircraft is considered a restricted category special purpose operation and provides procedures for designating other special purpose operations under FAR 21.25(b) (7).
SN 050-007-00638-1.
$1.75 Supt. Docs.

21-18
Bilateral Airworthiness Agreements
(8/20/82) (AIR-110)
Makes available to interested persons copies of all current U.S. Bilateral Airworthiness Agreements (BAA) together with an explanation of their intent.
SN 050-007- 00614-4.
$7.00 Supt. Docs.

21-19
Installation of Used Engines In New Production Aircraft
(4/26/82) (AIR-200)
Advises that under certain specified criteria, used engines may be used in new production aircraft.

21-20B
Supplier Surveillance Procedures
(4/22/96) (AIR-230)
Clarifies and revises methods acceptable to the Administrator for surveillance of suppliers by the Federal Aviation Administration Production Approval Holders. It applies to products and parts thereof, submitted for airworthiness certification or approval after design approval (e.g., type certificate) and a production approval has been granted.

21-21
Use Of Automobile Gasoline In Agricultural Aircraft
(8/24/84) (AIR-100)
Sets forth acceptable conditions under which automobile gasoline (autogas) may be used in restricted category agricultural aircraft powered by Pratt and Whitney R-985 and R-1340 radial engines, and being used in agricultural operations under Federal Aviation Regulations Part 137.

21-22
Injury Criteria for Human Exposure to Impact
(6/20/85) (AIR-120)
Describes a range of impact trauma which may be used to establish bases for acceptance levels or performance criteria in the evaluation of occupant survivability characteristics in civil aircraft.

21-23
Airworthiness Certification of Civil Aircraft Engine, Propellers, and Related Products
(7/7/87) (AIR-4)
Provides information on the Federal Aviation Administration's (FAA) objectives, regulations, and general practices for the United States of America airworthiness certification or acceptance of civil aeronautical products imported to the U.S.

21-24
Extending a Production Certificate to a Facility Located in a Bilateral Airworthiness Agreement Country
(4/14/89) (AIR-220)
Contains information and guidance concerning: (1) FAA production certificate (PC) holders located in the U.S. that plan to extend their PC to include a facility located in another country; (2) and the issuance of a PC to an applicant located in the U.S. when the applicant is engaged in a multinational coproduction program whereby major manufacturing facilities will be located in other countries.

21-25A
Approval of Modified Seats and Berths Initially Approved Under a Technical Standard Order
(6/3/97) (AFS- 610)
Provides information on approvals required for modifications to TSO'd seating systems. This revision incorporates guidance regarding TSO-C127 seating systems and additional information on marking and flammability testing requirements.

21-26
Quality Control for the Manufacture of Composite Structures
(6/26/89) (AIR-220)
Provides information and guidance concerning and acceptable means, but not the only means, of demonstrating compliance with the requirements of FAR Part 21, Certification Procedures for Products and Parts, regarding quality control (QC) systems for the manufacture of composite structures involving fiber reinforced materials, e.g., carbon (graphite), boron, aramid (Kelvar), and glass reinforced polymeric materials. Provides guidance regarding the essential features of QC systems for composites as mentioned in AC 20-107.

21-26, Chg. 1
(1/26/90)
Modifies the term "Rheometrics Dynamic Spectroscopy (RDS)," which has been shown to be specific to one manufacturer, to "Dynamic Rheological Analysis," which is more generic term.

21-27
Production Certification Multi-national/Multicorporate Consortia
(7/14/89) (AIR-220)
Provides information and describes criteria to be emphasized in evaluating and approving the quality control system of a multinational and/or multicorporate consortium seeking a production certificate (PC). This AC would not apply to a type certificate holds a PC. Production Certificated extensions are addressed in AC 21-24.

21-28
Airworthiness Certification of U.S. Produced Aircraft and Engine Kits Assembled Outside the United States
(6/20/90) (AIR-220)
Provides information and guidance concerning airworthiness certification requirements for aircraft or aircraft engines, assembled from kits by aircraft or aircraft engine manufacturers located in other countries.

6/15/00

21-29B
Detecting and Reporting Suspected Unapproved Parts
(2/20/98) (AVR-20)
Provides information and guidance to the aviation community for detecting and reporting Suspected Unapproved Parts.

✈21-29B, Chg. 1
(3/13/00) (AVR-20)
Implements revised FAA Form 8120, Suspected Unapproved Parts Notification, dated 11/99.

21-31
Quality Control for the Manufacture of Non-Metallic Compartment Interior Components
(11/15/91) (AIR-220)
Provides information and guidance concerning compliance with the requirements of Federal Aviation Regulations (FAR) Part 21, Certification Procedures for Products and Parts.

21-32A
Control of Products and Parts Shipped Prior to Type Certificate Issuance
(3/19/96) (AIR-230)
Provides a means, but not the only means, to control products and parts shipped prior to the issuance of a type certificate or supplemental type certificate by a manufacturer with an approved production inspection system or production certificate. This AC broadens the scope of AC 21-32 by including completed aircraft, aircraft engines, propellers, and parts thereof ship prior to TC/STC issuance.

21-33
Quality Assurance of Software Used In Aircraft or Related Products
(2/3/93) (AIR-220)
Provides an acceptable means, but not the only means, to show compliance with the quality assurance requirements of FAR Par 21, Certification Procedures for Products and Parts, as applicable to the production of software used in type certificated aircraft or related products (airborn software). Also provides supplemental guidance for the establishment of a quality control or inspection to control the development and production of software used in type certification aircraft.

21-34
Shoulder Harness-Safety Installations
(6/4/93) (AIR-120)
Provides information and guidance pertinent to an acceptable means, but not the only means, for installation of shoulder harness and safety belt restraint systems at all seat locations on all previously type certificated aircraft.

21-35
Computer Generated/Stored Records
(6/4/93) (AIR-220)
Provides information and guidance concerning controls for managing information systems that generate and store records used in the manufacture of products and parts. Describes an acceptable means, but not the sole means, of compliance with the Federal Aviation Regulations (FAR).

21-36
Quality Assurance Control for Products Acceptance Software.
(8/11/93) (AIR-200)
Provides information and guidance concerning control of software and related digital input/output data (used by production approval holders (PAH) and their suppliers during manufacture, inspection and/or test) designed for use in the acceptance of airborne products. Provides an acceptable means, but not the only means, of compliance with the applicable Federal Aviation Regulations.

21-37
Primary Category Aircraft
(6/14/94) (AIR-110)
Provides guidance for complying with Part 21 of Subchapter C, Chapter 1, Title 14 of the Code of Federal Regulations (CFR), which contains the certification procedures for products and parts.

21-38
Disposition of Unsalvageable Aircraft Parts and Materials
(7/5/94) (AIR-230)
Provides information and guidance to persons involved in the sale, maintenance, or disposal of aircraft parts. It provides one means, but not the only means, of complying with 14 CFR Part 21, Certification Procedures for Products and Parts, requirements for control rejected parts and materials.

21-40
Application Guide for Obtaining a Supplemental Type Certificate
(5/6/98) (AFS-610)
Intended as a certification guide and checklist for obtaining a Supplemental Type Certificate (STC). Title 14 of the Code of Federal Regulations (14 CFR) and Federal Aviation Administration (FAA) Directives (orders and notices) are the final authority and take precedence over this document.

✈21-41
Continued Use of MIL-S-8879C, General Specification for Screw Threads (2/26/99) (AIR-120)
Provides information, clarification, and procedural guidance concerning the Inactivation of MIL-S-8879Cm Screw Threads, Controlled Radius Root with Increased Minor Diameter, as it relates to the civil aviation industry.

21.17-1A
Type Certification-Airships
(9/25/92) (ACE-100)
Describes two acceptable criteria for the type certification of airships that may be used by an applicant in showing compliance with section 21.17(b) of the Federal Aviation Regulations (FAR), Part 21. General guidance relative to airship type certification is also provided.

21.17-1A, Chg. 1
(10/30/92)

21.17-2A
Type Certification-Fixed Wing Gliders (Sailplanes) Including Powered Gliders
(2/10/93) (ACE-112)
Provides information and guidance concerning acceptable means of showing compliance with Section 21.17(b) of Part 21 of the Federal Aviation Regulations (FAR) for type certification of gliders and

powered gliders. General guidance relative to glider type certification is also provided.

21.17-3
Type Certification of Very Light Airplanes Under FAR 21.17(b)
(12/21/92) (AIR-110)
Provides a means but not the only means for the type, production, and airworthiness certification of very light airplanes (VLA); and designates the "Joint Aviation Requirements for Very Light Aeroplanes" (JAR-VLA), issued April 25, 1990, by the Joint Aviation Authorities (FAA) of Europe as an acceptable airworthiness criteria that provides in equivalent level of safety under FAR 21.17(b) for Federal Aviation Administration (FAA) type certification of VLA as a special class of aircraft. Provides other acceptable uses of the JAR-VLA in the United States aircraft certification regulatory system.

21.25-1
Issuance of Type Certificate: Restricted Category Agricultural Airplanes
(12/1/97) (ACE-111)
Provides information and guidance for obtaining a type certificate in the restricted category under Title 14 of the Code of Federal Regulations (14 CFR) Part 21, Section 21.25, for small single-engine piston and turbo-propeller driven airplanes, which will be used for agricultural special purpose operations. It also provides an acceptable means, but not the only means, of meeting the requirements of 14 CFR part 21 for the issuance of a type certificate in the restricted category.

21.303-2H
Announcement of Availability: Parts Manufacturer Approvals--1992 (Microfiche)
(10/13/92) (AFS-610)
Provides information concerning how to obtain the latest edition of parts manufacturing approvals, which are valid through August 1992. PMAs since 1992 are available at internet site **http://av-info.faa.gov.**

21.431-1A
Designated Alteration Station Authorization Procedures
(12/19/85) (AIR-110)
Updates the FAA Designated Alteration Station (DAS) authorization program; provides acceptable means of compliance with the DAS eligibility, personnel qualifications, and procedural requirements; provides information on FAA's participation in design change approval projects conducted under DAS procedures; and describes the FAA's DAS audit procedures.

23-2
Flammability Tests
(8/20/84) (ACE-111)
Provides information and guidance concerning compliance with FAR Part 23 and CAR Part 3 applicable to flammability tests for various materials, components, and electrical wire.

23-3
Structural Substantiation of Secondary Structures (9/5/85) (ACE-111)
Provides information and guidance concerning acceptable means, but not the only means, of demonstrating compliance with the requirements of Part 23 of the Federal Aviation Regulations (FAR) applicable to the structural substantiation of secondary structures such as fairings, cowlings, antennae, etc.

23-4
Static Strength Substantiation of Attachment Points for Occupant Restraint System Installations
(6/20/86) (ACE-111)
Provides information and guidance concerning an acceptable means, but not the only means, of compliance with Part 23 of the Federal Aviation Regulations (FAR) applicable to the static strength substantiation of the attachment points for occupant restraint system installations which have both a safety belt and shoulder harness.

23-5
Cutouts in a Modified Fuselage of Small Airplanes
(8/6/86) (ACE-111)
Provides information and guidance concerning acceptable means of compliance with Part 23 of the Federal Aviation Regulations (FAR) applicable to the structural substantiation of a fuselage modified by incorporation of large or small cutouts.

23-6
Interpretation of Failure for Static Structural Test Programs
(9/2/86) (ACE-111)
Provides information and guidance concerning the interpretation of failure for small airplanes for static structural test programs.

23-7
Substantiation for an Increase in Maximum Weight, Maximum Landing Weight, or Maximum Zero Fuel Weight
(7/1/87) (ACE-100)
Provides information and guidance concerning acceptable means, but not the only means of compliance with Part 23 of the Federal Aviation Regulations (FAR) applicable to structural substantiation for an increase in maximum weight, maximum landing weight, or maximum zero fuel weight.

23-8A
Flight Test Guide for Certification of Part 23 Airplanes (2/9/89) (ACE-111)
Provides information and guidance concerning compliance with Part 23 of the Federal Aviation Regulations (FAR) concerning flight tests and pilot judgments.
SN 050-007-00817-1
$18.00 Supt. Docs.

23-8A, Chg. 1
(8/30/93)
SN 050-007-01013-3
$8.50 Supt. Docs.

23-9
Evaluation of Flight Loads on Small Airplanes with T, V, +, or Y Empennage Configurations
(1/27/88) (ACE-111)
Provides information and guidance concerning compliance with Part 23 of the Federal Aviation Regulations (FAR)

6/15/00

applicable to evaluation of empennage design flight loads on configurations where the horizontal tail surfaces are supported by the vertical tail, or have appreciable dihedral.

23-10
Auxiliary Fuel Systems for Reciprocating and Turbine Powered Part 23 Airplanes
(8/5/91) (ACE-111)
Provides information and guidance concerning acceptable means of showing compliance with Part 23 of the Federal Aviation Regulations (FAR), applicable to auxiliary fuel systems in Part 23 airplanes. It is intended to be used for auxiliary fuel system installations in the airplane including fuselage, wing, or external configurations.

23-11
Type Certification of Very Light Airplanes with Powerplants and Propellers Certificated to Parts 33 and 35 of the Federal Aviation Regulations (FAR) (12/2/92) (ACE-111)
Provides an acceptable means of compliance with Part 23 of the FAR for type certification of certain small airplanes.

23-12
Structural Substantiation of Part 23 Airplane Modifications Involving Increased Engine Power
(1/27/93) (ACE-111)
Provides information and guidance concerning acceptable means of demonstrating compliance with the requirements of Part 23 of the Federal Aviation Regulations (FAR) applicable to the structural substantiation of modifications involving increased engine power.

23-13
Fatigue and Fail-Safe Evaluation of Flight Structure and Pressurized Cabin for Part 23 Airplanes
(4/15/93) (ACE-111)
Provides information and guidance concerning an acceptable means of demonstrating compliance with the requirements of Part 23 of the Federal Aviation Regulations (FAR) regarding fatigue and fail-safe evaluation of metallic airplane structure.

23-14
Type Certification Basis for Conversion from Reciprocating Engine to Turbine Engine-Powered Part 23 Airplanes
(9/30/93) (ACE-100)
Provides information and guidance concerning an acceptable means of showing compliance with Part 23 through amdt.23-45 of the Federal Aviation Regulations applicable to replacing reciprocating engines with gas turbine engines (turbopropeller, turbojet, or turbofan).

23-15
Small Airplane Certification Compliance Program
(1/2/97) (ACE-111)
Provides a compilation of historically acceptable means of compliance to specifically selected sections of Part 23 of the Federal Aviation Regulations that have become burdensome for small low performance airplanes to show compliance. However, applicability of these means of compliance remains the responsibility of the certification manager for each specific project. Utilization of these means of compliance does not affect the applicability of any other certification requirements that fall outside the scope of this AC.

✈ 23-16
Powerplant Guide for Certification in Part 23 Airplanes
(9/21/99) (ACE-111)
Consolidates into a single document existing policy documents applicable to the powerplant installation in normal, utility, acrobatic, and commuter category airplanes; and, certain ACs that cover specific paragraphs of the regulations.
SN 050-007-01285-3
$14.00 Supt. Docs

✈ 23-17
Systems and Equipment Guide For Certification of Part 23 Airplanes
(4/25/00) (ACE-100)
Provides information and guidance concerning an acceptable means, but not the only means, for showing compliance with Title 14 Code of Federal Regulations (14 CFR) Part 23 for the certification of systems and equipment in normal, utility, acrobatic, and commuter category airplanes.
SN 050-007-01287-0
$21.00 Supt. Docs.

23.562-1
Dynamic Testing of Part 23 Airplane Seat/Restraint Systems and Occupant Protection
(6/22/89) (ACE-111)
Provides information and guidance regarding compliance with Part 23 of the Federal Aviation Regulations (FAR) applicable to dynamic testing of airplane seats.

23.607-1
Self-Locking Nuts on Bolts Subject to Rotation
(8/24/84) (ACE-111)
Provides information and guidance concerning compliance with Part 23 for self-locking nuts used on bolts subject to rotation in operation.

23.629-1A
Means of Compliance with Section 23.629, "Flutter"
(10/23/85) (ACE-111)
Presents information and guidance to provide one means, but not the only means, of complying with Section 23.629, Flutter (including flutter, airfoil divergence, and control reversal) of Part 23 of the Federal Aviation Regulations.

✈ 23.1309-1C
Equipment, Systems, and Installations in Part 23 Airplanes
(3/12/99) (ACE-111)
Provides guidance and information for an acceptable means, but not the only means, for showing compliance with the requirements of Section 23.1309(a) and (b) (amendment 23-49) for equipment, systems, and installations in Title 14 Code of Federal Regulations (14 CFR) Part 23 airplanes.

✈ 23.1311-1A
Installation of Electronic Displays in Part 23 Airplanes

(3/12/99) (ACE-111)
Provides an acceptable means of showing compliance with Title 14 of the Code of Federal Regulations (14 CFR) applicable to the installation of electronic displays in Part 23 airplanes.

23.1419-2A
Certification of Part 23 Airplanes for Flight in Icing Conditions
(8/19/98) (ACE-100)
Sets forth an acceptable means, but not the only means, of demonstrating compliance with the ice protection requirements in 14 CFR Part 23. The FAA will consider other methods of demonstrating compliance that an applicant may present.

23.1521-1B
Type Certification of Automobile Gasoline in Part 23 Airplanes with Reciprocating Engines
(3/2/95) (ACE-111)
Sets forth acceptable means of compliance with Part 23 of the Federal Air Regulations (FAR), for approval/certification to use automobile gasoline with or without oxygenates (alcohol, ethers, etc.) in Part 23 airplanes. These procedures also apply to those airplanes approved/certificated under previous regulations superseded by Part 23.

23.1521-2
Type Certification of Oxygenates and Oxygenated Gasoline Fuels in Part 23 Airplanes with Reciprocating Engines
(1/21/93) (ACE-111)
Provides information and guidance concerning an acceptable means of compliance with Part 3 of the Civil Air Regulations (CAR) and Part 23 of the Federal Aviation Regulations (FAR), applicable to approval procedures for certification of alternate fuels. Also apply to those airplanes approved under Part 4a of the CAR and Aeronautics Bulletin 7a.

23.1521-2, Chg. 1
(4/24/96) (ACE-111)
Clarifies the Scope and makes the Scope and Purpose of this AC consistent with AC 23.1521-1B, Type Certification of Automobile Gasoline in Part 23 Airplanes with Reciprocating Engines.

25-4
Inertial Navigation Systems (INS)
(2/18/66) (ANM-100)
Sets forth an acceptable means for complying with rules governing the installation of inertial navigation systems in transport category aircraft.

25-5
Installation Approval on Transport Category Airplanes of Cargo Unit Load Devices Approved as Meeting the Criteria in NAS 3610
(6/3/70) (AIR-120)
Sets forth an acceptable means, but not the sole means, of complying with the requirements of the Federal Aviation Regulations (FAR's) applicable to the installation on transport category airplanes of cargo load devices approved as meeting the criteria in NAS 3610.

25-7A
Flight Test Guide for Certification of Transport Category Airplanes
(3/31/98) (ANM-111)
Provides guidelines for the flight test evaluation of transport category airplanes.
SN 050-007-01214-4.
$33.00 Supt. Docs.

✈ 25-7A, Chg 1
(6/3/99) (ANM-111)
Provides updated guidance to ensure consistent application of certain airworthiness requirements adopted by Amendments 25-92 and 25-98

25-8
Auxiliary Fuel System Installations
(5/2/86) (ANM-112)
Sets forth acceptable means, but not the sole means, by which compliance maybe shown with auxiliary fuel system installation requirements in accordance with the Federal Aviation Regulations identified within.
SN 050-007-00741-8.
$4.00 Supt. Docs.

25-9A
Smoke Detection, penetrating, and Evacuation Tests and Related Flight Manual Emergency Procedures
(1/6/94) (ANM-111)
Provides guidelines for the conduct of certification tests relating to smoke detection, penetration, and evacuation and to evaluate related Airplane Flight Manual (AFM) procedures. These guidelines may be used to reduce the number of decisions based solely on judgment in conducting tests and evaluating test results. While not mandatory this AC offers a method of demonstrating compliance with the applicable airworthiness requirements.

25-10
Guidance for Installation of Miscellaneous Nonrequired Electrical Equipment
(3/6/87) (ANM-110)
Sets forth a method of compliance with the requirements of Part 25 of the Federal Aviation Regulations pertaining to installations of miscellaneous, nonrequired electrical equipment in transport category airplanes. Provides an example of a method of compliance that has been found acceptable.

25-11
Transport Category Airplane Electronic Display Systems
(7/16/87) (ANM-110B)
Provides guidance for acceptance of cathode ray tube (CRT) based electronic display systems used for guidance, control, or decision-making by the pilots of transport category airplanes.

25-12
Airworthiness Criteria for the Approval of Airborne Windshear Warning Systems in Transport Category Airplanes
(11/2/87) (ANM-111)
Provides guidance for the airworthiness approval of airborne windshear warning systems in transport category airplanes.

25-13
Reduced and Derated Takeoff Thrust (Power) Procedures
(5/4/88) (ANM-112)

6/15/00

Provides guidance for the certification and use of reduced thrust (power) for takeoff and derated takeoff and derated thrust on turbine powered transport category airplanes. Serves as a ready reference for those involved with airplane certification and operation.

25-15
Approval of Flight Management Systems in Transport Category Airplanes
(11/20/89) (ANM-111)
Provides guidance material for the airworthiness approval of flight management systems (FMS) in transport category airplanes. Is issued for guidance purposes and to outline a method of compliance with the rules. In lieu of following this method without deviation, the applicant may elect to follow an alternate method, provided the alternate method is also found by the FAA to be an acceptable means of complying with the requirement of Part 25.

25-16
Electrical Fault and Fire Prevention and Protection
(4/5/91) (ANM-111)
Provides information and guidance on electrically caused faults, overheat, smoke, and fire in transport category airplanes. Acceptable means are provided to minimize the potential for these conditions to occur, and to minimize or contain their effects when they do occur.

25-17
Transport Airplane Cabin Interiors Crashworthiness Handbook
(7/15/91) (ANM-114)
Provides acceptable certification methods, but not necessarily the only acceptable methods, for demonstrating compliance with the crashworthiness requirements of Part 25 of the FAR for transport category airplanes.
SN 050-007-00915-1.
$14.00 Supt. Docs.

25-18
Transport Category Airplanes Modified for Cargo Service
(1/6/94) (ANM-114)
Provides guidance for demonstrating compliance with the FAR pertaining to transport category airplanes converted for use in all-cargo or combination passenger/cargo (combi) service and the relationship of those regulations to the requirements of Parts 121and 135 of the FAR.

25-19
Certification Maintenance Requirements
(11/28/94) (ANM-113)
Provides guidance on the selection, documentation, and control of Certification Maintenance Requirements (CMR's).

25-20
Pressurization, Ventilation, and Oxygen Systems Assessment for Subsonic Flight Including High Altitude Operation
(9/10/96) (ANM-111)
Provides guidance on methods of compliance with the requirements of part 25 of the Federal Aviation Regulations pertaining to pressurization, ventilation, and oxygen systems, especially as they pertain to high altitude subsonic flight. As with all AC material, it is not mandatory and does not constitute a regulation. The applicant may elect to follow alternate methods provided that these methods are also found by the FAA to be an acceptable means of complying with the requirements of part 25. Because the guidance on the methods of compliance presented in this AC are not mandatory, the terms "shall" and "must" when used herein, apply only to an applicant that chooses to follow a particular method without deviation.

✈ 25-21
Certification of Transport Airplane Structure
(9/1/99) (ANM-110)
Provides guidance to airplane manufacturers, modifiers, foreign regulatory authorities, and FAA transport airplane type certification engineers and their designees.

✈25-22
Certification of Transport Category Airplane Mechanical Systems
(3/14/00) (ANM-112)
Provides methods acceptable to the Administrator for showing compliance with the type certification requirements for transport airplane mechanical systems and equipment installations.

✈25-23 ***Airworthiness Criteria for the* Installation Approval of a Terrain Awareness and Warning Sysstem (TAWS) for Part 25 Airplanes**
(5/22/00) (ANM-130L)
Describes an acceptable means for obtaining FAA airworthiness approval for the installation of a Terrain Awareness and Warning System (TAWS) that has been approved under Technical Standard Order (TSO)-C151a.

25.253-1A
High-Speed Characteristics
(12/27/76) (ANM-110A)
Sets forth an acceptable means, but not the only means, by which compliance may be shown with FAR 25.253 during certification flight tests.

25.335-1
Design Dive Speed
(10/20/97) (ANM-115)
Sets forth an acceptable means , but not the only means, of demonstrating compliance with the provisions of part 25 of the Federal Aviation Regulations (FAR) related to the minimum speed margin between design cruise speed and design dive speed for transport category airplanes.

25.562-1A
Dynamic Evaluation of Seat Restraint Systems & Occupant Protection on Transport Category Airplanes
(1/19/96) (ANM-14)
Provides information and guidance regarding compliance with the provisions of Part 25 of the Federal Aviation Regulations applicable to dynamic testing of seats intended for use in transport category airplanes.

25.571-1C

Damage-Tolerance and Fatigue Evaluation of Structure
(4/29/98) (ANM-115)
Provides guidance for compliance with the provisions of 14 CFR Part 25 of the Federal Aviation Regulations (FAR) pertaining to the damage-tolerance and fatigue evaluation requirements for transport catagory aircraft structure. It also provides guidelines for the evaluation of scatter factors for the determination of life for parts catagorized as safe-life.

25.629-1A
Aeroelastic Stability Substantiation of Transport Catagory Airplanes
(7/23/98) (ANM-115)
Provides guidance material for acceptable means for demonstrating compliance with the provisions of part 25 of the FAR dealing with the deisgn requirements for transport category airplanes to preclude the aeroelastic instabilities of flutter, divergence and control reversal.

25.672-1
Active Flight Controls
(11/15/83) (ANM-110B)
Sets forth an equivalent means of complying with the provisions of Part 25 of the Federal Aviation Regulations (FAR) pertaining to the certification requirements of active flight controls. The procedures set forth herein apply to load alleviation systems (SAS), and flutter suppression systems (FSS). These procedures provide compliance with Part 25 under the equivalent safety provisions of Section 21.21(b)(1) in addition to compliance with the applicable sections of Part 25.

25.703-1
Takeoff Configuration Warning Systems
(3/17/93) (ANM-111)
Provides guidance for the certification of takeoff configuration warning systems installed in transport category airplanes.

25.773-1
Pilot Compartment View for Transport Category Airplanes
(1/8/93) (ANM-111)
Provides guidance for demonstrating compliance with the airworthiness standards for transport category airplanes pertaining to pilot compartment view. These criteria include the properties of transport materials necessary to assure adequate visibility from the flight deck.

25.783-1
Fuselage Doors, Hatches, and Exits
(12/10/86) (ANM-110)
Sets forth acceptable means of compliance with the provisions of Part 25 of the Federal Aviation Regulations (FAR) dealing with the certification requirements of fuselage doors. Guidance information is provided for showing compliance with structural and functional safety standards for doors and their operating systems. The intent of the requirements and some acceptable means of compliance are discussed. Other means are acceptable if they meet the intent of the regulations. For the propose of showing compliance with section 25.783 of FAR, hatches and exits are also considered to be doors.

25.785-1A
Flight Attendant Seat and Torso Restraint System Installations
(1/6/94) (ANM-114)
Provides information and guidance regarding an acceptable means, but not the only means, of compliance with the portions of Sections 25.785 and 121.311 of the FAR which deals with flight attendant seats.

25.803-1
Emergency Evacuation Demonstrations
(11/13/89) (ANM-114)
Provides guidance material on a means, but not the only means, of compliance with the FAR concerning (1) conduct of full-scale emergency evacuation demonstrations, and (2) use analysis and tests for emergency evacuation demonstrations in lieu of conducting an actual demonstration.

25.807-1
Uniform Distribution of Exits
(8/13/90) (ANM-114)
Provides guidance material for acceptable means, but not the only means, of demonstrating compliance with the requirements for distributing required passenger emergency exits uniformly. Addresses only those passenger-carrying airplanes, including mixed passenger/cargo ("combi") configurations, with a type certification basis for Amendment 25-15 or later with respect to Section 25.807(c) or airplanes with an earlier type certification basis required by Section 25.2 to meet Section 25.807, Amendment 25-15. Does not address airplanes with only one pair of required exits.

25.812-1A
Floor Proximity Emergency Escape Path Marking
(5/22/89) (ANM-114)
Provides guidance material for use in demonstrating compliance with the provisions of Part 25 of the FAR requiring floor proximity emergency escape path markings.

25.812-2
Floor Proximity Emergency Escape Path Marking Systems Incorporating Photoluminescent Elements
(7/24/97) (ANM-114)
Provides guidance for use in demonstrating compliance with the provisions of part 25 of the Federal Aviaton Regulations (FAR) regarding floor proximity emergency escape path marking systems (FPEEPMS) which incorporate photoluminescent elements. Although mandatory terms such as "shall" or "must" are used in this AC, because the AC method of compliance is not itself mandatory, these terms apply only to applicants who seek to demonstrate compliance by use of the specific method described by this AC.

25.853-1
Flammability Requirements for Aircraft Seat Cushions
(9/17/86) (ANM-110)
Provides guidance material for demonstrating compliance with the Federal Aviation Regulations (FAR) pertaining to flammability of aircraft seat cushions.

25.939-1
Evaluating Turbine Engine Operating Characteristics

6/15/00

(3/19/86) (ANM-112)
Provides guidelines for the evaluation of turbine engine (turbojet, turboprop, and turboshaft) operating characteristics for subsonic transport category airplanes.

25.963-1
Fuel Tank Access Covers
(7/29/92) (ANM-112)
Sets forth a means of compliance with the provisions of Part 25 of the FAR dealing with the certification requirements for fuel tank access covers on turbine powered transport category airplanes. Guidance information is provided for showing compliance with the impact and fire resistance requirements of Section 25.963(e).

25.981-1A
Guidelines for Substantiating Compliance With the Fuel Tank Temperature Requirements
(1/20/71) (AIR-110E)
Sets forth some general guidelines for substantiating compliance with fuel tank temperature airworthiness standards section 25.981.

25.994-1
Design Considerations to Protect Fuel Systems During a Wheel-Up Landing
(7/24/86) (ANM-111)
Presents guidelines and methods for complying with the requirements of section 25.994 of the Federal Aviation Regulations (FAR). These guidelines pertain to protecting fuel system components located in the engine nacelles and the fuselage from damage which could result in spillage of enough fuel to constitute a fire hazard as a consequence of a wheels-up landing on a paved runway. This material is not mandatory and does not constitute a regulation.

25.1309-1A
System Design Analysis
(6/21/88) (ANM-112)
Describes various acceptable means for showing compliance with the requirements of section 25.1309(b), (c), and (d) of the Federal Aviation Regulations (FAR). These means are intended to provide guidance for the experience engineering and operational judgment that must form the basis for compliance findings.

25.1329-1A
Automatic Pilot Systems Approval
(7/8/68) (ANM-110A)
Sets forth an acceptable means by which compliance with the automatic pilot installation requirements of FAR 25.1329 may be shown.

25.1357-1
Circuit Protective Device Accessibility
(9/20/88) (ANM-111)
Describes acceptable means of compliance with the requirements of section 25.1357(d) and (f) of the FAR with respect to the accessibility of circuit protection devices (CPD), such as circuit breakers or fuses. An applicant may elect to use any alternative means found to be acceptable by the FAA for compliance with the FAR.

✈ 25.1419-1
Certification of Transport Category Airplanes for Flight in Icing Conditions
(8/18/99) (ANM-12)
Provides guidance for certification of airframe ice protection systems on transport category airplanes.

25.1455-1
Waste Water/Potable Water Drain System Certification
(3/11/85) (ANM-112)
Sets forth a specific method of compliance with the requirements of section 25.1455 of the FAR pertaining to draining of fluids through drain masts when the fluids are subject to freezing. This method is designed to verify that draining fluids will not accumulate as ice in sufficient quantity to be hazardous. Is for guidance purposes and to set forth one method of compliance that has been found acceptable.

25.1457-1A
Cockpit Voice Recorder Installations
(11/3/69) (ANM-110A)
Sets forth one acceptable means of compliance with provisions of FAR 25.1457 (b), (e), and (f) pertaining to area microphones, cockpit voice recorder location, and erasure features.

25.1523-1
Minimum Flight Crew
(2/2/93) (ANM-111)
Sets forth a method of compliance with the requirements of Section 25.1523 of the FAR which contains the certification requirements for minimum flight crew on transport category airplanes.

25.1529-1
Instructions for Continued Airworthiness of Structural Repairs on Transport Airplanes
(8/1/91) (ANM-112)
Provides instructions to ensure continued airworthiness of structural repairs on transport category airplanes. It addresses the approval procedures to follow when making structural repairs to structure certificated under the damage tolerance requirements of Section 25.571 of FAR, Amendment 25-45, and to type designs with Supplemental Inspection Documents which were based on these criteria.

25.1581-1
Airplane Flight Manual
(7/14/97) (ANM-111)
Identifies the information that must be provided in Airplane Flight Manual (AFM) under the airworthiness regulations and provides guidance as to the form and content of the approved portion of an AFM.

✈ 27-1B
Certification of Normal Category Rotorcraft
(9/30/99) (ASW-110)
Provides guidance regarding an acceptable means but not the only means of compliance with Part 27 of the Federal Aviation Regulations (FAR) applicable to certification of normal category rotorcraft. This revision renumbers paragraphs to correspond with FAR numbering. Also, it is divided by Subparts and the page numbers reflect the relevant FAR Subpart.
SN 050-007-01186-5
$57.00 Sup.Docs.

29-1
Approval Basis for Automatic Stabilization Equipment (ASE) Installations in Rotorcraft
(12/26/63) (AIR-160)
Gives means for compliance with flight requirements in various CAR's.

29-1, Chg. 1
(3/26/64)
Transmits revised information about the time delay of automatic stabilization equipment.

✈ 29-2C
Certification of Transport Category Rotorcraft
(9/30/99) (ASW-110)
Provides guidance regarding an acceptable means but not the only means of compliance with Part 29 of the Federal Aviation Regulations (FAR) applicable to certification of transport category rotorcraft. This revision renumbers paragraphs to correspond with FAR numbering. Also, it is divided by Subparts and the page numbers reflect the relevant FAR Subpart.
SN 050-007-01187-3
$67.00 Supt.Docs.

33-1B
Turbine-Engine Foreign Object Ingestion and Rotor Blade Containment Type Certification Procedures
(4/22/70) (ANE-100)
Provides guidance and acceptable means, not the sole means, by which compliance may be shown with the design and construction requirements of Part 33 of the Federal Aviation Regulations.

33-2B
Aircraft Engine Type Certification Handbook
(6/30/93) (ANE-110)
Contains guidance relating to type certification of aircraft engines which will constitute acceptable means, although not the sole means, of compliance with the Federal Aviation Regulations.

33-3
Turbine and Compressor Rotors Type Certification Substantiation Procedures
(9/9/68) (ANE-100)
Sets forth guidance and acceptable means, not the sole means, by which compliance may be shown with the turbine and compressor rotor substantiation requirements in FAR Part 33.

33-4
Design Considerations Concerning The Use Of Titanium In Aircraft Turbine Engines
(7/28/83) (ANE-110)
Provides guidance and acceptable means, not the sole means, by which compliance may be shown with the design requirements of Part 33 to minimize the probability of the occurrence of an internal fire when titanium is used in aircraft turbine engines.

33-5
Turbine Engine Rotor Blade Containment/Durability
(6/18/90) (ANE-110)
Provides guidance and acceptable methods, but not the only methods, that may be used by an applicant in showing compliance with the turbine engine rotor blade containment requirements of Part 33 of the Federal Aviation Regulations (FAR).

33-6
Weld Repair of Aluminum Crankcases and Cylinders of Piston Engines
(12/20/94) (ANE-110)
Provides information and guidance concerning acceptable means, but not the only means, for the development of process specifications for weld repairs on crankcases and cylinders of piston engines.

✈33.4-1
Instructions for Continued Airworthiness
(8/27/99) (ANE-110)
Provides guidance on acceptable methods, but not the only methods, of compliance with section 33.4 of the Federal Aviation Regulations, Title 14, Code of Federal Regulations.

✈ 33.15-1
Manufacturing Process of Premium Quality Titanium Alloy Rotating Engine Components (9/22/98) (ANE-110)
Provides guidance for compliance with the provisions under Title 14 under the Code of Federal Regulations, Part 33 (14 CFR 33) pertaining to the materials suitability and durability requirements, 33.15, as applicable to the manufacture of titanium alloy high energy rotating parts of aircraft engines.

33.47-1
Detonation Testing In Reciprocating Aircraft Engines
(6/27/88) (ANE-110)
Provides guidance material for acceptable means of demonstrating compliance with the requirements of FAR Part 33, relating to detonation testing for reciprocating aircraft engines.

33.65-1
Surge and Stall Characteristics of Aircraft Turbine Engines
(12/6/85) (ANE-110)
Provides guidance material for acceptable means of demonstrating compliance with the requirements of Part 33 of the Federal Aviation Regulations (FAR) relative to surge and stall characteristics and thrust response of turbine engines. These guidelines do not constitute a regulation and are therefore not mandatory.

33.74-92
Turbine Engine Continued Rotation and Rotor Locking
(2/14/97) (ANE-110)
Provides guidance and acceptable methods, but not the only methods, that may be used to demonstrate compliance with the continued rotation and rotor locking requirements of part 33 of the Federal Aviation Regulations (FARs).

✈ 33.78-1
Turbine Engine Power-Loss and Extreme Conditions of Rain and Hail
(2/8/00) (ANE-110)
Provides guidance and acceptable methods, but not the only methods, that may be used to demonstrate compliance with the requirements contained under Title 14 of

6/15/00

the Code of Federal Regulations (14 CFR), part 33, sections 33.78(a)(2) and 33.78(c).

33.83
Turbine Engine Vibration Survey
(2/14/97) (ANE-110)
Provides information and guidance concerning acceptable means, but not the only means, of compliance with part 33 of the Federal Aviation Regulation (FAR) applicable to vibration tests.

35.37-1
Composite Propeller Blade Fatigue Substantiation
(5/11/93) (ANE-110)
Provides guidance and an acceptable method, but not the only method, by which composite propeller blades can be fatigue for determination of safe vibrating loading, as required by FAR Part 35.37.

35.37-1, Chg. 1
(9/7/93) (ANE-110)

36-1G
Noise Levels for U.S. Certificated and Foreign Aircraft
(8/27/97) (AEE-110)
Provides noise level data for airplanes certificated under FAR Part 36. Noise level data for foreign airplanes certificated to ICAO Annex 16 standards are also provided in a separate appendix for informational purposes.

36-2C
Measured or Estimated (Uncertificated) Airplane Noise Levels
(2/12/86) (AEE-110)
Provides estimates of noise levels or measured noise levels from airplanes not certificated to FAR Part 36.

36-3G
Estimated Airplane Noise Levels in A-Weighted Decibels
(4/2/96) (AEE-110)
Provides lists of estimated airplane noise levels in units of A-weighted sound levels in decibels (dBA). A-weighted levels were estimated for each airplane as they might occur during type certification tests conducted under Appendixes A,B, and C of Federal Aviation Regulations Part 36.

36-4B
Noise Certification Handbook
(3/23/88) (AEE-3)
Promotes uniformity of implementation of the noise certification requirements of Part 36 of the Federal Aviation Regulations (FAR) by presenting technically acceptable test, analysis, and documentation procedures for subsonic turbojet airplanes that may be used by applicants for demonstrating compliance with Part 36. Where appropriate, FAA policy governing such certifications is reviewed.

39-1A
Jig Fixtures; Replacement of Wing Attach Angles and Doublers on Douglas Model DC-3 Series Aircraft Airworthiness Directive 66-18-2
(3/5/70) (AFS-340)
Describes methods of determining that jig fixtures used in the replacement of the subject attached angles and doublers meet the requirements of Airworthiness Directive 66-18-2.

✈ 39-6S
Summary of Airworthiness Directives, Announcement of Availability
(8/10/98) (AFS-610)
Announces the availability of the Summary of Airworthiness Directives 1998 edition in paper, microfiche, and electronic CD-ROM and bulletin board system, and also provides information for ordering these publications.

39-7C
Airworthiness Directives
(11/16/95) (AFS-340/AFS-613)
Provides guidance and information to owners and operators of aircraft concerning their responsibility for complying with airworthiness directives (AD) and recording AD compliance in the appropriate maintenance records

43-2B
Minimum Barometry for Calibration and Test of Atmospheric Pressure Instruments
(10/16/80) (AFS-343)
Provides guidance material which may be used to determine the adequacy of barometers used in the calibration of aircraft static instruments and presents information concerning the general operation, calibration, and maintenance of such barometers.

43-3A
Nondestructive Testing in Aircraft
(5/11/93) (AFS-330)
Reviews the basic principles underlying nondestructive testing.
SN 5007-00208-4.
$4.50 Supt. Docs.

43-4A
Corrosion Control for Aircraft
(7/25/91) (AFS-340)
Summarizes current available data regarding identification and treatment of corrosive attack on aircraft structure and engine materials.
SN 050-007-01044-3.
$13.00 Supt. Docs.

43-6A
Automatic Pressure Altitude Encoding Systems and Transponders Maintenance and Inspection Practices
(11/11/77) (AFS-310)
Provides information on the installation encoding altimeters based upon recently acquired operating experience and on the maintenance of ATC transponders.

43-7
Ultrasonic Testing for Aircraft
(9/24/74) (AFS-310)
Describes methods used in ultrasonic nondestructive testing, discusses the many advantages, and points out the simplicity of the tests. Contains many illustrations.
SN 050-007-00282-3.
$1.75 Supt. Docs.

43-9C
Maintenance Records
(6/8/98) (AFS-340)
Describes methods, procedures and practices determined to be acceptable for showing compliance with the general aviation maintenance record-making and

record-keeping requirements of Title 14 of the Code of Federal Regulations (14 CFR) parts 43 and 91. This material is issued for guidance and outlines several methods of compliance with the regulations.

43-10A
Mechanical Work Performed on U.S. and Canadian registered Aircraft
(2/25/83) (AFS-340)
Provides updated information and guidance to aircraft owners/operators and maintenance personnel concerning mechanical work performed on U.S. registered aircraft by Canadian maintenance personnel and on Canadian registered aircraft by U.S. maintenance personnel and on Canadian registered aircraft by U.S. maintenance personnel.

43-11
Reciprocating Engine Overhaul Terminology and Standards
(4/7/76) (AFS-340)
Discusses engine overhaul terminology and standards that are used by the aviation industry.

43-12A
Preventive Maintenance
(10/28/83) (AFS-340)
Provides information concerning preventive maintenance, who may perform it, the standards of performance applicable to it, authority for approving aircraft for return to service, and the applicable recording requirements. It also clarifies those areas most frequently misunderstood in the past, and explains the recent changes in the rules concerning preventive maintenance.

43-14
Maintenance of Weather Radar Radomes
(2/24/77) (AFS-350)
Provides guidance material useful to repair facilities in the maintenance of weather radomes.

43-15
Recommended Guidelines for Instrument Shops
(8/15/77) (AFS-350)
Provides guidelines concerning environmental conditions for instrument repair and overhaul shops and information on calibration of test equipment.
Provides information on obtaining printed copies of this document or electronic access to it.
Provides information on obtaining printed copies of this document or electronic access to it.

✈ 43-16A
Aviation Maintenance Alerts.
(9/3/99) (AFS-640)
Issued monthly, the Aviation Maintenance Alerts are prepared from information submitted by persons who operate and maintain civil aeronautical products. The Alerts provide a uniform means through which safety and service experience may be interchanged. The intent of this publication is to improve safety and service reliability of aeronautical products.
(Available on a subscription basis from the Superintendent of Documents, P.O. Box 371954, Pittsburgh, PA 15250-7954.)

43-17
Methods, Techniques, and Practices Acceptable to the Administrator Governing the Installation, Removal, or Changes of Identification Data and Identification Plates
(9/5/79) (AFS-340)
Provides information and guidance concerning the installation, removal, or change of identification data and identification plates on aircraft, aircraft engines, propellers, and propeller blades and hubs.

43-203B
Altimeter and Static System Tests and Inspections
(6/20/79) (AFS-350)
Contains acceptable methods for testing altimeters and static systems. Also provides general information concerning the test equipment used and precautions to be taken when performing such tests.

✈ 43-205
Guidance for Selecting Chemical Agents and Process for Depainting and General Cleaning of Aircraft and Aviation Products (9/25/98) (AFS-340)
Describes an acceptable means, but not the only means,, for selecting and testing alternatives to chemical agents and/or processes currently required by some manufacturers' maintenance instructions, including instructions for continuing airworthiness.

43.9-1E
Instructions for Completion of AA Form 337 (OMB No. 2120-0020), Major Repair and Alteration (Airframe, Powerplant, Propeller, or Appliance)
(5/21/87) (AFS-340)
Provides instructions for completing FAA Form 337, Major Repair and Alteration (Airframe, Powerplant, Propeller, or Appliance).

✈ 43.13-1B
Acceptable Methods, Techniques and Practices– Aircraft Inspection and Repair (9/8/98) (AFS-610)
Contains methods, techniques, and practices acceptable to the Administrator for inspection and repair of nonpressurized areas of civil aircraft only when there are no manufacturer repair or maintenance instructions.
SN 050-007-00806-6.
$55.00 Supt. Docs.

43.13-2A
Acceptable Methods, Techniques, and Practices Aircraft Alterations (Includes Chg. 1).
(6/9/77) (AFS-340)
Contains methods, techniques, and practices acceptable to the Administrator for use in altering civil aircraft.
SN 050-007-00625-0.
$9.00 Supt. Docs.

43.13-2A, Chg. 2
(10/30/89)
SN 050-007-00848-1.
$1.00 Supt. Docs.

45-2A
Identification and Registration Marking
(4/16/92) (AIR-230)

Provides guidance and information concerning the identification and marking requirements of Federal Aviation Regulations (FAR) Part 45, and describes an acceptable means, but not the sole means, of compliance with the regulations.

45-3
Installation, Removal, or Change of Identification Data and Identification Plates on Aircraft Engines,
(11/6/85) (AIR-200)
Provides information and guidance concerning the installation, removal, or change of identification data and identification plates on aircraft engines, and identifies an acceptable means, but not the only means, of compliance with FAR Part 45.

Airmen

Subject No. 60

60-4A
Pilot's Spatial Disorientation
(2/9/83) (AFS-840)
Acquaints pilots with the hazards of disorientation caused by loss of visual reference with the surface.

60-6B
Airplane Flight Manuals (AFM), Approved Manual Materials, Markings, and Placards Airplanes
(9/25/80) (AFS-820)
Calls attention to the regulatory requirements relating to the subject and provides information to aid pilots to comply with these requirements.

✈60-11C
Test Aids and Materials That May Be Used by Airman Knowledge Testing Applicants
(4/26/99) (AFS-630)
Provides information concerning test aids and materials that may be used by applicants taking airman knowledge tests.

60-22
Aeronautical Decision Making
(12/13/91) (AFS-800)
Provides introductory material, background information, and reference material on aeronautical decision making. Provides a systematic approach to risk assessment and stress management in aviation, illustrates how personal attitudes can influence decision

✈ 60-25D
Reference Materials and Subject Matter Knowledge Codes for Airman Knowledge Testing
(6/9/00) (AFS-630)
Appendixes 1 and 2 contain the latest list of reference materials and subject matter knowledge codes for airman knowledge testing.

✈ 60-26B
Announcement of Availability: Flight Standards Service Airman Training and Testing Information
(6/8/00) (AFS-630)
Provides Flight Standards Service on airman training and testing materials website information. The airman certification knowledge and skill testing information is critical to flight safety and comprises the FAA's standards for airman certification testing.

60-28
English Language Skill Standards Required by 14 CFR Parts 61,63, and 65
(9/23/97) (AFS-630)
Provides guidance for airman applicants, training organizations, designated examiners, and aviation safety inspectors in determining English language skills required for airman certification under Title 14 of the Code of Federal Regulations (14 CFR) parts 61,63 and 65.

✈60-29
Renumbering of Airman Training and Testing Publications
(2/1/99) (AFS-630)
Announces the renumbering of airman training and testing materials published by the Airman Testing Standards Branch, AFS-630, Oklahoma City, OK.

61-9B
Pilot Transition Courses for Complex Single Engine and Light, Twin-Engine Airplanes
(1/15/74) (AFS-630)
A guide to the procedures and standards to be followed for a thorough and comprehensive checkout in modern single- and twin-engine aircraft.
SN 050-007-00226-2.
$3.00 Supt. Docs.

61-10A
Private and Commercial Pilots Refresher Courses
(9/27/72) (AFS-630)
Provides a syllabus of study requirements and describes the areas of training that should be emphasized.
SN 050-011-00060-7.
$3.75 Supt. Docs.

61-23C
Pilot's Handbook of Aeronautical Knowledge
(7/10/97) (AFS-630)
Provides basic knowledge that is essential for pilots. Introduces pilots to the broad spectrum of knowledge that will be needed as they progress in their pilot training. Except for the Code of Federal Regulations pertinent to civil aviation, most of the knowledge areas applicable to pilot certification are presented. This handbook is useful to beginning pilots, as well as those pursuing more advanced pilot certificates.
SN 050-011-00078-1.
$13.00 Supt. Docs.

61-27C
Instrument Flying Handbook (Rev 1980).
(11/5/79) (AFS-630)
Provides the pilot with basic information needed to acquire an FAA instrument rating. It is designed for the reader who holds at least a private pilot certificate and is knowledgeable in all areas covered in AC 61-23B, "Pilot's Handbook of Aeronautical Knowledge."
SN 050-007-00585-7.
$11.50 Supt. Docs.

✈61-65D
Certification: Pilot and Flight Instructors and Ground Instructors

(9/20/99) (AFS-840)
Provides guidance for pilots and flight instructors on the certification standards, written test procedures, and other requirements contained in FAR Part 61.

61-67B
Stall Spin Awareness Training
(5/17/91) (AFS-840)
Explains the stall and spin awareness training required under FAR Part 61 and offers guidance to flight instructors who provide that training. Informs pilots of the airworthiness standards for the type certification of small airplanes prescribed in FAR 23.221 concerning spin maneuvers and emphasizes the importance of observing restrictions which prohibit the intentional spinning of certain airplanes.

61-83D
Nationally Scheduled FAA-Approved Industry-Conducted Flight Instructor Refresher Clinics (FIRC)
(9/20/95) (AFS-840)
Provides guidance for the preparation of training course outlines (TCO) for FAA-approved industry conducted FIRC's under Amendment 61-25 to the FAR, which was adopted 4/13/94.

61-84B
Role of Preflight Preparation
(3/18/85) (AFS-840)
Modifies and updates the flight information available to pilots as a result of changes in the basic Airmen Information Manual format.

61-89D
Pilot Certificates: Aircraft Type Ratings
(2/21/91) (AFS-840)
Provides a generic type rating curriculum that may serve as a basis for schools to develop a training requirements of Federal Aviation Regulations Parts 61 and 141.

61-91H
Pilot Proficiency Award Program
(4/26/96) (AFS-800)
Expands the Pilot Proficiency Award Program to 20 phases and makes special provision for seaplane-rated pilots to obtain "seawings."

61-94
Pilot Transition Course For Self-Launching Or Powered Sailplanes (Motorgliders)
(7/31/84) (AFS-840)
Provides recommendations, but is not the only means, that may be used by glider pilots who desire to transition into sailplanes or gliders with self-launching capability.

61-98A
Currency and Additional Qualification Requirements for Certificated Pilots
(3/26/91) (AFS-840)
Provides information for certificated pilots and flight instructors to use in complying with flight review required by FAR Section 61.56, the recent flight experience requirements of FAR Section 61.57, and the general limitations contained in FAR Section 61.31(d), (e), and (g). It also provides guidance regarding transition to other makes and models of aircraft.

61-107
Operations of Aircraft at Altitudes Above 25,000 Feet MSL and/or MACH numbers (Mmo) Greater Than .75
(1/23/91) (AFS-820)
Alerts pilots transitioning to complex, high-performance aircraft which are capable of operating at high altitudes and high airspeeds of the need to be knowledgeable of the special physiological and aerodynamic considerations involved within this realm of operations.

✈61-111A
Announcement of Availability: FAA-S-8081-4C, Instrument Rating Practical Test Standards (PTS) for Airplane, Helicopter, Power Lift
(12/15/98) (AFS-630)
Provides information on obtaining printed copies of this document or electronic access to it.

✈61-118A
Announcement of Availability: FAA-S-8081-14, Private Pilot Practical Test Standards (Airplane)
(3/1/99) (AFS-630)
Provides information on obtaining printed copies of this document or electronic access to it

61-121
Announcement of Availability: FAA-S-8081-10A, Aircraft Dispatcher Practical Test Standard
(5/17/95) (AFS-630)
Announces availability of this publication from the Superintendent of Documents.

✈61-122C
Announcement of Availability: FAA-S-8081-5C, Airline Transport Pilot and Aircraft Type Rating PTS for Airplane, Chg.1
(3/1/99) (AFS-630)
Provides information on obtaining printed copies of this document or electronic access to it.

61-123
Announcement of Availability: Practical Test Standards (Rotorcraft) FAA-S-8081-7A, FAA-S-8081-15, FAA-S-8081-16
(3/5/96) (AFS-630)
Announces the availability of FAA-S-8081-7A, Flight Instructor Practical Test Standards for Rotorcraft; FAA-S-8081-15, Private Pilot Practical Test Standards for Rotorcraft; FAA-S-8081-16, Commercial Pilot Practical Test Standards for Rotorcraft; and, provides information on obtaining printed copies or electronic access to these documents.

61-124
Announcement of Availability: FAA-S-8081-17, Private Pilot Practical Test Standards for Lighter-Than-Air (Balloon/Airship)
(5/15/96) (AFS-630)
Announces the availability of FAA-S-8081-17, Private Pilot Practical Test Standards for Lighter-Than-Air (Balloon/Airship), and provides information on obtaining printed copies or electronic access to this document.

61-125

6/15/00

Announcement of Availability: Commercial Pilot Practical Test Standards: FAA-S-8081-18 and FAA-S-8081-12A,
(4/30/97) (AFS-630)
Announces the availability of FAA-S-8081-18, Commercial Pilot Practical Test Standards for Lighter-Than-Air, and FAA-S-8081-12A, Commercial Pilot Practical Test Standards for Airplane; and provides information on obtaining printed copies or electronic access to these documents.

61-129
Announcement of Availability: FAA-S-8081-20, Airline Transport Pilot Aircraft Type Rating PTS for Helicopter
(8/12/98) (AFS-630)
Announces the availability of FAA-S-8081-20, Airline Transport Pilot and Aircraft Type Rating Practical Test Standards for Helicopter, from the Superintendent of Documents, and provides information on obtaining printed copies or electronic access.

(1/30/76) (AFS-640)
Provides information to prospective airframe and powerplant mechanics and other persons interested in FAA certification of aviation mechanics.
SN 050-007-00331-5.
$8.50 Supt. Docs.

65-5B
Parachute Rigger Senior/Master-certification Guide
(7/25/88) (AFS-630)
Provides information to persons interested

APPENDIX

IV

Aviation Business Marketing Suggestions

1. Tailor your marketing efforts to the specific needs of your customers. Doctors, farmers, businesspeople, college students, and homemakers all have different interests.
2. Stress aviation's value to the community: total payroll, total taxes paid, unusual services performed.
3. Series of interviews (newspaper, radio, TV) with local prominent citizen/flyers on "Why I Fly."
4. Interesting vacation or family trips taken by local aviators could be publicized.
5. "Create" news from the preparation efforts for an open house. Examples: painting or refurbishing your buildings (How many gallons of paint? How many worker hours? Who is doing the painting?); polishing up your planes for display; your staff meeting to discuss plans, and so on. Obtain a photographer for coverage.
6. Identify local newspeople/pilots and involve them in developing aviation promotions.
7. Schedule a cross-country competitive flight. Round-robin course, fuel stop, touch down points with the winner determined on the basis of time and fuel economy.
8. Fly your mayor to visit the mayor of an adjacent town to invite him or her to an aviation activity on your airport. Take along a newspaper or TV representative.
9. Provide free flight instruction to a local radio celebrity or public figure.
10. Erect a banner or streamer across a busy intersection in the downtown area or neighborhood shopping center for your open house.
11. Arrange a helicopter rescue demonstration in cooperation with your local hospital.
12. Plan a day honoring the oldest active pilot in your city, county, or state.
13. Working through a local supply source, arrange to "fly in" the refreshments for your (or some other) aviation activity.
14. Consider a planned group flight. Dawn patrols, breakfast flights, fly-ins have all been used successfully.
15. Plan a "March on the Shopping Center" where you supply posters, banners, pennants to turn the whole center into a promotion.
16. Get employees involved in the program by talking to their outside professional and social groups.
17. Join other operators in selecting a "Ms. or Mr. Aviation" from among local pilots. After he or she is selected, go after newspaper and broadcast publicity—"Head Table Guest" appearances at local business luncheons, dinners, and so forth.
18. Consider displaying a new aircraft in a bank lobby, shopping mall, department store, city park, or parking lot. (Arrange for security and salespeople).

19. Offer a special price on a flight instruction program given as a high school or college graduation present.
20. Don't forget the traditional "penny-a-pound rides" as a means of getting people to an open house.
21. Offer free flight instruction to the high school student who submits the best essay on "Why I'd like to learn to fly"; publicize the contest and winner.
22. Hold a week day open house just for women. Get any local 99's or local women pilots to hostess and give demonstration rides. Announce through women's clubs, garden clubs, church groups, and so on; invite the media.
23. When distributing invitations to aviation activities, distribute them where people are: downtown on a busy street corner, outside a local movie as it lets out, at drive-ins, at restaurants, at other types of activities.
24. Consider a "teaser" advertising program on billboards and newspapers. Give part of the message initially, and build upon it later.
25. Share the proceeds of contests and programs with charity or public service groups in order to get them working with you, promoting aviation activities.
26. Tourist or traveler guide published in the area? "What's going on" column in the newspaper? Be sure to get your dates listed with them.
27. Develop an "adult education course" on aviation and offer through a local school.
28. Get a senior high school class, a Boy Scout Troop, or other organization to sell tickets in advance of a promotion in return for a share in the proceeds.
29. If you have a local resort with a landing strip and a good restaurant, arrange a "Fly to Lunch" special. You sell special meal tickets that cover the cost of transportation and meal. Both you and the resort owner promote and benefit.
30. Place your advertisements in a different place—try the society page, the financial page, or maybe even next to the obituary column.
31. Contact local Air National Guard, Air Reserve, and Naval Air Reserve regarding static military aircraft displays and fly-bys. Include opportunity for recruiting booths.
32. Free shuttle bus to your special event from some large shopping center or congregation points.
33. Consider special interest groups. Special activities for doctors, undertakers, salespeople, executives.
34. Rent a tent, if necessary, for space or for other desirable reasons.
35. Get a radio or TV personality to do a remote broadcast from your lounge or line.
36. Try week night aviation activities. Consider "Moonlight Air Rides" to see the lights.
37. Get a local women's store or department store to conduct a fashion show in your hangar. Arrange a backdrop of cleaned and polished planes. Consider a drawing for free air rides.
38. For open houses and large crowds, identify everything in your facility with signs and explanation cards. Consider a mimeographed "Guide to a Walking Tour" so visitors can know what they should see.
39. A winter time (bad weather) activity: a series of movies on flying to keep interest up. May use a school facility or a restaurant's private dining room. Should consider light refreshments.
40. For public activities make your premises attractive: clean up, paint as needed, wear uniforms and jackets, have floral arrangements in office and lounge.
41. Hire a high school or veterans' band or drum and bugle corps for music at special programs.
42. Get a youth group to offer $1.00 car washes on your ramp while people visit the facility; publicize in advance.
43. Try ten-minute simulator "rides" for twenty-five cents.
44. At various professional programs and meetings display pilot aids and accessories. Have someone available to explain their use.
45. Make your lounge or ready room available to bridge groups.

46. Arrange for or provide babysitting service for flying parents.
47. Sponsor a photo contest—your airport, aircraft, or facility is the subject. Winner receives a number of free flying lessons.
48. Introductory business flights to the businessperson who has to travel during the week. He or she feels the convenience and discovers how easy it would be to learn to fly.
49. Consider a special program for flying farmers. Suggest that they each bring a nonflyer.
50. Develop a "trial order" package to promote air cargo shipments. Invite shipping agent or traffic manager to "ride the trip" with you.
51. Work with hospitals and doctors in developing an air ambulance service. Demonstrate with a trial run.
52. Get involved in an air education program with the local high school or junior college.
53. Develop a package of ideas to keep graduates of your flight schools in touch and proud of the association they have with you.
    - Regular meetings with films or slides to spark interest
    - Brochures and mail-outs to provide a regular source of information
    - Periodic special speakers on key aviation topics.

APPENDIX

V

Aviation Management Audit

Aviation Management Audit

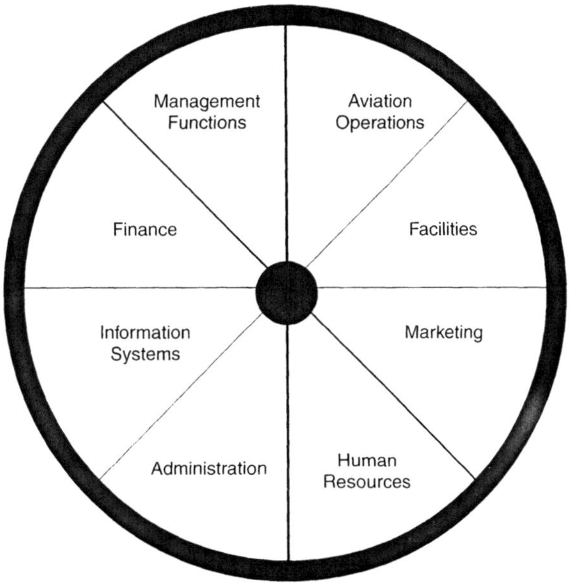

A Comprehensive Organizational Audit

Management Audit For Aviation Organizations

A systematic comprehensive organization review to be used by aviation managers in analyzing, evaluating and developing their business

Developed by:
John D. Richardson, Ph.D.

Introduction

The management audit is a systematic, checklist approach to the analysis of your organization, its functions, operations, and decisions. The audit reviews your whole business, as well as the separate components.

Just as a healthy person will go to his or her physician for a periodic check-up, managers can use the audit as a means of determining the condition of their businesses. It becomes the means for conducting a systematic, critical and unbiased review and appraisal. The main purpose is to help the manager better the position of his or her company; to improve the overall health of the organization.

There are three major steps in this audit:

1. The compilation of your business data, and the completion of the checklist.
2. The critical review, analysis, and evaluation of all information obtained by the audit.
3. Determining future action required to improve the health and position of the company.

The benefit derived from conducting an audit is directly related to the attitude of the participant. In order to maximize this benefit, you are encouraged to:

1. Consider each item in the audit seriously, thoughtfully, and with a view for the future.
2. Accept that every item may not apply 100 percent to your situation, but look for the value in each topic.
3. Make the audit a useful self-appraisal tool, sharing ideas and views when appropriate.

In order to make the audit a valuable part of your plan for the future, you are encouraged to use the following procedure in completing this booklet:

1. Complete the entire management audit, answering each question with as much objectivity as possible.
2. Next, start at the beginning and review your answers. Assign a plus (+) or minus (–) for each item you feel is a major strength or deficiency in your organization.
3. Complete the summary and evaluation sheet, list those areas in which you would like to initiate some action, and assign priorities to accomplish selected goals.
4. Establish future dates for reviewing the audit and determining your progress.
5. Follow through with additional audits on an annual basis.

It should be remembered that while the audit is comprehensive, it is only suggestive. The audit will not do the thinking for you. It compares your organization relative to a standard or to other organizations. You must then evaluate your findings and determine your action.

Can You??

- Set aside time to review the audit
- Have someone else take those incoming calls
- Review each item carefully and deliberately
- Remember, it's your business and your future you are evaluating

Contents

Part I—Management Functions Audit

Major concern should be focused upon the top-level managerial guidance provided the organization. Are the key management functions of planning, organizing, directing, and controlling being carried out? What is the status of long-range plans?

Management Functions

A. Planning

	Circle Answer	Evaluation (+) (–)
1. Do you regularly set aside time for planning?	1 **Yes No**	2 ______
2. Have you made a specific effort to set objectives for your organization?	3 **Yes No**	4 ______
3. List your current objectives:		

____

____

____

____

____

____

____

4. Are your objectives:		
a. definite	5 **Yes No**	6 ______
b. clear-cut	7 **Yes No**	8 ______
c. written	9 **Yes No**	10 ______
d. attainable	11 **Yes No**	12 ______
5. Are objectives understood by those involved in their attainment?	13 **Yes No**	14 ______
6. Are objectives accepted by those involved in their attainment?	15 **Yes No**	16 ______
7. Are your objectives current?	17 **Yes No**	18 ______
a. What is the date you last devoted time to listing objectives in writing?	______________	
b. Are your objectives responsive to change?	19 **Yes No**	20 ______
8. Do you make a specific effort to forecast future conditions?	21 **Yes No**	22 ______

Part II—Operations Audit

This portion of the audit is concerned with those activities primarily operational in nature.

Line Operations

Includes that portion of the business aimed at the incoming customer: the meeting, parking, and services of the aircraft.

	Circle Answer	Evaluation (+) (–)
1. Is your flight line visible and identified to incoming aircraft?	1 **Yes No**	2 ______
2. Is your flight line operational (easy to understand by the transient)?	3 **Yes No**	4 ______
3. Do tower personnel know the services offered by your business?	5 **Yes No**	6 ______
4. Can the tower direct the transient to your place of business?	7 **Yes No**	8 ______
5. Do you use radio assistance?		
a. for incoming planes?	9 **Yes No**	10 ______
b. for line personnel?	11 **Yes No**	12 ______
6. Do you use vehicles to assist incoming aircraft?	13 **Yes No**	14 ______
7. Do you provide training to line personnel on:		
a. aircraft servicing	15 **Yes No**	16 ______
b. appearance	17 **Yes No**	18 ______
c. attitude	19 **Yes No**	20 ______
d. local services	21 **Yes No**	22 ______
e. sales	23 **Yes No**	24 ______
8. Have you planned for line maintenance?	25 **Yes No**	26 ______
9. What courtesy services are available?		
a. line vehicle	27 **Yes No**	28 ______
b. luggage cart	29 **Yes No**	30 ______
c. courtesy car	31 **Yes No**	32 ______
d. refreshments	33 **Yes No**	34 ______

Part III—Facility Audit

The land, physical facilities, and major equipment.

Facilities

1. Are your facilities:
   a. self-owned? 1 Yes No 2 ______
   b. leased? 3 Yes No 4 ______
2. Is your lease for:
   a. one year? 5 Yes No 6 ______
   b. two years? 7 Yes No 8 ______
   c. five years? 9 Yes No 10 ______
   d. ten years? 11 Yes No 12 ______
   e. fifteen years? 13 Yes No 14 ______
   f. twenty or more years? 15 Yes No 16 ______
3. Is your lease with:
   a. airport commission? 17 Yes No 18 ______
   b. city board? 19 Yes No 20 ______
   c. county supervisors? 21 Yes No 22 ______
   d. private owner? 23 Yes No 24 ______
   e. other ______
4. You obtained assistance during lease negotiation from:
   a. lease manual 25 Yes No 26 ______
   b. lawyer 27 Yes No 28 ______
   c. aviation consultant 29 Yes No 30 ______
   d. none 31 Yes No 32 ______
   e. other ______
5. Your lease payments are:
   a. annual cash payments? 33 Yes No 34 ______

Part IV—Marketing Audit

This part deals with the many activities involved in the total marketing effort of the organization.

Market Facts

That necessary information required for the planning and development of an aggressive marketing program.

1. Do you have an overall plan for collecting market facts?	1	**Yes**	**No**	2 ______
2. Is this plan in writing?	3	**Yes**	**No**	4 ______
3. Was a proper market survey made when the business started?	5	**Yes**	**No**	6 ______
4. If not, should a market survey be made now?	7	**Yes**	**No**	8 ______
5. Have the basic sources of market survey data been studied?	9	**Yes**	**No**	10 ______
6. Does the population growth, new competition, or change in competitor methods justify new ways of serving the market?	11	**Yes**	**No**	12 ______
7. Is the major problem of your business a lack of sales?	13	**Yes**	**No**	14 ______
8. What has been the trend in your sales in recent years?				
a. rapid rise	15	**Yes**	**No**	16 ______
b. steady increase	17	**Yes**	**No**	18 ______
c. about level	19	**Yes**	**No**	20 ______
d. declining	21	**Yes**	**No**	22 ______

9. What factors have been determined as responsible for the trend in sales?

____

____

____

10. Have you identified your trading area?	23	**Yes**	**No**	24 ______
11. Has the character of the population in your trading area changed (aside from growth or decline)?	25	**Yes**	**No**	26 ______
12. Has this change affected sales?	27	**Yes**	**No**	28 ______
13. Does the future for your company, in your market, look:				
a. excellent	29	**Yes**	**No**	30 ______
b. good	31	**Yes**	**No**	32 ______

Part V—Human Resources Audit

The personnel in an organization should be considered its greatest asset. As such, the various programs dealing with personnel management become most important.

Staffing

The process of identifying human resource needs and providing for the steady flow of qualified personnel.

1. Do you have a firm procedure to follow in identifying human resource needs? 1 **Yes No** 2 ______

2. Do you have a personnel plan that is derived from the overall business plan? 3 **Yes No** 4 ______

3. Do you use a budget as part of your personnel planning process? 5 **Yes No** 6 ______

4. For the majority of employee positions:

a. do you use job descriptions? 7 **Yes No** 8 ______

b. do you utilize employee specifications? 9 **Yes No** 10 ______

5. List the recruiting techniques you use:

______

______

______

______

6. Do you use:

a. application blanks 11 **Yes No** 12 ______

b. weighted application blanks 13 **Yes No** 14 ______

c. interviewer's checklist 15 **Yes No** 16 ______

d. employment history form 17 **Yes No** 18 ______

e. education history form 19 **Yes No** 20 ______

f. military service form 21 **Yes No** 22 ______

g. request for information from references 23 **Yes No** 24 ______

h. request for medical examination 25 **Yes No** 26 ______

i. test score profile 27 **Yes No** 28 ______

j. contract of employment 29 **Yes No** 30 ______

Part VI—Administration Audit

Administration includes many key areas and becomes the focal point for most organizational activities.

Insurance

Every business is faced with many risks, ranging from minor to catastrophic. Managing these risks calls for an understanding of insurance principles and the selection of desired coverages.

1. **Has management truly analyzed all the major risks to which the company is exposed?** 1 **Yes No** 2 ______

2. **What protection has been provided against each of the risks?**

Risk	Protection
______	______
______	______
______	______
______	______
______	______
______	______
______	______
______	______

3. **Is self-insurance appropriate for your business?** 3 **Yes No** 4 ______

4. **What risks are being absorbed?**
   a. ______
   b. ______
   c. ______

5. **Why?**
   a. ______
   b. ______
   c. ______

6. **Are there any recommendations for reducing risks or getting protection more economically?** 5 **Yes No** 6 ______

Part VII—Information Systems

The manager needs a continuous flow of data to advise him or her of the organization's progress and to enable him or her to control its direction toward desired objectives.

Organization

A key element is the recognition of the need for the organization of information.

1. Have you systematically organized the information flow on your business activity?	1	**Yes**	**No**	2 ______
2. Does your information system cover:				
a. money?	3	**Yes**	**No**	4 ______
b. personnel?	5	**Yes**	**No**	6 ______
c. material?	7	**Yes**	**No**	8 ______
3. Does your information system:				
a. provide an accurate, thorough picture of operating results?	9	**Yes**	**No**	10 ______
b. permit quick comparison of current data with budgeted goals?	11	**Yes**	**No**	12 ______
c. provide a quick comparison of current data with prior years' operating results?	13	**Yes**	**No**	14 ______
d. reveal all possible employee frauds, thefts, waste, and record-keeping errors?	15	**Yes**	**No**	16 ______
e. provide the necessary data for the prompt filing of required reports?	17	**Yes**	**No**	18 ______
f. identify the contribution of each department to the overall organization?	19	**Yes**	**No**	20 ______
g. provide suitable financial statements for use by management and prospective creditors?	21	**Yes**	**No**	22 ______
4. Do you periodically review all procedures, records, forms, and reports that are part of your information system?	23	**Yes**	**No**	24 ______
5. Are your procedures, records, forms, and reports producing the required information at the lowest cost?	25	**Yes**	**No**	26 ______

Money

The information system should cover the movement of money into and out of the business, the reason for its movement and its availability.

6. Do you have a complete accounting system in operation?	27	**Yes**	**No**	28 ______

Part VIII—Finance Audit

Financial skill technically plays a major part in the operation and development of a business. A sound information system is a prerequisite to developing a high level of financial activity.

Financing the Business

A business man may obtain money from many sources to finance his business. He will need to answer questions of how? where? how much? when? why? and cost?

1. In financing your business do you use:

a. equity financing	1	**Yes**	**No**	2	______
b. loans	3	**Yes**	**No**	4	______
c. trade credit	5	**Yes**	**No**	6	______
d. business profits	7	**Yes**	**No**	8	______

2. To what sources do you turn for financing?

a. aircraft ____

____

b. building expansion ____

____

c. new shop equipment ____

____

d. receivables ____

____

____

3. Are you setting aside adequate reserves for the replacement of depreciating or obsolescent assets?	9	**Yes**	**No**	10	______

Financial Analysis

The manager must determine the tools needed for financial analysis, ensure that they are available in his organization and intelligently use them on a regular basis.

4. Have you determined the financial tools you need for the analysis of your business?	11	**Yes**	**No**	12	______

APPENDIX VI

Typical Data Inputs Used as Source Documents for Financial Management

This illustrates some typical business forms and source documents available for use by aviation businesses. For convenience of presentation, they are grouped into three areas; those for operational control purposes, those for marketing purposes, and those for financial purposes. The following pages suggest how these source documents may be organized.

Operational Control Purposes

- Aircraft scheduling books
- Line service slips
- Pilot check-out cards
- Plane cost records
- Applications for training
- Applications for employment
- Aircraft summary sheets
- Unicom log sheets
- Student pilot summary sheet
- Used aircraft appraisal report
- Instructor activity reports
- Contract forms (aerial applicator)
- Aircraft "squawk" card
- Air taxi reports; I, II, III
- Crew data sheets
- Repair tags
- Hangar lease agreement
- Tie-down lease agreement
- Student appointment form
- Flight reports (air taxi)
- Preflight and run-up checks

Marketing Purposes

- Advertising aids
- Student certificates
- Navigation worksheets
- Weather reporting forms
- Stickers and decals
- Aircraft sales calculation sheet
- Guest register
- Prospect worksheet and survey
- Sales department checklist
- Application for credit

Financial Purposes

- Aircraft revenue invoice
- Aircraft rental form
- Time and job ticket
- Time sheet
- Service order form
- Daily summary of shop time
- Invoice (aerial applicator)
- Lease forms
- Charter invoice
- Check forms
- Cash receipts
- Aircraft rental and invoice
- Tach sheets
- Supporting aircraft inventory schedule
- Daily line sales report
- Monthly aircraft report
- Aircraft depreciation record

> Aircraft summary
> Line service invoice
> Aircraft sales invoice
> Parts invoice
> Customer statement
> Bookkeeping system

Financial data of the business information system should move through the organization structure in a logical and efficient manner. The accounting system should receive information on all of the transactions that affect the company resources; and all individuals, both in and out of the organization, should understand the transaction so they can take appropriate action. The following pages contain activity flow charts for the overall system and the basic source documents used in aviation businesses:

> Aircraft rental and flight instruction
> Aircraft sales
> Aircraft charter
> Line sales
> Parts sales
> Service sales
> Payroll
> Cash disbursements and purchases
> Cash receipts

The flow chart graphically depicts the processing of data regarding each of the principal business activities. Individual organizations will vary, but the same basic steps should be followed.

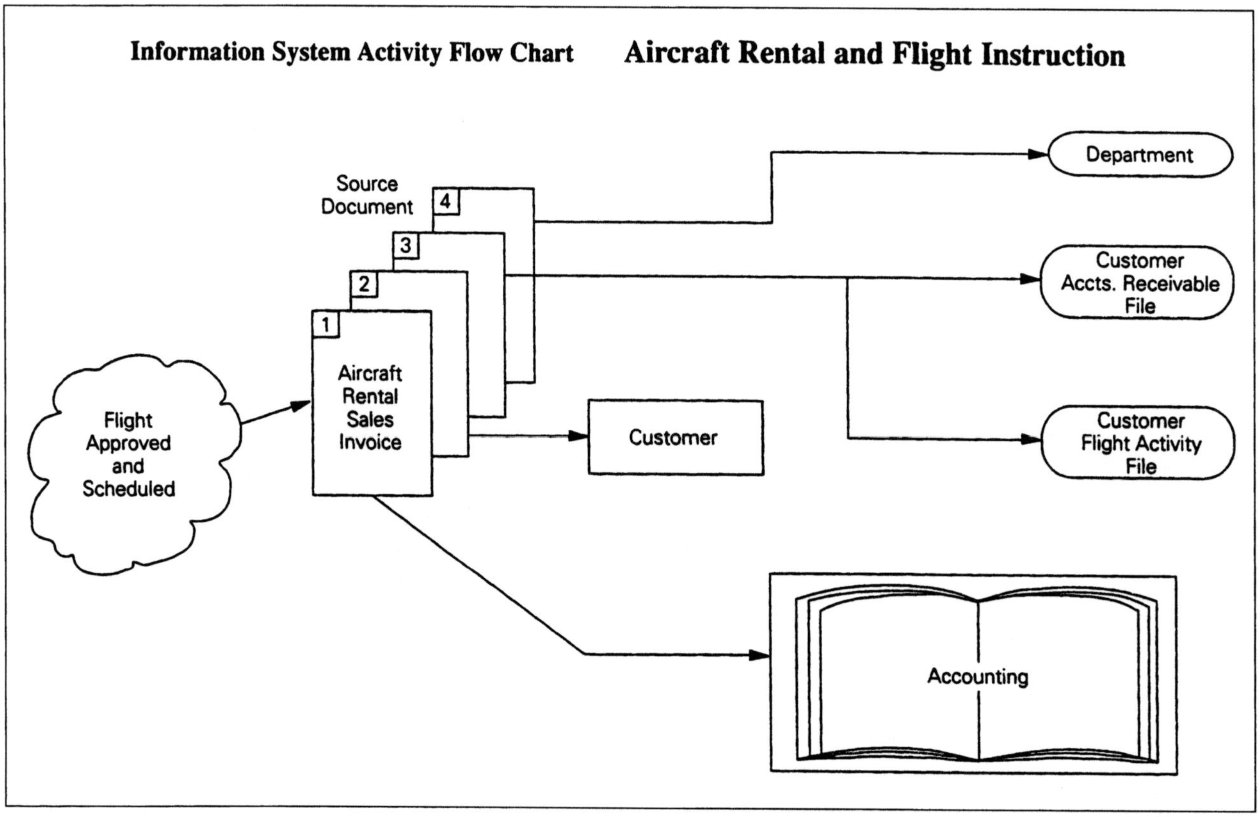

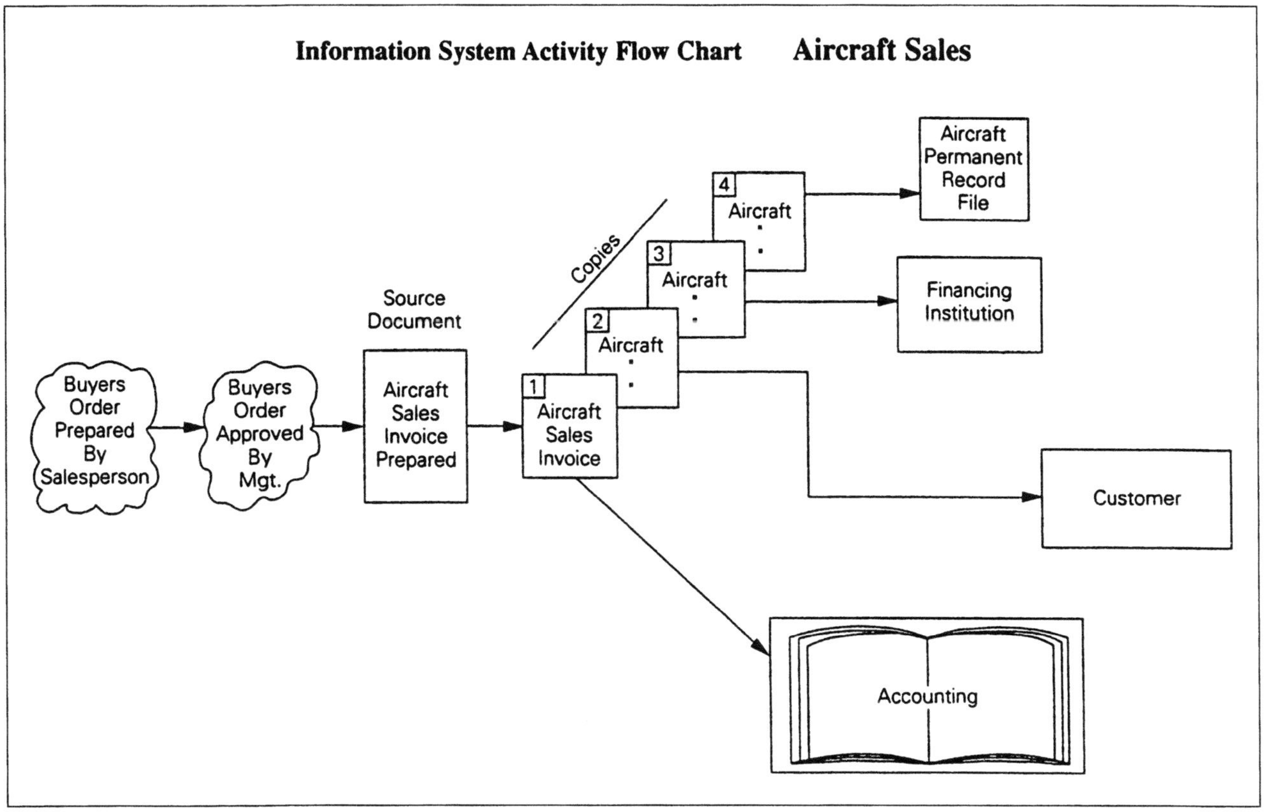
Information System Activity Flow Chart
Aircraft Sales
Buyers Order Prepared By Salesperson
Buyers Order Approved By Mgt.
Source Document
Aircraft Sales Invoice Prepared
Copies
1 Aircraft Sales Invoice
2 Aircraft
3 Aircraft
4 Aircraft
Aircraft Permanent Record File
Financing Institution
Customer
Accounting

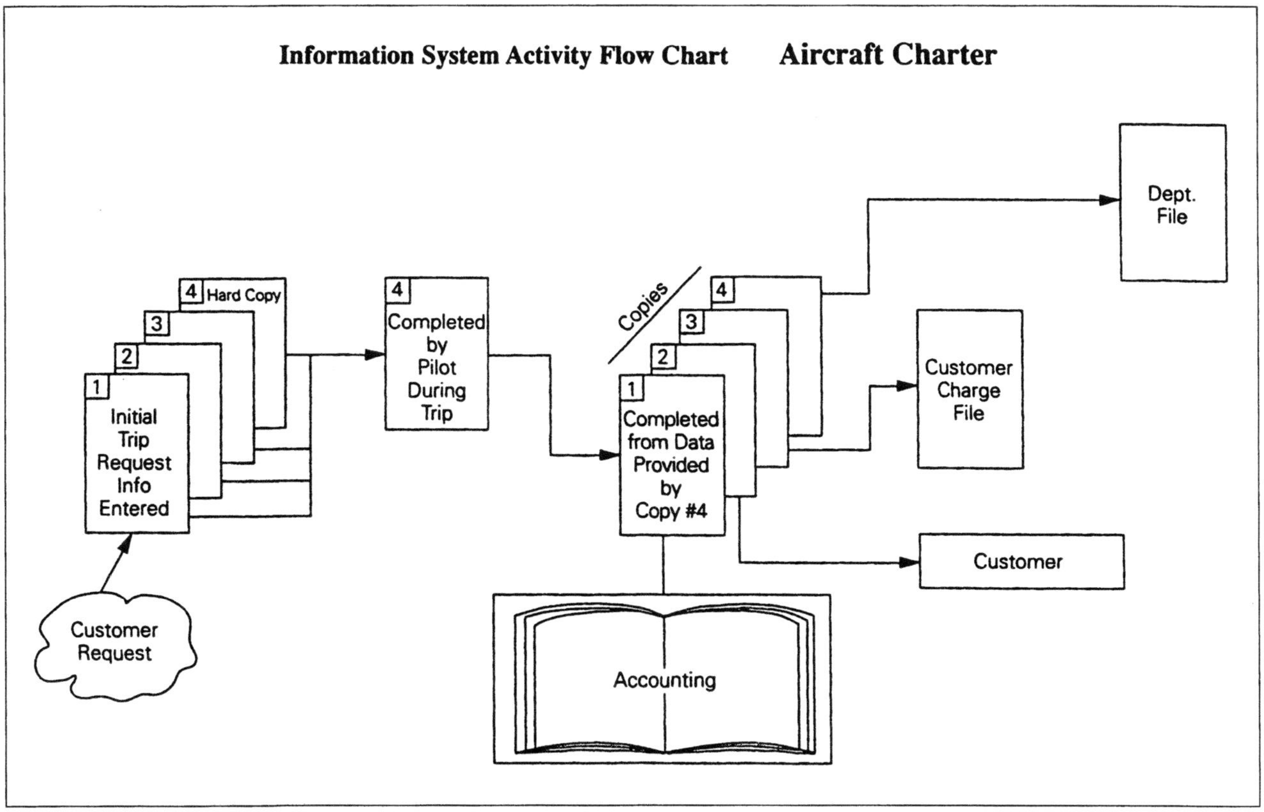
Information System Activity Flow Chart
Aircraft Charter
1 Initial Trip Request Info Entered
2
3
4 Hard Copy
Customer Request
4 Completed by Pilot During Trip
Copies
1 Completed from Data Provided by Copy #4
2
3
4
Dept. File
Customer Charge File
Customer
Accounting

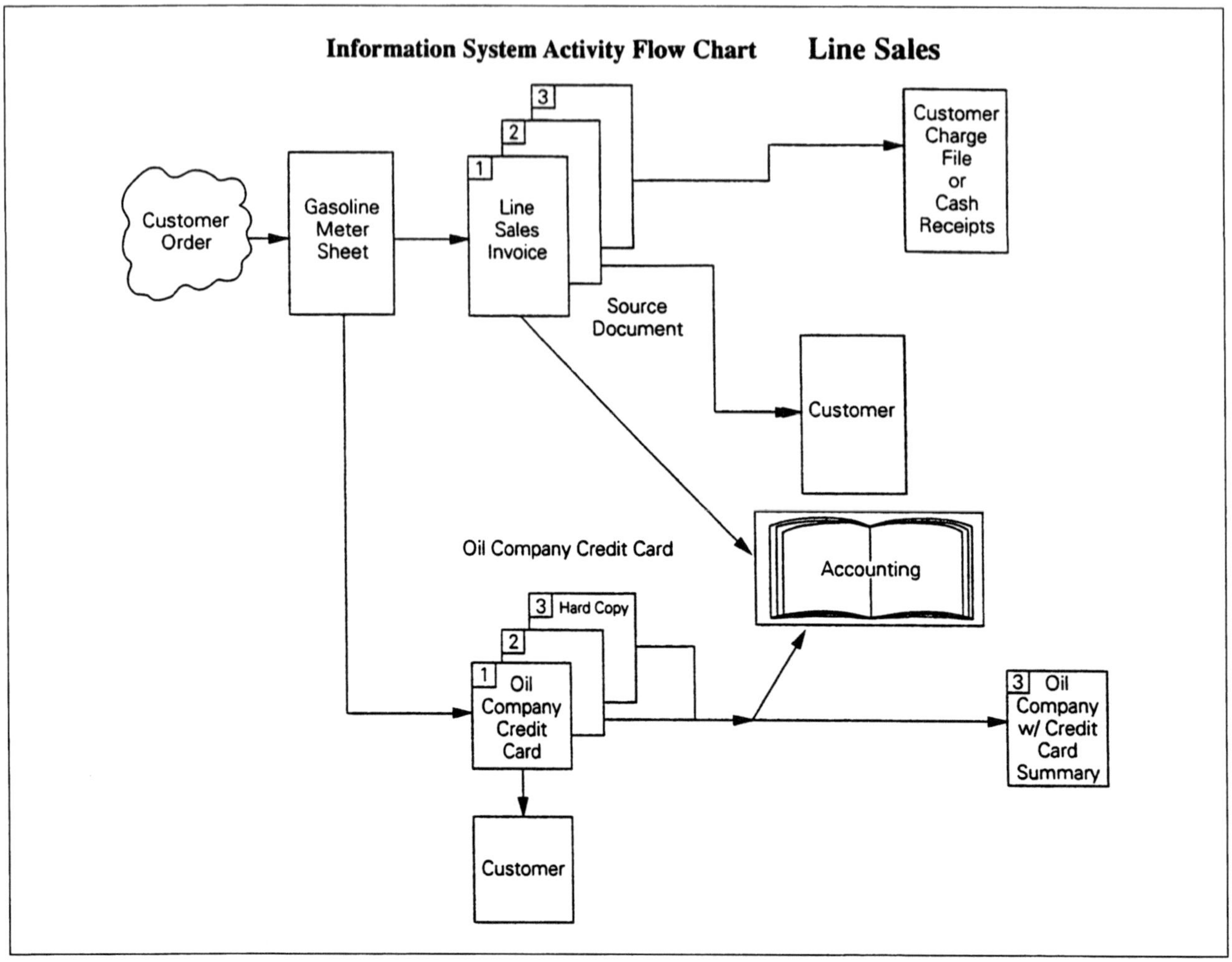
Information System Activity Flow Chart
Line Sales
Customer Order
Gasoline Meter Sheet
1
2
3
Line Sales Invoice
Customer Charge File or Cash Receipts
Source Document
Customer
Accounting
Oil Company Credit Card
3 Hard Copy
2
1 Oil Company Credit Card
3 Oil Company w/ Credit Card Summary
Customer

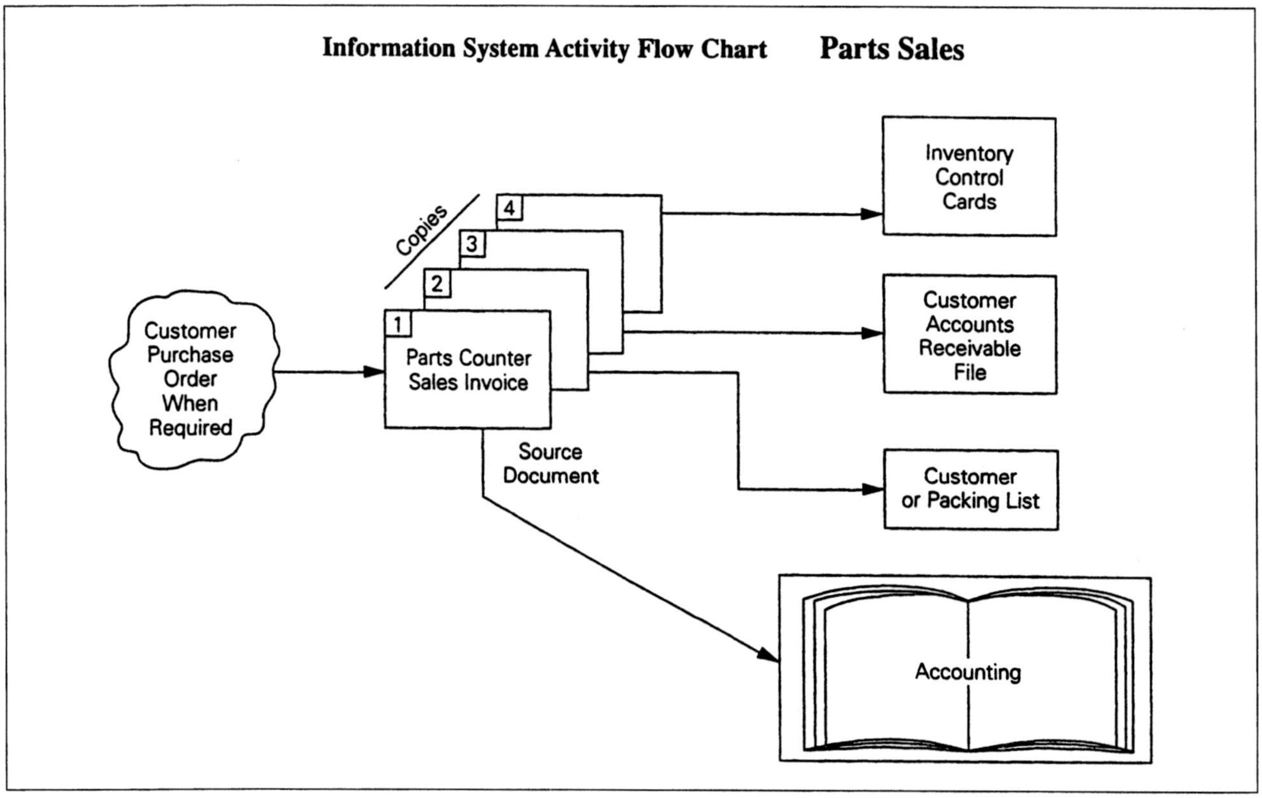
Information System Activity Flow Chart
Parts Sales
Copies
1
2
3
4
Customer Purchase Order When Required
Parts Counter Sales Invoice
Inventory Control Cards
Customer Accounts Receivable File
Customer or Packing List
Source Document
Accounting

Information System Activity Flow Chart Service Sales

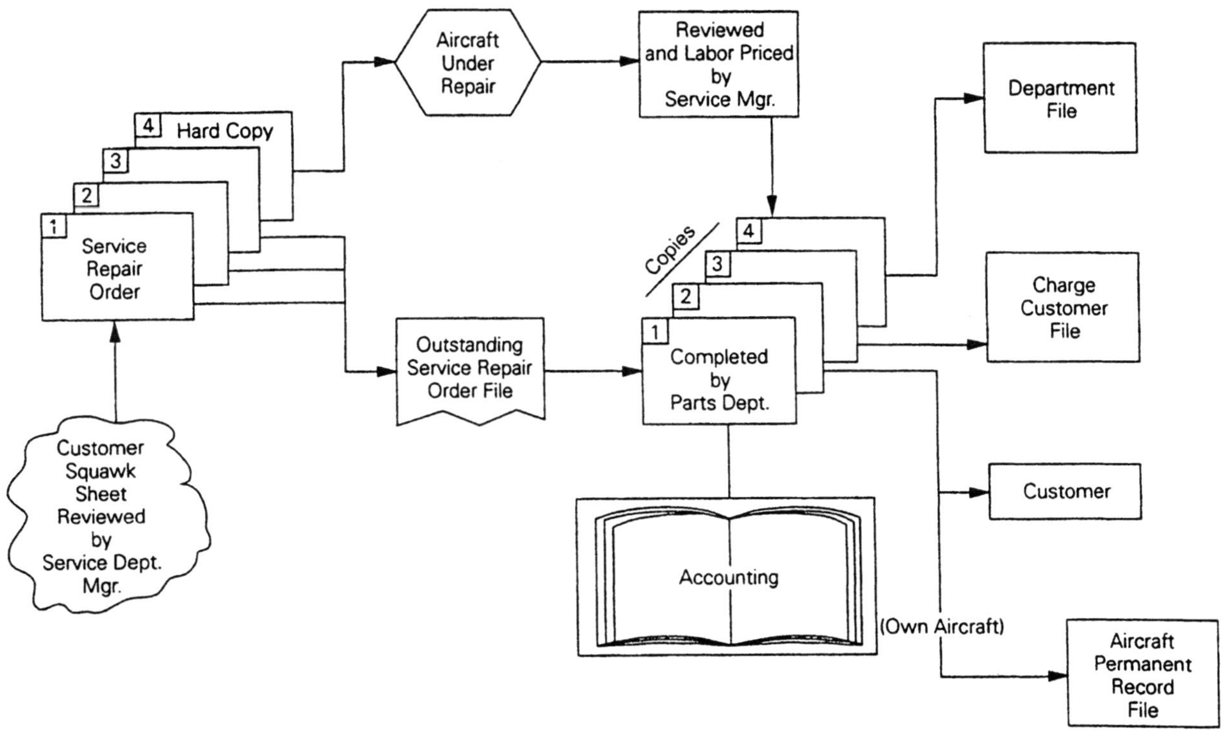

Information System Activity Flow Chart Payroll

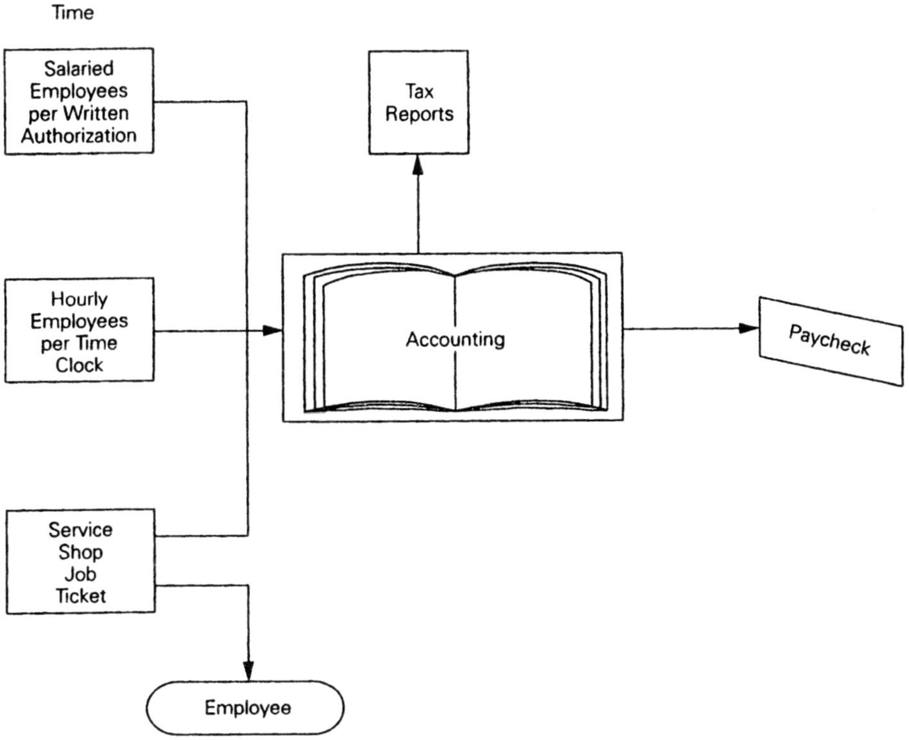

Information System Activity Flow Chart
Cash Disbursements and Purchases

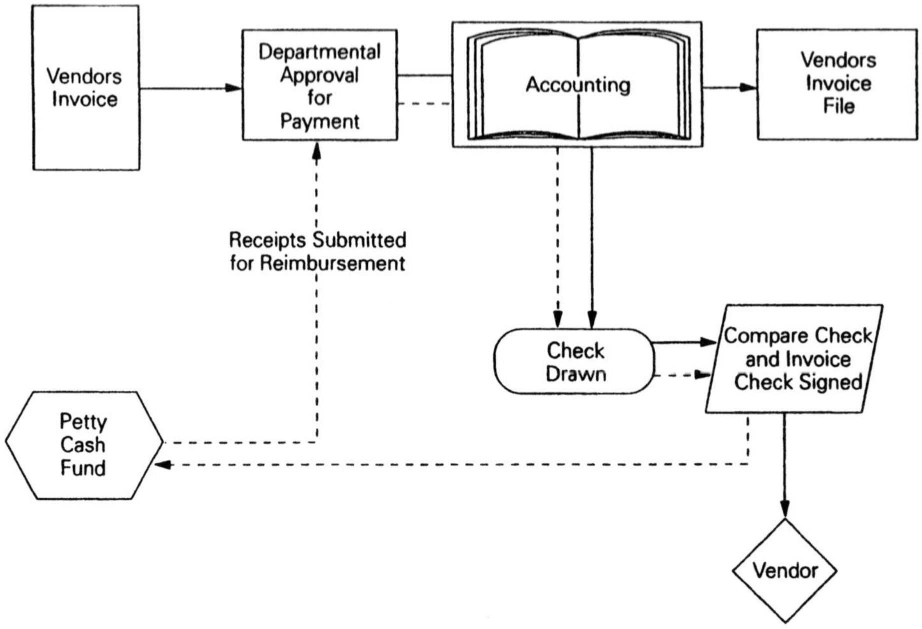

Information System Activity Flow Chart **Cash Receipts**

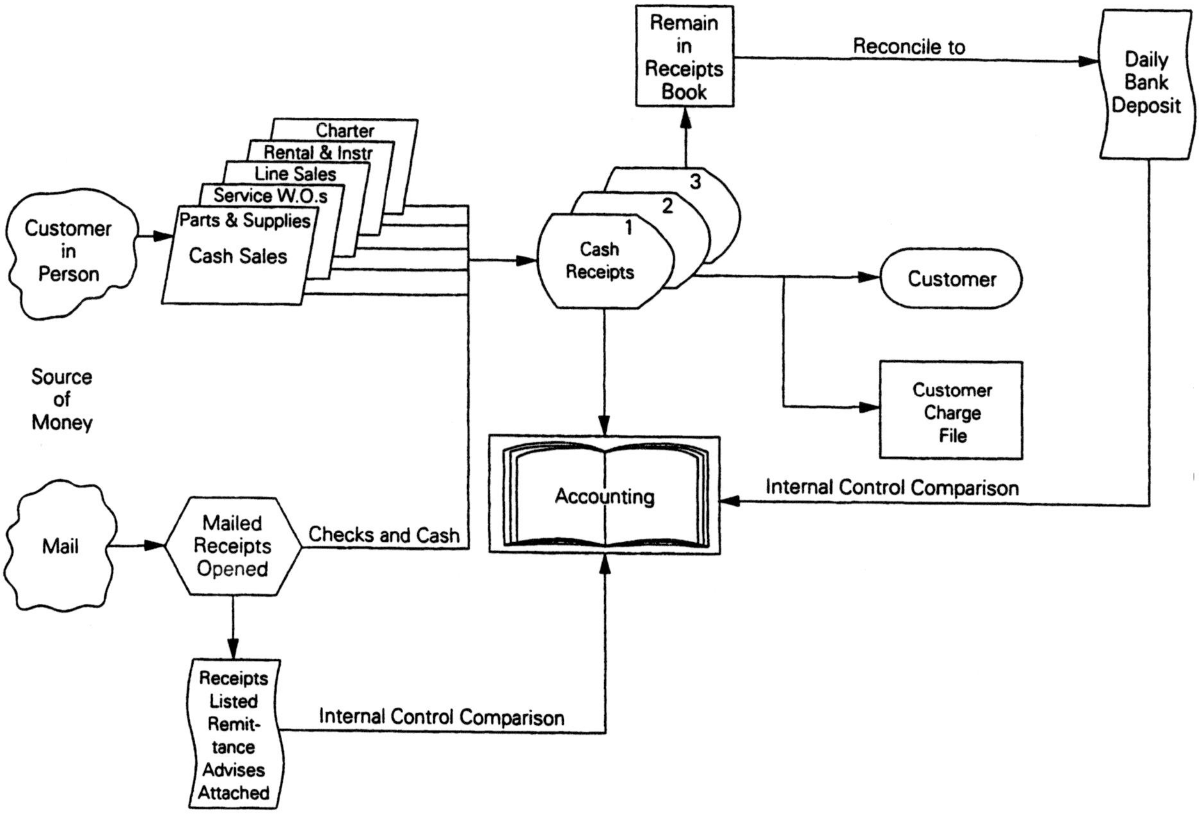

APPENDIX

VII

Front Desk Procedures Manual

Philosophy of Operation

The reception desk is the "front window" of an aviation business. As such, it represents the organization to the public, to the customer, and to the employees. The basic philosophy of the front desk should be to demonstrate to customers that everything possible will be done to give the best aviation service in the area. The reception desk is the hub for all business conducted by the company and is the public relations center. The primary goal is to see that the customer receives the most efficient and courteous service possible. The secondary goal is to ensure that all company procedures and guidelines are followed in achieving a successful front-desk operation.

Daily Operating Schedule

0000–0600	Reduced operations
0600	Limited services available to early customers
0700	Representatives for each department on hand
0800–1200	All departments and functions staffed at normal capacity
1200–1300	Lunch period
1300–1700	All departments and functions staffed at normal capacity
1700–2000	Limited services available, clean up, and prepare daily reports
2000–2400	Reduced operations

(The specific activity scheduled for each period of the day will be considerably more detailed and with specific activities and individuals indicated for the guidance of desk personnel.)

Customer Reception

The customer may approach the business by foot, by ground vehicle, or by aircraft. The front desk should regard all contacts, from any source, as customers and prepare to treat them in a courteous and efficient manner. Full recognition should be made of the fact that personnel staffing the desk, in the eyes of the customer, are "the company." In order to properly deal with the customer, it is mandatory that the contents of this manual be thoroughly understood and that the organization structure, activities, and personnel be known.

The physical aspects of the front office should be designed to be as attractive as possible and should be kept clean and operational at all times. All personnel should be trained in greeting and dealing with customers. Every effort should be made to ensure that a pleasant, courteous, and efficient image is projected at all times.

Information and materials shall be kept readily available for customers on:

- Services provided by the company
- Basic price information for materials and services offered
- Key organization personnel—telephone numbers and addresses

By permission, Montgomery Aviation Corporation, Montgomery, Alabama.

> City and local maps
> Motel and hotel accommodations
> Local restaurants, entertainment, and points of interest
> Local transportation services
> Aviation facilities
> Recreation facilities

Departmental Relationships and Responsibilities

In a very real sense the front desk is a representative of and a spokesperson for all the departments in the organization. As such, the front-desk personnel should be very cognizant of the personnel, capabilities, and responsibilities of the departments. The organizational relationships between various departments and the key personnel are depicted in the chart at the bottom of the page.

The assigned responsibilities of each of the departments includes the following:

1. *Administrative.* Personnel records and services, accounting, internal records.
2. *Customer services.* Line service, engine and aircraft service, parts, inventory.
3. *Instruction.* Syllabus, records, schedules, course sales.
4. *Flight service.* Rental, charter, special mission, air taxi.
5. *Sales.* New and used aircraft sales, avionics, and related equipment sales.

Information System Requirements

The internal information system has been designed and developed to provide management with the financial and operational data required for the efficient operation of the business. The front desk is instrumental in the initiation, collection and routing of much of the required data. In addition, front-desk personnel can do much to ensure that departmental data are accurate and timely.

Front-desk personnel will, in the course of work, come in contact with many forms and records. Familiarity with these forms is essential to the successful operation of the front desk.

Following are the forms and records most likely used:

> Gasoline credit cards
> Aircraft rental agreements

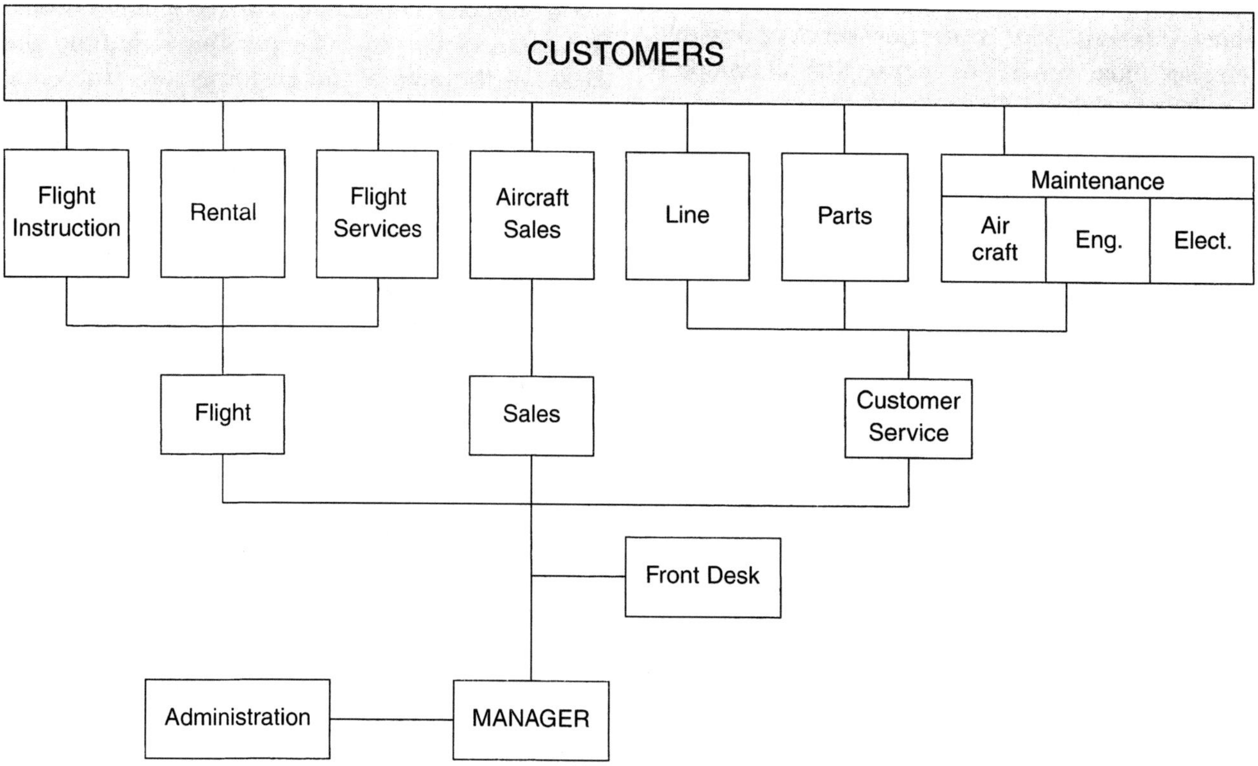

> Aircraft schedule sheets
> Aircraft record sheets
> Pilot licenses
> Automobile rental forms
> Cash sales tickets
> Cash drawer forms
> Accident reports
> Approved credit file
> Application for FCC license

Accounting System Information

Many of the forms handled by front-desk personnel must be completed using accounting system numbers and terminology. It is imperative that this be done consistently and accurately. The information system includes a chart of accounts, with assigned numbers, to be used in recording transactions and keeping the necessary records. The most frequently used account numbers for front desk personnel are:

No.	Description of Account	Form or Record	Departmental Codes
707	Pilot supplies	Cash sales	C—Aircraft sales
706	Tie down	Cash sales	D—Parts
701	Gas and oil—internal	Charge customers	E—Service
609	Flight service—internal	Gas sales summary	F—Flight
			G—Line
			Z—General and administration

Interdepartmental Billing

Many products and services normally billed to customers are also used by departments for internal consumption or use. It is necessary that this utilization be clearly identified and the proper billing procedure followed. Typical transactions might include:

Aviation fuel:
> Flight training activity
> Rented aircraft
> Air-taxi operations
> Aircraft sales
> Power line, forest patrol
> Charter
> Air ambulance

Vehicle fuel:
> Fuel trucks
> Line vehicles
> Courtesy car
> Rental car

Service activity:
> Washing aircraft
> Maintenance work
> Telephone charges

It is the responsibility of front desk personnel to ensure that proper action is taken to bill the correct department for each transaction, using the proper forms and the correct account number.

Company Policies and Procedures

The following company policies and procedures should be adhered to by all front-desk personnel:

1. Our company feels that the customer should receive the best aviation service in the area, and a major effort should be exerted to see that this is achieved.
2. Safety, in all aspects of the business, is of primary concern to the company. Safety of all employees, customers, and the public shall be regarded as the standard of operation for all departments.
3. The accident checklist shall be completed as expeditiously as possible for all accidents involving company personnel or equipment.
4. Credit can be extended only to those customers who have established an account with the company. Customers desiring to establish such an account must make application with the management. A list of established credit accounts will be maintained for the guidance of front-desk personnel and all departments.
5. Aircraft can be rented only to pilots who have been approved by a company check pilot. This approval must be based upon:
   a. Demonstration of knowledge of operational features and systems of aircraft (may require oral and written examination of specific aircraft)
   b. Flight check out in the aircraft for the specific type flight activity
6. Prior to each rental period, the individual at the front desk must check to see that the pre-

rental requirements have been complied with and the checklist completed. The post-rental checklist will be completed when the aircraft returns.

Emergency Procedures

As the hub of the activity for the organization, the front desk will undoubtedly observe or be notified quickly of emergencies involving company equipment or personnel. Possible emergency situations include:

1. Fire in buildings, equipment, or aircraft
2. Aircraft accidents involving customers, company aircraft, or personnel on the field or away from the field
3. Accidents involving company equipment, vehicles, and personnel
4. Impending hazardous weather situations
5. Loss of power or other utilities affecting business operations

In the event that an emergency situation is reported or observed, front-desk personnel will immediately take the action outlined in the Operational Checklist for the type of situation existing.

Company Personnel Guidelines

The company, in an effort to maintain the image of an efficient, professional activity and to provide individual employees with the opportunity to reach a high level of personal satisfaction, has developed personnel guidelines, procedures, and programs. The front desk has the specific responsibility for understanding and complying with these directives in the operation of front-desk activities and, as the center of activity for the overall organization, to monitor general compliance with the directives. Major emphasis should be given to the following checklists, job descriptions, and personnel programs:

> Handling incoming aircraft customers
> Servicing transient and local aircraft
> Front-desk manager job description
> Flight-line hostess job description
> Line-crew job description
> Front-desk operator job description
> Organization personnel assignments
> Departmental working schedules
> Employee personnel programs

Operational Checklist

To assist front-desk personnel in conducting an efficient and professional operation, the following Operational Checklists are provided. All personnel are encouraged to review these lists periodically and ensure that they are followed when conducting activities in either a normal situation or in an emergency:

A. Aircraft accident procedures
B. General accident procedures
   1. Equipment
   2. Personnel
C. Fire procedures
D. Hazardous weather procedures
E. Procedures for loss of power or other utilities
F. Cash handling procedures
G. Credit handling procedures
H. Renting automobiles
I. Interdepartmental billings
J. Transient pilot services
K. Detailed desk operating checklists:
   1. Cash check out
   2. Closing checklist for afternoon shift
   3. Checklist for night shift
   4. Checklist for early shift
L. Dealing with:
   1. Holdups
   2. Intoxicated persons
   3. Unhappy people
   4. Stolen aircraft

(Specific checklists for individual businesses should be added, similar to the following.)

A. Aircraft Accident Procedures

Accidents occur infrequently, but when they happen, events move rapidly, time is extremely important, and involved personnel can become very emotional. In order to ensure that all required and desirable action is taken as expeditiously as possible, the following steps should be taken:

1. Ensure that all personnel physically involved in the accident are provided immediate medical attention.
   Crash crew
      Telephone Number ________________
   Ambulance
      Telephone Number ________________

Doctor
Telephone Number ________________
Fire
Telephone Number ________________

2. Notify manager with pertinent details.
   What?
   Where?
   Who?
3. Initiate the following action if requested by manager. If unable to contact manager, complete as much as possible and advise manager later.
   a. Provide for physical security of damaged aircraft. Post guards as necessary. Notify nearest FAA GADO office.
   b. Develop a list of all personnel concerned. List eyewitnesses and observers. Obtain statements from witnesses.
   c. Have pertinent photographs taken.
   d. Notify insurance carrier
      Telephone Number ________________
   e. Notify company counsel
   f. Refer any requests for information from news media to FAA and/or to the manager. Maintain good relations.
   g. Cooperate with airport management, FAA, and NTSB in all matters related to accident.

B. General Accident Procedures

The organization is concerned with two categories of accidents: (1) those involving equipment and (2) those involving only personnel, such as personal injury due to falling, and so on. The procedures follow essentially the same guidelines:

1. Ensure that all personnel physically involved in the accident are provided immediate attention.
   First Aid
   Telephone Number ________________
   Doctor
   Telephone Number ________________
   Ambulance
   Telephone Number ________________
2. Notify the manager with pertinent details:
   What?
   Where?
   Who?
3. Initiate the following action if requested by manager. If unable to contact manager, complete as much as possible and advise manager later.
   a. Develop a list of all personnel concerned. List eyewitnesses and observers. Obtain statements from witnesses.
   b. Have photographs taken of equipment involved and the damage.
   c. Provide for security of equipment and for movement if required.
   d. Notify insurance carrier.
   e. Notify workmen's compensation agent.

C. Fire Procedures

In the event fire is noted, reported, or suspected in any of the company facilities, equipment, or spaces, comply with the following procedures:

1. Sound fire alarm. Report fire to manager and appropriate department.
2. Report fire to fire station.
   Telephone Number ________________
3. Assure that personnel on the scene are fighting or containing the fire using local equipment.
4. Provide for security of nearby equipment or material, moving if necessary.
5. Maintain constant vigilance for safety of personnel. Provide medical attention to all individuals requiring assistance.
6. After fire is under control, develop a list of all personnel involved, including eyewitnesses and observers—obtain statements from each.
7. Take photographs as needed to record pertinent information.

D. Hazardous Weather Procedures

Company operations, equipment, and personnel are influenced by weather factors, subjecting them to dangers of physical and personal damage. This includes high winds, freezing rain, snow, low visibility, flood, and blowing sand. The front desk, as part of the daily routine, should check the weather situation and remain cognizant of the trends as they might affect aircraft, equipment, buildings, and personnel. The following general procedures shall be used as a guide along with specific activities related to the particular type of weather.

1. Upon receipt of the notice that hazardous weather conditions are coming, alert all departments of the threat and advise the manager of this action.
2. Caution pilots flying or about to fly of the impending threat.
3. Check to see if student activity is being monitored by the flight department.
4. Tour ramp, hangar, and other areas to see if necessary precautionary action has been taken. Aircraft should be secured or stored, doors closed, loose articles or equipment secured or stored. Advise departments on recommendations.
5. Review rental aircraft activity and schedule. Consider canceling as necessary.
6. During period of hazardous weather, monitor the condition of aircraft and facilities to ensure that all possible action is being taken to properly maintain all company property.
7. Notify aircraft owners.

E. Loss of Utilities

The modern aviation activity as a sophisticated business depends heavily upon the uninterrupted supply of all utilities: electricity, water, oil, gas, or telephone. In the event of a utility loss, scheduled or otherwise, it is necessary that action be taken to minimize the effect of the disruption. The following guidelines should be reviewed and appropriate action taken:

1. Review the loss situation and determine the potential threats. For example:
   Loss of water—fire protection, restrooms, water fountains, washing aircraft, and so forth
   Loss of electricity—no lights, no refrigeration, no electric machines or test equipment, no power for doors, no air conditioning, and so on
   Loss of radio—effect on communication, traffic control
   Loss of oil, gas—effect on heat, air conditioning
   Loss of telephone—effect on scheduling, customers
   Loss of alarm systems—fire, security, and so on
2. Take action appropriate to type of loss.
   a. Advise all departments—time and duration, if anticipated.
   b. Alert customers if warning of loss is provided. Provide signs and notices for facilities not operating. Call appropriate utility service department if loss is unscheduled. Notify, request assistance, and attempt to determine time involved.

APPENDIX

VIII

Job Functions for Various Ratings

(a) An applicant for a Class 1, 2, 3, or 4 airframe rating must provide equipment and material necessary for efficiently performing the following job functions:

(1) **Steel structural components**

Repair or replace steel tubes and fittings, using the proper welding techniques when appropriate
Anti-corrosion treatment of the interior and exterior of steel parts
Metal plating or anodizing*
Simple machine operations such as making bushings, bolts, etc.
Complex machine operations involving the use of planers, shapers, milling machines, etc.*
Fabricate steel fittings
Abrasive air blasting and chemical cleaning operations*
Heat treatment*
Magnetic inspection*
Repair or rebuild metal tanks*

(2) **Wood structure**

Splice wood spars
Repair ribs and spars (wood)
Fabricate wood spars*
Repair or replace metal ribs
Interior alignment of wings
Repair or replace plywood skin
Treatment against wood decay

(3) **Alloy skin and structural components**

Repair and replace metal skin, using power tools and equipment
Repair, replace and fabricate alloy members and components such as tubes, channels, cowling, fittings, attach angles, etc.
Alignment of components, using jigs or fixtures as in the case of joining fuselage sections or other similar operations

---

Taken from *Federal Aviation Regulation, Part 145—Repair Stations,* U.S. Government Printing Office, Washington, D.C., 2002. http://ecfrback.access.gpo.gov/otcgi/cfr/otfilter.cgi?DB=3&query=14000000145&region=BIBSRT&action=view&SUBSET=SUBSET&FROM=1&SIZE=10&ITEM=1#Sec.145.39

Make up wooden forming blocks or dies
Fluorescent inspection of alloy components*
Fabricate alloy members and components such as tubes, channels, cowlings, fittings and attach angles etc.

(4) **Fabric covering**
Repairs to fabric surfaces
Recovering and refinishing of components and entire aircraft*

(5) **Control systems**
Renewing control cables, using swaging and splicing techniques
Rigging complete control system
Renewing or repairing all control system hinge point components such as pins, bushings, etc.
Install control system units and components

(6) **Landing gear systems**
Renew or repair all landing gear hinge point components and attachments such as bolts, bushings, fittings, etc.
Overhaul and repair elastic shock absorber units
Overhaul and repair hydraulic-pneumatic shock absorber units*
Overhaul and repair brake system components*
Conduct retraction cycle tests
Overhaul and repair electrical circuits
Overhaul and repair hydraulic system components*
Repair or fabricate hydraulic lines

(7) **Electric wiring systems**
Diagnose malfunctions
Repair or replace wiring
Installation of electrical equipment
Bench check electrical components (this check is not to be confused with the more complex functional test after overhaul)

(8) **Assembly operations**
Assembly of airframe component parts such as landing gear, wings, controls, etc.
Rigging and alignment of airframe components, including the complete aircraft and control system
Installation of powerplants
Installation of instruments and accessories
Assembly and fitting of cowling, fairings, etc.
Repair and assembly of plastic components such as windshields, windows, etc.
Jack or hoist complete aircraft
Conduct aircraft weight and balance operations (this function will be conducted in draft-free area)*
Balance control surfaces

(b) An applicant for any class of power plant rating must provide equipment and material necessary for efficiently performing the following job functions appropriate to the class of rating applied for:

(1) **Classes 1 and 2**

(i) **Maintain and alter power plants, including replacement of parts**
Chemical and mechanical cleaning
Disassembly operations
Replacement of valve guides and seats*
Replacement of bushings, bearings, pins, inserts, etc.
Plating operations (copper, silver, cadmium, etc.)*

Heating operations (involving the use of recommended techniques requiring controlled heating facilities)
Chilling or shrinking operations
Removal and replacement of studs
Inscribing or affixing identification information
Painting of powerplants and components
Anticorrosion treatment for parts
Replacement and repair of power plant alloy sheet metal and steel components such as baffles, fittings, etc.*

(ii) **Inspect all parts, using appropriate inspection aids**
Magnetic, fluorescent and other acceptable inspection aids*
Precise determination of clearances and tolerances of all parts
Inspection for alignment of connecting rods, crankshafts, impeller shafts, etc.
Balancing of parts, including crankshafts, impellers, etc.*
Inspection of valve springs

(iii) **Accomplish routine machine work**
Precision grinding, honing and lapping operations (includes crankshaft, cylinder barrels, etc.)*
Precision drilling, tapping, boring, milling and cutting operations
Reaming of inserts, bushings, bearings and other similar components
Refacing of valves

(iv) **Perform assembly operations**
Valve and ignition timing operations
Fabricate and test ignition harnesses
Fabricate and test rigid and flexible fluid lines
Prepare engines for long- or short-term storage
Functional check power plant accessories (this check is not to be confused with the more complex performance test of overhaul)*
Hoist engines by mechanical means
Install engines in aircraft*
Align and adjust engine controls*
Installation of engines in aircraft and alignment and adjustment of engine controls, when completed, must be inspected by either an appropriately rated certificated mechanic or certificated repairman. Persons supervising or inspecting these functions must thoroughly understand the pertinent installation details involved.

(v) **Test overhauled power plants in compliance with manufacturers' recommendations**
The test equipment will be the same as recommended by the manufacturers of the particular engines undergoing test or equivalent equipment that will accomplish the same purpose. The testing function may be performed by the repair station itself, or may be contracted to an outside agency. In either case the repair station will be responsible for the final acceptance of the tested engine.

(2) **Class 3**
Functional and equipment requirements for turbine engines will be governed entirely by the recommendations of the manufacturer, including techniques, inspection methods, and tests.

(c) An applicant for any class of propeller rating must provide equipment and material necessary for efficiently performing the following job functions appropriate to the class of rating applied for:

(1) **Class 1**

(i) **Maintain and alter propellers, including installation and replacement of parts**
Replace blade tipping

Refinish wood propellers
Make wood inlays
Refinish plastic blades
Straighten bent blades within repairable tolerances
Modify blade diameter and profile
Polish and buff
Painting operations
Remove from and reinstall on power plants

(ii) **Inspect components, using appropriate inspection aids**
Inspect propellers for conformity with manufacturer's drawings and specifications,
Inspect hubs and blades for failures and defects, using magnetic or fluorescent inspection devices*
Inspect hubs and blades for failures and defects, using all visual aids, including the etching of parts
Inspect hubs for wear of splines or keyways or any other defect

(iii) **Repair or replace components**
(Not applicable to this class.)

(iv) **Balance propellers**
Test for proper track on aircraft
Test for horizontal and vertical unbalance (this test will be accomplished with the use of precision equipment)

(v) **Test propeller pitch-changing mechanisms**
(Not applicable to this class.)

(2) **Class 2**

(i) **Maintain and alter propellers, including installation and replacement of parts**
All functions listed under paragraph (c) (1) (i) of this appendix when applicable to the make and model propeller for which a rating is sought
Properly lubricate moving parts
Assemble complete propeller and sub-assemblies, using special tools when required

(ii) **Inspect components, using appropriate inspection aids**
All functions listed under paragraph (c) (1) (ii) of this appendix when applicable to the make and model propeller for which a rating is sought.

(iii) **Repair or replace component parts**
Replace blades, hubs, or any of their components
Repair or replace anti-icing devices
Remove nicks or scratches from metal blades
Repair or replace electrical propeller components

(iv) **Balance propellers**
All functions listed under paragraph (c) (1) (iv) of this appendix when applicable to the make and model propeller for which a rating is sought

(v) **Test propeller pitch-changing mechanism**
Test hydraulically, propellers and components
Test electrically operated propellers and components
Test of constant speed devices*

(d) An applicant for a radio rating must provide equipment and materials as follows:

(1) For a Class 1 (Communications) radio rating, the equipment and materials necessary for efficiently performing the job functions listed in sub-paragraph (4) and the following job functions:
The testing and repair of headsets, speakers, and microphones
The measuring of radio transmitter power output

(2) For a Class 2 (Navigation) radio rating, the equipment and materials necessary for efficiently performing the job functions listed in sub-paragraph (4) and the following job functions:

The testing and repair of headsets

The testing of speakers

The repair of speakers*

The measuring of loop antenna sensitivity by appropriate methods

The determination and compensation for quadrantal error in aircraft direction finder radio equipment

The calibration of any radio navigational equipment, en route and approach aids, or similar equipment, appropriate to this rating to approved performance standards

(3) For a Class 3 (Radar) radio rating, the equipment and materials necessary for efficiently performing the job functions listed in subparagraph (4) and the following job functions:

The measuring of radio transmitter power output

The metal plating of transmission lines, wave guides, and similar equipment in accordance with appropriate specifications*

The pressurization of appropriate radar equipment with dry air, nitrogen, or other specified gases

(4) For all classes of radio ratings, the equipment and materials necessary for efficiently performing the following job functions:

Perform physical inspection of radio systems and components by visual and mechanical methods

Perform electrical inspection of radio systems and components by means of appropriate electrical and/or electronic test instruments

Check aircraft wiring, antennas, connectors, relays, and other associated radio components to detect installation faults.

Check engine ignition systems and aircraft accessories to determine sources of electrical interference

Check aircraft power supplies for adequacy and proper functioning

Test radio instruments*

Overhaul, test, and check dynamotors, inverters, and other radio electrical apparatus*

Paint and refinish equipment containers*

Accomplish appropriate methods of marking calibrations, or other information on radio control panels and other components, as required*

Make and reproduce drawings, wiring diagrams, and other similar material required to record alterations and/or modifications to radio (photographs may be used in lieu of drawings when they will serve as an equivalent or better means of recording)*

Fabricate tuning shaft assemblies, brackets, cable assemblies and other similar components used in radios or aircraft radio installations*

Align tuned circuits (RF and IF)

Install and repair aircraft antennas

Install complete radio systems in aircraft and prepare weight and balance reports* (That phase of radio installation requiring alterations to the aircraft structure must be performed, supervised, and inspected by qualified personnel)

Measure modulation values, noise, and distortion in radios

Measure audio and radio frequencies to appropriate tolerances and perform calibration necessary for the proper operation of radios

Measure radio component values (inductance, capacitance, resistance, etc.)

Measure radiofrequency transmission line attenuation

Determine wave forms and phase in radios when applicable

Determine proper aircraft radio antenna, lead-in and transmission line characteristics and locations for type of radio equipment to which connected

Determine operational condition of radio equipment installed in aircraft by using appropriate portable test apparatus

Determine proper location for radio antennas on aircraft

Test all types of electronic tubes, transistors, or similar devices in equipment appropriate to the rating

(e) An applicant for any class of instrument rating must provide equipment and material necessary for efficiently performing the following job functions, in accordance with pertinent specifications and manufacturers' recommendations, appropriate to the class of rating applied for:

(1) **Class 1**

(i) **Diagnose instrument malfunctions**

Diagnose malfunctioning of the following instruments:

Rate of climb indicators
Altimeters
Air speed indicators
Vacuum indicators
Oil pressure gauges
Fuel pressure gauges
Hydraulic pressure gauges
De-icing pressure gauges
Pitot-static tube
Direct indicating compasses
Accelerometer
Direct indicating tachometers
Direct reading fuel quantity gauges
Optical (sextants, drift sights, etc.)*

(ii) **Maintain and alter instruments, including installation and replacement of parts**

Perform these functions on instruments listed under paragraph (e) (1) (i) of this appendix.

The function of installation includes fabrication of instrument panels and other installation structural components

The repair station should be equipped to perform this function. However, it may be contracted to a competent outside agency equipped to perform the function.

(iii) **Inspect, test and calibrate instruments**

Perform these functions on instruments listed under paragraph (e) (1) (i) of this appendix, on and off the aircraft, when appropriate.

(2) **Class 2**

(i) **Diagnose instrument malfunctions**

Diagnose malfunctioning of the following instruments:

Tachometers
Synchroscope
Electric temperature indicators
Electric resistance type indicators
Moving magnet type indicators
Resistance type fuel indicators
Warning units (oil-fuel)
Selsyn systems and indicators
Self-synchronous systems and indicators
Remote indicating compasses

Fuel quantity indicators
Oil quantity indicators
Radio indicators
Ammeters
Voltmeters

(ii) **Maintain and alter instruments, including installation and the replacement of parts**

Perform these functions on instruments listed under paragraph (e) (2) (i) of this appendix.

The function of installation includes fabrication of instrument panels and other installation structural components. The repair station should be equipped to perform this function. However, it may be contracted to a competent outside agency equipped to perform the function.

(iii) **Inspect, test and calibrate instruments**

Perform these functions on instruments listed under paragraph (e) (2) (i) of this appendix, on and off the aircraft, when appropriate.

(3) **Class 3**

(i) **Diagnose instrument malfunctions**

Diagnose malfunctioning of the following instruments:

Turn and bank indicators
Directional gyros
Horizon gyros
Autopilot control units and components*
Remote reading direction indicators*

(ii) **Maintaining and alter instruments, including installation and replacement of parts**

Perform these functions on instruments listed under (e) (3) (i) of this appendix.

The function of installation includes fabrication of instrument panels and other installation structural components. The repair station should be equipped to perform this function. However, it may be contracted to a competent outside agency equipped to perform the function.

(iii) **Inspect, test and calibrate instruments**

Perform these functions on instruments listed under paragraph (e) (3) (i) of this appendix, on and off the aircraft, when appropriate.

(4) **Class 4**

(i) **Diagnose instrument malfunctions**

Diagnose malfunctioning of the following instruments:

Capacitance type quantity gauge
Other electronic instruments
Engine analyzers

(ii) **Maintain and alter instruments, including installation and replacement of parts**

Perform these functions on instruments listed under paragraph (e) (4) (i) of this appendix.

The function of installation includes fabrication of instrument panels and other installation structural components. The repair station should be equipped to perform this function. However, it may be contracted to a competent outside agency equipped to perform this function.

(iii) **Inspect, test and calibrate instruments**

Perform these functions on instruments listed under paragraph (e) (4) (i) of this appendix, on and off the aircraft, when appropriate.

(f) An applicant for a Class 1, 2, or 3 accessory rating must provide equipment and material necessary for efficiently performing the following job functions, in accordance with pertinent specifications and the manufacturers' recommendations:
   (1) Diagnose accessory malfunctions.
   (2) Maintain and alter accessories, including installation and the replacement of the parts.
   (3) Inspect, test, and, where necessary, calibrate accessories.

[Doc. No. 1157, 27 FR 11693, Nov. 28, 1962, as amended by Amdt. 145-14, 35 FR 19349, Dec. 22, 1970; Amdt. 145-19, 47 FR 33391, Aug. 2, 1982]

Note: When an asterisk (*) is shown after any job function listed in this appendix it indicates that the applicant need not have the equipment and material on the premises for performing this job function provided he or she contracts that particular type work to an outside agency having such equipment and material.

APPENDIX

IX

NATA's "Negotiating Aviation Agreements: Guidelines for Building and Protecting Your Business"

FOREWORD

This book was written by the National Air Transportation Association (NATA) to meet one of the most important but least explained areas of business for the Fixed Base and Air Taxi Operator: the leases and agreements by which a company conducts its activities.

During four years of research and preparation of the First Edition, released in 1980, contributors to this book studied leases and agreements from more than 250 airports of every size and description in the United States. The variables and provisions unique to each of them made it impossible to write universal standards and agreements that could be applied to every contractual arrangement.

Instead, we opted to compile in a single book the guidelines, recommendations, case studies, and examples to help the aviation business person structure agreements that will protect and, it is hoped, foster the growth of the company and the airport. While this publication is something of a "do-it-yourself" guide, it is intended to complement, and not replace, the expert legal, accounting, and insurance assistance needed to develop satisfactory binding agreements.

After three printings and six years of "field testing," *Negotiating Aviation Agreements* has become the proven industry standard with more than 2,000 copies now in use. This Second Edition embodies the many changes made necessary with the passage of time and the adoption of new laws and regulations.

NOTICE TO READERS

While this NATA publication is designed to provide accurate and authoritative information, it is distributed with the understanding that NATA is not engaged in rendering legal, accounting, or other professional advice. The sample agreements contained herein represent one approach to the situations covered, and may not comprehensively address all of the issues involved in any commercial transaction. Specifically, the sample agreements do not address any issues of federal or state income taxation. Therefore, the sample agreements are offered by NATA for guidance only and should not be used verbatim. Persons considering the use of these sample agreements should seek competent legal and tax advice.

Second Edition: First Printing
Printed in the United States of America

TABLE OF CONTENTS

CHAPTER 1
THE AIRPORT LEASE—THE DOCUMENT FOR PLANNED SUCCESS

"Throughout the following discussion the document to be discussed will be referred to as a 'lease.' However it must be clearly understood that it is considerably more than a mere lease of real estate; it is a composite agreement, a combination of a lease (as the term is understood by lawyers and laymen) and an operating agreement. Its terms set forth many obligations, duties, and restrictions which apply to the manner in which the aviation business operation will be carried on using the leased premises."

Reasons for A Long-Term Lease

Throughout the following discussion the document to be discussed will be referred to as a "lease." However it must be clearly understood that it is considerably more than a mere lease of real estate; it is a composite agreement, a combination of a lease (as the term is understood by lawyers and laymen) and an operating agreement. Its terms set forth many obligations, duties, and restrictions which apply to the manner in which the aviation business operation will be carried on using the leased premises.

The initial financing required to create a general aviation business operation can stagger the imagination! A small operation on a public airport can easily require several hundred thousand dollars of initial capitalization; financing a large base operation can easily run into millions of dollars. General aviation operators are usually committed by agreement to invest funds in buildings and other facilities at the airport as a condition of their lease and to enhance their business potential. Not only does such an operation require office space for its own administration, it requires a terminal facility for transient general aviation passengers. In addition, hangars, storage facilities, expensive maintenance and repair equipment are needed to handle the various types of aircraft which may require servicing, many of which are the same type as those used by the certificated air carriers.

As a result of the huge investments required, such improvements normally are financed to a large degree by borrowed funds. The usual sources of loan money, such as banks and other industrial lending institutions, lack enthusiasm for advancing funds upon improvements to be installed on publicly owned land simply because of the limiting characteristics of these improvements as collateral; improvements upon leased property are not readily marketable in the event of a default on the loan and subsequent foreclosure. In financial circles it is said that such a plan is not "bankable." Therefore, when creating a plan and setting the length of the lease and its terms, it is necessary to consider the practical requirements of potential lenders who will evaluate a loan proposal on a business investment.

This is true not only of banks, but of material suppliers, such as oil companies and other product distributors, who will frequently entertain proposals for loans to develop a market for their products, provided the anticipated business is attractive to them as businessmen.

Any potential lender will make his decision after an assessment of the financial return he can expect over the life of the loan as compared with other investment opportunities available to him. Thus, the amount loaned will be limited to that which can be adequately amortized from the funds generated by the business expected during the term of the lease. It is fundamental that a loan must be limited to the amount for which the collateral provides adequate security. Therefore, a lender will also evaluate the security of his investment in a business from the viewpoint of the adequacy of collateral and will insist on a reasonable expectation that the borrower can meet his continuing obligations to repay the loan. In analyzing this aspect he will take into consideration the fact that improvements usually have collateral value only over the life of the lease and diminish as the term of the lease expires. Collateral in the form of a lien upon improvements erected on the airport property leased by the operator is usually of value only if there is an assurance of continued occupancy in conjunction with the lease, or if the lease provides for compensation for the depreciated value of the improvements in the event of a premature termination of the lease. Representatives of lending institutions responsible for assessing the desirability of investing funds by loans to operators give prime consideration to potential sales volume, cash flow, and projected profits. It is obvious that subjecting any of these to unkown influences that could be detrimental to the business will restrict the incentive of a lender to make such investments.

Assignability Provisions

It must be recognized that a lending institution advancing funds will evidence a real interest in either a lease provision for the assignment of the rights for compensation for leasehold improvements or an assignment of the lease itself in the event of default. In either case, airport authorities frequently are requested to furnish evidence of consent to such assignments, which in themselves tend to assure continued availability of services at the airport. Once the lease is signed it becomes valuable property to the lessee, although since the lessor retains an interest in the lease, the lessee's freedom to exercise his business judgment may be limited. For example, a lessee may desire to assign or transfer the lease or parts of the rights established under the lease or assign, sublease, or transfer some portion of the land he holds on lease. Ordinarily, however, the lease will provide that he cannot exercise any of these options without the written consent of the landlord.

The lessee does have certain rights which should be specifically treated in the lease since they are vitally important in financing:

- The lessee should be empowered to assign the lease for financing purposes upon written notice to the lessor and approval thereof should not be unreasonably withheld. Assignment of the lease for financing purposes is a normal procedure, but the lessor then must recognize that the lending institution becomes the successor to the original lessee under the lease in the event of a default in payment or performance.

- It is desirable for the lease to state that the lessee has the right to sell without restriction to any corporation formed by it, or consolidated or merged with it, provided, however, that the purpose of the surviving organization is to perform under the lease for the same purpose -- as a Fixed Base Operation.

- Leases typically give a lessee the right to sublease part of the space covered by the lease, provided that the sublessee is subject to the same conditions and obligations as those in the basic lease and that the lessor's consent is first obtained. It should also be remembered that the original lessee is thereafter responsible for his sublessee's compliance.

Preliminary Planning

It is basic that any businessman proposing to operate a business does so with the reasonable expectation of deriving a financial profit; a businessman who does not make a profit simply does not survive. If constraints are posed which make his ability to derive a profit questionable, prudence would dictate that the business should not be entered into in the first place.

Furthermore, it is imperative that every businessman plan for the future growth of his business. Naturally, if he does not make enough profit to expand his operations in the future, his business cannot grow; and, when a business is unable to grow to meet growing demands, it cannot properly serve the community. If a Fixed Base Operator on leased property obtains loans from financial institutions, but because of contractual constraints placed upon him subsequently fails in business, it invariably becomes difficult, if not impossible, for a successor business to obtain funds from the same sources. This development can be harmful to the entire aviation business community. It is therefore vitally important that all parties entering into an airport lease agreement for a single or a variety of aeronautical activities understand all of the problems involved.

Move Slowly

A successful airport lease is a work of art. It must serve the best interests of both parties and at the same time be financially and practically sound. Not only must the terms of such a lease be reviewed and approved by several groups of attorneys representing the lessor and lessee, they must be acceptable to the attorneys of various financing institutions as well. The resulting document may contain terms which are not entirely satisfactory to the parties, but in any event it is imperative that they understand the import and meaning of all lease language before entering into such an agreement in the first place.

Lawyers

In all cases, it is absolutely necessary that the services of an attorney be obtained, and the attorneys, together with their clients, must spend considerable time acquainting themselves with the peculiarities and niceties of the problems involved. If possible, the proposed lessee and his attorney should study the lessor's previous agreements with parties involved in operating similar businesses. If the lessor is a public body, such leases are a matter of public record. Furthermore, if a certificated air carrier operates from the airport, the proposed lessee should study its lease as well. Attorneys representing air carriers are experienced in the field of lease negotiations and the form of their agreement should be analyzed thoroughly.

Acquire Information Prior to Negotiation

Before entering into negotiations, a proposed lessee should have his accountants develop a prospectus for the business and make financial projections which will give him a dependable guide for making judgments during every phase of the negotiations. He must be completely informed as to what lease costs can be contractually accepted without compromising his legitimate profit objectives. This can be determined by carefully reviewing the minimum operating standards or requirements for that airport.

Furthermore, the proposed lessee should ascertain prior to negotiating exactly what lease terms will be acceptable to the specific lending institutions from which he intends to borrow money. This is especially important in planning to build a hangar or other large facility on leased real estate.

A lessee who intends to sell aviation fuel should obtain the advice of his intended fuel supplier concerning lease or purchase agreements covering a fuel storage tank farm, fuel trucks, and fees related to fuel handling. This information also should be ascertained prior to instituting negotiations on the lease.

During negotiations the proposed lessee should constantly review his financial and business projections to maintain a clear picture of his objectives, the conditions under which he can operate, and what he can afford to pay for all the requirements sought to be imposed upon him by the lessor. He must comprehend clearly the limits of his financial abilities and of his business experience so that he will not accept contractural terms and commitments which he will be unable to meet. If acceptable terms cannot be reached between the parties within these clearly defined limits and the duties and obligations proposed in the lease under negotiation are recognized to be beyond the financial and business capabilities of the proposed lessee, it is to the advantage of both parties that such a lack of capability be clearly stated and frankly understood and, in the event that the proposed lessor insists that his demands be met, it is recommended that the proposed lessee break off negotiations.

Ownership

Early in the negotiations, the proposed operator should be certain that the people with whom he is negotiating have the legal capacity and authority to deal with him on behalf of the community. In addition, he and his attorney should conduct a title search to be absolutely satisfied that there is a clear title to the premises and that the ownership of the entire premises rests in the parties with whom he is negotiating. There have been many cases in which airports have extended over the boundries of two or three counties -- and, in some cases, across state lines -- and it is possible that a lessee may find himself in the unhappy position of having invested a great deal of money to improve premises which were not within the jurisdiction of the lessor in the first place.

It's a Partnership

Aviation, a unique and complicated business, is growing beyond the imagination of most Americans. In the United States there are approximately 4,000 fully attended airports. About 400 of these are served by the certificated air carriers; yet, all of them are served by general aviation. During the past 15 years the general aviation fleet has grown at an unprecedented rate.

In order for these aircraft to be useful for business and personal transportation to all communities, there must be a similar growth of airport support facilities.

The general aviation Fixed Base Operator and the airport operator are truly partners working for the benefit of all citizens in their community. Our composite "airport lease" is therefore more than a lease. It is a lease/operating agreement/partnership agreement which establishes a mutually beneficial relationship for all parties concerned -- and the people they serve. It cannot be entered into without a full realization of the implications of each phrase on the relationships of everyone concerned with the operation of the business. *The lease should be the document for planned success.*

CHAPTER 2
THE LEASE—PUTTING IT ALL TOGETHER

The Site

The language of the lease agreement itself must describe the premises clearly, fully and accurately; the official plot plan and survey drawing of the properties should be attached to the lease and incorporated by reference. The terms and objectives of the "master plan" for the airport should also be incorporated by explicit reference, and a copy of the master plan should be attached to the lease and also retained by all parties.

The lease may provide for future growth by specifying the lessee's option to expand to additional areas, even though such a provision may not be unreasonably restrictive and create a de facto exclusive operation. If the lessor receives an offer from a third party desiring to start a Fixed Base Operation on the potential "expansion area" during the term of the lease and its option period, the original lessee may be given the "first right of refusal" at the same rates which the new party has offered to pay. This first right of refusal is especially important with respect to adjacent areas not covered by the site description in the original lease.

In the site description, the lease must clearly and precisely describe the lessee's rights with respect to the use of landing areas, runways, taxiways, automobile and aircraft parking areas, aprons, ramps, and the use of navigational aids and terminal facilities. If aviation fuel is to be sold and dispensed, the lease should also provide for and describe a site to be used as a fuel storage area. The privilege to use these facilities ("appurtenant" privilege) must be discussed in the initial lease. It is suggested that the lessee obtain a clause ensuring him of "the general use of all public airport facilities and improvements of a public nature which are now or may hereafter be connected with or appurtenant to said airport."

The Term of the Lease

The primary term of the lease is established by setting the dates of the beginning and end of the lease period in the agreement itself. There are usually provisions for the extension of the term of the lease for an additional specified period by the exercise of an option by the lessee. To conform with the realities of the demands of lending institutions, the lease term should extend for a long enough period to permit the amortization of loans made for physical improvements on the property and the erection of hangars, terminal buildings, and other installa-tions. Financing experience has shown that 15 years is the absolute minimum accepted by most lending institutions for major improvements and a 20-year lease, with options to extend, is preferable.

Options

The options provision, whereby the lessee may extend the lease an additional term, should specify not only the length of the additional term and any additional option, it should also specify the maximum amounts by which rents, fees, and payments can be increased during the option period. Many leases specify that rents will not be increased by more than a stated percentage of value to be paid as rent for the option period.

Termination Before Expiration

Although a properly negotiated lease is instituted upon the premise that the business will be successful and will continue for the full term, the rights of the parties must be clearly set forth in the lease to cover the contingency that the lease may be terminated before its stated expiration date. It must be realized that either party can terminate (or "cancel") prematurely under certain conditions. The lessor can usually terminate for one or more of the following reasons:

A. For substantial non-performance (sometimes referred to as "breach of contract") under the terms of the document. The lessee must be careful in negotiations to prevent language which may be unreasonably restrictive, such as: "The lessee should conduct his business in a courteous manner, avoiding boisterous language, etc."

B. For the failure of the lessee to observe and conform to the terms and conditions of the lease and his continuing failure to bring his operations into compliance within 30 days after receiving written notice from the lessor to do so.

C. For the failure of the lessee to pay the rent when it is due. The lease should set a period of time (usually 30-60 days) during which the lessee may remedy the default.

D. If the lessee becomes bankrupt or if the lessee makes a general assignment of the lease for the benefit of creditors.

E. If the lessee abandons the premises. Under this circumstance the lessor generally has the right to remove the lessee's abandoned effects without being liable for damages.

Upon premature termination of the lease for any of the above reasons all rights of the lessee cease and he must vacate the premises. It must be reiterated that negotiators take care not to agree to overly restrictive language which may not be acceptable to lending institutions.

The lessee may terminate the lease prematurely for the following reasons:

A. If the lessor fails to perform substantially under the terms of the lease. Termination may require written notice to the lessor and the passage of a stated period of time (usually 30-60 days) before the actual termination.

B. If the lessor commits any act or engages in any activity that prevents the lessee from doing business for a period of time which should be specified in the lease.

C. In many cases a lessee can terminate the lease in event of civil commotion, acts of the military, acts of God, damage to runways, or such other causes as the issuance of a court order restraining the use of the airport, any of which may interrupt normal business for a specified period of time. In lieu of premature termination of the entire lease, it is recommended that the instrument provide for a moratorium on rent payments during such interruptions of operations and/or the extension of the primary term of the lease by an equivalent amount.

Rights After Termination

Some leases provide that upon termination of the lease, a lessor has the option to purchase, at a depreciated value, any improvements to the real estate constructed by the lessee. For this purpose, a depreciation schedule should be spelled out in the lease. Such provisions frequently indicate that the improvements shall revert to the lessor, who is then obligated to pay the lessee the depreciated value of the fixed improvement plus a premium of two percent a year of the undepreciated value for the unexpired term of the lease. The improvements then become the absolute property "in fee simple" of the lessor. Depreciation in such cases is ordinarily figured on the full term of the lease and the actual original cost of the improvements.

Release of Lease

Another way in which the lease may be terminated before the date of expiration is a mutually acceptable release. The lease itself should provide for situations in which the parties "agree to disagree," so they can, by a subsequent written agreement, terminate the original agreement. For example, the original agreement might provide that both parties terminate the lease if performance becomes impossible or impractical due to causes beyond the control of either party. Sometimes such impediments are corrected by the passage of time, so that a full release would not be indicated; under such circumstances a temporary release may be provided enabling either party to notify the other of its intent to resume performance when such impediment no longer exists. The provision can be negotiated so that the lease states that all obligations shall be held in abeyance during the period of interruption, and when operations under the lease are resumed the term of lease shall be extended for a period equal to the period of interruption.

Disputes on the Lease

It must be recognized that even the most thoroughly researched and meticulously drawn leases may not cover all problems and disputes which may arise. To settle such disputes (except on the payment of rent) the lease should provide for a three-person arbitration committee, with one arbitrator being picked by each of the parties to the lease and the two arbitrators so named selecting a disinterested third party to settle such disputes.

Rights and Obligations

It is imperative that the terms of the lease be designed to give the lessee sufficient latitude in operating his business to survive financially. For this reason, both parties must clearly understand their respective rights and duties. A "right" is what the lease says *may* be done; a "duty" (sometimes called an "obligation" or "undertaking") is what *must* be done. It must be reiterated that this section of an airport lease extends far beyond the normal real estate document. It is, in actuality, the basic operating contract which specifies what the base operator shall do and the functions he will be required to perform to satisfy the requirements of the airport owner and their mutual customers. It is important that all of the rights and obligations of both parties be clearly spelled out in the lease so that there is no room for misunderstanding.

Covenant not to Compete

Because this is an agreement covering a business operation, the lease should provide that the lessor will not compete with the lessee or, if the lessor intends to compete, the extent and character of the competition should be specifically set forth. In most situations, such competition is unfair and is to be avoided.

Insurance Requirements

It is normal that a lessor require indemnity insurance holding him harmless from all claims, risks, accidents, or injuries caused by the lessee or his employees acting in his behalf in the operation of the leasehold business. It is assumed (and recommended) that the services of a competent insurance consultant will be sought prior to determining the type and negotiating the amount of such coverage.

The lease must also give the lessee and his customers the rights of ingress, egress, and of free access to the premises, as well as "peaceful possession and quiet enjoyment" thereof. There should also be an assurance that the lessor will continue to operate the airport as a public airport consistent with government regulations, and there will be no restrictions on normal operations or contingent restrictions which might apply to the proposed leasehold operation during the term of the lease or option extensions thereof.

Duty to Make Improvements

Since, in most cases, the lease agreement will contain language which obligates the lessee to provide physical improvements and installations on the premises, including refurbishing existing structures and/or the erection of new structures, this matter deserves specific attention and discussion.

Examples of improvements and installations required of the lessee may include the erection of hangars (or the improvement of existing hangars), shop facilities, office facilities (including the installation of fixtures, decorations and office equipment), landscaping, paved parking areas for motor vehicles and aircraft, crating and paving taxi strips, ramps, aprons and erecting advertising displays and signs. The lessee may also be required to construct and maintain lounge and pilot facilities on the premises for the use and convenience of the general aviation public. The lessee must know the complete extent of all such requirements to be imposed on him by the terms of the lease before he negotiates or awards any construction contracts.

Right of Prior Approval

Frequently, the lease gives the lessor the right of prior approval of all architectural plans and designs for improvements, and also requires the lessor's prior approval of any contractor to be selected by the lessee to construct the improvements. It is recommended that the lessee take every precaution in this respect to prevent the development of arbitrary or capricious demands or restrictions by the lessor on landscaping, exterior design, paint schemes, heights of buildings and the number and type of signs to be erected. All of these matters should be carefully set forth in the proposed plan and specifically discussed during negotiations.

Minimum Criteria

Leases frequently specify the minimum fiscal expenditure expected on the part of the lessee for improvements. If it is financially unacceptable for the lessee to operate under the proposed requirements, it is recommended that this point be covered by alternative means, such as describing the required improvements in terms of size, e.g., the lease may specify a minimum of 4,000 square feet for a shop, etc. (see Chapter 4, "Preparation Guide for Establishing Minimum Operating Standards").

It is assumed that all parties recognize the necessity for complying with local laws, regulations and codes. Most leases state that "the lessee must abide by all regulations promulgated by the authorized officials of federal, state, county, city and airport authorities." The proposed lessee must seek the advice of an attorney and be carefully advised on such matters prior to executing the lease.

Deadlines

Frequently lessors will seek to insert terms in the initial lease which will establish a deadline or a series of deadlines for the construction of improvements required on the leasehold. It is recommended that the lessee in negotiating these terms try to have as much leeway as possible in the schedules for completing hangars, buildings and other improvements. Clauses requiring completion "within 30 days of signing the lease" or stating that "construction must be complete within six months of notice to begin" may be extremely dangerous for the lessee, especially when non-completion penalties are involved. It must be recognized that delays may be caused by situations beyond the control of the lessee and he should be protected by language in the lease which will excuse him in case of delays "caused by fire, earthquake, flood, military action, civil strife, strikes, picketing or other coercive activity by labor groups, action by a public agency or public officials, the enactment, enforcement or applicability of public laws or regulations, or any other cause beyond the control of the lessee."

Operating Equipment and Fixtures

Most leases provide that the lessee has the right to install at his own expense equipment and fixtures required to perform the functions of his operation and also provide that he has the right to remove them at any time (also at his own expense) sometimes subject, however, to the prior approval of the lessor. Under these circumstances, the lessee is expected to restore the premises to a condition satisfactory to the lessor. In this matter it is important that the lease terms either give the lessee unrestricted right to remove fixtures, machinery and furnishings at any time, or in the alternative, if the lessor's prior approval is required, that it will not be unreasonably withheld. Again, note the possible interest of lenders in removing such fixtures as collateral, and restrictions that may be imposed by them upon removal.

Maintenance and Repairs of Leasehold

The lease should clearly specify which party shall be financially responsible for repairs and maintenance of the leased premises. In some cases, the lessor pays for structural repairs and specific major items and the lessee pays for maintenance needed because of ordinary wear and tear. Under these circumstances, if the lessee does not perform the required maintenance and repairs the lessor ordinarily is given the right (usually within 30 days) to enter upon the premises to perform the necessary work at the lessee's expense.

Fire Loss

Most leases require the lessee to replace buildings or facilities destroyed by fire and to return them to the pre-damaged condition so that the replacement will be equivalent in value to the original facilities. This is another area in which the lease negotiators should discuss and understand the question of abatement of rent while the facilities are not in use and also consider the interests of lending institutions. Normally, the lease will require 75-80 percent fire and extended coverage and hangar keeper's liability coverage with insurance companies approved by the lessor. It is also common for the lessor, and frequently for lending institutions, to be named on the insurance certificates as additional insureds, with relative priorities established by negotiation while drafting the lease.

Ownership After Termination

During the initial lease negotiations, it should be agreed between the parties in whom title to the various improvements upon the leasehold will rest at termination. There are several possibilities which should be discussed and decided upon in advance of signing the lease.

1. The title to the improvements may pass to the lessor immediately upon the completion of construction. This can be an advantage to the lessee because it eliminates his need to pay real estate taxes on the facilities (except in certain cases). However, it can also be a serious disadvantage to the lessee because under such an arrangement he will not be able to use

the buildings as collateral for loans.

2. Some leases provide that title to improvements remains with the lessee at the termination of the lease. This arrangement may raise problems concerning their removal at that time, and this should be decided prior to executing the lease.

3. The title to improvements may remain with the lessee during the term of the lease, but then pass to the lessor at the end of the lease. This is a normal arrangement since the lessee will usually have depreciated the property and simultaneously will have satisfied the debt incurred with his lenders. Caution is urged that the parties ascertain the rights of lenders in the event of a premature termination.

Removal at Termination

The requirement for removal of fixtures or equipment on the site at the termination of the lease should be thoroughly discussed in negotiations. Ordinarily, a "reasonable" time (usually 30-60 days) is given to the lessee to exercise his option to remain on or to remove all possessions and vacate the premises. If the option to renew is not exercised and the lease is thereby terminated, the lessee should be given the right to remove certain clearly defined fixtures or equipment within a stated time. If the lessee fails to remove any fixtures, equipment or personal property within the stated time, many leases permit the lessor to remove the lessee's property with liability to the lessee, or provide that such property will become the property of the lessor.

Relocation of Site

With the growth of aviation and increasing demands on airport properties, it has been found that, from time to time, lessors may need the leased premises for the expansion or further development of the airport itself. Under such circumstances, the lessor may reserve the right, on six months' notice, to relocate or replace the lessee's improvements in substantially similar form at another generally comparable location on the airport. If this is done, the lessee's loss of income during the transition period should be considered, and all contingencies should be covered in the lease by abating the rent and/or extending the term of the lease itself.

In addition, the public authority owning the airport has an inherent right to condemn the leasehold and improvements in the usual manner provided by law under the right of eminent domain.

The Operating Agreement

All matters discussed thus far concerning the rights and obligations of the parties are reasonably commonplace to real estate lawyers. However, as stated before, part of this "lease" actually constitutes an "operating agreement" between the city and the general aviation base operator. In negotiating this area, which is so seldom understood by people outside of aviation, extreme caution is urged. The matters to be covered in the operating agreement should include but not necessarily be limited to the following:

Sales: The lessee should be specifically permitted to sell (in each case at retail and at wholesale) new and used aircraft, new and used radio and electronic equipment, aircraft parts, navigation equipment, and airman supplies and accessories. (Because of its importance, the sale of fuel is treated separately below.) In addition to the sale of aircraft, equipment, parts, and accessories, the lease should provide that the lessee has the right to finance and insure such aircraft and equipment, and contents, or to act as agent for another party for these purposes.

Flight Operations: The lessee should specifically be given the right to engage in flight operations, including the demonstration of aircraft for sale, charter flights (including air taxi and commuter airline operations), flight training (primary and advanced), the lease and/or rental of aircraft to qualified pilots, and flights to test the operation of aircraft and components in his custody and control. In the event that the lessor deems primary flight training activities unsuited for the airport, the lessee should not be prohibited from engaging in flight training activities away from the area. The specific airport exclusion "no primary flight training will be conducted off, on or at __________ Airport" may be acceptable, but, at the same time, another provision of the lease should permit the lessee to transport students by air to an outlying airport or practice area..

It is also recommended that although primary flight training might be excluded in the interests of safety, it should be acceptable to grant the lessee the right to conduct advanced, recurrent or periodic flight training of licensed pilots at the airport.

Maintenance, Repair, and Overhaul: It should be clearly and explicitly stated in the lease that the lessee has the right to maintain, repair and overhaul all types of aircraft, engines, instruments, radio and electronic equipment and to remove, install or reinstall such equipment in aircraft in his care, custody or control. It may also be advisable to spell out that the lessee has the right to maintain, repair and overhaul motor vehicles used in the business, such as courtesy buses, line support equipment, and fuelers.

Line Service: There has been a disturbing trend for some communities to engage in line service, including the fueling of aircraft, lubrication and provision of hangar, parking or tie-down areas for based and transient aircraft. Since income derived from aircraft fueling contributes significantly to the Fixed Base Operator's financial posture, it is strongly recommended that aircraft fueling and line service activities be reserved for him as a right. In some cases, this right may include servicing of military aircraft under into-plane contracts and performing turn-around servicing of large aircraft operated by certificated carriers which do not maintain their own servicing equipment on the airport.

In such an event, the locations where fueling and line service operations may be conducted on public-use aprons and/or transient aircraft parking ramps should be clearly defined in the lease. Under line service, the lease should also give the lessee the right to load and unload passengers and cargo and to transport passengers from transient aircraft parking areas to the terminal and other areas of the airport and also the right to charge a fee for such services, although this right may never be exercised. Some leases require the lessee to provide transportation service for general aviation travelers 24 hours a day. This can involve station wagons or similar equipment and usually requires a three-shift operation, including two-way radio equipment, all at the operator's expense. This should be considered in negotiating the lease.

Service Charges: The lessee must have the right to assess charges and fees to customers for services rendered, although it is sometimes provided that the lessee must agree to set charges at levels reasonably competitive with those in the surrounding area, and the lessor may be given the right to review the schedule of fees and charges periodically. (Landing and parking fees for transient aircraft are discussed under "rent.")

Towing Disabled Aircraft: The lessee should be given the right but not the obligation to tow disabled aircraft from or about the airport. In the event that the lessor insists that aircraft towing be included as an obligation, it is recommended that consideration be given to a restriction that such towing be required only for aircraft of less than a specified weight.

Police Duty: The lease may provide that the lessee has the duty to prevent unauthorized persons from transiting the facilities or entering into restricted flight areas. This might mean that the lessee has the financial obligation to provide fencing of a size and quality acceptable to the lessor, or to hire security personnel.

Snow Removal: The lease should be clear and explicit as to the duties and obligations of both parties to remove snow and should include (or refer to) a description or plot plan defining the various areas of responsibility.

Uniforms: Some lessors require the lessee's employees to be supplied with -- and wear -- uniforms, and sometimes also require the prior design approval of the lessor.

Parking Area For Motor Vehicles: The lease must also provide for adequate space for parking motor vehicles, not only those used by the lessee and his customers, but also trucks, refuelers, and ground support equipment.

Signs: The lessee should specifically have the right to install signs and advertisements promoting his name and the brand or names of any fuel, aircraft, and any other products or services he may offer. If the lease provides that the lessor's consent be required for the installation of signs it should also specify that such consent will not be unreasonably withheld.

Subleases: It is possible that the lessee may desire at some future time to operate an ancillary business on the leased premises: barbershops, gift shops, newsstands, restaurants, rental car agencies -- the same types of business carried on in the main airport terminal. It is recommended that approval of such subleases by the lessor be discussed in the lease and that approval not be unreasonably withheld.

Payment of Taxes: It must be remembered that a leasehold has a value as personal property and a trend has been noticed for some municipalties to assess personal property taxes on the value of the lease. To protect the lessee from financial overburden, it is recommended that the following clause be inserted in the lease:

"Lessee shall be liable for any and all taxes, penalties, and interest thereon assessed, levied or charged by any governmental agency against lessee's tangible personal property situated on the lessor's premises; however, rentals to be paid by the lessee to the lessor shall be reduced by an amount equal to the ad valorem taxes against the lessee's leasehold improvements under this agreement."

Inspection: There are many other important obligations which may be imposed upon a lessee.

The lessee may be required to give the lessor the right of access to the leased premises for inspection. The lease should specify that such rights should be exercised reasonably and not be abused to the detriment of the lessee's operation.

The lessee may also be required to open his books to the lessor at any time for the purpose of an audit, and may be required to maintain acceptable accounting records for at least three years after the expiration of each lease year. The examination of records and accounts of companies owned or controlled by the lessee may also be included in the lease for audit by the lessor. If such a requirement is included in the lease it is also recommended that the lease specifically provide that the lessor may not exercise this right to improperly harass the lessee, that reason be the criterion, and also that the lessor should pay the expenses of such an audit.

Caution must be exercised in creating provisions which could result in a very unfavorable business climate for the lessee. If the lessor's agent, or "airport manager," operates the airport and also operates an FBO in direct competition with the proposed lessee, the right to examine the books and records of a competitor will obviously give him an unconscionable business advantage. It is therefore recommended that the lease be designed to prevent a competitor's frequent and deep penetration of the lessee's day-to-day operation. Caution is urged in selecting any Fixed Base Operator as the airport operator.

Activities Not Covered in the Lease: For the protection of the lessee, the lease should provide that engaging in any general aviation activities not specifically covered in the lease may be approved by making a request in writing to the lessor, and that such approval shall not be unreasonably withheld. While negotiating the lease, the proposed lessee should be careful to avoid terms which require him to obtain the lessor's written approval of all prices and/or discounts created in dealing with his customers. The lessee should have broad latitude in exercising his own business judgment as to charges and inventory to be maintained and sold by him. In this respect, he should avoid lease terminology which would force him to invest in slow-moving items of merchandise, including some grades or types of aviation fuel or automotive fuel.

Exclusive Rights: From the viewpoint of any businessperson who has invested a huge amount of money in a general aviation business, it is desirable to limit destructive cut-rate competition as much as possible until business success becomes assured. Therefore, it is frequently requested by lending institutions and others that a restriction be imposed in the lease preventing additonal operations from entering on the airport for some specified period of time.

> Such a restriction is not acceptable to the Federal Aviation Administration and the existence of such language in any lease concerning an aeronautical activity on the airport will make the airport ineligible for federal funds - including funds for the installation of instrument approaches, approach light systems, control towers, or radar facilities.

Rent

It must be remembered that the airport operator not only collects rent on the real estate, improved and unimproved, and on the buildings and improvements situated thereon, but that as lessor, he also collects additional income exacted on his tenants' various sources of revenue. This area of concession fees and percentages is full of traps and must be explored carefully.

Rental Payments on the Real Estate

Rents, the fees charged for the use of real property upon which the business operates, should be specified in the lease as being levied on improved property, unimproved property, buildings, office space, terminal building space, aprons and ramps. The proposed lessee must ascertain if the proposed rates are competitive by checking the square footage rentals paid by other lessees in similar situations.

Using tie-down areas as an example, some recent leases provide that the airport owner install tie-down rings and the FBO install tie-down ropes. On a tie-down charge of $5.00 per day, for example, the operator acts as agent for the owner and the fee is split equally at $2.50 each. In the case of raw, unimproved ground which is not included in the long-term terminal building lease, some leases provide that the lessee pay a specified amount for each square foot for the first five years, then increase such rental payments pursuant to mutually agreed upon terms.

Sometimes a sliding scale of rentals is agreed upon for the relief of the lessee during the early years of operation. Although this may not, at first, appear to be a favorable arrangement for the lessor, it is favorable from a long-range viewpoint. The lessor must realize that his primary aim should not be the generation of immediate cash flow, but rather the establishment of a stable general aviation business operation for the performance of needed services. It is realistic, however, to anticipate that as such a business develops and grows, the lease may provide for increases in future rentals.

"Percentage of the Gross"

Here, we must start with a word of *CAUTION*. The examination of numerous leases under which lessees are encountering great financial problems reveals that many such leases provide for rent schedules based on a "percentage of the gross," with fixed minimum rental payments. These fees may range from two percent to five percent of the gross sales of the lessee, with an additional surcharge sometimes added. Whatever the percentage, this is a very critical item and unless properly negotiated, can unwittingly spell disaster for the lessee, since it may establish a system of charges so high that the lessee cannot operate at a profit.

Unfortunately, many lessors base their rent schedules on their experience in dealing with many types of airport lessees, such as car rental agencies, newsstands, etc., which, since they are supported for all practical purposes by a captive audience, can operate on a percentage of the gross rent formula because they can (and do) raise prices to meet the lessor's rent demands. However, a general aviation business operator is at a serious disadvantage under such terms. Most such businesses operate on a one to three percent margin and cannot possibly survive if, for example, a percentage of the gross revenue from aircraft sales is included in rent computations. It is vital that lease negotiators for the lessor understand the financial intricacies inherent in general aviation businesses.

However, if the lessor insists on gross sales revenues as an index for fixing rents, it is possible to use an "adjusted gross formula," that may be defined as the gross income, less taxes, less bad debts and less aircraft sales. Other items may be required to be added to such a formula.

Aircraft Sales

With respect to aircraft sales, in the case of wholesale sales by a distributor to his dealer, there should be no percentage taken in any case.

Some lessors encourage aircraft sales by taking no direct percentage on any sales (wholesale or retail) presuming that a long-range income benefit will result as a consequence of more aircraft operating more hours, requiring more maintenance, storage, and fuel. It must be noted that two percent of the wholesale aircraft price usually amounts to forty percent of the distributor's gross profit, so that a percentage charged by a lessor on such transactions results in an impossible situation for the wholesaler.

Fuel Sales

Fuel sales must be specially treated since they are a specialty business and part of the "line service" offered by the lessee to support transient aircraft. In lieu of charging a percentage of the gross income derived from fuel sales as a part of the "rent," some communities impose a "fuel flowage fee." Fuel flowage fees charged by lessors range from one-half cent, and up, on each gallon of fuel pumped through the lessee's storage tanks, known in the trade as "through-put." Some recent leases have provided as much as $.12 per gallon on fuel and $.50 per gallon on lubricating oil. Any flowage rate creates a heavy economic burden on the lessee, which is to the detriment of both parties. It is recommended that if the lessor insists upon a fuel flowage fee, some special considerations should be given to the practical problems involved. Accordingly, it is recommended that the lessee have the right to fuel his own aircraft, aircraft operated by the local, state, or federal government and certificated air carrier aircraft (under "turn-around" fuel contracts) free of such charges and that a specified sum (for example, two cents a gallon) be charged only for fuel sold at retail into transient aircraft.

The "Through Put" Requirement

Some airport authorities require that an operator not deliver fuel into any aircraft unless the fuel has first been placed in storage tanks at the airport, i.e., no fueling is permitted directly from a common carrier transport truck into a refueler truck on the airport.

It is frequently stated that this requirement is for the protection of both the lessee and the lessor on possible claims of fuel contamination, since it protects the ultimate user by providing a separate filtration system. However, consideration must also be given by the lessee to the fact that such a technique is normally used to collect fuel flowage fees, which are computed on fuel products delivered into and "put through" such storage facilities. This may create a heavy economic burden on the lessee by obligating him to pay fees upon fuel carried in inventory and from which he has not -- and may never -- derive any profit.

Tank Farms

Be careful of a situation in which an airport commission writes a bulk storage lease agreement with an oil company completely separate from the lease with the base operator who retails that brand of fuel. There have been situations where three or more operators sell different brands of fuel on the same airport and there are three tank farms. If one or more of the operators has a falling out with his supplier and makes a contract with another fuel supplier, the commission may suddenly find that it has more tank farms on the airport than FBOs. Some airport commissions have included provisions whereby any lease between the commission and a fuel supplier must have prior approval from the FBOs on the airport and further provide that in the event any operator selects a different fuel supplier at a later time, the new supplier may take over the existing tank farm at a fixed rate of depreciation, thereby eliminating the need for the installation of new facilities. Under such circumstances the depreciation schedules are created by negotiation.

The Right to Select Suppliers

The lessee should be given the *absolute* right to select his own fuel supplier. Consideration should also be given to the possibility that the lessee may, at some future time, propose to enter into an into-plane fueling arrangement with a certificated carrier. In such a case, the carrier may insist that it also has the right to select its own fuel supplier. Since this may cause some conflict with existing mutual aid arrangements (which are common between certificated air carriers) it is recommeded that a prospective lessee consult with the fuel department of any airline with which he may become involved to ascertain any conflict of policy which would prevent him from fueling another airline or transient, charter or non-scheduled flight.

Landing and Parking Fees

Although income derived from fees collected from transient and based aircraft is not truly rent in the legal connotation, it is part of the income expected to be paid to the lessor and must be carefully negotiated. Examination of many leases shows that, in most cases, the lessee collects fees as agent for the lessor and retains a percentage for himself. This may vary from 25 to 75 percent. It is recommended that if the lessee is required to collect parking fees on an area on which he has paid for paving or other improvements, he should be allowed to keep 100 percent of the parking fees until such improvements have been amortized, after which a percentage division formula may be applied. The amortization period should be clearly spelled out in the terms of the lease.

The imposition and collection of landing fees has always been a sticky matter. It is the experience of many airport operators that the administrative costs of collecting landing fees absorb most of the funds collected. In addition, most operators feel that the funds collected are so small that they do not contribute substantially to defraying overhead in operating the airport. It has also been found that landing fees may act as a deterrent to use of the facilities by itinerant pilots, a condition which is opposed to the airport's very purpose.

If landing fees are insisted upon, it is recommended that such fees not be collected for general aviation aircraft not "operating in commerce," or, in other words, if landing fees must be collected, they be collected only from commercial passenger or freight operations for hire, including air taxi and commuter airline flights.

Special Charges

Larger, and more progressive Fixed Base Operators may operate or sublease to such concessionaires as car rental agencies, shops, restaurants, and other small businesses similar to those at a main terminal building. During lease negotiations, fees and charges to be set on these business endeavors should be thoroughly discussed; although such ancillary businesses may not be immediately initiated, they should be provided for.

Lease Proposal Requirements Checklist

The airport owner will usually not accept, solicited or unsolicited, a request to lease land area and/or existing buildings unless the proposed lessee sets forth, in writing, a proposal which spells out the scope of the operation propsed and certain business qualifications.

Listed below are the items of information that are generally asked for in an airport owner's request for proposal (RFP) from a potential lessee. They form a basis for a checklist of items to be accomplished in the lease/bid proposal process.

- ❑ **Services to be offered**
- ❑ **Amount of land needed to be leased**
- ❑ **Building space that will be leased or constructed**
- ❑ **Number of aircraft to be provided**
- ❑ **Number of qualified and/or certificated employees**
- ❑ **Hours of proposed operation**
- ❑ **Types and limits of insurance coverage to be maintained**
- ❑ **Name of insurance carrier**
- ❑ **Evidence of financial capability to perform**
- ❑ **Evidence of level of competency and experience to perform**

CHAPTER 4
PREPARATION GUIDE FOR ESTABLISHING MINIMUM OPERATING STANDARDS

Preparation Guide for Establishing Minimum Operating Standards

The most fundamental, and perhaps the most important item for any airport to have available is an up-to-date set of minimum operating standards for each aeronautical activity that is to be conducted on or from the airport. These "rules of the road" should be tough, reasonable, and uniformly applied to all airport users on a non-discriminatory basis.

Minimum Operating Standards should not be subject to being lowered or waived to allow prospective lessees to conduct business on the airport. Such standards should be used to allow only those who are qualified to operate on the airport, thereby creating an atmosphere that is beneficial to the public interest.

The standards recommended in this chapter are for the typical aeronautical activities being conducted on airports of all size and are intended as a guide to develop new or update existing minimum operating standards. They include:

- ❑ Aircraft Rental
- ❑ Aircraft Sales
- ❑ Airframe and Power Plant Repair
- ❑ Air Taxi and Commuter Airline Operations
- ❑ Automotive Gasoline Self-Fueling Operations
- ❑ Aviation Fuels and Oil Dispensing Service
- ❑ Avionics, Instrument, and Propeller Repair Service
- ❑ Flight Training
- ❑ Flying Clubs
- ❑ Non-FBO Hangar and Aviation Fuel and Oil Dispensing Facilities
- ❑ Multiple Services
- ❑ Specialized Commercial Flight Services

AIRCRAFT RENTAL

Any lessee desiring to engage in the rental of aircraft to the public must meet the following minimum operating standards.

- ❑ **LAND**
  The leasehold shall contain an area of __________ square feet to provide space for all buildings, aircraft parking, paved ramp area, employee parking, and customer parking.

- ❑ **BUILDINGS**
  Lease or construct a building which will provide __________ square feet of properly lighted and heated space for work and office space, storage, and a public waiting area that includes indoor rest room facilities and a public telephone.

- ❑ **PERSONNEL**
  __________ commercial pilots, with appropriate ratings, currently certificated by the Federal Aviation Administration.

- ❑ **AIRCRAFT**
  __________ airworthy single-engine and/or multi-engine aircraft owned or leased in writing to the lessee.

- ❑ **HOURS OF OPERATION**
  The normal operating hours will be from __________ to __________, ___ days a week.

- ❑ **FEDERAL REQUIREMENTS**
  The lessee shall comply with all applicable federal statutes and all regulations including, but not limited to, those promulgated by the Federal Aviation Administration and federal environmental authorities.

- ❑ **STATE AND LOCAL REQUIREMENTS**
  The lessee shall comply with all applicable state and local statutes, rules, and regulations including, but not limited to, those relating to tax, environmental, fire, building, and safety matters.

- ❑ **INSURANCE COVERAGE**
  The following types of insurance coverage will be provided by the lessee:

Aircraft Liability	$ __________	each person
Bodily Injury	__________	each accident
Property Damage	__________	each accident
Student and Renter Pilot Coverage		
Comprehensive Public Liability and Property Damage		

Bodily Injury	__________	each person/	__________	each accident
Property Damage	__________	each accident		
Products Liability	__________	each accident		
Professional Liability	__________	each accident		
Environmental Impairment Liability	__________	each occurrence		

AIRCRAFT SALES

Any lessee desiring to engage in the sale of new or used aircraft must meet the following minimum operating standards.

- ❑ **LAND**
  The leasehold shall contain an area of __________ square feet of land to provide space for all buildings, aircraft parking, storage, aircraft display, employee parking, and customer parking.

- ❑ **BUILDINGS**
  Lease or construct a building which will provide __________ square feet of properly lighted and heated space for work and office space, storage, and a public waiting area that includes indoor rest room facilities and a public telephone.

- ❑ **PERSONNEL**
  __________ commercial pilots currently certificated by the Federal Aviation Administration, with ratings appropriate for the types of aircraft to be demonstrated.

- ❑ **DEALERSHIPS**
  It shall be at the discretion of the lessee: (1) whether or not to be an authorized factory dealer; or, (2) what manufacturers he chooses to represent. All aircraft dealers shall hold a dealership license or permit, if required.

- ❑ **AIRCRAFT**
  A dealer of new aircraft shall have available or on call at least one current model demonstrator and shall provide for demonstrations of additional models of the manufacturer for which a dealership is held, if any. A dealer shall provide an adequate supply of parts and servicing facilities to customers during aircraft and parts warranty periods.

- ❑ **SERVICES**
  Provide for adequate servicing of aircraft and accessories during warranty periods of new aircraft.

- ❑ **HOURS OF OPERATION**
  The normal operating hours will be from __________ to __________, __________ days a week.

- ❑ **FEDERAL REQUIREMENTS**
  The lessee shall comply with all federal statutes and all regulations including, but not limited to, those promulgated by the Federal Aviation Administration and federal environmental authorities.

- ❑ **STATE AND LOCAL REQUIREMENTS**
  The lessee shall comply with all state and local statutes, rules and regulations, including but not limited to, those relating to tax, environmental, fire, building, and safety matters.

AIRCRAFT SALES (continued)

☐ **INSURANCE COVERAGE**
The following types of insurance coverage will be provided by the lessee:

Aircraft Liability	$ ________	each person
Bodily Injury	________	each accident
Property Damage	________	each accident
Passenger Liability	________	each passenger
	________	each accident
Hangar Keeper's Liability	________	each accident
Products Liability	________	each accident
Professional Liability	________	each accident
Comprehensive Public Liability and Property Damage		
Bodily Injury	________	each accident
Property Damage	________	each accident

AIRFRAME AND POWER PLANT REPAIR

Any lessee desiring to engage in airframe and/or power plant repair service must meet the following minimum operating standards.

- ❑ **LAND**
  The leasehold shall contain an area of __________ square feet to provide space for all buildings, temporary parking of aircraft, employee parking, and customer parking

- ❑ **BUILDINGS**
  Lease or construct a building which will provide __________ square feet of properly lighted and heated space for work and office space, storage, and a public waiting area that includes indoor rest room facilities and a public telephone.

- ❑ **PERSONNEL**
  __________ people currently certificated by the Federal Aviation Administration, with ratings appropriate for work being performed.

- ❑ **HOURS OF OPERATION**
  The normal operating hours will be from __________ to __________, __________ days a week.

- ❑ **EQUIPMENT**
  Sufficient equipment, supplies and availability of parts to perform maintenance in accordance with manufacturers' recommendations or equivalent.

- ❑ **FEDERAL REQUIREMENTS**
  The lessee shall comply with all applicable federal statutes and all regulations, including but not limited to, those promulgated by the Federal Aviation Administration.

- ❑ **STATE AND LOCAL REQUIREMENTS**
  The lessee shall comply with all state and local statutes, rules and regulations including, but not limited to, those relating to tax, fire, building, and safety matters.

- ❑ **ENVIRONMENTAL REQUIREMENTS**
  The lessee shall comply with all applicable local, state and federal environmental statutes and regulations, including but not limited to, requirements for the disposal of waste oil and other potentially hazardous substances

- ❑ **INSURANCE COVERAGE**
  The following types of insurance coverage will be provided by the lessee:

Hangar Keeper's Liability $ __________ each accident

Products Liability __________ each accident

Professional Liability __________ each accident

Comprehensive Public Liability and Property Damage

Bodily Injury __________ each person/__________ each accident

Property Damage __________ each accident

Environmental Impairment Liability __________ each occurrence

AIR TAXI AND COMMUTER AIRLINE OPERATIONS

Lessees desiring to engage in air taxi and/or commuter airline operations must be certificated by the Federal Aviation Administration under Federal Aviation Regulation Part 135 and registered with the Department of Transportation under the Economic Regulations of Part 298 and meet the following minimum operating standards.

- ❑ **LAND**
  The leasehold shall contain an area of __________ square feet to provide space for all buildings, aircraft parking, paved ramp area, employee parking, and customer parking.

- ❑ **BUILDINGS**
  Lease or construct a building which will provide __________ square feet of properly lighted and heated space for work and office space, storage, and a public waiting area that includes indoor rest room facilities and a public telephone.

- ❑ **PERSONNEL**
  __________ commercial and/or airline transport pilots currently certificated by the Federal Aviation Administration, who are appropriately rated to conduct the air taxi and/or commuter airline service offered.

- ❑ **AIRCRAFT**
  It shall be left to the discretion of the lessee to provide the type, category, class, size, and number of aircraft to meet the scope and magnitude of the service performed. All aircraft will be owned or leased in writing to the lessee, and will be airworthy and meet all requirements of the certificate held.

- ❑ **HOURS OF OPERATION**
  The normal operating hours will be from __________ to __________, __________ days a week, and at all other times deemed appropriate by the lessee.

- ❑ **FEDERAL REQUIREMENTS**
  The lessee shall comply with all applicable federal statutes and all regulations including, but not limited to, those promulgated by the Federal Aviation Administration.

- ❑ **STATE AND LOCAL REQUIREMENTS**
  The lessee shall comply with with applicable state and local statutes, rules and regulations including, but not limited to, those relating to tax, fire, building, and safety matters.

- ❑ **ENVIRONMENTAL REQUIREMENTS**
  The lessee shall comply with all applicable local, state and federal environmental statutes and regulations, including but not limited to, requirements for underground storage tanks, for the disposal of waste oil and other potentially hazardous substances and for the refueling of aircraft and vehicles.

AIR TAXI AND COMMUTER AIRLINE OPERATIONS (continued)

❑ **INSURANCE COVERAGE**
The following types of insurance coverage will be provided by the lessee:

Aircraft Liability	$ __________	each person
Bodily Injury	__________	each accident
Property Damage	__________	each accident
Passenger Liability	__________	each passenger
	__________	each accident

Comprehensive Public Liability and Property Damage

Bodily Injury	__________	each accident
Property Damage	__________	each accident
Contingency Liability	__________	each accident
Professional Liability	__________	each accident
Environmental Impairment Liability	__________	each occurrence

AUTOMOTIVE GASOLINE SELF-FUELING OPERATIONS

The following requirements pertain to all airport users desiring to use automotive gasoline (mogas) in lieu of aviation gasoline (avgas) in their aircraft.

❑ **PERMIT**
All automotive gasoline self-fueling operations will be governed by a permit issued by the airport operator at a cost of $__________ and good for a period of __________. Such a permit must be issued for each aircraft subject to self-fueling operations.

❑ **FUEL**
Mogas must meet ASTM D-439-58 standards at the time of delivery into the aircraft. Mogas may be substituted for avgas in only those aircraft for which an individual Supplemental Type Certificate (STC) has been approved by the Federal Aviation Administration. A copy of the individually held STC must be on file with the airport operator.

❑ **REFUELING OPERATIONS**
Airport users not operating under a lease contract with the airport to conduct fueling operations, must refuel only in areas designated for that purpose. Refueling of aircraft in a hangar or building is strictly prohibited.

The maximum container size used for the transport and storage of mogas shall not exceed __________ gallons, and must be approved by the Fire Marshal or other appropriate authority.

Pumps, either hand or power operated, shall be used to transfer fuel from the storage vessel into the aircraft. Pouring or gravity flow transfer of fuel is not permitted. The transfer of fuel from the storage tank of a ground based vehicle (e.g. automobile gas tank) is not permitted.

The storage of mogas in any amount in a hangar, building or tie-down area is not permitted.

The transportation of mogas onto or off of the airport must be done in accordance with the regulations established by the Fire Marshal or other appropriate authority.

❑ **PERSONNEL**
Aircraft owners and operators engaged in refueling operations shall be properly trained in fuel handling and associated safety procedures and shall adhere to standard industry practice for aircraft refueling operations.

❑ **TAXES**
The lessee shall be responsible for the payment of the appropriate Federal Excise Tax on aviation gasoline and for all reports required by the Internal Revenue Service.

❑ **FLOWAGE FEES**
A flowage fee of __________ cents per gallon will be paid to the airport opertor by the lessee for each gallon of mogas as it is transported onto the airport. This will constitute a difference of __________ cents per gallon more than the highest per gallon flowage fee paid by tenant Fixed Base Operators.

❑ **FEDERAL REQUIREMENTS**
The leasee shall comply with all applicable federal statutes and all regulations, including but not limited to, those promulgated by the Federal Aviation Administration.

AUTOMOTIVE GASOLINE SELF-FUELING OPERATIONS (continued)

❑ **STATE AND LOCAL REQUIREMENTS**
The lessee shall comply with all state and local statutes, rules and regulations including, but not limited to, those relating to tax, fire, building, and safety matters.

❑ **ENVIRONMENTAL REQUIREMENTS**
The lessee shall comply with all applicable local, state and federal environmental statutes and regulations, including but not limited to, requirements for underground storage tanks, for the disposal of waste oil and other potentially hazardous substances, and for the refueling of all aircraft.

❑ **INSURANCE COVERAGE**
The following types of insurance coverage will be provided by the lessee:

Comprehensive Public Liability and Property Damage

Bodily Injury	$ ________	each person
	________	each accident
Property Damage	________	each accident
Environmental Impairment Liability	________	each occurrence

AVIATION FUELS AND OIL DISPENSING SERVICE

Lessees desiring to dispense aviation fuels and oil and provide other related services, such as aircraft tie-down and parking, must meet the following minimum operating standards.

- ❑ **LAND**
  The leasehold shall contain an area of __________ square feet to provide space for all buildings, aircraft parking, paved ramp area, employee parking and customer parking.

- ❑ **BUILDINGS**
  Lease or construct a building which will provide __________ square feet of properly lighted and heated space for work and office space, storage, and a public waiting area that includes indoor rest room facilities and a public telephone.

- ❑ **PERSONNEL**
  __________ properly trained persons shall be on duty during normal operating hours.

- ❑ **AIRCRAFT SERVICE AND SUPPORT EQUIPMENT**
  Aircraft service and support equipment will include all necessary equipment items that would be required to properly service and provide support for the aircraft that are based on and/or normally transiting the airport. Said equipment may include, but not be limited to, adequate fire extinguishers, aircraft tugs of various sizes, ground power starter and auxiliary power units.

- ❑ **SERVICES**
  Fuel, park, hangar, and tie-down aircraft.

  Other services may include aircraft grooming, engine oil changes, on-airport transportation for crews and passengers, and minor repairs and services not requiring a certified mechanic.

- ❑ **FUEL FACILITIES**
  __________ metered filter-equipped dispensers, fixed and/or mobile, for dispensing __________ octane and/or __________ jet aviation fuels from storage tanks having a minimum capacity of __________ gallons each. Mobile dispensing equipment shall have at least a total capacity of __________ gallons for each grade and/or type fuel.

- ❑ **HOURS OF OPERATION**
  The normal operating hours will be from __________ to __________, __________ days a week.

- ❑ **FEDERAL REQUIREMENTS**
  The lessee shall comply with all applicable federal statutes and all regulations including, but not limited to, those promulgated by the Federal Aviation Administration.

- ❑ **STATE AND LOCAL REQUIREMENTS**
  The lessee shall comply with all applicable state and local statutes, rules, and regulations including, but not limited to, those relating to tax, fire, building, and safety matters.

- ❑ **ENVIRONMENTAL REQUIREMENTS**
  The lessee shall comply with all applicable local, state and federal environmental statutes and regulations, including but not limited to, requirements for underground storage tanks, for the disposal of waste oil and other potentially hazardous substances, and for the refueling of all aircraft and vehicles.

AVIATION FUELS AND OIL DISPENSING SERVICE (continued)

❑ **INSURANCE COVERAGE**
The following types of insurance coverage will be provided by the lessee:

Comprehensive Public Liability and Property Damage

Bodily Injury	$ __________	each person
	__________	each accident
Property Damage	__________	each accident
Hangar Keeper's Liability	__________	each accident
Products Liability	__________	each accident
Professional Liability	__________	each accident
Environmental Impairment Liability	__________	each occurrence

AVIONICS, INSTRUMENT, AND PROPELLER REPAIR SERVICE

Lessees desiring to provide avionics, instrument, or propeller repair service must be certificated as a Repair Station, with appropriate ratings, by the Federal Aviation Administration and meet the following minimum operating standards.

❑ **LAND**
The leasehold shall contain an area of _________ square feet to provide space for all buildings, aircraft parking, paved ramp area, employee parking and customer parking.

❑ **BUILDINGS**
Lease or construct a building which will provide _________ square feet of properly lighted and heated space for work and office space, storage and a public waiting area that includes indoor rest room facilities and a public telephone.

❑ **PERSONNEL**
_________ people certificated by the Federal Aviation Administration, in accordance with the terms of the Repair Station Certificate.

❑ **HOURS OF OPERATION**
The normal operating hours will be from _________ to _________, _________ days a week.

❑ **FEDERAL REQUIREMENTS**
The lessee shall comply with all applicable federal statutes and all regulations including, but not limited to, those promulgated by the Federal Aviation Administration.

❑ **STATE AND LOCAL REQUIREMENTS**
The lessee shall comply with all applicable state and local statutes, rules and regulations, including but not not limited to, those relating to tax, fire, building, and safety matters.

❑ **ENVIRONMENTAL REQUIREMENTS**
The lessee shall comply with all applicable local, state and federal environmental statutes and regulations, including but not limited to, the disposal of waste oil and other potentially hazardous substances.

❑ **INSURANCE COVERAGE**
Comprehensive Public Liability and Property Damage

Bodily Injury	$ _________	each person
	_________	each accident
Property Damage	_________	each accident
Hangar Keeper's Liability	_________	each accident
Products Liability	_________	each accident
Professional Liability	_________	each accident
Environmental Impairment Liability	_________	each occurrence

FLIGHT TRAINING

Any lessee desiring to engage in pilot flight instruction shall meet the following minimum operating standards:

❑ **LAND**
The leasehold shall contain an area of __________ square feet to provide space for all buildings, aircraft parking, paved ramp area, employee parking, and customer parking.

❑ **BUILDINGS**
Lease or construct a building which will provide __________ square feet of properly lighted and heated space for work and office space, storageand a public waiting area that includes indoor rest room facilities and a public telephone.

❑ **PERSONNEL**
__________ commercial pilots currently certificated by the Federal Aviation Administration, with appropriate ratings to cover the type of training offered.

❑ **AIRCRAFT**
__________ airworthy, properly equipped single-engine and/or multi-engine aircraft owned or leased in writing to the lessee.

❑ **HOURS OF OPERATION**
The normal operating hours will be from __________ to __________, __________ days a week.

❑ **FEDERAL REQUIREMENTS**
The lessee shall comply with all applicable federal statutes and all regulations, including but not limited to, those promulgated by the Federal Aviation Administration and federal environmental authorities.

❑ **STATE AND LOCAL REQUIREMENTS**
The lessee shall comply with all applicable state and local statutes, rules and regulations including, but not limited to, those relating to tax, environmental, fire, building, and safety matters:

❑ **INSURANCE COVERAGE FOR OWNED OR LEASED AIRCRAFT**
The following types of insurance coverage will be provided by the lessee.

Aircraft Liability	$ __________	each person
Bodily Injury	__________	each accident
Property Damage	__________	each accident

Student and Renter Pilot Coverage,
Comprehensive Public Liability and Property Damage

Bodily Injury	__________	each person
	__________	each accident
Property Damage	__________	each accident
Products Liability	__________	each accident
Professional Liability	__________	each accident
Environmental Impact Liability	__________	each occurence

FLYING CLUBS

The following requirements pertain to all flying clubs desiring to base their aircraft on the airport and be exempt from certain minimum operating standards that apply to commercial operators.

❑ **REGULATIONS**
Each club must be registered as a non-profit corporation or partnership.

Each member must be a bona fide owner of the aircraft or stockholder in the corporation.

The club may not derive greater revenue from the use of its aircraft than the amount necessary for the actual operation, maintenance, and replacement of its aircraft.

The club will file and keep current with the airport owner, a complete list of the club's membership and the investment share held by each member.

The club's aircraft will not be used by other than bona fide members for rental and by no one for commercial operations.

Student instruction can be given in club aircraft to club members, provided such instruction is given by a lessee based on the airport who provides flight instruction or by an instructor who shall not receive remuneration in any manner for such service.

Aircraft maintenance performed by the club shall be limited to only that maintenance that does not require a certificated mechanic. All other maintenance must be provided by a lessee based on the airport who provides such service, or by a properly certificated mechanic who shall not receive remuneration in any manner for such service.

❑ **FEDERAL REQUIREMENTS**
The lessee shall comply with all applicable federal statutes and all regulations including, but not limited to, those promulgated by the Federal Aviation Administration.

❑ **STATE AND LOCAL REQUIREMENTS**
The lessee shall comply with all applicable state and local statutes, rules and regulations including, but not limited to, those relating to tax, fire, building, and safety matters.

❑ **ENVIRONMENTAL REQUIREMENTS**
The lessee shall comply with all applicable local, state and federal environmental statutes and regulations, including but not limited to, requirements for the disposal of waste oil and other potentially hazardous substances and for the refueling of all aircraft and vehicles.

❑ **INSURANCE COVERAGE**
The following types of insurance coverage will be provided by the lessee:

Aircraft Liability	$ __________	each person
Bodily Injury	__________	each accident
Property Damage	__________	each accident

Student Pilot Coverage, Comprehensive Public Liability and Property Damage

Bodily Injury	__________	each accident / __________ each person
Property Damage	__________	each accident
Environmental Impairment Liability	__________	each occurrence

NON-FBO HANGAR AND AVIATION FUEL AND OIL DISPENSING FACILITIES

Lessees desiring to operate from privately-owned or leased hangars and/or to dispense aviation fuels and oil and provide other related services for their own aircraft, such as aircraft tie-down and parking, must meet the following minimum operating standards.

- ❑ **LAND**
  The leasehold shall contain an area of __________ square feet to provide space for all buildings, aircraft parking, paved ramp area, employee parking, and official company visitor parking. All land shall be leased from the airport operator. Access to airport property from privately-owned land, commonly referred to as "through-the-fence" operations, is strictly prohibited.

- ❑ **BUILDINGS**
  Lease or construct a building which will provide __________ square feet of properly lighted and heated space for work and office space, storage, and an official company visitor waiting area that includes indoor restroom facilities and a public telephone.

- ❑ **PERSONNEL**
  __________ properly trained persons shall be on duty during all hours of operation.

- ❑ **SERVICES**
  The lessee may hangar, tie-down, adjust, repair, refuel, clean and otherwise service his own aircraft, provided he does so with his own employees in accordance with the established policies of the Federal Aviation Administration and standards of the airport operator relating to such work.

- ❑ **FUEL FACILITIES**
  __________ metered filter-equipped dispensers, fixed and/or mobile for dispensing __________ octane and/or __________ jet aviation fuels from storage tanks having a minimum capacity of __________ gallons each. Mobile dispensing equipment shall be of the bottom loading variety, and restricted to a total capacity of __________ gallons for each grade and/or type of fuel. Use of mobile dispensing equipment will be restricted to the demised premises of the lessee.

- ❑ **FLOWAGE FEES**
  A flowage fee of __________ cents per gallon will be paid to the airport operator by the lessee for each gallon of aviation fuel delivered to the lessee's storage facility. This will constitute a difference of __________ cents per gallon more than the highest per gallon flowage fee paid by tenant fixed base operators.

- ❑ **HOURS OF OPERATION**
  The normal operating hours will be at the discretion of the lessee.

- ❑ **FEDERAL REQUIREMENTS**
  The lessee shall comply with all federal statutes and all regulations including, but not limited to, those promulgated by the Federal Aviation Administration.

- ❑ **STATE AND LOCAL REQUIREMENTS**
  The lessee shall comply with all state and local statutes, rules and regulations, including but not limited to, those relating to tax, fire, building, and safety matters.

- ❑ **ENVIRONMENTAL REQUIREMENTS**
  The lessee shall comply with all applicable local, state, and federal environmental statutes and regulations, including but not limited to, requirements for underground storage tanks, for the disposal of waste oil and other potentially hazardous substances, and for the refueling of all aircraft.

NON-FBO HANGAR AND AVIATION FUEL AND OIL DISPENSING FACILITIES (continued)

❑ **INSURANCE COVERAGE**
The following types of insurance coverage will be provided by the lessee:

Comprehensive Public Liability and Property Damage

Bodily Injury	__________	each person
	__________	each accident
Property Damage	__________	each accident
Hangar Keeper's Liability	__________	each accident
Products Liability	__________	each accident
Environmental Impairment Liability	__________	each occurrence

MULTIPLE SERVICES

Lessees desiring to engage in more than one commerical aeronautical activity must meet the following minimum operating standards.

❑ **LAND**
The leasehold for multiple activities shall contain __________ square feet of land to provide space for specific use area requirements established for the service to be offered (specific use spaces need not be added where combination use can be reasonably and feasibly established), aircraft parking, paved ramp area, employee parking, and customer parking.

❑ **BUILDINGS**
Lease or construct a building which will provide __________ square feet of properly lighted and heated space for work and office space, storage, and a public waiting area that includes indoor rest room facilities and a public telephone.

❑ **PERSONNEL**
Multiple responsibilities may be assigned to personnel to meet personnel requirements for all activities, provided said personnel are properly certificated, rated and/or trained to carry out their assigned duties.

❑ **AIRCRAFT**
All requirements for aircraft for the specific activities to be engaged in must be provided; however, multiple uses can be made of all aircraft, except aerial applicator (agricultural) aircraft, to meet multiple service requirements. __________ aircraft must be owned or leased in writing to the lessee.

❑ **EQUIPMENT**
All equipment specifically required for each activity must be provided.

❑ **SERVICES**
All services specifically required for each activity must be provided during the hours of operation.

❑ **HOURS OF OPERATION**
The lessee will adhere to the operating schedule as required for each activity.

❑ **FEDERAL REQUIREMENTS**
The lessee shall comply with all applicable federal statutes and all regulations including, but not limited to, those promulgated by the Federal Aviation Administration.

❑ **STATE AND LOCAL REQUIREMENTS**
The lessee shall comply with all applicable state and local statutes, rules and regulations including, but not limited to, those relating to tax, fire, building, and safety matters.

❑ **ENVIRONMENTAL REQUIREMENTS**
The lessee shall comply with all applicable local, state, and federal environmental statutes and regulations, including but not limited to, requirements for the disposal of waste oil and other potentially hazardous substances and for the refueling of all aircraft and vehicles.

❑ **INSURANCE COVERAGE**
The lessee will obtain the amounts specified for each type of insurance required for the specific activity.

SPECIALIZED COMMERCIAL FLIGHT SERVICES

Lessees desiring to engage in specialized commercial aeronautical activities, including but not limited to, those listed below, must meet the following minimum operating standards.

- ❑ **COMMERCIAL SERVICES**
  Non-stop sightseeing flights that begin and end at the same airport within a 25-mile radius.

  Agricultural application.

  Banner towing and aerial advertising.

  Aerial photography and survey.

  Fire fighting.

  Power line or pipeline patrol.

  Any other operations specifically excluded from Part 135 of the Federal Aviation Regulations.

- ❑ **LAND**
  The leasehold shall contain an area of __________ square feet to provide space for all buildings, aircraft parking, paved ramp area, employee parking, and customer parking.

- ❑ **BUILDINGS**
  Lease or construct a building which will provide __________ square feet of properly lighted and heated space for work and office space, storage, and a public waiting area that includes indoor rest room facilities and a public telephone.

- ❑ **PERSONNEL**
  __________ commercial pilots certificated by the Federal Aviation Administration, who are appropriately rated to conduct the specialized flight services offered.

- ❑ **AIRCRAFT**
  __________ properly certificated aircraft owned or leased in writing to the lessee.

- ❑ **HOURS OF OPERATION**
  The normal operating hours will be from __________ to __________, __________ days a week.

- ❑ **FEDERAL REQUIREMENTS**
  The lessee shall comply with all applicable federal statutes and all regulations including, but not limited to, those promulgated by the Federal Aviation Administration.

- ❑ **STATE AND LOCAL REQUIREMENTS**
  The lessee shall comply with all applicable state and local statutes, rules and regulations including, but not limited to, those relating to tax, fire, building, and safety matters.

- ❑ **ENVIRONMENTAL REQUIREMENTS**
  The lessee shall comply with all applicable local, state and federal environmental statutes and regulations, including but not limited to, requirements for the disposal of waste oil and other potentially hazardous substances, and for the refueling of all aircraft and vehicles.

SPECIALIZED COMMERCIAL FLIGHT SERVICES (continued)

☐ **INSURANCE COVERAGE**

The following types of insurance coverage will be provided by the lessee:

Aircraft Liability		$ ______	each person
	Bodily Injury	______	each accident
Property Damage		______	each accident
Passenger Liability		______	each passenger
		______	each accident
Comprehensive Public Liability and Property Damage			
	Bodily Injury	______	each person
		______	each accident
	Property Damage	______	each accident
	Contingency Liability	______	each accident
Products Liability		______	each accident
Professional Liability		______	each accident
Environmental Impairment Liability		______	each occurrence

CHAPTER 5
AIRPORT COMPLIANCE REQUIREMENTS

Airport Compliance Requirements

Many people are not aware that the Federal Aviation Administration does not *approve* minimum operating standards or the actual lease and operating agreement. However, the FAA may, and often does, *disapprove* of certain minimum standards or lease provisions if interpreted to be unreasonable or exclusionary at the expense of an actual or potential new entrant desiring to engage in aeronautical activities. If that happens, the airport operator is likely to be directed by the FAA to make specific changes to the document in question in order to make it acceptable.

Negotiating Aviation Agreements was written with this in mind.

Specifically, the basis for much of the material contained in *Negotiating Aviation Agreements* complements the FAA handbook *Airports Compliance Requirements* (Order No. 5190.6). The handbook contains federal interpretations on such important items as:

- **Single Activity not Necessarily an Exclusive Right**
- **Restrictions Based on Space Limitations, Safety or on Self-Service**
- **Qualifications and Standards**
- **Examples of the Use of Standards**
- **Terms Applied to Airport Users**
- **Rentals, Fees and Charges**
- **Availability of Leased Space**
- **Agreements Granting Access from Adjacent Property**

NATA recommends that *Airports Compliance Requirements* be included as *required* reading for all airport tenants and airport managers doing business on a publicly-owned airport. While this publication is not generally available, it can be obtained directly from the FAA, or it can be made available through NATA.

In addition to this handbook, two very important Advisory Circulars should be considered in the relationship between the lessor and lessee. They are:

- AC 150/5190-1, *Minimum Standards For Commercial Aeronautical Activities On Public Airports*
- AC 150/5190-2A, *Exclusive Rights At Airports*

These Advisory Circulars have been reproduced in their entirety on the pages that follow for the convenience of the readers of *Negotiating Aviation Agreements*.

U.S. Department of Transportation
Federal Aviation Administration

Advisory Circular

Subject: MINIMUM STANDARDS FOR COMMERCIAL AERONAUTICAL ACTIVITIES ON PUBLIC AIRPORTS

Date: 12/16/85
Initiated by:

AC No: 150/5190-1A
Change:

1. PURPOSE. This Advisory Circular (AC) provides basic information and broad guidance material to assist the owners of public airports in developing and applying minimum standards for commercial aeronautical activities on public airports.

2. CANCELLATION. Advisory Circular 150/5190-1, Minimum Standards for Commercial Aeronautical Activities on Public Airports, dated 8/18/66, is cancelled.

3. RELATED READING MATERIAL.

a. Federal Aviation Agency Policy Statement "Exclusive Rights at Airports" as published in the Federal Register (30 FR 13661), October 27, 1965.

b. Order 5190.6, Airports Compliance Requirements.

c. Advisory Circular 150/5190-2, Exclusive Rights at Airports.

4. CONTENT. This AC discusses minimum standards in general, explains how they are developed, and illustrates how, through proper application, they can operate to the advantage of the airport owner, the operator of a commercial aeronautical activity, and the general public. Some examples of standards are offered to suggest how their various elements may be related to aeronautical activities commonly conducted at a public airport.

5. DEFINITIONS. As used in this AC:

a. Minimum Standards. The qualifications which may be established by an airport owner as the minimum requirements to be met as a condition for the right to conduct an aeronautical activity on the airport.

b. Aeronautical Activity - any activity which involves, makes possible, or is required for the operation of aircraft, or which contributes to or is required for the safety of such operations.

The following activities, commonly conducted on airports, are aeronautical activities within this definition: charter operations, pilot training, aircraft rental and sightseeing, aerial photography, crop dusting, aerial advertising and surveying, air carrier operations, aircraft sales and services, sale of aviation petroleum products whether or not conducted in conjunction with other included activities, repair and maintenance of aircraft, sale of aircraft parts, and any other activities which because of their direct relationship to the operation of aircraft can appropriately be regarded as an "aeronautical activity."

The following are examples of what are not considered aeronautical activities: ground transportation (taxis, car rentals, limousines); restaurants; barber shops; auto parking lots.

c. Land Use Identification Plan - a scaled, dimensional layout of the entire airport property, indicating current and proposed usage for each identifiable segment.

6. BACKGROUND. The owner of a public airport developed or improved with the assistance of funds administered by the FAA assumes certain responsibilities, among them the obligation to make the airport's facilities and services available on fair and reasonable terms without unjust discrimination. The grant of an exclusive right to conduct an aeronautical activity on one of these obligated airports is specifically forbidden by law. On an airport which is not so obligated, the grant of an exclusive right should also be avoided since it limits the usefulness of the airport and deprives the using public of the benefits of competitive enterprise. Where Federal funds have been expended on an airport the opportunity to engage in an aeronautical activity not provided by the airport owner should be made available to any person, firm or corporation meeting standards established by the owner which are relevant to the proposed activity, reasonable, and in the public interest. The owner of a public airport can restrict the commercial use of the airport, or the solicitation of business thereon, based on nondiscriminatory standards. He may insist, in return for the privilege of conducting an aeronautical activity on the airport, that the person, firm or corporation selected must meet the standards established by the airport owner governing the quality and level of services that are offered to the public in connection with the conduct of a particular aeronautical activity on the airport. These standards must, however, be reasonable, relevant to the proposed activity, and applied objectively and uniformly.

7. USE OF STANDARDS. The requirements of standards imposed on those proposing to conduct an aeronautical activity on a public airport should relate primarily to the public interest. As building and sanitary codes are enacted for the protection of the local community, airport standards should be designed to protect airport patrons from irresponsible, unsafe or inadequate service. Because the cost of meeting reasonable standards must be accepted as a normal business expense, no prudent operator will undertake the investment involved unless he foresees a volume of business that has not been fully developed. Thus, the use of reasonable standards, while safeguarding the public interest, has the additional effect of preserving the stability of an established business. Proper standards discourage the unqualified for the protection of both the established operator and the public.

8. NEED TO BE REASONABLE AND RELEVANT. If an airport owner adopts qualifications and standards which are capricious, irrelevant, or unreasonable, they could have the effect of perpetuating a monopoly. Since the situation is different at each airport it is not possible to provide rigid criteria to measure the reasonableness of standards. Each case must be evaluated on its own merits in the light of circumstances existing at that specific airport. The fairness and reasonableness of standards normally is judged against the background of general practices which have found acceptance at airports of comparable size and situation.

Similarly, proposed standards must be evaluated for their relevancy to the type of activity to which they apply. A requirement that may be perfectly reasonable when applied to a flight instruction school, for example, could be quite unreasonable if imposed on an air taxi operator. The elements of the standards selected should express the particular requirements to be met by each different type of aeronautical activity contemplated at the airport. Examples of how some elements may be shown in standards for certain common aeronautical activities are outlined in paragraph 9 below.

9. COMBINATIONS OF ACTIVITIES. A basic need at every airport is the provision of essential primary line services. Essential services include the sale of aviation fuel and oil, facilities for tie-down or other storage of aircraft, ramp services and some capability for minor flight line repairs. It would not be unreasonable for an airport owner to insist that, as a condition for the right to engage in any of these primary services, the standards relevant to all of them be met. Except for these primary services, however, if standards for one type activity incorporate requirements which obviously relate to another, the possibility of an implied monopoly is raised. A "package" of standards which is reasonable when applied to the operator conducting a variety of activities could be unfair and discriminatory if imposed on an operator proposing to engage in only one activity. For example, to require radio repair service to provide shop facilities for engine repair would be unreasonable, particularly so, if adequate shop facilities were already available on the airport.

A distinction should be made between a "standard" imposed as a prerequisite for all operators and contractual commitments made by the individual. However, the willingness of a commercial operator to provide a variety of aeronautical activities should benefit both the airport and its patrons.

10. ELEMENTS. A review of standards adopted by many communities reveals a frequent reliance on the financial commitment. This is usually expressed as a requirement to lease and develop minimum acreage or building space, or as an outright minimum dollar investment. Such a requirement, to be meaningful, should be clearly connected to other specific requirements which relate directly to the aeronautical activities proposed. Some of the elements that should be incorporated into standards at most airports would require the service operator to:

a. Arrange for suitable spaces, structures or facilities.

b. Provide adequate fixtures and equipment.

c. Maintain an adequate staff of employees with skills, licenses and certificates appropriate to the activities proposed.

d. Operate during specified minimum hours.

e. Conform to safety, health and sanitary codes.

f. Show evidence of financial stability and good credit rating.

g. Meet stated indemnity and insurance minimums.

11. LAND USE IDENTIFICATION PLANS. Land use identification plans are closely related to minimum standards. They offer a convenient and effective device for outlining the airport owner's program for development of balanced land usage. Such a plan indicates the airport owner's intention and capability to provide essential support services by allocating space for commercial aeronautical activities. To the prospective service operator the plan is evidence of the expected economic potential of the airport and it alerts him to other operations, existing or planned, which might be competitive. The plan should identify areas dedicated to aeronautical services, fuel storage, general aviation, passenger loading, air freight and cargo handling, common use aircraft parking, public automobile parking, etc.; plus parcels held for future expansion. It is an advantage to have the aeronautical services area platted, for it is often useful to make reference to the plat in the grant of leasehold rights. Indeed, land use plans quite properly can be made a part of the minimum standards themselves.

12. EXAMPLES. The examples below illustrate how the elements of a standard may be related to some of the aeronautical activities commonly found at a public airport. These should not, however, be considered as criteria for judging the reasonableness of standards. The level of qualifications to be imposed under each standard will vary, depending on the circumstances at each individual airport. The right to offer services and commodities to the users of a public airport might reasonably be conditioned on the ability to meet any combination of the following, adjusted to suit local circumstances. But care must be taken to make the standards realistic, especially to insure that they are not so demanding that they compel the service operator to extend his investment beyond the economic potential of the airport.

a. Fuel and Oil Sales.

(1) Suitable space in a convenient location to service the types of aircraft using the airport.

(2) Tank storage capacity, either above or below ground as mutually agreed upon, for a stated minimum capacity of both jet fuel and gasoline in specified grades.

(3) Mobile and fixed pumping equipment with reliable metering devices, and of sufficient capacity to refuel the largest aircraft likely to be serviced within a specified maximum time.

(4) Uniformed personnel on full time duty during the stated hours, which may range up to 24 hours, seven days a week, depending on local requirements.

(5) Demonstrated capability to perform minor repairs coupled with a requirement for tools, jacks, towing equipment, tire repair equipment, etc.

(6) Suitable aircraft parking and tie-down areas and the demonstrated capability to efficiently and safely move aircraft to such areas and store them in compliance with local regulations.

(7) A requirement that the operator install adequate grounding rods at all fueling locations to eliminate the hazards of static electricity.

(8) Provision of energizers, starters, passenger loading steps, oxygen, compressed air and such other equipment and supplies as may be required to serve the types of aircraft using the airport.

(9) Availability of conveniently located, comfortably heated waiting rooms for passengers and crew members of itinerant aircraft, including sanitary rest rooms and public telephone.

(10) A commitment to remove snow and otherwise clean up the fueling areas, coupled with the provision of the equipment necessary for this purpose.

(11) Provision of special fire detection or fire fighting equipment where justified, coupled with a commitment to have employees participate for a minimum number of hours in fire, rescue or other emergency training when provided for tenants by the airport owner.

b. Flight Training Activities.

(1) The availability, on a full time basis, of personnel and equipment appropriate to the types of training planned.

(2) The availability of a number of aircraft of specific types, compatible with the training proposed.

(3) The provision of a minimum amount of classroom space and related rest rooms, cloak rooms and arrangements for food service.

(4) The availability of specified minimum training equipment such as mock-ups, engine cut-aways, instrument flight trainers.

(5) The continuing ability to meet certification requirements of the FAA (and any pertinent state or local authorities) to conduct the training proposed.

c. Aircraft Charter and Taxi.

(1) Suitable arrangements for passenger shelter, rest rooms, public telephones, etc. However, where these and other convenience facilities are provided by the airport owner for public use, it would be unreasonable to require that they be duplicated by air carrier, air charter, or air taxi operators.

(2) Satisfactory arrangements for checking in passengers, handling luggage, ticketing and ground transportation.

(3) An assurance of the continued availability of suitable aircraft, with qualified operating crews, located at the airport (under acceptable separate arrangements) ready to depart within a specified maximum notice period.

d. Aircraft, Engine and Accessory Maintenance.

(1) Specific minimum hangar, shop and storage space.

(2) Availability of full time repairmen and mechanics in such fields as airframe and engine maintenance, electronics instruments, and others as required.

(3) Specified minimum equipment such as machine tools, jacks, lifts, and test centers.

(4) Arrangements for access to, or the provision of, specified minimum capacity for the storage of aircraft, coupled with a requirement to remove any nonairworthy aircraft from the airport premises within a reasonable time.

(5) Suitable facilities for washing and cleaning aircraft.

(6) A commitment to promptly remove from the public landing area (as soon as permitted by cognizant FAA and CAB authorities) any disabled aircraft; coupled with the availability of suitable tractors, tow bars, jacks, dollies and other equipment as might be needed to remove the largest type aircraft that normally could be expected.

(7) Provision of spaces and equipment meeting all applicable safety requirements for painting aircraft.

e. Crop Dusting and Spraying.

(1) Suitable arrangements for the safe storage and containment of noxious chemical materials.

(2) Availability of aircraft suitably equipped for agricultural operations with adequate safeguards against spillage on runways and taxiways or dispersal by wind force to other operational areas of the airport.

f. Aircraft Rental and Sales.

(1) Availability during specified hours of aircraft commensurate with the scope of the planned activity.

(2) Sales or distributorship franchise from an aircraft manufacturer for new aircraft, or adequate sources of used aircraft.

(3) Suitable sales and office facilities, leased, rented or constructed on the airport property.

(4) Satisfactory arrangements at the airport for repair and servicing of sales aircraft during the sales guarantee.

(5) Minimum stocks of spare parts peculiar to the aircraft types for which sales privileges are granted.

13. APPLICATION. Many communities choose to state their standards only in actual use agreements at the time they are executed. While standards can be effective in this form, it makes them vulnerable to challenge by prospective operators of aeronautical activities on the grounds that they are not objective. An airport owner can most closely approach complete objectivity by developing and publishing minimum standards before negotiating with any specific tenants. However, this is not always practicable. On occasion, a community finds it difficult to attract competent service agencies and, as an inducement, may elect to waive standards which, if applied at a later stage of airport development, might be perfectly reasonable. The owner of a public airport may quite properly increase the standards from time to time for the purpose of improving the quality of service to the public. But juggling of standards solely to protect the interest of an existing tenant would clearly be incompatible with this objective. In any event, any standard which a tenant operator is required to meet must be uniformly applicable to all operators seeking the same franchise privileges. A community may find it especially helpful to ask an FAA Airports program representative to comment on the relevance and reasonableness of standards it proposes to adopt.

Leonard E. Mudd
LEONARD E. MUDD
Director, Office of Airport Standards

AC NO: 150/5190-2A
DATE: 4 Apr 72

ADVISORY CIRCULAR

DEPARTMENT OF TRANSPORTATION
FEDERAL AVIATION ADMINISTRATION

REPRINTED MARCH 1976
INCORPORATES CHG 1

SUBJECT: EXCLUSIVE RIGHTS AT AIRPORTS

1. PURPOSE. This circular is issued to make available to public airport owners, and to other interested persons, basic information and guidance on this agency's policy regarding exclusive rights at public airports on which Federal funds, administered by the agency, have been expended.

2. CANCELLATION. AC 150/5190-2 dated 2 September 1966 is cancelled.

3. CONTENT. Included in this circular are discussions of the exclusive rights policy in general, the legislation requiring it, the history of its development and an explanation of how it applies to aeronautical activities conducted on public airports developed or improved with Federal assistance. Descriptions of some typical situations are presented to illustrate the agency's interpretation and administration of the policy. The material offered here is nonregulatory and is intended only to foster a better understanding of the exclusive rights policy by those public airport owners to whom it applies. For owners of public airports who have not received Federal aid, this circular will illustrate how they would be affected should they seek such aid in the future. Those engaged in a commercial activity on an airport should also find this information of interest.

4. REFERENCES.

   a. Policy Statement "Exclusive Rights at Airports" as published in the Federal Register (30 FR 13661), 27 October 1965.

   b. FAA Advisory Circular AC 150/5190-1, Minimum Standards for Commercial Aeronautical Activities on Public Airports. This circular can be obtained from the Department of Transportation (DOT) Distribution Unit, TAD-484.3, Washington, D.C. 20590.

5. LEGISLATIVE BACKGROUND.

a. There have been statutory prohibitions against the granting of exclusive rights at an airport ever since the enactment of the Civil Aeronautics Act of 1938. Section 303 of that Act provided "there shall be no exclusive right for the use of any landing area or air navigation facility upon which Federal funds have been expended." More recently, this identical language was incorporated in section 308(a) of the Federal Aviation Act of 1958.

b. During the course of World War II many civil airports were improved with Federal funds. This program was carried out under agreements requiring that these airports be operated "without the grant or exercise of any exclusive right for use of the airport within the meaning of section 303 of the Civil Aeronautics Act of 1938." Following World War II, a great many former military airports were conveyed to public agencies under the provisions of the Surplus Property Act of 1944. Initially, the deeds which transferred these surplus airports included a covenant that there would be no exclusive right contrary to the provisions of section 303. Subsequently, however, in 1947, the Surplus Property Act was amended by P.L. 80-289 which defined an exclusive right, but excluded from the definition the sale of gas and oil.

c. Since 1947, the Civil Aeronautics Administration (CAA) and its successors, the Federal Aviation Agency (FAA) and the Federal Aviation Administration (FAA), administered the Federal-aid Airport Program (FAAP) under the authority of the Federal Airport Act of 1946. The Federal Airport Act of 1946 was repealed by the Airport and Airway Development Act of 1970 and under the authority of the latter Act the Airport Development Aid Program (ADAP) was formulated. In approving grants of Federal funds under these programs, the CAA, and later the FAA, always maintained that there could be no exclusive right for any aeronautical activity which involved use of the airport's landing area. The acceptance of a grant under either of these programs prohibits the granting of an exclusive right of any aeronautical activity as long as the facility is operated as an airport. In recent years, the agency has refined and clarified its policies as referenced in paragraph 4. The following paragraphs explain how this policy will be administered and how it applies co specific circumstances frequently encountered.

6. DEFINITIONS. For the purpose of this circular, the following definitions apply:

a. Exclusive Right. A power, privilege, or other right excluding or debarring another from enjoying or exercising a like power, privilege, or right. An exclusive right may be conferred either by express agreement, by imposition of unreasonable standards or requirements, or by any other means. Such a right conferred on one or more parties but excluding others from enjoying or exercising a similar right or rights would be an exclusive right.

b. Aeronautical Activity. Any activity which involves, makes possible, or is required for the operation of aircraft, or which contributes to or is required for the safety of such operations.

(1) The following activities, commonly conducted on airports, are aeronautical activities within this definition; charter operations, pilot training, aircraft rental and sightseeing, aerial photography, crop dusting, aerial advertising and surveying, air carrier operations, aircraft sales and services, sale of aviation petroleum products whether or not conducted in conjunction with other included activities, repair and maintenance of aircraft, sale of aircraft parts, and any other activities which because of their direct relationship to the operation of aircraft can appropriately be regarded as an "aeronautical activity."

(2) The following are examples of what are not considered aeronautical activities: ground transportation (taxis, car rentals, limousines); restaurants; barber shops; auto parking lots.

c. Minimum Standards. The qualifications which may be established by an airport owner as the minimum requirements to be met as a condition for the right to conduct an aeronautical activity on the airport.

d. Federal-aid Airport Program (FAAP). A grant-in-aid program administered by the agency under the authority of the Federal Airport Act of 1946 (49 USC-1101), as amended, to assist public agencies in the development of a nationwide system of public airports. The Federal Airport Act of 1946 was repealed by the Airport and Airway Development Act of 1970.

e. Airport Development Aid Program (ADAP). A grant-in-aid program administered by the FAA under the authority of the Airport and Airway Development Act of 1970 (49 USC-1701) to assist public agencies in the substantial expansion and improvement of the Nation's airport system.

7. POLICY. The grant of an exclusive right for the conduct of any aeronautical activity, on an airport on which Federal funds, administered by the FAA, have been expended, is regarded as contrary to the requirements of applicable laws, whether such exclusive right results from an express agreement, from the imposition of unreasonable standards or requirements, or by any other means. However, the existence of an exclusive right to sell gasoline and oil will not be considered to be in violation of section 308(a) where such right has been specifically exempted by a deed under the Surplus Property Act, except where an agreement not to grant an exclusive right for the sale of gasoline and oil is controlling. (See subparagraph b.)

a. Agency Position. The agency considers that the existence of an exclusive right to conduct any aeronautical activity limits the usefulness of an airport and deprives the using public of the benefits of competitive enterprise. Apart from legal considerations, the agency believes it clearly inappropriate to apply Federal funds to improvement of an airport where full realization of the benefits would be restricted by the exercise of an exclusive right to engage in aeronautical activites.

b. Application of Law. The exemption contained in a surplus property deed permitting the grant of an exclusive right for the sale of gas and oil does not operate to confer a positive privilege. If the airport was already obligated by a prior agreement prohibiting an exclusive right, the deed does not relieve the owner from such obligation. Conversely, where such an exemption for gas and oil is in effect, any subsequent grant of Federal funds, administered by the agency, requires the airport owner to agree not to permit the establishment of an exclusive right to engage in aeronautical activities, including the sale of gas and oil, in the future and to terminate any existing agreement which permits such an exclusive right as soon as possible.

8. INTERPRETATION OF POLICY. The circumstances involved in arranging for the availability of adequate aeronautical services vary widely from airport to airport. The following material has been prepared in an effort to furnish general guidance based on experience with exclusive rights problems.

a. Single Activity. The presence on an airport of only one enterprise conducting aeronautical activities does not necessarily mean that an exclusive right has been granted. If there is no intent by express agreement, by the imposition of unreasonable standards, or by other means to exclude others, the absence of a competing activity is not a violation of this policy. This sort of situation frequently arises where the market potential is insufficient to attract additional aeronautical activities. So long as the opportunity to engage in an aeronautical activity is available to those who meet reasonable and relevant standards, the fact that only one enterprise takes advantage of the opportunity does not constitute a grant of an exclusive right.

b. Space Limitations. The leasing of all available airport land or facilities suitable for aeronautical activities to a single enterprise will be construed as evidence of an intent to exclude others. This presumption will not apply if it can be reasonably demonstrated that the total space leased is presently required and will be immediately used to conduct the planned activity. The amount of space leased to a single enterprise should be limited to that for which it can clearly demonstrate an actual, existing need. If additional space becomes necessary at a later date, it must be made available, not only to an incumbent enterprise, but at the same time to all qualified proponents or bidders. The advance grant of options or preferences on future sites to a single incumbent is evidence of an intent to grant an exclusive right. On the other hand, nothing in this policy should be construed as limiting the expansion of a single enterprise when it needs additional space, even though it may ultimately reach complete occupancy of all space available.

c. Restrictions Based on Safety. Under certain circumstances, it is sometimes necessary to deny the right to engage in an aeronautical activity at an airport for reasons of safety. Where this denial has the effect of shielding an established enterprise from competition, it should be carefully and thoroughly justified by the airport owner.

d. Restrictions on Self-Service. Any unreasonable restriction imposed on the owners and operators of aircraft regarding the servicing of their own aircraft and equipment may be considered as a violation of agency policy. The owner of an aircraft should be permitted to fuel, wash, repair, paint and otherwise take care of his own aircraft, provided there is no attempt to perform such services for others. Restrictions which have the effect of diverting activity of this type to a commercial enterprise amount to an exclusive right contrary to law. Local airport regulations, however, may and should impose restrictions on these activities necessary for safety, preservation of airport facilities and protection of the public interest. These might cover, for example, restrictions on the handling practices for aviation fuel and other flammable products, such as aircraft paint and thinners; requirements to keep fire lanes open; weight limitations on vehicles and aircraft to protect paving from overstresses, etc.

e. Monopolies Beyond Control of Airport Owners. The Federal Communications Commission, which authorizes the use of "UNICOM" frequencies for air-to-ground use at airports, will not license more than one ground station at the same airport. Although these and similar exclusive franchises unquestionably give the recipient an advantage over competitors, they do not constitute a grant of an exclusive right contrary to agency policy. Airport owners are encouraged to obtain the UNICOM license in their own names and through droplines to make the facility available to all fixed base operators on a required basis.

9. ENFORCEMENT.

a. Remedies. At any airport where there has been a grant of an exclusive right contrary to law and this policy, that airport and any other airport owned or controlled by the offending airport owner will be ineligible for assistance under the ADAP, and the agency will not expend Facilities and Equipment funds for installations designed to benefit traffic at such airports. No grant agreement may be executed, and no payment of funds due under prior grant agreements shall be made, nor shall any Facilities and Equipment funds be expended until the exclusive right has been terminated.

b. National Defense and National Interest. This policy shall not be construed as precluding the grant or expenditure of Federal funds when required for the national defense, or when determined by the Administrator to be in the national interest.

c. Application to Preexisting Agreements. On 17 July 1962, the agency defined the aeronautical activities prohibited by section 308(a) of the Federal Aviation Act. Prior to the publication of this definition, exclusive rights to conduct certain activities not involving the actual use of public landing areas were considered not to be in violation of the statute. Also, as noted in paragraph 7 hereof, the grant of an exclusive right to sell only gasoline and oil would not be in violation of the statute where the controlling agreement with the Government is a surplus property deed specifically exempting such sales from the activities otherwise prohibited on an exclusive basis. The agency will continue to participate in airport development in these instances if it can be demonstrated that an exclusive right agreement made prior to 17 July 1962, or pursuant to the exemption in a surplus property deed, will be effectively terminated as soon as possible. The termination date will in no event be later than the earliest renewal or cancellation date specified in the lease or agreement covering such an exclusive right agreement. However, in no case will ADAP participation in airport improvement be authorized where there exists an exclusive right which was prohibited under the interpretation prior to 17 July 1962.

4 Apr 72 AC 150/5190-2A

10. PROPRIETARY EXCLUSIVES. The public agency that owns and operates a public airport may engage in any proprietary aeronautical activity and deny the same right to others without violating this policy. This means that the public agency may provide aeronautical services on an exclusive basis, but only if it does so as a principal, using its own employees and resources. This exemption is not effective where an independent commercial enterprise is designated an "agent" of the airport owner.

11. ADMINISTRATION OF POLICY.

a. As a material part of any grant agreement in anticipation of financial assistance under the Airport and Airway Development Act, all applicants for such assistance will be required to:

(1) Certify that there is no grant of an exclusive right which would preclude expenditure of funds by the agency under applicable law and agency policy at any public airport owned or controlled by the applicant, and

(2) Give assurances that none will be granted on any airport now owned or controlled by the applicant.

b. It is the intent of this policy to promote fair competition at public airports and not to expose those who have undertaken to provide commodities and services to irresponsible competition. Prudent airport owners will adopt and enforce minimum standards to be met by those who propose to conduct a commercial aeronautical activity. Such standards, by expressing minimum levels of service that must be offered, relate primarily to the public interest, but appropriate requirements uniformly applied discourage substandard enterprises, thereby protecting both the established aeronautical activity and the airport patrons. The application of any unreasonable requirement, or standard not relevant to the proposed activity, or any requirement that is applied in a discriminatory manner shall be considered a constructive grant of an exclusive right contrary to applicable law and provisions of agency policy.

12. HOW TO OBTAIN THIS PUBLICATION. Obtain additional copies of this publication, AC 150/5190-2A, Exclusive Rights at Airports, from the Department of Transportation, Distribution Unit, TAD-484.3, Washington, D.C. 20590.

CHESTER G. BOWERS
Director, Airports Service

Sample Agreements

The agreements shown in this chapter are intended to provide insight into the importance and complex nature of such legal documents. They should be treated as sample agreements only.

The sample agreements shown in this chapter include:

- ❑ **Lease and Operating Agreement**
- ❑ **Aircraft Lease Agreement**
- ❑ **Aircraft Lease and Pilot Service Agreement**
- ❑ **Hangar Space Lease Agreement**
- ❑ **Hangar Lease Agreement**
- ❑ **Tie-Down Lease Agreement**
- ❑ **Aircraft Rental Agreement**

SAMPLE

LEASE AND OPERATING AGREEMENT

This Lease and Operating Agreement (this "Agreement") entered into as of the __________ day of __________, 19__, by and between the Anytown Airport Commission, a body politic and corporate created by the Council of Anytown ("Lessor"), and ______________________________ ______________________________, a ____________________ corporation with authority to do business in the State of ______________("Lessee").

Witnesseth:

WHEREAS, Lessor now owns, controls and operates the Anytown Airport (the "Airport") in the City and County of Anytown, State of ______________________;

WHEREAS, fixed base operation services are essential to the proper accommodation of general and commercial aviation at the Airport; and

WHEREAS, Lessor desires to make such services available at the Airport and Lessee is qualified, ready, willing and able to provide such services;

NOW, THEREFORE, in consideration of the premises and the mutual covenants contained in this Agreement, the parties hereby agree as follows:

ARTICLE ONE

TERM

The term of this Agreement shall be for a period of twenty-five (25) years, commencing on the _____ day of __________, 19__, and continuing through the _____ day of ______________, 20___ (the "Termination Date"), unless earlier terminated under the provisions of this Agreement. Lessee shall have the option, exercisable upon at least one hundred eighty (180), but not more than three hundred sixty-five (365), days' notice to Lessor prior to the Termination Date, to extend the term of the Agreement for an additional period of ____________ (_________) years from and after the Termination Date, upon the same terms and conditions as are contained in this Agreement.

ARTICLE TWO

LEASED PREMISES

Lessor hereby leases to Lessee, and Lessee hereby leases from Lessor, the following premises, identified and shown on Exhibit A, attached hereto and made a part hereof, including leasehold improvements constructed by Lessee pursuant to Article Five of this Agreement (the "Premises"), together with the right of ingress and egress for both vehicles and aircraft:

A. Real Property as follows:
(Legal description of real property)

B. Improvement on said real property, as follows:

1. **Hangar Number 1:** An area comprising approximately __________ (_________) square feet of usable space under roof (the "Hangar").

2. **Ramp and Apron Area:** An area adjacent to Hangar Number 1, comprising approximately __________ (_________) square feet.

SAMPLE

ARTICLE TWO (continued)

3. **General Aviation Terminal:**

   a. An area comprising approximately __________ (__________) square feet of space within the General Aviation Terminal.

   b. An area comprising approximately __________ (__________) square feet on the ramp side of the General Aviation Terminal.

   c. An area comprising approximately __________ (__________) square feet of space north of the General Aviation Terminal.

C. Fuel Storage Area: Above and below-ground fuel storage comprising approximately __________ (__________) square feet of land containing __________ (__________) __________ (__________) gallon fuel tanks.

ARTICLE THREE

RIGHTS AND OBLIGATIONS OF LESSEE

A. **Required Services.** Lessee is hereby granted the nonexclusive privilege to engage in, and Lessee agrees to engage in, the business of providing full and complete fixed base operation services at the Airport, __________ (__________) hours per day, every day, as follows:

1. Aircraft ground guidance within the uncontrolled areas adjacent to the Premises, and ramp service, including sale and into-plane delivery of aviation fuels, lubricants and other related aviation products.

2. Apron servicing of, and assistance to, aircraft, including transient parking, storage and tie-down service, for both based and transient aircraft upon or within facilities leased to Lessee or aircraft parking areas designated by Lessor.

3. Repair and maintenance of based and transient aircraft. Lessee agrees to maintain and operate a repair station approved by the Federal Aviation Administration (the "FAA"), with ratings as follows:

   a. Engine, airframe and accessories -- Classes I, II and III.

   b. Avionics -- Classes I and II.

4. Customary accommodations for the convenience of users, including pilot lounge area, information services, direct telephone service connections to the Flight Service Station and the United States Weather Bureau, and courtesy vehicle ground transportation to and from other terminals at the Airport.

5. Equipment and trained personnel to remove disabled aircraft with a gross landing weight of twelve thousand five hundred (12,500) pounds or less from those portions of the Airport provided and made available by Lessor for aircraft and related operations, including aircraft runways, taxiways, ramps, aprons and parking spaces, and areas directly associated therewith, which are not leased by Lessee or any other tenant on the Airport ("Air Operations Area"). Lessee shall perform such removal services on request.

6. Sales of avionic and engine parts and instruments and accessories.

SAMPLE

ARTICLE THREE (continued)

*7. Lessee acknowledges that no right or privilege has been granted which would operate to prevent any person, firm or corporation operating aircraft on the Airport from performing services on its own aircraft, with its own employees, including maintenance and repair services.

B. **Authorized Services.** In addition to the services required to be provided by Lessee pursuant to Paragraph A, above, Lessee is authorized, but not required, to provide the following services and to engage in the following activities:

1. Ramp service at other Airport locations, including into-plane delivery of aircraft fuel, lubricants and other related aviation products; loading and unloading of passengers, baggage, mail and freight; and providing of ramp equipment, aircraft cleaning and other services for air carriers and other persons or firms.

2. Special flight services, including aerial sightseeing, aerial advertising and aerial photography.

3. The sale of new and used aircraft, aircraft parts, navigation equipment, and new and used radio and electronic equipment.

4. The demonstration of aircraft for sale.

5. Flight training, including ground school.

6. Aircraft rental.

7. Aircraft charter operations conducted by Lessee or a subcontractor of Lessee.

8. Any other general aviation services not specifically provided for herein which are approved in advance by Lessor. Lessor's approval of such services shall not be unreasonably withheld.

C. **Operating Standards.** In providing any of the required and/or authorized services or activities specified in this Agreement, Lessee shall operate for the use and benefit of the public and shall meet or exceed the following standards:

1. Lessee shall comply with the minimum operating standards or requirements, promulgated by Lessor, applicable to each of Lessee's activities on the Airport.

*2. Lessee shall furnish service on a fair, reasonable and nondiscriminatory basis to all users of the Airport. Lessee shall furnish good, prompt and efficient service adequate to meet all reasonable demands for its services at the Airport. Lessee shall charge fair, reasonable, and nondiscriminatory prices for each unit of sale or service; provided, however, that Lessee shall be allowed to make reasonable and nondiscriminatory discounts, rebates or other similar types of price reductions to volume purchasers.

3. Lessee shall select and appoint a full-time manager of its operations at the Airport. The manager shall be qualified and experienced, and vested with full power and authority to act in the name of Lessee with respect to the method, manner and conduct of the operation of the fixed base services to be provided under this Agreement. The manager shall be available at the Airport during regular business hours, and during the manager's absence a duly authorized subordinate shall be in charge and available at the Airport.

---

* Must be included in all leases governing aeronautical services on airports receiving federal aid.

SAMPLE

ARTICLE THREE (continued)

4. Lessee shall provide, at its sole expense, a sufficient number of employees to provide effectively and efficiently the services required or authorized by this Agreement.

5. Lessee shall control the conduct, demeanor and appearance of its employees, who shall be trained by Lessee and who shall possess such technical qualifications and hold such certificates or qualifications as may be required by any governmental authority in carrying out assigned duties. It shall be the responsibility of Lessee to maintain close supervision over its employees to assure a high standard of service to customers of Lessee.

6. Lessee shall meet all expenses and payments in connection with the use of the Premises and the rights and privileges herein granted, including taxes, permit fees, license fees and assessments lawfully levied or assessed upon the Premises or property at any time situated therein and thereon. Lessee may, at its sole expense and cost, contest any tax, fee or assessment.

7. Lessee shall comply with all federal, state and local laws, rules and regulations which may apply to the conduct of the business contemplated, including rules and regulations promulgated by Lessor, and Lessee shall maintain in effect and post in a prominent place all necessary and/or required licenses or permits.

8. Lessee shall be responsible for the maintenance and repair of the Premises and shall keep and maintain the Premises in good condition, order and repair, and shall surrender the same upon the expiration of this Agreement, in the condition in which they are required to be kept, reasonable wear and tear and damage by the elements not caused by Lessee's negligence excepted.

9. It is expressly understood and agreed that, in providing required and authorized services pursuant to this Agreement, Lessee shall have the right to choose, in its sole discretion, its vendors and suppliers.

D. **Signs.** During the term of this Agreement, Lessee shall have the right, at its expense, to place in or on the Premises a sign or signs identifying Lessee. Said sign or signs shall be of a size, shape and design, and at a location or locations, approved by Lessor and in conformance with any overall directional graphics or sign program established by Lessor. Lessor's approval shall not be withheld unreasonable. Notwithstanding any other provision of this Agreement, said sign(s) shall remain the property of Lessee. Lessee shall remove, at its expense, all lettering, signs and placards so erected on the Premises upon termination of this Agreement.

E. **Trade Fixtures.** During the term of this Agreement, Lessee shall have the right, at its expense, to place in or on the Premises trade fixtures, furnishings, personal property, equipment and materials necessary to perform any services required or authorized hereunder. Said trade fixtures, furnishings, personal property, equipment and materials shall remain the property of Lessee.

*F. **Nonexclusive Right.** It is not the intent of this Agreement to grant to Lessee the exclusive right to provide any or all of the services described in this Article III at any time during the term of this Agreement. Lessor reserves the right, at its sole discretion, to grant others certain rights and privileges upon the Airport which are identical in part or in whole to those granted to Lessee. Lessor does, however, covenant and agree that:

1. It shall enforce all minimum operating standards or requirements for all aeronautical endeavors and activities conducted at the Airport;
2. Any other operator of aeronautical endeavors or activities will not be permitted to operate on the Airport under rates, terms or conditions which are more favorable than those set forth in this Agreement; and
3. It will not permit the conduct of any aeronautical endeavor or activity at the Airport except under an approved lease and operating agreement.

---

*Must be included in all leases governing aeronautical services on airports receiving federal aid.

SAMPLE

ARTICLE FOUR

APPURTENANT PRIVILEGES

A. **Use of Airport Facilities.** Lessee shall be entitled, in common with others so authorized, to the use of all facilities and improvements of a public nature which now are or may hereafter be connected with or appurtenant to the Airport, including but not limited to, the use of landing areas, runways, taxiways, navigational aids, terminal facilities and aircraft parking areas designated by Lessor.

B. **Maintenance of Airport Facilities. Lessor shall maintain all public and common or joint use areas of the Airport, including the Air Operations Area, in good repair, and shall make such repairs, replacements or additions thereto as it considers, in its sole discretion, necessary for the safe and efficient operation of the Airport.

C. **Aerial Approaches. Lessor reserves the right to take any action it considers necessary to protect the aerial approaches of the Airport against obstruction, together with the right to prevent Lessee from erecting, or permitting to be erected, any building or other structure on or adjacent to the Airport which, in the opinion of Lessor, would limit the usefulness of the Airport or constitute a hazard to aircraft.

D. **Noncompetition.** Lessor shall not engage directly or indirectly in any of the activities described in Paragraphs A and B of Article Three of this Agreement.

ARTICLE FIVE

LEASEHOLD IMPROVEMENTS

A. **Required Improvements.**

1. As part of the consideration for the privileges herein granted, Lessee agrees to construct or otherwise make improvements to the Premises in an amount not less than $__________, including all fees and costs associated therewith, but excluding the cost of tools, equipment, inventory or accessories installed or stocked on the Premises. The leasehold improvements are to include not less than __________ (__________) square feet of additional hangar space, major renovation and modification of existing office space, pilots' lounge, customer service, shop and maintenance areas. Lessee agrees that it shall, within ninety (90) calendar days from the effective date of this Agreement, submit to Lessor, for approval, detailed plans and specifications for all of the proposed leasehold improvements. Lessor agrees that it shall either approve the plans and specifications as submitted, or transmit proposed revisions to Lessee, within thirty (30) calendar days of receipt of the plans and specifications from Lessee.

2. Upon receiving final approval of the plans and specifications from Lessor, Lessee shall engage one or more qualified contractors to construct said improvements. Construction shall commence within sixty (60) calendar days of Lessee's receipt of Lessor's final approval of the plans and specifications and shall be scheduled for completion not later than one hundred eighty (180) calendar days after commencement of construction. It is agreed and understood that leasehold improvements undertaken pursuant to this provision shall become the property of Lessor upon final completion of construction.

3. **Ownership of Tanks.** Any underground storage tanks constructed by Lessee shall meet all local, state and federal requirements.

**Recommended for inclusion in all leases governing aeronautical services on airports receiving federal aid.

SAMPLE

ARTICLE SIX

PAYMENTS

A. **Rent and Fees.** In consideration of the rights and privileges granted by this Agreement, Lessee agrees to pay to Lessor during the term of this Agreement the following:

1. **Rent.** A rental of $____________ per annum for the Premises.

2. **Fees.**

a. A sum of $__________ per gallon on all aviation fuel sold by Lessee at retail, excepting federal (including military), state and municipal government contract and retail fuel and fuel used by Lessee in the operation of its business.

b. A sum equal to ____% of the adjusted gross receipts from all businesses conducted and carried on by Lessee at the Airport. The term "adjusted gross receipts" as used in this Agreement shall mean the aggregate amount of all sales made, and services performed, for cash, on credit or otherwise, of every kind, name and nature. Adjusted gross receipts shall also include the aggregate value of all goods, wares and merchandise received for property or services, at the selling price thereof, as if the same had been sold for cash. There shall be excluded from adjusted gross receipts (i) all fuel sales; (ii) all sales of new and used aircraft; (iii) all sales to federal (including military), state and municipal government entities; (iv) federal, state and municipal sales taxes, or other similar taxes, separately stated and collected from customers; and (v) bad debts.

B. **Payments.**

1. The rental payment specified in Paragraph A.1, above, shall be paid monthly in advance in the sum of $__________ per month, the first payment to be made on or before the first day of _________, 19__, and a like payment to be made on or before the first day of each month thereafter during the term of this Agreement. It is understood and agreed that the rental payments specified in Paragraph A.1, above, and in the preceding sentence, may be adjusted pursuant to Paragraph G, below, and that each such adjustment shall result in a change in the annual and monthly rental payments.

2. The fees specified in Paragraph A.2, above, shall be paid to Lessor on or before the twentieth (20th) day following the end of each month such fees are collected, together with a report of Lessee's retail fuel sales and adjusted gross receipts during the preceding month. It is understood and agreed that the fees specified in Paragraph A.2, above, may be adjusted pursuant to Paragraph G, below, and that each such adjustment shall result in a change in the calculation of the monthly payments of fees.

C. **Landing Fees.** Lessee shall collect landing fees from aircraft using Lessee's facility in accordance with a schedule of landing fees established by Lessor. Fees so collected shall be reported and paid monthly to Lessor, less a ____% handling charge to be retained by Lessee, at the same time as the fees paid to Lessor pursuant to Paragraphs A.2 and B.2, above.

D. **Parking Fees.** Lessee shall collect aircraft parking fees, in accordance with a schedule of parking fees established by Lessor, for all aircraft parked in public parking areas adjacent to the Premises, elsewhere on the ramp or apron area adjacent to the Premises, or on such areas as may be designated by Lessor from time to time. Fees so collected shall be reported and paid monthly to Lessor, less a _____% handling charge to be retained by Lessee, at the same time as the fees paid to Lessor pursuant to Paragraphs A.2 and B.2, above.

E. **Delinquency Charge.** A delinquency charge of ____% per month shall be added to payments required by Paragraphs A, B, C and D, above, which are rendered more than ten (10) days delinquent.

ARTICLE SIX (continued) **SAMPLE**

F. **Place of Payment.** All payments due Lessor from Lessee shall be delivered to the place designated in writing by Lessor.

G. **Renegotiation of Rent and Fees.** The rent and fees specified in Paragraphs A.1 and A.2, above, shall be renegotiated during the last six (6) months of each five (5) year period of this Agreement, the increases or decreases in the rent and fees resulting from such renegotiation to be effective as of the commencement of the succeeding five (5) year period.

It is understood and agreed that (a) no increase in such rental or fees shall exceed _____% of the rental or fees then being paid by Lessee hereunder, and (b) no such increases shall be required if Lessee is prohibited by law or regulation from passing such increase on to its customers.

H. **Records.** Lessee shall provide and maintain accurate records of retail fuel sales and adjusted gross receipts derived under this Agreement, and landing and parking fees collected, for a period of three (3) years from the date the record is made. Such records shall be maintained according to generally accepted accounting principles. Lessor or its duly authorized representatives shall have the right at all reasonable times during business hours, and at its own expense, to inspect the books, records and receipts of Lessee, and to verify Lessee's fuel sales and adjusted gross receipts, and landing and parking fees collected.

I. **Annual Statement.** Within sixty (60) days after the end of each calendar year, Lessee shall furnish to Lessor a statement of fuel sales and adjusted gross receipts generated, and landing and parking fees collected, during the preceding calendar year, certified by an officer of Lessee as to its accuracy. Lessor reserves the right to audit said statement and Lessee's books and records, including examination of the general ledger and all other supporting material, at any reasonable time during business hours, for the purposes of verifying the reported fuel sales and adjusted gross receipts, and landing and parking fees collected.

If the audit establishes that Lessee has understated or overstated fuel sales or adjusted gross receipts, or landing or parking fees collected, by ____% or more, the entire expense of said audit shall be borne by Lessee. Any additional payment due from Lessee shall forthwith be paid to Lessor, with interest thereon at ____% per month from the date such amount originally became payable to Lessor. Any overpayment by Lessee shall be credited against further payments due to Lessor. Either party may refer the results of the audit for resolution in accordance with Paragraph J, below.

J. **Disputes.** In the event that any dispute may arise as to fuel sales, adjusted gross receipts, or landing or parking fees collected, the amount claimed due by Lessor shall be paid forthwith and the dispute shall be submitted to a certified public accountant, agreeable to both parties, who shall determine the rights of the parties hereunder in conformity with generally accepted accounting principles. The fees due said accountant for such services shall be paid by the unsuccessful party, or in the event the determination is partially in favor of each party, the fee shall be borne equally by the parties.

ARTICLE SEVEN

SAMPLE

UTILITIES

Lessee shall have the right to use the utility service facilities located on the Premises at the commencement of the term of this Agreement. In addition, should Lessee's operations require additional utility service facilities, Lessor shall, at its expense, extend such facilities to the Premises. Lessor's obligation under this provision shall be limited to utilities extended by a public utility company to Lessor's property line, and nothing herein shall obligate Lessor to provide any utility to Lessee that is not otherwise available to Lessor at its property line. If Lessor is unable to provide utility service facilities due to the imposition of any limit on consumption or on the construction of additional utility facilities, or the allocation or curtailment of utility facilities or service by law or regulation, it shall have no obligation hereunder.

Lessee agrees to pay the cost of all utilities. In the event Lessee fails to pay any utility bill when due, lessor may, at its option, pay the same and collect from Lessee the amounts so disbursed, plus interest at the rate of ____% per month or fraction thereof.

ARTICLE EIGHT

INSURANCE

A. **Required Insurance.** Lessee shall obtain and maintain continuously in effect at all times during the term of this Agreement, at Lessee's sole expense, the following insurance:

1. **Comprehensive general liability insurance** protecting Lessor against any and all liability arising by reason of Lessee's conduct incident to the use of the Premises, or resulting from any accident occurring on or about the roads, driveways or other public places, including runways and taxiways, used by Lessee at the Airport, caused by or arising out of any wrongful act or omission of Lessee, in the minimum amount of $__________;

2. **Passenger liability insurance** in the minimum amount of $__________ per seat, and $__________ per occurrence;

3. **Hangar keeper's liability insurance** in the minimum amount of $__________;

4. **Product liability insurance** in the minimum amount of $__________;

5. **Professional liability insurance** in the minimum amount of $__________;

6. **Fire and extended coverage insurance** on all fixed improvements erected by Lessee on or in the Premises to the full insurable value thereof, and

7. **Environmental impairment liability insurance** in the minimum amount of $__________ per occurrence and $__________ total.

The insurance specified in Paragraphs A.2 through A.7, above, shall name Lessor as an additional insured.

B. **Notice.** Lessor agrees to notify Lessee in writing as soon as practicable of any claim, demand or action arising out of an occurrence covered hereunder of which Lessor has knowledge, and to cooperate with Lessee in the investigation and defense thereof.

ARTICLE NINE

INDEMNIFICATION

To the extent not covered by insurance carried in favor of Lessor, Lessee shall keep and hold harmless Lessor from and against any and all claims, demands, suits, judgments, costs and expenses asserted by any person or persons, including agents or employees of Lessor or Lessee, by reason of death or injury to persons or loss of or damage to property, resulting from Lessee's operations, or anything done or omitted by Lessee under this Agreement except to the extent that such claims, demands, suits, judgments, costs and expenses may be attributed to the acts or omissions of Lessor, its agents or employees.

ARTICLE TEN

CASUALTY

In the event that any fixed improvements erected on the Premises by Lessee, pursuant to Paragraph A of Article Five of this Agreement, are damaged or destroyed by fire or other casualty, Lessee shall immediately repair the improvements and restore them to a condition at least as good as existed immediately before the casualty. While the improvements are being so repaired and restored, the rent hereunder shall abate only if the Premises are rendered untenantable by such damage.

In the event that any fixed improvements erected on the Premises by Lessor are damaged or destroyed by fire or other casualty, the rent hereunder shall not abate provided the Premises are not rendered untenantable by such damage. If the Premises are rendered untenantable, and Lessor elects to repair the Premises, the rent shall abate for the period during which such repairs are being made, provided the damage was not caused by acts or omissions of Lessee, its employes, agents or invitees, in which case the rent shall not abate. If the Premises are rendered untenantable, and Lessor elects not to repair the Premises, this Agreement shall terminate.

ARTICLE ELEVEN

CONDEMNATION

If the entire leased Premises, or such portion thereof as will make the Premises unsuitable for the operation of Lessee's business, are taken under the exercise of the power of eminent domain by Lessor, Lessor shall pay to Lessee the sum of $__________, representing the fair market value of the leasehold, as liquidated damages, and not as a penalty.

ARTICLE TWELVE

LESSEE AS INDEPENDENT CONTRACTOR

In conducting its business hereunder, Lessee acts as an independent contractor and not as an agent of Lessor. The selection, retention, assignment, direction and payment of Lessee's employees shall be the sole responsibility of Lessee, and Lessor shall not attempt to exercise any control over the daily performance of duties by Lessee's employees.

ARTICLE THIRTEEN

ASSIGNMENT

This Agreement, or any part thereof, may not be assigned, transferred or subleased by Lessee, by process or operation of law or in any other manner whatsoever, without the prior written consent of Lessor, which consent shall not be withheld unreasonably.

ARTICLE FOURTEEN **SAMPLE**

*NONDISCRIMINATION

A. Notwithstanding any other provision of this Agreement, during the performance of this Agreement, Lessee, for itself, its heirs, personal representatives, successors in interest and assigns, as part of the consideration of this Agreement does hereby covenant and agree, as a covenant running with the land, that:

1. No person on the grounds of race, color, religion, sex or national origin shall be excluded from participation in, denied the benefits of, or otherwise be subjected to discrimination in the use of the Premises;

2. In the construction of any improvements on, over or under the Premises, and the furnishing of services therein or thereon, no person on the grounds of race, color, religion, sex or national origin shall be excluded from participation in, or denied the benefits of, such activities, or otherwise be subjected to discrimination;

3. Lessee shall use the Premises in compliance with all other requirements imposed by or pursuant to Title 49, Code of Federal Regulations ("C.F.R."), Department of Transportation, Subtitle A, Office of the Secretary, Part 21, Nondiscrimination in Federally Assisted Programs of the Department of Transportation -- Effectuation of Title VI of the Civil Rights Act of 1964, and as said regulations may be amended.

4. In the event of breach of any of the above nondiscrimination covenants, Lessor shall have the right to terminate this Agreement and to reenter and repossess the Premises and hold the same as if said Agreement had never been made or issued. This provision does not become effective until the procedures of 49 C.F.R. Part 21 have been followed and completed, including expiration of appeal rights.

**B. Lessee assures that it will undertake an affirmative action program, as required by 14 C.F.R. Part 152, Subpart E, to ensure that no person shall, on the grounds of race, creed, color, national origin, or sex, be excluded from participating in any employment, contracting or leasing activities covered in 14 C.F.R. Part 152, Subpart E. Lessee assures that no person shall be excluded, on these grounds, from participating in or receiving the services or benefits of any program or activity covered by Subpart E. Lessee assures that it will require that its covered organizations provide assurance to the Lessee that they similarly will undertake affirmative action programs and that they will require assurances from their suborganizations, as required by 14 C.F.R. Part 152, Subpart E, to the same effect.

Lessee agrees to comply with any affirmative action plan or steps for equal employment opportunity required by 14 C.F.R., Part 152, Subpart E, or by any federal, state, or local agency or court, including those resulting from a conciliation agreement, a consent decree, court order, or similar mechanism. Lessee agrees that a state or local affirmative action plan will be used in lieu of any affirmative action plan or steps required by 14 C.F.R. 152, Subpart E, only when it fully meets the standards set forth in 14 C.F.R. 152.409. Lessee agrees to obtain a similar assurance from its covered organizations, and to cause them to require a similar assurance of their covered suborganizations, as required by 14 C.F.R. Part 152, Subpart E.

---

* Must be included in all leases governing aeronautical services on airports receiving federal aid.
** Must be included in the leases of all lessees having fifty (50) or more employees and conducting aeronautical activities on airports receiving federal aid.

SAMPLE

ARTICLE FIFTEEN

*REQUIREMENTS OF THE UNITED STATES

This agreement shall be subject and subordinate to the provisions of any existing or future agreement between Lessor and the United States, or any agency thereof, relative to the operation or maintenance of the Airport, the execution of which has been or may be required as a condition precedent to the expenditure of federal funds for the development or operation of the Airport; provided, however, that Lessor shall, to the extent permitted by law, use its best efforts to cause any such agreements to include provisions protecting and preserving the rights of Lessee in and to the Premises, and to compensation for taking thereof, interference therewith and damage thereto, caused by such agreement or by actions of Lessor or the United States pursuant thereto.

ARTICLE SIXTEEN

DEFAULT AND TERMINATION

A. **Termination by Lessee.** This Agreement shall be subject to termination by Lessee in the event of any one or more of the following events:

1. The abandonment of the Airport as an airport or airfield for any type, class or category of aircraft.

2. The default by Lessor in the performance of any of the terms, covenants or conditions of this Agreement, and the failure of Lessor to remedy, or undertake to remedy, to Lessee's satisfaction, such default for a period of thirty (30) days after receipt of notice from Lessee to remedy the same.

3. Damage to or destruction of all or a material part of the Premises or Airport facilities necessary to the operation of Lessee's business.

4. The lawful assumption by the United States, or any authorized agency thereof, of the operation, control or use of the Airport, or any substantial part or parts thereof, in such a manner as to restrict Lessee from substantially conducting business operations for a period in excess of ninety (90) days.

B. **Termination by Lessor.** This Agreement shall be subject to termination by Lessor in the event of any one or more of the following events:

1. The default by Lessee in the performance of any of the terms, covenants or conditions of this Agreement, and the failure of Lessee to remedy, or undertake to remedy, to Lessor's satisfaction, such default for a period of thirty (30) days after receipt of notice from Lessor to remedy the same.

2. Lessee files a voluntary petition in bankruptcy, including a reorganization plan, makes a general or other assignment for the benefit of creditors, is adjudicated as bankrupt or if a receiver is appointed for the property or affairs of Lessee and such receivership is not vacated within thirty (30) days after the appointment of such receiver.

3. Lessee's abandonment of the Premises.

---

* Recommended for inclusion in all leases governing aeronautical services on airports receiving aid.

ARTICLE SIXTEEN (continued)

SAMPLE

C. **Force Majeure; Waiver.**

1. Neither party shall be held to be in breach of this Agreement because of any failure to perform any of its obligations hereunder if said failure is due to any act of God, fire, flood, accident, strike, riot, insurrection, war, or any other cause over which that party has no control; provided however, that the foregoing provision shall not apply to failures by Lessee to pay fees, rents or other charges to Lessor.

2. The waiver of any breach, violation or default in or with respect to the performance or observance of the covenants and conditions contained herein shall not be taken to constitute a waiver of any subsequent breach, violation or default in or with respect to the same or any other covenant or condition hereof.

D. **Payment for Leasehold Improvements.** In the event of any cancellation or termination of this Agreement, for any cause other than a breach or default by Lessee, Lessor shall, within thirty (30) days of the date of such termination or cancellation, pay Lessee, for all of the leasehold improvements installed or constructed by Lessee pursuant to Paragraph A of Article Five of this Agreement, a cash price equal to Lessee's unamortized costs for said improvements. Lessee agrees that, for purposes of this provision, it shall amortize the actual direct cost of such improvements on a straight-line basis, commencing with the effective date of this Agreement and extending for the twenty-five (25) year term hereof.

ARTICLE SEVENTEEN

ARBITRATION

Except as provided in Paragraph J of Article Six of this Agreement, all claims or disputes arising out of or relating to this Agreement shall be settled by arbitration in accordance with the Commercial Arbitration Rules of the American Arbitration Association then obtaining. Notice of the demand for arbitration shall be filed in writing with the other party to the Agreement and with the American Arbitration Association and shall be made within a reasonable time after the claim or dispute has arisen. The award rendered by the arbitrator or arbitrators shall be final, and judgment may be entered upon it in accordance with applicable law in any court having jurisdiction thereof.

Except by written consent of the person or entity sought to be joined, no arbitration arising out of or relating to the Agreement shall include, by consolidation, joinder or in any other manner, any person or entity not a party to the Agreement, unless it is shown at the time the demand for arbitration is filed that (a) such person or entity is substantially involved in a common question of fact or law; (b) the presence of such person or entity is required if complete relief is to be accorded in the arbitration; and (c) the interest or responsibility of such person or entity in the matter is not insubstantial.

The agreement of the parties to arbitrate claims and disputes shall be specifically enforceable under the prevailing arbitration law.

Pending final decision of the arbitrator or arbitrators, the parties shall proceed diligently with the performance of their obligations under this Agreement.

SAMPLE

ARTICLE EIGHTEEN

MISCELLANEOUS PROVISIONS

A. **Entire Agreement.** This Agreement constitutes the entire understanding between the parties, and as of its effective date supersedes all prior or independent agreements between the parties covering the subject matter hereof. Any change or modification hereof must be in writing and signed by both parties.

B. **Severability.** If a provision hereof shall be finally declared void or illegal by any court or administrative agency having jurisdiction, the entire Agreement shall not be void, but the remaining provisions shall continue in effect as nearly as possible in accordance with the original intent of the parties.

C. **Notice.** Any notice given by one party to the other in connection with this Agreement shall be in writing and shall be sent by registered mail, return receipt requested, with postage and registration fees prepaid:

1. If to Lessor, addressed to:

   ____

   ____

   ____

2. If to Lessee, addressed to:

   ____

   ____

   ____

Notices shall be deemed to have been received on the date of receipt as shown on the return receipt.

D. **Headings.** The headings used in this Agreement are intended for convenience of reference only and do not define or limit the scope or meaning of any provision of this Agreement.

E. **Governing Law.** This Agreement is to be construed in accordance with the laws of the State of ______________.

IN WITNESS WHEREOF, the parties have executed this Agreement as of the day and year first above written.

LESSOR: ______________________________

By: ______________________________

Title: ______________________________

LESSEE: ______________________________

By: ______________________________

Title: ______________________________

AIRCRAFT LEASE AGREEMENT

This AIRCRAFT LEASE AGREEMENT (this "Agreement") entered into as of the _________ day of __________, 19_____, by and between __________________________ ("Lessor") and __________________________ ("Lessee").

Witnesseth

WHEREAS, Lessor is the registered owner of an aircraft described as follows:

____

_________________ Registration Number

____ (the "Aircraft");

WHEREAS, Lessor desires to lease the Aircraft to Lessee in accordance with the terms and conditions herein contained; and

WHEREAS, the parties understand that Lessee intends to rent, charter and otherwise utilize the Aircraft in conducting its business;

NOW, THEREFORE, in consideration of the premises and the mutual covenants contained herein, and for other good and valuable consideration, the parties hereby agree as follows:

ARTICLE ONE

LEASE OF AIRCRAFT

Lessor agrees to lease to lessee the aircraft together with the accessories and equipment specified in the appendix attached hereto and made a part hereof.

ARTICLE TWO

TERM

The Agreement shall commence on the _____ day of __________, 19____, and shall continue in effect until _______________ _____, 19_____ unless earlier terminated under the provisions of this Agreement.

ARTICLE THREE

RENT

The rent payable by Lessee to Lessor shall be calculated on a per-flight basis at the rate of ________________________________ Dollars ($_______________) for each hour, or any portion thereof, the Aircraft is utilized by Lessee; provided, however, that Lessee shall not pay rent for the hours when Lessor utilizes the Aircraft, even if Lessee is providing pilot service for such flights.

ARTICLE FOUR

USE BY LESSOR

Lessor has the right to use the Aircraft subject to its availability for the period for which such usage is desired. The Aircraft must be piloted by either the Lessor, if qualified, or a pilot employed by Lessee.

SAMPLE

SAMPLE

ARTICLE FIVE

MAINTENANCE AND REPAIR

Lessee shall perform or cause to be performed all maintenance, repair, inspection and overhaul work necessary to obtain certification for the Aircraft pursuant to Part 135 of the Federal Aviation Regulations and to maintain such certification during the term of this Agreement. All such work on the Aircraft shall be performed in accordance with the standards set by regulations of the Federal Aviation Administration (the "FAA"). Lessee shall provide or cause to be provided at all times qualified personnel to perform all maintenance, repair, inspection and overhaul work on the Aircraft. All such personnel will be contracted for, or employed by, Lessee, and Lessor shall have no authority to direct, employ, discharge, or pay compensation to such personnel. Lessor shall rely wholly on the expertise of Lessee as to the necessity of the labor and materials required under this article.

ARTICLE SIX

OPERATING COSTS

Lessor shall be responsible for all costs and expenses incurred by Lessee in operating the Aircraft during the term of the Agreement including but not limited to the following:

A. **Maintenance:** All costs and expenses incurred by Lessee in performing or causing to be performed all maintenance, repair, inspection and overhaul work on the Aircraft pursuant to Article Five above, including but not limited to all costs and expenses associated with new parts and accessories utilized for such work.

B. **Fuel and Oil:** All costs and expenses incurred by Lessee in purchasing fuel and oil for the Aircraft.

C. **Insurance:** All costs and expenses incurred by Lessee in maintaining in force such passenger liability, public liability, property damage, baggage, and cargo insurance in such form, for such amounts, and with such insurers as shall be satisfactory to Lessor and Lessee, protecting Lessee and Lessor as co-insureds against claims for death of or injury to persons, and loss of or damage to property, in connection with the possession, maintenance, use and operation of the Aircraft.

D. **Pilots:** All costs and expenses incurred by Lessee in providing pilots to operate the Aircraft during the term of this Agreement.

E. **Taxes:** All taxes, fees, assessments, fines, and penalties due, assessed or levied by any taxing authority which relate in any way to the ownership, use or operation of the Aircraft, including, but without limitation, all sales taxes and personal property taxes, license and registration fees, and all use, excise, gross receipts, franchise, stamp or other taxes, duties or charges, together with any penalties, fines or interest thereon, imposed, or relating to activities conducted, during the term of this Agreement; provided, however, that Lessee shall be liable for all income taxes attributable to its income earned under this Agreement.

F. **Storage of the Aircraft:** All costs and expenses incurred by Lessee in storing the Aircraft.

ARTICLE SEVEN

LOG BOOKS AND RECORDS

Lessee shall maintain, at its sole expense, all log books and records pertaining to the Aircraft in accordance with FAA regulations. Such log books and records shall be made available for examination by Lessor or Lessor's duly authorized agents at Lessor's reasonable request. Lessee shall, at its sole expense, at the termination of this Agreement deliver such log books and records to Lessor.

SAMPLE

ARTICLE EIGHT

OPERATION OF AIRCRAFT

A. Lessee shall operate the Aircraft in accordance with this Agreement. During those times when the Aircraft has been chartered, Lessee shall have and maintain operational control of the Aircraft in accordance with Section 135.77 of the FAA regulations, 14 C.F.R. Section 135.77.

B. Lessee may operate the Aircraft only for the purposes, and within the geographical limits, set forth in the insurance policy or policies obtained by Lessee in accordance with Paragraph C of Article Six of this Agreement. Lessee shall not use the Aircraft in violation of any foreign, federal, state, territorial or municipal law or regulation and shall be solely responsible for any fines, penalties or forfeitures occasioned by any violation. If any such fine or penalty is imposed on and paid by Lessor, Lessee shall reimburse Lessor for the amount thereof within thirty (30) days after receipt by Lessee of written notice requesting such reimbursement. Lessee will not base the Aircraft, or permit it to be based, outside the limits of the United States of America, without the prior written consent of Lessor.

C. The Aircraft shall be operated only by licensed and qualified plilots. For charter flights, all pilots shall be employees of Lessee and shall be under the exclusive control of Lessee.

D. Lessee shall have sole control over dispatching and scheduling the Aircraft.

E. Lessor shall, at all times during the term of this Agreement, have the right to place its own qualified pilot, engineer, or other qualified employee on board the Aircraft during any flight operated hereunder for the purpose of monitoring the operation of the Aircraft and ensuring such operation complies with all applicable foreign, federal, state, territorial, or municipal laws or regulations.

ARTICLE NINE

ALTERATIONS

Lessee shall not have the right to alter, modify or make additions or improvements to the Aircraft, other than those necessary to obtain and maintain FAA certification, without prior written permission from Lessor. All such alterations, modifications, additions and improvements as are so made shall be subject to all of the terms of this Agreement.

ARTICLE TEN

TITLE

The registration of, and title to, the Aircraft shall be in the name of Lessor, and the Aircraft shall at all times bear United States registration markings.

ARTICLE ELEVEN

DEFAULT

A. Lessor shall be in breach of this Agreement if: (1) Lessor defaults in the performance of any of its obligations under this Agreement and such default shall continue for five (5) days after receipt by Lessor of notice thereof from Lessee; or (2) Lessor takes any action to prevent or hinder the performance by Lessee of any of its obligations under this Agreement. In the event of any breach, Lessee shall have the right to terminate the Agreement immediately and to pursue any other remedy available to Lessee in law or equity.

ARTICLE ELEVEN (continued) **SAMPLE**

B. Lessee shall be in breach of this Agreement if Lessee defaults in the performance of any of its obligations under this Agreement and such default shall continue for five (5) days after receipt by Lessee of written notice thereof for Lessor. In the event of any breach by Lessee, Lessor shall have the right to repossess the Aircraft without further demand, notice or court order, or other process of law and to terminate the Agreement immediately. Exercise by Lessor of either or both of the rights specified above shall not prejudice Lessor 's right to pursue any other remedy available to Lessor in law or equity.

C. The failure of either party to enforce strictly any provision of this Agreement shall not be construed as a waiver thereof and shall not preclude such party from demanding performance in accordance with the terms hereof.

ARTICLE TWELVE

PAYMENTS

A. The rent, as specified in Article Three, for each flight shall be due and payable to Lessor within thirty (30) days after each flight.

B. Payment for costs and expenses incurred by Lessee in the operation of the Aircraft, including but not limited to costs and expenses incurred for maintenance, repair, overhaul and inspection work, fuel and oil, pilots, storage and insurance, shall be due and payable to Lessee within ten (10) days following receipt by Lessor of a statement therefor from Lessee.

C. Payments made and statements furnished to a party shall be directed to the address specified in Paragraph D of Article Nineteen.

ARTICLE THIRTEEN

ASSIGNMENT

Lessee shall not assign this Agreement or any interest in the Aircraft without the prior written consent of Lessor. Subject to the foregoing, this Agreement inures to the benefit of, and is binding on, the heirs, legal representatives, successors, and assigns of the parties hereto.

ARTICLE FOURTEEN

ACCIDENT AND CLAIM

Lessee shall immediately notify Lessor of any accident involving the Aircraft, which notification shall specify to the extent known by Lessee, the time and place of the accident, the extent of the damage, the names and addresses of the parties involved, persons injured, known witnesses, and owners of properties damaged. Lessee shall advise Lessor of all correspondence, papers, notices, and documents received by Lessee in connection with any claim or demand involving or relating to the Aircraft or its operation, and shall aid in any investigation instituted by Lessor and in seeking the recovery of damages from third persons liable therefor.

SAMPLE

ARTICLE FIFTEEN

INDEMNIFICATION

Lessee shall be liable to Lessor for, and agrees to indemnify and hold harmless Lessor and its employees and agents from and against, any and all suits, claims, liabilities, settlements, losses and expenses (to the extent such are not covered by the insurance policies held pursuant to Paragraph C of Article Six above) arising out of or attributable to the operation of the Aircraft hereunder, including but not limited to, injuries to third parties, or employees of Lessee and Lessor, damage to property (whether of Lessee or any third party) and any consequential or incidental damages.

ARTICLE SIXTEEN

LOSS OR DAMAGE TO AIRCRAFT

Risk of loss of or damage to the Aircraft shall be borne by Lessor. If, during the term of this Agreement, the Aircraft is destroyed, lost or damaged beyond repair, this Agreement shall terminate immediately, provided, however, that Lessee shall continue to be bound by all obligations described in Paragraph C of Article Six and in Articles Twelve, Fourteen and Fifteen.

ARTICLE SEVENTEEN

RETURN OF PLANE TO LESSOR

On the termination of this Agreement by expiration or otherwise, Lessee shall, at its sole expense, return the Aircraft to Lessor at ______________________________________, in the same condition as when received, ordinary wear, tear and deterioration excepted.

ARTICLE EIGHTEEN

THIRTY (30) DAY TERMINATION

Either party to this Agreement shall have the right, with or without cause, to terminate this Agreement by giving thirty (30) days' prior written notice to the other party.

ARTICLE NINETEEN

MISCELLANEOUS PROVISIONS

A. The relationship between Lessor and Lessee shall always and only be that of lessor and lessee. Lessee shall never at any time during the term of this Agreement become the agent of Lessor, and Lessor shall not be responsible for the acts or omissions of Lessee or its agents.

B. This Agreement constitutes the entire understanding between the parties, and as of its effective date supersedes all prior or independent agreements between the parties covering the Aircraft. Any change or modification hereof must be in writing signed by both parties.

C. This Agreement is to be construed in accordance with the laws of the State of

________________________.

D. Any notice given by one party to the other in connection with this Agreement shall be in writing and shall be sent by certified or registered mail, return receipt requested:

ARTICLE NINETEEN (continued) **SAMPLE**

(1) If to Lessor, addressed to:

____

____

____

____

(2) If to Lessee, addressed to:

____

____

____

____

Notices shall be deemed to have been received on the date of receipt as shown on the return receipt.

E. Lessee shall have no right to consent, allow or permit any liens or encumbrances on the Aircraft. Lessee shall immediately remove from the Aircraft any lien or encumbrance arising or created by any act or omission on the part of the Lessee.

F. The rights and remedies with respect to any of the terms and conditions of the Agreement shall be cumulative and not exclusive, and shall be in addition to all other rights and remedies.

G. If a provision hereof shall be finally declared void or illegal by any court or administrative agency having jurisdiction over the parties to this Agreement, the entire Agreement shall not be void, but the remaining provisions shall continue in effect as nearly as possible in accordance with the original intent of the parties.

IN WITNESS WHEREOF, the parties have executed this Agreement as of the day and year first above written.

LESSOR: ______________________________

By: ______________________________

Title: ______________________________

LESSEE: ______________________________

By: ______________________________

Title: ______________________________

SAMPLE

AIRCRAFT LEASE AND PILOT SERVICE AGREEMENT

This AIRCRAFT LEASE and PILOT SERVICE AGREEMENT (this "Agreement") entered into as of the __________ day of ______________________, 19____, by and between ______________________ ("Lessor") and ________________________________ ("Lessee").

Witnesseth:

WHEREAS, Lessor is the registered owner of an aircraft described as follows:
____
______________ Registration Number ________________ (the "Aircraft");

WHEREAS, Lessor desires to lease the Aircraft to Lessee in accordance with the terms and conditions herein contained;

WHEREAS, the parties understand that Lessee intends to rent, charter and otherwise utilize the Aircraft in conducting its business; and

WHEREAS, Lessor desires to obtain and Lessee desires to provide pilot service for the Aircraft when it is flown for Lessor;

NOW, THEREFORE, in consideration of the premises and the mutual covenants contained herein, and for other good and valuable consideration, the parties hereby agree as follows:

ARTICLE ONE

LEASE OF AIRCRAFT

Lessor agrees to lease to Lessee the Aircraft together with the accessories and equipment specified in the appendix attached hereto and made a part hereof.

ARTICLE TWO

TERM

The Agreement shall commence on the _________ day of ________________, 19_____, and shall continue in effect until ____________________ _____, 19_____ unless earlier terminated under the provisions of this Agreement.

ARTICLE THREE

RENT

The rent payable by Lessee to Lessor shall be calculated on a per-flight basis at the rate of ____________________________ Dollars ($_____________) for each hour the Aircraft is flown, or portion thereof, during the term of the Agreement.

ARTICLE FOUR

CHARTER AND PILOT SERVICE FOR LESSOR

A. **Charter Service.** Lessee agrees to charter the Aircraft to Lessor on a per-flight basis for the fee of ________________________ Dollars ($__________) for each hour the Aircraft is flown, or portion thereof, for Lessor on a particular charter flight, subject, however, to the availability of the Aircraft for the period during which the Lessor desires the charter flight to operate.

ARTICLE FOUR (continued) **SAMPLE**

B. **Pilot Service.** Lessee agrees to provide to Lessor, and Lessor agrees to purchase, pilot service for those periods when Lessor charters the Aircraft, or any other aircraft, from Lessee for the set fee of ______________________ Dollars ($__________) per month.

ARTICLE FIVE

MAINTENANCE AND REPAIR

Lessee shall perform or cause to be performed all maintenance, repair, inspection and overhaul work necessary to obtain certification for the Aircraft pursuant to Part 135 of the Federal Aviation Regulations and to maintain such certification during the term of this Agreement. All such work on the Aircraft shall be performed in accordance with the standards set by regulations of the Federal Aviation Administration (the "FAA"). Lessee shall provide or cause to be provided at all times qualified personnel to perform all maintenance, repair, inspection and overhaul work on the Aircraft. All such personnel will be contracted for, or employed by, Lessee, and Lessor shall have no authority to direct, employ, discharge, or pay compensation to such personnel. Lessor shall rely wholly on the expertise of Lessee as to the necessity of the labor and materials required under this article.

ARTICLE SIX

OPERATING COSTS

In addition to the fee for charter service and pilot service specified in Article Four hereof, Lessor shall be responsible for all costs and expenses incurred by Lessee in operating the Aircraft during the term of this Agreement, including but not limited to the following:

A. **Maintenance:** All costs and expenses incurred by Lessee in performing or causing to be performed all maintenance, repair, inspection and overhaul work on the Aircraft pursuant to Article Five above, including but not limited to all costs and expenses associated with new parts and accessories utilized for such work.

B. **Fuel and Oil:** All costs and expenses incurred by Lessee in purchasing fuel and oil for the Aircraft.

C. **Insurance:** All costs and expenses incurred by Lessee in maintaining in force such passenger liability, public liability, property damage, baggage, and cargo insurance in such form, for such amounts, and with such insurers as shall be satisfactory to Lessor and Lessee, protecting Lessee and Lessor as co-insureds against claims for death of or injury to persons, and loss of or damage to property, in connection with the possession, maintenance, use and operation of the Aircraft.

D. **Taxes:** All taxes, fees, assessments, fines, and penalties due, assessed or levied by any taxing authority which relate in any way to the ownership, use or operation of the Aircraft, including, without limitation, all sales taxes and personal property taxes, licenses and registration fees, and all use, excise, gross receipts, franchise, stamp or other taxes, duties or charges, together with any penalties, fines or interest thereon, imposed, or relating to activities conducted during the term of this Agreement provided, however, that Lessee shall be liable for all income taxes attributable to its income earned under this Agreement.

E. **Storage of the Aircraft:** All costs and expenses incurred by Lessee in storing the Aircraft.

SAMPLE

ARTICLE SEVEN

LOG BOOKS AND RECORDS

Lessee shall maintain, at its sole expense, all log books and records pertaining to the Aircarft in accordance with FAA regulations. Such log books and records shall be made available for examination by Lessor or Lessor's duly authorized agents at Lessor's reasonable request. Lessee shall, at its sole expense, deliver such log books and records to Lessor at the termination of this Agreement.

ARTICLE EIGHT

OPERATION OF AIRCRAFT

A. Lessee shall operate the Aircraft in accordance with this Agreement. During those times when the Aircraft has been chartered, Lessee shall have and maintain operational control of the Aircraft in accordance with Section 135.77 of the FAA regulations, 14 C.F.R. 135.77.

B. Lessee may operate the Aircraft only for the purposes, and within the geographical limits, set forth in the insurance policy or policies obtained by Lessee in accordance with Paragraph C of Article Six of this Agreement. Lessee shall not use the Aircraft in violation of any foreign, federal, state, territorial, or municipal law or regulation and shall be solely responsible for any fines, penalties or forfeitures occasioned by any violation. If any such fine or penalty is imposed on and paid by Lessor, Lessee shall reimburse Lessor for the amount thereof within thirty (30) days after receipt by Lessee of written notice requesting such reimbursement. Lessee will not base the Aircraft, or permit it to be based, outside the limits of the United States of America, without the prior written consent of Lessor.

C. The Aircraft shall be operated only by licensed and qualified pilots. For charter flights, all pilots shall be employees of Lessee and shall be under the exclusive control of Lessee.

D. Lessee shall have sole control over dispatching and scheduling the Aircraft.

E. Lessor shall, at all times during the term of this Agreement, have the right to place its own qualified pilot, engineer or other qualified employee on board the Aircraft during any flight operated hereunder for the purpose of monitoring the operation and use of the Aircraft and ensuring such operation complies with all applicable foreign, federal, state, territorial, or municipal laws or regulations.

ARTICLE NINE

ALTERATIONS

Lessee shall not have the right to alter, modify or make additions or improvements to the Aircraft, other than those necessary to obtain and maintain FAA certification, without prior written permission from Lessor. All such alterations, modifications, additions and improvements as are so made shall become the property of Lessor and shall be subject to all of the terms of this Agreement.

ARTICLE TEN

TITLE

The registration of, and title to, the Aircraft shall be in the name of Lessor, and the Aircraft shall at all times bear United States registration markings.

SAMPLE

ARTICLE ELEVEN

DEFAULT

A. Lessor shall be in breach of this Agreement if: (1) Lessor defaults in the performance of any of its obligations under this Agreement and such default shall continue for five (5) days after receipt by Lessor of notice thereof from Lessee; or (2) Lessor takes any action to prevent or hinder the performance by Lessee of any of its obligations under this Agreement. In the event of any breach, Lessee shall have the right to terminate the Agreement immediately and to pursue any other remedy available to Lessee in law or equity.

B. Lessee shall be in breach of this Agreement if Lessee defaults in the performance of any of its obligations under this Agreement and such default shall continue for five (5) days after receipt by Lessee of notice thereof from Lessor. In the event of any breach by Lessee, Lessor shall have the following rights: (1) To repossess the Aircraft without further demand, notice or court order, or other process of law; and (2) To terminate the Agreement immediately. Exercise by Lessor of either or both of the rights specified above shall not prejudice Lessor's right to pursue any other remedy available to Lessor in law or equity.

C. The failure of either party to enforce strictly any provision of this Agreement shall not be construed as a waiver thereof and shall not preclude such party from demanding performance in accordance with the terms hereof.

ARTICLE TWELVE

PAYMENTS

A. The rent, as specified in Article Three, for each flight shall be due and payable to Lessor within thirty (30) days after each flight.

B. The amount specified in Paragraph A of Article Four for charter service performed by Lessee for Lessor shall be due and payable to Lessee within thirty (30) days following receipt by Lessor of a statement therefor from Lessee.

C. The amount specified in Paragraph B of Article Four for pilot service shall be due monthly in advance and shall be payable to Lessee on or before the first day of each month.

D. Payment for costs and expenses incurred by Lessee in the operation of the Aircraft, including but not limited to costs and expenses incurred for maintenance, repair, overhaul and inspection work, fuel and oil, and insurance shall be due and payable to Lessee within ten (10) days following receipt by Lessor of a statement therefor from Lessee.

E. Payments made and statements furnished to a party shall be directed to the address specified in Paragraph D of Article Nineteen.

ARTICLE THIRTEEN

ASSIGNMENT

Lessee shall not assign this Agreement or any interest in the Aircraft without the prior written consent of Lessor. Subject to the foregoing, this Agreement inures to the benefit of, and is binding on, the heirs, legal representatives, successors, and assigns of the parties hereto.

SAMPLE

ARTICLE FOURTEEN

ACCIDENT AND CLAIM

Lessee shall immediately notify Lessor of any accident involving the Aircraft, which notification shall specify to the extent known by Lessee, the time and place of the accident, the extent of the damage, the names and addresses of the parties involved, persons injured, known witnesses, and owners of properties damaged. Lessee shall advise Lessor of all correspondence, papers, notices, and documents received by Lessee in connection with any claim or demand involving or relating to the Aircraft or its operation, and shall aid in any investigation instituted by Lessor and in the recovery of damages from third persons liable therefor.

ARTICLE FIFTEEN

INDEMNIFICATION

Lessee shall be liable to Lessor for, and agrees to indemnify and hold harmless Lessor and its employees and agents from and against, any and all suits, claims, liabilities, settlements, losses and expenses (to the extent such are not covered by the insurance policies held pursuant to Paragraph C of Article Six above) arising out of or attributable to the use and or operation of the Aircraft hereunder, including but not limited to, injuries to third parties or employees of Lessee and Lessor, damage to property (whether of Lessee or any third party) and any consequential or incidental damages.

ARTICLE SIXTEEN

LOSS OR DAMAGE TO AIRCRAFT

Risk of loss of or damage to the Aricraft shall be borne by Lessor. If, during the term of this Agreement, the Aircraft is destroyed, lost, or damaged beyond repair, this Agreement shall terminate immediately, provided, however, that Lessee shall continue to be bound by the obligations described in Paragraph C of Article Six and in Articles Twelve, Fourteen and Fifteen.

ARTICLE SEVENTEEN

RETURN OF AIRCRAFT TO LESSOR

On the termination of this Agreement by expiration or otherwise, Lessee shall, at its sole expense, return the Aircraft to Lessor at ______________________________________, in the same condition as when received, ordinary wear, tear and deterioration excepted.

ARTICLE EIGHTEEN

THIRTY (30) DAY TERMINATION

Either party to this Agreement shall have the right, with or without cause, to terminate this Agreement by giving thirty (30) days' prior written notice to the other party.

ARTICLE NINETEEN

MISCELLANEOUS PROVISIONS

A. The relationship between Lessor and Lessee shall always and only be that of lessor and lessee. Lessee shall never at any time during the term of this Agreement become the agent of Lessor, and Lessor shall not be responsible for the acts or omissions of Lessee or its agents.

B. This Agreement constitutes the entire understanding between the parties, and as of its effective date supersedes all prior or independent agreements between the parties covering the Aircraft. Any change or modification hereof must be in writing signed by both parties.

SAMPLE

ARTICLE NINETEEN (continued)

C. This Agreement is to be construed in accordance with the laws of the State of ____________________.

D. Any notice given by one party to the other in connection with this Agreement shall be in writing and shall be sent by certified or registered mail, return receipt requested:

(1) If to Lessor, addressed to:

____

____

____

____

(2) If to Lessee, addressed to:

____

____

____

____

Notices shall be deemed to have been received on the date of receipt as shown on the return receipt.

E. Lessee shall have no right to consent, allow or permit any liens or encumbrances on the Aircraft. Lessee shall immediately remove from the Aircraft any lien or encumbrance arising or created by any act or omission on the part of the Lessee.

F. The rights and remedies with respect to any of the terms and conditions of the Agreement shall be cumulative and not exclusive, and shall be in addition to all other rights and remedies.

G. If a provision hereof shall be finally declared void or illegal by any court or administrative agency having jurisdiction over the parties to this Agreement, the entire Agreement shall not be void, but the remaining provisions shall continue in effect as nearly as possible in accordance with the original intent of the parties.

IN WITNESS WHEREOF, the parties have executed this Agreement as of the day and year first above written.

LESSOR: ______________________________

By: ______________________________

Title: ______________________________

LESSEE: ______________________________

By: ______________________________

Title: ______________________________

SAMPLE

HANGAR SPACE LEASE AGREEMENT

This HANGAR SPACE LEASE AGREEMENT (this "Agreement") entered into as of this ___________ day of _________________________ 19____ by and between ___________________________________ ("Lessor") and ______________________________________ ("Lessee").

In consideration of the mutual covenants contained herein, and for other good and valuable consideration, the parties hereby agree as follows:

1. **Lease of the Hangar Space:** Lessor hereby leases to Lessee hangar space in Hangar # _________ (the "Hangar") located at ___________________________ (the "Airport") and described as follows: ______________________________ (the "Hangar Space"). The Hangar Space shall be used and occupied by Lessee solely for the storage of the following aircraft: ____

____

_______________ Registration No. ______________________________ (the "Aircraft"), or any other similar aircraft owned or leased by Lessee (the "Substitute Aircraft"), provided Lessee has obtained the prior written consent of Lessor to store the Substitute Aircraft in the Hangar Space. In the event Lessee is permitted to store a Substitute Aircraft in the Hangar Space, all provisions of this Agreement applicable to the Aircraft shall also be applicable to the Substitute Aircraft.

2. **Term:** The term of this Agreement shall commence on ______________________ ______, 19_____, and shall continue in effect until ______________________, 19_____, unless earlier terminated under the terms of this Agreement. Thereafter, this Agreement shall continue in effect from month to month, being automatically renewed after each month, unless terminated under the terms of this Agreement.

3. **Rent:** For use of the Hangar Space, Lessee shall pay Lessor, at the address specified in Paragraph 20, the amount of ________________________________, ($___________) per month, payable in advance on the first day of each month. The amount of rent may be changed from time to time by Lessor upon thirty (30) days' prior written notice to Lessee.

4. **Substitution of Hangar Space:** Lessor shall make reasonable efforts to ensure that the Aircraft is stored in the Hangar Space during the term of this Agreement, provided, however, that Lessor shall retain the right to move, park and/or relocate the Aircraft to a new space within the Hangar in the event that Lessor, in its sole discretion, determines that such a move is necessary or appropriate and Lessee hereby authorizes Lessor to move, park or relocate the Aircraft. If Lessor elects to move, park and/or relocate the Aircraft to a new space, Lessor shall make a reasonable effort to notify Lessee of the change in the Aircraft's location.

5. **Services Provided:** Lessor will provide the service of moving the Aircraft from the Hangar Space onto the ramp area, and from the ramp area into the Hangar Space. It is expressly agreed that Lessee shall have no right to perform the above service unless Lessee receives written permission therefor from Lessor. Lessor will maintain the structural components of the Hangar, including doors and door mechanisms, and Lessor will provide light, water, electricity and normal building maintenance without additional cost to Lessee, provided, however, that Lessor reserves the right to assess an additional fee for consumption of utilities by Lessee beyond normal requirements as determined by Lessor.

6. **Use of the Hangar Space:** The Hangar Space shall be used only for storage of the Aircraft. No commercial activity of any kind whatsoever shall be conducted by Lessee in, from or around the Hangar Space or the Hangar. No maintenance on the Aircraft shall be performed in the Hangar Space or the Hangar without the prior written approval of Lessor, except such minor maintenance as would normally be performed by an aircraft owner without the benefit of an aircraft mechanic. If such minor maintenance work will immobilize the Aircraft for a period in excess of four (4) hours, Lessee shall give Lessor notice of its intent to perform such work. In the event that Lessee gives Lessor such notice, and Lessor determines in its sole discretion that the location of the Aircraft is such that it would be inconvenient or impracticable to perform such work at that location, Lessee shall refrain from commencing such work and Lessor shall move the Aircraft to another location where such work and immobility of the Aircraft will not hamper, impede or obstruct Lessor's operations., Lessee shall take steps to ensure that the performance of such maintenance work shall not damage the Hangar Space, the Hangar, or other area where the work is performed. Lessee shall control the conduct and demeanor of its employees and invitees, and of those doing business with it, in and around the Hangar and Hangar Space, and shall take all steps necessary to remove persons whom Lessor may, for good and sufficient cause, deem objectionable. Lessee shall keep the floor of the Hangar Space clean and free of debris at all times. In utilizing the Hangar Space during the term of this Agreement, Lessee agrees to and shall comply with all applicable ordinances, rules and regulations established by any federal, state or local government agency, by Lessor or by ________________ ________________________ (the "Airport Authority"). On the termination of this Agreement, by expiration or otherwise, Lessee shall immediately surrender possession of the Hangar Space and shall remove, at its sole expense, the Aircraft and all other property therefrom, leaving the Hangar Space in the same condition as when received, ordinary wear and tear excepted. Lessee shall be liable for any and all damage to the Hangar or to the Hangar Space caused by Lessee's use, including, but not limited to, bent or broken interior walls, damage to unsealed floors due to fuel spillage, or damage to doors due to Lessee's improper or negligent operation.

7. **Primary Lease:** It is expressly understood and agreed that if the primary lease between the Airport Authority and Lessor, which covers the Hangar and adjacent areas, is terminated, cancelled or for any reason abated as to any portion of the Hangar or adjacent areas, such termination, cancellation or abatement will operate as a cancellation of this Agreement, and Lessor will be relieved of liability for any and all damages Lessee may sustain as a result thereof.

8. **Sublease/Assignment:** Lessee shall have no right to sublease the Hangar Space or to assign this Agreement without the prior written approval of Lessor. The parking of aircraft not owned or leased by Lessee in the Hangar Space shall constitute a sublease.

9. **Condition of Premises:** Lessee shall accept the Hangar Space in its present condition without any liability or obligation on the part of Lessor to make any alterations, improvements or repairs of any kind on or about said Hangar Space.

10. **Alterations:** Lessee covenants and agrees not to install any fixtures or make any alterations, additions or improvements to the Hangar Space without the prior written approval of Lessor. All fixtures installed or additions and improvements made to the Hangar Space shall, upon completion of such additions and improvements, become Lessor's property and shall remain in the Hangar Space at the termination of this Agreement, however terminated, without compensation or payment to Lessee.

11. **Insurance:** Lessee agrees to maintain, at its own expense, for the benefit of itself and Lessor as co-insureds, insurance of such type and in such amounts as may be approved by Lessor, insuring against: (a) liability for damage to or loss of the Aircraft or other property; and (b) liability for personal injury or death arising from acts or omissions of Lessee, its agents and employees. Such policy or policies shall contain a provision whereby Lessee's insurer waives any rights of subrogation against Lessor, its agents and employees and providing that Lessor must receive at least ten (10) days' prior written notice of any cancellation of Lessee's insurance coverage. Prior to the commencement of this Agreement, Lessee shall deliver to Lessor certificates or binders evidencing the existence of the insurance required herein.

12. **Casualty:** In the event the Hangar or the Hangar Space, or the means of access thereto, shall be damaged by fire or any other cause, the rent payable hereunder shall not abate provided that the Hangar Space is not rendered untenantable by such damage. If the Hangar Space is rendered untenantable and Lessor elects to repair the Hangar or Hangar Space, the rent shall abate for the period during which such repairs are being made, provided the damage was not caused by the acts or omissions of Lessee, its employees, agents or invitees, in which case the rent shall not abate. If the Hangar or Hangar Space is rendered untenantable and Lessor elects not to repair the Hangar or Hangar Space, this Agreement shall terminate.

13. **Indemnity; Force Majeure:** Lessee agrees to release, idemnify and hold Lessor, its officers and employees harmless from and against any and all liabilities, damages, business interruptions, delays, losses, claims, judgments, of any kind whatsoever, including all costs, attorneys' fees, and expenses incidental thereto, which may be suffered by, or charged to, Lessor by reason of any loss of or damage to any property or injury to or death of any person arising out of or by reason of any breach, violation or non-performance by Lessee or its servants, employees or agents of any covenant or condition of the Agreement or by any act or failure to act of those persons. Lessor shall not be liable for its failure to perform this Agreement or for any loss, injury, damage or delay of any nature whatsoever resulting therefrom caused by any act of God, fire, flood, accident, strike, labor dispute, riot, insurrection, war or any other cause beyond Lessor's control.

14. **DISCLAIMER OF LIABILITY:** LESSOR HEREBY DISCLAIMS, AND LESSEE HEREBY RELEASES LESSOR FROM, ANY AND ALL LIABILITY, WHETHER IN CONTRACT OR TORT (INCLUDING STRICT LIABILITY AND NEGLIGENCE), FOR ANY LOSS, DAMAGE OR INJURY OF ANY NATURE WHATSOEVER SUSTAINED BY LESSEE, ITS EMPLOYEES, AGENTS OR INVITEES DURING THE TERM OF THIS AGREEMENT, INCLUDING BUT NOT LIMITED TO LOSS, DAMAGE OR INJURY TO THE AIRCRAFT OR OTHER PROPERTY OF LESSEE THAT MAY BE LOCATED OR STORED IN THE HANGAR SPACE, UNLESS SUCH LOSS, DAMAGE OR INJURY IS CAUSED BY LESSOR'S GROSS NEGLIGENCE OR INTENTIONAL WILLFUL MISCONDUCT. THE PARTIES HEREBY AGREE THAT UNDER NO CIRCUMSTANCES SHALL LESSOR BE LIABLE FOR INDIRECT, CONSEQUENTIAL, SPECIAL OR EXEMPLARY DAMAGES, WHETHER IN CONTRACT OR TORT (INCLUDING STRICT LIABILITY AND NEGLIGENCE), SUCH AS, BUT NOT LIMITED TO, LOSS OF REVENUE OR ANTICIPATED PROFITS OR OTHER DAMAGE RELATED TO THE LEASING OF THE HANGAR SPACE UNDER THIS AGREEMENT.

15. **Default:** This Agreement shall be breached if: (a) Lessee shall default in the payment of any rental payment hereunder; (b) Lessee shall default in the performance of any other covenant herein, and such default shall continue for five (5) days after receipt by Lessee of notice thereof from Lessor; (c) Lessee shall cease to do business as a going concern; (d) a petition is filed by or against Lessee under the Bankruptcy Act or any amendment thereto (including a petition for reorganization or an arrangement); or (e) Lessee assigns any interest in his/her property for the benefit of creditors.

In the event of any breach of this Agreement by Lessee, Lessor shall, at its option, and without further notice, have the right to terminate this Agreement and to remove the Aircraft and any other property of Lessee from the Hangar Space, using such force as may be reasonably necessary, without being deemed guilty of trespass, breach of peace or forceable entry and detainer, and Lessee expressly waives the service of any notice. Exercise by Lessor of either or both of the rights specified above shall not prejudice Lessor's right to pursue any other remedy available to Lessor in law or equity.

16. **Thirty (30) Day Termination:** Either party to this Agreement shall have the right, with or without cause, to terminate this Agreement by giving thirty (30) days' prior written notice to the other party.

17. **Governing Law:** This Agreement shall be construed in accordance with the laws of the State of ____.

18. **Relationship of Parties:** The relationship between Lessor and Lessee shall always and only be that of lessor and lessee. Lessee shall never at any time during the term of this Agreement become the agent of Lessor, and Lessor shall not be responsible for the acts or omissions of Lessee, its employees or agents.

19. **Remedies Cumulative:** The rights and remedies with respect to any of the terms and conditions of this Agreement shall be cumulative and not exclusive, and shall be in addition to all other rights and remedies available to either party in law or equity.

20. **Notices:** Any notice given by one party to the other in connection with this Agreement shall be in writing and shall be sent by certified or registered mail, return receipt requested:

(1) If to Lessor, addressed to:

____

____

____

(2) If to Lessee, addressed to:

____

____

____

Notices shall be deemed to have been received on the date of receipt as shown on the return receipt.

21. **Integration:** This Agreement constitutes the entire agreement between the parties, and as of its effective date supersedes all prior independent agreements between the parties related to the leasing of the Hangar Space. Any change or modification hereof must be in writing signed by both parties.

22. **Waiver:** The waiver by either party of any covenant or condition of this Agreement shall not thereafter preclude such party from demanding performance in accordance with the terms hereof.

23. **Successors Bound:** This Agreement shall be binding and shall inure to the benefit of the heirs, legal representatives, successors and assigns of the parties hereto.

24. **Severability:** If a provision hereof shall be finally declared void or illegal by any court or administrative agency having jurisdiction over the parties to this Agreement, the entire Agreement shall not be void, but the remaining provisions shall continue in effect as nearly as possible in accordance with the original intent of the parties.

IN WITNESS WHEREOF, the parties have executed this Agreement as of the day and year first above written.

LESSOR: ______________________________

By: ______________________________

Title: ______________________________

LESSEE: ______________________________

By: ______________________________

Title: ______________________________

HANGAR LEASE AGREEMENT

This HANGAR LEASE AGREEMENT (this "Agreement") entered into as of this ___________ day of ___________________________ 19_____ by and between _______________________________________("Lessor") and ___________________________________ ("Lessee").

In consideration of the mutual covenants contained herein, and for other good and valuable consideration, the parties hereby agree as follows:

1. **Lease of the Hangar:** Lessor hereby leases to Lessee Hangar # ____________ (the "Hangar") located at ____ (the "Airport") and described as follows: ____. The Hangar shall be used and occupied by Lessee solely for the storage of the following described aircraft: ______________________________________ ____ _________ Registration No. ___________________________ (the "Aircraft"), or any other similar aircraft owned or leased by Lessee (the "Substitute Aircraft"), provided Lessee has obtained the prior written consent of Lessor to store the Substitute Aircraft in the Hangar. In the event Lessee is permitted to store a Substitute Aircraft in the Hangar, all provisions of the Agreement applicable to the Aircraft shall also be applicable to the Substitute Aircraft.

2. **Term:** The term of this Agreement shall commence on _______________________ ___________, 19_____, and shall continue in effect until ___________________________ ___________, 19_______, unless earlier terminated under the terms of this Agreement. Thereafter, this Agreement shall continue in effect from month to month, being automatically renewed after each month, unless terminated under the terms of this Agreement.

3. **Rent:** For the use of the Hangar, Lessee shall pay Lessor, at the address specified in Paragraph 19, the amount of ____ ($_____________) per month, payable in advance on or before the first day of each month. The amount of rent may be changed from time to time by Lessor upon thirty (30) days' prior written notice to Lessee.

4. **Services Provided:** Lessor will provide the service of moving the Aircraft from the Hangar onto the ramp area, and from the ramp area into the Hangar. It is expressly agreed that Lessee shall have no right to perform the above service unless Lessee receives prior written permission therefor from Lessor. Lessor will maintain the structural components of the Hangar, including doors and door mechanisms, and Lessor will provide light, water, electricity and normal building maintenance without additional cost to Lessee, provided, however, that Lessor reserves the right to assess an additional fee for consumption of utilities by Lessee beyond normal requirements as determined by Lessor.

5. **Use of the Hangar:** The Hangar shall be used only for storage of the Aircraft. No commerical activity of any kind whatsoever shall be conducted by Lessee in, from or around the Hangar. No maintenance on the Aircraft shall be performed in the Hangar without the prior written approval of Lessor, except such minor maintenance as would normally be performed by an aircraft owner without the benefit of an aircraft mechanic. Lessee shall take steps to ensure that the performance of such maintenance work shall not damage the Hangar. Lessee shall control the conduct and demeanor of its employees and invitees, and of those doing business with it, in and around the Hangar and shall take all steps necessary to remove persons whom Lessor may for good and sufficient cause, deem objectionable. Lessee shall keep the Hangar clean and free of debris at all times. In utilizing the Hangar during the term of this Agreement, Lessee agrees to and shall comply with all applicable ordinances, rules, and regulations established by any federal, state, or local government agency by Lessor or by ____ (the "Airport Authority").

5. **Use of the Hangar (continued) :** On the termination of this Agreement, by expiration or otherwise, Lessee shall immediately surrender possession of the Hangar and shall , at its sole expense, remove the Aircraft and all other property therefrom, leaving the Hangar in the same condition as when received, ordinary wear and tear excepted. Lessee shall be liable for any and all damage to the Hangar caused by Lessee's use, including, but not limited to, bent or broken interior walls, damage to unsealed floors due to fuel oil spillage, or damage to doors due to Lessee's improper or negligent operation.

6. **Primary Lease:** It is expressly understood and agreed that if the primary lease between the Airport Authority and Lessor, which covers the Hangar and adjacent areas, is terminated, cancelled or for any reason abated as to any portion of the Hangar or adjacent areas, such termination, cancellation or abatement will operate as a cancellation of this Agreement, and Lessor will be relieved of liability for any and all damages Lessee may sustain as a result thereof.

7. **Sublease/Assignment:** Lessee agrees not to sublease the Hangar or to assign this Agreement without the prior written approval of Lessor. The parking of aircraft not owned or leased by Lessee in the Hangar shall constitute a sublease.

8. **Condition of Premises:** Lessee shall accept the Hangar in its present condition without any liability or obligation on the part of Lessor to make any alterations, improvements or repairs of any kind on or about said Hangar.

9. **Alterations:** Lessee covenants and agrees not to install any fixtures or make any alterations, additions or improvements to the Hangar without the prior written approval of Lessor. All fixtures installed or additions and improvements made to the Hangar shall, upon completion of such additions and improvements, become Lessor's property and shall remain in the Hangar at the termination of this Agreement, however terminated, without compensation or payment to Lessee.

10. **Insurance:** Lessee agrees to maintain, at its own expense, for the benefit of itself and Lessor as co-insureds, insurance of such types and in such amounts as may be approved by Lessor, insuring against liability for damage or loss to the Aircraft or other property, and against liability for personal injury or death, arising from acts or omissions of Lessee, its agents and employees. Such policy or policies shall contain a provision whereby Lessee's insurer waives any rights of subrogation against Lessor, its agents and employees and providing that Lessor must receive at least ten (10) days' prior written notice of any cancellation of Lessee's insurance coverage. Prior to the commencement of this Agreement, Lessee shall deliver to Lessor certificates or binders evidencing the existence of the insurance required herein.

11. **Casualty:** In the event the Hangar, or the means of access thereto, shall be damaged by fire or any other cause, the rent payable hereunder shall not abate provided that the Hangar is not rendered untenantable by such damage. If the Hangar is rendered untenantable and Lessor elects to repair the Hangar, the rent shall abate for the period during which such repairs are being made, provided the damage was not caused by the acts or omissions of Lessee, its employees, agents or invitees, in which case the rent shall not abate. If the Hangar is rendered untenantable and Lessor elects not to repair the Hangar, this Agreement shall terminate.

12. **Indemnity; Force Majeure:** Lessee agrees to release, indemnify and hold Lessor, its officers and employees harmless from and against any and all liabilities, damages, business interruptions, delays, losses, claims, judgements, of any kind whatsoever, including all costs, attorneys' fees, and expenses incidental thereto, which may be suffered by, or charged to, Lessor by reason of any loss of or damage to any property or injury to or death of any person arising out of or by reason of any breach, violation or non-performance by Lessee or its servants, employees or agents of any covenant or condition of the Agreement or by any act or failure to act of those persons. Lessor shall not be liable for its failure to perform this Agreement or for any loss, injury, damage or delay of any nature whatsoever resulting therefrom caused by any Act of God, fire, flood, accident, strike, labor dispute, riot, insurrection, war or any other cause beyond Lessor's control.

SAMPLE

13. **DISCLAIMER OF LIABILITY:** LESSOR HEREBY DISCLAIMS, AND LESSEE HEREBY RELEASES LESSOR FROM, ANY AND ALL LIABILITY, WHETHER IN CONTRACT OR TORT (INCLUDING STRICT LIABILITY AND NEGLIGENCE) FOR ANY LOSS, DAMAGE OR INJURY OF ANY NATURE WHATSOEVER SUSTAINED BY LESSEE, ITS EMPLOYEES, AGENTS OR INVITEES DURING THE TERM OF THIS AGREEMENT, INCLUDING BUT NOT LIMITED TO LOSS, DAMAGE OR INJURY TO THE AIRCRAFT OR OTHER PROPERTY OF LESSEE THAT MAY BE LOCATED OR STORED IN THE HANGAR, UNLESS SUCH LOSS, DAMAGE OR INJURY IS CAUSED BY LESSOR'S GROSS NEGLIGENCE OR INTENTIONAL WILLFUL MISCONDUCT. THE PARTIES HEREBY AGREE THAT UNDER NO CIRCUMSTANCES SHALL LESSOR BE LIABLE FOR INDIRECT, CONSEQUENTIAL, SPECIAL OR EXEMPLARY DAMAGES, WHETHER IN CONTRACT OR TORT (INCLUDING STRICT LIABILITY AND NEGLIGENCE), SUCH AS, BUT NOT LIMITED TO, LOSS OF REVENUE OR ANTICIPATED PROFITS OR OTHER DAMAGE RELATED TO THE LEASING OF THE HANGAR UNDER THIS AGREEMENT.

14. **Default:** This Agreement shall be breached if: (a) Lessee shall default in the payment of any rental payment hereunder; (b) Lessee shall default in the performance of any other covenant herein, and such default shall continue for five (5) days after receipt by Lessee of notice thereof from Lessor; (c) Lessee shall cease to do business as a going concern; (d) a petition is filed by or against Lessee under the Bankruptcy Act or any amendment thereto (including a petition for reorganization or an arrangement); or (e) Lessee assigns his/her property for the benefit of creditors.

In the event of any breach of this Agreement by Lessee, Lessor shall, at its option, and without further notice, have the right to terminate this Agreement and to remove the Aircraft and any other property of Lessee from the Hangar using such force as may be reasonably necessary, without being deemed guilty of trespass, breach of peace or forceable entry and detainer, and Lessee expressly waives the service of any notice. Exercise by Lessor of either or both of the rights specified above shall not prejudice Lessor's right to pursue any other remedy available to Lessor in law or equity.

15. **Thirty (30) Day Termination:** Either party to this Agreement shall have the right, with or without cause, to terminate this Agreement by giving thirty (30) days' prior written notice to the other party.

16. **Governing Law:** This Agreement shall be construed in accordance with the laws of the State of ____.

17. **Relationship of Parties:** The relationship between Lessor and Lessee shall always and only be that of lessor and lessee. Lessee shall never at any time during the term of this Agreement become the agent of Lessor, and Lessor shall not be responsible for the acts or omissions of Lessee, its employees, or agents.

18. **Remedies Cumulative:** The rights and remedies with respect to any of the terms and conditions of this Agreement shall be cumulative and not exclusive, and shall be in addition to all other rights and remedies available to either party in law or equity.

19. **Notices:** Any notice given by one party to the other in connection with this Agreement shall be in writing and shall be sent by certified or registered mail, return receipt requested:

(1) If to Lessor, addressed to:

____

____

____

____

SAMPLE

(2) If to Lessee, addressed to:

____

____

____

____

Notices shall be deemed to have been received on the date of receipt as shown on the return receipt.

20. **Integration:** This Agreement constitutes the entire agreement between the parties, and as of its effective date supersedes all prior independent agreements between the parties related to the leasing of the Hangar. Any change or modification hereof must be in writing signed by both parties.

21. **Waiver:** The waiver by either party of any covenant or condition of this Agreement shall not thereafter preclude such party from demanding performance in accordance with the terms hereof.

22. **Successors Bound:** This Agreement shall be binding on and shall inure to the benefit of the heirs, legal representatives, successors and assigns of the parties hereto.

23. **Severability:** If a provision hereof shall be finally declared void or illegal by any court or administrative agency having jurisdiction over the parties to this Agreement, the entire Agreement shall not be void, but the remaining provisions shall continue in effect as nearly as possible in accordance with the original intent of parties.

IN WITNESS WHEREOF, the parties have executed this Agreement as of the day and year first above written.

LESSOR: ____________________________

By: ____________________________

Title: ____________________________

LESSEE: ____________________________

By: ____________________________

Title: ____________________________

TIE-DOWN LEASE AGREEMENT

This TIE-DOWN LEASE AGREEMENT (this "Agreement") entered into as of the ______ day of ____________________ 19______, by and between ____ ("Lessor") and ____("Lessee").

In consideration of the mutual covenants contained herein, and for other good and valuable consideration, the parties hereby agree as follows:

1. **Lease of the Space:** Lessor agrees to lease to Lessee tie-down space # _______________ (the "Space") located at ____ (the "Airport"), and described as follows: ____. The Space shall be used and occupied by Lessee solely for the storage of the following described aircraft: ______________________ ______________________________ Registration No. _________________________ (the "Aircraft"), or any other similar aircraft owned or leased by Lessee (the "Substitute Aircraft"), provided Lessee has obtained the written consent of Lessor to store the Substitute Aircraft in the Space. In the event Lessee is permitted to store a Substitute Aircraft in the Space, all provisions of the Agreement applicable to the Aircraft shall also be applicable to the Substitute Aircraft.

2. **Term:** This Agreement shall commence on ______________________ _________, 19______, and remain in force until ____________________ ______, 19____, unless earlier terminated under the terms of this Agreement. Thereafter, this Agreement shall continue in effect from month to month, being automatically renewed after each month unless terminated under the provisions of this Agreement.

3. **Rent:** For use of the Space, Lessee shall pay Lessor, at the address specified in paragraph 18, the amount of _______________ ($____________) per month, payable in advance on or before the first day of each month. The amount of rent may be changed from time to time by Lessor upon thirty (30) days' prior written notice to Lessee.

4. **Lessee's Use of the Space:** The Space shall be used only for the storage of the Aircraft. No commercial activity of any kind whatsoever shall be conducted by Lessee in, from or around the Space. No maintenance on the Aircraft shall be performed within the Space without the prior written approval of Lessor except such minor maintenance as would normally be performed by an aircraft owner without the benefit of an aircraft mechanic. Lessee shall take steps to ensure that the performance of such maintenance work shall not damage the Space. Lessee shall control the conduct and demeanor of its employees and invitees, and of those doing business with it, in and around the Space and shall take all steps necessary to remove persons whom Lessor may, for good and sufficient cause, deem objectionable. Lessee shall keep the Space clean and free of debris at all times. In utilizing the Space, Lessee agrees to and shall comply with all applicable ordinances, resolutions, rules and regulations established by any federal, state or local government agency, by Lessor or by ____ (the "Airport Authority"). On the termination of this Agreement, by expiration or otherwise, Lessee shall immediately surrender possession of the Space and shall immediately remove, at its sole expense, the Aircraft and all other property therefrom, leaving the Space in the same condition as when received, ordinary wear and tear excepted.

5. **Services Provided by Lessor:** Lessor shall provide suitable ropes or chains and anchors for the purpose of securing the Aircraft to the Space. Lessor's employees may, from time to time, assist Lessee in securing the Aircraft; however, Lessee shall have the final responsibility for securing the Aircraft.

SAMPLE

6. **Primary Lease:** It is expressly understood and agreed that if the primary lease between the Airport Authority and Lessor, which governs the Space and adjacent areas, is terminated, cancelled or for any reason abated as to any portion of the Space or adjacent areas, such termination, cancellation or abatement shall operate as a cancellation of this Agreement, and Lessor shall be relieved of liability for any and all damages Lessee may sustain as a result thereof.

7. **Sublease/Assignment:** Lessee shall have no right to sublease the Space or to assign this Agreement without the prior written approval of Lessor. The parking of aircraft not owned or leased by Lessee within the Space shall constitute a sublease.

8. **Insurance:** Lessee agrees to maintain, at its own expense, for the benefit of itself and Lessor as co-insureds, insurance of such types and in such amounts as may be approved by Lessor, insuring against liability for damage or loss to the Aircraft or other property, and against liability for personal injury or death, arising from acts or omissions of Lessee, its agents and employees. Such policy or policies shall contain a provision whereby Lessee's insurer waives any right of subrogation against Lessor, its agents and employees, and providing that Lessor must receive at least ten (10) days' prior written notice of any cancellation of Lessee's insurance coverage. Prior to the commencement of this Agreement, Lessee shall deliver to Lessor certificates or binders evidencing the existence of the insurance required herein.

9. **Indemnity; Force Majeure:** Lessee agrees to release, indemnify and hold Lessor, its officers and employees harmless, from and against any and all liabilities, damages, business interruptions, delays, losses, claims, judgments, of any kind whatsoever, including all costs, attorneys' fees, and expenses incidental thereto, which may be suffered by, or charged to, Lessor by reason of any loss of or damage to any property or injury to or death of any person arising out of or by reason of any breach, violation or non-performance by Lessee or its servants, employees or agents of any covenant or condition of this Agreement, or by any act or failure to act of those persons. Lessor shall not be liable for failure to perform this Agreement or for any loss, injury or damage of any nature whatsoever resulting therefrom caused by any act of God, fire, flood, accident, strike, labor dispute, riot, insurrection, war or any other cause beyond Lessor's control.

10. **Condition of Premises:** Lessee shall accept the Space in its present condition without any liability or obligation on the part of Lessor to make any alterations, improvements or repairs of any kind within or to the Space.

11. **Default:** This Agreement shall be breached if: (a) Lessee shall default in the payment of any rental payment hereunder; (b) Lessee shall default in the performance of any other covenant herein, and such default shall continue for five (5) days after receipt by Lessee of notice thereof from Lessor; (c) Lessee shall cease to do business as a going concern; (d) a petition is filed by or against Lessee under the Bankruptcy Act or any amendment thereto (including a petiton for reorganization or an arrangement); or (e) Lessee assigns any interest in his/her property for the benefit of creditors.

In the event of any breach of this Agreement by Lessee, Lessor shall, at its option, and without further notice, have the right to terminate this Agreement and to remove the Aircraft and any other property of Lessee from the Space, using such force as may be reasonably necessary without being deemed guilty of trespass, breach of peace or forceable entry and detainer, and Lessee expressly waives the service of any notice. Exercise by Lessor of either or both of the rights specified above shall not prejudice Lessor's right to pursue any other remedy available to Lessor in law or equity.

12. **Thirty (30) Day Termination:** Either party to this Agreement shall have the right, with or without cause, to terminate this Agreement by giving thirty (30) days' prior written notice to the other party.

13. **DISCLAIMER OF LIABILITY:** LESSOR HEREBY DISCLAIMS AND LESSEE HEREBY RELEASES LESSOR FROM, ANY AND ALL LIABILITY, WHETHER IN CONTRACT OR TORT (INCLUDING STRICT LIABILITY AND NEGLIGENCE), FOR ANY LOSS, DAMAGE OR INJURY OF ANY NATURE WHATSOEVER SUSTAINED BY LESSEE, ITS EMPLOYEES, AGENTS, OR INVITEES DURING THE TERM OF THIS AGREEMENT, INCLUDING BUT NOT LIMITED TO LOSS, DAMAGE OR INJURY TO THE AIRCRAFT OR OTHER PROPERTY OF LESSEE THAT MAY BE LOCATED WITHIN THE SPACE, UNLESS SUCH LOSS, DAMAGE OR INJURY IS CAUSED BY LESSOR'S GROSS NEGLIGENCE OR INTENTIONAL WILLFUL MISCONDUCT. THE PARTIES HEREBY AGREE THAT UNDER NO CIRCUMSTANCES SHALL LESSOR BE LIABLE FOR INDIRECT, CONSEQUENTIAL, SPECIAL OR EXEMPLARY DAMAGES, WHETHER IN CONTRACT OR TORT (INCLUDING STRICT LIABILITY AND NEGLIGENCE), SUCH AS BUT NOT LIMITED TO LOSS OF REVENUE OR ANTICIPATED PROFITS OR OTHER DAMAGE RELATED TO THE LEASING OF THE SPACE UNDER THIS AGREEMENT.

14. **Governing Law:** This Agreement shall be construed in accordance with the laws of the State of ____.

15. **Relationship of Parties:** The relationship between Lessor and Lessee shall always and only be that of lessor and lessee. Lessee shall never at any time during the term of this Agreement become the agent of Lessor, and Lessor shall not be responsible for the acts or omissions of Lessee, its employees or agents.

16. **Remedies Cumulative:** The rights and remedies with respect to any of the terms and conditions of this Agreement shall be cumulative and not exclusive and shall be in additon to all other rights and remedies.

17. **Integration:** This Agreement constitutes the entire agreement between the parties, and as of its effective date supersedes all prior independent agreements between the parties covering the Space. Any change or modification hereof must be in writing signed by both parties.

18. **Notices:** Any notice given by one party to the other in connection with this Agreement shall be in writing and shall be sent by certified or registered mail, return receipt requested:

(1) If to Lessor, addressed to

____

____

____

____

(2) If to Lessee, addressed to

____

____

____

____

Notices shall be deemed to have been received on the date of receipt as shown on the return receipt.

SAMPLE

19. **Waiver:** The waiver by either party of any covenant or condition of this Agreement shall not thereafter preclude such party from demanding performance in accordance with the terms hereof.

20. **Successors Bound:** This Agreement shall be binding on and shall inure to the benefit of the heirs, legal representatives, successors and assigns of the parties hereto.

21. **Severability:** If a provision hereof shall be finally declared void or illegal by any court or agency having jurisdiction over the parties to this Agreement, the entire Agreement shall not be void, but the remaining provisions shall continue in effect as nearly as possible in accordance with the original intent of the parties.

IN WITNESS WHEREOF, the parties have executed this Agreement as of the day and year first above written.

LESSOR: ______________________________

By: ______________________________

Title: ______________________________

LESSEE: ______________________________

By: ______________________________

Title: ______________________________

AIRCRAFT RENTAL AGREEMENT

This AIRCRAFT RENTAL AGREEMENT (this "Agreement") entered into as of the ________ day of ____________, 19_____, by and between ____("Operator") and ____("Renter").

In consideration of the mutual covenants contained herein, and for other good and valuable consideration, the parties hereby agree as follows:

1. **Rental of Aircraft:** Operator hereby rents to Renter the following described aircraft: ____________
____
___________ Registration Number
____(the "Aircraft").

2. **Rental Period:** The rental period shall commence at ______________________________ on ____________________, ______, 19______, and shall continue until __________________________ on ______________________, ______, 19______, at which time Renter shall return the Aircraft to Operator at ____ ______.

3. **Rental Fee:** Renter shall pay Operator a rental fee for Renter's use of the Aircraft according to the following schedule: ____ ______ ____. Such rental fee shall be due and payable immediately following the rental period.

4. **Route:** The Aircraft shall be flown during the rental period only over the following route: ____________
____
____________.

5. **Sole Pilot:** Renter shall be the sole pilot of the Aircraft during the rental period. Renter must complete an Aircraft Renter Primary Data Sheet ("Sheet") attached as Appendix A to this Agreement. The information and representations made on that Sheet are hereby incorporated by reference into this Agreement.

6. **Certificates:** Renter must hold valid and current Federal Aviation Administration ("FAA") pilot and medical certificates, and have passed a biennial flight review within the last twenty-four (24) months. The validity and currency of such certificates and review shall be determined by Operator in its sole discretion.

7. **Pre-Flight:** Renter shall personally conduct a pre-flight inspection of the Aircraft as prescribed by the manufacturer of the Aircraft, including checking the fuel from all sumps and determining that the fuel and oil on board the Aircraft are sufficient.

8. **Check-Lists:** Renter shall use the aircraft manufacturer's recommended pre-takeoff, cruise and pre-landing check-lists, which shall be supplied by Operator.

9. **Weather:** Renter shall obtain weather reports or forecasts for the proposed route prior to commencing a flight. The Aircraft shall only be operated when present and forecasted aviation weather indicate that Visual Flight Rule weather conditions are present both locally and enroute. Instrument Flight Rule operations must be approved in writing by Operator prior to any flight.

SAMPLE

10. **Runways:** Renter shall utilize only established, hard-surfaced runways, except in cases of emergency.

11. **Accidents:** Renter agrees to report to Operator any accident, mishap, incident or physical damage to the Aircraft as soon as practicable, but in no case later than twenty-four (24) hours after its occurrence.

12. **Compliance with Laws:** Renter shall file an FAA flight plan for all flights of more than twenty-five (25) nautical miles in one direction. The Aircraft shall only be operated in accordance with all federal, state and local air regulations and laws.

13. **Physical Condition:** The Aircraft shall not be operated if Renter has used intoxicating liquor, tranquilizers or sleep-inducing drugs within twenty-four (24) hours prior to the commencement of a flight.

14. **Inspection:** Renter certifies that he/she has inspected the Aircraft or has caused it to be inspected and certifies that the Aircraft is in good mechanical condition.

15. **Prohibited Activities:** The Aircraft shall not be used (a) to carry persons or property for hire; or (b) in any race, test, contest or acrobatics.

16. **CONDITION OF AIRCRAFT:** RENTER HEREBY ACKNOWLEDGES THAT OPERATOR IS NOT THE MANUFACTURER OF THE AIRCRAFT OR THE MANUFACTURER'S AGENT, AND THAT OPERATOR MAKES NO WARRANTY OR REPRESENTATION, EITHER EXPRESS OR IMPLIED, AS TO THE FITNESS, WORKMANSHIP, DESIGN, CONDITION, OR MERCHANTABILITY OF THE AIRCRAFT, ITS FITNESS FOR ANY PARTICULAR PURPOSE, OR THE QUALITY OR CAPACITY OF THE MATERIAL IN THE AIRCRAFT.

17. **Sublease/Assignment:** Renter agrees not to sublease the Aircraft or assign this Agreement without the prior written approval of Operator.

18. **Alterations:** Renter agrees not to make any additions, alterations or improvements to the Aircraft without the prior written approval of Operator.

19. **Indemnity; Force Majeure:** Renter agrees to release, indemnify and hold Operator, its officers and employees harmless from and against any and all liabilities, damages, business interruptions, delays, losses, claims, judgments of any kind whatsoever, including all costs, attorneys' fees, and expenses incidental thereto, which may be suffered by, or charged to, Operator by reason of any loss of or damage to any property, or injury to or death of any person, arising out of or by reason of any breach, violation or non-performance by Renter of any covenant or condition of the Agreement or by any act or failure to act of Renter. Operator shall not be liable for its failure to perform under this Agreement or for any loss, injury, damage or delay of any nature whatsoever resulting therefrom caused by any act of God, fire, flood, accident, strike, labor dispute, riot, insurrection, war or any other cause beyond Operator's control.

20. **DISCLAIMER OF LIABILITY:** OPERATOR HEREBY DISCLAIMS, AND RENTER HEREBY RELEASES OPERATOR FROM, ANY AND ALL LIABILITY, WHETHER IN CONTRACT OR TORT (INCLUDING STRICT LIABILITY AND NEGLIGENCE), FOR ANY LOSS, DAMAGE OR INJURY OF ANY NATURE WHATSOEVER SUSTAINED BY RENTER, ITS EMPLOYEES, AGENTS OR INVITEES DURING THE TERM OF THIS AGREEMENT, UNLESS SUCH LOSS, DAMAGE OR INJURY IS CAUSED BY OPERATOR'S GROSS NEGLIGENCE OR INTENTIONAL WILLFUL MISCONDUCT. THE PARTIES HEREBY AGREE THAT UNDER NO CIRCUMSTANCES SHALL OPERATOR BE LIABLE FOR INDIRECT, CONSEQUENTIAL, SPECIAL OR EXEMPLARY DAMAGES, WHETHER IN CONTRACT OR TORT (INCLUDING STRICT LIABILITY AND NEGLIGENCE), SUCH AS, BUT NOT LIMITED TO, LOSS OF REVENUE OR ANTICIPATED PROFITS OR OTHER DAMAGE RELATED TO THE RENTING OF THE AIRCRAFT UNDER THIS AGREEMENT.

21. **Damage to Aircraft:** At the termination of the rental period, Renter shall return the Aircraft to Operator in the same condition as when received, excepting reasonable wear and tear. Renter shall be liable to Operator for any and all loss or damage sustained by the Aircraft during the rental period.

22. **Emergency Repairs:** Emergency repairs shall be defined as repairs to the Aircraft which, due to statute, regulations, mechanical failure or damage, should be made to the Aircraft before further flight. Should the Aircraft require emergency repairs, Renter shall comply with the following procedures: (a) Contact Operator for instructions; (b) If no contact can be made and repair can be effected for One Hundred Dollars ($100.00) or less, Renter may authorize and make payment for the repairs, for which Renter shall be reimbursed by Operator. Under no circumstances shall Renter authorize repairs to the Aircraft unless no contact with the Operator can be effected and the repairs can be made for One Hundred Dollars ($100.00) or less, and under no circumstances shall the Aircraft be flown by Renter without repair if to do so would violate any govennmental statute or regulation or compromise the safety of the Renter, his/her passengers or the Aircraft.

23. **Default:** If Renter defaults in the performance of any of his/her obligations under this Agreement, Operator shall, at its option, and without further notice, have the right to terminate the Agreement and to repossess the Aircraft using such force as may be reasonably necessary without being deemed guilty of trespass, breach of peace or forceable entry and detainer, and Renter expresssly waives the service of any notice. Exercise by Operator of either or both of the rights specified above shall not prejudice Operator's right to pursue any other remedy in law or equity.

24. **Governing Law:** This Agreement shall be construed in accordance with the laws of the State of ______________.

25. **Relationship of Parties:** Renter shall never at any time during the term of this Agreement become the agent of Operator and Operator shall not be responsible for the acts or omissions of Renter, its employees, or agents.

26. **Remedies Cumulative:** The rights and remedies with respect to any of the terms and conditions of this Agreement shall be cumulative and not exclusive, and shall be in addition to all other rights and remedies available to either party in law or equity.

27. **Integration:** This Agreement constitutes the entire agreement between the parties, and as of its effective date supersedes all prior independent agreements between the parties related to the renting of the Aircraft. Any change or modification hereof must be in writing signed by both parties.

28. **Waiver:** The waiver by either party of any covenant or condition of this Agreement shall not thereafter preclude such party from demanding performance in accordance with the terms hereof.

29. **Successors Bound:** This Agreement shall be binding on and shall inure to the benefit of the heirs, legal representatives, successors and assigns of the parties hereto.

30. **Severability:** If a provision hereof shall be finally declared void or illegal by any court or administrative agency having jurisdiction over the parties to this Agreement, the entire Agreement shall not be void, but the remaining provisions shall continue in effect as nearly as possible in accordance with the original intent of the parties.

SAMPLE

IN WITNESS WHEREOF, the parties have executed this Agreement as of the day and year first above written.

OPERATOR: ______________________

By: ______________________

Title: ______________________

RENTER: ______________________

By: ______________________

Title: ______________________

APPENDIX A

AIRCRAFT RENTER PRIMARY DATA SHEET

I. Personal Information

A. Name ______________________
B. Home Address ______________________
____
C. Home Phone Number ______________________
D. Spouse's Name ______________________
E. Employer's Name ______________________
F. Business Address ______________________
____
G. Business Phone Number ______________________
H. Name, Address & Phone Number of Person to Contact in an Emergency ______________________
____
____
____
I. State Driver's Lic. # ______________________
J. Date of Birth ______________________
K. Soc. Security Number ______________________

II. References

A. Name, Branch & Address of Bank ______________________
____
____
B. Credit Cart References:
(1) Name & Acct. # ______________________
(2) Name & Acct. # ______________________
(3) Name & Acct. # ______________________
C. Personal References:
(1) Name, Address & Phone ______________________
____
(2) Name, Address & Phone ______________________
____

III. Flight Experience

A. Total Time PIC ______________________
B. Total Time PIC Last 90 Days:

(1)	Make	Model	Day	Night
a.	______	______	______	______
b.	______	______	______	______
c.	______	______	______	______
d.	______	______	______	______

(2) No. of Take-Offs & Landings:
PIC Last 6 Months ______________________
a. Actual ______________________
b. Simulated ______________________
c. No. of Approaches ______________________

IV. Airman Information

A. Airman Cert. # ______________________

(1) Ratings & Limitations ______________________

____

(2) Date of Issuance ______________________

B. Medical Cert. # ______________________

(1) Limitations ______________________

(2) Class ______________________

(3) Date of Expiration ______________________

C. Bienniel Flight Review ______________________

(1) Date of Expiration ______________________

V. Renter's Insurance

A. Name of Insurance Policy ______________________

B. Policy Number ______________________

C. Limits of Liability ______________________

VI. Aircraft Pilot Qualification

Date	Check Pilot Initials	Make	Model

VFR	IFR	Day	Night

VII. Renter's Warrenties

A. I am a certified pilot under the laws of the United States of America and am rated and qualified for the flight in the aircraft I desire to rent.

B. I have a valid and unexpired medical certificate. I have passed a Bienniel Flight Refiew within the last 24 months.

C. I warrant that the information contained on this data sheet is correct. I understand that the Operator is relying on this information to rent the Aircraft *only* to me.

D. I understand that false information might invalidate insurance policies rendering me personally liable for loss or damage resulting from an accident.

____

RENTER'S SIGNATURE AND DATE

Case Studies

The following case studies are presented in synopsis form to facilitate a quick review and comparison of circumstances of a variety of cases that may be similar to your own. The full text, consisting of court records, correspondence or reprints of printed articles, can be obtained from NATA for a nominal cost of $.10 per page plus $5.00 for computer search and shipping and handling. The actual cost of each case study varies, depending on the number of pages to be photocopied.

NATA Case Study File 00103
City of Kalamazoo v. Bartelt Aviation, Inc. (Decision)

The defendant was found to be engaging in certain commercial aeronautical activites on the Kalamazoo Municipal Airport without a proper lease and not in compliance with established minimum standards.

While the Court found the aggregate space requirements to be unreasonable in this instance, the concept and principle of minimum standards were upheld.

The defendant was required to enter into a lease to conduct commercial aeronautical activities on the airport, and to payover to the City the percentage (rent) that would have been required from June 1, 1979 to the present.

NATA Case Study File 00104
Community Communication Company, Inc. v. City of Boulder, Colorado (Decision)

The Supreme Court of the United States ruled in January, 1982 that "home rule" municipalities may be sued for violating federal antitrust laws when they regulate cable television or other private business activity. The ruling in this case could have an impact on municipalities that operate airports and their relations with FBOs and other contractors.

NATA Case Study File ER00106
Niswonger v. American Aviation (Decision)

In 1969, the airport operator leased all currently available facilities suitable for aeronautical activities to the incumbent FBO and revealed it took this action to exclude all other FBOs.

Another company applied to the airport operator in 1973 to become the second, or new FBO specializing in air taxi operations, and wanted to locate on the new ramp space soon to become available. The bid request was denied on the basis that all available space was under lease, and the new space was contractually committed to the established FBO. The matter went to litigation.

In its findings, the Court ruled that an exclusive right was being enjoyed by the established FBO. The Court, in a declaratory judgement, ruled in favor of the second FBO. "The leasing of all available aipon land or facilities suitable for aeronautical activities to a single enterprise is evidence of an intent to exclude others. . . The amount of space leased to a single enterprise should be limited to that for which it can clearly demonstrate an actual, existing need," the judgement read.

NATA Case Study File MD 00115
Availability of Federal Funds for Airport Development, Albany County Airport, Albany, New York (FAA Opinion Letter)

Funding for the airport was made available contingent on positive steps to correct unresolved compliance problems.

The FAA "strongly suggested" that the airport operator issue minimum standards for the conduct of aeronautical activities on the airport on a fair and reasonable basis and directly issue lease agreements for a proposed business.

NATA Case Study File FC 00119
State of Ohio v. National Flyers's Association (Decision)

The State of Ohio Tax Court ruled that a non-profit flying club, operating on a commercial basis, be assessed and required to pay tax on income.

NATA Case Study File FA 00122
Airport Sponsor Relinquishes Exclusive Right To Sell Fuel

The City of Columbus, Georgia turns fuel sales responsibility over to its FBOs.

NATA Case Study File FC 00130
FAA Upholds Minimum Standards, Leesburg Municipal Airport, Leesburg, Virginia (FAA Opinion Letter)

The FAA agreed with city officials that all potential users of the airport are subject to the same requriements and restricitions, including the charging of certain fees.

NATA Case Study File ME 00136
Pocono Mountains Municipal Airport Authority v. Stroudsburg-Pocono Airways, Inc. (Opinion)

The Court ruled that Stroudsburg-Pocono Airways cannot operate without first entering a lease agreement. The decision followed an investigation by the FAA that concluded that Stroudsburg-Pocono Airways should be allowed to operate at the airport, but only if it made a lease arrangement and met minimum operating standards.

NATA Case Study File GO 00142
Travel Air West v. Hughes Aviation Services (Directed Verdict)

Three independent aircraft mechanics wanted to conduct airplane repair and servicing on the North Las Vegas Airport without full compliance with the minimum standards. the mechanics brought suit against Hughes claiming the minimum standards were discriminatory and illegal. On a preliminary matter, the Court ruled that the minimum standards were not unreasonable or anti-competitive.

NATA Case Study File FC 00147
FAA Upholds Minimum Standards, Nampa Municipal Airport, Nampa, Idaho (FAA Opinion Letter)

The airport commission received FAA support on the minimum standard that prohibits remuneration of flying club members.

NATA Case Study File FA 00151
Airport Sponsor Relinquishes Exclusive Right to Sell Fuel

The city of Raleigh-Durham, North Carolina turns fules sales responsibility over to its FBOs.

NATA Case Study File TF 00162
FAA Reviews Minimum Standards, Sonoma County Airport, Santa Rosa, California (FAA Opinion Letter)

In its review of the airport's minimum standards, the FAA was very specific with regard to through-the-fence operations. The FAA recommended that the following statement or similar statement be added to the minimum standards:

"County will obtain FAA approval on any proposal from adjacent land onto the airport. No person, partnership, or corporations located on privately-owned property shall be permitted access to the airport's runway/taxiway system without first obtaining the approval of and any permit from the Board of Supervisors and agreeing to fully compensate the county for use of the airport facilities."

NATA Case Study File 00164
Atlantic Richfield Company v. William M. Razumic (Decision)

An automotive service station operator/franchisee refused to vacate the premises after being served an eviction notice by the owner. The Supreme Court of Pennsylvania ruled in favor of the operator/franchisee and remanded the case for a new trial.

NATA Case Study File FA 0166
Airport Sonsor Relinquishes Exclusive Right To Sell Fuel

The Purdue University Airport turned fuel sales responsiblity over to its FBOs.

NATA Case Study File AT00171
Greyhound Renta-A-Car, Inc. v. City of Pensacola and Dollar Rent-A-Car System, Inc. (Decision)

A bid by Greyhound Rent-A-Car to operate a car rental concession was rejected by the city. The Court agreed with the city in that it was free to establish standards for potential concessionaires and to refuse to deal with those who do not comply with those standards.

APPENDIX

X

FAA's "Guidelines for Leases or Agreements"

Guidelines for Leases or Agreements Granting Commercial Franchise Privileges for Aeronautical/Non-aeronautical Activities at Public Airports Affected by Federal Agreements

1. Background
   a. The federal interest in promoting civil aviation and the FAA responsibility related thereto has been established and augmented by various legislative actions which authorize programs for granting funds, property, and other assistance to local communities for the development of airport facilities. In each instance, the recipient public agency assumes certain obligations, either by contract or by restrictive covenants in deeds, pledging it to maintain and operate its airport facilities safely and efficiently and in accordance with specified conditions.
   b. The legal obligations and conditions assumed by airport owners in consideration of the federal benefits arise through the following:
      (1) Grant agreements issued under the Federal Airport Act of 1946 or the Airport and Airway Development Act of 1970.
      (2) Surplus airport property instruments of transfer, issued pursuant to Section 13g of the Surplus Property Act of 1944, as amended by Pl. 80-289 in 1947. [Surplus airport property conveyances prior to 1947 were handled by WAA (now GSA) as prescribed in Regulation 16, generally referred to as WAA—Reg. 16.]
      (3) Deeds of conveyance issued under Section 16 of the Federal Airport Act of 1946 or under Section 23 of the Airport and Airway Development Act of 1970 (nonsurplus federal land).
      (4) AP-4 Agreements and Section 308a of the Federal Aviation Act of 1958 (exclusive rights).
2. General
   a. The prime obligation of the owner of a federally assisted airport is to operate the airport for the use and benefit of the public. Coincidental with that obligation are the legal obligations of the agreements imposed by the federal government. The sponsor, through these agreements, provides, among other assurances, that with regard to leases or other agreements at the airport.

Source: FAA, Airports Division NW/Mountain Region. Seattle, WA 1985

(1) The airport will be available for public use on fair and reasonable terms and without unjust discrimination.

(2) Airport users will be charged for facilities and services under a fee and rental structure which will make the airport as self-sustaining as possible under the circumstances.

(3) No exclusive right will be granted or permitted which is prohibited by Section 308(a) of the Federal Aviation Act of 1958 and its successors.

(4) The airport will be bound by the assurances contained in Title VI of the Civil Rights Act of 1964, as implemented by Part 21 of the Regulations of the Office of the Secretary of Transportation.

(5) All revenue derived from the use of the obligated airport property will be used for the operation, maintenance, or development of the airport. Fair market rental values must be charged for the use of federal surplus property.

b. The sponsor's responsibility for operation is to make available to the public the landing areas, taxiways, parking areas, and other public areas. There is, however, no requirement that the use of the airport be provided free of charge. A cost or fee may be imposed on users in order to recover the costs of providing these facilities. The charge may be a landing fee (which is similar to the toll charge on a highway, bridge, or tunnel) or an indirect charge. Quite frequently the airport owner recovers this use charge indirectly as part of the consideration received from commercial tenant operators who provide direct services to users of the public areas. It may, for example, take the form of a gallonage fee, in which case fuel consumption is regarded as a measure of relative usage or benefit derived from the availability of the public landing area. It may also take the form of a monthly flat charge or a variable charge using the volume of business—rather than fuel gallonage—as the yardstick of benefit derived by patrons from the availability of the public landing areas.

In addition to those charges usually sought to be recovered from a user and/or tenant, there is normally an intent to recover some element of rent for the occupancy of specific premises granted by the airport owner to a private enterprise by lease, license, permit, or other contract.

3. Agreements for leasing airport property

a. The type of document, form of lease, or other written instrument used to grant airport privileges is the sole responsibility of the airport owner. Because of the variety of state laws affecting this type of agreement and because of possible infringement upon the realm of authority of the legal profession, the FAA has not deemed it wise to attempt to prepare and publish a model form of lease. Also, it is quite likely that the provisions required in any one particular lease may be of little value or concern in a lease at another location for various reasons. However, it has been found through experience that generally a lease for a fixed-base operation and other commercial activities on an airport should adequately cover certain points.

b. Typically, any document for the leasing of airport land or facilities should include the following elements:

(1) Airport property to be leased

(a) The lease agreement should adequately describe the specific portion of the airport property leased. (The leased premises should consist of only that portion of the airport property necessary for the lessee's business operation, such as a hangar, shop, office, and gasoline storage space and must *not* include landing, taxiing, or other common use facilities.)

(b) Aeronautical leases should provide the lessee the right to ingress and egress to and from the leased area.

(2) Rights and privileges granted to aeronautical lessees include, among others:

(a) For FBOs, the non-exclusive right to conduct certain specified aeronautical activities at the airport.

(b) The non-exclusive right to use, in common with others, all public airport facilities and improvements of a public nature which are now, or may hereafter be, connected with or appurtenant to landing, taxiing, parking areas, and other common use facilities.

(c) The right to construct facilities such as hangars, ramps, office, shop, buildings, improvements, and so on required in connection with the services to be provided.

(3) Obligations assumed by lessee include, among others:

(a) To operate the premises leased for the use and benefit of the public, and

1) To furnish said service on a fair, equal, and not unjustly discriminatory basis to all users thereof[1]

2) To charge fair, reasonable, and not unjustly discriminatory prices for each unit or service, provided that lessee may be allowed to make reasonable and nondiscriminatory discounts, rebates, or other types of price reductions to volume purchasers

(b) The (grantee, licensee, lessee, or permittee, as appropriate) for himself, his heirs, personal representatives, successors in interest, and assigns, as part of the consideration hereof, does hereby covenant and agree (in the case of deeds and leases add "as a covenant running with the land") that in the event facilities are constructed, maintained, or otherwise operated on said property described in this (deed, license, lease, permit, as appropriate) for a purpose for which a DOT program or activity is extended or for another purpose involving the provision of similar services or benefits, the (grantee, licensee, permittee) shall maintain and operate such facilities and services in compliance with all other requirements imposed pursuant to 49 CFR Part 21, Nondiscrimination in Federally Assisted Programs of the Department of Transportation, and as said Regulations may be amended.

The lessee, for himself, his personal representatives, successors in interest, and assigns, as part of the consideration hereof, does hereby covenant and agree, as a covenant running with the land, that (1) no person on the grounds of race, color, or national origin shall be excluded from participating in, be denied benefits of, or otherwise be subjected to discrimination in the use of said facilities, (2) that in the construction of any improvements on, over, or under such land and the furnishing of services thereon, no person on the grounds of race, color, or national origin shall be excluded from participation in, be denied benefits of, or otherwise be subjected to discrimination, (3) that the lessee shall use the premises in compliance with all other requirements imposed or pursuant to Title 49, Code of Federal Regulations, Department of Transportation, Subtitle A, Office of the Secretary, Part 21, Nondiscrimination in Federally-Assisted programs of the Department of Transportation—Effectuation of Title VI of the Civil Rights Act of 1964, and as said Regulations may be amended.[2]

That in the event of breach of any of these nondiscrimination covenants,

_______*(Name of Sponsor)*_______ shall have the right to terminate the license, lease, permit, etc., and to re-enter and repossess said land and facilities thereon, and hold the same as if said lease had never been made or issued; provided, however, that the (licensee, lessee, permitee) allegedly in breach shall have the right to contest said alleged breach under applicable Federal Aviation Administration procedures, and any sanctions under or termination of (license, lease, permit), shall be withheld pending completion of such procedures.

(c) To provide and maintain sufficient fixtures and equipment to meet public demand for services offered.

(d) To provide and maintain an adequate staff of employees with skills, licenses, and certificates appropriate to the activities conducted.

- (e) To maintain accurate and acceptable records which are to be made available for examination by the lessor.
- (f) To operate during specified minimum hours and to conform to all rules, regulations, fixed-base operator's standards and ordinances adopted by the lessor or other applicable government bodies including, but not limited to, safety, health, and sanitary codes.
- (g) To demonstrate evidence of financial stability and good credit rating.
- (h) To meet indemnity and insurance minimums.

(4) Rights and privileges reserved to the lessor include, among others:

- (a) For FBO leases, the right to further develop or improve the landing area of the airport as the lessor sees fits, regardless of the desires or view of the lessee, and without interference or hindrance.
- (b) The right, but not the obligation, to maintain and keep in repair the landing area of the airport and all publicly owned facilities of the airport, together with the right to direct and control all activities of lessee in this regard.
- (c) The right to take any action the lessor considers necessary to protect the aerial approaches of the airport against obstruction, together with the right to prevent the lessee from erecting, or permitting to be erected, any building or other structure on the airport which, in the opinion of the lessor, would limit the usefulness of the airport and constitute a hazard to aircraft.
- (d) The right to temporarily close the airport or any of the facilities thereon for maintenance, improvement, or for the safety of the public.
- (e) The right to approve or deny any sub lease of the premises leased.

(5) Other rights and obligations of the lessee and lessor to be ascertained include:

- (a) Who is to provide maintenance of leased area.
- (b) Who is to provide utilities (such as heat, electricity, and water) to the leased area and who is to pay charges therefor.
- (c) The disposition of structures and improvements erected by the lessee. (Is title to pass to lessor at some future time?)
- (d) The period of the lease and whether options for renewal are to be granted. Typically, lease periods should not exceed five years unless substantial capital investments are involved.
- (e) The amount of the rent to be charged and the method of computation: monthly, yearly, or percentage of lessee's gross net sales.
- (f) Frequency of review and basis of adjustment of rental amount.
- (g) Provisions for termination and surrender of lease, including:
    - 1) Grounds on which lease may be terminated.
    - 2) Rights and obligations of parties upon termination.
    - 3) Obligation of lessee to surrender premises upon termination.
    - 4) Right of lessor to re-enter premises upon termination.
- (h) Provisions for breach of covenants, including:
    - 1) Procedure by which either party is to give other party notice of breach.
    - 2) Length of time allowed to rectify breach.
    - 3) Method for settling dispute as to whether breach has occurred.
- (i) Provisions covering fire damages to premises, including:
    - 1) Responsibility for restoration and/or repair of damaged premises.

2) Time allowed for restoration and repair.
3) Abatement of rent if premises rendered untenantable.

(6) Other provisions to be included in lease agreements for aeronautical use:

(a) It is clearly understood by the lessee that no right or privilege has been granted which would operate to prevent any person, firm, or corporation operating aircraft on the airport from performing any service on its own aircraft with its own regular employees (including, but not limited to, maintenance and repair) that it may choose to perform.[1]

(b) It is understood and agreed that nothing herein contained shall be construed to grant or authorize the granting of an exclusive right forbidden by Section 308 of the Federal Aviation Act of 1958 or for aeronautical activities, such as, but not limited to:[2]

1) Charter operations
2) Pilot training
3) Aircraft rental
4) Aerial photography
5) Crop dusting
6) Sale of aviation petroleum products
7) Air carrier operations
8) Aircraft sales and services incidental thereto
9) Any other activity which, because of direct relationship to the operation of aircraft, can be regarded as an aeronautical activity.

(c) During the time of war or national emergency, lessor shall have the right to lease the landing area or any part thereof to the United States Government for miliary or naval use and, if such lease is executed, the provisions of this instrument insofar as they are inconsistent with the provisions of the lease to the government, shall be suspended.[3]

(d) This lease shall be subordinate to the provisions of any existing or future agreement between the lessor and the United States relative to the operation or maintenance of the airport, the execution of which has been or may be required as a condition precedent to the expenditure of federal funds for development of the airport. Failure of the lessee or any occupant to comply with the requirements of any existing or future agreement between the lessor and the United States, which failure shall continue after reasonable notice to make appropriate corrections, shall be cause for immediate termination of lessee's rights hereunder.[4]

(7) Other considerations

(a) Airport manager and/or related duties should not be incorporated in FBO lease agreements. The airport should establish standard rental/lease rates and apply them equally to all and handle the airport manager duties by separate contract. This allows the airport owner to change airport managers or his duties without affecting the basic lease rates.

(b) Provisions not specifically *NOTED* in b. of "agreements for leasing airport property" are not mandatory, but are strongly recommended as being in the best interests of the airport and the sponsor.

(c) Leases not containing the required provisions [1], [2], [3], or [4], should be amended at the first opportunity.

4. Through-the-fence-operations

a. There are instances when the owner of a public airport proposes to enter into an agreement which permits access to the public landing area by aircraft based on land adjacent to, but not part of, the airport property. This type of an arrangement has frequently been referred to as a "through-the-fence-operation," even though the perimeter fence may be an imaginary one.

The obligation to make an airport available for the use nd benefit of the public does not impose any requirement to permit access by aircraft from adjacent property. On the contrary, the existence of such an arrangement has been recognized as an encumbrance upon the airport property itself. Orders governing administration of ADAP indicate that a sponsor's title to airport land so encumbered does not meet the land interest requirement for a federal aid project unless the sponsor retains the legal right to, and in fact does, require the off-site property owner or occupant to conform in all respects to the requirements of any existing or proposed grant agreement.

b. The owner of a public airport is entitled to seek recovery of his initial and continuing costs of providing a public use landing area. Historically, he has been urged—in the interests of promoting general aviation—to refrain from direct assessment of user charges except for those engaged as common carriers for hire. Since enactment of the Airport and Airway Development Act of 1970, the owners of airports receiving federal funds have been required to establish a fee and rental structure designed to make the airport as self-sustaining as possible. Most public airports seek to recover a substantial part of airfield operating costs indirectly, through various arrangements relating to commercial activities. The development of aeronautical enterprises on land uncontrolled by the owner of the public airport cannot but result in a competitive advantage to the detriment of on-base operators on whom the airport owner relies for service to the flying public. To equalize this imbalance, the airport owner should attempt to obtain from any off-base enterprise a fair return for its use of the landing area.

c. Arrangements that permit aircraft to gain access to a public landing area from off-site properties introduce safety considerations with additional hazards, and complicate the control of vehicular and aircraft traffic. The construction of additional taxiways, the protection of additional intersections along airport perimeter roads, and frequently the basic airport layout itself, when designed to accommodate landing area access from multiple perimeter locations, presents a substantial and continuing burden for the sole benefit and convenience of such landholding neighbors. Depending on the volume and type of flight activity, the hazards of such an arrangement may well result in severe curtailment of the user potential of the airport.

d. The FAA, almost without exception, discourages and opposes any agreements which grant access to the public landing areas by aircraft normally stored and serviced on adjacent property. Typically, exceptions are considered in the following circumstances:

   (1) Where a bona fide airport tenant has already leased a site from the airport owner and has negotiated airfield use privileges, but also desires to move aircraft to and from a hangar or manufacturing plant on adjacent off-airport property. In this case, actual access will be gained through the area provided by the airport.

   (2) Where an individual or corporation actually residing or doing business on an adjacent land tract proposes to gain access to the landing area solely for aircraft used incidental to such residence or business without offering any aeronautical services to the public, provided that the airport owner is prepared to accommodate the normal expansion of aeronautical services to the public on publicly owned areas of the airport. This situation is commonly encountered where an industrial airpark is developed in conjunction with the airport.

   (3) Where there is insufficient land for further development of aeronautical activities.

e. Any agreement for a "through-the-fence-operation," in addition to the normal lease provisions above, must include a provision making the lease and such operations subject to the same obligations (present and future agreements with the federal government, rules, regulations, and so on) as tenants on airport property (see (6)(d) above).

   (1) Provision must also be made to assure that the lessee contributes his or her fair share toward the cost of operation, maintenance, and improvement of the airport, and that no benefits accrue to the lessee which would give him or her an advantage over an on-airport operator.

One method of determining a fair return to the airport from off-airport use would be to utilize a percentage of the on-airport tiedown rate, if no other equitable method is available, such as percentage of gross sales, etc. This type of arrangement has the advantage of an automatic inflation factor that would keep off-airport charges in line with on-airport charges.

(2) It is suggested that on all airports having or anticipating agreements with the federal government, any such proposal be submitted to the FAA for review and comment prior to its finalization.

(3) A suggested permit is included as Exhibit A.

Notes

1. Required in leases/agreements for aeronautical services at airports subject to continuing obligations under FAAP/AIP agreements.

2. Required in all leases/agreements involving federal agreements executed after July 2, 1964.

3. Only required leases/agreements at airports acquired in whole or in part under a Federal Surplus Property Transfer (unless the National Emergency Use Provision of the Surplus Transfer document has been specifically released by the FAA).

4. Required in leases in aeronautical operations from adjoining non-airport property ("through-the-fence-operations").

Language provided in [2], [3], and [4], should be used verbatim.

Exhibit A

INGRESS AND EGRESS PERMIT

______________________________ AIRPORT

The (Grantor) for the consideration hereinafter specified, grants to ______________________, (Grantee) the right of ingress and egress into and upon a portion of the ______________________ Airport in ______________ County, ______________________, from property owned or occupied by Grantee which adjoins said Airport on the ______________ side near the ______________ end. The boundaries of said Airport are described in ______________ recorded in Volume _____ of Deed Records for ________ County ______________, at Page _____ thereof. Ingress and egress hereunder shall be limited to a ______________ foot portion of the ______________ Airport boundary, as shown on drawing attached hereto marked Exhibit A.

This permit shall be for a term of ____________ ( ) years commencing on the ________ day of ____________, 19 ____, and terminating on the _____ day of ______________, 19 _____.

As part of the consideration for granting this permit, Grantee agrees to pay Grantor [____________ (______¢) per gallon for all aviation fuel sold or used by Grantee]. [The sum of $ ____________ per month] or [$ ____________________] or [other basis]. Payment shall be made on or before the ________________ of each month. Grantee agrees to permit Grantor to audit books and records at any reasonable time and place for the purpose of verifying the amount due the Grantor.

Grantee agrees to comply with all airport rules and regulations adopted by the Grantor relative to the ______________________________ Airport.

Grantee shall save and hold Grantor harmless from any claim or liability arising out of its activities, and shall procure and continue in effect public liability and property damage insurance in minimum amounts as follows:

(a) $__________ when the claim is one for damage to or destruction of property and $_____ to any claimant in any other case.

(b) $_______ for any number of claims arising out of a single occurrence.

Certificate evidencing such insurance and bearing endorsements requiring _____ days' written notice to Grantor prior to any change, cancellation, or expiration shall be furnished to Grantor prior to exercise by Grantee of its right of entry hereunder. However, Grantee assumes no tort liability either to Grantor or to any other party for damages or injury other than through its own negligence or lack of due care.

Grantee agrees to observe all applicable federal and state statutes and rules and regulations in its operations upon the property abutting said ______________ Airport and in any operation carried on by Grantee or under its supervision or direction upon the airport. Grantee further agrees and covenants to at all times maintain its abutting property, and the improvements thereon, and to conduct its operation, both on and off the Airport, in a reasonably neat and clean fashion, and not to permit the accumulation of rubbish or junk airplane or automobile parts or other material in an unsightly manner. Grantee agrees that if it fails to so maintain its abutting property, Grantor shall have the right, after ________ days' written notice, to come upon the property of Grantee and cause the same to comply with this provision, and to charge the expense thereof to Grantee, or, at the option of the Grantor, to terminate the rights of Grantee hereunder.

Grantee further agrees not to use any portion of the Airport property for the permanent storage of aircraft or other personal property of Grantee, or of personal property for which Grantee is acting as bailee, and Grantee agrees that if Grantor shall at any time demand the removal of personal property located upon the Airport, which personal property is under the control of Grantee and grantee shall fail to remove the same within a period of ________________ ( ) hours after such demand, then Grantor may remove the same and charge the cost of such removal to Grantee.

This permit shall not be sold, assigned, or otherwise transferred by operation of law or otherwise by Grantee to any other person, corporation, association, partnership, municipal corporation or body politic, and this permit shall not pass with any sale, lease, or other disposal of land abutting upon said ______________________________ Airport, and shall automatically terminate in the event of the bankruptcy or dissolution of Grantee, or in the event Grantee shall dispose of its interest in said lands abutting upon the ____ Airport, provided, however, the Grantor may by its express written approval permit the assignment hereof.

Grantee agrees to conduct its operation, both on Airport and on adjoining premises, for the use and benefit of the public, and particularly[a]:

a. To furnish good, prompt, and efficient services adequate to meet all the demands for its serve at the Airport;
b. To furnish said service on a fair, equal, and nondiscriminatory to all users thereof; and
c. To charge fair, reasonable, and nondiscriminatory prices for each unit of sale or service, provided that the Grantee may be allowed to make reasonable and nondiscriminatory discounts, rebates, or other similar types of price reductions to volume purchasers.

The Grantee, for himself, his personal representatives, successors in interest, and assigns, as part of the consideration hereof, does hereby covenant and agree, as covenant running with the land, that (1) no person on the grounds of race, color, or national origin shall be excluded from participation in, be denied the benefits of, or otherwise subjected to discrimination in the use of said facilities, (2) that in the construction of any improvements on, over, or under such land and the furnishing of services thereon, no person on the grounds of race, color, or national origin shall be excluded from participation in, denied benefits of, or otherwise subjected to discrimination, (3) that the lessee shall use the premises in compliance with all other requirements imposed by or pursuant to Title 49, Code of Federal Regulations, Department of Transportation, Subtitle A, Office of the Secretary, Part 21, Nondiscrimination in Federally-assisted programs of the Department of Transportation—Effectuation of Title VI of the Civil Rights Act of 1964, and as said Regulations may be amended. That in the event of breach of any of the preceding nondiscrimination covenants, ________*(Name of Sponsor)*________ shall have the right to terminate the license, lease, permit, etc., and to reenter and repossess said land and the facilities thereon, and hold the same as if said lease had never been made or issued.

It is clearly understood by the Grantee that no right or privilege has been granted which would operate to prevent any person, firm, or corporation operating aircraft on the Airport from performing any services on its own aircraft with its own regular employees (including, but not limited to, maintenance and repair) that it may choose to perform.

It is understood and agreed that nothing herein contained shall be construed to grant or authorize the granting of an exclusive right forbidden by Section 308 of the Federal Aviation Act of 1958 or for aeronautical activities such as, but not limited to:

a. Charter operations
b. Pilot training
c. Aircraft rental
d. Aerial photography
e. Crop dusting
f. Sale of aviation petroleum products
g. Air carrier operations
h. Aircraft sales and service incidental thereto

i. Any other activity which, because of its direct relationship to the operation of aircraft, can be regarded as an aeronautical activity

Grantor reserves the right to further develop or improve the landing area of the Airport as it sees fit, regardless of the desires or view of the Grantee, and without interference or hindrance.

Grantor reserves the right, but shall not be obligated to Grantee, to maintain and keep in repair the landing area of the Airport and all publicly-owned facilities of the Airport, together with the right to direct and control all activities of Grantee in this regard.

During the time of war or national emergency, Grantor shall have the right to lease the landing area or any part thereof to the United States Government for military or naval use and, if such lease is executed, the provisions of this instrument insofar as they are inconsistent with the provisions of the lease to the Government, shall be suspended[b].

Grantor reserves the right to take any action it considers necessary to protect the aerial approaches of the Airport against obstruction, together with the right to prevent Grantee from erecting, or permitting to be erected, any building or other structure on or adjacent to the Airport which, in the opinion of the Grantor, would limit the usefulness of the Airport or constitute a hazard to aircraft.

This permit shall be subordinate to the provisions of any existing or future agreement between Grantor and the United States, relative to the operation or maintenance of the Airport, the execution of which has been or may be required as a condition precedent to the expenditure of Federal funds for the development existing or future agreement between Grantor and the United States, which failure shall continue after reasonable notice to make appropriate corrections, shall be cause for immediate termination to Grantee's rights hereunder.

IN WITNESS WHEREOF the parties hereto set their hands and seals this ________________ day of ____________________________, 19 ____.

GRANTOR:

____

____

GRANTEE:

by ________________________________

[a] Required where aeronautical services are to be provided.

[b] Required where airport was acquired in whole or in part under Federal Surplus Property Transfer (unless National Emergency Use Provision has been specifically released by the FAA).

APPENDIX

XI

National Air Transportation Association's "Community Relations Toolkit"

Table of Contents

By permission, National Air Transportation Association

Preface

The National Air Transportation Association recognizes the need for expanding community outreach efforts to airport neighbors and key stakeholders. This toolkit has been developed to provide a guideline for community relations efforts.

In developing this toolkit, a key philosophy has been the need to think beyond the traditional methods of relating to airport neighbors. This does not necessarily mean that the tools discussed here have changed. What it does mean is we need to rethink how we choose the tools and why.

This manual emphasizes the importance of spending time evaluating the issues and concerns of local airport neighbors. In the past, we have pointed to the economic benefits derived from a general aviation airport and expected that local officials and residents should automatically appreciate an airport's value. What we are realizing is that, as important as they are, these benefits need to be translated into quality of life benefits that mean something to neighbors at your particular airport. These benefits will vary from airport to airport, but what is consistent will be the need to link the airport to the community. Access becomes an important message—medical access, transportation access, business access, and public safety access, among others. But as with economic benefits, it is critical to link this to specific needs in your community.

In addition, this manual emphasizes the importance of delving into the concerns identified by airport neighbors. This serves two purposes. In researching the concerns, solutions may be identified that will reduce or eliminate the concern. Evaluating concerns also provides an opportunity to explore what mechanisms might be most effective in reaching out to the community to address issues in your specific situation.

We are pleased to offer this toolkit and hope you will find it helpful.

James K. Coyne
President

Introduction

Background

While in many ways the future of air transportation has never been brighter, there are threats to the value, growth and prosperity of the aviation system. Of greatest concern are isolated groups of vocal airport opponents who fail to recognize the importance of universal access to the air transportation system. This growing trend is placing many airports in jeopardy.

A significant number of airports are facing restrictions on the operations of certain types of aircraft as a response by local communities to these anti-airport activists. Taken individually, these restrictions would be worrisome; when considered in the larger context of a national air transportation system, they are significant barriers to our nation's economic prosperity. Congestion and delays are symptoms of this problem.

In a recent report, the U. S. General Accounting Office (GAO) stated, "As airports grow and balance their growth with its effects on the environment, the primary environmental concern and challenge facing them now and for the foreseeable future is noise, specifically noise generated by aircraft operations."

National Air Transportation Association's (NATA) study on the public's attitude toward improving airports found that over three-quarters of those polled either supported or did not oppose improving these facilities. Unfortunately, the study also revealed that many people do not understand the benefits that aviation brings to their community. To the extent that local political leaders reflect their constituencies, the aviation industry must overcome this lack of knowledge if communities are to prosper and thrive through access to the national air transportation system.

It has also become evident that general aviation aircraft have become the travel method of choice for a growing number of air travelers. As the quality of service by the scheduled airlines has deteriorated, travelers are appreciating the value and flexibility that on-demand air charter and private aircraft provide. Due to congestion and the location of air carrier airports, many of these general aviation flights are conducted at smaller regional airports.

Regrettably, access restrictions or insufficient facilities often limit the use of these airports to fully access the aviation system.

General aviation has already proven itself to be an intricate and vital part of this nation's infrastructure. Today your airport stands to be a true force in the 21st century as well, whether it's located in an area better known for rolling farmland than shopping malls or part of a bustling metropolis.

Because of the vital imperative to be linked to the air transportation system, communities and individuals suffer when air travel becomes difficult or unavailable. It is the responsibility of managers of aviation businesses to take steps necessary to proactively counter this trend.

The Role of Community Relations

More and more airports are including community relations as an integral part of operating an airport. Community relations play a vital role in ensuring good relations with local neighbors, businesses and public officials. It is through an effective community relations plan that an aviation business owner or airport manager can detect, in the early stages, concerns or issues within the local public that need to be addressed.

Involvement in local community activities is an important aspect in developing the two-way conduit desired in any community relations program. It is essential for an aviation business's management staff to take time for civic activities and to encourage other airport tenants and pilots to do the same. This involvement also opens the door to the two-way communications process, enhancing the potential for long-term compatibility with local communities.

Today, community relations is *not* just public relations. Public relations is promoting your facility or the airport. It is "selling" the benefits of the airport to surrounding communities. It includes publicity and media relations, all intended to improve the image of the airport. Community relations goes beyond this by inviting the public to participate in the airport.

Involving the Community

Developing a comprehensive community relations plan is an important first step toward establishing a conduit with your community. This plan needs to provide mechanisms that most effectively provide outreach into local communities. The community relations plan should be defined in terms of goals and objectives. It identifies target audiences, methodology and mechanisms for measuring success. Special events, public forums, a speakers bureau and airport friends groups are some of the tools that are discussed in this manual and have proven to be effective.

Community relations can be viewed on several levels. Through workshops, hearings, small group meetings and one-on-one involvement, interested community members are provided opportunities to comment and provide input on airport projects and activities. A community relations plan can help you gain understanding and future support for airport projects within the community you serve.

Being Involved In Your Community

A good community relations program will help surrounding communities better understand the airport and its projects by involving them in airport activities and making the airport an integral part of community activities. Community outreach efforts include such activities as establishing an airport tenant and users association, developing plans for assisting in a community disaster and developing an observation area on the airport. It includes involvement in local civic organizations and sponsoring local youth organizations. Most important, a good community relations program makes members of the community feel like the airport is their airport.

Dealing With Crisis

Even with an effective community relations program, an airport is often faced with a crisis. In the context of this manual, "crisis" is defined as any community situation that has escalated to the degree that it has the potential of jeopardizing an airport project or the operation of the airport itself.

A "How To" Toolkit

This manual is meant to be a "how to" toolkit which will assist in developing various aspects of a community relations program.

A few simple steps can go a long way toward assuring the talk about your airport or aviation business—whether it's on the evening news or around the family supper table—is positive. The general aviation industry can both benefit from and drive this nation's growing economy of opportunity. But a large part of assuring general aviation lives up to its potential as an engine for economic prosperity depends on promoting the notion that your airport is a critical community resource.

Broken down into four phases, this kit provides suggestions for building community support for your airport and aviation business.

In **Phase 1: Developing a Community Relations Program**, you'll find the first steps necessary to get out the good news about your airport and the services you provide:

1. Finding value for your airport and the general aviation system;
2. Locating friends and gaining support;
3. Developing an airport users group;
4. Working with public officials;
5. Working with the media; and
6. Coordinating with the FAA and airport staff

In **Phase 2: Implementing Community Outreach Elements**, you will enhance the relationships developed in Phase 1:

1. Developing a speakers bureau;
2. Staging special events;
3. Supporting local education;
4. Assisting in a disaster; and
5. Developing an airport friends group

In **Phase 3: Communicating Effectively and Resolving Conflicts**, you will learn about ways to enhance communication with airport neighbors and key stakeholders:

1. Using conflict resolution techniques;
2. Developing guidelines for crisis management; and
3. Gathering input from the public

In **Phase 4: Pulling It All Together—Strategies for Action**, you will find ideas and strategies for implementing the tools and techniques provided in this manual.

Phase 1: Developing a Community Relations Program

A. Finding Value for Your Airport and the General Aviation System

Today, airports are a fixture in this nation's transportation system. What is less certain is whether or not airports and the communities they serve will see their futures as inextricably linked and work together to promote their shared goals.

Every community in this country is unique, with special qualities that define it as home to the people who live there. So it makes sense that the first step toward improving your airport's stature in the community is to demonstrate just how many ways the airport is involved with the day-to-day lives of people who make up the community. Equally important, you must show that your airport is a critical force in building the kind of future that keeps them wanting to call it home.

The following steps will help you get started. Consider these steps as you evaluate your airport and your community and how to better connect them.

1. Take an inventory of your community and what makes it attractive to the people who live there and the businesses that may want to move there. Good schools, state-of-the-art hospitals, a highly trained workforce, low unemployment, safe neighborhoods, thriving industries, a strong agricultural base, and responsive government are just a few of the ways people define an attractive community.

2. Now do an accounting of your airport. What services does your airport provide to the community? Who depends on your airport for access? How many new businesses has your airport played a role in attracting? General aviation airports across the country provide access to numerous sectors of the community including:

- Business and community leaders
- Commercial cargo and package operations
- Crop protection and other agricultural services
- Emergency medical aircraft and helicopters
- Fire fighting and wildlife tracking
- Law enforcement officers
- Military personnel
- Students in flight schools
- Television and radio crews
- Weather and traffic reporters

3. Now go back and compare your two lists. You should be able to see how your airport contributes directly to the very qualities that make your community special.

Does your community boast about state-of-the-art hospitals? The access your airport provides to emergency medical aircraft and helicopters plays a critical role. How about the low unemployment rate your town has experienced lately? The new businesses that located in your region because the airport provided them with easy access to their plants across the country is a major factor in those plunging unemployment figures. Does your community take pride in preserving its agriculture traditions? The crop protection your airport provides is a factor in assuring agriculture continues to reap profits, enabling the town to maintain its historic character.

That's the story you have to start telling. Remember, you're not just selling a runway—you're selling a better quality of life.

Propelling a Vision of your Airport

For most people in your community general aviation means a world of private planes, pilots, and technicians far removed from their day-to-day lives. Your job is to show them that your world of general aviation and theirs aren't so far apart. The following information is the kind of information that you may be able to provide that will give members of your community another perspective about general aviation activity.

- No one airplane, airport or operator defines general aviation. General aviation is made up of many different kinds of planes, from single-engine two-seaters to regional airliners to turbine-powered jets. And you'll find people from all walks of life coming through the doors of these airports, from students in pilot schools to company CEOs to union workers at the local plant to the aviation businesses who provide fuel and services to the aircraft. The truth is aviation affects just about everyone in your community, from the food they eat to the clothes they wear to the medical care they receive.

- When people get in their cars and head off down the highway, they get a sense of being connected to another place further down the road. Remind them that your airport puts them just a short ride away from the other 5,415 public-use airports in America, connecting them to every state in the nation.
- There are 181,000 general aviation aircraft flying four billion miles each year, guaranteeing transportation for packages and people, linking major cities and rural communities, and putting your community on the map of easily accessible tourism and business destinations.
- General aviation is a $17 billion industry that generates more than $51 billion annually in other economic activity. So as your airport prospers, so too does your community, from increased home starts to expanding church congregations to higher retail sales.
- General aviation aircraft fly over 26 million hours, assuring that 145 million passengers reach their destinations, from CEOs of Fortune 500 companies to law enforcement officers to medical personnel to family vacationers. And approximately 600 of these airports are served by commercial airlines, which means general aviation is the answer to more and more questions about how your community makes itself accessible to goods, services and visitors.
- No matter what they're selling, companies are buying into aviation. They understand air travel allows them to erase the miles between their plants and their customers. That's why 70 percent of general aviation flights are flown for business purposes.
- In studies from Oregon to New Jersey, findings have shown that communities without an airport are less likely to bring new jobs from outside the region and that general aviation airports are a major factor in relocation decisions by companies both large and small.
- Because businesses see aviation as part of the solution, they're willing to invest in air travel, with nearly 7,000 U.S. companies writing 9,715 turbine-powered aircraft into their annual budgets.
- General aviation airports are the training ground for pilots all across the country from weekend fliers to commercial pilots. The majority of the pilots hired by domestic airlines get their start at general aviation airports.

- General aviation knows how to have fun, too. That's why millions of visitors come out to air shows every year, making the shows the nation's second most popular spectator event, just behind major league baseball.
- Members of your community should know that general aviation has a stellar safety record. For the past five years, general aviation has experienced the lowest number of accidents since record-keeping began.

B. Locating Your Friends and Initiating Support

From the students logging flight hours to the emergency response team saving precious hours, each person who relies on the airport knows first-hand that it's about more than terminals, fuel, runways and landing systems: it's about providing people with an opportunity to lead safer and more fulfilling lives. They understand that the airport is a vehicle for accomplishing their goals, from getting their goods into the global marketplace to providing up-to-the-minute traffic reports.

A first step is to determine who's out there and what kind of potential they have for promoting the airport. Do they already support the airport? Are they key stakeholders in the local community? Think about possible friends of the airport including the following:

- Airport tenants and employees
- Businesses that rely on the airport
- Suppliers and contractors
- Agricultural agents
- Emergency medical teams
- Firefighters
- Law enforcement officers
- Military personnel
- Student pilots and flight instructors

Also, consider the organizations these people may belong to, including the Chamber of Commerce, Rotary clubs, labor unions, Flying Doctors, National Guard, Fraternal Order of Police, or the Farm Bureau, just to name a few.

Once you've identified key stakeholders and possible supporters, make contact and cultivate at least one representative from each group who can serve as a contact. Through one-on-

one meetings, phone calls, emails or regular mailings, remind them:

- How much the airport has aided them in the past;
- How a thriving airport will continue to help the region compete both nationally and internationally; and
- How working as a team, you can move forward together.

Ask them to serve as an advocate for the airport, giving speeches, providing reporters with supportive quotes, and sending letters to local representatives on behalf of the airport.

Before asking them to make a presentation or phone call on behalf of the airport, make sure you've provided your team with the information they need to succeed. Giving a speech at their organizational meetings is just one way you can personalize the information about your airport to their special needs, educating and energizing them at the same time. Provide them with talking points that incorporate their business or hobby into the airport's profile. Be sure that when called on to promote the airport, they've got the facts.

C. Developing an Airport Users and Tenants Association

Establishing an Airport Users and Tenants Association at an airport can enhance communications and understanding between the airport, its tenants and its neighbors. Because the airport tenants actually develop the Association, getting the local pilots, airport operators and tenants involved is the place to start.

Tenant and User Objectives

- Gain better communication and understanding with airport and area residents.
- Enhance communications and relationships with local, regional and state officials and agencies that impact airport tenants and operators.
- Conduct business in an atmosphere of increased cooperation through enhanced understanding with officials, airport staff and residents, tenants and users.
- Promote growth of aviation interests in the airport area consistent with the interests of the local residential community, through better cooperation.

Goals

- Develop short-term and long-term strategies and goals for the Association in relationship to the airport and the surrounding communities.

- Initiate meetings with local officials and agencies affecting airport owners and operators to increase rapport and communication.
- Increase positive awareness of the airport and positive benefits in the local and regional media.
- Assist airport in developing a "Friends of the Airport Group" to promote a positive image in the surrounding communities and gain positive visibility.
- Enhance the positive image of the airport and the Association through use of promotional tools to gain greater positive awareness of the airport in the surrounding communities.
- Attend public meetings, directly or indirectly impacting the airport to gain information regarding strategies and policies that will, or potentially could, impact the airport, tenants and operators.
- Evaluate the short- and long-term goals stated in the airport's existing planning documents such as the Master Plan, the Federal Aviation Administration's Part 150 Noise and Compatibility Study or Part 161 Cost Benefit Study.
- Interface with community and key stakeholders on a one-on-one basis as requested and appropriate, to assist in diffusing problems and increase cooperation between the Association, the airport and residents.

Plan of Action

- Maintain ongoing communication with numerous individuals and organizations that impact the airport.
- Set up meetings and lunches with officials and agency representatives that affect the airport.
- Establish a friends group through local business, community and airport interests that will provide a positive forum for demonstrating airport benefits.
- Develop a media plan to better provide positive story angles concerning the airport and its operators.
- Develop events in cooperation with the airport and/or the Chamber (pancake breakfast, barbeque, black-tie event, etc.).
- Establish a speakers bureau with presentations on operations and benefits of the airport.
- Work with airport staff to monitor, evaluate and reduce noise and safety calls to the airport.

➤ Work with airport staff, FAA and tenants to educate pilots regarding noise abatement.

In addition, media contacts need to be cultivated and greater interface maintained to improve relationships with local newspapers. Story angles can be developed from tenants and operators to be pitched to media representatives that highlight operations and benefits derived from the airport.

The local Chamber of Commerce can be included to an increased degree for both positive publicity and to enhance understanding in the business community. The Chamber can provide significant support and credibility for the tenants and operators in difficult times. There may also be a number of events or publicity tools that can be developed in conjunction with the Chamber.

Many local service organizations offer tremendous opportunities to develop friendships and gain support. This can be accomplished through speaking to numerous organizations as well as supporting their cause and, where appropriate, becoming involved in the organizations.

Finally, increased cooperation and credibility must come by establishing positive communication with local residents. This can be accomplished in a number of ways, including tours, orientation flights, one-on-one conversations, invitations to your local neighbors to special events or parties, and an increased desire and effort to resolve problems.

To be even moderately successful in this endeavor requires a combined effort in all of these areas. It will necessitate assistance and interest from local pilots and a majority of airport tenants.

Through an enthusiastic team effort, a negative, "us against them" attitude with airport neighbors can begin to shift to a more cooperative spirit. Just as there are always new pilots and operators to educate about flying neighborly, so there will also be new neighbors to involve in the airport and its activities.

D. Working with Local, State and Federal Public Officials

Today, it's critical for you to develop—or strengthen—your relationships at the local, state and federal levels of government, including commissioners, mayors, council members, state representatives, congressional delegations, and governors. Make them a part of your team. The following ideas will assist you in cultivating these relationships:

1. Identify the staff member most likely to handle aviation issues. Set up a meeting and provide that person with background information about the airport and its importance to the community, whether it is keeping a rural area connected to much-needed services or pulling in new industry to the region.

2. Arrange for an on-site visit. Your first choice is to have the public official visit the airport. But it is also very beneficial to have key staff tour your facility as well. Not only do these staff members play a key role in any decision-making processes, but their visit can also lead to a visit by the public official.
3. If a public official does tour your facility, if possible, turn the visit into a media event. Use this as an opportunity to demonstrate the airport's role in the community. For example, include representatives from businesses or organizations that rely on the airport. If your airport was used recently to rush a life-saving organ to a constituent, invite the family to the airport. Once officials see first-hand how your airport affects the day-to-day lives of their constituents, they'll be more likely to offer a helping hand when you need it.
4. Identify those committees on which your representatives—both state and federal—serve. Representatives on appropriations or authorizing committees with jurisdiction over aviation matters can do a tremendous job of helping secure funds. Keep informed about the committees' legislative schedules from hearings to floor debates. This way you can provide members with up-to-date information to include in testimony or floor statements.
5. Even if your representatives aren't on one of these key committees, they're still your best source for cutting through government red tape and making connections to the members that are on these committees.
6. By including government representatives—from mayors to governors—as part of your team, they'll also serve as a way of promoting your airport in their own speeches, press releases and newsletters.

Public officials can play a key role in the success of your airport. By recognizing and including these individuals in special events as well as operation planning, an airport manager or an aviation business owner is taking the first step toward nurturing a relationship that will establish the airport as an integral member of the community.

Staying in touch with public officials and their staff is an important vehicle by which you can influence the long-term viability of your airport.

Public Officials as a Target Audience

Although public officials at the local, state and federal levels are important to the airport, the major concentration of the efforts discussed here focus on local officials. Remember that public officials operate within a very busy schedule. Establishing a contact with a key assistant or staff member may be the best avenue in developing a dialogue with public officials.

When corresponding with officials, keep it concise, state your objective, and identify early on how you may be able to assist them in resolving an issue. Include them in local airport events and find ways to give them greater visibility.

Involve Officials in Airport Issues

When you realize you may have a potential crisis looming, it is important to initiate a dialogue to avert a political reaction. Keep the officials and their staff apprised of any important airport issues and potentially volatile situations, offering alternatives and possible solutions to them before an issue escalates into a crisis.

It is when officials are left out of the loop that they, just like their constituents, become frustrated, resentful and distrustful. It is up to not only the airport administration but also aviation businesses to include local officials in periodic updates and posted on activities. This is a way to keep elected officials involved and aware of the airport.

A Positive Working Relationship

Inviting local officials to participate in an airport or aviation meeting is an effective way of gaining their interest and awareness. Remind them of your business concerns. Join with other airports or aviation interests to present not only the economic benefits derived from your airport but also the critical element of access that the airport offers.

Developing a personal relationship with public officials is also important. Crisis is not the best time to introduce yourself and ask for support or try and educate them about an airport issue. You need to become a familiar face and resource prior to a negative situation. This means, in addition to attending city council meetings, commission meetings and Airport Advisory Committee meetings, it is important to:

1. Join the chamber of commerce and attend meetings on a regular basis.
2. Participate in other local civic activities.
3. Establish periodic breakfast meetings with public officials.
4. Invite public officials to all special airport events.
5. Invite a local official to be master of ceremonies at an airport event.
6. Invite an appropriate official to be honorary chair of major airport-related events.
7. Invite a local official or staff person to join you at airport-related conferences.
8. Respond to complaints and inquiries quickly and responsibly.

Be an information resource for your elected officials. Listen and respond quickly to public officials and their constituents' issues and concerns. Get involved in community meetings and programs. In time, you will gain credibility with your local public officials as well as the trust of your community.

It is important to establish a positive relationship between the airport and local officials as well as the airport manager and FAA staff in order to work together to address local issues and concerns. The result will be public officials who look to the aviation businesses for input and expertise, rather than in an adversarial or confrontational manner. Frustration and suspicion can give way to trust, credibility and a willingness to work cooperatively.

E. Working with the Media

You don't want your airport's name in the local paper or on the evening news for the first time because of some controversy. Instead, you want to position your airport to receive the best media coverage possible, both when you've got good news to tell and when you need to get your side of the story out during a dispute.

1. It's very important to develop a relationship with your local media outlets before you actually want to get news out. This includes newspapers, television, radio, and wire services. Most of these outlets will have someone on staff who covers business issues. Reporters appreciate this kind of contact because it helps them develop their sources.

2. Don't limit yourself to only using business or trade reporters. Remember, you're not just selling a product or a business. You're telling a story. Your airport is tied to nearly every person in the community, helping to put services that once were out of reach right in their backyard. Many of your stories will have a human-interest angle that will sell easily to the lifestyle or community section of your papers.

3. Don't forget newsletters put out by local organizations. Groups like the Chamber of Commerce, labor unions, Rotary, police, National Guard, hospitals, and the Farm Bureau all have regular newsletters and are always looking for ideas, and they reach hundreds of households. A university paper is also an important venue for getting out information and reaching not just a student audience but also the university administration, support staff and faculty.

4. Keep a photo file. Many local papers and newsletters will use photos you send them with a tag line explaining who is in the picture and the occasion.

5. Get some standard quotes about the airport from your natural base of support, such as business owners or aviation students. Also get a quote from someone less directly

attached to the airport but who still feels its influence. For example, a worker at a local plant that moved to the area because of the airport.

6. Have some B roll footage produced of the airport. This doesn't have to be extensive or costly. It can be used by the media for advertising and for promoting the airport in other forums.
7. Develop a web site including pictures, video footage and listings of local businesses and national organizations.
8. Be available to reporters and ready to provide them with information. If they know they can depend on you to answer their questions, they're more likely to respond when you're trying to pitch a story.
9. Don't forget radio. Too often, the power and reach of radio is forgotten. In addition to getting to know news directors and reporters, be aware of any programs that might provide a forum for you or one of the many players on your team to talk about the airport.

Positive exposure in the media is a great way to stimulate airport interest as well as enhance aviation business owners' image. The news media will continue to pursue stories on aviation, some good and some having a negative impact. A well thought out media management plan set up prior to a crisis saves a lot of time and frustration while instilling a feeling of confidence in the airport's staff and airport tenants.

Working with the Media Includes:

- Becoming an industry resource.
- Helping reporters find interesting story angles about the airport.
- Remembering the five W's (who, what, when, where and why).
  They must be clear and complete.
- Assigning a spokesperson.
- Knowing each publication's deadline.
- Remembering that the media will ask "what if" questions and speculate if not provided information.
- Notifying the appropriate staff or public officials if you have talked with a reporter or expect a negative story.
- Offering experts that can be connected to a story to help substantiate the facts.

- Keeping public meetings open to media.
- Being truthful.

Develop a Plan

By establishing a system for handling routine media calls, it is easier to meet the demands of crisis situations. Being prepared and understanding the local media's style in covering aviation issues is a must and will better prepare you in the future. Identify who your media spokesperson(s) is and ensure that all staff are aware of communication protocols in dealing with the media.

Know Your Local Media

Develop a media list and update it on a regular basis. This is necessary because there are frequent changes in reporters and assignments. Developing contacts in the local area and maintaining them is equally important. Remember to not overlook the local newspapers. Local papers are more likely to print your press releases. They are also what local airport neighbors read.

Talking with Reporters

When being interviewed by reporters, it is important to know your audience and avoid speaking in aviation industry jargon that could confuse the general public. If there is time, outline a few main topics on which to comment and give as brief and complete answers as possible.

Avoid the phrase "no comment" because this answer gives the media the feeling that you are hiding something. Reporters will ask "what if" questions and speculate. Be prepared with facts. Do not agree to speculate. If you do not have the information at hand, or are not sure of the facts, tell the reporter you will call back. Find out when the reporter's deadline is and get back to him or her before then. Do not state something "off the record."

Always assume that everything you say will be quoted. If you do not want to be quoted, do not say it. Most importantly, be honest and up front in an interview. Credibility is essential to good relations.

Routine Releases for Newspapers

Many options are available for getting news to the surrounding communities. Sending a press release to the newspapers is the most common way to get stories printed. Press releases briefly describe the who, what, when, where, why and how of an upcoming event. Submitting photos along with your press release is suggested whenever possible. Be sure to include a photo caption naming each person from left to right and identifying what the photo is showing. Begin the caption in all capital letters followed by lower case letters for the remainder of the sentence. Another way is to begin the caption with a phrase in all capital letters, followed by a dash, with the remainder of the caption in lower case letters.

Avoid photos with more than three or four people whenever possible. Always use rubber cement to secure the photo, never tape or staples. Action photos that tell stories are more likely to get printed. Keep in mind that the local weekly newspapers are many times more valuable than the larger ones. The community reads these more than the larger regional newspapers. Use press conferences sparingly and only when you have a major news event to announce.

Overall Guidelines

- Distribute releases to all publications simultaneously.
- If appropriate, put releases out across city wire services 24 hours before the event—email and facsimile are also good means of distribution.
- Be sure the release is accurate and newsworthy.
- Be conscious of deadlines.
- Do not editorialize; submit facts only, and attribute quotes to company spokespersons.
- Make sure there are no typos or errors in names, etc.; double-check spelling of names.
- Do not forget the weekly newspapers.
- Place follow-up calls after the release has gone out.
- Do not ask to review the story prior to publication.
- Use a headline that summarizes the story.
- Use slug lines at the top left of second and all other additional pages; sluglines can be the two key words in the headline.
- Get quotes approved. If it is a questionable source or quote, get a signed approval.

News Release "How To's"

- Follow the who, what, when, where, why and how format in order of most important to least important.
- Leave a wide margin for the editor.

- Always double space.
- Keep the release as brief as possible.
- Always type on a standard 8 1/2" x 11" letterhead page on one side only.
- Use email whenever appropriate.
- Start the copy one-third of the way down the first page.
- Double-space for newspapers; triple-space for electronic media.
- Use a contact line which includes your name and phone number, including facsimile number.
- Use "For Immediate Release" or date to be released.
- Put "-more-" at the end of the page to indicate additional pages; use ### to indicate the end of the story.

News Release Format

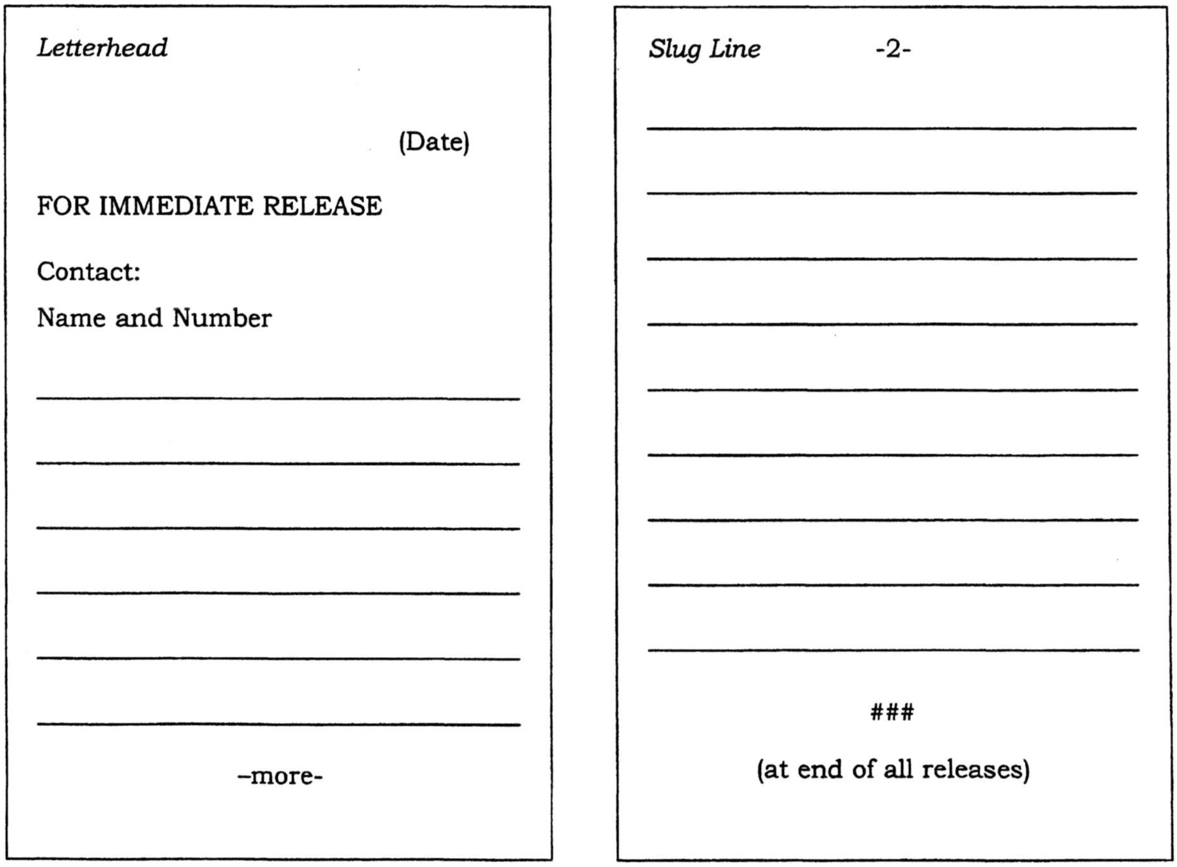

Letterhead
(Date)
FOR IMMEDIATE RELEASE
Contact:
Name and Number
-more-
Slug Line
-2-
###
(at end of all releases)

Radio and Television

In preparing news releases or announcements for radio, most of the same rules apply as for newspaper stories. Stories are submitted to television stations in the form of fact sheets which are similar to press releases but shorter. You can assume that a story longer than 8 to 15 lines will not appear. Also, remember that the news announcer will "speak" your story. Therefore, sentences must be brief and simple so that they sound conversational. As in the case of newspaper articles, radio and television stories should always be written in the present active tense, using tight, simple language.

Public Service Announcements

Another way to deliver information to the community is through public service announcements, which are accepted by both radio and television stations. These are very similar to media releases, but shorter. Most public service announcements average 10 to 60 seconds in length and usually publicize information or events sponsored or co-sponsored by a non-profit organization.

Airports can take advantage of public service announcements for events such as an Airport Awareness Day or one that offers free rides to disabled children. Even though public service announcements are not guaranteed to be read, there is a good chance they will be if they are written correctly and submitted at the right time. Different radio and television stations accept public service announcements in different forms. Call in advance to see if they prefer a copy in script or a pre-recorded copy on tape.

Public Service Announcement Guidelines

- Use 8 1/2" x 11" white bond paper only.
- Use both upper- and lower-case typing, double space, and punctuate simply.
- Do not hyphenate at the end of a line, separate sentences with a series of dots or use abbreviations.
- Do not staple copy together or fold several sheets of copy separately.
- Do not mention prizes to be given away or drawings of any kind.
- When soliciting donations of any kind other than money, arrange for collection at a non-commercial place of business. No station will donate free advertising to a commercial establishment.
- Copy must reach stations at least two weeks prior to the desired air-date unless otherwise requested by individual stations.

- If submitting a live copy on tape, it must be professionally recorded.
- Stop date on copy must be the day before the event.
- Only include one announcement per page.
- Always write in an advertising copy style.

Public Access/Cable Television

Local public access TV can be a valuable community involvement tool. Services available vary from station to station, but, generally, most offer several ways of publicizing airport activities. Cable advertising can be considered an effective tool for publicizing airport or aviation business activities of interest to local neighbors. The cable company's production staff is usually available to assist in developing still-frame ads as well as more sophisticated productions. Fees for these services are usually very reasonable. Still-frame ads (for meeting announcements, etc.) average $150.00 a month.

In addition to basic advertisements, local cable TV stations often have community programs, which provide excellent opportunities for airport tours, interviews, etc. On some stations, the local chamber of commerce has a weekly program. On other stations, local public officials or community leaders host programs. In either format, sponsors are anxious to have interesting topics and are likely to welcome airport-related programs.

Possible story angles for airport topics could include:

- A tour of the airport
- An interview with the airport manager
- A visit to the FAA's air traffic control tower
- History of the airport
- Different types of aircraft located at the airport
- Interviews with local pilots
- What is an FBO?
- Learning to fly
- How the airport benefits local residents
- How local citizens are involved in the airport
- Maintaining an airport

- The airport's noise abatement program
- Current airport projects

Another opportunity that most public access stations offer is production for videotapes. Production rates vary, but usually average $125.00 an hour for either commercial or in-studio productions, depending on number of cameras, audio dubbing, computer graphic design, etc. This can be a very economic way to develop a video regarding the airport, often at half or a quarter of commercial rates. If the airport plans to run the video as a half-hour cable program, rates can be even more competitive.

Just as weekly "throw away" newspapers are often not taken seriously, public access TV is often discounted with comments that "no one watches local cable TV." On the contrary, local residents, especially community activists, are more likely to read local "throw-aways" as well as watch cable TV to learn of local news and issues of interest.

Announcing airport meetings, participating on local cable programs and producing an airport program are all excellent opportunities to gain visibility with local residents. It is important to take advantage of public access television programs on a regular basis, not just when an airport or aviation business wants to promote a project. Frequent visibility signifies a commitment to the local community.

To explore possibilities, call your local public access TV station and set up an appointment with the production manager. In most cases, the production of an advertising commercial or program will be handled by the production department and the actual airtime will be negotiated with the sales staff.

Public Service Announcement Format

<u>ORGANIZATION:</u>	<u>CONTACT:</u>
name	name
address	phone number
phone number	
Start Use ____________	
Stop Use ____________	
READING TIME	___ SECONDS
______________________________	
______________________________	
______________________________	
______________________________	
______________________________	
______________________________	
______________________________	
SOCIAL SERVICE # ______________________	

Normal Process for Media Coverage of Event

3-4 weeks prior:	Initial release in locals, trade publications and public service announcements.
2-3 weeks prior:	Announcement for majors, photo caption for locals.
1-2 weeks prior:	Phone call follow-up, release for directories/planning guides.
1 week prior:	Complete media kits as appropriate, finalize phone calls.
1-2 days prior:	Put over wire services, call assignment editors of broadcast.
During event:	Supervise photographer, assist media, update own publicity records with names and notes for future contacts.
Following event:	Get staff photos produced ASAP, written within hours if possible; "Today's news is tomorrow's old news," so get release with photo caption out immediately, especially to majors.

Using the Internet

Many airports and aviation businesses today are accessing the Internet and using the many services that are becoming available through this technology. Aviation business owners can communicate almost instantly with airports and other aviation businesses across the country and around the world. Clipping services are available through the Internet, as well as news groups and mailing lists that also provide valuable information. Users can access developments at the FAA and other federal agencies by reading public documents.

"Chat rooms" and "aviation forums," as they are more commonly called in this industry, can be established for your own airport users, neighbors, or others with similar airport interests. Many national and regional aviation organizations are using chat rooms for users to stay in touch and talk about subjects that most interest them.

One of the most important functions available through the World Wide Web is web sites and home pages that can be developed to promote and educate interested individuals about a specific airport, aviation business, airport project or event.

The National Air Transportation Association (NATA) has developed a web site and offers a variety of services to its members. Through NATA's web site (http://www.nata-online.org), members can stay in touch and stay current on industry issues.

The Internet can play a significant role in community outreach and community involvement. Local residents are able to become informed regarding airport activities and stay involved through the use of e-mail, chat rooms, aviation forums, home pages and access to airport and government documents. A government agency recently used teleconferencing to gain significant public input on a national issue when workshops were not feasible. Such technology, in conjunction with use of the Internet, greatly expands the possibilities for public interaction with airports in the future.

Conclusion

Working with the media does not have to be a struggle. By preparing your staff with a media management plan, maintaining media contacts and assisting reporters in finding interesting story angles, you can cultivate good relationships with members of the media.

F. Coordinating with the FAA and Airport Staff

In the myriad of issues facing the general aviation industry today, many technical concerns are readily discernable: airspace, procedures, flight standards, and safety—the list goes on. On another front, an equally difficult issue continues to wear away at our ability to conduct business and have this industry grow and prosper—community resistance to the growth and expansion of airports.

Unfortunately, community concerns are often not taken into consideration soon enough. This may occur because issues are often difficult to recognize and even less tangible in solving. These issues are not technical, but psychological, and require a different mindset, different methods for solution, and different players. In addition to the obvious reasons of flight altitude, routes, and the unique sound of specific aircraft, a primary reason for frustration is the airport neighbors' sense of invasion of privacy and lack of control over their own backyards.

Handling Grievances

Invasion of privacy is an issue well known by those who have sat through countless public meetings. Early turns, run-ups, touch and goes, late night and early morning flights—the list of grievances is long. Difficulty in getting an adequate response to complaints and inquiries adds to the frustration and anger of the affected residents. Longtime airport activists are tired of bureaucratic answers—enter a new age of community activism and a growing concern. Citizen anger and frustration are only partly due to the actual aviation noise or potential safety incidents. Many concerned citizens are fed up with the bureaucratic run-around and lack of adequate response from officials. Unfortunately today, general aviation often receives a great deal of this pent-up anger and frustration.

When residents feel that they have been given inadequate explanation by the airport or the FAA for a particularly disturbing operation, their level of frustration will grow to where they just "aren't going to take it anymore."

FAA and Airport Management Involvement

As the aviation industry promotes airports and expansion, it is important to involve airport management and the FAA, encouraging them to employ new solutions. They can be essential links in our community relations efforts. It can help the situation if an aviation business owner appreciates an airport manager's perspective. As an airport manager related, "I get the brunt of all community aviation noise concerns, whether they are landing at my airport or not." It is not that the airport or the FAA are necessarily the bad guys. But today's environment requires new approaches and new solutions that include a renewed spirit of cooperation and sensitivity to all sides.

Public officials are listening more and more to individual citizens and homeowner groups. In particular, airport management is feeling the impact of citizen groups. As overall airport concerns increase, it often seems that restrictions on aviation users are convenient responses.

Finger pointing within general aviation itself is also an all too prevalent problem. Other aviation interests are glad to take a breather and have community "heat" directed elsewhere. In the midst of these kinds of airport-community issues that affect operations, both airport management and the local and regional FAA offices can quickly become a friend or foe. And as mentioned above, surprisingly, the solutions utilized in the past may not be the most effective methods toward reaching resolution. To truly resolve concerns and "quiet" neighbors requires innovative thinking, a dedication of time, and the willingness on all sides to explore alternatives.

Proven community relations techniques can help educate community members regarding operations. These include speaker bureaus, aviation awareness days, and operator involvement in local Chamber of Commerce activities. Providing information to residents as to why and how aircraft fly where they do, and about existing safety concerns, is a long-term, but valuable community relations tool.

It is advantageous for aviation business owners to take a lead role and, if necessary, encourage both airport and FAA staff to become more responsive. Possible actions for resolving community-airport concerns, by working directly with FAA and airport staff, include:

1. **Communicate with airport management to eliminate the old finger-pointing syndrome.** Work with your airport manager to monitor complaints and community concerns. In conjunction with other operators and aviation businesses, develop and conduct a regional workshop for airport managers to discuss many of these issues. Facilitate meetings between airport neighbors and pilots. This will help reduce or eliminate the old "finger-pointing" syndrome between staffs or operators who try to put the problem on someone else. The typical response of "it isn't our fault" or "we can't do anything about it" only increases the frustration on the part of airport neighbors. As an operator, let your airport manager know that you are willing to work with community members.
2. **Increase cooperation between airport management, the FAA, and airport operators.** Involve FAA air traffic controllers to develop new noise abatement ideas by periodically attending team briefings and weekly meetings. Invite the tower chief, controllers, and

airport manager to pilot and airport association meetings. Act as facilitator to increase communication between the tower and airport staff in working with operators. Encourage a change in everyone's thinking to enhance proactive attitudes and a desire to solve problems that require creative, innovative thinking and communication.

Request greater involvement from FAA tower, FSDO and regional office personnel to enhance communication and cooperation with airport staff and operators. In the long run, the time and cooperation devoted to working with pilots has also reduced FAA time spent on community concerns.

Too often, aviation business owners are reluctant to meet with either the airport or local FAA staff, not realizing the help that these staffs can offer. It is becoming more common for citizens to go directly to either the FAA or request a "congressional" action that the FAA needs to investigate. Aviation businesses can help themselves if they have established and cultivated relationships with FAA offices. Just as they might set up periodic meetings with local elected officials to acquaint them with aviation issues of interest and develop a positive relationship, this same outreach is needed with FAA staffs and airport managers.

3. **Establish an effective "Community Response Line" to provide feedback.** Most airports have complaint lines, but how they are utilized and managed is the key to effective results vs. frustration for both residents and operators. Residents need to provide specific information that will assist in understanding the incident time, location, type of aircraft, color/paint scheme, and what it was doing. Ensure that the monthly report of complaints/incidents gets out to pilots and operators. Too often, the report is circulated to "interested parties," which usually means public officials and the same people that are complaining. It makes them feel good, but does little to resolve the problem. Operators can assist in managing the report to find trends and perpetrators, and take action. Operators should also monitor the reports to identify early warning signals of increasing concerns.

4. **In working with local communities, recognize that any effort is a long-term endeavor.** Do your homework and know your audience. A foundation of education is the key. It is important to get everyone talking the same language. Listen more than you talk, especially early on. Accept the fact that it takes continual education and explaining the same issues over and over to an ever-changing community. Ensure that good neighbor efforts and new noise abatement policies get publicized.

5. **Educate transient pilots to local noise-sensitive areas.** Work with transient pilots and tower personnel to increase communication and understanding of local flight procedures. As transient pilots get tuned in to local noise abatement techniques, they will probably be more comfortable in asking the tower for specific information. As controllers gain insight into airport tenant/community concerns, they will be able to recognize transients and more readily assist them in avoiding noise sensitive areas.

6. **Encourage periodic evaluation of established routes and altitudes.** Work with the FAA and airport staff to periodically review flight paths and procedures. This could involve reviewing recent noise complaint records or citizen comments to determine troublesome areas or escalating concerns. This evaluation requires cooperation, insight, and sensitivity from all parties to obtain the most benefit. It can be a great opportunity to remind airport operators, tenants and local pilots about noise sensitive areas, noise abatement procedures and airport neighbors' concerns.

These are but a few of the techniques and opportunities to enhance communication and cooperation between airport tenants, airport management, the FAA, and community members. Used in conjunction with more traditional community relations efforts that provide excellent opportunities for positive public interface, these methods will assist in developing greater trust and credibility between aviation operators and local citizenry. In today's environment of community activists, who call for "shutting down the airport" or restrictive curfews, it is important for aviation businesses to find ways to work more effectively to resolve mutual concerns.

As the days of avoiding public scrutiny draw to a close, it is up to pilots and operators to encourage and educate the FAA and airport managers to find cooperative alternatives. It is the general aviation industry's livelihood at stake. Airport management and the FAA hold valuable opportunities for this industry in helping to educate and enhance positive relations with communities. But the key for initiating changes in attitudes and methods lies with pilots, operators, and manufacturers. This industry, in a spirit of open communication and desire to resolve mutual concerns, can lead the way to a new and higher level of understanding and ultimately, compatibility.

Phase 2: Implementing Community Outreach Elements

With Phase One underway, you should have a solid base of support in place—from the people who come through the gates of your airport on a regular basis to the government leaders who recognize your airport as an important economic development tool. Now you need to expand that awareness to other parts of your community, so when someone is asked what makes their community special, the airport will be on their list.

In **Phase 2: Implementing Community Outreach Elements** you'll find the next steps necessary to make your airport a positive household name:

A. Developing a speakers bureau;

B. Staging special events;

C. Supporting local education;

D. Assisting in a disaster; and

E. Developing a friends of the airport group

Everyone has a different vision of the perfect community. And while each would probably look different, they would have many elements in common. We all want to ensure our families' safety and health, build an economically secure future, and have the time to enjoy the rewards of our hard work. Your challenge is to show that the airport holds all of these pieces together, connecting rural areas to every corner of the world, bringing the latest medical technology to their front door, bringing new jobs and opportunities, and making them feel good about the place they call home.

A. Developing a Speakers Bureau

A Speakers Bureau can be a very positive public relations tool for the airport. Once guidelines for the Bureau are established, and volunteers trained, it can work to establish the airport as an important member of the community.

The face-to-face contact with members of your community is a direct and effective means of communicating and helps personalize the airport and its programs. It also allows for some give and take during question and answer sessions, which helps to demonstrate the airport's openness. If your airport does not have a Speakers Bureau, consider developing one with the airport or through the users association.

Guidelines for an Effective Speakers Bureau

First and foremost, it is important that the Speakers Bureau does not represent the airport management in any way. It is simply a forum to provide interesting information regarding the airport for the benefit of clubs and organizations. It is offered free of charge.

Topics are to be predetermined. The organization requesting a speaker can select the topic from an established list. It is important that topics be light in nature and not invoke heated discussion or controversy. This program can almost be viewed as entertainment. Airport topics for presentation could include the following:

- A History of General Aviation
- A History of the Airport
- Flying, A Fun Hobby
- General Aviation Airports—Access to the World
- Emergency Air Medical Services
- The Purpose of the Civil Air Patrol
- The Role of the Helicopter
- The Economic Impact of General Aviation
- Air Traffic Control Tower Operation
- Airplane Repair and Restoration

Speakers Bureau volunteers must be well trained. Because airport issues are often controversial, speakers must make it clear to the organization they are addressing that they will only speak on the topic selected. If questions are asked of the speaker that they cannot address, a speaker should be trained to say "I can't answer that for you; however, if you give me your name and number, I will have Mr. Doe at the airport get back to you right away." Or "Mr. John Doe of the airport can best answer that question, his number is XXX-XXXX."

To find interested groups, compile a list of civic organizations in your community. Examples of these are Girl Scouts, Boy Scouts, business clubs, Kiwanis, labor unions, Rotary International, Soroptimists, senior citizen groups, etc.

The effectiveness of the Speakers Bureau rests in how committed its members are. A public relations disaster would be to accept a speaking engagement and not show or make an unprepared presentation. A good way to handle this issue is to assign one coordinator for a specified period of time. All bookings can be scheduled through this person only. The coordinator would then be responsible for confirming speakers and rotating them so that individual speakers do not get burned out and become a liability.

A simple brochure on the purpose and availability of the Bureau is essential. This brochure can outline how to schedule a speaker, and what topics are available. Once the brochure is developed, a mass email and/or regular mailing to appropriate clubs and organizations can be conducted.

If a formal Speakers Bureau seems overwhelming, an airport could consider an annual or semi-annual round of speaking engagements to local civic groups. Aviation businesses could help organize and participate in these presentations.

B. Staging Special Events

Staging a special event at the airport is an effective way of bringing the community to you and you to them. It provides an opportunity to showcase the airport's facilities, its users, and its capabilities. It pulls airport supporters, users and tenants into your community relations projects as an active participant; and when promoted, the special event opens the door to positive press in the community at large.

While organization and attention to detail are important in your execution of the event, gathering volunteers often becomes one of the most important things you can do to ensure a successful event. Airport users and tenants understand the importance of community relations to the airport's long-term viability and are often eager to help. It is through these special events that you can provide them with an opportunity to contribute.

Finally, a special event does not have to be a negative cash drain on the airport. If the special event is well conceived, well publicized and of interest to the community, the event can often pay for itself and, in some circumstances, generate funds for future events.

Special Events Ideas

Pancake Breakfast, Tour, and Raffle

Develop a theme for the event such as Airport Appreciation Day, Civic Day, or Airport Awareness Day. If there is access to antique airplanes, design the event around the history of flying and place antique aircraft near the breakfast site for viewing. This event can span a four-hour period on a weekend morning. The event begins with the pancake breakfast, followed by a fun and informative airport tour which includes stops at airport businesses. A per-person charge should be levied for the breakfast and volunteers can sell raffle tickets throughout the morning. When possible have something for the kids to take home such as a paper airplane, wings pin, placemat with the history of aviation outlined, etc.

The event can be promoted through the local Chamber of Commerce, local press, local radio stations, with posters, airplane banners and in your local schools. At one general aviation airport, the breakfast was used as a fund-raiser for the local YMCA. Be sure to solicit volunteer help from the sponsored charity and use them to promote and sell tickets to the event.

Black-Tie Fundraiser to Support Local Charity

Given the right charity, an airport black tie fund-raiser is a terrific special event. Airport personnel, friends and users, public officials, and community members alike can participate.

Staging such an ambitious event requires development of a planning committee and extensive pre-party planning. Be sure to include community members and public officials in the planning committee. This will ensure selecting an appropriate charity and help in promoting the event to the public. A detailed action plan and timeline should be developed and used.

Paper Airplane Contest as Part of Aviation Day

A paper airplane-flying contest is a fun way to generate funds and excitement at an existing airport event. Proceeds from the event can be donated to a local charity, support local school programs, or be used to offset the main event's cost. Plus, the uniqueness of this event is a good media story to draw attention to your main event.

All you need to conduct this event is a timer, a whistle, a referee, a target (like a big tire from an old airplane), and colored construction paper. For a fee (maybe a dollar a page), each participant receives a piece of paper that has lines for name and address. Each contestant makes their own paper airplane design and attempts to fly it into the center of the target. Participants can buy as many pages of paper as they want. Adults and kids alike will want to compete. You can even stage this mini event several times during the course of the main event. Aviation businesses can contribute prizes for the winners.

Air Shows

Planning an air show can be one of the most challenging, yet most rewarding of all events that an airport hosts. When done correctly, a well-planned air show brings with it tremendous media involvement, consistent audience participation, and numerous opportunities for cross promotion.

Second only to baseball, air shows continue to be one of the most popular spectator events in North America. More than 26 million people attend air shows in North America annually. No other airport event brings such a large portion of the community together on airport grounds than an air show.

Planning an air show takes a great deal of time and commitment. Just as every airport is unique, so is every air show. But the majority of all well planned air shows take the same factors into consideration—media, safety, displays, transportation, insurance, concessions, VIP guests, etc.

If hosting an air show is something of interest to you and your airport, it is recommended that your airport join the International Council of Air Shows. This council consists of many experts knowledgeable in the mechanics of planning an air show. Upon joining, you will receive a manual that contains an abundance of information with specific tasks and checklists on the guidelines for hosting an air show.

If your airport is considering hosting an air show, keep in mind that a show which has only an agenda of flying will not be as successful in encouraging community involvement and participation as one which contains ground exhibits as well. An air show which emphasizes the fun of flying, job opportunities and the history of aviation will not only improve the image of the airport, but can also encourage young people to choose a career in aviation.

To truly involve the public and local communities, an airport may want to involve local civic organizations and the Chamber of Commerce. In addition, community leaders may be interested in hosting community events in conjunction with the air show. Examples of this might include a pancake breakfast, barbeque, an evening fireworks display or special downtown events before or during the actual air show. These can be great local economic incentives and can expand the air show to a broader community focus. At Air Show Canada for example, the local community hosts a "picnic in the park" the evening before the air show and invites air show exhibitors and pilots. It has become a very popular community event with dancing and contests as well as many food booths and other entertainment.

C. Supporting Local Education

A fun and effective way of gaining publicity and grassroots support for an aviation business or airport is through your community's educational system. You will not find a more receptive audience. Teachers and students often get excited about the field of aviation and careers in aviation.

Whether you work with one facility in an Adopt-A-School program or with local educators across all educational levels to design Aviation Teaching Modules, an educational program's only limits are your staff's imagination and creativity.

The key to the success of all aviation educational programs is the successful collaboration of teachers and aviation experts as they work together to develop the presentation materials. Achieving this end requires early consultation with educators about their curriculum objectives, their teaching techniques and their classroom needs. It also requires obtaining their input on whether existing airport printed and audio-visual material (such as videos, slide shows, brochures, posters, etc.) can be effective teaching tools. Through this partnership, it is hoped that the final program materials, both existing and newly developed, are widely accepted by the educational community and thus used at all levels within the educational system.

Become a Partner in an Adopt-A-School Program

Often, school districts have an Adopt-A-School program that match schools with businesses in an effort to enrich educational programs for students and help the community prepare for its economic future.

The program involves meeting with your adopted school's principal and staff and outlining mutually agreeable goals for the program. A key element of the program can be the providing of role models for students and the creation of special aviation events such as student career days, writing contests, and airport tours. This represents a commitment of time, but not a big financial commitment by the airport itself. Such volunteer efforts more often than not become mutually satisfying as the partnership is an investment in the future of the community and to many children in the area.

Design an Aviation Teaching Module

Another approach is to consult with local educators (teachers, administrators, science instructors and career counselors) to develop Aviation Teaching Modules for use at elementary schools, junior high schools and high schools.

You can achieve these objectives by conducting an Educators Workshop at your airport. At the workshop, you can determine the educators' interest level in an Aviation Teaching

Module and the adaptability of current airport material to the program, and get their input on what materials are needed, what subjects should be addressed, and how these new programs can be cost effectively developed and produced.

Elementary Schools

An elementary program is designed to promote general interest in the field of aviation. The format is informative and fun. All children attending the kickoff assembly could receive a pair of wings. Components of the elementary program could include airport tours, coloring books, teacher-designed lesson material, a poster contest for Aviation Days, classroom speakers, field trips to the airport or children's museum, and aviation films.

Junior High Schools

A Junior High School program, while still fun, is more sophisticated and is primarily for use in science and modern history classes. Sample components of this program are airport tours, teacher-designed lesson material, trips to an aviation museum, an essay or poster contest and aviation films.

High Schools

High school programs are geared primarily for use in career workshops but are also included in social studies programs. Program components could include aviation films, an essay or poster contest, Aviation Days and career day speakers.

Working with Young People

Young Aces

Taking a different approach, one general aviation airport started up a non-profit program for at-risk juveniles through their Young Aces program. The program gives at-risk youths an opportunity to fly a high-performance aerobatic aircraft. The ride is a thrill, but also provides a chance for teens to prove their mettle.

Churches, group organizations and juvenile diversion programs recommend participants. Mentor pilots guide youths through a two and one-half hour military style flight experience, safety demonstrations and the 45-minute flight.

Young Eagles

The Santa Monica Chapter (Chapter 11) of the Experimental Aircraft Association (E.A.A.) originated the Young Eagles program that operates similarly to the Young Aces program. The goal of E.A.A.'s program is to give one million first flights to youngsters all over the world by the 100th anniversary date of the very first flight of the Wright Brother's "Flyer" (the year 2003).

Held quarterly, the Saturday event draws youngsters from the entire Los Angeles basin, with the majority being reached through area service groups looking for positive directions for young people. Each youth is not only given a ride, but is encouraged to participate in all aspects of the flight. It is hoped that this first ride can foster a lifelong interest in aviation.

D. Assisting in a Disaster

During a major public emergency such as a serious earthquake or hurricane, emergency facilities will be strained and probably overloaded. Well-coordinated general aviation volunteer pilots, operators and support personnel can significantly contribute to emergency relief efforts. This can supplement and complement existing resources by using the extensive fleet of airplanes and helicopters and the highly trained pilots and other personnel involved in general aviation. Thus, every airport can serve as a new major resource, providing disaster relief capabilities for the families and the surrounding communities.

General Aviation Capabilities During Emergencies

Often able to operate when other transportation facilities are disabled or destroyed, general aviation volunteers can transport injured victims, medical personnel and vital supplies, supplementing the medevac and airlift capabilities of the public agencies and the National Guard. General aviation aircraft can be especially useful for bringing regular and supplemental emergency service workers into a stricken community that may be isolated because of disrupted ground transportation infrastructure. Another important role is the evacuation of non-critical injury cases and patients with chronic medical conditions that would add to the workload of already overburdened medical and rescue personnel. Likewise, smaller aircraft can transport the specific supplies and equipment needed directly to the affected communities, reducing the need for ground transportation and on-site distribution during the frantic circumstances of an emergency situation.

General aviation helicopters can rescue stranded personnel from buildings, parks and other tight spaces and bring in emergency personnel and supplies. General aviation airplanes can link up with the helicopters, handling intermediate and medium range tasks using local airports and disabled stretches of freeways, roads and fields.

The general aviation community can also supply many additional supplementary services. Small aircraft can be invaluable for surveying damaged areas and spotting isolated victims. Their sophisticated multichannel radio equipment can provide a complete, parallel communications network independent of telephones and existing emergency services. Local, state and federal personnel will be freed to perform vital administrative and interagency surveying, reopen airfields, assist FAA personnel in reestablishing air traffic control facilities and services and assist activities and loading and unloading of aircraft.

Existing Preparedness Programs

Most of the emergency plans associated with airports have to do with the treatment of injured at the airport and the continuation of airport operations based on the Federal Aviation Administration Advisory Circular 150/5200-31. How the continued operation of the airport relates to aiding the community during a disaster is left to local preparedness plans to define. The role of airports is often included in statewide plans, but overlooked in local plans.

Many airports take it upon themselves to coordinate a disaster preparedness program. The Fullerton City Council in California has approved a "Volunteer Pilot Service Program" submitted by Fullerton Municipal Airport, which would allow pilots to volunteer their time and aircraft to assist fire and rescue personnel in observing local disasters. The city council also agreed to add pilots wishing to join the program to their Workers' Compensation coverage while they are engaged in pre-approved activities solely on the city's behalf.

Airports or aviation businesses with an interest in assisting in a community disaster and disaster planning can offer support to local and regional planning agencies. Some airports have taken an active role in disaster planning. For example, this could include helping develop the plans necessary to make a fleet of general aviation airplanes, helicopters and jets available to assist a city in the event of a disaster that would require air transportation assistance. Airports and airport tenant associations have also sponsored events on disaster preparedness for local communities as well as events to assist airport tenants in learning how to cope in a disaster.

E. Developing an Airport Friends Group

Results from a study of public attitudes toward airports revealed both nationally and locally a lack of understanding of the benefits of general aviation airports and local plans for improvements. A volunteer community support group can be a good way to develop positive promotion for the airport. These support groups, frequently called Airport Friends Groups, represent and promote the airport in the community through assorted activities. Airport Friends Groups can increase the effectiveness of an airport's community relations effort by including and involving large numbers of the general public who either support the airport or are interested in learning more about the airport. Some Friends of the Airport Groups are advocate groups with the specific objective of gaining support for airport issues. Other groups are more interested in reaching the many local residents and businesses that know little about the airport but would like to learn more about it.

In setting up and implementing such an organization, keep in mind the following:

- Make sure each member knows and understands the purpose of the organization and its role in the community.
- Be sure that the group's goals are stated so that they can be understood, accepted and supported by each member of the organization and, in the end, the general public.
- Keep all members well briefed on how the Airport Friends Group's interests coincide with those of specific target audiences and the general public.
- Conduct year-round activities or mailings to maintain ongoing support and interest from both members and the public.

In the end, the real challenge of the group is to seize the initiative and develop a positive, coordinated program in which communications with the community help achieve its long-term objectives.

The Steering Committee

Members of an appointed Steering Committee can spearhead the organization. To start, a Steering Committee can be drawn from any airport associations already established, the local Chamber of Commerce, airport business owners and airport staff. This Steering Committee will structure the "Friends Group" and develop the necessary procedures to be an effective organization.

In choosing organization goals and the appropriate subcommittees, it is helpful for the Steering Committee to concentrate its efforts on the uncommitted public. The airport's firm supporters and irrevocable opponents are recognized as such and, while not ignored, should not be given the majority of the group's attention. In most cases, non-aviation people are the group's ultimate audience in most Friends Groups.

General Membership

Once the Friends Group is well established, a direct mail piece can be sent to the community at large and a membership drive can begin. Fertile ground for conducting a membership drive is most likely to be found in the airport's surrounding residents, local businesses, educators, government officials, and schools. Membership will, of course, be open to all members of the community. Most likely, members will have a general interest in aviation.

Airport Friends Groups Program and Events

Programs and events should be interesting and entertaining to capture the attention of the community and encourage positive interest in the airport. It is also important that there be a regular schedule of programs and activities as a means of maintaining year-round interest. Possible programs and event opportunities are:

Air Corp

The Air Corp would involve high school students dedicating a set number of hours per month to responsibilities at the airport. Active students would receive a jacket or cap to signify participation. The Airport Friends Group could even award scholarships to outstanding Air Corp members who are interested in pursuing careers in aviation.

Airport Traveling Exhibit

The Airport Friends Group could sponsor an Airport Traveling Exhibit. A historical look at aviation or the development of the airport are but two of many potential ideas. The exhibit would travel to schools, libraries, malls and civic centers.

Community Open House or Aviation Day

Another type of activity could be an Airport Open House for the surrounding community, featuring aviation displays, food booths, and entertainment.

In addition to the ideas above, a Friends Group could be the coordinator for the Speakers Bureau outlined earlier in this section. The Friends Group could also be the focal point for tours of the airport, air traffic control tower, or an FBO or other aviation business to familiarize members with different aspects of the airport. Another idea would be to have membership meetings focus on specific airport groups such as the 99s or the local EAA chapter. If the group is well organized and ambitious, it could take on improvement projects to beautify the airport, such as clean-up day, or they could work with airport management to develop an airport observation area to view arriving and departing aircraft. The ideas are unlimited, but it is important that whatever is undertaken can be accomplished so that the group enhances the image of the airport, not detracts from it by unsuccessful efforts.

Meetings

The Steering Committee would meet monthly with subcommittee meetings to be held as needed. relative to planned programs and events. General membership meetings or social events could be held quarterly, or at least semi-annually with several special events planned at appropriate intervals. A location at the airport is an appropriate meeting place, as this will ensure focus on airport issues. Whenever possible, try to establish a permanent location for the meetings. This makes arrangements for the meetings easy to accomplish and should enhance attendance.

Things to Consider Before Organizing a Friends Group

- You can start small and build the group. Don't formulate such an overwhelming organization that it is nearly impossible to orchestrate or coordinate. Keep it as simple as possible.
- What type of group do you want and would the community want to meet both your needs? A strong advocates group might be needed in one situation, but only further alienate residents in another situation.
- Can the group be maintained once it is organized? Are there sufficient resources to keep it going, especially the first year or two? It may not be an instant success, and it may require enough resources to see it through a start-up phase. Also, are there enough businesses and airport groups to keep the interest alive? This is primarily a concern for small airports, but could be of concern even at a larger airport if your airport's management or business owners are skeptical of the idea.
- Is there sufficient support or interest for such a group? You may want to test the possibility before committing to a group, or try it small scale before announcing it publicly.
- Will the formulation of a support group activate the anti-airport forces to create an all out anti-airport campaign? In considering a Friends Group, it is important to not create an "us vs. them" atmosphere. If the group is perceived as drawing the battle lines, it will be seen as a threat by those opposed to the airport who are then likely to escalate their efforts. This should not stop the formation, but it must be considered by the founders.

Phase 3: Communicating Effectively and Resolving Conflicts

In **Phase 3: Communicating Effectively and Resolving Conflicts**, you'll find the next steps necessary to make your airport a positive part of the community:

A. Using Conflict Resolution techniques;

B. Developing Guidelines for Crisis Management, and

C. Gathering input from the Public

The last thing you want is for the community to define your airport with negatives, whether it's over noise, development, or other factors. You need to be prepared to bridge differences, calm fears and dispel myths, before these negative words escalate into lawsuits, political decisions and state or federal intervention.

1. Lay the groundwork for consensus *before* you move forward with your plans. If you're planning changes at the airport or with your operation at the airport, consider the impact of those changes on the local community. This is just as important as the work put into securing grant money and selecting a contractor.

   - Give your local officials from council members to the mayor to local state and federal representatives a heads-up on what your plans are, along with the negative impacts. They'll appreciate not getting blindsided, especially if you've come to them for help on the project.

   - Enlist the support of others who stand to benefit from the changes. Whether it's a company using the new terminals or an aircraft operator that will be able to land on a longer runway, ask them for their support writing letters, attending meetings, and making phone calls.

- Provide a presentation on your plans at a neighborhood association or property owners meeting. Again, let them know about your proposed plans, where you foresee problems and ask for their input. Don't leave them with the impression that you'll ram through the changes without their support.

- Ask these groups to appoint someone that you can use as a contact. Follow up and keep them informed at each step of the way.

- Look at how other airports and aviation businesses have worked through these kinds of problems. Learn from the mistakes they've made. Consider bringing someone from this airport and the effected neighborhood in to talk to your neighborhood groups.

2. Convey what is at stake. Be sure those concerned understand whether safety issues, meeting new federal regulations, increasing access, or drawing new business is at stake with these changes. If failing to extend a runway means losing an important employer and the jobs that come with it, let them know. Remember, the airport is about improving their quality of life.

3. Don't discount their concerns, especially when it comes to objections to airport noise. Remember not only is noise a subjective issue, but you want the airport to be considered a positive in the community, not a negative.

   - Take the time to explain the science behind measuring noise, so you're all talking in the same language. It may be a good opportunity to bring in a noise expert to provide a presentation on noise metrics. This expert could address the three physical factors used to measure aircraft noise: time duration, sound intensity, and frequency content. Once you agree on the appropriate measurements, you can assure consistency in your discussions.

   - Present different options. If possible, create noise abatement air traffic control procedures and day/night noise abatement programs.

   - Generate a noise exposure map for the airport to define problem areas and acceptable noise standards. For example, noise above 65 dB in a residential area is unacceptable.

   - Look to the FAA for guidance. They can help you prepare an Airport Noise Compatibility Plan through their Part 150 Airport Noise Compatibility Program.

4. Plan to respond. If you want to be a bigger part of the community, be prepared to modify your plans to meet their needs and concerns. In the long term, these accommodations will pay off in good will and good words.

A. Using Conflict Resolution Techniques

Conflict is defined as the existence of opposing or differing points of view. Another, more complex definition states, "Conflict is the interaction of interdependent people who perceive incompatible goals and interference from each other in achieving those goals." (Fink, 1968) This definition aptly describes many airport-community conflicts today.

Individuals bring unique information, perceptions, values and goals to every situation. Conflict is to be expected in situations that involve more than one person. That is to say, conflict is normal. Most people perceive conflict as a negative thing, mainly because it brings uncertainty. But not all conflict is bad.

Conflict can provide us with opportunities to air important issues, to consider new and creative ideas, and it can lead organizations to re-evaluate and clarify goals and missions. Therefore, it is important to understand processes that can be used in order to resolve conflicts more effectively. There may be airport issues or conflicts that could benefit from the expertise and experience of a professional facilitator or mediator. While a formal mediation process is not discussed in this overview, many airport issues can be facilitated through the formation of an informal working group. These groups can use an informal style of mediation to resolve issues of concern.

Facilitating Conflict Resolution

In general, suggestions for facilitating conflict resolution include:

- Respond to frustrations and address concerns
- Try to not react or become defensive when faced with strong emotions
- Stay focused on issues
- Ask clarifying questions
- Address needs rather than positions
- Determine areas of agreement
- Listen carefully to other perspectives
- Review main points

- Determine where each party is stuck
- Discourage scenarios which pit one side against the other
- Take a break
- Agree to maintain communication
- Help the parties find ways to "save face"

The Four C's Approach

The "four C's" approach is used to assist groups who recognize there is a problem and would like to initiate a conflict resolution process but are unsure of how to proceed. The four C's are as follows:

- Catalysts
- Communication
- Cooperation
- Compatibility

Catalysts

The catalysts element involves recognizing and responding early to problems and issues. Early warning signs are usually evident. Escalating complaints, political pressure, increasing polarization and increased frustration are a few indicators of a conflict in the making. Airport officials, tenants, community leaders and the FAA need to stay in touch with the local residents. It is important to listen to community activists and be responsive to their concerns. There are usually a limited number of individuals in any community that have a pulse on what is happening.

The catalysts stage of the conflict resolution process helps to identify conflicts and stakeholders as well as help parties to develop and maintain compatibility. This is done by recognizing and responding early to problems and issues as well as keeping in touch with the citizens and organizations affected.

Identifying the participants who will work together to resolve the issue is an important part of the catalysts stage. Stakeholders are the catalysts to bring about change. Determining key issues and concerns as well as establishing the potential for initiating a resolution process are critical components of issue resolution. Representatives of all affected organizations and individuals need to be recognized and involved. Forming a working group to study an issue and jointly develop recommendations through mediated agreement can often facilitate resolving airport conflicts. A critical element is that each individual involved realizes that they can make a difference.

Communication

The communication element of issue resolution involves several aspects. First are the logistics for establishing a forum for effective dialogue between stakeholders in the conflict. Logistics include selecting a neutral location for bringing together interested parties, establishing a comfortable setting, keeping the group size workable and selecting a facilitator or mediator who can foster trust and openness. The role of facilitator or mediator is a key ingredient in the positive resolution of an issue. The situation may require the skills of a professional, but this is not always the case. The perfect facilitator could be a respected individual or business leader in the community or on the airport. It is important that the individual be considered a neutral party and has the respect and credibility of the conflicted parties.

Next is the actual communication process, which hinges on recognizing that conflict resolution is often a long-term effort. It takes time to develop trust and credibility between conflicting interests.

The communications part of the process involves the following phases for a group to resolve an issue:

- Education
- Brainstorming
- Recommendations
- Evaluation
- Approval
- Implementation

Education allows different interests to provide their side of the story as other members listen. This phase is essential in order to keep the group on equal ground. The information that the members present to the rest of the group will provide a baseline and will prove indispensable as the process progresses. It may be necessary or desirable to bring in outside experts to assist in this phase.

During the brainstorming phase, new ideas for solutions can be explored. The key to success in this phase is to allow all input to be made without judging it. The facilitator should be versed in brainstorming techniques and be able to assist the committee in exploring options.

The recommendation phase is when viable alternatives are explored and evaluated. Consensus may not be necessary depending on the group involved. In some instances, it may be preferable to not insist on consensus, but instead, submit a number of feasible alternatives to the deciding party for evaluation. In either case, avoid a voting situation when possible, especially if the issue is extremely contentious and it is evident consensus cannot be reached.

Upon completion of the evaluation phase, the changes will either be fully approved and implemented, refined or further committee work may be required to develop a compatible environment. It is often desirable to keep the working group together for periodic meetings to monitor the situation. This reduces the likelihood of another crisis.

Cooperation

Cooperation and collaboration are important ingredients in successful negotiation and, therefore, conflict resolution. In situations where frustrations have accumulated, it will take time to build a trusting relationship. It will require the airport and the tenants to display a willingness to resolve the issues with local neighbors or the community at large. Through this collaborative attitude, trust and credibility will develop and be reflected by members of the community.

Collaboration encompasses:

- Acknowledging concerns of all parties involved
- Encouraging joint fact finding
- Separating the people from the problem
- Distinguishing interests from positions and focusing on interests
- Looking forward for solutions rather than focusing on the past
- Accepting responsibility as well as sharing ownership in the process
- Helping each party find ways to "save face"
- Building trusting relationships
- Establishing long-term relationships

Compatibility

Compatibility is defined as being capable of existing or operating together in harmony. Compatibility is listed as one of the four C's because it represents the results of a successful conflict resolution process. In order to maintain compatibility, ongoing communication must be present between the once conflicting individuals or organizations.

Important Aspects of Compatibility

Written guidelines, including the following, can often be helpful in keeping the group on track:

- Develop and adopt a Statement of Intent and Commitment to the process
- Develop ground rules by which the group will function and on which it can rely when needed
- Develop a process design to assist members understand the steps to resolution
- Draft documents can be developed by the facilitator or a committee to be discussed and approved by the entire group

Airports can survive conflicts and grow as a result. Leadership in conflict resolution requires:

- Focusing on "needs" rather than "wants"
- Focusing on facts, not personalities
- Demonstrating equality to all parties
- Steering the parties away from a win-lose solution using a mutual gains approach

By adopting these leadership qualities and utilizing the four C's process, effective airport managers and aviation business leaders can dispel the fears that conflict has generated in the past with neighbors. Properly managed conflict will then become an opportunity, not a deterrent.

B. Developing Guidelines for Crisis Management

The most common reaction to a crisis is the "fight or flight" syndrome. This is when an individual feels backed into a corner and acts defensively or avoids dealing with the problem. Working with appropriate officials, concerned parties, and the media early in a crisis or conflict is often the difference between a disaster and an averted crisis. Many times in today's highly publicized and politicized environment, how the issue itself is resolved is less important than how you handle the crisis.

For purposes of community relations, "crisis" is defined as any community situation that has escalated to the degree that it has the potential of jeopardizing an airport or aviation business project or the operation of the airport itself.

DECIDE

An effective way to begin the process of handling a crisis is to use the DECIDE method. DECIDE is an organized process for decision making in an emergency response situation. The six steps are as follows:

Step One	**D**etect change
Step Two	**E**stimate the need to respond
Step Three	**C**oordinate with and involve appropriate parties
Step Four	**I**dentify actions needed
Step Five	**D**o something positive
Step Six	**E**valuate effects

The DECIDE method encourages directed action. Beyond this, it is helpful to have an outline and clear directives that identify the manner and method for handling any airport crisis.

Crisis Management Guidelines

Being prepared to respond efficiently and effectively in the event of a crisis is crucial. Whether it is negative community reaction to an airport project or to the airport itself, it is important to have set guidelines which the staff understands and can follow before a crisis arises.

While every community incident is unique and there is no way to predict how a community or resident will respond to a given situation, the following should be considered in developing crisis management guidelines:

- Assign a spokesperson(s) who is authorized to talk with the media and public officials
- Talk with local officials, including FAA, airport commission and city council members as early as possible in the crisis
- Provide the facts
- Correct inaccuracies
- Alert your network of supporters
- Avoid assigning blame
- Avoid defensiveness
- Be in the problem-solving mode with the desire to correct misinformation

- Do the necessary homework to understand the issue(s), interests and parties involved
- Encourage communication and initiate communication where possible
- Readily apologize and/or admit mistakes
- Demonstrate willingness to alter plans, projects and philosophies to incorporate new and different possibilities

Communicating Under Pressure

There are several key principles to apply in order to communicate effectively under pressure. The time to learn them is before a crisis occurs. The time to practice communication skills is in everyday situations. It is too late for preparation after a situation escalates.

Every airport will face a difficult communication situation. This can represent an opportunity to strengthen public image and credibility, or it can add to the airport's troubles. The key to a successful outcome is early recognition of warning signs and preparation for the opportunity to initiate dialogue.

When participating in a public dialogue, be guided by three principles: truth, completeness and position.

Truth is the only effective way to gain trust and reduce suspicion. Trust and credibility grow given honesty in answers, even those answers that are not pleasant news to the audience.

Give the complete story to the reporter or group. The background of an issue can sometimes be helpful to place events in historic perspective. Attempt to fully meet the information needs of the audience by the end of the meeting. Remember that every question asked is another chance to get a beneficial point across.

Position answers by coupling straight "Yes" or "No" with solid reasons or evidence for the answer. Inform the audience why the action was taken or how and why the policy was established. Connect the dialogue to the answer so the explanation is not drowned out by the next question as well as guaranteeing that it is not easily edited in segments for short tape spots on the news.

Handling an Interview with the Media

Being interviewed during non-crisis times can create anxiety. Being interviewed during a crisis takes on additional pressure dimensions. Suggestions for the successful interview under pressure are:

- Choose descriptive words carefully. There is a big difference between the word "crisis" and the word "disaster."

- Do not speculate. Use the phrase "I can't speculate" when reporters ask you to speculate on facts yet to be determined. The place to hypothesize is not in front of the cameras.
- When possible, discredit rumors and challenge questionable information the media has already received.
- Remain calm.
- Don't rush.
- Before meeting with the media, determine two or three brief points to make. Outlining an agenda before the interview can alleviate a defensive answer.
- Remember that full disclosure with plans for corrective action is the quickest way to handle a crisis.

Dealing with Difficult People

- View the public as customers and assume that your objective is to have the airport be a compatible neighbor. Research shows that one unsatisfied customer tells at least nine others about their treatment. In an airport operation, frustrated residents can instigate a crisis.
- Keep smiling and remain pleasant, no matter how heated the situation becomes. Remember that upset people are not attacking the speaker personally, even though it seems like it at the moment.
- Continue to listen. Let the other person vent their frustrations before attempting to address the problem. Listen with the intent of learning the details about the issue, not with the intent of forming an answer or defending your position.
- Acknowledge the person's frustration. Try and find an area of agreement, even if it is only that the person is disturbed or frustrated by an incident or situation. Rather than trying to convince them otherwise or "sell" them on the benefits of the airport, it is important to first recognize their annoyance and acknowledge it.
- Ignore the person's style of delivery and personality. Focus on the problem being explained and handle the problem with a calm and concerned approach.
- Use language appropriate to the person's level of understanding. Never use technical jargon and always be concise, to the point and uncomplicated.
- Speak slowly and quietly. Bringing your voice level down can assist the other person to do the same.

- Gather all the facts that have created the situation. An issue cannot be resolved until you understand all the facts (and perceptions) surrounding problem. Ask clarifying questions.
- Contact a person immediately once an answer or resolution is found. Thank them for bringing the problem into the light. Determine if this is an isolated incident and, if it is not, take action to alleviate further complaints.

Diffusing Negative Situations

It is in the early stages of a negative situation that there is the most opportunity to avert a real crisis. The sooner a problem is recognized, identified, and responded to, the more likely a crisis can be averted. Conflict resolution techniques are most valuable in the early phase of a crisis. There may also be time to implement a Working Group or mediation process during the early phase to resolve the issue.

It is critical to maintain an open attitude. Too often community residents hear, "We can't do that" or "We've never done it that way." This only further frustrates and alienates them. As long as there is an openness and willingness to consider options, most citizens and public officials respond.

Last, be proactive. It is important to be one step ahead of any problem. If a problem is anticipated, it can be dealt with early. Alert appropriate agencies and public officials of a possible conflict or potential crisis. If public officials and, in some cases, the media are aware of the building conflict, the issue is somewhat diffused. It creates an opportunity to prepare and involve interested parties and, thus, eliminates the often negative element of surprise. Additionally, dealing with the situation puts one in the position of managing the message, not reacting to a sensationalized story.

Dealing with a Crisis

Remember, the best way to avoid crisis situations is by using community involvement methods and conflict resolution techniques to avert or resolve conflict in its early stages.

The following is a list of possible negative situations that could arise as part of an airport project. Suggestions are provided on how to best respond. There is no "best" answer in any given crisis, except good communication and cooperation. Most crises take a long period of time to become volatile. When allowed to fester, it will take even more time to diffuse them. Initiating a dialogue and maintaining a channel of communication are the most critical elements in most crises.

Negative Media Story/Inaccuracy in Story or Negative Letter to the Editor

Possible actions to diffuse or resolve the impact include the following:

- Discuss inaccuracies with reporter/editor
- Submit letter clarifying inaccuracies, giving another perspective
- Be truthful
- Do not become emotional or defensive

Formation or Escalation of Anti-Noise, Anti-Operator Group Mobilizing Citizens Against Project or Airport

Possible actions to diffuse or resolve the impact include the following:

- Research the issues
    - — Is it noise, is it safety?
    - — Is it invasion of privacy? Is it a feeling of no control over situation?
    - — Do individuals want more information?
- Meet with local citizens
- Discuss with airport and FAA staff
- Alert officials. Discuss options
- Attempt to include citizens in an airport forum
- Develop options to meet citizen needs

Increased Number of Complaints

Possible actions to diffuse or resolve the impact include the following:

- Evaluate complaints to determine the trends (geographic, time of day, type of aircraft, day of the week, etc.)
- Discuss with Airport Steering Committee or Advisory Council
- Discuss complaints with affected residents/callers
- Discuss with local airport staff
- Discuss with pilots/tenants to determine possible change in operations
- Discuss with ATC tower chief

- Coordinate possible resolution if appropriate and required

Negative Letter/Call to City Council, County Commissioner or Other Public Official Regarding Project or Airport

Possible actions to diffuse or resolve the impact include the following:

- Investigate complaint
- Do not react emotionally or defensively
- Remain open to all issues
- Meet with any individuals who wrote letters as well as with public officials if appropriate
- Respond in writing, if there are major inaccuracies, and copy officials
- Discuss with FAA, Airport and appropriate local officials

Negative Comments at Public Meeting, City Council or Commission Meeting

Possible actions to diffuse or resolve the impact include the following:

- Ask questions to determine the circumstances and to clarify issues
- Do not react emotionally or defensively
- Commit to investigating the situation
- Offer to discuss with the individual or group outside the meeting
- If negative comments are overwhelming, suggest establishing a working group to explore options

C. Gathering Input from the Public

Before any meeting with the public, whether it is in the form of a workshop, small working group, or public hearing, there are a number of key steps that must be accomplished to ensure the meeting's objectives are met. While each step may vary slightly depending on the size of the group and the goal of the meeting, the following methodology demonstrates key aspects in meeting planning. These guidelines are included in this toolkit because there are many factors involved in setting up a productive meeting with members of the local community. Too often, proper coordination and attention to detail are overlooked, hampering the actual conduct of a good meeting.

General Guidelines for Meeting Planning Coordinate Logistics. Most meeting planning begins with determining a date, securing room(s), ordering coffee and coordinating other logistics. This is fairly basic, but in public outreach programs, the date, time and location of a meeting can take on important ramifications if not handled carefully with knowledge of various interests' perspectives.

Develop Meeting Materials. Meeting notices will need to be developed as well as written material used during the public meeting. These documents need to be written in easy to understand layperson terms. For public meetings, material such as fact sheets, questions and answers, and flow charts can be developed to help answer questions. The form of these written materials varies with the audience and with meeting objectives.

Develop Direct Mail. Adequate mailing lists and sufficient notice are probably the two most common questions and concerns at the beginning of any public meeting. Therefore it is important to develop an extensive mailing list to include all residents and other interests within the designated outreach area. This direct mailing, in addition to advertisements and media releases, can be used for the large public meetings and mailed three to four weeks before the event. In addition, a stakeholder mailing list can be developed, consisting of key individuals. For smaller meetings, individual mailings can be used to notify people.

Develop Proposed Agenda. The agenda is a pivotal instrument in the flow and outcome of any meeting. It is especially important in public meetings and can require input from several stakeholders as well as staff and the consulting team (if used) to be sure it meets the needs of those attending.

Coordinate with Key Players. Among the most important aspects for planning any meeting are to communicate and coordinate with the various interests and stakeholders prior to a meeting. These become especially important before a public meeting. Often in pre-meeting discussions, questions and concerns can be addressed before the day of the event.

Finalize and Publish the Agenda. As the meeting gets closer, it will be necessary to finalize and possibly publish the agenda. Pre-distribution of the agenda depends on the audience, the focus of the meeting, and the meeting goals.

Work with the Media. Some meetings will attract the attention of the media. Occasionally, it may be appropriate to send out a release regarding a meeting with community members or regarding an airport issue or project. Normally, the airport manager would do this. One of the worst things that can happen is for either the community or the public to consider a meeting a "secret" meeting. Expect the media to show up at virtually any meeting you have with members of the community. Sufficient notification in the local media is one of the most critical elements in planning a meeting.

Rehearse Presentations. The flow of a public meeting is important, whether it is with 25 people or 500 people. It will be important that all meeting participants are comfortable with the flow and their portion of the meeting. This is the time to be sure common questions that members of the community or elected officials might pose have an answer.

Finalize Arrangements. A last-minute check of all the details and logistics is imperative. Reviewing the availability of audio-visual equipment, seating, refreshments, as well as invited participants can be crucial. This check needs to be done sufficiently in advance so that there is the opportunity for changes.

Facilitating Meetings

Facilitation is a multifaceted process requiring astute abilities to derive maximum input and meaningful dialogue. Aviation business owners may be given an opportunity to act as a facilitator in an airport meeting. This could be a formal request to act as a facilitator or, more likely, the recognition of the need for facilitation during an existing meeting. Business leaders can be on the lookout for misperceptions, misinformation, frustration and highly charged emotional statements during public meetings. Any of these indications could signify that the group might benefit from the skills of a facilitator as well as use of conflict resolution skills. Meetings that are highly charged with misperceptions and frustration are not going to be productive or beneficial. There are a number of important factors to providing effective facilitation.

The most important factor is good communications. Inherent in effective communications is the ability to gain trust and credibility. This will result in the participants' willingness to share issues and concerns at a deeper level. It provides the forum for meaningful dialogue to take place, which is critical to obtaining significant input, thereby maximizing the success of the entire strategic plan.

Knowing how to listen, knowing for what to listen, and being able to understand what is not said as well as what is said by the various interests, requires skills and expertise in communication and facilitation. While rudimentary in many peoples' minds, these skills and expertise can make a large difference in the outcome of a discussion, a meeting and a project.

It is this critical aspect that can lend depth to the input received from the public. Keying into peoples' underlying concerns as well as what they are verbally expressing can help clarify their needs and interests. These underlying issues are often not readily apparent, even to the individual, but once identified can often be addressed effectively to not impede the process and project.

It is also important to recognize that there will be different and unique dynamics during the myriad types of meetings that an airport may hold. Each will require specific mechanisms to provide participants with the feeling of ownership of the process, without allowing them to overwhelm the group dynamics or dictate results.

It is in the best interests of an aviation business owner to consider the flow of a meeting, the needs of the public and any dynamics that may impede the successful outcome of a meeting. To the degree possible, it is worthwhile to keep an open mind to what the public or other stakeholders are saying as well as how the meeting is being conducted.

In sum, public meetings bring people together to speak and listen to facts and feelings regarding issues and allow an exchange of viewpoints. It provides an opportunity to present information to citizens who have shown an interest and is an excellent opportunity to listen to stakeholders' concerns.

Careful planning and use of good facilitation skills are essential elements in assuring that effective, two-way communication takes place. Meetings need not be a "necessary evil," but can give airport managers or an airport business owner valuable input regarding the public's views.

Phase 4: Pulling it all Together— Strategies for Action

Now that you have read each section in this manual and evaluated the various tools and techniques for use at your airport, it is time to consider how to most effectively implement an action plan. In **Phase 4: Pulling it All Together**, you will learn strategies for putting the tools to work for you.

How to Implement an Action Plan

There is no way to predict exactly the right approach for each airport or each situation. Because each airport and each situation is unique, the right strategies and right action plan must be carefully considered and evaluated depending on the issues, the parties involved and the objectives desired.

With this in mind, the following sample strategy can be considered to see if it would be an effective approach to issue resolution and community relations in your situation. There are several things to remember as you consider the best way to use the tools identified in this toolkit.

- Don't develop a strategy or action plan in a vacuum. Involve as many stakeholders as is appropriate to your situation. Find interested supporters who will assist you to achieve success.
- Just because a tool or strategy worked in the past, or for another airport, does not mean it is automatically the right action for this situation.
- When the plan is developed, keep it fluid and flexible. Review it periodically and consider what changes are needed.
- Don't think that your plan has to be comprised of numerous tools. It may be most effective to choose one or two tools and implement those. Undertaking an action plan that is

too complex can be overwhelming. It is better to take simple steps that are achievable based on resources you have available.

- As any event or tool is implemented, be sure to evaluate its effectiveness. Take steps to modify the action if needed to achieve your objective.
- The right tool at the wrong time or at the wrong airport is not effective. Timing and choice of the most effective outreach tool based on the community and its issues are very important.
- Effective community outreach takes time and continued effort to develop trust and credibility. This will not happen after one event. It may take years. Consider it a long-term commitment. It is also a philosophy—believing that you are an integral part of the community. Developing an appropriate approach takes time, input and careful consideration.

Strategy A

This strategy may be an appropriate plan if you are interested in developing a comprehensive outreach plan. It will also be most appropriate if you are looking to maximize the input and participation of local citizens. This strategy uses the desire for more community outreach as a primary objective, not only of the plan but as the focal point for the outreach itself. This is a most desirable strategy, but does take time to develop and initiate. If implemented successfully, it is also most likely to have long-term benefits.

1. Determine that you want and or need more community outreach.
2. Review "Community Relations Plan Outline" in this section.
3. Begin to consider what you are trying to achieve and why you need to achieve it.
4. At this point, do not jump to the conclusion of what ideas or tools would be most effective.
5. Now is the time to begin to talk with other stakeholders in informal ways to get initial input and feedback
6. Set up a series of input sessions to involve a variety of stakeholders. These focus group sessions will be used to explore the needs and opportunities for a community outreach effort and should include the following:
    - Airport staff
    - Aviation business owners
    - Pilots and other airport groups
    - Other city/county departments

- ➤ Chamber of Commerce and other civic groups
- ➤ Homeowner groups, neighborhood activists and residents
- ➤ Airport Authority/Commission

7. Based on the input received from these sessions, determine the key issues and concerns that need to be addressed.

8. Next, determine the most effective means of addressing the key concerns. This could be determined by a small group of key representatives, or additional sessions could be held to brainstorm the most effective tools to achieve results. If not feasible, key stakeholders from the input sessions could review tools you recommend.

9. Using the "Community Relations Plan Outline," develop a draft action plan based on resources available and within budget and staff requirements.

10. Share this draft plan with as many stakeholders as possible to obtain buy-in.

11. Once it is approved, begin to implement the plan, drawing on the support of appropriate stakeholders.

The key to this strategy is the involvement and buy-in of local residents and other key stakeholders. Inviting them into the process is a key strategy in itself. But there must be a commitment on the airport's part that the residents' participation will be reflected in the outcome. If the airport or aviation business owner is not prepared to listen carefully and incorporate some of the ideas generated, this approach could end up being more damaging than the status quo.

Strategy B

This strategy focuses on the formation of a Tenants/User group, which then develops and implements the community relations action plan. It can be an important strategy if developing a cooperative effort with a single focus is necessary before reaching out to the general public.

1. Determine that you need support to be able to implement an effective Community Relations Plan.

2. In conjunction with other aviation business owners and/or the airport staff, develop an Airport Tenant and User Association.

Strategy C

This strategy is similar to strategy B, except rather than forming an on-airport group before initiating an action plan, you would form an Airport Friends' Group. A key goal of this Friends Group would be the community outreach effort, not the advocacy aspect discussed in Phase 2, Section E "Developing an Airport Friends Group." This Friends Group would then initiate a strategy similar to either A or B above, or a combination of both, as deemed appropriate to the airport and community situation.

Strategy D

Another strategy could focus on an outreach effort to a specific audience such as the media (Phase 1, Section E) or elected officials (Phase 1, Section D) or even the FAA and airport staff (Phase 1, Section F). It is very likely that all three of these groups could be cultivated in parallel efforts.

One example of when this could be an appropriate strategy is if you have an extensive community relations effort underway, but negative publicity or a small number of anti-airport activists continue to have a negative influence on the media and public officials against the airport. In such a case, a carefully crafted campaign to meet with key members of the media and public officials would be critical. Carefully crafted messages would need to be developed and effective spokespersons chosen to meet with the various entities. One important message would be to demonstrate efforts that have been undertaken to reduce community concerns regarding the airport, as well as ongoing outreach efforts you have established. While one meeting will probably not bring significant change, cultivating these relationships and becoming a resource will help reduce misinformation and one-sided perspectives.

Implementation of Other Strategies

The above examples are but a few of the possible strategies. Each airport and each community is unique and requires an application specific to its needs. Once a strategy is determined, the most appropriate tool(s) can be selected. In some cases, that could be one tool, at least to start. This may lead to a more comprehensive strategy.

Developing a Community Relations Plan

The following outline provides a format for developing a Community Relations Plan. Using the tools and strategies provided in this tool kit, this outline is intended as a starting point for discussions and evaluation for developing and adopting a plan that is most effective for an airport.

One of the sample strategies provided in the section above may also be helpful in providing guidance for developing a plan. It is important to remember that tools should be selected based on identified goals and objectives, stakeholders involved, their issues and concerns as well as resources available to undertake each strategy.

The intent of this community relations plan outline is to assist in carefully considering the many factors involved in outreach efforts. It often seems easier to just choose a tool or technique without evaluating the overall goals, stakeholder needs and underlying issues. But without this careful analysis of the situation and community issues, any community relations plan will be less effective.

Therefore, it is beneficial to spend time delving into community concerns, problems, opportunities and what is needed to improve the relationship with airport neighbors. Questions such as the following ones may be helpful in determining significant issues with the local community and then developing the best strategy for the circumstances:

- Is there existing support in the community that can be cultivated?
- Does the community need to have better access to and more involvement in the airport?
- Is there misinformation or misperceptions about the airport that could be detrimental?
- Do the airport neighbors have a lack of trust of the airport or you?
- Is there an airport project underway or coming soon that will impact local neighbors?

These kinds of questions are important to ask before filling out the Community Relations Plan outline. The more an airport staff, the aviation businesses and users of the airport can examine and analyze community needs, (when possible in conjunction with airport neighbors), the more effective the outcome will be.

Do not forget to find ways to measure the success of the strategies you choose. While it is difficult to quantify the results of some tools, it is important to find some way to determine if it was effective. At times, community relations' efforts feel either fruitless or minimally effective. This is because the effect is cumulative. To achieve maximum results and the full effect of your efforts will require years. Rather than expecting instant results, it helps if you understand that it is a long-term endeavor.

Outline for Developing a Community Relations Plan

Organization

Date

Developed By

WHAT ARE YOUR COMMUNITY RELATIONS GOALS AND OBJECTIVES?

1.

2.

3.

4.

WHY ARE YOU PROPOSING THIS INVOLVEMENT?
(Address Issues and Concerns)

WHAT RESULTS WOULD YOU LIKE TO SEE THROUGH THE SUCCESS OF YOUR OBJECTIVES? (Be as specific as possible)

1.

2.

3.

4.

5.

LIST YOUR TARGET AUDIENCES	IDENTIFY THEIR ISSUES AND CONCERNS
1.	
2.	
3.	
4.	
5.	

STRATEGIES TO ACCOMPLISH THIS OBJECTIVE?

Outreach Tool/Strategy	Person Responsible	Implementation Date	Budget Estimate

WHAT IS REQUIRED TO ACHIEVE EACH STRATEGY? (Methodologies)

1. ______
2. ______
3. ______
4. ______
5. ______

MECHANISMS TO MEASURE SUCCESS

Measurement Technique	How Measured	Level Desired to Achieve Success

(Measurement is often associated with the number of community calls, comments, complaints, editorials, number of participants at an event, etc.)

Good luck in your endeavors to involve and connect with your community. With patience, persistence and continuing communication, positive changes will happen.

Index

Note: Page numbers followed by f indicate figures.

B

C

D

Q

R

V

W

Y

Z